HAMMER FILMS

THE BRAY STUDIOS YEARS

HAMMER FILMS

THE BRAY STUDIOS YEARS

WAYNE KINSEY

Reynolds & Hearn Ltd
London

Harvey Clarke

To Cathy – for her unselfish loyalty
and forgiveness of my guilty pleasures.

FRONTISPIECE:
The Evil of Frankenstein (1963)

OPPOSITE:
Bray's ballroom stage today (now a viewing theatre)
at the back of the house facing the Thames' grassy bank.

First published in 2002 by
Reynolds & Hearn Ltd
61a Priory Road
Kew Gardens
Richmond
Surrey TW9 3DH

© Wayne Kinsey 2002
reprinted 2010

A CIP catalogue record for this book is available from the British Library.

ISBN 1 903111 44 7

Designed by Peri Godbold.

Printed and bound in Malta by Melita Press.

Contents

Introduction

In the 1950s, a large house on the banks of the River Thames was the source of one of the British film industry's greatest success stories. There, Hammer Film Productions made pictures that are now revered the world over, igniting the imaginations of filmmakers as well as filmgoers. To date, Hammer has produced 152 theatrical feature films (not counting featurettes and television specials). Among them are horror pictures, science fiction fantasies, psychological thrillers, prehistoric extravaganzas, gritty war dramas and colourful adventures both historical and fantastical.

Many agree that Hammer's 'classic' period ran from The Quatermass Xperiment in 1954 to The Phantom of the Opera in 1961, at which time a number of key personnel left the company. Some consider that the first nail in Hammer's coffin came with their departure from Bray Studios in 1966. The Hammer that faced the 1970s was not the same. It was ill-prepared, and the films, with a few memorable exceptions, were pale shadows of those produced at Bray.

This is what makes the present book different to other Hammer histories. Rather than plough through the entire Hammer story again, as has been done in a number of highly recommended books, I've decided to concentrate on one slice of Hammer's history, the so-called Golden Era when Hammer occupied Bray. The book also places greater emphasis on the talented team that made these films the cult classics they are today. The approach is essentially that of an oral history, told by the many who worked on these films in order to give a greater insight into what it was like working for Hammer during this period. We will see how the team developed, why certain individuals were absent from certain productions and why some projects had to be located at larger studios.

Focus puller Harry Oakes kept a personal diary of his days at Hammer between 1953 and 1961 and he shares it with us here. I have also reproduced much of the Hammer file held at the British Board of Film Classification, which offers tremendous insights into how the projects developed from script to screen, verifying once and for all whether certain hotly debated 'lost' scenes were actually filmed or not.

This work would be incomplete without the efforts of those who have recorded the history of Hammer over the years, and I am grateful for the use of their interview materials in the text. They're all referenced and I urge you to catch up with the superb original interviews in their entirety. In particular, I would like to thank Dick Klemensen and his inspirational magazine Little Shoppe Of Horrors. May I also acknowledge two other excellent journals, Mike Murphy's Dark Terrors and Marvel's Hammer Horror, edited by Marcus Hearn, as well as the three definitive books on Hammer history: Hammer Films An Exhaustive Filmography by Tom Johnson and Deborah Del Vecchio (McFarland 1996), A History of Horrors by Denis Meikle (Scarecrow Press 1996) and The Hammer Story by Marcus Hearn and Alan Barnes (Titan Books 1997).

I am also grateful to the many who have talked to me about their far-off Hammer days: Roy Ashton, Len Harris, Aida Young, Val Guest, Margaret Robinson, Don Mingaye, Michael Reed, Neil Binney, Harry Oakes, Derek Whitehurst, Hugh Harlow, Basil Keys, Bert Batt, Bill Lenny, Alfred Cox, Eric Boyd-Perkins, Chris Barnes, Claude Hitchcock, Gordon Thompson, James Bernard, Renée Glynne, Marjorie Lavelly, Pauline Harlow, John Jay, Roy Field, Kit West, Ian Scoones, Brian Johnson, Jackie Cooper, Peter Diamond, Ray Harryhausen, Peter Graham Scott, Christine Stevens, Marje Hudd, Christopher Lee, Yvonne Monlaur, Janina Faye, Geoffrey Bayldon, Harold Goodwin, Edward De Souza and Geoffrey Toone. In particular, I would like to thank Harry Oakes, who spent hours scribbling notes from his diaries, which proved immensely helpful in nailing down elusive facts (notably the date of the Bray fire in 1961, which has so far escaped Hammer historians).

The Hammer team relaxes during the shooting of Murder by Proxy (1953). Left to right: Jimmy Sangster, Michael Carreras, Percy Britten, Don Alton, Bill Salter, Jack Curtis, Jimmy Harvey, an electrician, Len Harris, Terence Fisher, Harry Oakes and Renée Glynne.

My sincere thanks go to the British Board of Film Classification, particularly David Barrett, for their unselfish help in opening their Hammer files to me. Thanks also to Ian Crane for compiling the index. And a book like this can't get out without the support of one's friends, so thanks to Harvey Clarke, Marcus Hearn, Richard Reynolds, Peri Godbold, Don Fearney, Simon Greetham and Norman J Warren. Finally, a special 'thank you' to my parents (and ATV) for exposing me to Hammer horror back in 1971 at the impressionable age of nine, Sue & Colin Cowie and Keith Dudley for introducing me to the wonderful world of film conventions, and, of course, to my lovely wife, Cathy.

Don Sharp and his camera crew on location in Black Park for Rasputin the Mad Monk (1965).

ONE

Hammer's Origins

A talent show in Hammersmith, and a comic double-act are asked in the wings what they want to be introduced as. Only then do they realise that they have no stage name. Tongue in cheek, they draw instant inspiration from the London suburb they're performing in and call themselves 'Hammer and Smith'. Such is the legend behind the origin of Hammer films.

Whether the story is apocryphal or not is irrelevant. What's important is that amateur stand-up William Hinds' stage name was Will Hammer, and this man was partly responsible for the establishment, not to mention christening, of Hammer Films.

William Hinds (born 1889) was a shy and retiring man despite his penchant for amateur variety. Starting as a successful businessman in his family's jewellery retailing business (F W Hinds the jewellers, founded in 1856), his passion for the stage eventually led him to branch out, renting and buying a series of seaside theatres and opening his own booking agency. Hinds would hire music hall performers and stage his own seaside summer shows, in which he would sometimes perform under the pseudonym Will Hammer. It was only a matter of time before Hinds' theatrical interests merged with the new force in entertainment, the motion picture.

In November 1934 he registered his own film company, Hammer Productions Ltd [1,2]. This was a different company to the one we know today and was based in a three-room office suite at Imperial

House in London's Regent Street. Hinds was chairman, joint managing directors were George Gillings and Henry Fraser Passmore, and company directorships were held by George Mozart (stage name of comedian-cum-actor David Gillings, brother of George) and art director James Elder Wills. They immediately set to work on a modest 60-minute comedy called *The Public Life of Henry the Ninth* (starring George Mozart) at the MGM/ATP studios, which finished shooting on 2 January 1935 [3].

Around this time William Hinds bumped into Spanish émigré Enrique Carreras (born 1880) in Hammersmith. Carreras, like Hinds, was a reserved businessman who, forsaking his family's cigarette firm, had arrived in England in 1907 with his brother Alphonse and been involved in several unsuccessful ventures before stumbling upon the film industry. In 1913 Enrique and Alphonse built a cinema in Hammersmith called The Blue Hall. It was a prototype of today's cinemas in that it had two screens, each housing 1000 patrons, and soon a chain of seven picture houses was set up. Enrique also staged the first cinematic Royal

LEFT: Enrique Carreras, surrounded by Vera St John Carreras (wife of James), actress Constance Smith and Violet Goodlatte (wife of Jack) on the set of *Room to Let* in 1948.

OPPOSITE: The introduction to the earliest Hammer films featured Bombardier Billy Wells striking an anvil.

Stanley Lupino and a spotted friend in a scene from Sporting Love *(1936).*

Prophetic casting: Hollywood's Dracula star Bela Lugosi in The Mystery of the Mary Celeste *(1935), long before Hammer ever entertained the idea of Gothic horror.*

Command Performance, when he rented out the Albert Hall for a showing of *Quo Vadis* to members of the Royal family, including the King and Queen.

In 1932 Carreras sold off his chain of Blue Hall cinemas to Associated British Cinemas (ABC) in order to concentrate on a toothpaste venture which ultimately left him bankrupt [4]. Wounded, Carreras decided to return to the relative safety of the film world with plans to develop a distribution company. By then, William Hinds already had a foothold in around 30 companies, so what did one more matter? On 10 May 1935, they formed Exclusive Films Ltd [1], together with Jack Spratling, James Dawson and secretary Mrs Burnham, operating from a single office at 60-66 National House, Wardour Street. They kicked off by distributing the two-reelers *Snowhounds* and *Spilt Salt*. As Enrique's grandson, Michael Carreras, explained, "They joined forces and started off with a marvellous deal that got the company on its feet – they managed to get the reissue rights to many of Alexander Korda's London Film Productions which included some of Laurence Olivier's earliest films." [5]

Between 1935 and 1937 the Hammer company produced a further four films released by Exclusive; *The Mystery of the Mary Celeste* (1935; produced by Henry Fraser Passmore, art director J Elder Wills, starring Bela Lugosi and George Mozart), *The Song of Freedom* (1935; director J Elder Wills, producers Will Hammer and Enrique Carreras, production supervisor Henry Fraser Passmore, starring George Mozart and Will Hammer), *Sporting Love* (1936; director J Elder Wills) and *The Bank Messenger Mystery* (1936; starring George Mozart). However, a massive slump in the British film industry soon forced Hammer into bankruptcy and the fledgling company went into liquidation in 1937. Exclusive survived and on 20 July 1937 purchased the leasehold on 113-117 Wardour Street to use as their base [6].

LEFT: *Genial host and expert deal-maker James Carreras was the managing director of Hammer during its most successful era.*

ABOVE: *Producer Tony Hinds confers with director Terence Fisher during production of* Stolen Face (1951) *at Riverside Studios.*

In 1938 Enrique's son, James Carreras (born 30 January 1909), an outspoken former car salesman, joined Exclusive after working as an assistant manager to the ABC chain of theatres. He was closely followed by Will Hammer's son, Anthony Hinds (born 19 September 1922), who joined as a booking-and-barring clerk the following year. On the outbreak of war in September 1939, James left to join the Honourable Artillery Company (HAC) while Anthony joined the Royal Air Force.

Meanwhile, Exclusive continued to struggle on in a limited capacity and, in 1943, James' son, self-confessed jazz fanatic Michael Carreras (born 21 December 1927), joined not only Exclusive's booking department but also its accounts, sales and publicity departments, in charge of issuing stills and posters to cinemas showing Exclusive's releases. Michael remembered, "I had the advantage of going through all the various departments – logging, buying, accounts – ending up in the publicity department, which was responsible for sending out the posters to the cinemas that were playing the various Exclusive releases. That was during the war and we were in Wardour Street. I remember that the secretary of the company was a woman who had a dog and insisted on bringing it to the office every day. So it was part of my job to walk down seven flights of stairs with this dog four times a day, at the same time as the doodle-bugs were dropping. It was a fairly exciting period." [7]

On demobilisation, Lt Col James Carreras (awarded the MBE by George VI for extraordinary service in the defence of London) returned to the company in 1946. In March of that year, the 18-year-old Michael was seconded into the Grenadier Guards for National Service. The company was also rejoined, after much persuasion from James Carreras, by Tony Hinds. With a whisper in his ear from Jack Goodlatte, booking manager of the ABC chain of cinemas, James was convinced to relaunch the company into film production with programme-fillers for the 'quota quickie' market. Hammer was accordingly resurrected as Exclusive's production arm and kicked off with a few modest features in 1947: *Death in High Heels*, *The Dark Road* (starring a young Michael Ripper, a familiar face in some 33 Hammer movies), *Crime Reporter* and *Dick Barton Special Agent*, all shot at Marylebone Studios.

Hammer Productions
—— 1947-48 ——

1947:
- ✦ *DEATH IN HIGH HEELS*
- ✦ *THE DARK ROAD*
- ✦ *CRIME REPORTER*
- ✦ *DICK BARTON SPECIAL AGENT*

1948:
- ✦ *RIVER PATROL*
- ✦ *WHO KILLED VAN LOON?*
- ✦ *DICK BARTON STRIKES BACK*
- ✦ *DICK BARTON AT BAY*

Dick Barton (Don Stannard) is bound and gagged, watched by the sinister Fouracada (Sebastian Cabot) in Dick Barton Strikes Back (1948).

The last of these underlined the key approach that Hammer/Exclusive would adopt in choosing their future projects. *Dick Barton* was a successful radio show and it was only common sense that a film version would be just as successful with its in-built audience. Don Stannard came in as Dick and the feature proved successful enough to spawn two sequels the following year, *Dick Barton Strikes Back* (shot at Viking Studios) and *Dick Barton at Bay* (back at Marylebone).

Hammer's second production of 1948, *Who Killed Van Loon?*, was a rather impromptu affair which unexpectedly saddled Tony Hinds with the position of regular producer for the company. He explains, "A would-be producer started the film and almost immediately ran out of money and disappeared. Some time later, Jim Carreras was asked if Exclusive Films would like to complete the film and distribute it. I was given the job of producing the thing. Unfortunately no copies of the original script were available, so I had to devise a plot that could incorporate the existing footage and make some sort of sense. To further complicate things, very few of the original cast were available, or willing, to complete the film. In fact, one of them had committed suicide partially, if not completely, because he had not been paid. I finished the thing on a budget that would just cover the wages of a clapper/loader nowadays."[8]

Michael Carreras, who had returned to the company in the summer of 1947, initially worked as general dogsbody, experimenting in a number of departments before finally being appointed assistant to producer Tony Hinds in November 1948. "When I rejoined the company," Carreras remembered, "the idea in the minds of the elder statesmen – Tony's father and my grandfather – was that Tony would go into production and I would be introduced to the distribution and sales side. Distribution is a very complex thing – in real terms you obviously cannot just turn up in a van with a film for the cinema. There have to be bookings and so on. So they actually tempted me into going into the distribution side of things. My natural inclination was not to get onto that and I think that I probably made it difficult enough – so they allowed me to go and join Tony ... I had the marvellous opportunity, which everyone longs for, of doing anything I wanted as long as I didn't get in anybody's way. I wasted a lot of time fiddling about with electrics, in which I was interested at one time, and I made it a particular interest of mine in getting into the cutting rooms."[9]

Enter another character who would 'grow up' in step with the company. Jimmy Sangster (born 2 December 1927) had returned from National Service to work as third assistant (ie, gofer) on a film for producer Mario Zampi called *Third Time Lucky*. Exclusive/Hammer approached Zampi to produce their next film, *Dick Barton Strikes Back*, and Zampi's crew were transferred to Exclusive's payroll.

However, Zampi went AWOL and Tony Hinds had to produce the picture. Sangster stayed on as third assistant and the years to come would see him rise through the ranks from second to first assistant, then to production manager, scriptwriter, producer and finally director. Sangster and Michael Carreras got on immediately. "We became best mates forever," Sangster explains. "We both joined the company at the same time. I think he had done a little bit of work for the company before his National Service, but he came out of National Service the same time as I did and we were shooting a Dick Barton picture. That's when I first met him and we both liked jazz, girls and drink, and it was just best friend material from then on."

On location for *Dick Barton Strikes Back* in Blackpool, chief electrician Jack Curtis planted a seed in Tony Hinds' mind. Why not save money by renting out a country house to make the movies instead of hiring expensive stage space at the larger film studios?[10] Consequently, for their next production, *Dr Morelle – The Case of the Missing Heiress* (starting on 15 November 1948), Hammer moved to Dial Close, an unfurnished 23-bedroom mansion overlooking a bend in the River Thames at Winter Hill, Cookham Dean near Maidenhead. It was then being used as a furniture store. Michael Carreras recalled the move: "Tackling his assignment in an unusual way, Tony rented as the studio base for the Hammer programme an unfurnished country mansion at Cookham Dean. He collected together a group of knowledgeable technicians who, under his guidance, transformed the empty house into a practical and economical working studio, as well as a very comfortable residence, complete with butler, for those who wished to live on the job."[11]

Dr Morelle was based on another popular BBC radio show and Godfrey Grayson, who had directed the last two Dick Barton adventures, was brought back to direct. The film was a murder mystery with Valentine Dyall playing the famous radio sleuth. Filming concluded in December and, on 12 February 1949, Exclusive finally registered Hammer Film Productions Ltd, with company directors named as Enrique and James Carreras and William and Tony Hinds. James Dawson was company secretary and Anthony E ('Brian') Lawrence (who had come to Exclusive in 1945 from the Anglo American Film Corporation) sales manager. Exclusive's offices were still located at 113-117 Wardour Street and now Hammer joined them on the fifth floor; the building would soon be christened Hammer House. James Carreras (or the Colonel, as everyone called him) was now in over-all charge and *Dr Morelle* was designated as Hammer's first 'official' film.

The Hammer team that arrived at Cookham Dean for *Dr Morelle* included producer Tony Hinds, his assistant Michael Carreras, sound mixer Edgar Vetter, camera operator Peter Bryan (later to

The start of a lasting friendship. Third assistant Jimmy Sangster and Michael Carreras pictured in South Kensington, London.

Hammer Productions at Dial Close

1948:
+ DR MORELLE – THE CASE OF THE MISSING HEIRESS

1949:
+ THE ADVENTURES OF PC 49
+ CELIA
+ MEET SIMON CHERRY

RIGHT:
Dial Close was Hammer's first 'house' studio.

BELOW:
Exclusive's stills photographer John Jay with producer Michael Carreras.

become scriptwriter on several of Hammer's fantasy films), focus puller Neil Binney (later to become a camera operator), lighting cameraman Cedric Williams, Jimmy Sangster (now promoted to second assistant), production manager Arthur Barnes, chief electrician Jack Curtis (who would stay on in that capacity throughout Hammer's years at Bray), chief carpenter Freddie Ricketts (later to become studio manager at Bray) and musical director Frank Spencer.

After *Dr Morelle*, Hammer shot another three films at Dial Close in 1949, all based on popular BBC radio shows: *The Adventures of PC 49, Celia* and *Meet Simon Cherry*. On *The Adventures of PC 49*, they were joined by make-up man Phil Leakey, hair-stylist Monica Hustler (later to marry Jimmy Sangster), assistant editor Alfred Cox (later to become an editor/sound editor on Hammer's fantasy films), continuity supervisor Renée Glynne and clapper Michael Reed (later to become a lighting cameraman). Moray Grant (born 13 November 1917) took over as camera operator on the film, but Peter Bryan would be back in that role from the next film, *Celia*. Grant would return to Hammer as camera operator in the sixties and as director of photography in the seventies.

Phil Leakey was born in London on 4 May 1908. His break into the film industry came about in very odd circumstances when his father, a doctor, was asked to supervise a boxing match at the Stoll Studios. Leakey accompanied him and went up to the studio manager, Joe Grossman, to ask his permission to watch, only to be stopped in his tracks by Grossman telling him to start work Monday at eight o'clock. Though it was obviously a case of mistaken identity, the bemused and intrigued Leakey kept his appointment. Of course, Grossman was equally bemused but set him to work in the sound department nevertheless. After a studio fire, Leakey found himself moved across to the make-up department. He watched the resident make-up men at work and was later given a break when American actress Bebe Daniels arrived to make a film accompanied by her very own personal make-up artist. Fortunately, he was looking for an assistant and took Leakey on, training him in Hollywood make-up techniques. After a brief spell at Shepperton Studios, Leakey joined the newly formed Hammer company. His pioneering make-up work would make a major contribution as Hammer entered its horror period.

Continuity girl Renée Glynne had already worked on Exclusive's first film, as she explains: "It was 1947 and I had a call from Tony Hinds asking me to go to Marylebone Studios to work on Exclusive's *Death in High Heels* and part of a Dick Barton. Some time later I worked on Vernon Sewell's film *Jack of Diamonds* at Carlton Studios for Exclusive. Having done those led me on to *The Adventures of PC 49* at Dial Close. Having found me, I was continuously employed by them for something like eight years. We were in our rented house studios and I just went from film to film, on the payroll, off the payroll, on the payroll."

Michael Reed was born in Wandsworth in 1928. He left school at the age of 15 and became an assistant at the Studio Film Laboratories in Wardour Street. "I worked there for about a year and got my union ticket," remembered Reed. "I then transferred through to Southall studios in 1946 as a clapper boy on a film called *Dancing with Crime*, which starred Dicky Attenborough, Bill Owen, Sheila Sim and Barry K Barnes. I worked at Southall just under a year. Alliance Film Studios were running it at the time and they had three studios, Southall, Riverside and Twickenham. I did the Just William films with Val Guest (*Just William's Luck* in 1947 and *William Goes to Town* in 1948) and then I left there and became freelance around 1948. I worked on two or three pictures as a clapper boy. I did *Murder at the Windmill*, again with Val Guest. Then I went to Exclusive, again as clapper boy, on *The Adventures of PC 49*."

Stills photographer John Jay (later to become stills photographer on Hammer's fantasy films, as well as countless big-budget classics such as *Born Free* and *Star Wars*) would join the team on *Celia*. "I was with Gainsborough for many years," he recalled, "and when they moved from Islington Studios to Shepherds Bush Studios, I became their head photographer and ran the stills department until they closed the building down. I then freelanced and joined Hammer at Cookham Dean under the banner of Anthony Hinds. It was very much a family atmosphere but, despite that, everything was very well-run, with Tony Hinds at the helm. We shot the films in the rooms and used the grounds for exteriors." He remembers the primitive stills unit at Dial Close: "It was just me. I developed my own negatives but did not do any printing as there were no facilities there. By developing my own negatives I then knew that all was OK before sending them for printing."

Celia also gave a break to future Hammer focus puller Harry Oakes (born 16 January 1921). "After I got out of the army I managed to get a job with a small documentary company called Merlin Films. It was difficult getting a job – one didn't need a union really for the camera department in those days, you just had to know people. I did know one or two, because basically the chaps in the Army Photographic unit with me were professionals in one way or another, stills or cine. It was rough going at first. Then it so happened that our production manager, Arthur Barnes, went to work as production manager for Hammer at Dial Close and when he wanted an assistant with a Newman-Sinclair for a couple of days on *Celia*, he rang his old company up at Merlin Films and I got loaned out with the camera. Rather coincidentally, later on Hammer bought Merlin Films – the name – because they used to make films under different company names for taxation purposes." Harry would return to the company on *The Man in Black* later in the year.

Director Francis Searle also joined the team on *Celia*. He would go on to direct nine pictures for the company, alternating with Godfrey Grayson.

Renée Glynne remembers that, at Dial Close, "We were a very tight-knit crew, with regular directors Frank Searle and Godfrey Grayson. I remember us all going down to the river in the evenings, swimming, punting, sailing. There was a tennis court and we played lunchtime and in the evening. We stayed in the house during the week and went home at the weekend. That period was the beginning of Monica Hustler and Jimmy Sangster's love affair, which led to their marriage. Monica and I became friends and we shared a room." Neil Binney added, "Dial Close was perched up on a hill overlooking the Thames. A very nice atmosphere, we had a cook there that cooked our lunches and gave us tea. Also we were able to stay overnight or stay there the whole week if we wished, because in those years not many people had cars."

It was at Dial Close that Hammer developed the quaint custom of transporting their staff to the studio each morning. "Dial Close was miles out in the country," explains John Jay, "a difficult place to get to, but good for location work." Hammer's solution was simple. "We had a bus, an old London transport bus," recalls Renée Glynne. "They hired it at first, then they bought it." Michael Reed adds, "We used to meet up in Hammersmith to catch the coach that took us to the studio and then they would take us back at night. Transport was very difficult, because the train service was erratic and you couldn't rely on it, so it was far better for them to coach us all down there. It made sure everyone was on time."

Every inch of the house was used for filming, including the grounds, and Hammer now began to develop the method of converting existing rooms into sets and shooting within their confined spaces. Neil Binney remembers, "In those years they were ahead of their time. I don't recall films ever being made in houses before. It was a question of covering up scaffolding and lamps with curtains etc, which is quite common now, but in those years it was most unusual. I remember they had a lot of sound damping around; they put blankets up to dampen down the hollow, oak-panelled rooms." These makeshift sets were, of course, not sound-proofed and the sound department had numerous headaches thanks to the planes flying regularly overhead.

The Hammer team's ability to shoot within the confines of a country house was largely down to the resourcefulness of lighting cameraman Cedric Williams, who had to sling his lamps across low ceilings, concealing them with canvas, or else hang them from the tops of ladders; he frequently lit sets from ground level too. Michael Reed recalls, "Cedric Williams was the cameraman and he made a marvellous job of them. He was the one who put rails up and hung lamps through the ceiling. It was quite an experience actually; with a house you couldn't hang a gantry or a catwalk around any of the areas, because the ceilings were so low compared with a studio height, and so he used to set up his own little gantries as it were."

On Saturday 9 July 1949, Dick Barton actor Don Stannard was killed in a car accident on his way home from a garden party at Dial Close to celebrate the release of *Dick Barton Strikes Back*. The crash occurred on Winter Hill, a notorious black spot. On 14 July, *Kinematograph Weekly* described the terrible events: "The vehicle was seen to swing out of the drive running down the twisted incline which links the house with the main road into Cookham village. It got out of hand on a bend and overturned. Stannard was killed instantly, and all the passengers were taken to Maidenhead Hospital. Mrs Stannard was unhurt, but the other passengers all suffered severe shock and lacerations." Also injured were music director Frank Spencer and actor Sebastian Cabot (the film's villain) and his wife. The tragedy brought to an end the trio of successful Dick Barton adventures, as Tony Hinds felt it imprudent to continue the series with another actor.

In August 1949, Hammer were eventually hounded out of Dial Close when the locals complained about the noise of the generators and the arc lamps used for night filming. Hammer now sought refuge at Oakley Court, a Gothic folly on the banks of the Thames between Windsor and Maidenhead, and shot a further five films there over 1949 and the early part of 1950: *The Man in Black, Room to Let, Someone at the Door, What the Butler Saw* and *The Lady Craved Excitement*.

With the team's arrival at Oakley Court came a minor reshuffling of Hammer's 'cabinet'. Jimmy Sangster was promoted to first assistant director on *The Man in Black*, becoming the youngest in the country at just 21. "They had to get a new first assistant," he explained. "I was second assistant at the time and Tony Hinds said, 'Come on, this Sangster chap hasn't been around much, has he? He's only a second assistant and he's only 21 years old. Are we really going to make him first assistant?' Arthur Barnes was the production manager, Jack Curtis was the chief electrician and Tommy Money was the head prop man and they said, 'We'll make sure he's all right. If he messes up, we'll cover for him and see to it he's all right.' And because those three principal characters were backing me up, Tony

Hammer Productions at Oakley Court

1949:
+ THE MAN IN BLACK
+ ROOM TO LET
+ SOMEONE AT THE DOOR

1950:
+ WHAT THE BUTLER SAW
+ THE LADY CRAVED EXCITEMENT

said, 'Fine, all right. I'll give him a shot.'"

After *Meet Simon Cherry*, focus puller Neil Binney left to go into National Service. Michael Reed was now promoted from clapper to focus puller for *The Man in Black* and Harry Oakes, who had worked a few days on *Celia*, returned as the new resident clapper/loader. Scriptwriter John Gilling (later to write and direct Hammer fantasy films) also joined the team on *The Man in Black*. Gilling (born 1912) started in the film industry in 1933 as an assistant to his uncle, director W P Kellino, at British International Pictures. He later did some freelance work as second then first assistant director until 1937, when he joined Gainsborough. After the war, he wrote his first screenplay, *Black Memory* (1946), notable only in that it launched Sid James' career. Gilling's next screenplay, *House of Darkness* (1947), was Lawrence Harvey's first film.

Oakley Court stands on the banks of the Thames. Nowadays it is a luxury hotel.

Room to Let is an interesting film, given Hammer's later direction; it's about a Victorian family who believe their sinister lodger, Dr Fell (Valentine Dyall), is Jack the Ripper. Editor James Needs joined the team on this film. Needs had entered the film industry in the editing department of Islington Studios in 1935. After the war, he joined Gaumont-British at the old Shepherds Bush studios, initially as assembly cutter, eventually progressing to editor in 1948. John Jay remembers introducing Needs to Hammer: "Tony Hinds was looking for an editor and I suggested Jimmy for the job. I had worked with him many times at Gainsborough Studios." Needs would later become Hammer's resident supervising editor in 1957.

On *The Man in Black* and *Room to Let*, Cedric Williams had continued to modify his lighting styles, often daubing the windows with gelatinous paint to control the light and designing a special exposure meter for rapid light-readings and a stand capable of holding six movable lamps, which he called 'the octopus', built by chief electrician Jack Curtis and his assistant Percy Harms. Lighting cameraman Walter (Jimmy) Harvey, elder brother of half-German movie star Lilian Harvey, would take over regularly from Williams on *Someone at the Door*. The film's director, Francis Searle, explains, "I knew lighting cameraman Jimmy Harvey for a long time, because he used to do freelance when I was at Gaumont-British and he did some 2nd unit work on *Celia*. So, after Cedric Williams left, Jimmy came in on lighting." [12]

The Hammer team were now afforded Oakley Court's elaborate Victorian furnishings. While the ground floor and large staircase were deployed for filming, they modified as best they could the first floor for the staff. The bedrooms were used by the live-in staff and stills photographer John Jay remembers having to work from a converted toilet: "Funny what you do, isn't it? I had taken a tank down there and processed my negatives there. They were big toilets actually, with plenty of room in them. I had one as a dark room." However, such alterations had to be limited as Harry Oakes explains: "The existing ownership wouldn't let any major construction go on there."

Then there were the lovely grounds and gardens that sprawled down to the banks of the Thames. An outhouse was converted into the carpenters/paint shop and a makeshift viewing theatre, while the generator was set up in an old boathouse on the river. According to Harry Oakes, "We had no canteen, apart from a couple of girls making cups of tea, so we used to go into Bray village for lunch." Renée Glynne concurs: "Every lunchtime we piled into our famous bus, had a drink in the pub, then lunched at the Hinds' Head Hotel."

According to John Jay, "Oakley Court was owned by an eccentric old Frenchman who dressed in top hat and evening suit even when just walking around the place. He did not understand us at all. There was an organ in the entrance hall in a massive glass case. This was often used in films; however, it made a terrible noise, similar to a fairground steam organ!" Renée Glynne also has

Hammer Productions — at Gilston Park —

1950:

- ✦ *BLACK WIDOW*
- ✦ *THE ROSSITER CASE*
- ✦ *TO HAVE AND TO HOLD*
- ✦ *THE DARK LIGHT*

vivid recollections: "It was totally Gothic. Our room there was wonderful. Up in the turret. Monica and I had a four-poster bed with ladybirds on the ceiling, bats in the room and a bolster down the centre of the bed so we didn't touch each other. That was a fantastic period; baronial dining, a billiard room, beautiful grounds..."

During their stay at Oakley Court, Hammer became attracted to the neighbouring property of Down Place, a ramshackle mansion that also stood on the banks of the Thames. During the shooting of *The Lady Craved Excitement*, the film's director, Francis Searle, approached a friend in the RAF who owned a flat there. He was going away for a few weeks and allowed Searle to shoot a few scenes there. But there was to be yet another port-of-call before Down Place came into its own...

It was time to move again and the next productions were shot at Gilston Park, a country club in Harlow, Essex: *Black Widow, The Rossiter Case, To Have and To Hold* and *The Dark Light*. The move to Gilston Park was proudly proclaimed on the cover of *The Cinema Studio* on 15 March 1950 during the shooting of *The Lady Craved Excitement* at Oakley Court:

EXCLUSIVE PRODUCTION TO BE INCREASED 50 PER CENT: NEW STUDIO AND SECOND UNIT.

> With production slumped to a very low level in most of the studios remaining open in this country at the present time, Jimmy Carreras, managing director of Exclusive Pictures, announces that he is to increase production at their studios by fifty per cent. Already eight pictures have been scheduled for the next twelve months and this is now to be increased to twelve. For the purpose of meeting this rise in output, Exclusive are not only moving to another building, Gilston Park Country Club near Harlow, Essex, for filming but will be putting a second unit into operation at regular intervals at their present studio at Bray [Oakley Court]. Mr Carreras told Cinema Studio yesterday that their last ten productions have been so successful, with seven having had circuit deals and three more yet to be released, that they decided to step up production whilst ensuring that the high level of quality and entertainment was maintained, if not further improved upon.

This meant that Hammer's policy of five weeks' shooting and two weeks off had to be modified to accommodate the increase in production; the respite between films was accordingly reduced to one week. Two large rooms were used as stages and the building could also accommodate the workshops. "We constructed a bit there – put cantilevers in for the lamps," explained Harry Oakes, "whereas at Oakley Court it was all from the floor." Renée Glynne adds, "It was in parkland and animal land, so lunchtime was wonderful: a walk around the grounds, a witty discourse with assistant director Bill Shore. The house was way across London in Hertfordshire. Again we went by our bus. The house had a lovely staircase and open fireplaces."

On 15 October 1950, Enrique Carreras died and his son James therefore became the biggest shareholder in the company, taking over as managing director with William Hinds as chairman. Michael Carreras now stepped up onto the board of directors. William Hinds had no real interest in film production and James now found himself controlling the company with Tony Hinds as his producer and Michael as assistant producer.

Michael, though not always seeing eye-to-eye with his father, was always complimentary about him: "He was a salesman par excellence, a man who as they say could sell refrigerators to the Eskimos, and he had a tremendous outgoing personality. When I was a child, I think a lot of my energy was drained by just watching my father perform. He was a great sportsman, a great cricketer, a great rugby football player – never used to stop. He also loved social occasions and was at ease in any class of society or size of group. This was illustrated very much by his activities in the Variety Club, which developed later. He was an incredible extrovert as opposed to the older generation." [13]

Actor Christopher Lee agrees: "Jimmy Carreras was a businessman and a brilliant entrepreneur. He was a brilliant salesman and a brilliant showman and, believe you me, we sadly need people like Jimmy Carreras around today to try to get this industry back on its feet. Jimmy was a genius at this sort of thing." Lee also affectionately remembers Tony Hinds and Michael Carreras: "Michael was always living in the shadow of his father, which I think was very difficult for him, because he wanted to be a producer as opposed to an executive. Michael was far more film-minded than his father and was more involved in the film itself, as producer and later as director. Michael looked far more Hispanic than his father. Both Jimmy Carreras' parents were Spanish. I knew Jimmy Carreras' mother and she didn't speak English. Tony was very quiet, with a very dry sense of humour and a very good one. He was very unobtrusive and had an enormous amount of control. He *was* Hammer. Michael was much more up-front, more obvious, more on show. They were total opposites, but I suppose you could say that one didn't function very well without the other."

Gilston Park, another of Hammer's house studios, was a country club in Harlow, Essex.

At the end of 1950, Michael Carreras produced his first film, *The Dark Light*, at the age of 23. He recalled, "Then there came a time when Tony discovered what producing a picture was about and we suddenly realised that I was wasting my time assisting him because he didn't need an assistant, as he knew what he was doing. For a period I took full advantage of getting into what was laughingly called the Story Department, which was mainly reading or listening to the radio, because all those early productions came from known material. Then I got into the casting bit and it developed from there. I suppose that I became a bit itchy and they gave me my first film to do, which was an extraordinary film which Vernon Sewell directed." [14]

As 1950 drew to a close, Hammer was on the brink of one of its most significant deals, one which would finally lead to the acquisition of a permanent studio.

Hammer Moves to Bray

(1 9 5 1 - 1 9 5 2)

As their 1950 programme came to an end, Hammer were still intrigued by Down Place, which stood proudly on the banks of the River Thames just off the main Maidenhead to Windsor road (now the A308), flanked on one side by Water Oakley Farm and on the other by the estate of Oakley Court. Hammer approached the owners, the Davies family, who were then only living in the south west wing of the house, and arranged to lease the property for a year as their next base. Consequently, Hammer filmed a few scenes of their last production of 1950, *The Dark Light*, at Down Place before moving there permanently, beginning their 1951 programme with *Cloudburst*.

Hammer found Down Place virtually derelict when they moved in. As Tony Hinds explained, "My chief electrician and my master carpenter told me that they had noticed a house which was known locally as 'duffel coat manor', because it had been used after the war for storing duffel coats. The roof had leaked and the duffel coats had taken up so much water that the weight had caused the whole of the inside to collapse. So really it was a shell. I went back to look at this and we decided that we could turn this into a sort of studio." [1]

Harry Oakes also remembers the house: "When we were there the building was a bit of a shambles and it was stocked up with ex-WD coats. Now at that time there was no end of shops all over the place selling ex-WD gear, duffel coats and so on – it was only five years after the war, you see. There was a bit of a row afterwards because a lot of the duffel coats got nicked. Anyway, they must have liked the place since Oakley Court had its limitations, because they couldn't construct there. We only had the house to begin with and we used to have to cart everything up the stairs, tracks as well, because in those days there was no hand-held stuff."

Hammer shot eight films in 1951. The first five of these were shot at Down Place: *Cloudburst, A Case for PC 49, Death of an Angel, Whispering Smith Hits London* and *The Last Page*. Gradually a special team began to take shape – one that would very soon grasp the baton in Hammer's horror renaissance. Still with the team, and working on all five of the films at Down Place that year, were first assistant director Jimmy Sangster, camera operator Peter Bryan, Harry Oakes (now promoted from clapper/loader to focus-puller on *Cloudburst*), director of photography Walter Harvey, make-up artist Phil Leakey, continuity girl Renée Glynne, production manager Arthur Barnes and music director Frank Spencer. Anne Box now joined the roster as hairstylist on all five.

Whispering Smith Hits London caused a rift between writer John Gilling and Hammer's boss James Carreras when Gilling's screenplay (based on his original story *Where is Sylvia?*) was credited to Whispering Smith's creator Frank H Spearman; Hammer had just bought a series of Whispering Smith stories. Gilling sent Carreras a solicitor's letter and Carreras warned him that he would never work for Hammer again. Gilling disappeared for a time but would return to the company in 1960 to write and direct a number of their fantasy films.

For their last picture that year at Down Place, *The Last Page*, a thriller starring George Brent, Marguerite Chapman and Diana Dors, Hammer made a significant appointment in director Terence Fisher (born 23 February 1904). He had first entered the film industry at the age of 28 – as Fisher described it, he was "the oldest clapperboy in the business". After spending some time editing, he turned to directing relatively late in his career at Rank and Gainsborough, before joining Hammer. "I made two films with Sydney Box at Pinewood," remembered Fisher. "Then, of course, Rank began to be very wary about their investment in films and the whole industry in Britain began to go through a very bad time – apart from Hammer, who were applying themselves very seriously to improving

Hammer Productions
—— 1951-52 ——

1951:
+ *CLOUDBURST*
+ *A CASE FOR PC 49*
+ *DEATH OF AN ANGEL*
+ *WHISPERING SMITH HITS LONDON*
+ *THE LAST PAGE*
+ *WINGS OF DANGER*
+ *NEVER LOOK BACK*
+ *STOLEN FACE*

1952:
+ *LADY IN THE FOG*
+ *THE GAMBLER AND THE LADY*
+ *MANTRAP*
+ *FOUR SIDED TRIANGLE*
+ *THE FLANAGAN BOY*
+ *SPACEWAYS*

Sheila Burrell, Robert Preston and Elizabeth Sellars in Cloudburst (1951), the first film Hammer shot at Bray. Sellars' only other Hammer film would be The Mummy's Shroud (1966), the last film the company shot at the studios.

Opposite: An aerial shot of Bray Studios, on the banks of the River Thames.

Brian Reece reprises his role as radio's favourite policeman in *A Case for PC 49* (1951).

their product. And so I joined Hammer." [2]

Sound recordist Bill Salter and editor Maurice Rootes also joined the company on *The Last Page*, while music director Frank Spencer would finally leave after this production. Rootes would now effectively alternate productions with James Needs.

One problem Hammer faced during this period was the limited acceptability of their all-British films to an international audience, particularly in the US. James Carreras overcame this by forging his first international deal in 1951 with American producer/distributor Robert L Lippert. A deal was struck with Lippert whereby he would supply minor American stars to Hammer and then distribute the films throughout America via his association with 20th Century-Fox. In return, Exclusive would release some of Lippert's films in England (including *Rocketship XM*, *The Steel Helmet*, *Lost Continent* and *Catwomen of the Moon*). The deal lasted four years, opening with *The Last Page* in 1951 and ending with *Women Without Men* (aka *Prison Story*) in 1955.

The original lease on Down Place expired at the end of 1951. Consequently, the last three productions of 1951 and the first of 1952 moved elsewhere: *Wings of Danger*, *Stolen Face* and *Lady in the Fog* were filmed at Hammersmith's Riverside Studios and *Never Look Back* was shot at Manchester Film Studios. Throughout 1951, Michael Carreras had taken on the mantle of casting director before returning as mainline producer later that year on his second feature, *Never Look Back*, giving Tony Hinds another respite. Thereafter he continued in his role as assistant to Tony Hinds, but now began to take over more regularly as mainline producer. Anthony Nelson Keys came in as associate producer on *Never Look Back* for a one-picture deal – he would return regularly in the spot from *The Steel Bayonet* (1956) onwards.

After *Stolen Face*, the last production of 1951, the team would fragment somewhat with the loss of Jimmy Sangster, Arthur Barnes, Peter Bryan and Harry Oakes. Sangster had married Hammer hairstylist Monica Hustler in 1950 and now they emigrated to Montreal. "The country was still in pretty dire straits even this long after the war," Sangster stated in his autobiography. "Food was still rationed and there was a general shortage of everything, including confidence. So we packed our bags, paid our money, and emigrated to Canada. To Montreal, where the only job I could get was selling insurance while Monica worked in a department store. Very depressing!" [3]

Camera operator Peter Bryan had succumbed to a car accident and would be replaced over the next two productions by Moray Grant. Bryan would return to Hammer to produce, write and direct a short called *Operation Universe* in 1957 before turning his hand to writing some of their later horrors. Focus-puller Harry Oakes left to rejoin his old unit, Merlin Films, but would return in 1953. John Green and Victor Wark would now take over from Arthur Barnes as production manager, effectively alternating productions.

By this time, Hammer's success was on the increase and, to accommodate the new programme of films, secret plans were in hand to stay on at the Riverside Studios in Hammersmith and thereby return to a more conventional, studio-based operation. However, Hammer was forced to reconsider when its proposals led to a dispute with the Association of Cinematograph Technicians. Consequently, just as Down Place began to look for new tenants, James Carreras made an offer to buy the freehold of the property. As part of the deal the Davies family were allowed to stay on in the south west wing of the house, which is today converted to luxury private flats. Hammer moved back to Down Place for their second film of 1952, *The Gambler and the Lady*. Soon the estate would be renamed Bray Studios after the nearby village of Bray. It would remain Hammer's principal production base until 1966.

FOUR SIDED TRIANGLE

PRINCIPAL PHOTOGRAPHY: August to September 1952
DISTRIBUTION:
　UK: Exclusive; certificate 'A'
　US: Astor Pictures
81 minutes; b/w
UK RELEASE: 25 May 1953 at the Rialto
US RELEASE: 15 May 1953

DIRECTOR: Terence Fisher; PRODUCERS: Michael Carreras, Alexander Paal; SCREENPLAY: Paul Tabori, Terence Fisher, based on the novel by William F Temple; DIRECTOR OF PHOTOGRAPHY: Reg Wyer; CAMERA OPERATOR: Len Harris; EDITOR: Maurice

Rootes; ART DIRECTOR: J Elder Wills; PRODUCTION MANAGER: Victor Wark; ASSISTANT DIRECTOR: Bill Shore; CONTINUITY: Renée Glynne; MUSIC COMPOSER: Malcolm Arnold; SOUND RECORDIST: Bill Salter; DIALOGUE DIRECTOR: Nora Roberts; MAKE-UP: D Bonner-Moris; HAIR STYLIST: Nina Broe

Barbara Payton (Lena/Helen); James Hayter (Dr Harvey); Stephen Murray (Bill); John Van Eyssen (Robin); Percy Marmont (Sir Walter), Jennifer Dearman (young Lena); Glyn Dearman (young Bill); Sean Barrett (young Robin); Kynaston Reeves (Lord Grant), John Stuart (solicitor), Edith Saville (Lady Grant)

ABOVE: John Van Eyssen with Hollywood bad girl Barbara Payton in Hammer's first attempt at science fiction, Four Sided Triangle (1952).

LEFT: Len Harris (camera operator), Reg Wyer (director of photography) and Terence Fisher (director) on location near Lulworth Cove outside Weymouth for Four Sided Triangle (1952).

Throughout the remainder of 1952, Hammer churned out four more films at Bray: Mantrap, Four Sided Triangle, The Flanagan Boy and Spaceways. More Hammer regulars joined the fold on Mantrap: future producer Aida Young started as second assistant director, Len Harris as camera operator and Molly Arbuthnot as costume supervisor.

Len Harris (born 19 May 1916) was another descendant of Gainsborough, where he had operated for director Terence Fisher on Portrait from Life (1948) and The Astonished Heart (1949). Moray Grant, who had taken over from Peter Bryan after his accident, was not available for Mantrap and Hammer accordingly wrote to Len Harris. "I'd been freelancing for different companies," remembered Len. "Hammer asked if I would help them on a film and indicated there might be more work to follow. The terms were good and I knew some of the people there, so I agreed to try it. The first film was Paul Henreid's Mantrap. They had a good art director and the sets were good. It was a very polished production and a good job, so I decided to stay with them. I stayed for ten years. I was on a yearly contract with Hammer. Another firm I had worked for offered me a job as director and cameraman on documentaries and they offered me more money. I went to talk to Michael Carreras about it and he said, 'No! We have big plans for you. You can't leave us now. As long as we are making pictures, you've got a job. Always.' He called the secretary in and had her draw up a new contract. I was between contracts at the time. He gave me more money, too. Not a fortune, but reasonable. I liked them and the atmosphere there and I was happy. So I turned down the other job, but it would have been a break." [4]

In 1952 Michael Carreras produced Hammer's first two science fiction films, Four Sided Triangle and Spaceways.

SPACEWAYS

PRINCIPAL PHOTOGRAPHY: 17 November 1952 to January 1953
DISTRIBUTION:
UK: Exclusive; 76 minutes; certificate 'U'
US: Lippert; 74 minutes
b/w
UK RELEASE: 21 December 1953
US RELEASE: July 1953

DIRECTOR: Terence Fisher; **PRODUCER:** Michael Carreras; **SCREENPLAY:** Paul Tabori, Richard Landau, based on the BBC radio play by Charles Eric Maine; **DIRECTOR OF PHOTOGRAPHY:** Reg Wyer; **CAMERA OPERATOR:** Len Harris; **EDITOR:** Maurice Rootes; **ART DIRECTOR:** J Elder Wills; **PRODUCTION MANAGER:** Victor Wark; **ASSISTANT DIRECTOR:** Jimmy Sangster; **CONTINUITY:** Renée Glynne; **MUSIC:** Ivor Slaney; **SOUND RECORDIST:** Bill Salter; **Make-up:** D Bonnor-Moris; **HAIRSTYLIST:** Polly Young; **Dialogue DIRECTOR:** Nora Roberts; **SPECIAL EFFECTS:** The Trading Post Ltd; **PROCESS SHOTS:** Bowie, Margutti & Co

Howard Duff (Stephen Mitchell); Eva Bartok (Lisa Frank); Andrew Osborn (Philip Crenshaw); Anthony Ireland (General Hays), Alan Wheatley (Dr Smith); Michael Medwin (Toby Andrews); David Horne (minister); Cecile Chevreau (Vanessa Mitchell); Hugh Moxey (Colonel Daniels); Philip Leaver (Dr Keppler); John Webster-Brough (Mrs Daniels); Leo Phillips (Sgt Peterson), Marianne Stone (Mrs Rogers)

Howard Duff is suited up for his ill-fated space mission in Spaceways (1952).

Four Sided Triangle tells of two scientists who duplicate the woman they both love. Shot over August and September 1952, it was a forerunner of Frankenstein but made little impact on its release, despite Robert Lippert's acquisition of Hollywood bad girl Barbara Payton to spice things up. Len Harris recalled, "We went down to Weymouth for a few days on Four Sided Triangle. We had to shoot a few swimming sequences with Barbara Payton from a yacht. On board was Terence Fisher, Victor Wark, the skipper, his wife, and myself. Suddenly the wind picked up and nearly capsized us. The production manager, fortunately a keen yachtsman, was hanging over the side trying to balance us, and he was going right under the water at times. I was holding a Newman Sinclair camera with one hand and holding on for dear life with the other!"[5]

Barbara Payton would stay on for Hammer's next outing, The Flanagan Boy. Also back was Jimmy Sangster; his move to Canada had lasted five months, as he explained in his autobiography. "Finally I wrote to Monica's father and asked if he could loan us the money to come home where I was prepared to go to work for him as a bookmaker's clerk in Dorking."[3] It wasn't long before Sangster was enticed back to his old job at Hammer: "I was about to start on a novel when Tony Hinds called me. Hammer was about to start shooting a movie called The Flanagan Boy. Tony wanted a man named Basil Keys as assistant director, but Basil couldn't or wouldn't do it. Basil was a top assistant director and I believe he had been offered the same job on a much bigger picture. The devil you know is better than the devil you don't, and Tony offered the job to me."[3]

Spaceways was a murder mystery with a doomed space flight thrown in. Michael Carreras later commented: "I think because of the success of the distribution of that very minor picture [Robert Lippert's Rocketship XM, which Exclusive distributed in England] in America and in England, we decided to go into a science fiction picture and we made Spaceways. This was really lunacy as the budget was the same as it would have been if it was about two people in bed – a domestic comedy type of thing. We tried to make this picture which suffered from an obvious lack of funds. In those days we only had one stage, and one cylinder set which was the interior of the rocket."[6]

Spaceways also saw the first appearance at Hammer of special effects pioneer Les Bowie. Born in Vancouver Canada, Bowie had been taken prisoner during World War II and found time to develop his artistic skills. As well as helping out on stage shows by painting the background scenery and adding some simple special effects such as snow and rain, his versatility was put to use for more pressing matters when he was called upon to forge passports for escape attempts, manufacturing German rubber stamps from potatoes and making German uniforms from blankets (dyeing them with vegetable and fruit dyes), as well as engineering air pumps for tunnel digging and building decoys to keep the captors occupied during escape attempts. Bowie was later introduced to matte painting (the process by which glass paintings are incorporated with live action, either by putting them in front of the camera as a 'foreground glass' or merging them optically as a 'matte') by Percy 'Poppa' Day at Highbury Studios and went on to develop the technique with Bill Warrington at Pinewood before going freelance. He later set up a company with Vic Margutti (Bowie-Margutti Ltd), operating from a small studio at Stoke Court in Stoke Poges. Alas, not even Vic and Les could save *Spaceways*.

The new team at Bray continued their time-honoured routine. Each morning the old London Transport bus would pick up the crew at Hammersmith Broadway to get them to the studio for 8.20. "We used to catch the coach at Hammersmith every morning at 7.30 and pick up some people en route," remembered Jimmy Sangster. "We'd stop for breakfast in Windsor and the café would have our bacon and eggs on the table waiting for us. What's interesting is there was no motorway then. We used to leave Hammersmith Broadway dead on 7.30 and go down the Great West Road, have breakfast in Windsor, drive to the studio and still be on set by 8.30!"

John Jay concurs. "Often we would stop at Windsor at a workman's café for breakfast. In the early days there were no facilities at Bray for food, until later, when the canteen was introduced. On foggy days our accountant, who rode a motorcycle, used to guide the coach by riding ahead, though how he could see any better in the fog remains a mystery." Renée Glynne recalls: "I used to travel on the bus when I lived in Willesden Green. Then I moved to my house in Harrow, where I still am, and I went by car. Sometimes it was Jimmy Harvey's car, sometimes mine. We used to pick up Len Harris on the way."

Hammer and its regular crew had found a home. And then, the BBC had a hand in changing the family company's fortunes forever.

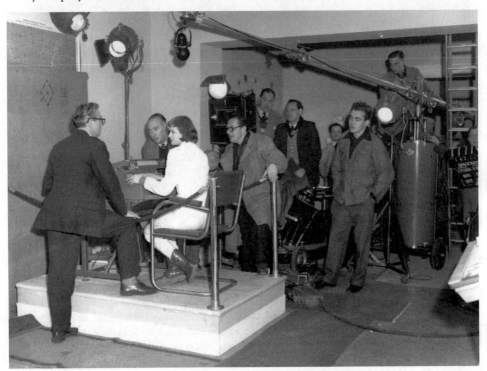

Filming Spaceways (1952). From left to right, Alan Wheatley, Reg Wyer, Eva Bartok, Terence Fisher and Len Harris. Jimmy Sangster stands with his hands in his pockets and Percy Britten operates the sound boom.

THREE

A New Era

(1 9 5 3 - 1 9 5 5)

"If it's successful on TV or radio, then a film version ought to be just as successful." This was the philosophy that had kept Hammer afloat for years, a low-risk approach that clearly worked for them. So when Nigel Kneale's groundbreaking BBC serial *The Quatermass Experiment* started its pub-emptying run at 8.15 pm on Saturday 18 July 1953, they could hardly fail to take notice.

Kneale had written a modest thriller with the working title of 'Bring Something Back'. In it he explored fears common to many at the dawn of the Space Age. Man was being hurled into a new universe – what would he meet out there? What might he bring back? The tale focused around British experimental rocket scientist Bernard Quatermass, who had just launched Britain's first manned rocket from Australia. His experiment confirmed our deepest fears and brought back an alien intelligence capable of destroying our world.

Tony Hinds watched the first episodes with great interest and urged James Carreras to catch up with it too. As Britain became hooked on the exploits of Bernard Quatermass and the horror he had brought back, Hammer rubbed their hands together and approached the BBC. Contract writer Kneale was, however, not party to the deal: "They bought the first one from the BBC. I was glad to see it go. I said, 'Can I have a nice big share of the money you are going to get from Hammer?' They said, 'No!'" [1]

For the time being, however, Professor Quatermass had to wait his turn amid Hammer's already overflowing schedule. A massive eight films were produced at Bray in 1953; even Michael Carreras made a guest appearance, playing his trumpet, in *Face the Music*. Harry Oakes returned to Hammer as focus puller on *The Saint's Return*, the first film of the year. This would unite him with camera operator Len Harris and together they would create a formidable team which would continue through all the classic Hammer horrors, right up until the end of 1961 when they both left after *The Phantom of the Opera*.

Hammer Productions 1953-55

1953:
+ THE SAINT'S RETURN
+ BLOOD ORANGE
+ 36 HOURS
+ FACE THE MUSIC
+ THE HOUSE ACROSS THE LAKE
+ LIFE WITH THE LYONS
+ MURDER BY PROXY
+ FIVE DAYS

1954:
+ THE STRANGER CAME HOME
+ THIRD PARTY RISK
+ MASK OF DUST
+ THE MEN OF SHERWOOD FOREST
+ THE LYONS IN PARIS
+ THE GLASS CAGE
+ BREAK IN THE CIRCLE
+ THE QUATERMASS XPERIMENT

1955:
+ WOMEN WITHOUT MEN
+ CYRIL STAPLETON AND THE SHOWBAND *
+ JUST FOR YOU *
+ THE RIGHT PERSON *
+ THE ERIC WINSTONE BAND SHOW *
+ PARADE OF THE BANDS *
+ A MAN ON THE BEACH *
+ DICK TURPIN – HIGHWAYMAN *
+ ERIC WINSTONE'S STAGECOACH *
+ THE EDMUNDO ROS HALF HOUR *
+ COPENHAGEN *
    * INDICATES FEATURETTE

OPPOSITE: *Richard Wordsworth as the tragic Victor Carroon in* The Quatermass Xperiment *(1954).*

ABOVE: *The trumpeting trio of Kenny Baker, Alex Nicol and Michael Carreras are accompanied by pianist Stan Tracy at the music recording session for* Face the Music *(1953) at Riverside Studios.*
BELOW: *Camera operator Len Harris and his focus puller Harry Oakes film a scene from* Thirty Six Hours *(1953) watched by continuity supervisor Renée Glynne.*

To the right of the ballroom stage today. The ground floor of the arched tower was the staff canteen (now the bar). Above this was the art department. To the right of this is the stairwell. The window top right was the location of producer Anthony Nelson Keys' office.

Val Guest (born 1911) was introduced to Hammer on their comedy spin-off *Life with the Lyons*. He was already a seasoned veteran of screen comedy, having penned numerous Will Hay and Crazy Gang comedies. His arrival at Hammer came by complete chance: "I first met Ben and Bebe Lyon at Gainsborough Pictures when I and Marriott Edgar wrote the script for *Hi Gang*. Then years later, in Wardour Street, I met Ben walking along, and he said he'd been signed up to do his *Life with the Lyons* radio series for Hammer and he asked me, 'Would you like to write and direct it for us?' So that's how I got involved with Hammer."

Up to this point Bray housed no proper stages. As with their country houses before, the rooms of Down Place were transformed into sets which were redressed for each production. They filmed largely in eight rooms of the house, which were tentatively called Stages A-H. 'Stages' A-D were a cluster of rooms on the ground floor, one of which was the old ballroom whose arched French windows faced the grassy knoll on the banks of the Thames. Stages E-G were in the opposite wing and Stage H was where the future general stores would be positioned. These were of course not proper soundproofed stages by any means and the crew often found themselves compromised by the cramped spaces. To make extra space, camera crews were regularly suspended outside the windows.

As producer Aida Young explains, "It was a joke when you look back on it, but it was just wonderful – we never knew any difference. I mean I can remember the sound crew standing outside the window, because there was no room in the room, and poking the boom through the window with a tarpaulin over the top of them, because it was raining. And that's how we worked. The design people were incredible – I mean every time you see a Hammer film, the quality of it is first class, and how they managed it I don't know, because it was just a large house."

Now Phil Leakey also found himself working from a toilet. "My first make-up room was an old bog, can, privy, WC, toilet or whatever you might like to refer to it as. It was halfway up a back staircase and of the kind that when it was used for the purpose for which it was built – when one arose from the seat – one would doubtless bump one's head. Rather small, in fact. Anyway, the throne was boxed over and my store cupboard set on it. A mirror was stuck on one wall with a few quite inadequate lights put around it and a small platform was put in the middle of the room (if one could call it that) and a small chair was placed on that. Couldn't have a proper tip-up or up-and-down

How many Lyons does it take to change a light bulb? Ben Lyon in Val Guest's Life with the Lyons (1953).

chair, the ex-bog not being large enough. Anyway, that was my first make-up room and I grew to love the place ... I then moved on to a bigger and better room next door to Ken Gordon's cashier office." [2]

By 1953 Hammer obviously felt the need for more extensive stage space. In the autumn of that year, they knocked Stages B, C and D into one big rectangular stage. Stage B-C-D, as it now became known, again incorporated the old ballroom and gave a camera run of 110 by 25 feet. This newly converted stage was already in operation when Kine Weekly reported on the studio during filming of Murder by Proxy on 8 October. It was not soundproofed, which meant a deathly hush still had to be cast over the rest of the house during filming, leaving the crew at the mercy of riverboats surging down the Thames and planes zooming through the sky on their way back and forth from nearby Heathrow. As if that wasn't enough, being just a room, the 'stage' had a low ceiling, which meant lights still couldn't be rigged in the normal way and had to be strung from the ceiling or from a ladder, or the scenes simply had to be lit from the floor. Many of the techniques that had been pioneered over previous years by lighting cameraman Cedric Williams still had to be applied.

Next, a purpose-built brick stage was erected at the front entrance of the manor house, which now afforded Hammer the luxury of a proper functioning sound stage. A Kine Weekly article of 8 August 1953 reported that it was "nearing completion" and the finished stage was formally opened in November for the shooting of Five Days, the final film of the year, by its American star Dane Clark. The stage was designed by Orman and partners of Guildford at a cost of over £10,000. It stood 48 by 40 feet and, at 16 feet high, allowed Hammer the luxury of actually rigging their lights from the ceiling. This new stage was also fireproof and would later house many of Hammer's infamous fire scenes. The shooting schedule for the first production of 1954, The Stranger Came Home, calls this stage the 'New Stage', which is how it was referred to until being rechristened Stage 2 when the new Stage 1 opened in September 1957.

The 'New Stage' encroached on the old circular driveway at the front of the house (sacrificing a tree which stood there) and created a makeshift courtyard bordered on the right by the stage itself and on the left by the side wing of the house, containing the main entrance. The bottom right-hand corner of the courtyard contained the entrance to Stage B-C-D and an impressive wisteria twisted itself up the wall. This area would be used to good effect in later horror films. It would double as the prison courtyard seen in the opening moments of The Curse of Frankenstein (1956) and

RIGHT: *The driveway and tree were sacrificed for the construction of the new stage on the right. Note the large wisteria crawling up the front of the house. This photo was taken during the filming of* The Camp on Blood Island *in 1957. The panels resting against the wall on the left were for the camp huts erected on the Bray lot.*

A rare view of the front of Down Place during the filming of Mantrap *(1952) before the new brick stage was built. The staff bus is ariving at the front of the house. Note the circular driveway with tree.*

the main entrance would become the door through which Christopher Lee exits the monastery carrying Suzan Farmer in *Dracula Prince of Darkness* (1965). The main entrance led to the reception area, switchboard and studio manager's office; director Francis Searle also had a flat here. The reception area conveniently led to the restaurant and artists' dressing rooms, so that the actors could collect messages en route.

With their schedule crammed to capacity, Hammer produced a further eight films in 1954. Incredibly, the first seven were shot in just nine months. Michael Carreras wrote his first script for *The Stranger Came Home*. Jimmy Sangster was promoted to production manager on the film, which also gave assistant editor Bill Lenny (born 1928) his editing break at Hammer. "Terry Fisher gave me my first full editing job," Lenny remembered. "I've always loved him for giving me that first job." [3] They would team up later in the year on *Mask of Dust* and, more significantly, on Hammer's classic *Dracula* in 1957.

Also for *Mask of Dust*, John Hollingsworth (born 1916) was appointed music director at Hammer. In 1948 he had begun a ten-year association with the Royal Opera House Convent Garden, conducting operas and Sadlers Wells ballets, and in 1949 he become associate director of the Henry Wood promenade concerts, a position he held for ten years. He also became the principal conductor for the Tunbridge Wells Symphony Orchestra. Around the same time he became acquainted with film work and was appointed assistant musical director to Muir Matheson, working on such films as *Brief Encounter* and *Jungle Mariner* (both 1945).

John Jay now started to expand the stills department. "When we moved there I built a laboratory. There were two large garages and one was made into a cutting room with Jimmy Needs in it. The other garage was made into a stills department, which I was allowed to fit out with the equipment I needed such as enlargers, contact printers, zinc sink etc. My assistant was Tom Edwards, who eventually took over from me when I left. Upstairs in the main house there was a projection room where they used to show the rushes. Through that was another large room which I turned into a studio for doing portraits of artists." His assistant Tom Edwards remembered: "I joined Hammer/Exclusive when they moved into Riverside Studios Hammersmith [*Wings of Danger* and *Stolen Face* in 1951], to do the processing for their stills man, John Jay. When the unit returned to Bray, I was unable to join them as the studio did not have a stills darkroom, so I continued to work from a small London photographic studio in which John had an interest. This arrangement must have lasted for something like two years, when we were able to organise a darkroom at Bray." [4]

Chief carpenter, then construction manager, Freddie Ricketts was Bray's first studio manager and would be followed by Arthur Kelly in October 1955. Pauline Wise, later to become a continuity supervisor and marry assistant director Hugh Harlow, started as a receptionist at Bray straight from school in 1954, while *The Stranger Came Home* was on the floor, also acting as secretary to studio managers Ricketts and Kelly. "I worked in the reception for a couple of years, also doing letters for the studio manager, Mr Ricketts," Pauline remembers, "and then I think he must have retired, because he left and Mr Kelly joined us. The studio was getting much busier then and it was too much for me to do the jobs of being telephonist, receptionist and looking after the office, so Mr Kelly got some-one in to take over the reception and the telephone and I moved in as his secretary, which I enjoyed.

"I was replaced by Maureen Osborne. She started in reception and then went on to become a producer's secretary, so a vacancy came up again for telephonist/receptionist and Christine Addaway (now Stevens) came to be interviewed and she got the job in 1957. She was a trained telephonist and she stayed for a few years." Pauline would later become secretary to Anthony Nelson Keys when he became general manager of the studio in April 1959, before being persuaded by Michael Carreras and Tony Hinds to take up continuity work.

Pauline's future husband, Hugh Harlow, joined the company around the same time as 'office junior' at Hammer House, but soon had duties at Bray as well, where he worked as a runner on the production floor. "I came straight in from school – I was a lad of 16," Hugh remembers. "I was going to go into engineering with my father, who had his own company, but I had no real desire to go into that, much to his disappointment, and I duly responded to a request passed down through one of the old boys at Exclusive Films for an office junior in the distribution department. It wasn't a publicised advert. Hammer Films was then just a small production arm of Exclusive Films, working with Robert Lippert on these sort of B-features that would go out in a twin-feature role in the cinemas. I went for the interview and so started at Hammer House within a few weeks of finishing school.

'Hammer were then just getting a bit bigger and had never had an office boy before. Exclusive Films were on the second floor of Hammer House and Hammer were on the fifth and I was sent up to the fifth floor. I was only there for a week, or two weeks at the most, sticking on stamps, when I was seconded to Michael Carreras and Tony Hinds and from there I used to make the odd trip down to their home studio at Bray – catch the train from Waterloo down to Windsor Riverside, a fantastic outing that was – and was launched into the colourful world of film making, to see the other side of the business. As time went on, I spent longer times there and in between I was actually attached to a film as a runner, a gofer, and when that finished I would go back to the office."

Break in the Circle in 1954 was the first film on which Hugh served as a runner. He would become a 3rd assistant director in 1956 on *X the Unknown*.

1954 proved to be a busy year for Val Guest at Hammer. He started by taking Don Taylor through his paces in Hammer's first colour feature, *The Men of Sherwood Forest*, followed by writing and directing two other pictures: a Lyons sequel, *The Lyons in Paris*, and Hammer's second colour

Val Guest prepares a scene for Break in the Circle (1954). Len Harris is behind the camera in the helicopter.

THE QUATERMASS XPERIMENT

PRINCIPAL PHOTOGRAPHY: 18 October to December 1954
DISTRIBUTION:
  UK: Exclusive; 82 minutes; Certificate 'X'.
  USA: United Artists; 78 minutes; US title: The Creeping Unknown
b/w
UK RELEASE:
  TRADE SHOW: 25 August 1955 at Studio One
  PREMIÈRE: 26 August 1955 at London Pavilion, Piccadilly Circus with The Eric Winstone Band Show
  GENERAL RELEASE: 20 November 1955, on the ABC circuit with Rififi
US RELEASE:
  June 1956, with The Black Sleep

DIRECTOR: Val Guest; PRODUCER: Anthony Hinds; SCREENPLAY: Richard Landau, Val Guest based on the BBC television play by Nigel Kneale; ART DIRECTOR: J Elder Wills; DIRECTOR OF PHOTOGRAPHY: Walter Harvey; CAMERA OPERATOR: Len Harris; FOCUS PULLER: Harry Oakes; ASSISTANT DIRECTOR: Bill Shore; 2ND ASSISTANT DIRECTOR: Aida Young; EDITOR: James Needs; ASSISTANT EDITOR: Henry Richardson; MUSIC: James Bernard; MUSIC SUPERVISOR: John Hollingsworth; SOUND RECORDISTS: H C Pearson, John Woodiwiss; SOUND CAMERA OPERATOR: Don Alton; BOOM OPERATOR: Percy Britten; CLAPPER: Tommy Friswell; MAKE-UP: Phil Leakey; HAIRSTYLIST: Monica Hustler;

PRODUCTION MANAGER: T S Lyndon-Haynes; CONTINUITY: Renée Glynne; WARDROBE: Molly Arbuthnot; SPECIAL EFFECTS: Les Bowie; SPECIAL EFFECTS ASSISTANTS: Vic Margutti, Roy Field, Ray Caple; STILLS PHOTOGRAPHER: John Jay; Production SECRETARY: Dora Thomas; CONSTRUCTION MANAGER: Freddie Ricketts; CHIEF ELECTRICIAN: Jack Curtis; MASTER PLASTERER: Arthur Banks; PROP MASTER: Tommy Money; PROPS BUYER: Jim Day; CASHIER: Ken Gordon; ACCOUNTANT: Larry Edmunds

Brian Donlevy (Prof Quatermass); Jack Warner (Inspector Lomax); Margia Dean (Judith Carroon); Richard Wordsworth (Victor Carroon); David King-Wood (Dr Gordon Briscoe); Thora Hird (Rosie); Gordon Jackson (TV producer); Harold Lang (Christie); Lionel Jeffries (Blake); Maurice Kaufmann (Marsh); Gron Davies (Green); Stanley Van Beers (Reichenheim); Frank Phillips (BBC announcer); Arthur Lovegrove (Sergeant Bromley); John Stirling (Major); Eric Corrie (young man); Margaret Anderson (Maggie); Henry Longhurst (Maggie's father); Michael Godfrey (fireman); Fred Johnson (Inspector); George Roderick (local policeman); Ernest Hare (firechief); John Kerr (laboratory assistant); John Wynn (Best); Toke Townley (chemist); Bartlett Mullins (zookeeper); Molly Glessing (mother at zoo); Mayne Lynton (zoo official); Harry Brunsing (night porter); Barry Lowe (Tucker); Jane Aird (Mrs Lomax); Sam Kydd (station sergeant); Arthur Gross (floor boy); James Drake (sound engineer); Edward Dane (station policeman); Basil Dignam (Sir Lionel); Betty Impey (first nurse); Marianne Stone (second nurse); Jane Asher (girl)

feature, the thriller Break in the Circle, with Forrest Tucker. Tony Hinds thought he was the obvious choice to lead his Quatermass project, as Guest explains. "Tony Hinds had bought the TV series and they were going to make a film of it and he asked would I read it. I said, 'We're just going on holiday now to Tangiers.' And he said, 'Oh, all right, take it with you.' And he arrived at Northolt airport with an enormous stack of scripts, all six episodes, which was all I needed on the plane, and he said, 'Read them.' I wasn't all that excited – it wasn't my cup of tea at all."

On holiday Guest tossed the scripts into a corner and forgot about them, and there they would have stayed but for the intervention of his wife, actress Yolande Donlan. "They were at the side of the bed for about a week. Suddenly Yolande said, 'What's this?' I said, 'It's something Tony Hinds wants me to read.' 'Well, have you read it?' she asked. 'I said no, it's science fiction or horror. I don't want to do that.' She said, 'Since when have you been ethereal?' I said, 'All right, I'd better read it then', so I read it on the beach at Tangiers and I thought it was very exciting stuff." Val Guest was on board.

Richard Landau wrote the screenplay, condensing Kneale's teleplay to a more manageable length. Landau's script was further streamlined and adapted by Guest. Landau was no stranger to Hammer, having already written six scripts for them, including the early foray into science fiction, Spaceways, in 1952. Guest completed the process, trawling the best from Nigel Kneale's three-hour teleplay. It was a difficult task and one that Kneale has never forgiven him for. Guest nonchalantly explains, "I don't think he's very happy with anything I did on his films. He's a brilliant writer, but he was inclined to get too verbose and we had to cut that down, condense it, for the screen."

The plot line Landau and Guest are most criticised for leaving out is the one concerning the central character of Victor Carroon; in Kneale's story he is three men in one – he has absorbed the characteristics and knowledge of his fellow astronauts. Moreover, they are still alive within him. This formed the basis of Kneale's conclusion, where Quatermass literally 'talks' the monster to death in Westminster Abbey by appealing to the remnants of the three astronauts to defeat the thing they have become. Guest instead settled on the customary torching of the thing as it drapes itself around the Abbey scaffolding, which admittedly does make for a very exciting climax. He also skimped on Kneale's original premise in the scene where Carroon concocts a catalytic potion in the

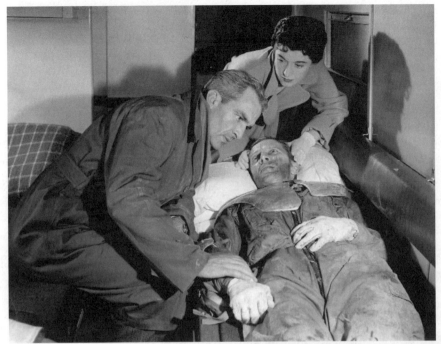

LEFT: Dr Briscoe (David King-Wood) examines the traumatised astronaut Victor Carroon (Richard Wordsworth). Judith Caroon (Margia Dean) shows concern for her husband, who has become the third victim of The Quatermass Xperiment (1954).

BELOW: Professor Quatermass (Brian Donlevy), Briscoe (David King-Wood) and Inspector Lomax (Jack Warner) inspect one of Carroon's victims in The Quatermass Xperiment (1954).

chemist shop, utilising the chemistry know-how of his absorbed colleague Charles Greene.

With such 'horror' pictures, Hammer developed the custom of submitting the script to the British Board of Film Censors (BBFC) for their opinion prior to shooting. The script would be sent to the Board Secretary, who would pass it down to his team of readers/examiners (readers and examiners being one and the same: they 'read' scripts and 'examine' films). He would then summarise their views in a final report, which he would send back to Hammer for guidance. This was a voluntary process and the Board's advice, though sometimes ignored, gave Hammer early notice of scenes that should

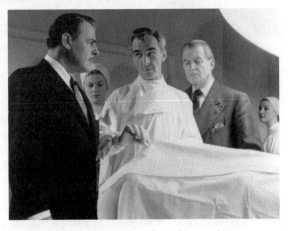

be modified or omitted. There would follow a similar but more formal process where the examiners would demand the cuts necessary to achieve the desired certificate. Many of the Board's records still exist, giving a tremendous insight into the social and moral standards of the time, showing what was permissible and what Hammer could, and tried to, get away with.

Production manager Tommy Lyndon-Haynes passed on a copy of the script for The Quatermass Xperiment to Board Secretary Arthur Watkins on 27 August 1954 and received a reply from him on 10 September:

"We have now read the screenplay of The Quatermass Experiment which was enclosed with your letter of the 27th August. I must warn you at this stage that, while we accept this story in principle for the 'X' category, we could not certificate, even in that category, a film treatment in which the horrific element was so exaggerated as to be nauseating and revolting to adult audiences. Nor can we pass uncut, even in the 'X' category, sequences in which physical agony and screams of pain or terror are unnecessarily exaggerated or prolonged. Most of the following points of detail relate to these two general observations.

P.6. There should be no shot of a horse 'wild with fright' running towards the flames.

P.24. The references to 'crucifying' and 'a cross' should be omitted.

P.49. Carroon's 'knotted hands'; P.80. his fingers twisting in time with the heartbeats; P.89. his hands opening and closing violently, etc. There is some danger in these sequences of shots of the gradually transforming hands which will be too repulsive for 'X': this applies particularly to any close-ups.

P.53, 79, 89. Shots of Carroon's convulsive movements and agonised face should not be prolonged.

P.86. Ramsay's screams should not be unreasonably prolonged; there should be no shot of him on fire and the statement that the driver has been burned alive should be omitted. [NB This is a reference to a gang of crooks who kidnap Carroon. The scene was part of the television version, but went unused in the film.]

P.96. Care should be taken that Christie's dead body, and all other corpses in the film, are not too gruesome; P.98. It is stated that a dead face 'looked like a punctured balloon', and anything of this kind would not be acceptable. On P.108 the fungoid growth on the dead chemist's face is likely to be too horrible.

P.103 and elsewhere. While we recognise that Carroon, in his plight, must 'look pretty terrible', there is an obvious need for discretion in all shots of Carroon, of his fungoid arm and of the mass of writhing vegetation which he finally becomes. (cf. P.133, 142, 148)

P.120. The noise of terrified animals [in the zoo sequence] should not be overdone or too prolonged.

P.124. 'What a mess ... all grey ... and the blood ... and alive.' These words seem unnecessarily nauseating. (Here and elsewhere, reasonable restraint should be used in describing the Thing, even if the visuals are discreet.)

As I told Colonel Carreras on the telephone yesterday, I think it would be helpful if we had a talk with the producer before the completion of the shooting script, which we should see in due course. I am returning the copy of the screenplay in the meantime."

Following some night shooting at Chessington Zoo on Tuesday 12 October, the cameras rolled on *The Quatermass Xperiment* (Hammer eventually dropping the 'E' in Experiment to emphasise the film's 'X' certificate) on Monday 18 October 1954 at Bray Studios, with a ridiculously low budget of £42,000. Val Guest conducted the show with a deliberate documentary-style approach, which added to the film's stark realism and stopped it from degrading into another clichéd monster on the loose vehicle. As he explained, "When I first agreed to do it, I said, 'I will do it, but only if you let me treat it as though I was taking a newsreel and we had a correspondent on the story who followed it up – and I would like to use a lot of handheld cameras, unsteady here and there.' They were very reluctant, but finally they did let me have it."

Guest's camera crew were more than competent in realising his dream. Behind the camera was the stalwart Len Harris and his focus puller, Harry Oakes, both of whom would continue through the Gothics to follow. Walter Harvey's stark black-and-white photography added to the tension, in particular highlighting and intensifying Phil Leakey's weird and startling make-up for Richard Wordsworth. The film was shot in the rooms of Down Place (Lomax's office was one of the upstairs rooms facing the Thames) and Bray's first two stages. The art director was none other than James Elder Wills, one of the directors of the original Hammer company in the 1930s.

Throughout his years at Bray, Harry Oakes kept a personal diary of events off and on. For *The Quatermass Xperiment*, having noted the 12 October pre-production shooting at Chessington, he recorded rocket site filming on the 25th, night exteriors in Bray on the 27th, and day exteriors on Westminster Bridge on Saturday the 30th. He also noted, as late as 31 December, meeting Elmo Williams (director of the next production, *Women Without Men*) at Hammer House and shooting *Quatermass* crowd scenes with Len Harris prior to continuing work after dinner on *Women Without Men*, then called *Prison Story*.

Location work took Hammer into Bray village for the opening scenes in which fire engines rush past Bray garage to the crashed rocket. Sadly, the garage has been pulled down in recent years. Producer Aida Young was then a young second assistant director. "I remember how difficult that was, because we did our exteriors in Bray village. It was my first time, I think, on a genuine location and we had such trouble, and quite rightly, with the people who lived there, because we were turning lights on and making such a noise, and of course it was part of my job to make sure that everybody was quiet and nice about it. It was very, very difficult, but Val Guest and the crew were so nice to work with."

The actual ship was erected in a field on Water Oakley farm, next door to Bray Studios, and clever camera angles hid the fact that it was conveniently leaning against a tree. Continuity supervisor Renée Glynne remembers the location work with the rocket: "It was in the field, which is on the left as you drive in. [Female lead] Margia Dean sat at the back of the control van on my customised continuity stool and I had to stand writing my notes until the props found a replacement stool for me." The crew went into nearby Windsor for some of the street shots, which included the chemist shop, 'Woods of Windsor Pharmacy', on Queen Charlotte Street – the establishment still exists – and Goswell Hill (leading down from Windsor Central Station), where the trail of slime climbed the 30-foot wall.

Jimmy Sangster was 2nd unit production manager and was left in charge of arranging the scene where the lights go out all over London. "I wasn't actually working on The Quatermass Xperiment," recalled Sangster. "I was doing another picture and I took a second unit out. The idea was that we were going to switch all the lights out, because all the electricity was going to be diverted to Westminster Abbey to kill the monster. I remember I went to Battersea Power Station, which was fully operative in those days, and arranged with the guy in charge that exactly at 10 o'clock, or some specified time, he would turn off the floodlights in front of the station. We synchronised our watches and I went back across the river to the camera crew and about 30 seconds to whatever this time was I said, 'Roll them.' They rolled them and we were photographing the power station and sure enough, exactly on time, the lights went out. I was about to say 'Cut' when they started going out everywhere else all along the river. The guy had misunderstood and he started switching off the main power. There was a little article in the paper about it the next day saying there was a slight blip in the electricity currents in London last night. Nobody quite knew what it was."

A pensive Joan Rice in Women Without Men (1955). The film was shot at Bray under the working title Prison Story.

Robert Lippert brought in 55-year-old US star Brian Donlevy to play Quatermass. According to Val Guest, "He was all right, no problem at all once you kept him sober! Nigel Kneale was expecting to find Quatermass like he was on television, a sensitive British scientist, not some American stomping around, but to me Donlevy gave it absolute reality." Kneale's views are very different. "He was a tragic creature – Hollywood story. He was a good heavy comedian who'd played in a lot of films directed by Preston Sturges, a Hollywood director of the 1940s. He'd starred in a film called The Great McGinty – Donlevy was the star – and he was very, very good, and you see him again and again in those pictures and he could really do it, but he became a total drunk, as a lot of Hollywood people did at that time, and it finished poor old Donlevy off. When he came onto the set, he couldn't remember the name of the film or the scene or any of his lines, he was prompted all the way. He would just get through it with a burst of anger – that was the only thing that sustained him – anger and shouting at people. That helped him remember his lines, but he was truly terrible. He had no notion of what the character could be and he wasn't interested."[1]

Father David (Toke Townley), Lady Alys (Eileen Moore), Sir Guy Belton (David King-Wood) and Hubert (Harold Lang) greet Robin Hood (Don Taylor) in Val Guest's *The Men of Sherwood Forest* (1954).

In stark contrast, Richard Wordsworth's portrayal of the tormented Victor Carroon steals the show. The pathos and anguish he injects into the role is awesome, aided and abetted by Phil Leakey's subtle make-up, exaggerated by the atmospheric lighting of Walter Harvey. Wordsworth remembered that "My part in the film had been over about 20 minutes when the monster attacks Westminster Abbey. In that sequence the monster has become a great round blob of rubber solution draped over everything. A landlady up north said to me, 'Mr Wordsworth, you were so good. And in the Abbey scene – your make-up! It was marvellous!'" [5] Jack Warner played a likable Lomax 'by arrangement with J Arthur Rank Organisation', to whom he was then contracted. Warner was a popular character actor on the verge of his successful *Dixon of Dock Green* TV show, which would be launched by the BBC the following year. A believable Dr Briscoe, David King-Wood had already starred in two Val Guest/Hammer films that year, *The Men of Sherwood Forest* and *Break in the Circle*. Margia Dean was allegedly girlfriend of Fox president Spyros Skouras and had secured the role through his association with Robert Lippert.

Val Guest inserted an interesting scene which was strangely prophetic of things to come at Hammer. Guest obviously saw a parallel between Kneale's tragic man-made monster and Mary Shelley's Frankenstein creature. This prompted him to write a scene, which is not in Kneale's original story, in which Victor Carroon, increasingly twisted by the alien influence within him, meets a little girl played by Jane Asher – a scene clearly borrowed from James Whale's immortal *Frankenstein*. Little did Hammer know that within another two years they would be turning to Frankenstein themselves to begin an unparalleled series of Gothic shockers.

The film's focus puller, Harry Oakes, remembers quite vividly an incident involving make-up man Phil Leakey's 'cactus arm'. "We were pals, you know, Phil and I. He was very good to me because I didn't have transport in those days and when we worked at Gilston Park, I used to get a bus to the North Circular Road and he used to pick me up there. Otherwise I would have had a hell of a journey getting down to Hammersmith to get onto Hammer's coach. This particular week we were shooting in the East India Docks in London. My wife was looking after our small daughter then and she was down in Chichester. I explained to Phil that I was going down there and sure enough he gave me a lift to Victoria Station. He lived at Walton on Thames, you see. So I sat in the car and I said, 'What's this I'm sitting on?' And it was horrible – it looked horrible without touching it – this arm with bits sticking out of it. I had an empty stomach as well, so it didn't go down very well!"

Tony Hinds brought back the Bowie-Margutti company for the special effects. Les Bowie created the monster at the end out of tripe and rubber, but the wires that control it are all too visible. Bowie told *Kine Weekly*: "We went to the slaughterhouse, got some tripe, and cut it up. We made a wooden frame with lots of joints. After photographing it in miniature, we married it up with paintings on foreground glass – and eventually made it look like the monster in Westminster Abbey. Tripe is flabby, you see. Anything else and we'd have had wrinkles in it. As it was, we used to have to warm up the stuff before photographing it."

Bowie's assistant on the film, Roy Field, remembers, "Oh that horrible creature. It was a mixture of everything, that was. Les and Ray Caple made that. They stitched up rubber and bits and pieces to make these octopus-type tentacles. They made about three of them at different scales. The largest was about eight to ten feet across, then one approximately three feet across, and the smallest one was about 12 inches across. Then we built a model of the tubular scaffolding in the Abbey and Vic Margutti and I were the ones who photographed it. The model was about eight to ten feet across. It was quite large really for a model, but it had to be to get the actions and the sparks, because it had to be electrocuted, so we had to have a lot of spark effects and it has to be quite big scale to make that look reasonable. They were pyrotechnics, little fuses that burn rather quickly. Les made all those up, I didn't have anything to do with that. We made some of the tubular scaffolding out of rubber, so it would melt and bend and twist."

Michael Carreras added "I can still remember the conference following the screening of the *Quatermass* rough cut, prior to the screening of the final special effects shots. The monster hanging over Westminster Abbey at the end was a bit of a gooey mess. Out of that conference came the decision to give the monster some semblance of humanity in its last moments, to reflect the man it had once been. It was decided to incorporate within the sludge a faint image of a human eye, although of enormous proportions, and to have a distant, final human scream. That improved the Quatermass monster, and in a strange way, it also foreshadowed the human monsters who were featured in the horror cycle." [6]

Roy Field discusses the rocket effects: "The field out at Bray where the rocket lands was full of corn. Les thought that if he could set it alight with petrol, it would look as if the heat from the rocket landing had set fire to it. However, it poured with rain that night, so it was a bit of a disaster. The rain beat us, so we had to do it in miniature instead. That model wasn't very big actually. It was only five to six feet high and it had to include the model of the rocket too.

"The last shot of the picture is interesting, because we showed the model of the rocket taking off and going into the sky. We had difficulty in doing that, because we couldn't find any building high enough to pull it up, so Les came up with the idea of pivoting it on an arc, so we didn't have to pan right up and look straight up into the sky. We just had to pan up to about 90 degrees and then it looked as if it went away from us. It was quite a cunning little rig that worked very well. We got away with it because it was night and very dark and really all you see are the lights from the bottom of the rocket. Vic Margutti arranged to have some special bulbs made that burn very hot in the bottom and we put some little pyrotechnics in there as well to give it a bit of spark and life, and that's how it was done, very quickly and very simply."

The Quatermass team toiled for five weeks before the fruits of their labour were handed over to post-production for editing, sound recording/editing and music scoring/recording. James Bernard (born 20 September 1925) composed a sombre and uneasy score to perfectly complement the action in this, his inaugural flight with Hammer. As a pupil at Wellington College, Bernard had been introduced to Benjamin Britten, who took an interest in the young hopeful. After serving four years in the Royal Air Force, he received a government grant and entered the Royal College Of Music, studying piano and composition. It was during his three years at the Royal College that he realised he would never achieve the proficiency needed to be a concert pianist and concentrated instead on his composing. This was facilitated by Bernard's continuing association with Benjamin Britten, spending a year with him copying out the vocal score for his opera Billy Budd. An interesting sideline grew from his love for the theatre and his relationship with author and film critic Paul Dehn, with whom he shared a flat. Dehn and Bernard together wrote the original story for *Seven Days to Noon* (1950), for which they won the Oscar for 'best original story'. Despite this, it was

Bernard's passion for music that carried him onwards and he was soon introduced to the BBC by a friend of Dehn called Patric Dickenson, where he began to score a number of their radio plays.

However, Bernard's employment on The Quatermass Xperiment came about quite by chance. "I first met John Hollingsworth when he conducted my very first score for radio, The Death of Hector," Bernard explained. "In those days they played the music live in the studio while the play was going on. I did quite a lot of radio plays in the early fifties and John conducted a few of them. The final play I scored for BBC Radio was an all-star production of The Duchess of Malfi by John Webster. It is a marvellous play and this production contained Peggy Ashcroft, then at the peak of her career, Paul Scofield and other equally illustrious actors. I wrote the music for strings and percussion and asked John Hollingsworth if he would conduct. It is a real horror play, full of murders, poisoning and stabbing, and luckily by then they were actually recording the music on tape. It was not long after this that Anthony Hinds rang up John Hollingsworth from Bray studios and said, 'John, we've almost finished our current film, The Quatermass Xperiment, and John Hotchkiss, the composer who was going to do it, is ill and can't do it. It's getting rather urgent, because we'll soon be ready for the music. Have you any young composers you might recommend?' John knew I was longing to get into films, so said, 'Yes, I think I have somebody who might suit you.' Fortunately I had done this score for The Duchess of Malfi, which is, as I say, rather horrific, and he had it on tape, so he rushed down to Bray Studios and played the tape to Tony Hinds, who said, 'Yes, fine. Ask him to do the score.' So that was the beginning and I got paid a hundred pounds."

Bernard discussed his approach to this first Hammer horror. "I went down to Hammer's plush little viewing theatre in Soho and watched the film several times to get the feel of it. Then finally we had a music session, stopping after each reel to discuss exactly where we felt music was needed. The editor and his assistant would be there, and the sound editor, because he would know where there was going to be a thunder storm or horses' hooves, etc. So you could plan out the music reel by reel, exactly where the music would start and stop, and it was the taxing job of the long-suffering assistant editor to note all this down, measure it out, and send you lists of what were called time sheets. One had to be severely practical and decide what was the feeling one needed to get. With science fiction stories one wanted weirdness and I often found that a single line of music worked better than a great big symphonic sound. John said, 'Well, as you did so well with strings and percussion on The Duchess of Malfi, let's use the same combination again for The Quatermass Xperiment.' I agreed and the result was apparently okay." It was more than okay; it would ensure the composer's participation in many of the Gothics to come. James Bernard would soon define the very sound of Hammer horror.

Now Hammer held their collective breath. It was not a good time for a British film producer. The interest in TV had grown, independent television was looming on the horizon for a September 1955 start date and cinema box-offices were starting to suffer. As Quatermass finished, Hammer had seven features on their shelves yet to be distributed. They had to continue with Women Without Men, which was already in preparation while The Quatermass Xperiment was on the floor and which brought the Lippert deal to a close. But the production schedule was brought to a halt right there. Instead they invested in a series of featurettes, which gave Michael Carreras an opportunity to experiment in widescreen. It came as no surprise that the subjects he chose were largely jazz-oriented. Such short features were cheap and in demand – sufficiently so for Hammer to tread water with them while they waited for the climate to change and, of course, for the response to Quatermass.

Harry Oakes recalls: "When widescreen first started, they shot in Cinemascope and the films were two to two and a half hours long, so there was a market for small three-reelers. Hammer cashed in on this and they made several three-reelers, including musicals such as The Eric Winstone Band Show." Michael Carreras remembered, "At the time the Cinemascope lens came out we had an association with 20th Century-Fox. The lens was like a huge piece of glass and everybody was showing it to everybody else and didn't know what to do with it. This was a period when Hammer was undergoing a transition. We only made one picture that year and were making loads of shorts as we were approaching the period of The Curse of Frankenstein and were gearing ourselves to that. Someone came along with this huge lens, put it on the table and said: 'Do you know, we charge thousands of pounds a week to loan this out? But if you would like to use it and we can see what the film looks like, you can have it for nothing!' We did use it – very badly as no one told us how to use it!" [7]

Hammer made sure their widescreen tests were not wasted. They began work on a short feature, *The Right Person*, on 9 March 1955 and, as Harry Oakes explained, made good use of location. "On *The Right Person* we went to Denmark for a week, to Copenhagen. The film needed scenes of Copenhagen and there was no library material in Cinemascope, so Michael Carreras, Len Harris and myself had to go to there and, while we were at it, we shot a small travelogue as well, called *Copenhagen*."

Between 23 March and 29 April, principal photograpy took place on *Women Without Men*. On 18 July, they began work on an interesting little thriller called *A Man on the Beach*, from a screenplay by Jimmy Sangster, about a robbery

Michael Ripper and Michael Medwin slug it out in Joseph Losey's A Man on the Beach *(1955). The short film marked the writing debut of Jimmy Sangster.*

at a casino in the South of France with Michael Medwin, Michael Ripper and Donald Wolfit. The film was directed by American blacklisted director Joseph Losey. Harry Oakes recorded in his diary that location work using the Rolls-Royce 'getaway' car took place between 3 and 5 August: "Len, an assistant and I left Hammer House 4.00 pm. [Producer?] Mickey Delamar drove us to Dover in the old Rolls-Royce! Stayed at 'The White Cliffs'. Early call to Hythe to fly the old Rolls and up to Ostend. Arrived 9.10, met Joe Losey and Tony Hinds. Shots between Zoote and Ostend."

Around this time the favoured few, including Len Harris and Harry Oakes, found themselves on a retainer at Hammer. Harry Oakes explained: "That was quite generous of them really. We went from picture to picture and about 1955/56 the idea was that in between pictures you would be on a retainer. We would be on two days a week as it were, half a week's pay. So if we were off three weeks, we would get half a week's pay each week. If we wanted to work any of the other days, they were quite willing to let us provided that they got first call. I did one or two jobs like that. For instance, Len and I worked on the second unit on a picture called *The Baby and the Battleship* and we got clearance from Hammer and we had a nice two or three weeks in Malta and places."

Len and Harry would often be farmed away from Hammer when they weren't needed. "And there was a time too when we were hired out in the summer of 1955 to *Jack Hylton Presents*, filming stage shows for commercial television at the Adelphi. It was good for me because I was living in Highgate and it was just a case of getting on the Northern line. It was a luxury for me instead of traipsing 30 miles to Bray Studios. Mickey Delamar came to see us one evening and said they've got a picture coming into Bray about Dick Turpin and they wanted Len to light it. I thought that would be great, Len could light it and I could operate on it, but no, he didn't want to light, so in the end he went on the picture to operate and I finished doing the operating on these shows at the Adelphi."

Dick Turpin – Highwayman was another widescreen short, but in colour, starring Philip Friend as Dick Turpin.

Throughout 1955, one by one Hammer put out its remaining films. *The Quatermass Xperiment* was submitted to the BBFC on 3 June and was eventually granted its 'X' certificate. It was tradeshown at Studio One on Thursday 25 August and premièred at the London Pavilion, Piccadilly Circus the following day, supported by one of Michael Carreras' jazz shorts, *The Eric Winstone Band Show*. The film received mixed reviews, but they were generally favourable. "Val Guest directed and A Hinds produced. None of these – if I may put it so – are classed among our swells; but they have done their job well, and the result seems to me a better film than either *The War of the Worlds* or *Them*" (*New Statesman*); "That TV pseudo-science shocker *The Quatermass Xperiment* has been filmed. And quitermess they've made of it, too" (*Reynolds News*). More importantly, however, the public loved it and the success continued on general release across Britain on the ABC circuit from 20 November, supported by the 'X'-rated French thriller *Rififi*. The touch paper was lit and Hammer began production again in earnest. All they needed was a story and a script...

═══ F O U R ═══

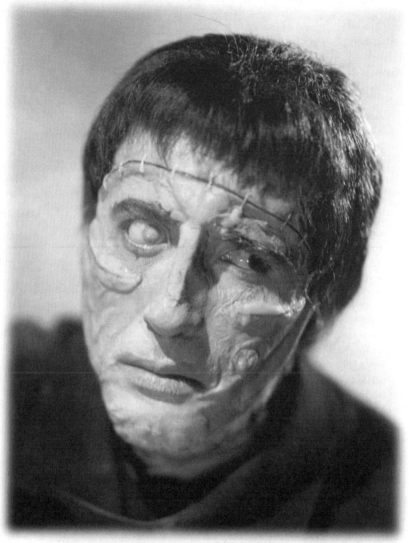

Enter Frankenstein

(1 9 5 6)

Faced with the huge success of their *Quatermass* venture, Tony Hinds, Michael Carreras and Jimmy Sangster were the participants in an informal story conference held in late 1955. "The *Quatermass Xperiment* had just come out and it was a big success," Sangster recalls. "And they said, 'Let's do another science fiction film right away.' But there wasn't anything around at that moment. Tony, Michael and myself were sitting around the office one day and I said, 'Instead of a monster coming from outer space, how about a monster that comes from the centre of the earth?' Then Tony said, 'Oh yeah and maybe so and so.' Then Michael said, 'So and so', and I said 'So and so.'

"And in the end of an hour we got sort of a rough story together and Tony said, 'You came up with the most ideas, go away and write it.' I said, 'I'm not a writer for Christ's sake, I'm a production manager.' He said, 'Well no, write it. We'll pay you as a production manager. Go and write it and if we like it, we'll pay you as a writer as well.' So I went and wrote the treatment. They liked the treatment and the same thing happened. Tony said, 'All right, go and write the script. If we like it we'll pay you.' So I went and wrote the script and they paid me £450 and I was production manager on the film as well. And that's how I became a writer."

The project became *X the Unknown*, the story of an unstoppable mass of radioactive slime which emanates from a fissure on a lonely Scottish moor during a routine army training exercise. Atomic scientist Adam Royston must stop the thing before it hits Inverness in its hungry search for radioactivity. Hammer asked Nigel Kneale if they could use the character of Professor Quatermass. Kneale refused – he had his own plans for his favourite rocket scientist.

> # Hammer Productions
> ## — 1956 —
>
> ✦ *X the Unknown*
> ✦ *Quatermass 2*
> ✦ *The Steel Bayonet*
> ✦ *The Curse of Frankenstein*
>
> FEATURETTE:
> ✦ *Day of Grace*

OPPOSITE: *Christopher Lee as the Creature in* The Curse of Frankenstein *(1956).*

Tony Hinds submitted a draft script to Arthur Watkins, Secretary of the BBFC, on 23 November 1955: "Please find enclosed script of *X the Unknown* which I am to produce in January, and for which I would like an 'X' certificate."

Reader/examiner Audrey Field (AOF or AF in some reports) was not impressed and commented on 24 November: "These people, having prospered exceedingly on the proceeds of Quatermass, now appear to have been looking at *Quatermass II* [Nigel Kneale's second TV serial, which ended its BBC run two days later], which goes in for shots of leprous-looking sores and of people engulfed in lethal oil. This epic is described by the BBC as 'not for children or nervous persons', but I think most grown-ups would find it disgusting rather than frightening – certainly I found certain shots pretty nauseating: and *X – the Unknown* is heading in the same direction. I think the film company should be strongly cautioned on treatment: we cannot stop them making the film, but I think it will revolt many people – even *The Quatermass Experiment* did this, and it was mild compared with the present subject. The free use of the words 'evil' and 'obscene' is ominous."

"Well, no one can say the customers won't have had their money's worth by now. In fact, someone will almost certainly have been sick. We must have a great deal more restraint, and much more done by onlookers' reactions instead of by shots of 'pulsating obscenity', hideous scars, hideous sightless faces, etc, etc. It is keeping on and on in the same vein that makes this script so outrageous. They must take it away and prune. Before they take it away, however, I think the President should read it. I have a stronger stomach than the average (for viewing purposes) and perhaps I ought to be reacting even more strongly."

A further reader added on 30 November: "This is a mixture of scientific hokum and sadism in equal parts without benefit of wit or humour and incidentally a wretched exploitation of the 'X' certificate. I'm upset that we cannot reject it. Our only course, as AF suggests, is to insist on drastic pruning when they make a shooting script."

Watkins passed on the bad news to Tony Hinds in a letter dated 4 December.

"We have now read the draft script of *X – the Unknown* which was enclosed with your letter of 23rd November. While we have no basic objection to the story for the 'X' category, we consider that a great number of details will prove too nauseating even for that category and that much more restraint will be necessary in preparing the shooting script, which we should see. This applies particularly to shots of 'the unknown', which are too numerous and in many cases likely to be too revolting, and to the shots of its victims, alive and dead. The following is a complete list of the details which will need to be treated with greater discretion or, in some cases, to be deleted altogether:

P.21. The 'angry blisters and sores' on Lancing's burnt body. These burns should be more discreetly suggested. The same applies to, P.22, the burn scars on the old soldier.

P.35. The ten-year-old boy's terror, and his scream, call for particular restraint.

Privates 'Haggis' (Ian MacNaughton) and 'Spider' (Anthony Newley) watch as Sergeant Grimsdyke (Michael Ripper) hides the radioactive sample in X the Unknown (1956). The location was a very wet and muddy Gerrards Cross.

X THE UNKNOWN

PRINCIPAL PHOTOGRAPHY: 9 January to February 1956
DISTRIBUTION:
  UK: Exclusive; certificate 'X'
  US: Warner Bros
78 MINUTES b/w
UK RELEASE:
  PREMIÈRE: 21 September 1956 at London Pavilion, Picadilly Circus
  GENERAL RELEASE: 5 November 1956, on the ABC circuit with Les Diaboliques
  US RELEASE: May 1957, with The Curse of Frankenstein

DIRECTOR: Leslie Norman; PRODUCER: Anthony Hinds; EXECUTIVE PRODUCER: Michael Carreras; SCREENPLAY: Jimmy Sangster; DIRECTOR OF PHOTOGRAPHY: Gerald Gibbs; ART DIRECTOR: Ted Marshall; DRAUGHTSMAN: Don Mingaye; CAMERA OPERATOR: Len Harris; FOCUS PULLER: Harry Oakes; ASSISTANT DIRECTOR: Chris Sutton; 3RD ASSISTANT DIRECTOR: Hugh Harlow, EDITOR: James Needs; ASSISTANT EDITOR/SOUND EDITOR: Alfred Cox; MUSIC: James Bernard; MUSIC SUPERVISOR: John Hollingsworth; SOUND RECORDIST: Jock May; MAKE-UP/SPECIAL MAKE-UP EFFECTS: Phil Leakey; PRODUCTION MANAGER: Jimmy Sangster; CONTINUITY: June Randall;

WARDROBE: Molly Arbuthnot; SPECIAL EFFECTS: Bowie Margutti Ltd, Jack Curtis; SPECIAL EFFECTS ASSISTANTS: Roy Field, Ray Caple, Brian Johncock; CONSTRUCTION MANAGER: Freddie Ricketts; CHIEF ELECTRICIAN: Jack Curtis; MASTER PLASTERER: Arthur Banks; PROP MASTER: Tommy Money

Dean Jagger (Dr Adam Royston); Edward Chapman (Elliot); Leo McKern (Inspector McGill); Anthony Newley (Pte 'Spider' Webb); Jameson Clark (Jack Harding); William Lucas (Peter Elliot); Peter Hammond (Lt Bannerman); Marianne Brauns (Zena); Ian MacNaughton ('Haggis'); Michael Ripper (Sgt Grimsdyke); John Harvey (Major Cartwright); Edwin Richfield (old/burnt soldier); Jane Aird (Vi Harding); Norman Macowan (Old Tom); Neil Hallet (Unwin); Kenneth Cope (Pte Lancing); Michael Brook (Willie Harding); Frazer Hines (Ian Osborne); Max Brimmell (hospital director); Robert Bruce (Dr Kelly); Brown Derby (vicar); Archie Duncan (Sgt Yeardye); Lawrence James (second guard); Edward Judd (second soldier); Stella Kemball (nurse); Stephenson Lang (reporter); Philip Levene (security man); Brian Peck (first s oldier); Anthony Sager (gateman); Barry Steel (soldier in trench); John Stirling (police car driver); John Stone (Gerry); Frank Taylor (PC Williams); Shaw Taylor (police radio operator); Neil Wilson (Russel)

P.41. The shot of the boy's burns should be omitted altogether.
P.67. The love-making sequence [between Unwin and Marianne] (in which we are told that the girl 'swarms all over' her lover) should be treated with reasonable discretion.
P.68-9. The whole sequence in which the Thing advances upon Unwin and kills him will require much more restraint: there should be no shot of 'horrible blisters' after the oil has

flowed over his hand; and the final shots, in which his face runs into 'horrible blodges of
formless flesh' and the eyeball loosens in its socket, are quite prohibitive.

P.74. Nutty [NB this character is assumed to be one of the soldiers] gives a 'sudden,
terrifying, ear-splitting scream'. Here and elsewhere, it should be remembered that screams
are a powerful ingredient in horror and that, even for the 'X' category, there is a limit.

P.93. The proposed shot of the soldier Haggis in the crevasse ('the skin hangs loosely over the
skeleton, two large empty eye-sockets stare unwinkingly at Peter') is too repulsive.

P.94. The Unknown, as here described ('a dark, seething, putrid mass, writhing with
corruption and hideous rottenness', displaying 'unctuous, oily bubbles' and described as 'this
obscene thing'), is likely to give trouble when the film is submitted for censorship. The 'Thing'
in The Quatermass Experiment – which, incidentally, appeared much less frequently – caused us
some misgivings on viewing the film, and 'the Unknown' in the present script seems likely to
be infinitely more repulsive. The sound-effects, as well as the shots, will call for reasonable
restraint. (Cf. also p. 102, 111, 114, 115, 116, 121, 122, 136, 137, 138, 139. We think that the
shots of it are too numerous, as well as too unpleasant.)

P.115. The shot of the Security Guard 'engulfed in black, viscous slime' should be omitted, and
also, P.116, the close shot of 'the shell of the Security Man', looking like the earlier shot of the
sightless corpse of the soldier in the crevasse.

"It is difficult to assess the quality of this type of film in advance of seeing it, and we can give no
positive guarantee at this stage that the treatment will be acceptable. We should certainly see a
shooting script and, if you think it would be helpful, by all means consult us in the preparation
of it. However, I think I have said enough to indicate our anxiety less the cumulative effect of
repulsive and nauseating shots should go beyond what is acceptable to adult audiences. You might
perhaps find it helpful, in this particular case, to show us a few 'rushes' before shooting is too far
advanced. I return the draft script herewith."

Jimmy Sangster's maiden horror script had certainly struck a raw nerve with the censor, something he would continue to do for years to come. Tony Hinds replied to Watkins on 6 December:
"Thank you for your letter of December 4th and for returning the script. I have noted all your
comments and will act accordingly. The 'angry blisters' on the boy's body will be handled with
care; the 'burn scars' on the Old Soldier will not be in any way horrific; the love-making will be
played for comedy and will not be distasteful; and the shots of the 'Unknown' will be cut down to
the minimum (I only wish I thought it could look half as exciting as the writer has described it!).
With regard to the two horror sequences, Unwin being attacked by the 'Unknown' and the body of
the soldier in the fissure, I think the only thing we can do is shoot them and then show them to you.
The shot of the Security Guard engulfed in slime will simply be a shot of a man sprayed with chocolate blancmange and I do not think it will be upsetting. Thank you for reading the script so quickly."

Hinds wouldn't always be as accommodating with the censor, but he was new to the game and
would harden with experience. It's difficult to tell, though – knowing Hinds' dry sense of humour
– whether his comment about chocolate mousse was intended as a practical solution or just an
elaborate joke.

As Christmas came around, the weather turned perishingly cold. Joseph Losey, however, was
unperturbed. It was the time of the McCarthy witch hunts in America and Losey had been
blacklisted as an alleged Communist by the dreaded House Un-American Activities Committee.
He had already directed a short for Hammer in 1955, A Man on the Beach, Jimmy Sangster's first stab
at scriptwriting, and was now busy casting and scouting locations for X the Unknown (under the
pseudonym Joe Walton). But Hammer couldn't afford to alienate their US associates; indeed, the
man their American backer Sol Lesser had picked to play Dr Royston, Dean Jagger, was a staunch
anti-Communist. It is believed that they asked Losey to step down, saving his face by telling the
crew he had developed pnuemonia while choosing locations in the freezing cold. In his stead Tony
Hinds brought in Ealing director Leslie Norman (father of film critic Barry) literally days before the
start of filming, on the strength of his The Night My Number Came Up.

Filming began at Bray on Monday 16 January. The team of Harris and Oakes were back behind the
camera (Harry Oakes celebrating his 35th birthday on the first day of shooting), joined this time by

director of photography Gerald Gibbs to carry on the monochrome mood of Quatermass. Jimmy Sangster was back as production manager with the regular support of Jock May, Molly Arbuthnot, Phil Leakey and James Needs. Hugh Harlow was now promoted to regular third assistant. Ted Marshall took control of sets, while Hammer introduced continuity girl June Randall to their ranks.

In his diary, Harry Oakes noted on Monday 30 January: "Location call. The fissure has collapsed so back to the studio." Also that the Bray church material was shot on Tuesday 21 February and that the "close-up of melting hand" followed on Saturday the 25th. The diary also gives some insight into the stages used. On Friday 10 February he refers to filming in Adam's Workshop on G stage and on Monday 20 February records, "Upstairs on 'F' stage – police station. Then tower set on 'A'."

It must have been a coup for Hammer, having an Oscar-winning actor among the ranks; Dean Jagger had won the Best Supporting Actor award in 1949 for his performance in the acclaimed war picture, Twelve O'Clock High. But Hammer still had a strict schedule to keep to. They had already agreed to rent out Bray to Motley Films for the next six months for The Errol Flynn Theatre, a television drama series hosted by the Hollywood megastar, to begin in February. Sangster, in his last stint as production manager, scheduled the film so that the unit would vacate the warm confines of the studio for the freezing wastes of Beaconsfield and Gerrards Cross, in time for the TV company to move into Bray. As a result, Hammer would have to stage their next production, Quatermass 2, at the newly built Danziger studio, New Elstree, before returning to Bray in November for The Curse of Frankenstein.

Leslie Norman was inclined, by all accounts, to be a little 'difficult'. Camera operator Len Harris explained: "The director was rather trying for everybody. He was a very good technical director. With artists he was very tough. It was all right if they could stand up to it, but some of them couldn't. I think it made things very difficult. But the whole unit had a row with him at some time or other." [1] His focus puller Harry Oakes agreed. "He was a natural antagonist. He wasn't happy until he'd made somebody cross and then he'd grin like mad. Leslie didn't like it at Hammer and didn't want to do the film. He was contracted out to Ealing and looked down on Hammer."

As if this wasn't enough, there was more to follow when they went out on location. The weather was still bitterly cold. Torrential rain poured down on Beaconsfield gravel pits, the unit's home for the next few weeks. The pits flooded, the pits froze, the pits turned into a sea of sinking mud. Art director Ted Marshall remembered that "On this film we had two weeks shooting at night at a quarry near Beaconsfield in midwinter, which was not a very pleasant experience, especially since the frozen ground suddenly thawed out and became a quagmire, necessitating the removal to high ground to film the cracking of the Earth's fissure out of which 'X' – looking rather like a mess of boiling porridge – slowly oozed." [2]

The nightmare was indelible for Len Harris, who recalled it as his worst memory at Hammer. "I'll never forget that one. Working out of doors so much and really up to it in mud. We worked in some gravel pits near Beaconsfield Studios. And after all the rain, they were actually flooded. Well … the picture had to start. Bitterly cold – cold winds – horrible." [1] Harry Oakes recalled Leslie Norman adding to the misery: "Joe Losey was going to direct it originally and he had a wonderful idea of how he was going to shoot the scenes at Gerrards Cross gravel pits on a forklift tractor with a rostrum top so we would have a mobile camera unit, but because of this political thing which we didn't know about at the time – we were told he was ill – Leslie Norman came along from Ealing and of course he didn't want any of this. No, we had to track everywhere. Oh, it was awful, the mud! Those mud scenes were like pictures of Flanders in the First World War. Poor old Molly Arbuthnot, the wardrobe mistress – all the gumboots for the artists. They work very hard, these wardrobe ladies and their assistants."

Long night shoots were undertaken as the ground froze around them. Harry Oakes remembers, "There was a lot of night work. Several weeks, all night long. From about six till dawn next day and that can be quite long with the winter mornings." For the young third assistant director, Hugh Harlow, it was no picnic either. "It was one of the worst pictures I've worked on. It was a very unhappy film. Tony Hinds was the producer and went sick on it, Jimmy Sangster went sick for a while, the first assistant was ill. There were two or three weeks of night shooting in slush in the winter. I seem to remember. Leslie Norman, who was the director, no longer with us, was a bit of a tyrant and was an ex-Ealing director, and the chemistry between people was not gelling very

well. It became an unhappy experience, I remember that."

Harry Oakes remembers escaping the carnage early. "I got off the last week, because it went over schedule and I had to go back to Bray to operate on *The Errol Flynn Theatre*. Hammer had loaned out the camera and the studio to these people making this series you see, while they were on location. Motley Films wanted someone who could use the Vinten-Everest camera and Hammer sent me across to operate since Len was unavailable. He was still operating on *X the Unknown* – I didn't mind missing it, because it was still these exteriors in the gravel pits. After *X the Unknown* had fin-

ished, Len joined us. We only left the series so we could go straight onto *Quatermass* 2." Hugh Harlow would also move across to join the unit at Bray temporarily: "I was a clapper/loader for a while and then a runner on *The Errol Flynn Theatre*, but I didn't work on all of the episodes."

And then, of course, there was the fissure itself. "I can remember that we shot it, or were about to shoot it, in one of the wettest winters that we'd ever had in this country," remembered production manager Chris Sutton. "Every time we built a fissure – one of the things where the monster came out – it collapsed because of the rain. This was the usual thing sent to us: it's always the wettest time ever or it's the hottest time ever. When you're on location, these are the problems that you have. This was at night, and freezing cold nights, and pouring rain. It didn't make for easy location." [3]

Draughtsman Don Mingaye was assistant to art director Ted Marshall and was left in charge of the fissure. "The fissure was scripted to be 50 feet. So I was standing on a ridge looking down on a plateau below thinking, 'This is ridiculous, 50 feet is nothing.' So I had two stakes put in to mark the length of the 50 feet and I drew Tony Hinds' attention to the fact that it was a bit ridiculous. So he looked and said, 'I see what you mean. Yes, it's not really a crack in the ground at this distance.' So we ended up with something like about a thousand yards or more, digging out the trench, which constantly collapsed under the torrential rain we enjoyed at that point. That was quite a task

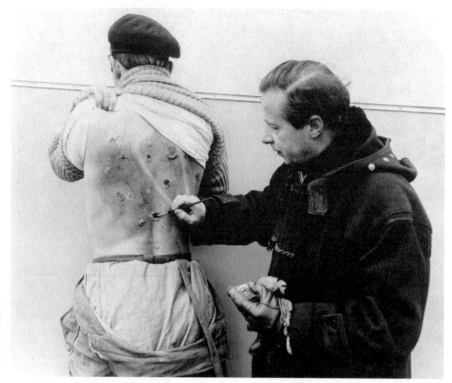

Make-up artist
Phil Leakey applies
'radiation burns' to
the back of Edwin
Richfield back for
X the Unknown
(1956).

and, to shore it up, Mr Banks with his merry men would come along. Can you imagine – this is the only industry that would do daft things like this – there we were trying to make a crack in a pot of porridge, holding the sides up and putting plaster cladding on and painting it as though it was solid. It was absolutely crazy!"

Mingaye also remembered the difficulties with Leslie Norman. "Oh yes, he was a bit of a tartar to work with. This is where poor old Ted Marshall used to shake in his boots, hoping he wouldn't get sworn at that day." The quiet and reserved Ted Marshall was in full agreement: "One previous slight 'disaster' occurred when producing the effect of an underground explosion at the first 'fissure' site. Explosives were placed under the dummy section of ground, made by stretching thick brown paper across the 'fissure' and covering it with earth and dummy rocks. With the special effects man, I was down in the fissure – about five foot deep – and at the first attempt the explosion blew sheets of torn brown paper in the air and I heard the furious scream of Les Norman as I peered over the edge of the fissure. 'You've just ruined my f***ing shot – that's all!' he cried. When the thaw set in, I got a certain amount of satisfaction from seeing Les Norman up to his knees in mud as he struggled to lift his rubber boots out of the quagmire. But, despite his loud mouth, he was a pleasant man to work with and had a nice sense of humour." [4]

Harry Oakes remembers testing this sense of humour. "I used to get on quite well with Leslie, but he liked to antagonise people. At this time all the construction boys were on a six-day week and they couldn't get their hair cut. It was early closing day on a Wednesday in Windsor, so the hairdresser used to come over to Bray Studios and set up shop in the electrician's workshop. I thought it was a good idea and I'd get my hair cut. Of course Leslie noticed it and took me to task over this, it was lovely bait for him: 'What do you mean, using the production's time?' I said, 'Well, it grows during the film time, doesn't it, Leslie?' He was good-natured though, he laughed about it."

This was the first film in which Phil Leakey took credit for his 'special make-up effects', on which he worked very closely with the special effects department. To depict the radiographer whose face melts under the heat of the thing, Leakey made a cast of the actor's face and constructed a paraffin wax replica into which was inserted a plaster skull containing heating elements. The heat was turned on and the wax melted to reveal the skull. Another example was the victim's arm which deflates under the energy of the thing. This was achieved by pumping red dye acetone into a foam hand. The scene was then played backwards to give the final impression of the arm collapsing.

The special effects were again attributed to Bowie-Margutti Ltd, this time with the help of Hammer's chief electrician Jack Curtis. For the title monster, Bowie had to be inventive. As he explained to *Kine Weekly*: "First we tried tapioca pudding. Worms are the most successful so far. We photograph them and magnify them. The kind of worms you feed tropical fish."

Bowie's assistant on the film, Roy Field, explains further. "A lot of it was done with these tiny little worms you use for fishing, mixed in with something that looked like polycell paste. It wasn't actually that paste, but it was the basis of it, without the glue substance in it, to give it body, because it didn't go hard and it wasn't a glue. You got the movement, because all these little worms were always moving and gave this lovely feeling that the whole lot was moving. Les came up with that one and Tony Hinds said, 'Well, shoot me a bit and let me see.' So we did a few little test shots and they loved it! Les wanted to pour these things, this mixture of stuff, so that it could run down roads. The set was built and then lowered into a glass tank about six feet by six feet in size. It was then filled with paraffin and we filmed through the glass front. It was all to get the movement really, because it needed to be poured against something. You couldn't just pour it free, because it ran like water, but if you poured it against something, which was a liquid, it bunched up and gave a lovely rolling effect. And of course all the sets were built on a slope, so it would always roll down. Although the camera always made it look level, the model sets were built to get the gravity.

"To get the 'monster' to flow down the road with the police car heading towards it, we filmed the action of the police car against a blue screen at Bray and then the roadway model with the monster was added to the police car scene." More tricky was the scene where the monster fells a power cable, which electrocutes it. "The pylon etc was a Les Bowie painting," recalls Field. "The monster was filmed on a small set some 15 inches wide and the cables were all photographed separately with heated tungsten wire to make them glow and pyrotechnics for the sparking. These were again shot separately, then all the elements were combined in a bi-pack camera by me, to make a composite negative."

Editor James Needs and his assistant, Henry Richardson, then took X the Unknown into post-production and James Bernard put his percussion and strings to the test again with another nail-biting, edge of the seat score conducted by John Hollingsworth. For recording purposes (both sound and music), Hammer usually used Ken Cameron's Anvil studios at Beaconsfield.

In 1956 Bray's editors were still located in rather primitive surroundings. Editor Bill Lenny explains, "During shooting we used to go down to the studio at Down Place, where they had a room around the back – it's now the gardener's cottage, I believe, or the gardener's room – it's attached to the house, a tiny little room, big enough for a bench, a Moviola, a couple of chairs and a bin. We used to edit while they were shooting there, but as soon as they finished shooting we would move up to Hammer House."

The cramped editing facilities at Bray meant that only one production at a time could occupy the cutting room there. Consequently, after shooting, the editor would have to vacate the premises and move up to Hammer House to make way for the editor on the next production at Bray, which was never that far away. Up at Hammer House in Wardour Street, James Carreras and Brian Lawrence could be found on the second floor, Michael Carreras and Tony Hinds had their offices on the fifth, and the editing facilities were situated on the fourth. Sound editor (and subsequently editor) Alfred Cox explains the set-up at Hammer House: "It had three cutting rooms. We had a much better theatre for screening in the basement and of course we were central to everything, rather than being way outside of other facilities." As for Bray's viewing theatre, it could be found above the ballroom stage and stills cameraman John Jay had a portrait studio tucked away behind it.

X the Unknown was Jimmy Sangster's last film as production manager; although he would still be engaged at his office at Bray, breaking down scripts and scheduling potential projects (which would soon include The Curse of Frankenstein), he would now turn to writing.

As noted above, Britain's TV viewers had in the meantime been spellbound by Nigel Kneale's BBC follow-up to The Quatermass Experiment. Quatermass II seems a logical title when viewed today in the light of modern sequel-mania, but back then it also carried another meaning – it was the name of Quatermass' second spaceship. 'Q1' had returned with what Hammer's US distributors had called *The Creeping Unknown*. Now for the sequel, Kneale envisaged an alien menace falling to Earth in the form of meteorites, subjugating human minds while being acclimatised in large steel domes in a bogus food plant. Enter Quatermass to spoil their fun and destroy the asteroid from whence they came using said 'Q2'. Quatermass horrors were coming from all sides, the second teleplay coinciding with the theatrical release of Hammer's *The Quatermass Xperiment*. Quatermass was never more popular and Hammer inevitably sought the rights to *Quatermass II*.

With the rights to *Quatermass II* came its creator Nigel Kneale; he was no longer on the BBC payroll so Hammer had to go to him direct to secure his story. Kneale worked on the first draft and Val Guest was again brought in to refine it and direct it. Once more the six-part telecast had to be pared down. Like its predecessor, the climax was rewritten: Quatermass no longer goes into space to destroy the asteroid at close range. Instead, Quatermass' dying sidekick, Brand, launches the unstable 'Q2' as a makeshift warhead to blast the asteroid to smithereens. The end justifies the means and the Earth is saved one more time.

Tony Hinds submitted the script to the BBFC's Arthur Watkins on 27 April 1956. Reader Audrey Field was not amused (again) and reported on 2 May: "What nonsense. Sillier than *Quatermass I*, or the other recent effusion from Hammer Films on the same lines. However, it is the sort of nonsense which aims at an 'X' certificate and is quite disgusting, if not frightening enough, to get it. I think I am right in saying that *Quatermass II* on television was preceded by the customary caution about children and nervous people; and the only part I saw (which involved engulfing people with slime) was quite sickening enough to be kept away from the very young or the moderately squeamish. For 'X', there should be the customary general caution that the sky is not the limit, either in sights or sounds. But I think most of what is in the script could be done in a way which would not be prohibitive." She went on to list her objections, closing with: "<u>P.165</u>. In a climax to this long crescendo of destruction, four colossal things sway about above the broken domes and machinery. All this sort of thing is trying to ordinary nerves, but people with ordinary nerves shouldn't come: publicity on the TV serial has warned them not to. Cf. final dissolution of the Things on p.166."

Arthur Watkins summarised his readers' opinions in a letter to Hinds on 11 May.

"We have now read the script of *Quatermass II* which was enclosed with your letter of the 27th April. There does not appear to be much here which need be prohibitive for the 'X' category, but, as in previous productions of this type, everything will depend upon reasonable discretion of treatment. Even for 'X', the sights and sounds indicating terror and agony, and the portrayal of what is horrific and nauseating, can go too far. I think our standards are by now well known to you; however, it may be helpful at this stage if we draw attention to the following points:

<u>P.9-10</u>. Discretion should be exercised in Ben's screams of pain – also the shots of his face when it has been marked by the meteorite. (The same applies to this mark wherever it appears throughout the film.) [NB This refers to the man that appears in the pre-titles sequence.]

<u>P.36</u>. Marsh's coughing and cries after gas from the meteorite has affected his lungs should not be too harrowing or protracted.

<u>P.38</u>. There should be no shot of the impact of the rifle-butt on Quatermass' face.

<u>Pp.84-86</u>. Great discretion will be needed in all shots and sounds of the horrible death of Broadhead.

<u>P.87</u>. The presence of dead bodies in the car should be very discreetly suggested and the shot of the little boy's blood stained arm hanging out of the car should be omitted.

<u>P.122</u>. The scene in which Sheila is attacked and marked by the 'thing' inside the meteorite calls for particular discretion.

<u>P.129</u>. There should be no shot of the station wagon actually going over the body of the guard.

<u>Pp.135, 160, foll</u>. It is a little difficult to advise you on shots of such an unusual object as the 'bubbling, heaving, monstrous' slimy Thing which escapes from the storage domes. We can only repeat that, even for the 'X' category, the nauseating and horrible can be carried too far and there is an obvious case here for reasonable restraint.

<u>P.148</u>. The clubbing of Peterson with the rifle-butt should not be too brutal.

Quatermass (Brian Donlevy) and Broadhead (Tom Chatto) are met by the PRO (John Van Eyssen) for a visit to the so-called food plant in Quatermass 2 (1956).

QUATERMASS 2

PRINCIPAL PHOTOGRAPHY: 21 May to 13 July 1956
DISTRIBUTION:
United Artists; 85 minutes; b/w
UK: certificate 'X'; US title: Enemy from Space
UK RELEASE:
TRADE SHOW: 22 March 1957 at the United Artists' Wardour Street Theatre
PREMIÈRE: 24 May 1957 at London Pavilion, Piccadilly Circus
GENERAL RELEASE: 17 June 1957 on the ABC circuit with And God Created Woman

DIRECTOR: Val Guest; PRODUCER: Anthony Hinds; EXECUTIVE PRODUCER: Michael Carreras; SCREENPLAY: Nigel Kneale and Val Guest, from the story by Nigel Kneale; ART DIRECTOR: Bernard Robinson; DRAUGHTSMAN: Don Mingaye; DIRECTOR OF PHOTOGRAPHY: Gerald Gibbs; CAMERA OPERATOR: Len Harris; FOCUS PULLER: Harry Oakes; ASSISTANT DIRECTOR: Don Weeks; THIRD ASSISTANT DIRECTOR: Hugh Harlow; EDITOR: James Needs; ASSISTANT EDITOR/SOUND EDITOR: Alfred Cox; MUSIC: James Bernard; MUSIC SUPERVISOR: John Hollingsworth; SOUND RECORDIST: Cliff Sandell; BOOM OPERATOR: Claude Hitchcock;

MAKE-UP: Phil Leakey; PRODUCTION MANAGER: John Workman; PRODUCTION SUPERVISOR: Anthony Nelson Keys; CONTINUITY: June Randall; WARDROBE: Renée Cope; SPECIAL EFFECTS: Bill Warrington, Henry Harris, Frank George; SPECIAL EFFECTS ASSISTANT: Brian Johncock; MATTES: Les Bowie; CONSTRUCTION MANAGER: Freddie Ricketts; CHIEF ELECTRICIAN: Jack Curtis; MASTER PLASTERER: Arthur Banks; PROP MASTER: Tommy Money

Brian Donlevy (Quatermass); John Longden (Lomax); Sydney James (Jimmy Hall); Bryan Forbes (Marsh); William Franklyn (Brand); Vera Day (Sheila); Charles Lloyd Pack (Dawson); Tom Chatto (Broadhead); John Van Eyssen (The PRO); Percy Herbert (Gorman); Michael Ripper (Ernie); John Rae (McLeod); Marianne Stone (Secretary); Ronald Wilson (Young Man); Jane Aird (Miss McLeod); Betty Impey (Kelly); Lloyd Lamble (Inspector); John Stuart (Commissioner); Gilbert Davis (Banker); Joyce Adams (Woman MP); Edwin Richfield (Peterson); Howard Williams (Michaels); Philip Baird; Robert Raikes (Lab Assistants); John Fabian (Intern); George Merritt (Super); Arthur Blake (Constable); Michael Balfour (Harry); Alastair Hunter (Labour MP); Barry Lowe (Chris); Henry Raynor (Drunk); Joan Schofield (Woman shopper); Vernon Greeves; Ronald Wilson (1st and 2nd men)

P.158. The very macabre episode of the blood dripping from the pipe should be indicated as discreetly as possible.
P.159. Shots of Ernie's and Gorman's bloodstained faces will need care.
P.161, 163. The shots of the slimy tentacle grasping or slapping the terrified workmen may well give trouble in the completed film.
"As you know, we are always willing to look at 'rushes' if we can help you in this way before the completed film is submitted for censorship. I return the script herewith."

The scene that particularly offended the readers related to a sequence in the serial where the 'zombie' guards murder a family who are having a picnic on the beach. The scene, on page 87 of the script, had the guards drive the family's car through the gates of the plant just as Quatermass is escaping after the death of Broadhead – and, rather disturbingly, called for the bloodstained arm of the boy to be hanging out of the car. Miss Field had naturally taken exception to this and so had reader Newton Branch when he read the scene on 5 May, necessitating him to make the file note: "Do we need this?" Hammer obviously complied; in the final film the car is still driven through the gates, but there is no longer any explanation as to whose car it is and certainly no sign of any dead family members. Censor documentation on the cutting of the final film is no longer available, so it is difficult to say whether the scene was pruned at the script or editing stage.

Nigel Kneale may have had a bit more say in the sequel, but he was powerless to stop Brian Donlevy reprising his role as Quatermass. The budget was double that of the original – £92,000. This boost had come from a deal struck with United Artists, who had just agreed to pick up *The Quatermass Xperiment* for US distribution. Robert Lippert had been desperately trying to get *The Quatermass Xperiment* distributed in the States. First Columbia were interested but then pulled out when they thought it would compete with their own Ray Harryhausen thriller, *It Came from Beneath the Sea*. Lippert desperately changed the title to the rather abstract *Shock* (in fact it went on release in Germany as *Schock*) and eventually changed it again to *The Creeping Unknown*. It was finally taken up by United Artists in March 1956 for a flat fee of $125,000. United Artists pared it down by four minutes and released it Stateside in June with Reginald LeBorg's *The Black Sleep* (starring Bela Lugosi, Lon Chaney Jr, John Carradine and Basil Rathbone). Now United Artists secured worldwide distribution of *Quatermass 2* (Kneale's title slightly adjusted by Hammer), but only after agreeing to finance a substantial part of the budget; they contributed £64,000 as well as $25,000 for Donlevy, plus his return air fare.

Just as *Quatermass 2* was being lined up for shooting on 21 May, something more important was happening behind the scenes at Hammer House. The end of the Lippert deal now meant Hammer had to find another American partner willing to put money up front, promote the films in the States and secure the necessary distribution deals. This took James Carreras to Eliot Hyman, head of Associated Artists Pictures (AAP), through their mutual association with the Variety Club. The timing was opportune because it brought the company *Frankenstein*.

Strange as it may seem, Hammer's decision to tackle Mary Shelley's anti-hero was not a direct consequence of their three science fiction shockers. Two young Americans, Milton Subotsky and Max J Rosenberg, had just produced their first film, a rock 'n' roll musical called *Rock, Rock, Rock*. Following this Subotsky wrote a treatment of *Frankenstein*, which he maintained was very close to the original novel, and took it to Hyman and his partner, David Stillman, at their New York office. Hyman was not prepared to back a horror movie made by a team which had only produced one film, and a musical at that, but told them that he knew a man in England who could pull it off. Hyman sent the script to James Carreras at Hammer House and the rest as they say, is history.

The story has an ironic postscript. The two men who were deemed incapable of producing a horror film went on to form Amicus Productions, Hammer's latterday rival in the horror stakes. Amicus always seemed to lack the sweep and polish of their rivals, however, so it was fortunate indeed that the Frankenstein story was passed to James Carreras.

The subject touched a nerve with Carreras and he hurriedly brought it to the attention of his son Michael, as Tony Hinds was busy preparing the second Quatermass adventure. Michael had immediate reservations about Subotsky's script and his correspondence with Max Rosenberg was far from complimentary:

"FRANKENSTEIN: Unless an incident is mentioned in the book *Frankenstein* by Mary W Shelley, it must be very carefully checked that there is no parallel in the original film (Universal 1931). It is not sufficient to take the book and write an original from it; if this is done you will find that at least 80 % of the good ideas were used in the original. Wherever the new screenplay deviates from the book it must use ideas well-clear of the original. We suggest that the screenplay is carefully checked against the original film by somebody competent to recognise infringement of copyrights.

"The script as it stands at present has a running time in the region of 55 minutes. A further 35 minutes must be added to bring the picture up to the required length for UK distribution (90 min).

This extra time must be brought in to existing sets or locations with no increase on night locations if possible.

"The script is badly presented. The sets are not marked clearly on the shot headings, neither is DAY or NIGHT specified in a number of cases. The number of set-ups scripted is quite out of proportion to the length of the screenplay, and we suggest that your rewrites are done in master scene form.

"The 'construction' of the monster is too quick. As we have got to increase the length, a large proportion of this increase should deal with the creation of the monster. This is the whole crux of the story; it should be dwelt upon.

"VICTOR spends an enormous amount of time and energy in creating the monster. Finally, after months of painstaking work he completes his task with the exception of the brain. He insists that the brain should be a first class one, and he steals WALDMAN'S. After the accident where he drops and destroys WALDMAN'S brain he turns straight round and takes the first brain that comes to hand. This is bad. The mistake in brains should be just that, a mistake by which he THINKS he is taking WALDMAN'S brain, whereas in fact he is taking the brain of a criminal lunatic.

"We attach herewith a suggested story line amending the 1st section of the Subotsky script:

1) INSANE ASYLUM: KREMPE visits insane asylum and meets VICTOR. VICTOR commences his tale (as per script).

2) FRANKENSTEIN HOME: VICTOR takes leave of his family to commence his studies (as per script).

3) UNIVERSITY TOWN AND LODGINGS: VICTOR arrives, asks his landlady for a room he can use as a laboratory.

4) UNIVERSITY: VICTOR meets KREMPE and gives him his letter of introduction. After their conversation as per script (pages 15-19), VICTOR goes to the DISSECTING ROOM, as opposed to the lecture hall, and commences work.

5) Montage: VICTOR studying. Scenes in DISSECTION room, LODGINGS, LABORATORY, etc.

6) KREMPE'S OFFICE: WALDMAN visits KREMPE and tells him he is disappointed in VICTOR'S progress (as per script).

7) VICTOR'S LODGINGS: KREMPE goes to see VICTOR and tells him he is disappointed in VICTOR'S progress (as per script).

8) Montage: This time mainly in VICTOR'S LAB. And we see the monster beginning to take some sort of shape.

9) FRANKENSTEIN HOME: Parents are worried and decide to write to KREMPE.

10) VICTOR'S LODGINGS: KREMPE sees VICTOR again. VICTOR tells him of his experiments and says all he needs now is a master brain (as per script).

11) GRAVEYARD: The stealing of the brain. NB. please read remarks in para 6 of general remarks.

12) VICTOR'S LABORATORY: The monster comes to life, breaks loose as VICTOR tries to explain to KREMPE what he has done (as per original script).

"NOTE: After this point the script can in general follow the Subotsky line with added length in the scenes themselves."

Subotsky and Rosenberg were invited to Hammer House to discuss the project on Wednesday 9 May and met with James Carreras. Rosenberg replied to Michael Carreras the following day:

"We are writing to you at the request of your brother James [an unfortunate diplomatic blunder on Rosenberg's part], with whom we had a most pleasant meeting yesterday. He outlined the changes desired in the script of FRANKENSTEIN. The expansion and revision of the script will take about two weeks. We will send you a copy of the revised script as soon as it is ready.

"In reply to the specific questions raised in your memo, please note the following:

1) The script has been checked by several people against the first FRANKENSTEIN film made by Universal in 1931 and its sequels. Except for sequences taken from the book (and Universal used very few of those except in their second picture, BRIDE OF FRANKENSTEIN), there is no resemblance between our script and scenes in any of Universal's FRANKENSTEIN films.

2) The script will be expanded to a running time of 90 minutes, utilising existing sets and locations.

3) The script will be presented better with sets and NIGHT or DAY marked clearly on each shot.

4) MASTER SCENES: It is not the number of set-ups that are out of proportion to the length of

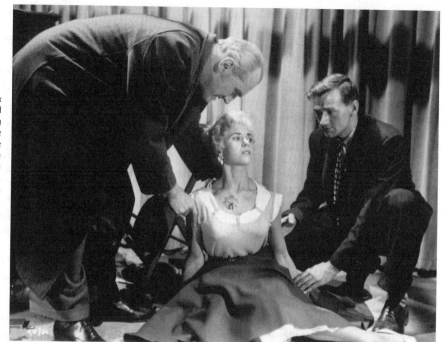

RIGHT: Lomax (John Longden) and Gorman (Percy Herbert) find the alien mark on the chest of Sheila (Vera Day) in Quatermass 2 (1956).

BELOW: Quatermass (Brian Donlevy) is abducted by guards as he tries to rescue his assistant at Winnerden Flats (on location on the South Downs near Brighton) in Quatermass 2 (1956).

the screenplay, but the number of CUTS. Almost every sequence in the picture is designed to be shot from no more than five set-ups: A master full shot, two favouring shots and two close-ups. However, the cutting back and forth between the shots is probably much too rapid. In the revised screenplay, this will be reduced.

5) The scenes allotted to the construction of the monster will be extended. This will not only extend the length of the picture, but should also increase the suspense.

6) The problem of the exchange of brains is a difficult one to solve. First – it is the one part of the picture which is not taken from the book and which resembles in idea, if not in incident, the first Universal picture. Second – while exchanging the brain may make for an additional thrill, it is artistically dishonest, since Mary Shelley's intention in the novel was to show the creature as a really superior being who turns monster when hurt and rejected by society. We may write alternate versions of this part of the script and send them to you and let you decide which to use.

7) In rewriting the script, Subotsky will follow as closely as possible the suggested outline on the second page of your memorandum.

"In conclusion, I would like to say, whatever suggestions and ideas you have concerning either point six in my letter and, for that matter, anything else that has to do with the script or the other points listed in this letter, do advise immediately. We believe we have a most interesting project here, and we hope to have it before the cameras in July. We are certain that we will have a close and harmonious relationship so that we can get the best possible picture."

While deliberations at Hammer House continued, movements were afoot at the Shell Haven Refinery as Val Guest readied himself for Quatermass 2, which started on Monday 21 May, the very day America dropped her first H-bomb from a plane over Bikini Atoll. Much of the team from *X the Unknown* returned including Gerald Gibbs, Len Harris, Harry Oakes, James Needs, June Randall, Phil Leakey and Hugh Harlow. Don Weeks joined the ranks as assistant director. (He was brother of wardrobe supervisor Molly Arbuthnot.) John Workman replaced Jimmy Sangster as production manager, Cliff Sandell gave Jock May a respite for this and the next production as sound recordist and Renée Cope was brought in to look after wardrobe for this one film.

One notable addition to the regular Hammer team was art director Bernard Robinson (born 1912). He entered the film industry in 1935 as a draughtsman at Warner Bros' Teddington Studios, where he would soon become one of the industry's youngest art directors, aged 26. He went on to work at Apollo Films and joined Pinnacle Productions in February 1955, before moving to Hammer. His cost-cutting, no-nonsense approach to set design would hide Hammer's tiny budgets and set them apart from their cash-strapped rivals. Draughtsman Don Mingaye, who would later become Robinson's regular art director at Hammer, remembers their first meeting on *Quatermass 2*: "Bernard came in and I was introduced to him. He made me feel totally relaxed and I thought, 'What a nice guy.' And from there on, we sailed into the business. He didn't come in in the old-fashioned way as a new broom who was going to sweep clean and make drastic changes, he made gradual ones. He was an absolute gentleman."

Brian Donlevy flew into London Airport from New York four days into production on Thursday 24 May. For seven days the crew recorded the action at the vast oil refinery which had already played host to the original serial. Focus puller Harry Oakes remembers filming there: "It was still in operation. We had to use our Newman Sinclair clockwork camera, because it was very toxic and inflammable where we were and they didn't like anything electrical. I remember one day there, while we were shooting, the riggers lined up this thing, which was a bit like a crane that swung horizontally over a vast area between a couple of gantries, to use as a camera position. Somehow the riggers had been up there making it stable, otherwise as it moved along it would sway slightly, so they put great lengths of tubing all the way down across it. Anyway, Len and I got up there and they did a dummy run, but they'd overlooked some cables and we felled them. There was a terrific flashing and banging as they blew all the electricity up and we lost the power to this crane business. They couldn't move it, so we had to get out of it, but it was still some distance from the side – I suppose about 12 or 15 feet from the crane to the gantry and it was quite a drop down below – about 40 foot down to these big turbines at the bottom.

"We were due at Scotland Yard that evening to do some shooting and of course Tony Hinds was very worried and got hold of the rigger, who put a ladder across, one of those aluminium ladders, which were quite new then. He was a marvellous chap and he got halfway along the ladder and I managed to pass the gear to him. So we got everything out and it was just Len and myself left to crawl across the ladder, but poor Len, who was about 16 stone, said, 'No, I'm not doing that.' I said, 'Well, I'm going.' In the end we eventually managed to coax Len across. One problem was of course that these aluminium ladders creaked like mad, which apparently is a good thing – if they creak they're all right. Anyway, with the aid of this rigger, who had no fear of heights, we managed to coax him across, but poor old Len, he had his eyes closed, his teeth clenched, and bit by bit we got him across."

The story made good use of the refinery's vast steel domes but yet larger domes were necessary, courtesy of Les Bowie's matte paintings. Guest recalls that they had problems shooting the scene where Tom Chatto emerges from one of the domes covered in a corrosive substance, which necessitated four takes. Chatto was at the time married to one of Britain's leading casting directors and defused the situation perfectly by joking to the crew: "Remind me to talk to my wife!" Special effects man Bill Warrington topped off Chatto's gooey appearance by pouring the smoking chemical titanium tetrachloride onto his protective jacket. The substance was later banned by health and safety watchdogs on both sides of the Atlantic.

The crew moved to Stages 2 and 5 of the Danziger Brothers' New Elstree Studios on Monday 28 May, where they filmed for another three weeks until Monday 18 June. Further location work took place at Hemel Hempstead, covering as Winnerden Flats, and the climactic hurricane scene was shot on the South Downs near Brighton. The latter was fondly remembered by Val Guest, owing to a humorous incident involving Brian Donlevy's hairpiece: "We were up on the hills somewhere and we needed a cyclone or tornado or something and we had the wind machines for it up there. We had to try to make sure that Brian always faced the machines and they were never behind him. When we had got one particular shot, I said, 'Cut, that's fine.' Brian turned around and, of course, the machines just blew his toupée off and it took forever to catch it. It floated around like a bat." It would be Donlevy's last performance for Hammer.

Once again Val Guest conducted a tight ship, running his story along at a nail-biting pace. Guest used an early story-boarding technique that kept all the crew well aware of the rigours of the day. As third assistant Hugh Harlow remembers, "Val was one of the first directors I ever met. When I came into the business, he was then the resident director. Break in the Circle was the first film I worked on with Val, when I started as a runner. He was a very experienced and polished man, with very much an air of efficiency about him. I worked on a number of films with him, not only with Hammer but films away from them as a freelance production manager, and he kept the same format throughout.

"He would do his homework very thoroughly, to the extent that he would always have a caravan on the stage or location and he would be one of the first people on the set in that caravan early in the morning, preparing his pages of script for that day's work. He'd have his master script on the table and a second script from which he would extract the relevant pages of those scenes for the day, all marked up to the angles he wanted to shoot, and then he would transfer that information onto a large sheet of paper on a board and easel on the set or location and anybody could go up to that board and see what angles he was going to shoot and what scene numbers were relative to what angles – were they tracking shots, close-ups or pans. He kept to it religiously. It was a tremendous system and invariably he'd finish the day's work with that relevant portion of the script completed. He certainly helped me in my early years, little titbits about working, and he was a very kind person."

Principal photography ended on Friday 13 July after eight weeks. Editor James Needs and sound editor Alfred Cox then took Quatermass 2 into post-production at Hammer House. John Hollingsworth again brought in James Bernard for the score.

As Quatermass 2 went into post-production, Tony Hinds was now drawn into the Frankenstein debate in order to release Michael Carreras for the company's next production, a war film called Observation Post, which would finally go out as The Steel Bayonet. This gritty drama set in North Africa in 1943 had the British taking on a German tank regiment and was again financed by United Artists. Producer Michael Carreras asked to direct it, his wish was granted and he directed this, his first feature (in Scope, to boot) in August. Production manager John Workman and assistant director Don Weeks carried over their respective duties from Quatermass 2. This was, however, Don Weeks' last film as assistant director; from The Curse of Frankenstein on, he would become Hammer's regular production manager. His sister, Molly Arbuthnot, was back in charge of wardrobe after a brief respite, and the film also saw the welcome return of Hammer's veteran continuity girl Renée Glynne and editor Bill Lenny.

The sandy-haired and charismatic Anthony Nelson Keys had returned to Hammer as production supervisor on Quatermass 2. He now moved into the associate producer slot for The Steel Bayonet, a position he would now hold regularly at Hammer, lending support to the main-line producer. Keys was son of music hall comedian Nelson 'Bunch' Keys. His elder brother was noted director John Paddy Carstairs (famous for his comedies, including the Norman Wisdom vehicles), who would direct one film for Hammer, another comedy called A Weekend with Lulu in 1960. Of his younger brothers, Basil Keys would work for Hammer as production manager on Ten Seconds to Hell and associate producer on The Old Dark House, The Phantom of the Opera and Paranoiac, while the youngest, Roderick Keys, was a film editor. In fact they had all worked together on Dancing with Crime in 1946: director John Paddy Carstairs; assistant producer Rod Keys; first assistant Basil Keys and production manager Anthony Nelson Keys.

Tony Keys had come to Hammer fresh from Daniel Angel's Pinnacle Films and would be instrumental in attracting a number of key personnel to Hammer. One was art director Bernard Robinson, with whom he'd worked on a number of impressive productions for Angel, including Albert RN (1953), The Sea Shall Not Have Them (1954) and the classic Reach for the Sky (1956). Although Robinson had taken over from Ted Marshall on Quatermass 2, Marshall was back for The Steel Bayonet and would be initially appointed art director on The Curse of Frankenstein. Keys would bring back Robinson as 'production designer' for the latter to work above Marshall. Fortunately for

Jack Asher looks down the camera to set up a shot for The Steel Bayonet (1956). To his right are Len Harris, Michael Carreras and Harry Oakes (with soldier's hat). Leading man Leo Genn can be seen on the left.

THE STEEL BAYONET

PRINCIPAL PHOTOGRAPHY: 13 August to 20 September 1956
UK DISTRIBUTION: United Artists; 85 minutes; b&w;
  Hammerscope; certificate 'A'
UK RELEASE:
  TRADE SHOW: 14 May 1957
  GENERAL RELEASE: 3 June 1957

DIRECTOR/PRODUCER: Michael Carreras; ASSOCIATE PRODUCER: Anthony Nelson Keys; SCREENPLAY: Howard Clewes; ART DIRECTOR: Ted Marshall; DIRECTOR OF PHOTOGRAPHY: Jack Asher; CAMERA OPERATOR: Len Harris; FOCUS PULLER: Harry Oakes; ASSISTANT DIRECTOR: Don Weeks; EDITOR: Bill Lenny; SOUND RECORDISTS: Cliff Sandell and Maurice Askew; SOUND EDITOR: Alfred Cox; MUSIC: Leonard Salzedo; MUSIC SUPERVISOR: John Hollingsworth; MAKE-UP: Phil Leakey; PRODUCTION MANAGER: John Workman; CONTINUITY: Renée Glynne; WARDROBE: Molly Arbuthnot;

DIALOGUE DIRECTOR: Howard Clewes; SPECIAL EFFECTS: Frank George and Sid Pearson; STUNT SUPERVISOR: Jock Easton

Leo Genn (Major Gerrard); Kieron Moore (Capt Mead); Michael Medwin (Lt Vernon); Robert Brown (Sgt Gill); Michael Ripper (Pvt Middleditch); John Paul (Lt Col Derry); Shay Gorman (Sgt Gates); Tom Bowman (Sgt Nicholls); Bernard Horsfall (Pvt Livingstone); John Watson (Cpl Bean); Arthur Lovegrove (Pvt Jarvis); Percy Herbert (Pvt Clark); Paddy Joyce (Pvt Ames); Jack Stewart (Pvt Wentworth); David Crowley (Pvt Harris); Barry Lowe (Pvt Ferguson); Michael Dear (Pvt 'Tweedle'); Ian Whittaker (Pvt Wilson); Michael Balfour (Pvt Thomas); Raymond Francis (General); Anthony Warren (wounded German); Rolf Carston (German NCO); Gerard Green (German company commander); Wolf Frees (German staff officer); Jeremy Longhurst (German sniper); David Ritch (Mahomet); Abdul Noor (Arab); Victor Platt (sapper sentry); John Trevor (sapper captain)

Hammer, Robinson would then stay on as their regular production designer and would be responsible for much of the Hammer magic during the Gothic revival.

Keys also brought in brilliant lighting cameraman Jack Asher (born 29 March 1916) on The Steel Bayonet, with whom he had also worked with on Albert RN and Reach for the Sky. Both Asher's parents worked for Fred Karno's vaudeville empire, his father as assistant stage manager and his mother as a 'Karno girl'. Asher became resident camera operator at Gainsborough's Shepherds Bush studios in 1940 and was eventually promoted to director of photography in 1947 on Jassy. Although restricted to black-and-white at Hammer for the time being, it would be his vivid colour photography that breathed life into the Gothic horrors to come.

Harry Oakes recalled, "Shooting started on 13 August under its original title of Observation Post. It was all shot on location. We were working on observation posts in Aldershot at the army training area. The area in which we shot was called Long Valley and we noticed that the paras used to do field craft there. The officer and the Sergeant Major would stand on this hill and the chaps had to go all through the undergrowth in camouflage without being seen. It was part of their testing and this was going on while we were filming."

Stunt man Captain Jock Easton joined the team to help with the film's many action sequences. Easton put together Britain's first stunt agency and ran it with his partner Joe Powell from an office at Silver Place in Soho. As Harry Oakes remembers, "Jock Easton was a fabulous character. Of course he was a master stuntman then, he was like the Godfather among stuntmen. He was a captain in the SAS, if I remember rightly, in Italy. On *The Steel Bayonet* we were working on location in Aldershot and we had a lot of real troops as extras. Unfortunately, it must have put a hell of a cost on the film, because the Suez Canal war started and all the troops who were allocated to us had to be withdrawn, so we had to use a load of extras. Jock was amongst them."

The completed *X the Unknown* then made it onto the nation's screens. Like its predecessor, it exploited the controversial 'X' certificate. The film premièred on Friday 21 September at the London Pavilion and went on general release on the ABC circuit from Monday 5 November, supported by *Les Diaboliques*. The response was good, making it one of the year's most successful thriller double-bills. *Kine Weekly* on 16 August called it "Gripping science fiction. The picture builds up big suspense and ends spectacularly." *Variety* on 10 October called it "A highly imaginative and fanciful meller, with tense dramatic overtones."

It would seem, however, that Exclusive's branch managers were not entirely content with the film's 'X' certificate, complaining bitterly to both James Carreras and the BBFC in March 1957. Their representative, prints manager F E Richens, wrote to the BBFC on 25 March 1957: "Re: *X the Unknown*. The above subject was originally granted an 'X' certificate, and we now desire to resubmit this subject to you, in view of granting an 'A' certificate. A copy of this will be made available for viewing at any time you desire."

The protest was supported by James Carreras, who began to realise the limited bookings his 'X' pictures were getting (some cinemas still refused to book them) and accordingly wrote to John Nicholls, the new Secretary of the BBFC, the following day: "Many months ago we made the above picture and tried very hard to get an 'X' certificate for it. Through the kindness of Arthur Watkins, who stretched everything for us, we achieved an 'X' certificate. Our branch managers are now telling us that the picture is not an 'X' picture and should really have an 'A' certificate. We would therefore like to resubmit the picture to you and we are confident that with only a couple of small cuts, you will be able to give us an 'A' certificate, which will enable us to play the picture in so many situations we cannot get it into now."

John Nicholls was having none of it. He replied to Richens on 26 March: "I write in reply to your letter of 25th March about *X the Unknown*. We have carefully considered what you say, but I am afraid no useful purpose would be served by our seeing this film again with a view to granting an 'A' certificate, since both story and treatment are in our view inescapably 'X'."

We've already seen the censor's less than charitable response to the draft screenplay of *X the Unknown*. Sadly, no documentation remains at the BBFC regarding the censor's reaction to the finished product. In the above correspondence, James Carreras seems to imply that, despite all the initial fuss over the script, the censor ultimately struggled to give Hammer their 'X' certificate when faced with the movie itself. Perhaps Tony Hinds was right – if chocolate blancmange was the best they could muster, the written word and its implications would always seem more disturbing. Or were Carreras' comments in this letter merely a clever ploy to catch a new Secretary off his guard in order to wheedle an 'A' certificate out of him? If so, it didn't work.

X the Unknown was destined for RKO, but the distribution rights ultimately switched to Warner Bros in America, when it was released on a double-bill with *The Curse of Frankenstein* in May 1957.

On 13 June 1956, James Carreras submitted the latest draft of the Subotsky script, which now had the working title *Frankenstein – The Monster!* (sometimes simply referred to as *Frankenstein* in correspondence), to Arthur Watkins, who was then still Secretary of the BBFC: "We are re-making in colour, and with our tongue in both cheeks, 'FRANKENSTEIN'. Herewith, a script, which we have received from America, and which I know we must submit to you. Upon receipt of your twenty page reply, I will make an appointment to see you."

Baron Frankenstein (Peter Cushing) implores his friend Paul Krempe (Robert Urquhart) to declare his innocence to the priest (Alex Gallier) in The Curse of Frankenstein (1956).

THE CURSE OF FRANKENSTEIN

PRINCIPAL PHOTOGRAPHY: 19 November to 3 January 1956/7
DISTRIBUTION:
  Warner Bros.; 82 minutes; Eastman Colour.
  UK: certificate 'X'
UK RELEASE:
  PREMIÈRE: 2 May 1957 at the Warner Theatre, Leicester Square
  GENERAL RELEASE: 20 May 1957, with *Woman of Rome*
US RELEASE: May 1957, with *X the Unknown*

DIRECTOR: Terence Fisher; PRODUCER: Anthony Hinds; ASSOCIATE PRODUCER: Anthony Nelson Keys; EXECUTIVE PRODUCER: Michael Carreras; SCREENPLAY: Jimmy Sangster; PRODUCTION DESIGNER: Bernard Robinson; ART DIRECTOR: Ted Marshall; DRAUGHTSMAN: Don Mingaye; DIRECTOR OF PHOTOGRAPHY: Jack Asher; CAMERA OPERATOR: Len Harris; FOCUS PULLER: Harry Oakes; ASSISTANT DIRECTOR: Derek Whitehurst; 2ND ASSISTANT DIRECTOR: Jimmy Komisarjevsky; 3RD ASSISTANT DIRECTOR: Hugh Harlow; EDITOR: James Needs; ASSISTANT EDITOR: Roy Norman; MUSIC: James Bernard; MUSIC SUPERVISOR: John Hollingsworth; SOUND RECORDIST: Jock May; SOUND CAMERA OPERATOR: Michael Sale; BOOM OPERATOR: Jimmy Perry; MAKE-UP: Phil Leakey; MAKE-UP ASSISTANT: George Turner; HAIRSTYLIST: Henry Montsash; PRODUCTION MANAGER: Don Weeks; CONTINUITY: Doreen Soan;

WARDROBE: Molly Arbuthnot; CASTING: Dorothy Holloway; MATTES: Les Bowie; CONSTRUCTION MANAGER: Freddie Ricketts; CHIEF ELECTRICIAN: Jack Curtis; ELECTRICIANS: Bob Palmer, Harold Marland; MASTER PLASTERER: Arthur Banks; PROP MASTER: Tommy Money; PRODUCTION SECRETARY: Faith Frisby; STILLS CAMERAMEN: John Jay, Tom Edwards

Peter Cushing (Victor Frankenstein); Hazel Court (Elizabeth); Robert Urquhart (Paul Krempe); Christopher Lee (Creature); Melvyn Hayes (young Victor); Valerie Gaunt (Justine); Paul Hardtmuth (Professor Bernstein); Noel Hood (Aunt Sophia); Fred Johnson (Grandpa); Claude Kingston (little boy); Alex Gallier (priest); Michael Mulcaster (warder); Andrew Leigh (Burgomaster); Anne Blake (Burgomaster's wife); Sally Walsh (young Elizabeth); Middleton Woods (lecturer); Raymond Ray (Uncle)

The following were listed in the film's pressbook but not in the on-screen credits: Marjorie Hume (mother); Henry Caine (schoolmaster); Patrick Troughton (Kurt); Joseph Behrman (Fritz); Raymond Rollett (Father Felix); Ernest Jay (undertaker); Bartlett Mullins (a tramp); Eugene Leahy (second priest). The pressbook also includes different artists in the roles of the Burgomaster (Hugh Dempster) and the uncle (J Trevor Davis). The voice of Patrick Troughton was retained in the charnel house scene when the Baron purchases a pair of eyes.

Watkins rose to the 'twenty page' bait and jokingly replied to Carreras on 14 June, "All I want to know is whether you or Arthur Abeles are playing the part." (To explain the gag, Arthur Abeles was managing director of Warner Bros in England at the time.) The response of the Board's readers was less jocular, however, setting the tone for the turbulent years to come. Reader Frank Crofts (FNC for short) wrote on 16 June: "Exclusive Films say they are going to make this film in colour and 'with tongue in both cheeks'. Whatever contortions their tongue may perform, such a film will obviously be 'X', so I have only to list what may be too strong for that category ... The American author called the script *Frankenstein*. Exclusive apparently intend to call it *Frankenstein the Monster*. Anyone who goes to a film of this name cannot complain that he has not been warned, but that should not mean that the film should give even sensation-hunters nightmares. I think this is the first horror film to be made in colour in this country, and a good deal will depend on what use is made of the colour."

Reader Audrey Field concurred on 21 June: "As FNC says, people who come to a new *Frankenstein* should know what to expect – There is, however, a tendency to exaggerate what is brutal and nauseating, as opposed to what is merely good, tense horror, and several warnings of a general nature will be necessary. I have not much to add to FNC's note, but it may be worth remarking that excessive cruelty and brutality is no more welcome in horror films than anywhere else, and even a monster, when helpless and tied upside down on a pole, is entitled not to be teased and singed with lighted torches (see p.48)."

One of Watkins' team replied on his behalf to James Carreras on 22 June.

"Mr Watkins has asked me, in his absence from the office, to let you have the readers' observations on the draft script of *Frankenstein* which you sent us on 13th June. We have the following details to mention from the point of view of the 'X' category:

P.3. The asylum attendant should not thrust a torch against an inmate's arm.

P.6. The 'rotting corpse' should not be too gruesome or disgusting (the same applies to corpses throughout the script).

Pp. 14, 25, 35, 36. (The scenes in which Frankenstein is working on the corpse which is eventually transformed into the monster.) These scenes will obviously call for discretion and in particular there should be no close or clearly identifiable shots of human organs, either being worked upon by the scientist or in jars. The monster's face, here and elsewhere, could be too repulsive, even for 'X', if reasonable discretion were not used: this applies particularly to any shots of the face streaming with blood.

P.23. The shot of the mallet being brought down on the live worm is rather unpleasant, and does not seem to be really necessary.

P.31. The shot of the rat scurrying across Professor Waldman's dead body should be omitted. The whole of the body-snatching episodes will call for reasonable restraint.

Pp. 41, 46, 56, 66, 67. Screams should not be too piercing and blood-curdling. Apart from the scream, the whole incident of the frightened child (p.41) will need care. The same applies to the whole incident of Elizabeth being carried by the monster and falling to her death, and she should not be heard to 'hit bottom'.

Pp.45, 50, 55-6. The scenes in which the monster strangles a man and two guards and half-strangles Frankenstein's friend, Henri, should not be overdone.

P.48. The breaking of the dog's neck should not be clearly visible. In the ensuing scene, when the creature is captive and carried along tied to a pole, it should not be too viciously tormented, and the captors should not be shown actually singeing it with their torches.

P.59. The caution in regard to pp.14, etc., applies equally to shots of Frankenstein working on the second creature.

"I am sure the foregoing points were already obvious to you, but I have set them down in detail for convenience of reference. If we can give any further help on the shooting script, we shall be pleased to read it. I return the draft script herewith."

Meanwhile, the Frankenstein project had now been handed on to Tony Hinds, who liked the Subotsky script even less than Michael Carreras and was apparently unsympathetic to James Carreras' grand design, intending to 'knock it off' in black and white. Len Harris remembered this well: "I was getting a lift back from some location with Tony Hinds. He's a very chatty sort of fellow – very nice. 'Our next picture is going to be *Frankenstein*. We'll knock it off in three weeks. I don't think it'll amount to anything'. He said, 'There's some talk of it being in colour, but we don't want it distributed in colour. We'll get our money back over here in black and white.'" [4]

Uninspired by the screenplay in hand, Hinds commissioned Jimmy Sangster to write an alternative script, concerned that Subotsky's too much resembled Universal's films. Indeed, the BBFC had already highlighted concerns on page 48, where the monster was to be held upside down and tormented – a similar scene had appeared in The Bride of Frankenstein. "I remember Jimmy told me how he came to write that," recalls stills photographer John Jay. "They used to have a break between productions, do two or three films with a month's break. During that break they were going to do Frankenstein and Jimmy Sangster said to Michael Carreras, 'I wouldn't mind having a go at writing that. Would they mind?' And he said, 'No, see Tony Hinds.' And Tony said, 'If you want to do the script, we'll have a look at it.' And it was so good they bought the script from him."

More than that, Sangster's new approach had fired Hinds' enthusiasm and now, with his associate producer Tony Keys, they decided to give the project the full attention it deserved. Cinematographer Jack Asher recalled, "The Curse of Frankenstein was originally scheduled as a quick, inexpensive follow-up on the Hammer treadmill, but I suspect that Tony Keys, who had been assigned to this film, thought otherwise. He influenced, after many discussions with me, an expanded shooting schedule, an enlarged budget and the eventual shooting in colour."[5]

Preproduction work on The Curse of Frankenstein took place under the shadow of Universal, who were ready to initiate legal proceedings at every turn. Hammer's lawyer Edwin Davis set to work and a letter to James Carreras on 24 August explained the situation:

"With reference to our conversation over the telephone yesterday, I have made investigations and find that the work entitled Frankenstein by Mary Wolstoncraft [sic] Shelley (the wife of the poet) was published in 1818. Mrs Shelley was born in 1797 and died in 1851 and therefore this particular work is in the public domain and you are entitled to make a film based thereon together with such alterations and additions thereto as you may desire."

This of course still meant that Hammer could not lift any ideas from the Universal series. Carreras wrote to Eliot Hyman on 23 August after his call from Davis:

"1. 'FRANKENSTEIN' by Shelley is in public domain.

2. If our screenplay is based on the book, 'FRANKENSTEIN', nobody on earth can do anything about it and we are entitled to use the title 'FRANKENSTEIN'.

3. Whatever original ideas are added to the book are in order.

4. If we use any ideas in the Universal International pictures on 'FRANKENSTEIN' then we are headed for trouble.

5. It is our intention that the script shall be as per the book backed by original ideas and having nothing whatsoever to do with the Universal International pictures, which puts us 100% in the clear.

"We do not think that any insurance brokers will have anything to do with the proposed film unless assured of the above, in which case we don't need them at all. Tony Hinds is being meticulous about this and I believe we can get out a script which can be called 'FRANKENSTEIN AND THE MONSTER' without any danger from anyone, which is still international box office, and which will show a very big return for the money invested ... Your second paragraph [with] reference [to] the cast. I thought it was agreed that the picture would be made with a completely competent British cast under the title of 'FRANKENSTEIN AND THE MONSTER'. We have not considered any American actors for this picture as we thought that the title alone would ensure distribution but we are quite happy to be guided by you on this and if you want an American actor in it we are willing to have one."

Hyman replied to Carreras on 28 August:

"I have noted all of your remarks in regard to paragraph three of my letter and the only additional precaution that I would suggest would be that your Mr Tony Hinds and your director view those 'FRANKENSTEIN' films produced by Universal in order that duplication be eliminated. It would seem as though you should be able to procure prints in London, but if this cannot be accomplished I would arrange to obtain 16mm prints here and forward them to you via Air Express for this purpose, providing they are returned promptly and providing it remains a completely confidential matter.

"I don't believe we ever discussed cast, and when you use the expression 'competent British cast' you must bear in mind that there are British casts and British casts. You still have not told me what the cast consists of and it is needless for me to point out to you that although the people themselves may be British, just how British are they by way of accent as the effect will be upon the acceptance of the picture in America."

HAMMER FILMS · THE BRAY STUDIOS YEARS

Carreras' reply on 3 September gave an early indication of Hammer's choice of script:

"Tony Hinds has viewed *Frankenstein*, *The Bride of Frankenstein* and *The Son of Frankenstein* and we believe that the script which Tony Hinds has prepared uses nothing that Universal-International have put into these pictures that is not in the book, which being in public domain we can use. My lawyer Edwin Davis suggests that Tony Hinds' script should be submitted to Universal-International, advising them that we are going to make the picture and asking if they have any comments on the script. The London representative of Universal-International has already been advised that the picture is going to be made this winter and has advised Hollywood of the same.

"When Tony Hinds saw *The Bride of Frankenstein* he found that many of the original ideas that Universal-International had put into this picture were used in the Subotsky script and so I would suggest that we agree to use Tony Hinds' script, which in my opinion is a far safer way of doing things."

And so Hammer decided to go with Sangster's script. In the final movie Subotsky would of course get no formal script credit, but he always maintained that he received a percentage of the profits for his work and this is confirmed later in the same letter: "Reference Max Rosenberg. I agree that he should recieve 15% of the profits after all normal deductions, production, distribution, etc etc, and I also agree that $5,000 should be added to the budget for his services to date."

As to casting, Hammer seemed to be backing down slightly: "... Reference cast, rest assured that the British cast will be absolutely first class and will have no trace whatsoever of British accent. Now, whether you want Professor Frankenstein to be an American is entirely up to you, if so please let me have suggested names to play this part. Obviously he will have to be a middle man and in my opinion should cost no more than $20,000. In our budget we have allowed £1250 for this part, for which we would get a very competent actor but of course with no name, relying upon the title 'FRANKENSTEIN' to sell the picture world-wide. However if you want an American actor please let us have some names to choose from."

Jimmy Sangster had prepared his screenplay under the title *The Curse of Frankenstein*, adapting Mary Shelley's story in line with Hammer's modest set-up. Sangster explains his approach to the script: "Basically, Tony told me to write the script for *Frankenstein*. I asked him, 'How much are you going to spend on this picture?' I was a production manager at the time, so I knew about budgets and I did tailor it to a certain extent to Hammer's financial restrictions. In every Frankenstein film there's always peasants storming the castle at the end to burn it down. Tony said, 'You can hear the peasants, you can see the torchlight on the trees, but you can't see the peasants. We can't afford it. So you have to be a bit imaginative.'"

The basic storyline contained a major flaw, however. The whole plot revolves around the story Victor tells a priest in order to avoid the guillotine. Victor has been condemned to death for the alleged murder of his maid, Justine. Yet in declaring his innocence, he openly admits to not only killing Professor Bernstein, but also to being an accessory to Justine's murder after all. Sangster dismisses this quibble by pointing out that it's the sort of thing people would only pick up on after repeated viewings – and he could well be right.

Sangster himself submitted his screenplay to the BBFC on 9 October: "Please find enclosed herewith a copy of our current screenplay *The Curse of Frankenstein*. I am forwarding it on behalf of Mr Tony Hinds and would be grateful if you would send your observations direct to him."

The response from the readers was again predictable.

Audrey Field, 10 October: "This is infinitely more disgusting than the first script. In fact, really evil. A lip-smacking relish for mutilated corpses, repulsive dismembered hands and eyeballs removed from the head, alternates with gratuitous examples of sadism and lust. While the general outline of the story cannot be rejected for 'X', a great many details will have to be modified or eliminated."

Frank Crofts, 11 October: "This is certainly a monstrous script. It is ludicrously written, with a complete disrespect for history. Frankenstein and his monster were merely medical figures, yet we find the former reading Darwin's *Origin of Species* (p.9). The dialogue is modern jargon. None of the details of the creature's birth and activities bears much resemblance to what I have read of him and the author has done his best to pile horror on horror in a way that, in my opinion, makes it unlikely that we should be able to pass such a film as this. With very considerable changes it might get through, but I should prefer to see an amended script ... I agree with AOF's objections, but I go

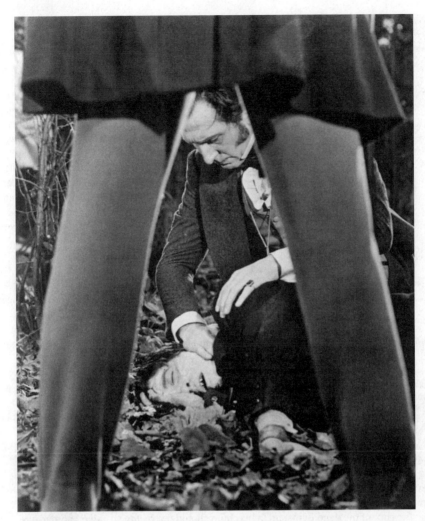

Baron Frankenstein (Peter Cushing) examines the Creature (Christopher Lee) after it has been shot in The Curse of Frankenstein (1956).

further and suggest that we should hold out no hope of passing a film based on this script, which is far worse than the one sent in by Exclusive Films. If the present company (Hammer Films) wants to proceed, I think they should have the script re-written and send it in again. It seems to me that a film that is even somewhat watered down from this script might give many adults a nightmare: people who go to a Frankenstein film expect horror but a horror based on a fairly well-known legend and not this sort of stuff."

'SWH', 16 October: "This is a loathsome story and I regret that it should come from a British team. We have had some horrors from America, but none in my experience without some saving humour or light interlude. The writer of this script seems to think that the 'X' category is a depository for sewage."

Strong words. Audrey Field's report (on behalf of secretary Arthur Watkins, who was on leave) to Tony Hinds on Friday 19 October was no more flattering:

"We have now read the script entitled 'THE CURSE OF FRANKENSTEIN' which was enclosed with Mr Sangster's letter of 9th October. As we told Mr Carreras on the telephone last Friday, this script differs considerably from the script entitled *Frankenstein* which he sent us on 13 June and we must treat the subject de novo.

"We are concerned about the flavour of this script, which, in its preoccupation with horror and gruesome detail, goes far beyond what we are accustomed to allow for even the 'X' category. I am afraid we can give no assurance that we should be able to pass a film based on the present script, and a revised script should be sent us for our comments, in which the overall unpleasantness should be much mitigated. In particular, the following points should be noted:-

P.10. The profession of atheism by the ten year old boy seems a gratuitously ugly touch.

P.12. The attempts of the child to vivisect rabbits (the second of which obviously succeeds, though it is not seen) should be omitted.

Pp.20-21. Shots of the dog's corpse will be offensive to many: they should be brief and not detailed, and the shot of the hypodermic needle being plunged home should be omitted.

P.25. The scene of the cutting down of the corpse from the gibbet should be brief. Close shots and details should be avoided – also the shots of it dancing around wildly.

Pp. 27, 28. The dialogue about the head having been mutilated by birds, the cutting off of the head out of frame, and the brief shot of the mutilated head, are all liable to give trouble. The dialogue should be drastically modified and the shot of the head omitted.

Baron Frankenstein (Peter Cushing) kisses his maid Justine (Valerie Gaunt) in The Curse of Frankenstein. The BBFC had concerns about the scene in Sangster's original script and insisted that it "should be discreetly indicated: she should not kiss him with open mouth."

Pp.29, 30. There should be no more than brief flashes in long shot of the headless body floating in the tank.

P.34. There should be no shot of the amputated hands.

P.41. The love making between Justine and Victor (unpleasant in the circumstances of this story) should be discreetly indicated: she should not kiss him with open mouth.

P.45. The talk about bodies mutilated by fish should be omitted.

Pp.46, 49. There should be no shots of the eyeballs.

P.50 and elsewhere. The proposed shots of the horrible composite body, whether alive or dead, sound very likely to be too much for even the 'X' category, as here described, particularly the proposed shots of the face.

P.61. The shot of the dead Bernstein in his coffin should not be too sustained or macabre.

Pp.69 and 77. There should not be too much brutality in the attacks by the creature on Victor and the old man. On p.78, the shot of the old man's body should not be too horrible, and the shot of the little boy's body should be omitted.

P.84. The shot of the creature when it is dug up – eyes and ears full of dirt, and a gaping wound in its face – may well be prohibitive in the completed film.

P.86. The rather gross dialogue about Justine's pregnancy is particularly offensive in the context of this story and should be toned down.

P.90. The present implications that Justine is murdered by the creature are too much. There should be no more than a brief shot of her terrified face – the scream should be omitted – and the sounds of the creature growling and bumping about as it worries her off screen should be omitted.

P.96. This shot of the creature with a blood stained bandage round its face and the appearance of a raving lunatic may well be troublesome in the completed film.

P.98. The statement that Victor cut the creature's vocal cords because it made a noise during the operation should be omitted.

P.100. The death of the creature (half its face is blown away by a bullet; it is then hit by a lamp and catches fire; it then falls into the acid and disintegrates in agony) will not pass. It should not fall into the acid while alive; the shot of its face half blown away is unlikely to pass; and there should be no more than a flash of it catching fire.

<u>P.109</u>. There should be no undue brutality in Victor's attack on Paul.

"We hope the foregoing points will help you in the preparation of a revised script, which we will read for you at short notice as soon as it is ready. If, in the meantime, there are any details which you wish to discuss, I am sure Mr Watkins will be glad to help you on his return to the office next week."

Tony Hinds was having none of it and wrote to Watkins on 24 October 24: "I have made note of the cuts and alterations requested by yourselves. However, as I am setting out to make a 'blood chiller' I must incorporate a certain amount of visual horror as that is what the public will be paying to see. However, based on my experience with *Quatermass* and *X the Unknown*, I think that I can assure you that I will not include anything too horrid or offensive."

Hinds would go on to supervise the shooting of Sangster's script pretty much as it was submitted, with only minor rewrites by himself. As for Jimmy Sangster – it was an exciting time. *X the Unknown*, his first full feature screenplay, had been released to favourable reviews and now his script for *The Curse of Frankenstein* was about to go before the cameras. Now he had prospective employers knocking at his door, but it was a sympathetic friend who finally gave him his break.

"If Michael Carreras hadn't made me the offer that he did I probably wouldn't have become a writer," Sangster recalls. "On the back of *X the Unknown* I'd been asked to do a script for Irving Allen and Cubby Broccoli at Warwick Films based on *The Day of the Triffids*. They never used it and they never made it. I remember I was working on it in my office at Bray one day when Michael called by and caught me burying it under my desk like a naughty schoolboy. He said, 'What are you doing?' I said, 'I'm doing this script for Warwick Films.' He said, 'Come on, you're a production manager working for us. You've got to make up your mind what you want to be. Do you want to be a production manager or do you want to be a writer?' I said, 'I'd better be a production manager because I get a weekly salary.' I think it was £35. I'd just had a kid and I'd got a mortgage on a house and so I said I'd stick to being a production manager. He said, 'I tell you what, I'll make you an offer. I guarantee you one script a year for the next three years at £750 a time.' Believe it or not, that was enough to pay my mortgage and so I could afford to become a writer."

And so Jimmy Sangster finally left Hammer's permanent payroll. He received a golden handshake from Will Hammer (the first time Sangster had met him) and an inscribed gold cigarette case. However, *The Day of the Triffids* fell through and the months to follow would not bode well for the fledgling writer.

With a projected budget of £65,000, Tony Hinds gradually assembled the film's brilliant technical crew. Terence Fisher was brought in to direct, supported by Jack Asher as cinematographer, Len Harris as camera operator, Harry Oakes on focus, Bernard Robinson as production designer, James Needs as editor, Don Weeks as production manager, Jock May on sound and Molly Arbuthnot on costumes; a formidable team that worked well together and would continue to do so on the Gothic renaissance to come.

In fact, Fisher, Asher and Harris had already worked together on two productions at Gainsborough: *Portrait from Life* (1948) and *The Astonished Heart* (1949). Jack Asher remembered, "Terry and I met for the first time some years previously at the old Gainsborough studio, Islington, London, where he served an apprenticeship in the editing department whilst I was an assistant cameraman. We were both attached to the permanent staff, a circumstance that prevailed in those far-off days. We worked on the same film for the first time later at the same studio when he was elevated to director and I became a director of photography. I remember the film well – it was titled *Portrait from Life* and starred Mai Zetterling, Herbert Lom and Guy Rolfe. This partnership must have shown promise because it was repeated again but this time at Pinewood Studios, Iver, Bucks under the J Arthur Rank banner when they absorbed both the Gainsborough and Gaumont British companies' key technicians. *The Astonished Heart* was a more sophisticated movie and boasted a cast starring Noël Coward, Celia Johnson and Margaret Leighton. There was a lapse of time before our third meeting. We were brought together when Anthony Nelson Keys, whom we both knew from our old Gainsborough days, decided to team Terry and myself in the 'megging' and 'lensing' position on the first Hammer Frankenstein vehicle which was in preparation." [6]

Sadly, it would seem that Fisher felt he was only given the picture because Hammer literally owed him one. Tony Hinds saw it very differently: "I was rather sorry to discover that he thought the only reason Hammer engaged him to direct the first of their Gothic horrors was that they owed him a [picture on his existing] contract: it is not true. I asked to have him. We had worked on two shows together before and had got on so well that I knew that he would at least understand what sort of films I wanted the Hammer horror shows to be – rich-looking, slow, deliberately paced, bursting with unstated sex but with nothing overt – no nudity, no dolly girls – and he did." [7]

Fisher (then a veteran aged 52) embraced the subject in his own modest way. "I found the project very exciting not only because it was in colour, but because it was a new version of a film classic. It proved to be the start of a new cycle in this genre of film making. It had a very modest budget. Really, I've worked with medium budgets all my life. I've learned how to be economical in the way that I've shot. I trust I've not become poverty stricken in the way I've expressed myself. The big money wasn't there, but one had to use one's brain … practically or largely cutting in the camera, rather than supplying the cutting room with a colossal amount of waste shots." [8]

Next, Hinds, together with casting director Dorothy Holloway, assembled his 'competent British cast'. 43-year-old Peter Cushing was already an accomplished British television actor, having had won the *Daily Mail* National TV Award in both 1953 and 1954 and the Guild of Television Producers and Directors Award in 1955, the latter for his interpretation of Winston Smith in Nigel Kneale's adaptation of Orwell's *Nineteen Eighty-Four* for the BBC. "At the time there was quite a strong rivalry between the film and television companies," Cushing recalled. "The film people did not really want to employ anyone associated with television and vice versa. The exception however was Hammer films. In 1956 I was reading the various trade papers and read that Hammer were preparing to film *Frankenstein* in colour. Having seen the original James Whale version and loved it, I telephoned my agent and said, 'As I now have some spare time, this is something I would like to do. Are Hammer interested in my services?' They were, I was, so that is how it all began." [9]

James Carreras arranged a private screening of *X the Unknown* for Cushing in order to show what Hammer were capable of. Cushing was impressed and signed his contract on 26 October. He would become the screen's definitive Baron Frankenstein, returning to the role for a further five Hammer adventures.

Cushing explained his approach to the Baron: "I've never seen him as a madman … I place him on an even par with Robert Knox the anatomist. As you know, Knox was a real person. Knox only had one eye and used to close it when Burke and Hare brought him freshly killed people, rather like turning a blind eye in a different way. His whole point was that to cure a sick body you had to know how it functioned and the only way to find out was to experiment on an actual body, and to do this you had to have a supply of cadavers, which Burke and Hare were only too willing to supply for a price … I always feel he [Frankenstein] is experimenting for the same reason as Robert Knox but in reverse, by taking pieces of bodies and making one…" [10]

Cushing was a perfectionist and never more so than when attacking the role of Baron Frankenstein. Perfectionism for Cushing meant playing the role as legitimately as possible, especially the laboratory scenes, requiring a rudimentary but practical knowledge of anatomy and how to handle instruments, as well as certain medical procedures, some more unorthodox than others. This often meant a visit to his general practitioner: "I must know what I am doing and you have to allow for any medical viewers who may be annoyed by any incorrect procedures. It's the same as driving a car. You would not take it on the road unless you were fully conversant with the knowledge of how to handle the vehicle properly. My doctor is always delighted to see me and often says it makes a change to see someone who is not ill, but just wants to know how to remove a brain!" [11]

For the role of the Creature, Hammer looked for a suitably tall actor. Comic actor Bernard Bresslaw (fondly remembered today as a member of the Carry On team) was initially considered, but the role eventually went to a tall and relatively unknown 34-year-old called Christopher Lee. What is not commonly appreciated is that *The Curse of Frankenstein* was his 42nd film. He made his film debut in *Corridor of Mirrors* in 1947 and continued with a succession of small character parts in impressive movies like *Scott of the Antarctic, Captain Horatio Hornblower RN, The Crimson Pirate* and *The Dark Avenger*. Prophetically, he also appeared in Peter Cushing's first two films in England (though they never met), *Hamlet* (1947) and *Moulin Rouge* (1952), as well as a film directed by Terence Fisher called *Song for Tomorrow* (1948). He also supplemented his film work with numerous television

Phil Leakey tests
his designs for
Creature make-up
on Christopher
Lee during
pre-production of
The Curse of
Frankenstein
(1956).

appearances including *Douglas Fairbanks Presents*, *Colonel March of Scotland Yard* (his first encounter with Boris Karloff) and *The Errol Flynn Theatre* (his first work at Bray Studios).

"All I know is that I had been told for years that I was too tall and too foreign-looking," recalls Lee. "I had no name and no experience, although I must say those first 10 years had been priceless, because I was learning, which is something that they don't even bother to do now. Then my agent just rang up one day and said, 'They're looking for somebody who's very tall and who has experience in mime.' I said, 'Well, what is it?' He said, 'They're going to do *Frankenstein* and they want you to play the Creature.' I thought, 'Well, I haven't been getting anywhere looking like I do, so if I cover myself in peculiar make-up and it's a success, people will wonder what I really look like.' So I took it."

While in the wrong hands the Creature might have come across as a robotic stumbling brute (as in *The Evil of Frankenstein*, Hammer's third entry in the series), Lee tackled the role intelligently. With the oppressive gaze of Universal ever-present, Hammer had to make sure that their 'Creature' bore no resemblance to the Universal 'Monster' immortalised by Boris Karloff. The end result of Phil Leakey's countless make-up tests has been described by Lee on several occasions as "something resembling a road accident."

The task of coming up with something completely different to the Universal 'look' was a daunting one for Leakey, as he explained: "We tried several versions, some getting a little too close to Jack Pierce's, and they were scrapped. One which we tried was with a completely bald head, but nobody liked it, least of all Christopher ... Then we tried something that looked like a cross between a man and a gorilla that had had an argument with a truck. A few variations like this and, remember, all this against the clock. We were due to start shooting in 20 hours' time and nothing settled. All very worrying and much conferring between Terry, Tony, Christopher and myself. Then we came to a sort of consensus of opinion – more or less. That we would try and forget all about monsters and other people's films and anything else that was worrying us. The idea evolved that we would just try sticking lumps of flesh on a skeleton or skull and stitch it all up. That is what happened. I felt that another week and it would have been much better." [12]

Lee remembers the tests: "There are a series pictures of me being made up in *The Curse of Frankenstein*. That was not the make-up in the film, it was one of the tests. One of the pictures is a

Christopher Lee clowns around with Hazel Court in the canteen during the shooting of The Curse of Frankenstein (1956).

profile shot with Phil Leakey and there is a white lump on the front of my nose. Now that was one of the three dreadful make-up tests that were done on me and I remember that particular one made me look like the elephant man. Then there was another one that made me look like a cross between a wild boar and a wolf – all very bizarre. Then somebody came up with the idea, and I think I was partially involved, of just putting bits and pieces on my face, which probably would be the case if you were putting somebody together from bits and pieces. It was very crude and very obvious in some respects, but it probably would look like that."

Assistant director Derek Whitehurst even remembered Leakey frantically testing on him. " I remember Phil experimented on me while we were doing the preproduction. He shoved a whole lot of it on my face one day. For quite a while they were trying out all sorts of formulas, because they had this thing, as you know, that they couldn't use the Universal make-up. The original Karloff make-up is probably the most perfect make-up and it will never go away. So for a long time Phil was working this out and trying many experiments, but I think what he did was pretty good actually. He just tried the one on me. I can't think what he did now, I think my eye was in my forehead or something like that. I think he was just trying it out to see how the thing would cling to one's face, because the make-up wasn't too sophisticated in those days, but he did a wonderful job on Chris. It was terrific and Chris was very good about it, because it was not the most comfortable thing to have done each morning by any means."

Phil Leakey was far from impressed by the whole exercise. "Although I had a good chap helping me on that film called George Turner, he didn't want to know anything about Christopher Lee's make-up. In fact, he swore that he developed a stomach ulcer as a result of that first Frankenstein. It was all such a mad rush with no proper preparation, no understanding from the producers of what the job entailed to do it as it should have been done, and none of the materials to make up the parts to stick to poor old C Lee's face. A bit of a cock-up, in fact, as far as I was concerned." [13]

The basic premise involved bits of flesh crudely sewn together with the right eye blinded by a cataract. The make-up was later modified when Paul Krempe shoots half the Creature's face away in the forest, resulting in a balding scar where Frankenstein performed his makeshift brain surgery. The make-up was extremely uncomfortable for Lee to wear and, with his right eye obscured by the cataract, his facial movements were very limited. Instead, Lee concentrated on the bodily expression of the creature – without proper control of his limbs, adopting a sad spastic gait.

Lee explains his approach: "As far as I was concerned, I was doing a film and playing a character which had been played many times before – most famously of all by a very dear friend of mine, Boris Karloff. I only had one thought in my mind and it had nothing to do with Mary Shelley. I thought that this being, this creature, didn't ask to be born. He's been put together from bits and pieces of somebody else and the brain, which controls everything, has been damaged, so the movements, the head, the body, the hands or the legs, are not co-ordinated. That's why in that scene where I'm chained sitting on the floor in front of Robert Urquhart, I was like a spastic trying to get to my feet and trying to sit down. I wasn't using that as a model, I just wanted to convey the feeling that he was disconnected. That was the only thought in my mind. I didn't set out to frighten people."

The make-up also made it difficult for Lee to eat or drink. A number of publicity stills were released showing him at lunch with co-star Hazel Court in the canteen. So disguised was Lee by the make-up that Peter Cushing was apparently bemused by the tall handsome stranger who used to greet him by name at the studio, not recognising him as the hulking brute he was bringing to life in the film. The make-up took two and a half to three hours to apply and, to relieve the boredom, Lee and Leakey listened to the Olympic games, which were currently taking place in Melbourne Australia, on the radio.

For Hammer's first two Gothic 'scream queens' they chose two West Midlands girls: 30-year-old Black Country native Hazel Court as Elizabeth, Frankenstein's fiancée, and 23-year-old Birmingham-born Valerie Gaunt as Justine, the maid. Court had been in films since 1944 and was married to actor Dermot Walsh. Their six-year-old daughter Sally was called upon to play the young Elizabeth at the beginning opposite Melvyn Hayes' young Frankenstein. Janina Faye, soon to play little Tania in the following year's *Dracula*, also auditioned for the role, but the family resemblance between mother and daughter presumably won the day. For Valerie Gaunt, Justine was her first film role. Hammer's publicity department would have us believe she was chosen for her screaming abilities after Tony Hinds had seen her scream her way through a TV play, *Chance Meeting*.

Shooting began on *The Curse of Frankenstein* on Monday 19 November, yet a letter from James Carreras to Eliot Hyman on 21 November showed that Universal International were still fighting: "I hear that Universal International have objected to the registration of the title 'THE CURSE OF FRANKENSTEIN'. Fight this with everything you have got because we are advised here that being in public domain anybody can call a film 'FRANKENSTEIN' and 'THE CURSE OF...' is an original addition of our own." The letter also throws light on a developing distribution deal being negotiated with Warner Bros: "Please let me know when the Warner deal is signed and settled." Hyman was a good friend of Ben Kalmenson, the Warner Bros president, and already had personal dealings with Warners through his AAP outfit.

Meanwhile, the financial backing for Hammer's first Frankenstein was proving far from ideal. Initially, Eliot Hyman agreed to take a 50 per cent interest in the film's financing and profits while Carreras arranged additional financing from his friend Jack Goodlatte at Associated British Pictures (ABPC). However, Hyman's unpredictable handling left Hammer in a constant state of insecurity and at various times production on *The Curse of Frankenstein* nearly had to close down. Hammer got no preproduction cash in advance from their American financiers, as promised, and only after numerous pleading letters did they receive the first instalment – a full 12 days after shooting began. James Carreras was far from impressed as his letter to Eliot Hyman of 1 October attests: "Hysterical you suggest. After looking through our correspondence file, it's a wonder I'm not biting lumps out of the carpet. Before the film started we wrote you five pleading letters and sent you four cables requesting your share of the budget. Stillman arrived one week after production had started with the agreement and after that was signed your share arrived. No pre-production cash from you and your share twelve days after the shooting starts – what sort of a 50/50 partnership is that?"

While films are usually shot out of sequence, the first scenes shot just happened to be the first in the film, namely the long shot of the priest riding up the hill (with an impressive Les Bowie matte painting in the background), followed by his arrival at the prison courtyard. The latter was in fact the front courtyard entrance of Down Place. The prison gates were erected flush with the doors of the brick 'New Stage' (out of sight on the right) to create the walled-off courtyard; the two boarded windows we see at the bottom of it, positioned either side of the wisteria, were the windows of the studio manager's office and that of his secretary. The area either side of the concrete drive that led up to the main entrance then lay empty and undeveloped. Soon this would become Hammer's back lot, blossoming with a number of external sets that were left to stand between productions and reused. Stage 1 would be erected on the right side of the drive by the car park and a large village square complex would soon grow up on the left side.

The two long shots of the castle at night, the first after Frankenstein and Krempe bury the Creature and the other after Frankenstein tells Justine to pack her bags, were actually views of nearby Oakley Court. The window we fade to as Cushing bends over the tank to implant the brain is at Down Place and looms above what today are Bray's canteen and bar, overlooking the lawn on the side of the Thames and the ex-ballroom stage (now a viewing theatre). It was here, alongside the Thames in a secluded wooded area backing onto Oakley Court, that the Creature killed the blind man and was ultimately shot by Paul and buried.

Bray at that time still only had two stages and the rest of the house had to be deployed for other scenes. Third assistant Hugh Harlow remembers the arrangement of the sets: "Frankenstein's prison cell was on the Ballroom Stage. Frankenstein's lounge, hall and stairs, and the laboratory, were on the New Stage'. The scene where the Creature falls through the skylight, was filmed in two sections over different days. The exterior was shot at night on a constructed set over the ceiling of the ballroom's bay window steps – this being the part in which the Creature crashes through the skylight – and the second shot was on the New Stage, bringing him through the skylight into the tank of acid." Though the sets for *The Curse of Frankenstein* were modest compared with the Gothics to follow (owing to the opening of Bray's large Stage 1 in 1957), they were still pretty remarkable, especially the laboratory set on the New Stage, an intricate collection of bubbling jars with vibrant colours and pseudo-Victorian wizardry, including an exquisite Wimshurst machine.

Ted Marshall was first appointed as art director on the movie, but was later demoted to assisting Bernard Robinson when the latter was brought onto the project late. Draughtsman Don Mingaye, who himself would soon be working alongside Robinson as art director, remembered the shuffle: "Ted Marshall actually started that [film]. I really don't know what happened in the front office to this day, but there was obviously a need for a change." The change would seem to have been imposed by Robinson's buddy, associate producer Anthony Nelson Keys: "I brought Bernie with me really," he confessed. "He was one of the greatest, he really was. Built sets out of nothing." [14]

The sets were erected by Hammer's construction crew led by Master Plasterer Arthur Banks. Jack Curtis was chief electrician-cum-electrical special effects man and contributed to the magic of Frankenstein's lab. Hugh Harlow remembers him: "He was a stalwart old trouper, salt of the earth, chief electrician and general hands-on. He knew everything mechanical around the studio. He was one of the original people that Michael and Tony brought into Hammer Films as it was in the very early days, virtually at the beginning." John Jay remembers his major contribution to Bray: "The head electrician was Jack Curtis, a very clever man. He was also a great engineer and a master at such skills as welding etc. He built a power station and had a generator brought in which supplied power to the stages."

Curtis, assisted by his team of Bob Palmer and Harold Marland, created the electrical special effects as Frankenstein's lab hummed, throbbed and crackled into life. Hammer fan Stephen Pickard remembered Jack Curtis telling him about the construction of the Wimshurst generator, which would later reappear in the sequel, *The Revenge of Frankenstein*: "It consisted of a thick wooden base and an attractively carved axle. The counter-rotating wheels were perspex and the fins were made of ordinary silver foil, which provided the eye-catching stroboscopic pattern when turning. The spark gap over the top of the wheels was devised with two long, half-inch, copper tubes from the base and curving at the top parallel to the wheel, with a gap of 14 inches. The tips were made up of two spherical objects, one an eight-inch ballcock and the other a brass poker knob. Two armatures, positioned halfway at the widest point between the two wheels, were each connected to a coil entering two enclosures made up of toilet brush containers covered with foil, also attached to the base. Thin long pieces of glass piercing the wooden axle contributed to the support of the

Frankenstein
(Peter Cushing)
conducts an
experiment to
revitalise a dog in
The Curse of
Frankenstein
(1956).

half-inch copper tubing." [15] The machine was fully operational and Curtis had to supervise Peter Cushing very carefully as he generated potentially lethal voltages to create the stunning effects.

Third assistant Hugh Harlow remembers what it was like working at Bray during this time. "It was a very happy routine, I know that. I have to say it because, today, film's aren't always that way. They were very tightly scheduled and budgeted and they just seemed to go like clockwork. They were shot in five weeks, invariably on a very low budget, something like £60,000 – peanuts then. We were a regular crew and continued to be. We would shoot for five weeks and there would be about a two-week lay-off while they were revamping the main set to another set, while the village on the lot was becoming Dracula's castle or another Transylvanian village setting. Without striking the entire set they would just revamp it. So there was this turnaround which just happily went on. The working day would start at 8.30. There would be a big coach leaving Hammersmith at 7.30 picking up a good chunk of the crew en route, going down the Great West Road, the Bath Road – there was no M4 then. Got there at 8.20, washed your hands, put your overalls on, start at 8.30. Finish at 5.50 on a Wednesday and Friday or 6.20 on a Monday, Tuesday and Thursday ... all union hours, and into the coach by half past the hour or six o'clock and back up to Hammersmith. That was week in week out. No Saturdays or Sundays, occasionally the odd late day in the evening or over to Black Park, for coaches going through country roads or Transylvanian forests. And it was a happy family, I always remember that. Everyone knew everybody and Mrs T, who ran the restaurant and canteen with a rod of iron, did superb cooking."

Producer Tony Hinds' routine was just as gruelling: "Up early so as to be at the (generally bitter cold) studio before the first actor arrived (and with some of the make-ups required for our shows, that meant arriving pretty damn early!). Onto a soundstage for the first set-up (everybody always takes it easy at first, then panics in the afternoon, trying to get the day's schedule done. I was there to remind them to start panicking first thing!). Into the Art Department to see what Bernie Robinson was drawing. We never agreed (he always won). Into the office to phone my secretary in London to see what was happening at the head office (I never had a secretary at the studio). Back to the stage to breathe down the director's neck (they took it very well, really, particularly Freddie Francis and Terry Fisher, both of whom are still speaking to me). Possibly the writer of the next show would come down (if I was not writing it myself), and we'd have a session discussing it

Christopher Lee
enjoys a tea break
at Bray during the
shooting The
Curse of
Frankenstein
(1956). Note the
blood on his face;
he has just
completed the
scene where he is
shot in the head.

(falling about with laughter most of the time, I have to confess). Back to the floor for more heavy breathing. Rushes ... Then lunch (we always had marvellous food at Bray). A brief kip, then back to work, breathing down their necks again. Et al." [16]

From his office on the left-hand side of the courtyard, Tony Hinds kept a silent vigil with his finger very much on the pulse. As Hugh Harlow explains: "Tony Hinds had a microphone sitting on his desk which was wired through to the sound console on the floor and the boom (which picks up all the dialogue from the artists and any other miscellaneous dialogue), and this would come right through to Tony's loudspeaker. Mind you, it could be switched off from the set, so we used to play around with that and sometimes switch it off and say what we wanted to say, so that Tony wouldn't hear us." First assistant Derek Whitehurst did not much care for it either: "They had a microphone linked up to Tony Hinds' office, so they could hear everything that was going on on the set. I didn't like it actually, because one was aware that you were being listened to and you just had to keep things moving. You couldn't waffle about and make excuses. Once a shot was done, it was, 'Quick please, let's have the viewfinder. Let's line up the next shot. Where are the actors? Shall we rehearse them? Do you want this Terry?' It was all like that."

Given the cult status of Hammer today and its rich heritage of genre films, it can be very easy to take for granted the one that started it all – *The Curse of Frankenstein*. It must be remembered, however, that Britain had never before produced a colour horror film, nor had the Frankenstein saga been afforded anything but shadowy black and white. It must therefore have taken a courageous and determined group of filmmakers that winter to forge what was then a totally unprecedented motion picture, with a new, liberal approach to horror. (And, though relatively 'under wraps' for the time being, sex.) Pivotal to the film's success was director Terence Fisher, who, with a highly talented group of technicians and actors at his disposal, brought to life a classic of the genre, sparking off a horror renaissance which continues to this day.

The success and high production values of Hammer's Gothics were the result of a talented team of technicians who could work together like a well oiled machine in spite of undue pressures imposed by the less than sympathetic producers. The core team on *The Curse Of Frankenstein* consisted of the camera crew headed by the director of photography (Jack Asher), camera operator (Len Harris) and focus puller (Harry Oakes). The director of photography or lighting cameraman is responsible for creating the mood of the picture and although Jack Asher was deemed a little slow, he was exemplary in his field. Harry Oakes recalls, "Jack would use a lot of lamps. For example, if there were four or five people in a scene, Jack would light them individually and light the back wall separately, so that when the artist moved there weren't a lot of shadows on the wall. It was a matter of time, you see. He used to tell me, 'Harry boy, it's what lights you leave off that counts!' And sure enough, always with every lamp, he'd have what we call a flag, which would start from the top and cut right down to lose all the light possible for that lamp which wasn't necessary, so it didn't spill onto the set."

The camera operator's job is to frame the shots and capture the action. Len Harris was a perfectionist and director Terence Fisher trusted him implicitly as Harry Oakes explains, "He had such a good rapport with Len that he trusted him absolutely. He would look up and down the track and look at these different positions and so on, and would tell Len what he wanted, but once he had OK'd it, it was all Len." Harris adored his Vinten/Everest camera. "*The Curse Of Frankenstein* went to the Warner Bros. cinema in the West End of London," he remembered. "Had a good run there. A technically interesting thing, the chief projectionist there told one of our representatives, 'This is the sharpest focusing film I've had for many, many years.' This reflects well on the Vinten camera. Excellent camera. They didn't make a large number of them, because it didn't look like a camera. It didn't look very exciting. Jack Asher was against it the first time he saw it. 'Can't we get a Mitchell or something?' I said, 'Jack, I've used this camera a lot and I like it.' And he said, 'Well, if you like it, we'll try it.' And he was absolutely sold on it." [4]

Focus puller Harry Oakes describes the process of focusing the movie camera, "One has to stand by the camera during all the rehearsals to know what the shot is. The number boy marks the positions of the feet of the artists on the floor when possible. Having made a note of all that, when you finish with the main artists and call in the stand-ins, you get your tape measure out and just measure up the various positions. The operator would be doing much the same for himself through his viewfinder. Sometimes it would be necessary to split the focus, for example if you've got someone in the foreground and someone up stage a bit and they both need to be sharp. This would be done by altering the depth of field. The more the aperture stops down the greater the depth of field. For tracking shots, the focus puller has a little seat on the side of the velocelator or dolly and you generally have marks on the floor at a certain position, for example where 10 feet is and so on. Different chaps had different ways of doing it. I don't like marks on the floor myself, because something may happen while you're looking on the floor. I find it best to look at the artists and take positions where the artists are at a certain time. Artists are pretty good and so once you've got it taped it doesn't really vary a great deal. They knew they had to be spot on themselves."

Supporting the camera crew are the clapper/loader (who loads the film magazine), the camera grip (who moves the camera along its tracks) and the sound boom operator. Sound boom operator on *The Curse Of Frankenstein* was Jimmy Parry and Harry Oakes recalls the problems he faced, "Then of course you have the boom operator. That was always a problem for the lighting cameraman to light beyond the boom and the microphone. The boom operator used to get quite skilful actually. He would ask what lens you were using and if it was a 28, wide angle, then he would know he had to sky his microphone higher. Some cameramen were kinder than others in the way they lit the set to miss the microphone all together."

The director Terry Fisher is essentially there to get the best out of his actors and he decribed his approach, "I've had my call sheet. I know what scenes are to be shot – I know what they mean. I've thought about them within context – it could even be one of the last scenes in the picture, but it could be the most important. On every day of shooting, I've a complete overall development of the story, so you go on the floor and know what to do. I know exactly how many shots I've got to do, where I'm going to put the camera. In other words, once you have the overall picture and the overall movement of actors, you then have your first physical rehearsal, get a real pattern and from there, the thing just progresses. There's a lot of spontaneity I think and intuitional feel when you start getting physical rehearsal. I can never understand directors who say six shots for this scene and so and so will move from there to there to keep them in, and virtually having in their minds eye what they think they are going to do before physical rehearsal. This I don't understand – treating actors as puppets then manipulating them. Purely mechanical things are wrong, because some of the most brilliant ideas come out of physical rehearsal, when actors and actresses get together and the chemistry starts working. Movements come out of their rehearsal, which one could never think of beforehand. This is the basis I think and this is the way I work. Everybody has a different way of working. One of the gravest mistakes is to pre-plan to the point where an actor merely becomes a mechanical puppet and movement .... it's playing the scene and feeling the scenes and movements you could not think of. You can't evolve it in cold blood beforehand – I can't anyhow. You can guide them sometimes and stop them from doing the wrong things, but they have got to have their heads to start the chemistry of things going." [17]

John Jay concurs, "He used to let the artists do it. He'd have a scene to do and stand there and say, 'Well run it for me.' And they used to run it and he would make very few alterations. He would do the set ups, because he was a very good director, but he would give them a complete free hand to do how they thought it should be done and most of the time it was correct and he didn't have much to do, but just set it all up and do the camera angles and his close-ups and things. He was a very good director that way and I think the artists adored him for giving them such a free hand. It was the right way to direct, because you really got out of people what they could do then."

Peripheral to the process are first, second and third assistant directors. The first assistant director is the director's right hand man. For 25-year-old first assistant Derek Whitehurst, it was a learning experience. This was his first feature as first assistant, having been plucked by Tomy Nelson Keys from the Bray filming of *The Errol Flynn Theatre*. "It's a coordinating job really. Standing by the director, having everything ready, being able to take rehearsals with actors, being able to break down a script. In general, knowing your script back to front and being able to plan out the day's shooting. Logistics was the main thing of the job, but I felt very young at the time. When I look back on it, I realise how much knowledge I lacked, and working with someone like Terry, it was quite an education.

"Jack Asher was the cameraman. I'd worked with Jack at Gainsborough studios – I was his camera assistant – but of course it's a different thing when suddenly you're confronted with being the assistant director and you have to push people. I wasn't used to this at all. I often wonder how good I was at the job at the time, because there were inquests by Tony Nelson Keys at the end of the day about how far behind we had got and the schedules and budgets, and it was terrible when he would say to me, 'Now Derek, what do you think of Jack's work today? Are you pushing him hard enough?' And I was only 25. At 25 today, most people are very sophisticated, but certainly I wasn't then. 25 was considered quite young in the industry then – most directors were in their late thirties and forties – so I felt very much a novice on the picture, but I like to think I got through it all right."

The second assistant director, Jimmy Komisarjevsky, was the link between the production office and the floor, in charge of producing the daily call sheets. Derek Whitehurst remembers him: "Jimmy was on the Errol Flynn series with me and his father was a famous impresario, who had quite a reputation. Jimmy was a good 2nd assistant. He was very, very worldly, knew a lot about life."

Third assistant director Hugh Harlow was the gofer and he recalls, "That was Christopher Lee's first picture for Hammer as the creature. I always remember him getting very annoyed with me, because I was forever hounding him to get onto the set. He was spending so much time in the make-up chair under the auspices of Phil Leakey, putting on this fantastic make-up. He put in these contact lenses and they were so painful and I was too young to appreciate what he was going through. I know Christopher Lee quite well now and every so often we talk on the phone or meet with each other and he says, 'Do you remember when you ..?' So I remember hounding Chris and being hounded by Chris for hounding him."

Sound recordist Jock May was another colourful character. Hugh Harlow recalls, "He lived in a riverside house near Bray in Maidenhead and because the studio backed on to the river, Jock would canoe down. He'd got this big bushy red beard and red hair and abhorred socks, so he was regarded as one of the characters of the unit as he came off the banks of the Thames with his canoe on his back reporting for work." Harry Oakes remembers that, "The sound camera operator [Michael Sale] was often not on the set at all at Bray. He would be in the sound truck, which was parked outside. A cable went through to it from the sound camera and he would sit and operate it. He'd have his headphones on to make sure it was all going okay. The Mitchell was operated on the floor of course. The actual sound recordist on the set would give the turn over and signal the sound camera operator in the truck with a little buzz and when the sound camera was running, he would give us a little buzz as well. We would say 'camera running' and that was the cue for the director. The clapper boy would announce the take and the director would shout 'action!'"

The process of making movies is a slow and laborious business, so much so that James Carreras generally kept well out of the way, finding it too painful to watch people whose wages he was paying standing around for much of the time. "I remember once when he came down," remembers John Jay. "You know how you stand around in between takes and there's nothing to do until they're ready for most of us? He said to Tony Hinds, 'What are they all doing? They're reading the paper, they're all sitting around.' He couldn't stand it – he didn't understand it took a long time to set it up. I don't think he could stand the slow pace, but he was a very charming and a very clever man."

Gifted lighting cameraman Jack Asher recalled that "I was convinced from the beginning that The Curse of Frankenstein, being a dramatic production, should be photographed as such. Even my photo colleagues were sceptical about my plans to shoot ... an overall majority low-key scene, but with very vivid and vibrant colours always present among the highlights. As the production progressed, I realised, not without some satisfaction, that my outlandish theories were correct. This evidence viewed every day in the rushes made filming ever more interesting and absorbing. It was also interesting to note the reaction from management as the rushes unfolded happily before their eyes."[5]

Asher remembered well his difficulties within the rather confined spaces at Bray. "When I first arrived at Bray Studios, I was surprised to learn that the only sound stage was quite small. I also found, to my dismay, that the rooms in the adjoining house would be our other stages. I never did get quite used to the idea of calling a room Stage 3 or 4. It was lucky that I had experience while shooting Young Lovers in using tubular portable rigging. This was necessary in some of the beautiful town houses used for that story. This enabled me to place my lamps strategically but unobtrusively. This was useful knowledge at Bray, where it was a way of life. The sets just fit within the four walls of the rooms, with the loss of any space for catwalks for the electricians to manoeuvre my lamps. I remember setting up. A metal ladder was brought in and set up, then taken away for each lighting adjustment. Only the support I got from George Robinson, the gaffer, and his entire electrical crew, made it possible to proceed with any speed or efficiency."[5]

Terence Fisher was always complimentary. "Jack Asher makes a very stylised use of colours. He can never resist juxtaposing red and green and he does it marvellously. But he can also create a highly surreal atmosphere with very little means. He believes in the dramatic use of colours."[18] Len Harris agreed: "Jack would use a gelatin film and put it over a lamp to shine on a certain part of a set to very good effect. Sometime or other, he would say to me, 'I hope you are getting that effect.' He tended to paint the set in light and colour. Where blood was featured, he would try and get a red glow into it."[1]

The Curse of Frankenstein was an experiment in colour. In the scene where the boy disappears in the woods, the ground was still covered with autumn leaves and Fisher remembers further exaggerating the colour: "I can remember painting leaves or twigs red, because I wanted in the foreground a suggestion of red. If people were conscious of it, I don't know. The leaves' red indicating danger and blood as the little boy went away and disappeared, and you were left there staring at that little foreground of foliage with blotches of red in it. I have a feeling we shot that scene in the autumn and I got the idea purely by chance, because the leaves were just turning darker and I thought we'd turn them a bit redder than they were. If anybody really got it, I don't know. It's the sort of psychological thing without realising it they might get. This is picture making – the hidden meanings."[19]

Harry Oakes also remembered the almost obsessional attention to colour detail: "Jack was very extravagant with colour, because it was colour. I remember when we were doing some tests with the dog on *The Curse of Frankenstein*. When Terry Fisher saw the dog, he said, 'Oh, it's a colour film. What are we doing with a black and white dog?' And we had to take it back and get a black and tan one. I remember we'd just moved house ... It was quite quiet in the house and my daughter was only five or six and she wanted a puppy, so to save the buyer taking him back, I bought him. We called him Badger." Sure enough the episode is recorded in Harry Oakes' diary on 15 November: "Brought a puppy home for Christine. We were doing tests for *Frankenstein*. Terry Fisher said it was a colour film so he didn't want a black-white dog. I bought it off the buyer for £1-10-0."

The replacement dog also got a good home, courtesy of co-star Robert Urquhart. "Do you remember the little puppy, one of the first experiments? Well, I had that for the rest of its life. We have, I think, had three or four generations from Frankie. I remember seeing Hazel Court years afterwards and we were talking about the picture. I said that the film had been on the telly and she said, 'Oh yes.' And I said, 'What on earth did you watch that for?' Of course, she watched it for her daughter. She said, 'Why did you watch it anyway?' And I said, 'For the dog!' That was the only reason I ever watched it!" [20]

The film saw the beginning of a great friendship between co-stars Cushing and Lee. "Chris Lee used to pop in singing opera and complaining that he hadn't any lines, to which I replied 'You haven't read the script'," Cushing remembered. "It was a rather ropey script at that time. It did need a little attending to. You could always tell when Christopher arrived at the studio, because you could hear his great voice singing, but when he got all this make-up stuff on, it did keep him a little quieter." [21] Lee adds, "It's true I used to sing to him and we did do dances at the rushes in front of the screen for the benefit of the crew and cast. We used to link arms and do softshoe shuffles and things like that."

The production was not without its problems. One painful moment Lee remembers well is the scene where he is shot in the face. He had to press a handful of fake blood to his eye to simulate being shot in the head, and the blood got into his eye. "It was like someone had put a red hot poker into my eye." Ted Marshall recalled other problems: "There was another anxious day on that film when the Frankenstein Monster – plaster dummy wrapped in bandages – was first put into the glass-sided tank. My first anxiety had been the strength of the toughened glass to withstand the pressure of a tank filled with water, but this was soon forgotten when the plaster could not be made to float face upwards and kept on sinking to one side. There were a few angry glances from the producer at the time being wasted, but finally nylon thread and some well-placed weights did the trick. The director on this film was, of course, Terence Fisher, a very pleasant man to work with and very quiet and methodical in his approach. But I can't say I much enjoyed preparing for the 'operation' sequences, with the daily order of goats' eyes from the local abattoir and the exacting demands of Peter Cushing to have all the correct medical equipment at hand." [2]

To prevent major mishaps, stuntman Jock Easton was on hand for the more risky scenes. His first big scene was as the highwayman Frankenstein cuts down from the gibbet. At the end of the first day's shooting, strung up by a parachute harness, Easton had to hold his breath so that it didn't show in the crisp November air. He later supervised one of his colleagues making Professor Bernstein's death plunge from the top of the staircase onto a trampoline in a cut-out section of the marble floor below. According to Terence Fisher, "Originally I thought he had killed himself. He only had half the size of the rug on paper capra to fall on. He missed the edge and he badly bumped himself, but we got the camera in the right spot for it." [19]

The shooting extended into the Christmas festivities that year. More of a problem for burly Scotsman Jock Easton was that his most dramatic scene, the death of the Creature at the climax, interfered with his Hogmanay celebrations – it was filmed on New Year's Day. With nursing sister Yvonne Parke from Putney standing by, the hung-over Scotsman was subjected to Phil Leakey's full Creature make-up and then smeared with anti-flash paste. He was then dressed as the Creature, daubed in petroleum jelly and set alight. His 'inhuman torch' as he falls through the skylight into the vat of 'acid' looks most convincing.

Harry Oakes remembers filming the scene: "We had two cameras on it and I operated the bottom camera. Len did the master shot and I had the one that was tilting down into the acid. I was rather

LEFT: Nurse Yvonne Parke watches over stuntman Jock Easton behind the Creature make-up before his fiery plunge at the climax of The Curse of Frankenstein (1956).

BELOW: Jock Easton doubles for Christopher Lee during the Creature's death-fall in The Curse of Frankenstein (1956).

pleased about that actually because dear old Len hated two cameras on a shot. It was his professionalism, you see; he liked to think he did every shot and, as so often, he would be on the master shot. They actually shot it on New Year's Day, because it wasn't a Bank Holiday in those days. Years ago we worked on Christmas Eve and finished at four o'clock, so New Year's Day was just another day, but poor old Jock Easton, he was in a bit of a state being a Scotsman. How he managed to do that as he was – 'the morning after the night before' – I found quite amazing, but he did it perfectly well."

Stills photographer John Jay remembers his difficulties with the scene: "I remember when they did the first Frankenstein, where the monster falls through the roof into a tank of acid. When they did that I had two cameras on a single release and the release didn't work, and I got no shots. The next day, when I took the contact prints in to show Tony Hinds what we'd done, he said, 'Where's the shots of him falling into the tank?' I told him what had happened and he dropped his pen and said, 'You're joking, aren't you?' I said, 'No, I'm terribly sorry, Tony. It's never happened before.' He said, 'I don't care about that, but how can you come in here and be so honest? Someone else would have said, "My camera fell over" or something.' I said, 'No, no, no. I'm too old for that and I'm too honest.' He said, 'You're all right boy, because we didn't get it either.' And they had to shoot it again. Something went wrong with their camera, so I was bloody lucky."

As the year closed, principal photography on The Curse of Frankenstein was coming to an end. 1957 was ushered in with the Creature plunging to his death, after which the film entered post-production. 1957 would prove to be a pivotal year for the company – their endeavours on Frankenstein would be amply rewarded and they would mount their most significant production, Dracula, at the end of the year.

... and Dracula

(1 9 5 7)

As 1957 began, the expanding film company at Bray was making plans for a new sound stage. To accommodate the snow scenes in the forthcoming *The Abominable Snowman*, they would have to move to the more expansive stages of Pinewood. On Sunday 13 January, Hammer submitted plans for a new stage to Berkshire County Council and the contract was signed on Wednesday the 30th. Building of the new stage would go ahead in July and would be completed in September for *The Snorkel*.

Meanwhile, shooting on *The Curse of Frankenstein* finally wrapped on Thursday 3 January. The end of filming had overlapped with Peter Cushing's preparation for his role as the villainous Mr

Manningham in the BBC's revival of *Gaslight*, which was finally broadcast on Sunday 13 January. In it, Cushing was still sporting the modest beard he had grown for the prison scenes in *The Curse of Frankenstein*, which suggests that these were among the last scenes to be shot.

After shooting, James Needs and his assistant Roy Norman undertook the final editing at Hammer House. Enter the composer, in this case James Bernard, to stamp his signature on the film. "The music director would usually ring me while the film was being shot or when it was just about to be shot," explained Bernard. "You can't do the music really until the film is finished, because of all the measurements. So I would simply wait until the film was finished and then go down and see it in the viewing theatre." *The Curse of Frankenstein* gave Bernard a chance to develop the sound that would soon define Hammer Horror. "My first three films, *The Quatermass Xperiment*, *X the Unknown* and *Quatermass 2*, were all science fiction and it was only when I came to do *The Curse of Frankenstein* that I felt I needed more – for instance, brass and woodwind – and said to John Hollingsworth, 'On this one, can we please have a bigger orchestra?' To which he acceded, so that was my first score with a full orchestra."

Bernard described the process of composing, which began on his piano at home. "Of course nowadays one has the luxury of having the film on video with the time code on it, so one can time it frame by frame, but in those days I didn't have that. I would be sent the assistant editor's typed lists of all the timings and could then go to work. I always like to do my own orchestration, all the suspense and horror and romance, because that's what gives the music its own special flavour. It's probably why my music is apparently so recognisable, because I never learnt orchestration. I had to teach myself and several of my ideas are perhaps a little unorthodox. You write what you call the full score. You start at the top where you have the woodwind section, flutes, oboes, clarinets, bassoons and any other woodwind instruments you might need like bass clarinet or cor anglais, and then you have the brass section, the horns, trumpets, trombones, tuba and any others you might be using, and then the percussion section and piano if required, and then at the bottom of the page the string section, first violins, second violins, violas, cellos and double bases. You as the composer have to write out the full score, from which the conductor will be conducting, but the individual parts are then copied by professional copyists."

Meanwhile, John Hollingsworth, the music supervisor, would be securing the orchestra and arranging a recording date at Beaconsfield. Bernard explained: "Hammer were always quite firm about the numbers that I could have. I mean 35 players was stretching it a bit. I always wanted more strings, but in those wonderful recording studios at Beaconsfield [Anvil Studios, run by Ken Cameron and Eric Tomlinson], they had marvellous sound. Well, you know from hearing those earlier scores I did, like *Dracula* and *The Curse of Frankenstein*, it sounds like an orchestra about twice the size. I knew I couldn't have more than 35 or 36 musicians, so it was up to me to decide what I needed and in the Gothic horrors I needed the heaviness and bite of brass. Then, of course, I wanted strings for the more lyrical parts; strings can be sinister or romantic, they can do anything, so they're a marvellous general ingredient because they can play so many different roles. And I always needed a good percussion team. I like using plenty of percussion and then some woodwind also, for the quieter or more romantic moments, or to add to the general excitement at climactic moments."

Of the recording sessions Bernard remembered: "Hammer were always working on a small budget – tiny by today's standards – therefore they liked to get things done in two sessions if they could. You were not allowed to record more than 20 minutes' worth of music in a three-hour session, then you

Hammer Productions
— 1957 —

HAMMER PRODUCTIONS:
+ *THE ABOMINABLE SNOWMAN*
+ *THE CAMP ON BLOOD ISLAND*
+ *THE SNORKEL*
+ *UP THE CREEK* ⋆
+ *DRACULA*

FEATURETTES:
+ *OPERATION UNIVERSE*
+ *CLEAN SWEEP*
+ *DANGER LIST*
+ *MAN WITH A DOG*
+ *SEVEN WONDERS OF IRELAND*
+ *ITALIAN HOLIDAY*

⋆ CREDITED ON SCREEN TO BYRON FILMS

OPPOSITE: Christopher Lee as the definitive Count in Terence Fisher's classic Dracula (1957).

could do an hour's overtime." The years to come would be rewarding for Bernard. "We had all the top players of the time – I couldn't believe that I had such players playing my music. We'd often have Leon Goosens on first oboe (the famous oboe soloist); Jack Brymer, the famous clarinetist, on first clarinet; Hugh Bean on first violin, and many other players of equal calibre. In fact, I think they enjoyed these sessions because it gave them a change from playing the classics and it was good quick money. John Hollingsworth conducted. I cannot conduct myself, although some composers do like to conduct their own scores. For each section of music, the film, with all the timings superimposed, is shown on a large screen behind the orchestra, so that the music can be synchronised with the action."

Tony Hinds now submitted a black-and-white print of the first cut of *The Curse of Frankenstein* to Arthur Watkins at the BBFC and his examiners commented on it on 11 January:

"Reel 3. Reduce to one brief shot the severing of the head out of frame, and remove all sounds. Resubmit, so that we may see if the remainder of this sequence is then acceptable."

On the report, Watkins also made a note of his own:

"Reel 5. (a) No sound effects when Frankenstein removes brain from head in coffin. (b) No screams when monster ignited, please."

Watkins spoke to Tony Hinds on 15 January and made further comment: "Spoke to Mr Anthony Hinds, who confirmed that there will be no sound effects with (a). There will be screams with (b), therefore see the dubbed reel."

Not surprisingly, the scene that caused most offence was Cushing lowering the highwayman's severed head into the acid bath. Make-up artist Phil Leakey remembered: "The one that caused the most mess in my home (I used to do most of this kind of thing at home before we had a small laboratory at the studio) was the making of the beheaded head. It was supposed to be the head of a man who had been hanged from a gallows, cut down and his head removed from his body. Eyes bulging, face disfigured and generally a bit of a mess and the crows had been pecking at his face. Someone in the story needed a skull. I made a model in plaster and clay; the skull in plaster and the face in clay, distorted it, then made another plaster mould. Into this was put a skin – then liquid paraffin wax and before it set, the plaster skull, eyes etc. I tied the three-piece mould together and let it set in the fridge. There was much more to it than that, but that is the general idea.

"After a few hours I took it out of the fridge, put another skin on it and a few hair whiskers, blood, etc. The neck looked as though it had been hacked off – bits of gullet, windpipe and neck bone showing. The wax in the face was filled with a blood-reddy dye and Alka-Seltzer. This was to be thrown into a glass-sided booth of 'acid', which was in fact boiling water. The effect was that the 'acid' melted the wax, the dye turned everything red and the Alka-Seltzer fizzed like acid. Quite effective. Now the funny part was this – I made the model at home and had to take it to the studio. I laid it on the back seat of my car on a newspaper and it was very gory. On the way to the studio about 6.00 am, I stopped at a shop for a newspaper and some cigarettes. While I was there a man on a bicycle arrived beside my car and stopped with the idea of entering the shop. However, he didn't. He must have seen the head, let out a gasp, grabbed his cycle and set off at a rate of knots for the police station. The shopkeeper said, 'What's the matter with that bloke?' I replied 'Can't imagine' and went on my way."[1]

Derek Whitehurst also remembered the scene. "I always remember we did this shot in the tank. There was meat slapped on the stump of the neck of this false head and I remember everybody saying, 'This is for the Japanese version.' It was horrible and I always remember the continuity girl, Doreen Soan, was quite ill at the whole thing, because it was shot in a glass tank. As far as I can remember, that was the only thing done specially for the Japanese version."

Tales of such 'Japanese versions' are legendary among Hammer employees, although interestingly Terence Fisher always viewed the issue from a different standpoint: "I must insist in saying that there are no South American versions, nor are there any Japanese versions or any other versions. This is what happens: we shoot the scenes up to the point where we say, 'This is it; no further; this is how it should be.' Subsequently, the complete integral version is submitted to the censors of each country, whereupon they decide what should be cut and what should be left in. I do my job the way I think it should be done and the distributors and censors do theirs, that's all."[2]

Minor cuts were undertaken by James Needs, as instructed by Tony Hinds, and the offending Reel 3 resubmitted, but the slight slimming-down did not appease Arthur Watkins, who reported in an

LEFT: *Right up to the last moment the BBFC objected to the Creature's blood-smeared face in* The Curse of Frankenstein *(1956).*

BELOW: *A rare view of the* Curse of Frankenstein *prop head that caused a sensation at the BBFC.*

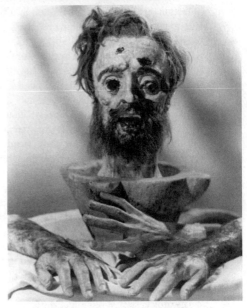

internal memo dated 28 January: "Reel 3 was seen again on 25th January by the President, GRS, JC and AW. It was agreed that the shot of the actual severing of the head could still be reduced a little further and that the actual shot of the head itself, just before it is dropped into the acid tank, should be removed. I spoke to Mr Hinds (Exclusive) today and asked him to look into these two points. He said that he could certainly shorten the severing, but he would like us to consider an alternative shot of the head in which it was not nearly so distinct. I said that we would do this and that Reel 3 should be resubmitted at the same time as Reel 5 was sent in to check on the screams when the monster is ignited."

Needs gently pared away at the scene again and a sound copy of Reels 3 and 5 were now submitted on 5 February with fingers crossed. Alas, the censor's comments were again discouraging, as Watkins' letter to Hinds the next day explained:

"We saw two reels of *The Curse of Frankenstein* again yesterday.

Reel 3. There still appears to be a slight sound when Frankenstein is cutting off the head. There must be absolutely no sound whatever. We cannot, I am afraid, allow the shot of the head being dropped in the bath and this must be removed.

Reel 5. We saw this again, in order to reach a decision about the screams when the monster is set on fire. As viewed by us yesterday, there was one scream at the end of the sequence and to this we have no objection. But the monster had been on fire for some little time and it would seem natural to suppose that he would scream during the earlier process of his discomfiture. Would you please let us know whether the absence of these screams was due to a defect on the soundtrack or whether, in fact, there is only one scream at the end.

"Although reference was made as far back as the 13th June last in a letter from Colonel Carreras, to the fact that the film would be in colour, no step was taken to remind us of this when a black and white print was submitted on 11th January, 1957. We are prepared to view intended colour films in a black and white version if we are approached and asked to do so. When we view such versions we bear in mind the fact that the completed film is to be in colour and frequently ask for certain reels to be resubmitted when colour has been added.

"As regards *The Curse of Frankenstein*, it will certainly be necessary for us to see the whole film again in colour, in order to determine whether there is anything visually too unpleasant which we have overlooked at the black and white stage. There is one cut which I feel we shall have to ask you to make and you might as well do it now – and that is the shot in Reel 3 of Frankenstein wiping the blood off on his overall after severing the head. It is also the colour factor which has influenced our request, made above, for the shot of the head being dropped in the tank to be removed."

Accordingly, Hinds submitted the reels in colour on Friday 8 February. Watkins wrote back to Hinds on the Monday:

"Further to my letter of 6th February, I write to say that we saw the colour pilots of *The Curse of Frankenstein* on Friday. There are only three places where there might be trouble from our point of view in the completed film. They are these:-

(1) The close-up of the two hands lying on the table.

(2) The close-up of an eye observed through a magnifying glass.

(3) The shot of the monster's face with a blood smear across one cheek when he is standing facing the maid.

"I believe you would be wise to shorten all three of the above, so that only the minimum is left in the completed film. I confirm that we still wish the complete film in colour to be submitted to the Board when it is ready."

Watkins finally passed the film on 8 April. For the first of their blood-soaked Gothic chillers, Hammer got around the censor relatively unscathed. It would not always be so, as Tony Hinds would soon learn.

The BBC had just cause to be proud of the team of writer Nigel Kneale and producer/director Rudolph Cartier. They had created many notable dramas together, none more significant than *The Quatermass Xperiment* and *Nineteen Eighty-Four*. On Sunday 30 January 1955, the same team brought another thriller to the screen, *The Creature*, a single-episode morality play (transmitted live – and repeated live on Thursday 3 February) about the search for the legendary Abominable Snowman of the Himalayas. In it Peter Cushing played Dr John Rollason, whose pursuit of the creature arises from scientific curiosity. His partner Tom Friend, played by Stanley Baker, has more commercial reasons for the expedition and intends 'bringing one back'. Sadly, the original teleplay is no longer with us. Later in the year Kneale and Cartier would collaborate again on *Quatermass II*. Hammer had been quick to snap up the Quatermass sequel, but their version's release would now be held up in the excitement over *Frankenstein*. On Friday 2 November 1956, some two weeks before the cameras were due to roll on *The Curse of Frankenstein*, Hammer had also bought the rights to *The Creature* from the BBC.

Val Guest was the natural choice of director for this, his third Hammer/Kneale production. This time Kneale adapted his own story for the screen, but Guest still had cause to do an uncredited rewrite. "It was great writing, but I had to pare it down enormously to get it to size and that didn't go down well with Nigel at all. You can't have long speeches with people on the screen unless it's a closing argument in a court case or something."

The project started out under the title *The Snow Creature* but soon resorted to the more familiar *The Abominable Snowman*; the Americans would expand it still further to *The Abominable Snowman of the Himalayas*. Hammer took immediate advantage of their acquisition of Peter Cushing. After Baron Frankenstein, he would have only a month to prepare for his reprise of Kneale's Dr Rollason. Though the Lippert deal was over, Robert Lippert was nevertheless instrumental in bringing Forrest Tucker over to play Tom Friend; Tucker would take top billing. He had previously starred in Hammer's *Break in the Circle* in 1954, which was also directed by Val Guest. Returning, like Cushing, from the television play were Arnold Marle as the Lama and Wolfe Morris as Kusang. For the film version some romantic interest was deemed necessary and a strong-willed Mrs Rollason was written in accordingly.

THE ABOMINABLE SNOWMAN

PRINCIPAL PHOTOGRAPHY: 28 January to 5 March 1957
DISTRIBUTION:
UK: Warner Bros; 91 minutes; certificate 'X'
US: 20th Century-Fox; 85 minutes; US title: *The Abominable Snowman of the Himalayas*
b/w; Regalscope.
UK RELEASE:
TRADE SHOW: 7 August 1957, at Studio One
GENERAL RELEASE: 26 August 1957, on the ABC circuit with *Untamed Youth*
US RELEASE: November 1957

DIRECTOR: Val Guest; PRODUCER: Aubrey Baring; ASSOCIATE PRODUCER: Anthony Nelson Keys; EXECUTIVE PRODUCER: Michael Carreras; SCREENPLAY: Nigel Kneale; PRODUCTION DESIGNER: Bernard Robinson; ART DIRECTOR: Ted Marshall; DRAUGHTSMAN: Don Mingaye; DIRECTOR OF PHOTOGRAPHY: Arthur Grant; CAMERA OPERATOR: Len Harris; FOCUS PULLER:

Harry Oakes; FOCUS ASSISTANT, CLAPPER/LOADER: Ted Cutlack; ASSISTANT DIRECTOR: Robert Lynn; 2ND ASSISTANT DIRECTOR: Tom Walls; 3RD ASSISTANT DIRECTOR: Hugh Harlow; EDITOR: Bill Lenny; MUSIC: Humphrey Searle; MUSIC SUPERVISOR: John Hollingsworth; SOUND RECORDIST: Jock May; MAKE-UP: Phil Leakey; HAIRSTYLIST: Henry Montsash; PRODUCTION MANAGER: Don Weeks; CONTINUITY: Doreen Soane; WARDROBE: Molly Arbuthnot; DRESS DESIGNER: Beatrice Dawson; MATTES: Les Bowie, CONSTRUCTION MANAGER: Freddie Ricketts; CHIEF ELECTRICIAN: Jack Curtis; MASTER PLASTERER: Arthur Banks; PROP MASTER: Tommy Money

Forrest Tucker (Tom Friend); Peter Cushing (Dr Rollason); Maureen Connell (Helen Rollason); Richard Wattis (Peter Fox); Robert Brown (Ed Shelley); Michael Brill (McNee); Wolfe Morris (Kusang); Arnold Marle (Lama); Anthony Chin (Majordomo); Jock Easton, Joe Powell (Yetis); Fred Johnson (Yeti face)

Shooting started on Monday 14 January, for two weeks (through to Thursday the 24th) in the French Pyrenees, where Guest took his second unit up to La Monge, situated above the Po Valley, to record the mountain-climbing scenes. Harry Oakes remembers the trip: "We had a full camera crew. Arthur Grant, Len Harris of course, Val Guest the director. It wasn't easy with all the gear because Molly Arbuthnot and continuity girl Doreen Soan also had to go. None of the principal actors went, they were all doubles. We went across the Channel on a ferry and then we took a sleeper from Paris to Tarbe near the French border and got cars from there. It was a place called La Monge, which had just opened as a ski resort on the French Peak du Midi, the highest point in the French Pyrenees."

The film's producer Aubrey Baring also joined the crew on location, as Oakes explains. "Aubrey Baring was a lovely bloke. Looking back over the years, that few weeks' location in the Pyrenees was one of the happiest moments I can remember. It was a lovely location. Aubrey – I think he was the Honorable Aubrey Baring – was a fighter pilot during the war and spoke French fluently, which was great out there. What the French loved about him was that he would ski in his ski trousers, his raincoat and a trilby hat. They loved him for that. I think really, as far as they were concerned, he was the only Englishman out there."

Peter Cushing reprised his television role of Dr Rollason for The Abominable Snowman (1957), Hammer's adaptation of Nigel Kneale's The Creature.

Each day the team travelled up by cable car, through the clouds, to film around the Peak du Midi observatory at around 8000 feet. To the chagrin of the crew, they first had to watch as the cable car was sent up ahead each morning to break the ice off the cables. Some shots were even filmed from the vantage point of the cable car itself. Doubles for the actors were used, which gave Cushing extra breathing space between Frankenstein and Rollason. Val Guest always laughs when he remembers Tucker's double: "It was very funny because in later years Forrest Tucker used to tell

RIGHT: On location at La Monge for The Abominable Snowman (1957). Len Harris is behind the camera with Harry Oakes and director Val Guest (with cigar).

BELOW: Third assistant Hugh Harlow clowns around with stuntmen Joe Powell and Jock Easton, who played the Yeti, outside the courtyard entrance to the ballroom stage during the shooting of The Abominable Snowman (1957).

everyone about what he went through up there – but he was never there. He did all his suffering at Pinewood on a big stage!"

Harry Oakes discusses the cameras that were chosen to cope with the snowy location shooting: "We used a clockwork camera, a Newman-Sinclair – it had been adapted. It was strange, because the French unit (they had a strong union and had to double up) had their own cameraman with a big BFC Mitchell, but it was so cold there they had a lot of trouble getting up to speed and hardly shot anything, whereas our clockwork camera, a marvellous camera really, didn't give us any trouble. The only problem we had was on the very first day, when we soon learnt that if you take a warm camera into the cold it's all right, but coming into lunch on that very first day – it took ages to dry out, because of the condensation when we brought it into the warm."

The film was shot in Regalscope, an anamorphic process which took in the mountain shots spectacularly. As Harry Oakes recollects, "Hammer had their own anamorphic lens which was converted to go on the Sinclair. We did one or two early Cinemascope films, but after that we bought our own lens and called it Hammerscope. But the system was the same. Panavision now uses anamorphic lenses and you just need the one focus puller, but back then on a Scope picture you had the regular focus puller, who was looking after the camera lens, the objective lens, and the anamorphic lens had to be focused separately, so you needed two focus pullers." Ted

Cutlack was his focus assistant: "Ted was clapper/loader basically, but assisted me with the focus pulling. He was getting on a bit for an assistant. He'd worked in the labs for a long time and decided to get out. I suppose when I was in my early thirties, he was in his mid forties."

On Monday 28 January, Guest started the main shoot at Bray Studios. There, cast and crew would toil for the next three weeks. Production designer Bernard Robinson, art director Ted Marshall and draughtsman Don Mingaye had converted the back-lot into a Tibetan monastery. Ted Marshall remembered: "The Abominable Snowman was an enjoyable film to work on, because of the preparatory research into the Tibetan background, where the story began, and we built some quite elaborate sets in the rather restricted space of Bray Studios."[3] Don Mingaye also remembers the preparation: "I did quite a bit of research for it, again out of books and libraries, to build the monastery and the prayer wheels."

A central core team now formed that would continue over the next four Hammer pictures at Bray (The Camp on Blood Island, The Snorkel, Dracula and The Revenge of Frankenstein). This consisted of assistant director Robert Lynn, 2nd assistant Tom Walls, 3rd assistant Hugh Harlow, sound recordist Jock May, and the cheerful team of Harris and Oakes fresh from location in France. Robert Lynn (born 1918) was the son of the famous farceur Ralph Lynn and had entered the film industry in 1936 as a camera assistant. Curiously, Tom Walls was the son (and namesake) of Ralph Lynn's equally famous collaborator in the Aldwych farces.

Arthur Grant (born 1915) stepped in as lighting cameraman. Grant left school when he was 14 to join the local silent film studio of pioneer Cecil Hepworth. He worked through many departments, eventually becoming a camera operator after the war in 1947 on The Master of Bankdam (Terence Fisher's last film as editor) and then progressed to cinematographer on The Second Mate in 1951. His faster, more commercial style of lighting would soon bring him into competition with Jack Asher for Hammer's top spot and in later years he would become Hammer's most prolific cinematographer. He would also light three of Hammer's short featurettes later in 1957: Clean Sweep, Danger List and Man with a Dog. For now, Grant's black-and-white photography complemented Guest's documentary-style approach. "Nigel had written it as a moralistic thriller very well but it might very easily have turned into Godzilla, you know," observes Guest. "But again I tried to give it an almost documentary approach of someone going on an expedition with a camera for Panorama or something."

The crew would be constantly entertained and amazed by Peter Cushing's improvisation with props. "Oh, Peter was a dream. Great fun, enormous fun, and he was very good," remembers Val Guest. "We used to call him 'Props Cushing', because he was forever coming out with props. When he was examining the Yeti tooth, he was pulling these things out totally unrehearsed and we found it very difficult keeping quiet." Hugh Harlow, too, reminisces about the maestro: "He was a lovely man. He was fastidious with his props and continuity – he was a continuity girl's delight, because he would make copious notes in his script per scene of what he was wearing, how he was wearing it, any changes that he would make or apply, if he had a button undone or a button done up... little touches like that, and he was just very efficient, a very professional person."

Guest insisted that his Yeti should not be seen, preferring to leave them to the imagination of the paying public. Thus he tantalises us by only showing the arm of the creature when it is shot dead, followed by a dramatic shot of another great clawed hand as it fumbles around beneath the tent, picking up a rifle like a toy gun. Nigel Kneale saw it differently. He had shown the dead beast in his teleplay and thought that Hammer should have done the same. Guest was forced to show the Yeti at the climax, but again insisted on only a brief and very tight close-up on the eyes of actor Fred Johnson, which Guest thought were "full of worldly understanding." Johnson had first appeared for Hammer in The Saint's Return in 1953 and would go on to be a regular face in Hammer's fantasy pictures. Again, Kneale's teleplay had been more graphic, even resorting to using a dwarf dressed as Peter Cushing to convey the great size of the creature. Hugh Harlow remembered Hammer's two Yeti, put together by Phil Leakey in conjunction with the wardrobe department: "They were two stunt men. One was Jock Easton and the other was Joe Powell, the brother of Eddie Powell, who would later become Christopher Lee's regular stunt double."

While the unit beavered away at Bray, Bernard Robinson's team had scrutinised the location footage from La Monge and designed corresponding indoor snowscapes, which had to be erected on the more spacious stages at Pinewood. Don Mingaye remembered, "To vary the snowscapes we built them on rostra, which are telescopic wheels, so you could take bits out and move them around a bit to make different shapes with a panoramic backing all around. It's still done today for all sorts of projects like commercials and so on."

The unit transferred to Pinewood on Monday 18 February for the two remaining weeks of shooting. The main problem for the crew was the artificial snow, particularly during the blizzard scenes. Don Mingaye remembered the magic ingredient: "Polystyrene and salt, which caused a bit of a problem at Pinewood. We didn't realise that we used quite a quantity of salt on foreground work and of course it started to make all the metalwork and runners rusty quite quickly." Ted Marshall also recollects the problem. "There was a daily call for milk to combat the unpleasant effect of the powdered foam that filled the air for the blizzard scenes, to say nothing of the effect of mounds of salt on the stage floor on one's shoe leather."[3] Not even the crew's protective gear could keep it out, as Len Harris complained. "I recall the artificial snow. It was everywhere. Although we had masks and goggles, it could still get down your throat. It was unpleasant when it was blowing all about in the storms."[4]

Principal photography ended at Pinewood on Tuesday 5 March. As the film entered post-production, Hammer set to work on three short featurettes, all using a core team of producer Tony Hinds, associate producer Anthony Nelson Keys, executive producer: Michael Carreras, production manager Don Weeks, director of photography Arthur Grant, camera operator Len Harris, focus puller Harry Oakes, sound recordist Jock May, art director Ted Marshall, supervising editor James Needs and editor Alfred Cox. First came *Clean Sweep*, a 29-minute featurette directed by Maclean Rogers, which started production on 11 March at Bray. Starring Eric Barker, Thora Hird, Vera Day and Wallas Eaton, the story told how George Watson (Barker) is sent to the doghouse by his wife Vera (Hird) for gambling, only to be forgiven when he wins a fortune on the Irish sweep.

This was immediately followed on 15 March by *Danger List*. Directed by Gainsborough veteran Leslie Arliss, this 22-minute thriller told how a killer drug is accidentally dispensed to three patients by a hospital pharmacy. Philip Friend (star of *Dick Turpin – Highwayman* in 1955) played the doctor and Honor Blackman the distressed pharmacist. Mervyn Johns played the tragic Mr Ellis, who uses the drug to end his wife's suffering. Arliss returned to direct the next featurette, *Man with a Dog* on 25 March. A mere 20 minutes in length, it had a solid cast of some interest to Hammer fans: Maurice Denham, Sarah Lawson, Clifford Evans, John Van Eyssen, Marianne Stone and Jan Holden. It was another medical/human drama about an elderly war veteran who only consents to an emergency operation when he has found people to look after his dog, plants and fish! Filming finished on 29 March.

Meanwhile, Bill Lenny continued editing *The Abominable Snowman* at Hammer House. He had already worked with Val Guest on *Break in the Circle* and it would be the start of a lasting professional partnership. "Oh, Val was fabulous," remembers Lenny. "He was a great character to work with and had an amazing sense of humour. One of those guys who knew exactly what he wanted and how he wanted it. I think I did 15 or 16 pictures with him over the years. Every now and again he liked to see what I'd put together as a sequence. We'd work on the moviola in the evening after filming – with some coffee and sandwiches, and smoking his trademark 'big cigars' – and we adjusted the scenes as he felt we wanted it. Then when it was all done that way, we would have a few days to polish the final cut at the end of a shoot. He was a very one-man-band show. After a couple of films with him, I got to know his style and he didn't stay very long for the final edit, because I was putting it together as I knew he visualised it. He shot it the way he wanted it, so he didn't waste a lot of time like I'm afraid a lot of directors do, who shoot all around the clock. He just shot really what he basically wanted and invariably it just fell together as it were.

"I got on extremely well with Val. He was very honest and very fair and had a great memory for movies. I remember on *The Abominable Snowman*, they flew over the Pyrenees in a helicopter and shot miles of footage for title backgrounds, which I had to plough through to put something together. Val would come along and say, 'Use the bit where the camera went just round the corner over that hump.' And you'd go back and plough through it all again and sure enough, there was a shot similar to that!"

Lenny also remembers Guest's strict style of directing. "He had a blackboard with a diagram of every set drawn by the art department as a bird's eye view and he'd mark on it all his set-ups, with the continuity numbers according to the scene numbers, with a little 'V', which denoted the camera position, and a little dotted line to another 'V' if it was a panning shot or tracking shot. And anybody at any time could come up and see how many more shots he'd got left, because he used to cross them off when he'd done them and everybody knew basically what the next shot was going to be. There was none of this 'Shall we try the camera here, shall we try the camera there?' nonsense – it was right here. He would be open to offers, but he basically started off with his preconceived idea."

With The Abominable Snowman in post-production, Hammer were now busy preparing The Curse of Frankenstein for distribution. James and Michael Carreras, together with Tony Hinds, flew to America in April to show the film to the Warner Bros executives. They were so impressed that they allegedly had a copy sent straight to their president Jack L Warner in California. Warner Bros arranged worldwide distribution on a scale usually reserved for the bigger Hollywood pictures. The film opened in America in late spring (supported by Hammer's X the Unknown) and had its UK première at the Warner Theatre in London's Leicester Square on Thursday 2 May. After reaping record box-office takings on its first weekend, it smashed its own record the following week at the Warner, resulting in the film opening simultaneously at another cinema in Leicester Square, the Ritz. The film went on general release from Monday 20 May with Woman of Rome.

Christopher Lee with Hazel Court at a special press reception held in Brooks Wharf, Lower Thames Street, London, to publicise The Curse of Frankenstein (1956).

With Frankenstein out of the way, Hammer now turned their attention to Quatermass 2. Despite a trade show at United Artists' Wardour Street Theatre on Friday 22 March, the première was held back until Friday 24 May at the London Pavilion, where its predecessor had opened. It later went on general release on the ABC circuit from Monday 17 June with And God Created Woman. They formed a successful double-bill, but it was Frankenstein that got all the attention. Quatermass 2 was released later in the States as Enemy from Space.

On 3 June, The Steel Bayonet opened at the Odeon Leicester Square. Despite their domination of the West End, this was also a sad time for Hammer. Founding father William 'Hammer' Hinds had died as a result of a cycling accident just two days before, on 1 June. He had been present at the première of The Curse of Frankenstein a mere month before. Publicity photos show a shocked and bemused Will Hammer hamming it up as James Carreras jokingly throttles Peter Cushing next to a tank containing a mock-up of the Creature.

With the huge success of The Curse of Frankenstein, Hammer were already planning the sequel. In a letter to Eliot Hyman at AAP, James Carreras wrote from his Costa Brava hotel, the Hostal de la Gavina, on Sunday 7 July 1957: "I enclose a new batch of figures which are quite fantastic. England is sweltering in a heat-wave and NOTHING is taking any money except The Curse of Frankenstein. I've seen the first Warner advertisements in the American papers, which are quite first class, and I'm confident of a terrific gross in all territories handled by Warners. Tony Hinds and Michael are busy on the Blood of Frankenstein and I feel sure that we have another terrific winner on our hands. When I get back on July 22nd I'll let you have the starting date and budget. If we give Warners the world for distribution on Blood of Frankenstein – without them putting up any production cash – can you get an advance guarantee of $500,000? Not, of course, to include Japan. This must be done through Hammer. Reply before July 22nd please. P.S. DRACULA???"

Dracula indeed. Hammer already had their hands on a document passed on from Associated-Rediffusion Ltd, dated 31 October 1956:

"We desire to adapt the novel by Bram Stoker for a seven-part serial for live transmission. The copyright situation is extremely complicated and it would take a long time and a lot of money to carry out the necessary investigations. However, I think that there is a quick cheap way of doing this if our American attorneys could obtain the co-operation of Universal Pictures Inc, as I feel sure that that Corporation would have in its archives all the relevant information as it produced a motion picture of DRACULA in 1947 [sic], and I see that Universal procured an assignment from Florence A L Stoker, the executrix of Abraham Stoker, Hamilton Deane and J L Balderston in September 1930.

"American Corporations do not usually embark upon spending a large sum of money on the making of a motion picture unless and until they have thoroughly investigated the rights, which can sometimes take a year and the expenditure of a great deal of money. In this case Universal went to a great deal of trouble to investigate the rights because it appears from the said assignment that they procured Hamilton Deane and J L Balderston to join in. The reason for this was that Hamilton Deane made the first dramatisation of the novel, which was performed in 1924 (after Bram Stoker's death). Now it is obvious that Hamilton Deane must have acquired certain rights to enable him to make this dramatisation and the question is did he obtain the sole and exclusive world performing rights?

"Next we find that in 1927 a new version of the Hamilton Deane play was written by John Balderston and the question arises did Balderston take over Hamilton Deane's rights or what rights did he get?

"The next question that arises is what rights did Universal acquire in the novel and in the two plays. We are not interested in Deane's and Balderston's dramatisations but it is essential for us to discover whether Mrs Bram Stoker granted either of them exclusive dramatic performing rights. If she did not then we would only have to deal with Mrs Bram Stoker subject to whatever rights she may have granted to Universal. If she did then we will have to get a clearance from the estates of Hamilton Deane and J L Balderston and perhaps also from Samuel French [publisher of play texts], to whom they may possibly have passed on their rights."

The television project had been abandoned in light of the tangled rights the novel still held, but this ground work would prove useful and paved the way for Hammer, who now badly needed to secure those rights. Hammer's lawyer, Edwin Davis, sought the answer in Universal's archives and eventually, after many months of negotiating, drew up a lengthy and intricate contract between Universal Pictures and Hammer via one of Hammer's subsidiary companies, Cadogan. This agreement also granted Universal distribution rights to the finished film throughout most of the world. So complex was this agreement that it was still being finalised as *Dracula* went into production. The final legal document, 80 pages in length, was not completed till 31 March 1958, by which time the film had already been shot and the finishing touches were being put to it.

James Carreras announced *Dracula* to the press on Friday 26 July 1957. *To-Day's Cinema* picked up the story that Monday: "Jimmy Carreras told me on Friday that Exclusive, who have the rights on *Dracula*, are planning a big-scale re-make of the famous thriller. To be made in colour, *Dracula* will go on the floor at an early date. *The Curse of Frankenstein*, by the way, is now the sixth highest grosser in America – this picture can't go wrong!"

Hammer started shooting their next movie the very same day...

The Camp on Blood Island would deal with the horror and brutality of a Japanese prisoner of war camp. The project had been taking shape at Hammer House for some time, although there are differing accounts of its origins. According to the brochure accompanying its world première on 18 April 1958, it all started one morning when an ex-Japanese POW called on Michael Carreras at his Wardour Street office and presented him with a foolscap envelope containing a report of an episode that had occurred at his POW camp in Malaya at the end of the war. Michael Carreras continues in the article: "There was something about this particular caller, and what he told me, which aroused my interest and curiosity. As soon as he had gone I opened the envelope he had given me. Inside I found a mass of notes written in pencil. I began reading, and quickly realised that I had in my possession one of the most extraordinary documents to come out of World War II. I was so excited I immediately commissioned Jon Manchip White, the author, to write a draft screenplay based on what I had read.

THE CAMP ON BLOOD ISLAND

PRINCIPAL PHOTOGRAPHY: 14 July to 11 September 11 1957
UK DISTRIBUTION: Columbia; 82 minutes; b/w;
Megascope. UK: certificate 'X'
UK RELEASE:
TRADE SHOW: 10 April 1958, at the Columbia Theatre
PREMIÈRE: 18 April 1958, at the London Pavilion,
Picadilly Circus
GENERAL RELEASE: 20 April 1958
US RELEASE: 8 September 1958, with *The Snorkel*

DIRECTOR: Val Guest; PRODUCER: Anthony Hinds; ASSOCIATE PRODUCER: Anthony Nelson Keys; EXECUTIVE PRODUCER: Michael Carreras; SCREENPLAY: Jon Manchip White and Val Guest from a story by Jon Manchip White; ART DIRECTOR: John Stoll; DRAUGHTSMAN: Don Mingaye; DIRECTOR OF PHOTOGRAPHY: Jack Asher; CAMERA OPERATOR: Len Harris; FOCUS PULLER: Harry Oakes; FOCUS ASSISTANT: Edward Cutlack; CAMERA GRIP: Albert Cowland; ASSISTANT DIRECTOR: Robert Lynn; 2ND ASSISTANT DIRECTOR: Tom Walls; 3RD ASSISTANT DIRECTOR: Hugh Harlow; SUPERVISING EDITOR: James Needs; EDITOR: Bill Lenny; MUSIC: Gerard Schurman; MUSIC SUPERVISOR: John Hollingsworth; SOUND RECORDIST: Jock May; BOOM OPERATOR: Jim Perry; SOUND CAMERA OPERATOR: Michael Sale; SOUND CAMERA MAINTENANCE: Charles Bouvet; MAKE-UP: Tom Smith; HAIRSTYLIST: Henry Montsash; PRODUCTION MANAGER: Arnold Brettell; CONTINUITY: Doreen Dearnaley; WARDROBE: Molly Arbuthnot; PRODUCTION SECRETARY: Cynthia Maugham; PROPERTY MASTER: Tommy Money; FLOOR PROPS CHARGEHAND: Peter Allchorne; PROPERTY BUYER: Eric Hillier; STILLS CAMERAMAN: Tom Edwards; PUBLICITY: Douglas Railton; PRODUCTION ACCOUNTANT: W H V Able; CASHIER: Ken Gordon; STUDIO MANAGER: Arthur Kelly; Construction Manager: Mick Lyons; Chief Electrician: Jack Curtis; Master Painter: Lawrence Wren; MASTER PLASTERER: Arthur Banks; TRANSPORT DRIVERS: W Epps, Wilfred Faux

Carl Mohner (Piet Van Elst); André Morell (Colonel Lambert); Edward Underdown (Major Dawes); Walter Fitzgerald (Cyril Beattie); Phil Brown (Lt Bellamy); Barbara Shelley (Kate Keiller); Michael Goodliffe (Father Anjou); Michael Gwynn (Tom Shields); Richard Wordsworth (Dr Keiller); Edwin Richfield (Sergeant Major); Ronald Radd (Colonel Yamamitsu); Marne Maitland (Captain Sakamura); Wolfe Morris (interpreter); Lee Montague (Jap Officer Nangdon); Peter Wayn (Lt Thornton); Michael Brill (Lt Peters); Barry Lowe (Corporal Betts); Max Butterfield (Corporal Hallam); Jack McNaughton (1st prisoner); Howard Williams (2nd prisoner); Michael Dea (3rd prisoner); Michael Ripper (Jap driver); Anthony Chin (Jap sentry); M R Takaki (Jap patrol); S Goh (Jap radio officer); Jimmy Raphael (1st Jap soldier); Don Lee (2nd Jap soldier); Mary Merrall (Mrs Beattie); Lillian Sottane (Mala); Grace Denbeigh Russell (thin woman); Geoffrey Baledon (Foster); Jan Holden (nurse); Betty Cooper (1st woman prisoner); Anne Ridler (2nd woman prisoner); Jacqueline Curtiss (Jennie – sick girl)

Ronald Radd as the villainous Colonel Yamamitsu in *The Camp on Blood Island* (1957).

Mr Manchip White was equally excited. Within a few days he had completed the draft script. I called in the ex-POW who had submitted the story idea and showed him the script. He suggested a few alterations in the interests of accuracy and fact, and gave us a lot of advice. This time, when he left my office, he had a contract in his pocket covering our acquisition of his story and calling on his services as technical adviser."

Bearing in mind that this brochure was aimed purely at publicity, it is perhaps not surprising that Tony Nelson Keys remembered events somewhat differently: "I took a number of projects to them such as *The Camp on Blood Island*. I took that to them – actually I took it to Michael at first and said, 'Michael, this is a fabulous story – a true story – the story of my great chum who was a Jap POW for three and a half years. I managed to get the story out of him – it took me a long time.' Michael took it to see the board and they agreed to do it for Columbia."[5]

Whatever happened, Michael Carreras asked Jon Manchip White to write a treatment of the story. The torrid tale tells of the sadistic camp ruled over by Colonel Yamamitsu. He has

Filming The Camp on Blood Island (1957). Len Harris is behind the camera with his focus puller Harry Oakes next to him. In front of the camera are Michael Gwynn and Carl Mohner. Behind clapper boy are Edward Underdown and André Morell.

threatened that if Japan loses the war he will massacre every man, woman and child in the camp. The allies' leader, Colonel Lambert, is hiding a terrible secret. They have intercepted a radio signal – the war is over, Japan has lost. Desperately they must now try to keep the truth from Yamamitsu until help arrives, but their reprisals only lead to further bloodshed. Eventually the prisoners have no choice but to retaliate and the camp is turned into a bloody killing field. Heavy casualties are incurred on both sides, but Lambert prevails – just as the allies arrive. At the risk of opening old war wounds, Hammer turned the picture into a showcase piece for the company – their 50th production, if, like Hammer, you start counting from *Dr Morelle – The Case of the Missing Heiress*.

Given the film's sensitive theme, James Carreras was wise to send a copy of the draft script to the BBFC in November 1956. The new secretary of the Board, John Nicholls, replied to the Colonel on 20 November (the second day of shooting on *The Curse of Frankenstein*):

"As I told you on the telephone this morning, we have now read the story treatment entitled *The Camp on Blood Island* and we liked it very much, except for the ungracious behaviour of the Major in charge of the rescuing detachment of paratroopers, which does not seem to ring quite true. I think some change along the lines you suggested would be all to the good.

"To turn to censorship: this type of story of cruelty in Jap prison-camps is necessarily strong meat, and you obviously will not want the film to overstep the bounds of the 'A' category. Restraint in details is therefore particularly necessary. The following is a full list:

Pp.2, 5, 15. The word 'bastards' should be omitted; also the word 'bloody' (p.2)

P.4. The 'cuffing and clubbing' of the prisoners must be no more than suggested.

Pp.5, 51. The word 'Christ' should be omitted here, and wherever else it might occur.

P.5. The 'vicious' beating back of the prisoners by the guards' rifle butt should be brief, and close shots should be avoided.

P.18 -19. There should be no shot of the impact of the 'smashing blow' from the rifle butt which sends the American sprawling back into the truck.

P.50. The 'spine tingling shriek' when the dispatch-rider is knocked off his motor-bike should not be too horrible.

P. 51-52. There should be no more than one shot of Yamamitsu striking his helpless prisoner, Colonel Lambert, and that should not be too brutal. The shot of something unspecified being thrown in Lambert's face should be omitted.

P. 67. The 'cuffing' of the bound prisoners should be briefly indicated and close shots should be avoided; the kicks should be omitted.

P. 70. There should be no shots of the 'kicking and battering to death' of the three Japs. Needlessly brutal details should be avoided in the fight which precedes the rescue of the prisoners.

"I think it would be advisable in this case to send us a shooting script."

Tony Hinds took over as producer, with Tony Nelson Keys as his associate producer. Val Guest was brought in to finish the screenplay and direct. In the première brochure, Guest is on record as saying, "I knew that this was one film I just had to make. I'll tell you why. First, the story it told was based on fact. Secondly, up to that time no-one had made a Jap POW picture that didn't pull punches. Thirdly, producer Anthony Hinds and executive producer Michael Carreras insisted that this was to be one film which was to be handled without kid gloves. Fourthly, many of my greatest friends are ex-POWs of the Japs. Their stories of their lives in Japanese camps so appalled and angered me that here, I felt, was a chance to tell the world of the hell they suffered. Now, I have nothing personal against the Japs, the Germans, or anyone who was our enemy during the last war. But I, along with everyone else, will always feel a great bitterness towards the unprincipled, unethical, and barbarous members of the warring nations; and it is as a living protest against the inhumanities they practised that I launched into this film." Strong stuff, but these words were embellished by Hammer's publicity machine.

Hinds submitted the final screenplay to the BBFC on 22 July 1957, a mere week before shooting was scheduled to begin at Bray. By the time he got a reply from the Board's secretary on 30 July, the film was already underway:

"We have now read the script entitled The Camp on Blood Island which was enclosed with your letter of the 22nd July. As you probably know, Exclusive Films sent us a treatment of this subject in November last, when we expressed the opinion that the film could qualify for the 'A' category. However, the developed script emphasises the potentially 'X' elements in the story and, without guaranteeing the category in advance of seeing the film, we agree with you that this picture will probably be 'X'. From that point of view, there is little in the present script which seems likely to give trouble, provided the treatment is reasonably discreet, but obviously treatment is even more than usually important when there are so many tense and harrowing moments in the story and when the possibility of brutal action is ever-present. The following details call for a particular caution –

P.4. The death of the prisoner (bullets thudding into his body, blood flowing from his mouth).

P.10. The incident of the Jap Colonel spitting in Lambert's face: any close shot of spittle on Lambert's face might well give trouble.

Pp. 12, 19 and elsewhere. Close or other brutal shots of the impact of blows should be avoided.

P. 28. The slap on the woman's face by the Jap Officer should not be too violent. The same applies (p. 68, 70) to the slaps on Bellamy when he is held and helpless.

P. 77. We would enter a caution on the shots of Bellamy's back and face after he has been beaten up.

P. 96. There should be no close or prolonged shots of the throttling of the driver.

P. 107. The killing of the Jap by Bellamy is potentially troublesome as here scripted – particularly the shot of the knife making contact with the Jap's throat, and subsequent shots of the girl covered with blood. Care should be taken that the disarray of the girl's dress is not indecent. P. 109. Shots of the Jap's dead body should not be too gruesome or horrible. We do not like the dialogue about hiding the corpse in Maya's bed, or Maya's screaming revulsion from the suggestion: we would look at this in the completed film, but we think you should be prepared for a cut.

P. 111, 118. A caution on the death of Van Elst, and on shots of his body displayed in camp afterwards."

Jack Asher was back as lighting cameraman. "The film reunited me with Val Guest, with whom I had worked at Gainsborough. He had introduced me to a type of shooting which I was happy to accept. It consisted of shooting all the scenes in the script that faced a particular set or direction; ideal from my point of view. It saved breaking down an intricate lighting pattern and reusing it again an hour later. It saved me much time, effort and headache."[6] The same core team from *The Abominable Snowman* returned, with the notable exceptions of Arnold Brettell replacing Don Weeks as production manager and John Stoll taking over from Bernard Robinson as art director. In any case, the film didn't require the lavish set designs that Robinson would soon be associated with. It called for sombre wooden huts and weatherbeaten palms as the camp took shape on the Bray lot. Ted Cutlack returned to assist focus puller Harry Oakes with the widescreen process, now called Hammerscope.

Shooting began on Monday 29 July, finishing on Wednesday 11 September after just over six weeks. While the film was being made, the construction of the new stage was taking place at Bray. *Camp* was fitted around this with minimal interior work at Bray and was mostly shot on the Bray external lot, with location work at a local sand quarry and at Black Park in Slough, just behind Pinewood Studios. The latter would become a popular locale for Hammer, with its fine woods and large lake, but for now it would do for darkest Malaya. Hugh Harlow recalls, "A lot of it was shot at some sand pits out at Gerrards Cross, where we shot *X the Unknown*. I don't recall it being a grim picture to do. It was a very dirty production certainly. It was a very hot summer when we shot that and we used a lot of oil and grease for make-up for the artists."

Guest was to pull no punches in presenting the dreadful atrocities. Nightmarish images included a man digging his grave before a chuckling firing squad, six POW hostages being decapitated and women being beaten. This was to be no ordinary war film and boasted a strong cast headed by Carl Mohner and André Morell, with another haunting performance from Richard Wordsworth as the emaciated doctor who is callously shot down while crawling to see his wife (played by Barbara Shelley in her first Hammer genre outing, after appearing briefly for them under her maiden name of Kowin in *Mantrap* in 1952). Guest had a hand in the casting: "They were mostly hand picked. I had a lot of actors that I used almost as my own repertory company. I would write them into my films."

Being an editor at that time was an all-encompassing job. Bill Lenny explains, "Basically on every film, when we come to put it together, there was a fair amount of 2nd unit stuff left over and Jimmy Needs and I would always go out and shoot them and direct them for our own pictures, whether it be a police car going past or whatever. That was part of the norm. We would direct them with a 2nd unit camera unit. Not with Len Harris, unless it was that fortnight after the picture when we would get the main camera unit, because they were on payroll, checking out, repairing and cleaning their equipment, so we used to nick them for a day or two or bring in a special 2nd camera crew – it was only probably a two-man crew."

On *Camp*, Lenny remembers photographing the parachute sequence at the end when the allies arrive: "The production office had arranged it with the army and the parachute people from Abingdon and when I got there I said, 'The picture is set in 1944/45, I'm told you've got these oblong-shaped parachutes now?' They said, 'Yeah.' I said, 'That's no good to me, they weren't invented then, were they?' So we had to be very careful how we shot it. We shot it from underneath as the planes came over. Just as their parachutes were opening, before they had fully opened, I planned to cut down below to the guys in the camp reacting, followed by a library shot with the real round mushroom types, and that's how we managed to get it over. We went up there one day, then stayed overnight and shot first thing in the morning and came home that night – big location!"

Editing the scenes of torture and brutality had to be handled carefully. "Things like the sword chopping off the head, I think the censors were a bit squeamish about that," Lenny recalls. "That's where we had a lot of fun getting the sound. Sometimes those sound effects are so important that when the sound editors are shooting sound effects, I like to go along to watch and see what they're up to and put my two penn'orth in if I feel it could be bettered. That's one of the effects which the sound editor and myself had a lot of fun making, with a cabbage wrapped up in a piece of hessian or something, chopping it with a big chopper and experimenting on the sound desk to make it echo, back-echo and all that sort of thing."

It was on this film that Hammer decided to bring in the post of supervising editor. James Needs, who had been the longest-serving editor at Hammer, fitted the bill. "I think the bosses felt that they'd like to have the editing, especially the post-production, under one person," explained Lenny. "They were always worrying about 'Who's cut this one? Who's cut that one? Have the titles been made?' – and they wanted to centralise it under a one-person banner."

It was a busy time for Hammer. While the atrocities on Blood Island were being filmed, they continued preparations in earnest for both Blood of Frankenstein and Dracula. It would prove an equally busy time for Jimmy Sangster. Since his departure from Hammer, a long and desperate six months had followed in which he got no work. He was about to ask Michael Carreras for his old job back at Hammer when he finally got a call from an Independent Television company to say they would take a serial he had written called Motive for Murder. Saved by the bell, he was then rung by Michael Carreras with a plethora of writing jobs. In late June he began his adaptation of Dracula; Sangster read Bram Stoker's novel twice and then completed his first draft in four weeks. On 24 July, he was contracted to write the first draft of Blood of Frankenstein, which had now fallen behind Dracula in the schedule. Around the same time he was also asked to rewrite Peter Myers' script for The Snorkel. Sangster's future at Hammer was secured.

Meanwhile, Hammer finally launched The Abominable Snowman. After a trade show on Wednesday 7 August, it finally went on general release on Monday the 26th on the ABC circuit with Untamed Youth, to moderate success. It would open in the States in November.

However, despite all the excitement, the atmosphere was not good at Hammer House. The Camp on Blood Island had been set up in conjunction with Eliot Hyman, who had promised to come up with 50 per cent of the production costs. By 23 July no funds had arrived and the desperate Carreras had to write to his silent partner to demand his share by 30 August. Still no money had appeared as the film went before the cameras on 29 July. By 16 August Carreras had had enough and wrote to Hyman:

"A few facts as at August 16th, 1957, to bring up to date all matters between us ... Camp On Blood Island You are not in this film, unless you contribute half the production costs before Friday, August 30th, as explained very fully in my letter to you dated July 23rd. The Snorkel Starts September 7th. You are not in this as confirmed by your cable dated July 2nd. By not coming in on The Camp on Blood Island or The Snorkel you forced us to finance 100% ourselves. Therefore as every major distributor is trying to get Blood of Frankenstein we are insisting that whoever gets it also takes The Camp on Blood Island and The Snorkel by either contributing towards the production costs and thereby buying a percentage of the profits, or on a straight guarantee against distribution. Please read all the above carefully and confirm to me so that we are up to date with all our facts on these pictures."

It was a wonderful coup. Distributors were indeed falling over themselves to secure the Frankenstein sequel. Now Hammer offered it up for grabs providing they picked up the two projects Hyman had reneged on. Hammer dangled the carrot, Columbia took the bait and a deal was eventually finalised on Friday 6 September 1957. A proud announcement was splattered across the front page of To-Day's Cinema on the 9th, showing the full extent of James Carreras' brilliant wheeler-dealing:

THE PERFECT PATTERN FOR BRITISH INDEPENDENTS
BIG INTERNATIONAL DEAL FOR BRITISH PRODUCTIONS
HAMMER PRODUCTIONS' THREE PICTURE DEAL WITH COLUMBIA
A deal which will give three British films an international showing and which represents yet another triumph for an independent British company was announced on Friday by M J Frankovich, Columbia chief in Britain. Columbia, he said, will distribute worldwide The Camp on Blood Island, The Snorkel and Blood Of Frankenstein. These are Hammer Film Productions' fiftieth, fifty-first and fifty-second productions. Blood

Island, just off the floor at Bray Studios, should be released by Columbia early in January next year, added Mr Frankovich. The corporation also had a 50-50 financial partnership in this film and The Snorkel.

The article was explicit about the emerging plans for *Dracula*: "This arrangement in no way cut across their deal with Universal-International for worldwide distribution of the fourth forthcoming production *Dracula*, which they financed 100% themselves."

In fact, Hammer had still to organise the financing of *Dracula*. Initially Universal were not interested, so Hammer had to look elsewhere. Their desperate search (hard to believe in view of their recent successes) took them back to Eliot Hyman at his other company, Seven-Arts. On 15 October, Hammer drew up a contract through their subsidiary, Cadogan Films Ltd, with Seven-Arts Productions and Seven-Arts International Inc 're Horror of Dracula'. The proposal was a 50-50 deal, Cadogan to foot £42,000, Seven-Arts Productions £31,875, and Seven-Arts International £10,625. The deal was never realised, however, and sources suggest that the film was ultimately funded with £33,000 from the National Film Finance Corporation (NFFC) and the rest via a change of heart from Universal in return for worldwide distribution rights[7]. But Hammer still had two productions to go before *Dracula* came to pass.

Betta St John as Jean Edwards in The Snorkel (1957).

The first of these was *The Snorkel*, a neat little thriller about a psychotic killer (Peter Van Eyck) who gases his wife in an airtight room while he lies beneath the floorboards breathing life-giving air through a snorkel. The death is assumed to be suicide, but his stepdaughter suspects him and that he is also responsible for the death of her father in an earlier 'accident'. He is finally caught out when trying to dispose of the stepdaughter the same way he killed his wife. The film was directed by Guy Green, who had previously won an Oscar for his black-and-white photography on David Lean's *Great Expectations* (1946). Sangster's script had left his killer callously trapped beneath the floorboards, but Green decided to soften the ending with a visit by the stepdaughter to the police to disclose the facts. The film was in many ways a forerunner of Sangster's series of Hammer suspense thrillers in the sixties.

Second unit location work began on *The Snorkel* in Alassio, Italy, on Saturday 7 September. Harry Oakes

THE SNORKEL

PRINCIPAL PHOTOGRAPHY: September to 22 October 1957
DISTRIBUTION:
  UK: Columbia; 90 minutes; certificate 'A'
  US: Columbia; 74 minutes
b/w
UK RELEASE:
  PREMIÈRE: May 1958 aboard the *Queen Elizabeth* on a
    trans-Atlantic crossing
  GENERAL RELEASE: 7 July 1958 on the ABC circuit
US RELEASE: September 1958

DIRECTOR: *Guy Green;* PRODUCER: *Michael Carreras;* ASSOCIATE PRODUCER: *Anthony Nelson Keys;* SCREENPLAY: *Peter Myers and Jimmy Sangster;* ART DIRECTOR: *John Stoll;* DIRECTOR OF

PHOTOGRAPHY: *Jack Asher;* CAMERA OPERATOR: *Len Harris;* ASSISTANT DIRECTOR: *Robert Lynn;* SUPERVISING EDITOR: *James Needs;* EDITOR: *Bill Lenny;* MUSIC: *Francis Chagrin;* MUSIC SUPERVISOR: *John Hollingsworth;* SOUND RECORDIST: *Jock May;* MAKE-UP: *Phil Leakey;* Hairstylist: *Henry Montsash;* PRODUCTION MANAGER: *Don Weeks;* CONTINUITY: *Doreen Dearnaley;* WARDROBE: *Molly Arbuthnot;* SPECIAL EFFECTS: *Sydney Pearson*

Peter Van Eyck (Paul Decker); Betta St John (Jean Edwards); Mandy Miller (Candy Brown); Gregoire Aslan (the Inspector); William Franklyn (Wilson); Henry Vidon (Italian gardener); Marie Burke (gardener's wife); Flush ('Toto'); Irene Prador (French woman); Robert Rietty (station sergeant); Armand Guinie (waiter); David Ritch (hotel clerk)

UP THE CREEK

Exclusive presents a Byron Film
PRINCIPAL PHOTOGRAPHY: November to December 1957
DISTRIBUTION:
  UK: Exclusive; certificate 'U'
  US: Dominant Pictures
83 minutes; b/w; Hammerscope
UK release:
  PREMIÈRE: 7 May 1958 at the London Warner
  GENERAL RELEASE: 2 June 1958 on the ABC circuit
  US RELEASE: 10 November 1958

DIRECTOR: Val Guest; PRODUCER: Henry Halstead; SCREENPLAY: Val Guest, John Warren; ART DIRECTOR: Elven Webb; DIRECTOR OF PHOTOGRAPHY: Arthur Grant; CAMERA OPERATOR: Moray Grant; ASSISTANT DIRECTOR: John Peverall; EDITOR: Helen Wiggins; MUSIC: Tony Fones, Tony Lowry; SOUND RECORDIST: George Adam; MAKE-UP: Alec Garfather; PRODUCTION SUPERVISOR: Fred A Swann; TECHNICAL ADVISOR: Lt Cmdr J H Pidler, RN

David Tomlinson (Lt Fairweather); Peter Sellers (Bosun); Wilfrid Hyde White (Admiral Foley); Vera Day (Lilly), Liliane Sottane (Suzanne); Tom Gill (Flag Lt); Michael Goodliffe (Nelson); Reginald Beckwith (publican); Lionel Murton (Perkins); John Warren (Cooky); Lionel Jeffries (Steady Barker); Howard Williams (Bunts); Peter Collingwood (Chippie); Barry Lowe (Webster); Edwin Richfield (Bennett); David Lodge (Scouse); Max Butterfield (Lefty); Malcolm Ransom (boy); Sam Kydd (Bates); Frank Pentingell (station master); Donald Bissett (labourer); Leonard Fenton (policeman); Basil Dignam (Coombes); Peter Coke (Price); Jack McNaughton (Reg Petty Officer); Larry Noble (Chief Petty Officer); Patrick Cargill (Commander); Michael Ripper (decorator)

remembers, "While we were travelling over there, they were still shooting the last week on The Camp on Blood Island at Bray, so Len stayed behind. They didn't intend them to overlap; The Camp on Blood Island must have gone over a few days, and after about the seventh day of The Snorkel, Len finally came over. What was funny was that on The Camp on Blood Island they had prop palm trees and these were floated all over the place, so that when you changed your angle you could cheat like mad. As soon as they finished, Len came literally straight over to join us in Italy and he went on the camera the same day he arrived. We were standing outside this house and he called out to Bob Lynn or Tom Walls, 'Oh, that palm tree there. Get it floated a bit to the right.' Of course they looked at him in amazement. He hadn't really come off the previous picture and he was terribly confused and apologised. After two or three days of Len being in Italy he suddenly became ill and I operated for a couple of days on the second unit camera."

David Tomlinson and Peter Sellers head the cast in Val Guest's maritime comedy Up the Creek (1957).

Shooting took place in the grounds of the Villa Pergola, home of Mrs Daniel Hanbury, widow of the late drugs manufacturer. The villa was also used for a number of interiors. Other scenes were shot in the streets, public squares, bars and hotels of Alassio. The crew returned to pick up interiors at Bray later in September and the production christened the new Stage 1. The stage was in fact a disused soundstage bought from the old Walton on Thames studios and rebuilt on the side of the car park at Bray. It became Hammer's largest stage, standing 90 by 80 feet, and could house Bernard Robinson's increasingly grandiose Gothic sets. With the new stage came a change to the numbering system of the existing stages. The previously designated 'New Stage' now became 'Stage 2' and Hammer's ballroom stage (B-C-D), facing the Thames, was now relegated to 'Stage 3'. Soon a fourth stage would appear on the left-hand side of the driveway on the lot.

While plans were going full steam ahead on Dracula at Bray, Hammer engaged themselves in a co-production with Byron Films. Up the Creek, an inoffensive maritime comedy, was the brainchild of Val Guest, written to launch famous radio 'Goon' Peter Sellers. James Carreras was unconvinced of

DRACULA

PRINCIPAL PHOTOGRAPHY: 11 November to 24 December 1957

DISTRIBUTION:

UK: Rank; certificate 'X'

US: Universal-International; US title: Horror of Dracula

82 minutes; Eastman Colour processed by Technicolor

UK RELEASE:

TRADE SHOW: 1 May 1958

PREMIÈRE: 22 May 1958, at the Gaumont Haymarket

GENERAL RELEASE: 16 June 1958, on the Gaumont circuit with There's Always a Price Tag

US RELEASE:

WORLD PREMIÈRE: 8 May 1958, at the Warner Theatre, Milwaukee, Wisconsin.

NEW YORK PREMIÈRE: 28 May 1958 at the Mayfair Theatre

DIRECTOR: Terence Fisher; PRODUCER: Anthony Hinds; ASSOCIATE PRODUCER: Anthony Nelson Keys; EXECUTIVE PRODUCER: Michael Carreras; SCREENPLAY: Jimmy Sangster; PRODUCTION DESIGNER: Bernard Robinson; DRAIGHTSMAN: Don Mingaye; DIRECTOR OF PHOTOGRAPHY: Jack Asher; CAMERA OPERATOR: Len Harris; FOCUS PULLER: Harry Oakes; ASSISTANT DIRECTOR: Robert Lynn; 2ND ASSISTANT DIRECTOR: Tom Walls; 3RD ASSISTANT DIRECTOR: Hugh Harlow; SUPERVISING EDITOR: James Needs; EDITOR: Bill Lenny; MUSIC: James Bernard; MUSIC SUPERVISOR: John Hollingsworth; SOUND RECORDIST: Jock May; MAKE-UP: Phil Leakey; MAKE-UP ASSISTANT: Roy Ashton; HAIRSTYLIST: Henry Montsash; PRODUCTION MANAGER: Don Weeks; CONTINUITY: Doreen Dearnaley; WARDROBE: Molly Arbuthnot, Rosemary Burrows; SPECIAL EFFECTS: Sydney Pearson; MATTES: Les Bowie; TITLES: Les Bowie and Studio Film Laboratories; PROPERTY MASTER: Tommy Money; PROPERTY BUYER: Eric Hillier; STILLS CAMERAMAN: Tom Edwards; PUBLICITY: Douglas Railton; PRODUCTION ACCOUNTANT: W H V Able; CASHIER: Ken Gordon; STUDIO MANAGER: Arthur Kelly; CONSTRUCTION MANAGER: Mick Lyons; CHIEF ELECTRICIAN: Jack Curtis; MASTER PAINTER: Lawrence Wren; MASTER PLASTERER: Arthur Banks; MASTER CARPENTER: Charles Davis

Peter Cushing (Dr Van Helsing); Christopher Lee (Dracula); Michael Gough (Arthur Holmwood); Melissa Stribling (Mina Holmwood); Carol Marsh (Lucy Holmwood); Olga Dickie (Gerda); John Van Eyssen (Jonathan Harker); Valerie Gaunt (vampire woman); Janina Faye (Tania); Barbara Archer (Inga); Charles Lloyd Pack (Dr Seward); George Merritt (policeman); George Woodbridge (landlord); George Benson (frontier official); Miles Malleson (undertaker); Geoffrey Baledon (porter); Paul Cole (lad)

EXTRA NAMES ON THE PRESSBOOK INCLUDED:

Guy Mills (coachdriver); Dick Morgan (driver's companion); Judith Nelmes (woman in coach); Stedwell Fulcher (man in coach); William Sherwood (priest); Humphrey Kent (fat merchant); John Mossman (hearse driver) stunt double for Melissa Stribling: Daphne Baker

Sellers' pulling-power but was pacified by the casting of David Tomlinson. Filming took place over November and December at Elstree, with location shooting on the Thames Estuary and in Weymouth. The film was the last feature to be released by Hammer's parent company, Exclusive. With Hammer's new success, the Board now felt it was time to dismantle the family distribution company and concentrate full time on film production. Hammer would now wind down the Exclusive operation with a number of shorts throughout the rest of the fifties, some of which were produced by Hammer.

Tony Hinds submitted Jimmy Sangster's second draft screenplay of Dracula to John Nicholls, Secretary of the BBFC, on 8 October. The comments of Audrey Field on 14 October in an internal report were far from flattering:

"The uncouth, uneducated, disgusting and vulgar style of Mr Jimmy Sangster cannot quite obscure the remnants of a good horror story, though they do give one the gravest misgivings about treatment. I never read the original story, and do not remember the first film, though I know it had a great effect on me when I saw it at the age of 16 or thereabouts. It seems to me that there is nothing censorable in the story as a whole, but a good deal to complain of in details. The curse of the thing is Technicolor blood: why need vampires be messier feeders than anyone else? Certainly strong cautions will be necessary on shots of blood. And of course, some of the stake-work is prohibitive."

Nicholls detailed the objections in his letter to Hinds of 21 October:

"We have read the script of Dracula which you sent us with your letter of the 8th October, and I would enter a very strong caution at this stage on the treatment of this subject. Many of the details in the present script are unacceptable, in particular the shots of vampires and their victims smeared with blood, and the writhings and screams of agony when the vampires are pinned down by stakes driven through the heart. The following is a list of details which should be mentioned; but the final decision on all details must of course rest with the examiners when the completed film is submitted for censorship.

P.10, 29, 45, etc. It is important that the women in the film should be decently clad, not seen in transparent nightdresses or with bared breasts, or in unduly suggestive garments. I would

One of Tom
Edwards' famous
publicity shots of
Christopher Lee
and Melissa
Stribling from
Dracula (1957).

add that anything which cross-emphasises the sex aspect of the story is likely, in a horror
subject of this kind, to involve cuts in the completed film.

P. 22. When the woman embraces Jonathan, she should not be seen to sink her teeth in his
neck. Here and elsewhere, the appearance of the vampires should not be too revolting; and
neither they nor their victims should be shown with clothes or faces smeared with blood
(cf. pp. 28, 75, 78, 102, etc.) Dracula should not hurl the woman across the room by the hair.

P. 23. The attempted throttling of Jonathan by Dracula is much too long and full of close-ups.

P. 24. The sharp scream of the woman out of frame should be omitted.

Pp. 28, 79-80. There should be nothing more to indicate that the various vampires are to be
transfixed by a stake through the heart than a shot of the mallet and stake being picked up,
followed, if necessary, by a shot of the stake being driven home out of frame. Shots of it being
planted on the corpse, shots of the corpse while it is being driven in or after, and all shots of
the vampire writhing, and sounds of its screams, should be omitted.

P. 37. Shots of Jonathan's dead face should not be too horrible.

P. 48. The word "unnatural" should be changed – to, eg, "excessive".

P. 110. There should be no shot of the driver's cut throat.

"I return the script herewith."

It would seem that Tony Hinds had little interest in any observations the Board might have to offer, because, while Nicholls and co were busy deliberating over the draft script, Hinds had Jimmy Sangster present him with a final shooting script, dated 18 October. However, the Board would take exception to Hinds' blatant disregard of their script advice when the film was later submitted for certification. A credit to Sangster was the way in which he condensed Stoker's novel into a storyline still steeped in Gothic menace yet fast-paced and above all well within the economical constraints of Hammer's production capabilities. As a result of this literary concentration, various scenes and characters had to be either reduced or omitted altogether. Gone were the numerous gypsies and wolves that littered the Transylvanian countryside. Dr Seward was reduced to a virtual walk-on and Dracula's three wives became one. The character of Renfield was omitted and Dracula's sea voyage to Whitby was exchanged for the much more economical coach ride to nearby Carlstadt.

With a budget of £81,412, Tony Hinds brought back the same crew that had just worked on *The Snorkel*, apart from director Terence Fisher and production designer Bernard Robinson. It included most of the successful team that had worked on *The Curse of Frankenstein*, apart from Robert Lynn and Tom Walls, who were now Hammer's regular 1st and 2nd assistant directors, Bill Lenny as editor and Doreen Dearnaley as continuity. Also back from *Curse* were Peter Cushing, Christopher Lee and scream queen Valerie Gaunt. Cushing was again the main star, but *Curse* had kickstarted Lee's career and he came to *Dracula* fresh from playing the Marquis St Evremonde in Rank's *A Tale of Two Cities*.

On 9 October, Terence Fisher signed a contract to shoot *Dracula* and *The Revenge of Frankenstein* (the new title for *Blood of Frankenstein*) back-to-back. Hammer had been justly pleased with his work on *The Curse of Frankenstein* and he was the obvious choice to lead their next two Gothic shockers. "For both *The Curse of Frankenstein* and *Dracula*, Hammer suggested that I should look at the original Universal prints," remembered Fisher. "I wouldn't do this, because I felt one had to take the idea out of the new script and not from what had been done before."[8] Fisher would inject the fresh approach of *Curse* into *Dracula* too. "We weren't influenced at all by the old Universal horror films when we started ours," Fisher went on. "I didn't screen them or refer to them at all. I was uninterested in them. I started from scratch. You can't go back and remake a film; you can remake a subject but that's different. There was a long period of time between theirs and ours. The whole way of living had changed so it would have been pointless to try and copy them. You can't go back. I have seen Universal's films since then. I think they're melodramatic. I wouldn't call mine melodramatic."[9]

The first actor to sign his contract for the film was Peter Cushing, also on 9 October, which called for him to be available for shooting "on or about 7 days before or after 4th November for 5 consecutive weeks." The contract further stipulated that "prior to shooting" he was to be available for one week from 28 October for "rehearsals, testing, fitting of clothing and other pre-production matters." Christopher Lee signed up on 29 October for six weeks to begin "on or about" 11 November. The rest of the cast signed up during November: Melissa Stribling, Michael Gough and George Benson on the 5th, George Woodbridge on the 6th, Janina Faye on the 19th, John Van Eyssen and Valerie Gaunt on the 20th and Geoffrey Bayldon on the 29th.

Contracts also exist for some of the characters in the legendary coach scene included at the beginning of Sangster's final script of 18 October. This was an introductory scene (very similar to the one in Universal's 1930 version) where a man, woman, priest and merchant try to convince Harker not to go on to the castle. The contracts asked the artists to be available on or about 19 November; Stedwell Fulcher (man in coach) signed his contract the day before that, while William Sherwood (priest), Judith Nelmes (woman in coach) and Humphrey Kent (fat merchant) all signed on 27 November, a full week, oddly enough, after their proposed shooting date. This sequence has always been the subject of debate; was it shot and later edited out, or just omitted by Fisher altogether? Certainly the film's British publicity folder and Universal-International's New York press sheet include these extra characters in the cast list and at the beginning of the film we do see a coach in transit, albeit briefly, with people just about visible inside (including a driver and companion, the two other characters in this sequence), suggesting that the actors did at least attend the location. But no one, including Terence Fisher and camera operator Len Harris in later interviews, can remember the rest of the sequence being shot.

Shooting was initially scheduled to begin on Monday 4 November; Fisher's and Cushing's contracts both say that the film was to start then, while the budget statement clearly states on its

Jonathan Harker (John Van Eyssen) makes his fateful entrance into Castle Dracula in Terence Fisher's Dracula (1957).

cover that the film was to have a six-week shoot, from Monday 4 November to Friday 13 December. The date eventually slid back to the 5th when the trade papers excitedly proclaimed its coming:

"NOV 5 IS NO ORDINARY DAY
       IS A DAY TO REMEMBER
       IS GUY FAWKES DAY
       IS THE DAY WILLIAM OF ORANGE LANDED AT TORBAY
       IS POLLING DAY IN THE USA
BUT most important of all TODAY is the day Hammer Film Productions' Dracula commences shooting at Bray Studios."

However, last-minute problems put filming back another week and shooting finally commenced at Bray on Monday 11 November. Bernard Robinson erected his magnificent sets during the three weeks before the start of the film's six-week shooting schedule. That November Britain was succumbing to a bitter winter and the unit had to contend with freezing cold on the back lot and on location. Actor Geoffrey Bayldon still vividly remembers going to the studio for his day's shooting: "My first memory is that it was bitterly cold when I made that early morning journey to Bray Studios, where the heating system offered little comfort. Perhaps that is why I remember so well that piping-hot, delicious meat-and-two-veg that Peter, Christopher and I collected from the cheery ladies in white aprons at lunch time."

Melissa Stribling also remembered the cold, particularly in the scene where Dracula was to bury her in a freshly dug grave. "It was one of those funny things where I kept saying, 'When are we going to shoot that sequence where I'm in the grave?' The film happened to be shot at a time when it was so cold I can't tell you – it was miserable, miserably cold. I kept saying, 'When are we going to shoot that scene?' I thought the grave was going to be in a corner of the set and nobody ever said – they kept on putting me off and it became sort of a joke! Then one day when we were going to have lunch – and to go to lunch we had to go across open ground, and I was always in thin nightdresses and petticoats and things – I suddenly passed a great big six-foot open grave half-filled with water. I turned round and said, 'You stinking rotten lot, that's where I'm going. That's why you haven't shot it, 'cos I might die! You'll have to shoot it at the end.' And that's what they did. The girl they threw in for the long shot obviously wasn't me [it was stunt double Daphne Baker]. They threw her in, but at least she

RIGHT: *The undead Lucy (Carol Marsh) abducts little Tania (Janina Faye) in the Holmwood Crypt in this scene from* Dracula *(1957).*

BELOW: *Bernard Robinson's set was recycled for the dining room and stairs of Castle Dracula.*

had a mattress underneath. When it came my turn to go in, in that thin nightdress, they took the mattress out and I was lying in the bottom of the grave, and Chris Lee was nothing if not keen. I had to wake up suddenly and see him and scream, and as I screamed a great big clod of earth came right in my face ... so there are some very funny shots somewhere of me swearing at Chris Lee from the bottom of a grave!"[10]

Many, including the present author, regard this as Hammer's finest work. Even Terence Fisher once said, "Everything was right about that film; the script, the casting, everything just clicked. The chemistry just worked the whole way. A wonderful experience."[11] This says it all: brilliant direction, photography, editing, set design, music, acting – everything fell into place to make an undisputed classic.

Jack Asher's rich colour photography gives extra depth to Bernard Robinson's ornately dressed sets. "*The Curse of Frankenstein* was a try-out, a debut of my ideas for photographing colour," Asher remembered. "In retrospect, just to realise that it worked so well is really great. When we started *Dracula*, I felt a settling down, a maturing of style. I began to feel that we had something special, perhaps transcending all previous visions."[6] Though his perfectionist slowness often irritated the producers, he was nevertheless well respected by them and his lighting of *Dracula* didn't pass without comment. As he explained, "My relationship with Tony Hinds was always mutual and full of respect. One always had to admire his executive strength and tenacity, but we never saw eye to eye on artistic, photographic procedures. Time and cost studies were his details. Undoubtedly he appreciated my contributions to the films and said so. He pointed out a good review in the Hollywood Reporter on Dracula, which said, in part, 'superb camerawork by Jack Asher.' This came to me in a telegram, which said 'Congratulations! Love, Tony' – and in parentheses at the bottom, 'This does not mean more money.'"[6]

This was the first time audiences were exposed to the full splendour of Bernard Robinson's immaculate sets. Terence Fisher was always complimentary: "They were a joy to work on because wherever you went on a Bernie Robinson set you could shoot with effect. They were designed in such a way that no matter where you stood and looked you had interest."[12]

So radical were Robinson's designs for Dracula's castle interior, however – contrasting so starkly with the heavily cobwebbed Universal version – that Hammer almost got cold feet and took him off the project. His wife Margaret explains: "When he designed the first Dracula sets, he found out later that there had been a discussion as to whether or not to pay him off and get another art director, because those sets were so different from anything they expected. They were scared of them. And then, I suppose, thrift got the better of them and they decided to risk it and go ahead and keep the sets he'd designed. I must say, I found those sets a bit puzzling myself. I said, 'Bernard, there were no cobwebs. Who did the cleaning?' I told Bernard that it didn't seem very logical. 'Of course it is,' he said. 'Magic!'"

Don Mingaye, draughtsman on the movie (there was no art director), concurs. "They were concerned about it, because the Lugosi film was the only yardstick they had. But we were talking about colour and the Lugosi one wasn't, so we had a lot more going for us. But we were not briefed in any detail whatsoever as to what they wanted."

Luckily, Robinson's floor designs for the Dracula sets on the newly constructed Stage 1 still exist, allowing us to piece together the progression and revamping of the sets throughout the production and illustrate his clever and economical approach to set design. First he erected the exterior graveyard set where Van Helsing would rescue the little girl from Lucy's clutches. This is a wonderfully atmospheric set; a decaying staircase leading down to a sombre garden of tombstones dressed with fallen leaves and partly obscured by billowing dry ice. After filming was completed there, rather than tearing it down and starting from scratch, it was revamped into the impressive dining room set complete with staircase and first floor balcony, twisting pillars, Gothic and Baroque arches, and grand fireplace, all soon to become characteristic trademarks of Robinson's interiors. Thus the bedraggled steps that had once led down to the graveyard were now redressed into the ornate staircase on which Dracula first appears.

The carefully detailed floor was made of hessian, papered and painted. Saving money, the window and fireplace from the Italian villa in The Snorkel were reused. This set also doubled as the entrance hall to the castle we see at the beginning as Harker enters. Here the staircase was hidden by drapes and a row of arches added. Robinson's floor plans also show that behind this set, hidden from view, was Harker's bedroom set.

The floor plans also give details of the final revamp to the library where Harker would first encounter Dracula in his vampire guise and where, in the final moments, Van Helsing would destroy him. This concurs with the accounts of cast and crew, who agree that Van Helsing's leap from the table to pull the curtains down was one of the last scenes, and makes sense of the fact that the library set would reappear almost unchanged in the next production, The Revenge of Frankenstein. The stairs were again hidden by drapes, while a note on the floor plan explains: "Book shelves glue in here for Gothic room conversion." (The library was referred to as the 'Gothic room' in Sangster's original script). This meant that the windows of Harker's room, concealed behind the library, would effectively open onto the door through which Dracula bursts into the library to attack Harker. Indeed, Harker's room would itself be revamped into Dracula's crypt.

The brick Stage 2 now housed the interiors of the Holmwood household. The Holmwood cellar was revamped into the undertaker's parlour and Van Helsing's hotel room was also built on Stage 2. The rectangular ballroom Stage 3 was the ideal shape to house Hammer's many inns and Dracula started the ball rolling, introducing Cushing's wily vampire hunter and the understandably paranoid villagers led by veteran George Woodbridge.

Robinson and Mingaye were also responsible for the impressive exterior sets on the back lot. The external castle set was constructed close to the main gates of the studio just to the left of the entrance road which led up to the house. This set was small in comparison to its immense stature when seen on screen, particularly in the opening minutes of the film when Harker arrives at the castle and we are granted our first impressive view of it in long shot, with its great towers and snow-capped peaks in the background. This appearance was created by incorporating the actual standing set with a Les Bowie glass painting which contained the turrets and mountains. The set was complete with a lodge and gravel pit, which led up to the main entrance of the castle. To the left of the great door stood a flight of steps, which descended to the entrance of the mausoleum. Opposite the steps was a low wall containing two tapering pillars. Afoot each pillar stood a large stone eagle, wings spread as if to ward off unwanted visitors. This part of the set was used effectively in the film's opening credits.

So impressive was the external set that, instead of being cleared after Dracula, it was used in other productions over the next year. Suitably disguised each time, the set reappeared in The Revenge of Frankenstein, became Baskerville Hall for The Hound of the Baskervilles and even became part of an Indian village in The Stranglers of Bombay. The set would finally be struck in 1959 following the latter film and another erected in its place.

Most of the inherent Gothic mood of the film is, however, down to the expert judgement and skill of Terence Fisher. He once explained why he found the character so fascinating: "Because he's basically myth and superstition. Because he's basically sexual. He has the power of evil to prey on the female victim's sexual feelings, so that they at the moment he bites it is the culmination of a sexual experience. This is only because Dracula is the personificaton of evil and will always play on the weakness of every victim, no matter whether it's greed or sexuality. He is the personification temptation, preying on the needs of each victim.

"Even when I came to shoot the Dracula films," Fisher maintained, "I still did not consult Bram Stoker's novel or the Transylvanian vampire legends. I think my greatest contribution to the Dracula myth was to bring out the underlying sexual element in the story. I also believe that the first Dracula film is just about the best thing I have ever done for Hammer and it still looks a very successful film; everything seemed to hang together for once during the shooting."[14] Of the Lucy/Dracula seduction scene, Fisher commented: "It's almost ballet the way she opens the doors, goes back and lies down again, her eyes focused, waiting for him to appear … You know, it's a distortion of the so-called 'true love', and this is the power of evil working from a distance. Dracula could cause himself to appear there right at the moment when he realised that any resistance to him she might have had was gone."[15]

The film's sensuality is taken even further with Dracula's seduction of Mina. "Dracula preyed upon the sexual frustrations of his woman victims," Fisher explained. "The [Holmwood] marriage was one in which she was not sexually satisfied and that was her weakness as far as Dracula's approach to her was concerned. When she arrived back after having been away all night she said it all in one close-up at the door. She'd been done the whole night through, please! I remember Melissa saying, 'Terry, how should I play the scene?' So I told her, 'Listen, you should imagine you have had one whale of a sexual night, the one of your whole sexual experience. Give me that in your face!' And she did, of course."[16]

Further insight into the moral code of the vampire is given as Van Helsing listens to the phonograph recording of his notes. Interestingly, Sangster here compares the vampire's hold on his victim to that of a drug addict yearning for his next fix, making the supernatural seem that much more tangible. To further embellish the reality of the story, he took away Dracula's ability to turn into a bat, fobbing it off as "a common fallacy". Sangster explains: "One of my reasons was that it had never been done very well, and I tried to ground the script to some extent in reality. I thought that the idea of being able to change into a bat or a wolf or anything like that made the film seem more like a fairy tale than it needed to be. And, fortunately, everybody agreed with me."[12]

Fisher would change a number of key scenes as he shot the movie. The unforgettable entrance of Dracula was not what Sangster envisaged in his final shooting script, where he had intended Harker to suddenly turn in response to Dracula's voice calling his name from a doorway. In the film, Harker, sensing Dracula's presence, turns to see the dark-cloaked shadow of the Count standing in silhouette at the top of the stairs as James Bernard's Dra-cu-la motif crashes in. "It's a physical thing, horror," Fisher explained. "The first time you see Dracula is up at the top of the staircase, in silhouette – and the audience, the ones you want to laugh, start to laugh, because they think that they're going to see ... what? Instead, they see this very handsome man, the perfect host, come down the stairs into close-up. I did it this way, not just to tease the audience but to show them that the whole idea of evil is very attractive. It's one of the great cards that evil holds!"[17] The visual impact of this scene is realised further when we compare it to the Count's entrance in the later *Scars of Dracula* (1970), which introduces Dracula in much the same way Sangster intended in his original *Dracula* script. In *Scars*, one is momentarily startled by the sudden arrival of the Count, but the sheer shock and sensation of the original film is sadly missing.

Foreshadowing Hitchcock's *Psycho*, Harker, the character we have come to identify with, is unexpectedly killed and Van Helsing discovers his body stretched out in Dracula's sarcophagus. Again Fisher made minor amendments to the script at this point. Sangster's screenplay describes Harker's corpse as "Completely drained of blood, what is left is merely skin over a skeleton. The skeleton hands are crossed in mock reverence over the chest, and the skull grins up at HELSING malevolently." A dummy of the shrivelled Harker was accordingly assembled for the scene but Fisher wisely chose not to use it, replacing it with a shot of John Van Eyssen with added fangs. This is more consistent with the overall concept; Harker has only just become a vampire so there is no need for his appearance to have changed so drastically. Hammer were careful, however, not to lose out on the dummy altogether, capturing it for posterity as a publicity still.

Fisher offered his own interpretation of the staking of Lucy. The script called for Arthur to deliver the first two blows, with Van Helsing taking over only when Arthur is unable to continue. Fisher condensed this, allowing Van Helsing to handle the staking unaided. However, the American version remains far more graphic than the scene which appears in British prints. In the UK print, the doctor lines his stake over Lucy's heart and we cut to Arthur cringing against the wall as the stake is driven home off-screen. In fact, the only blood we see is a smear on Van Helsing's hand, which he wipes away on a handkerchief as he beckons the stricken Arthur to his sister's side. From Arthur's shocked reaction as he gazes on, we cut to Lucy's peaceful face, the cross burn on her forehead gone and Bernard's 'good' motif taking momentary control on the soundtrack. We still do not see any blood or even the stake in position. The American censor would allow a slightly extended scene, which includes close-up shots of Lucy as she screams in agony, as well as a shot of the stake entering her body, complete with blood gushing around its sides. The problems this scene posed with the British censor will be discussed later.

Focus puller Harry Oakes remembers, "They shot three different versions of the staking for overseas markets. If I remember rightly we used to have a close-up of a stake with a mallet hitting it, then a bit more for the American set-up, penetrating the flesh or the make-up, but there was to be blood for the Japanese market. I remember also I was 2nd unit cameraman on the Frank Langella *Dracula* in 1978 at Shepperton and we were doing the same thing then, we had two versions of it."

Fisher always insisted on the necessity of showing the stakings graphically. As he explained, "The critics who attacked me for being explicit never understood that what I wanted to show in the vampire films was the triumph of good resulting from the act of staking; that it was a release for the victim tainted with vampirism. I filmed the first staking in 'Dracula' using shadows because it would have been far less exciting to have filmed them all the same way. But you can't show the destruction of the vampire solely by shadows or implications; you've got to be explicit since it is important that the release from vampirism be shown, just as it's important to show the resulting look of peace upon the victim's face."[16]

The finale of the movie, which was played out on the new Stage 1, is superbly choreographed by Fisher and cut by the Needs/Lenny team, qualifying as one of the most memorable endings to any horror film. Yet the dynamic confrontation between Van Helsing and Dracula was strangely muted in Sangster's script:

117. <u>INT. GOTHIC ROOM. DAWN</u>
This is the room where Jonathan had the encounter with the woman in sequence one.
The light through the stained glass windows is just beginning to pick out the colours of the window on the dust covered floor.

In the centre of a raised dais DRACULA is lifting a heavy stone trap in the floor.

C. S. HELSING

He sees what is happening. Quickly he closes the door behind him and locks it with the large key that is in the lock. He runs towards DRACULA taking a crucifix from his pocket.

M. S.

DRACULA is just heaving the trap fully open when HELSING reaches him and holding the crucifix in front of him he forces a snarling DRACULA to let go of the trap which slams shut again. Then HELSING plants himself over the trap, looking at DRACULA.

C. S. HELSING

Staring steadily at DRACULA

C. S. DRACULA

He is looking at HELSING, his blood red eyes flooded with anger, unable to do anything for a moment.

Then even while he is standing there a ray of sunlight creeps across his face.

He clasps his hand to his face and screams, then he turns.

M. S.

HELSING uses the crucifix to force DRACULA back into the pool of light.

He looks up towards the stained glass window.

C. S. WINDOW

The sun is now beaming through the whole window, the colours sparkling and then beaming in the dust laden room.

C. S. DRACULA

He stands where he is for a moment not knowing what to do. Then he runs for the door that HELSING has locked. In so doing he passes through the light.

Before he can reach the door he falls headlong.

As he starts to try and scramble to his feet, we hear an ominous splintering, cracking sound.

C. S. DRACULA'S LEGS.

The trousered legs, scrabbling for a foothold, seem suddenly to no longer contain leg at all. The solidity inside the trouser seems to dissolve, and as the boots fall from the end of the trouser leg, a little pile of whitish powder cascades from both the boot and the trouser leg.

C. S. DRACULA

His face has started to powder too, the flesh drying fast and falling from the skull in the form of dust.

C. S. DRACULA'S HANDS

The hands which are scrabbling along the floor trying to reach the door. Suddenly the fingers start to break off, snapping at the joints, and they too start to dissolve into powder and dust.

C. S. DRACULA

The last sight of his face before it is no more. Before it dries up completely, and spreads itself in powder form across the room.

After the exciting chase sequence, the events in Sangster's finale appear rather anticlimactic. His conclusion is less than spectacular and somewhat frustrating in that it denies us any sort of physical contact between Van Helsing and Dracula, which we have been led to expect in this energetic movie. Instead the crew were wise only to use Sangster's framework. In addition to the exciting fight sequence inserted, a vital contribution was made by Peter Cushing. "In the first Dracula picture I suggested that it is always a good idea to have some sort of almost Douglas Fairbanks scene – to have a jolly good leap or jump." Remembered Cushing, "Towards the end, just before Chris Lee disinte-grates in that wonderful bit of special effects, the script just said that Van Helsing gets out his crucifix and forces Dracula into the sunlight. I said that it would be absolutely marvellous if they could jump off a balcony onto the curtains ... but they couldn't construct a balcony because it would be frightfully expensive and they'd shot already and they had already built the set. What we did have was a long, long refectory table. I ran along it and leapt as far as I could and pulled the curtains down, which was much more effective than just running to them and pulling them down."[19] Accordingly the scene was revamped, with Cushing's double making the climactic leap for the curtains.

Van Helsing (Peter Cushing) warns Arthur Holmwood (Michael Gough) of the threat to his wife in Dracula (1957).

Cushing's second suggestion regarded the crucifix with which he forces the vampire into the light. He explained, "In the original script Van Helsing was sort of like a salesman for crucifixes. He was pulling them out of every pocket. He was giving them to children to protect themselves, and putting them in coffins and so on. At the end of the film, he pulled out another one, so I asked if we couldn't do something exciting instead. I remembered seeing a film years ago called *Berkeley Square*, in which Leslie Howard was thought of as being the Devil by this frightened little man who suddenly grabbed two big candlesticks and made a sign of the cross with them. I remembered that this had impressed me enormously. I suggested the run along the refectory table to jump onto the curtains and hit Dracula square in the face with the sunlight. He would, of course, be trapped. Then I could come along like a hero, grab the two candlesticks and make the cross with them in his face. They agreed. Originally the candelabra they had were the type with four candles on each base. You could tell what I was doing, but it didn't look like a cross, but they changed to the ones you see in the film. At least it wasn't another crucifix coming out of my pockets. I think it was quite an effective ending to that picture, especially with what the special effects boys did."[20]

The climactic special effects may be outdated by today's standards, but they are still visually striking. Harry Oakes remembers the simple technique used in producing the shaft of light that destroys Dracula: "It was done very quickly actually. Jack Asher, I presume, must have organised it all before, because the carpenter appeared with a sheet of glass in a frame, I suppose roughly two feet by 18 inches or bigger, and he nailed it to a couple of light stands. He put it in front of the lens and he angled it down slightly and to the right. Jack looked through to make sure that the glass covered completely. Then he got Len to look behind the camera. With a light pencil he made marks on the glass, which turned out to be the beam of light that was coming from the curtain to Christopher Lee's stand-in on the floor. Having drawn that very lightly, he then covered the rest of the glass up with black paper and then the stand-by chip [carpenter] came along and very softly gave a light spray with white paint over the slot that was left over the glass. Jack then got an electrician to put a 2kw spot light on the floor and shone it onto the glass at an angle, which didn't affect the glass in any way, it only illuminated this white spray. The lamp was left on but covered up and Jack took all the surrounding paper off the glass and, sure enough, when you looked through the camera it was such a light spray you couldn't notice it except when the light was put on, which illuminated it.

"We did rehearsal and then Peter Cushing pulled the curtain back and at the same time the electrician uncovered the spotlight. And it all happened in about 10 minutes. I was amazed. It was quite simple really. The trick was having it just light enough so that you didn't notice it looking through without any light on it and then angling the glass sufficiently so that the light caught it, but at the same time that it didn't pick up any other reflections in the studio lights. You know, I've been doing special effects for years, I was second unit on *Aliens*, but I've never seen anything done so effectively so quickly."

In fact, so impressed were writer Chris Columbus (later to direct the first two *Harry Potter* movies) and director Joe Dante with this climax that they adapted it for the ending of their movie *Gremlins* (1984).

Many remember fondly Bray's canteen/restaurant and the fabulous home cooking of Mrs Thompson and Mrs Croft. Charles Lloyd Pack, who played Dr Seward, remembered: "I enjoyed working at Bray Studios and I particularly remember the food they used to serve us for lunch. You see, we at Hammer didn't get paid very much money, in fact the whole of their budget was very confined, but they still made first class films. Anyway, they made up for not paying us much by having a first class chef. They never had big casts in these horror films – a very limited number of people – so there was always plenty of food. When you went into the dining room you had the local ladies cooking and they used to cook such splendid food. In fact, we could hardly move afterwards and work was very scarce in the afternoons. We always looked forward to our roasts and treacle pudding – real home cooking."[21]

Christopher Lee recalls, "I was determined not to see the Lugosi film and I didn't for years. I didn't want to do any of the things he'd done and I thought the idea of someone in the wilds of Tyransylvania, in full evening dress, a little bit incongruous ... So I never copied him in any way. I played the part by reading the book, by reading the script and putting into it what I thought needed to be done. So the first time I played it, I enjoyed it and we had a lot of fun. Peter Cushing and I used to giggle a lot and behave disgracefully. You have to keep your sense of humour in situations of that kind. All the time we'd keep saying to each other, wouldn't it be marvellous if I could do this, if I could do that, because it would get a big laugh, and the director says, 'That's not quite the intention of the picture!' ... And there were times with those wretched contact lenses in my eyes – I couldn't see a thing. I'd start to cry, and charge past the camera, knocking everybody over, tears falling down my cheeks. *That* wasn't intended."[20]

Lee describes his approach to the character, "I saw him as a decisive, charming, heroic, erotic figure – irresistible to women, unstoppable by men – a sinister but aristocratic nobleman. He also had a tragic quality to him – the curse of being immortal by being undead. But I don't think very much of the sadness of Count Dracula came out in the first film, apart from brief glimpses, because he had relatively little screen time. He was more of a juggernaut, building to that ferocious confrontation with Peter's Van Helsing at the end."[22]

Lee continues, "Well, as you know, I've always tried to put this element of sadness into this kind of role. I've termed it 'the loneliness of evil', which I think is the truth. This element of sadness I always try, and I portray these bad, wicked characters with a slightly sad, pathetic look or quality to them. Dracula is not exactly pathetic, but there is a terrible dark sadness about him. He doesn't want to live, but he's got to, he doesn't want to go on existing as an undead, but he has no choice."[23]

Terence Fisher was always complimentary about Lee's performance. "The emergence of Christopher Lee as the new Dracula was an instant success. His performance was superb in every respect. It is not a part that is dependent upon dialogue. Its interpretation relies largely upon physical movement and facial expression, in other words, on a very real understanding of the art of mime. This, Christopher Lee possesses. He knows how to project mood and inner feeling – particularly the supernatural quality of Dracula. I have great respect for his professionalism and always enjoy working with him."[24]

The relationship between Lee and Fisher was one of mutual respect. Lee explains, "Terry was a very nice person, a lovely character with a terrific sense of humour. He started as an editor, of course. Good directors usually do. They should be, it's how you put a picture together. I've always said this about Terry – he was the easiest man in the world. He knew what he wanted. He didn't let it go if it wasn't what he wanted. What's on the screen is what Fisher wanted and intended that it should be.

He would listen to us and very often he would
agree. He also would disagree, but he was a
brilliant arranger. Very often he would say,
'Well now, you make your entrance in there and
show me what you can do.' So we had a
rehearsal and if there was dialogue, we could
even change that. You would come in and he
would say, 'No, maybe you should come in
from there and stop before you do that.' He
was a brilliant arranger, but I don't remember
Terry giving me a great deal of specific direction. 'Come in there, say this line, emphasise
that word, then walk over there whilst saying
the rest.' That's specific direction and Terry
was never like that. Some directors are, but the
really good ones are intelligent enough to
realise that you are instinctively going to do
something and they like to see what it is first."

Valerie Gaunt in a relaxed
publicity pose for Dracula
(1957).

Lee and Cushing had strong support.
Michael Gough played the stiff-upper-lipped
Arthur Holmwood and during filming, on 23
November, celebrated his 40th birthday. On
the same day Boris Karloff turned 70. There
had been early rumours that Karloff would
play Dracula. To-Day's Cinema on Tuesday 13
August had reported, "Hammer also point out that stories which have appeared
in the Press ... stating that Boris Karloff will star in their Dracula film are entirely
without foundation." The confusion probably arose because American producer
Richard Gordon was planning a film called Dracula's Revenge, to star Karloff. He nixed the idea
when Hammer got in ahead of him.

This time Melissa Stribling and Carol Marsh joined Valerie Gaunt in providing the glamour.
Melissa Stribling remembered Carol Marsh's vampire teeth: "Carol Marsh had her vampire teeth
after she had been vampirised. She didn't like them because they didn't make her look pretty – and
they made her lisp when she talked. She would say to Terence Fisher, 'They really wouldn't show
when I had them in. They really wouldn't show.' But he would say, 'Yes, my dear, but they would.
You still have to have them.' And she cried and cried when she had them put in. I would smile at
her and say in a sneaky way, 'Well, I don't have to have them.'"[25]

Janina Faye was then a child star of nine. Her first speaking part was as the young Heather Sears
in the opening scenes of The Story of Esther Costello. She had been pipped at the post for the part of
the young Elizabeth by Hazel Court's daughter, Sally Walsh, in The Curse of Frankenstein, but proved
ideal casting for the part of Tania in Dracula. She still has vivid recollections of the film: "I was nine
and I suppose initially it wasn't scary, because it was just acting and, because everybody else was
very concerned that I might be scared, they were so protective of me. Terence Fisher was a very
cuddly sort of chap and he would go through the scenes with me and explain them to me. There
are pictures of me talking to Terence Fisher while reading the 'Jack and Jill' comic. It was a very
protective instinct that they had.

"I remember in one scene I had a very heavy costume on, made of this thick pink material, and I
can remember sitting under the lights and I was so hot! I had a little nightdress on when Peter
Cushing put the coat round me in the graveyard. He would say to me, 'I'm going to put this coat
round you, but you mustn't be scared, because it's not real.' I remember thinking, 'Oh, what a nice
man.' And I can still feel that coat, I can still feel that collar and smell that collar, because it was a
black coat and it had this brown fur collar, and I remember sitting there thinking, 'Wow, this is big
time, this is the movies!' And then they blew all this dry ice at us, but they never took me into the bit

RIGHT: The library set, inside which the climax of Dracula (1957) took place, was a redressed version of a set that had first appeared as the Holmwood Crypt and the dining room.

BELOW: When Harker stakes the vampire woman she ages into an old crone in Dracula (1957). The senior actress did not take to her coffin easily.

where the coffin was. They kept me away from that." She never got chance to see the finished film, because of its 'X' certificate. "The first time I saw Dracula was on television. The first time I saw it on the big screen was at the Barbican's Hammer festival in 1996."

The film provided the first in a series of Hammer cameos for veteran character actor and ad-libber Miles Malleson as the chuckling mortician, J Marx, whose grim banter and jokes includes drumming his hands on a coffin lid as he absent-mindedly tries to locate Dracula's coffin. Christopher Lee remembers his co-star affectionately: "Yes, the human windmill! Miles Malleson did things in front of the camera which nobody else has ever done, without any warning. And we had to keep a straight face, which is not easy!"[26]

Geoffrey Bayldon played a cameo as the hotel porter who surprises Van Helsing with his prototype Dictaphone. He vividly remembers his make-up session. "At the age of 33, as I was then, I had done very few films and in my ignorance I had not thought it in any way odd that I had been cast to play an 'Old Hotel Porter'. After all, in the theatre I had made a speciality of playing old men – to the point of boredom. But when I entered the make-up department to meet the brilliant Phil Leakey for the first time, I realised that perhaps I was lucky to have got the job at all. 'You're playing the old hotel porter?' Phil said incredulously. 'For God's sake get in that chair right away. There's one hell of a lot to be done!' An hour or so later I emerged, my hair crimped and whitened and my face a convincing 70.

"There had been a temporary interruption to the make-up when there was an urgent need for an elderly woman to take my place and become a most convincing corpse – and one not in the best state of preservation at that! She left the make-up chair quite contentedly and was ushered down to the studio. But a few minutes later we heard that there had been a most distressing scene when she realised with horror that all she had to do was lie still – in a coffin! Someone had forgotten to tell her that little detail." Terence Fisher remembered saving the day: "She suggested that she remove her false teeth to draw in her face. The only thing she didn't like one little bit was getting into the coffin. She was very upset about that, so I gave her a kiss which reassured her it was all in fun; a sweet lady." [15]

Despite the fact that the film was shot in colour, the rushes were viewed in black and white. Editor Bill Lenny explains, "In the early days of colour, we never saw anything in colour till the first print. It was always processed in black and white with what they call two colour frames of each shot. Two frames before the clap and two frames at the tag end of the shot were printed in colour, so you had these strips and you could see what the colour looked like. The cameraman had to say to himself, 'OK, that's fair enough.'" Fisher explained: "I love black and white. In a way it is more obviously 'fantastic' than colour. When I made Dracula, I worked on the editing with Tony Hinds for quite a long time. As you may know, we work with a non-colour copy (a bit yellowish, in fact), and I must admit that some of the scenes were even more effective that way! But then again colour is more realistic, and that, too, can enhance a horror film, depending, of course, on how you use the colour process. Personally, I choose a precise, but not too realistic, use of colour. I use it to the maximum with the sets; laboratories, castles etc. Not dominating colours, but just the ones that manage to convey the proper atmosphere."[27]

Bill Lenny remembers an amusing tale involving Christopher Lee. "I was in the little theatre, which didn't have a door; it had a closed double curtain. I was in there looking at a reel one day with Dracula doing his business. All of a sudden this voice, almost over my shoulder, said, 'I like that.' I looked around and it was Chris in his gory make-up with fang teeth, looking through the curtains. It really shook the hell out of me. I said, 'Chris, for God's sake come in.' He said, 'Do you mind, dear boy?' I said, 'No, I don't mind at all. You frightened the life out of me.' He said, 'Oh, I'm terribly sorry. I didn't realise.' So he sat down and then up comes another scene, where he'd bit this girl and I'd cut away to a shot of an owl with a terribly loud screech, and that's what made him jump. I got my own back then."

Principal photography with the actors ended on Christmas Eve. Meanwhile, Hammer were working on new projects. American novelist Richard Matheson, author of The Incredible Shrinking Man, had arrived in London on Wednesday 18 September for two months to start work on a screenplay based on his successful novel, I Am Legend. He penned a script called Night Creatures, a disturbing story about one man left alive following a mass plague epidemic, trapped in his house by vampire-like creatures. The Cinema on Thursday 12 December 1957 reported that Val Guest would direct it the following summer. However, the BBFC was horrified and threatened to ban it outright if it was made. Hammer had no choice but to back down – an alienated censor could mean ruin for the company, particularly with the risqué type of film they were producing – and they sold the property to Lippert Films in America. There Matheson wrote another screenplay, but the director Sidney Salkow brought in William P Leicester to revise it. Mortified, Matheson insisted that only his pen name, Logan Swanson, be used in the screenplay credits. The film went out in 1964 as The Last Man on Earth, with Vincent Price as the beleaguered hero, and was remade in 1971 as The Omega Man, starring Charlton Heston.

As Hammer's association with Columbia flourished, plans were hatched for a proposed television series called Tales of Frankenstein, a co-production between Hammer and Screen Gems, Columbia's television subsidiary. If the pilot was successful it was to spawn a series of 26 half-hour shows, 13 episodes to be shot in Hollywood and the other 13 at Bray. Tony Hinds went out to Screen Gems in Hollywood but returned frustrated when it became clear that they had no understanding of Hammer's approach to horror. Michael Carreras took up the negotiations and on Tuesday 12 November flew out to Hollywood in his turn. German actor Anton Diffring was chosen to front the show as Baron Frankenstein, but clues to the disaster that was brewing can be seen in a letter from Tony Hinds to Diffring dated 31 December:

Dear Mr Diffring,
Many thanks indeed for your Christmas card. May I take this opportunity of wishing you a very happy and successful New Year? I am leaving for Hollywood in a few days' time. At the moment, I am rather in the dark as to how the Frankenstein pilot is being set up, but by the time you arrive in Hollywood, I hope to be 'in the picture'. In the meantime, if you have any questions, my partner, Michael Carreras, has just returned from there and will be pleased to answer them for you. I look forward to seeing you in Hollywood.

Hammer was becoming big business, even if their break into US television was proving problematic. And the year ahead would be even bigger.

SIX

The Hound from Hell

(1 9 5 8)

January 1958 was a busy time for Hammer as *Dracula* went into post-production and the long awaited sequel to *The Curse of Frankenstein* took to the floor at Bray.

As previously noted, principal photography had ended on *Dracula* on Christmas Eve. "The artists left the film and then we carried on with inserts and pick-ups after Christmas," remembers Harry Oakes. Then Syd Pearson completed the special effects for the climax, assisted by make-up artist Phil Leakey. Pearson described the process of disintegration: "When we were given the script of *Dracula*, I can assure you that the disintegration interested me immensely. At that time, I really had

no idea how to tackle the problem, but I think I must have
a macabre sense of humour, because it seemed to evolve
itself extremely quickly, and on discussions with Terry
Fisher, the director, we decided we would attempt the
sequence in a series of cuts – we would cut back to
reaction shots of Peter Cushing as Van Helsing, then Chris
Lee in his dying throes, once the shaft of light had hit him."[1]

Stills were taken of Lee's exact position as he had collapsed
on the floor, slumped across the painted Zodiac, so that
Pearson could faithfully reproduce his position afterwards. To
film the disintegration of the leg, a dummy leg was used consisting basically of a skeleton, around which was impacted
Fuller's Earth and dust. The final movements of the leg as it
disintegrated was then achieved by Pearson himself lying flat
on the floor with his hand inside the trouser leg.

As the scene continues, Dracula's hand disintegrates also.
Pearson used his own hand in the initial scenes: "I coated my hands with a paste
which I made out of Fuller's Earth – ladies' mud pack, actually – and warm paraffin
wax. I dipped my hands into this paste and made a coating with this grey dust. As
the paste was made with acetone, it evaporated very quickly and it soon began to
drop away from the hands. Before this happened, I quickly dipped my hands into a
flesh-coloured paraffin wax, just molten – wasn't hot, didn't hurt. My hands then became, after
several dippings, coated in this paraffin wax. I had a make-up man standing by who applied artificial
fingernails to my hands, which were completely solidified in wax, with an undercoating of that grey
powder. Then, to camera requirements, I did the gesticulations that Chris was doing in the master-
shot, with his hands in front of his face in sheer horror and terror, as his body started to disintegrate,
and you saw my hands and my fingers moving and as they moved the flesh cracked, dropped away and
dust fell to the ground. Once again we cut away and we came back – this time my hands were removed
and I had an articulated pair of skeleton hands, again made up with the powder. And I moved those by
a series of levers, remote-controlled, and the fingers were then showing through as bones."[1]

The last stages of Pearson's disintegration sequence involved the final dissolution of Dracula's
face. A skull was made up with latex rubber solution complete with articulated jaw. To achieve the
last glimmer of life fading from Dracula's face, small medical endoscopic lamps were put within
the eye sockets which shone faintly and were then faded out. "Then we cut away from the skull
and you saw the chest collapse," Pearson continues. "Well, again this was done by one of my
colleagues, lying full-length on the floor just out of camera range and, with the aid of balloons and
his own hands, he was able to collapse the chest. Then we cut back again to Peter and then back
again to the remains. Eventually we end up with just the clothes lying there, a pile of dust, the ring
that Dracula wore and a tuft of hair, because hair is one thing that doesn't disintegrate – through
the centuries it always remains – and then I merely turned on the wind machine, which was again
just off screen and just out of camera range. We had a large night wind blowing through the set,
blowing across this powder and this ring and we faded out on that. We never used any stop-motion
cameras, we did it entirely with a series of dissolves and cuts."[1]

Fisher had already shot the necessary covering angles for this sequence, including the close-ups
of Lee in agony, in varying states of decomposition thanks to Phil Leakey's superb make-up. For this
movie, Leakey was joined by Roy Ashton, an Australian-born make-up man who would soon take
over the make-up department from him. Ashton recollected his involvement in the disintegration
sequence: "I can remember going down onto the floor there. It was Phil's film with his ideas. I did
actually help in putting the stuff on Dracula's face in the disintegration sequences, the various
pieces of treated paper and one thing and another. The further stages of the disintegration were
principally the special effects boys' job."[2]

Then there was the legendary Japanese scene where Lee tore at his face. Lee remembers, "There
were extra make-ups I had, which did not appear in the story. If they appeared in the Japanese

Hammer Productions
——— 1958 ———

+ THE REVENGE OF
  FRANKENSTEIN
+ TEN SECONDS TO HELL
+ FURTHER UP THE CREEK
+ I ONLY ARSKED
+ THE HOUND OF THE
  BASKERVILLES
+ THE MAN WHO COULD
  CHEAT DEATH

OPPOSITE: Sir Hugo
Baskerville (David Oxley) slays
the servant girl (Judi Moyens) in
The Hound of the
Baskervilles (1958).

Jonathan Harker (John Van Eyssen) declares his intentions as he writes in his diary in Dracula (1957).

version or not, I'm afraid I don't know. Progressive deterioration of my face is all I can tell you. That was all there was. There was some left out for the version in this country and maybe left in for other countries." [3] Syd Pearson concurred: "We had Chris made up with a composite latex rubber face mask over him so that we were able to pull the flesh away from his face and allow a certain amount of dusty powder – Fuller's Earth – to drop to the floor, but I know it was not in the British version, because it was considered too gruesome for the censor." [1]

An internal memo from Don Weeks to Tony Keys, James Needs, Terence Fisher and Bernard Robinson on 21 January disclosed that seven pick-up shots were still outstanding – four exteriors of the Holmwood house, a letter (Dracula's welcome note for Harker), a woodland gravestone and a close-up on Harker's diary. These shots were picked up while The Revenge of Frankenstein was on the floor. Indeed, Harry Oakes' diary on Wednesday 5 March verifies, "Worked on Dracula. Shots on the owl then to Marlow for exterior night woodland shots."

Editors Bill Lenny and James Needs now took Dracula into post-production at Hammer House in order to vacate Bray's cutting rooms for Revenge. The opening credits were put together (over exterior castle footage already filmed) on 28 January by Studio Film Labs while John Hollingsworth brought back his friend James Bernard to compose his most memorable score. Bernard's thunderous opening theme is dominated by his classic three-note motif based on the word 'Dra-cu-la' and immediately sets the mood of the movie, which is then carried on at a blistering pace by a score rich in suspense, punctuated by pounding chase themes and brought to the boil with a haunting good motif as evil is finally vanquished. Forty years later, I asked James what his lasting memories of scoring the film were. "My main memory is of the total rush and panic to get it finished on time! From the moment of receiving the first batch of timings, I probably had about four weeks to complete the job – and I always did my own orchestration, which for me is an essential part of composing. So I went into complete seclusion and worked more or less round the clock till it was finished. At the same time I was thrilled to be doing it as Dracula (which I read in a cold and gloomy vicarage in midwinter during my time in the RAF) was one of my favourite books. Little did I think the score would still be alive and kicking 40 years later!" Hammer sent a black-and-white cut of the film to John Nicholls, Secretary of the BBFC, on 5 February. His examiners were not amused by Hammer's blatant disregard of their earlier recommendations on the script. Audrey Field commented on the same day:

"This is yet another version of Dracula, but with such a strong infusion of horror comic element injected into considerable parts of it as to make them acceptable conventions within the horror film genre. The version we saw had six scenes missing and was in black and white. The final version will be in colour and its addition, in our opinion, will make certain scenes intolerable. The producers have ignored the script letter and, also, have deviated from the script. We consider that the president and other examiners should see this film."

On 6 February, John Nicholls made a note of his own:

"I have told Col Carreras and Nelson Keys that we shall have to view again. They both confirm that we are seeing the American version and that they have alternative shots for points objected to in script letter. Please arrange." He made a further note the following day: "I have advised Mr Nelson Keys to include covering shots for all sequences to which we took exception at script stage, for next viewing."

On his return from supervising the pilot episode for the Tales of Frankenstein TV series in Hollywood, Tony Hinds wrote to John Nicholls on 11 February:

"I have just returned from America and heard of the objections raised by the Board in connection with this film. I have today been through the whole picture with my cutter, Mr James Needs, and we have made the following alterations in accordance with your requirements:

REEL 2: The shot of the vampire woman sinking her teeth into Jonathan's neck has been removed entirely.

REEL 7: All shots of the stake being driven into the girl's heart have been removed entirely.

REEL 9: The disintegration of Dracula: (i) The shot of his hand tearing the flesh from his face has been removed entirely. (ii) All further shots of disintegration have been trimmed to the minimum. I trust you will find this satisfactory when you see the film tomorrow."

Hinds resubmitted the film. The examiners watched it on 12 February and John Nicholls reported back to James Carreras the following day:

"The film *Dracula*, with the amendments referred to in Mr Hinds' letter of 11th February, 1958, was seen by the Board yesterday. Further treatment is required to certain sequences to which we have already referred before we view the colour version for certification. In view of the accentuation of certain obvious features in the film by the addition of colour and full sound we are unable to promise an 'X' certificate until the completed version of the film has been viewed. The following cannot, in any case, be allowed:-

Reel 7. The whole episode of a stake being driven into Lucy, together with her screams, writhing and agonised face. The scene can retain only shots of Dr Van Helsing taking up the stake and mallet, possibly one blow on the mallet as seen from outside the coffin, followed by him and Arthur looking at Lucy's peaceful face.

Reel 8. The whole episode of Dracula and Mina together whenever either of them shows sexual pleasure. There must, for instance, be no kissing or fondling.

Reel 9. We have severe doubts about the disintegration of Dracula. In any case the shot of the disintegrating ankle between trouser and boot must go and any shots where flesh seems to disintegrate. If handled with care the middle distance shots of clothing and dust blowing away from them can be acceptable.

"We would advise the greatest caution about blood – on faces, necks and clothes and in, or immediately after, the blood transfusion scene. Caution is also required with regard to the music effects, especially 'shock' music, and sound in general. If you would like us to have another look at the reels referred to above when they have been dealt with, before the colour version is completed, I shall be very pleased to arrange a viewing."

James Carreras was not happy, and replied to Nicholls the following day, the 14th:

"Just a few general observations on 'horror pictures'.

These pictures get an 'X' certificate which immediately bars everybody under sixteen years of age from seeing them.

The 'X' certificate also means that approximately 800 cinemas who call themselves family houses will not book the pictures.

The horror audience is a very specialised one and many people who go to "X' for sex' pictures will not go to see a horror film.

Naturally those who do go to see horror films expect to see something out of the ordinary, although quite often the horror mis-fires and they laugh at it.

With the very poor state our industry is in it would be a terrible thing if the horror addicts go to see horror pictures and there is no horror in them, in other words, we will lose this audience. There has always been a horror audience since movies began and nobody has ever been the worse for it.

Dracula is acknowledged the granddaddy of them all and, as you know, has been made at least a dozen times.

The specialised audience who will go to see 'DRACULA' will expect thrills but the cuts that you are asking us to make, in our opinion, are taking every thrill out of the picture, in fact, it is not as horrific as any of the past Draculas and we cannot believe that that is your intention.

"We have once again today resubmitted the three reels that you have objected to and I am seeing you at 4.15 this afternoon to discuss the matter."

Before the meeting, the Board watched the film again on 14 February to prepare themselves and define how far they were willing to go. Examiner Newton Branch (NKB in some reports) commented:

"Reel 7. There are still shots of stake pressing into Lucy's breast and his blows are struck with accompanying screams, moans and sighs. We are prepared to see this in colour with the warning that reduction may well have to be made on final viewing in accordance with our letter of 13th February.

Reel 8. There is still a strong sex element in this scene. This is due to Mina's anticipating expression in close-up and Dracula's face (and expression) as it 'hovers' over Mina's before he applies himself to her neck. We are very doubtful whether this sex element can be removed ... cut the scene from immediately after Mina gets on the bed to shot of owl screaming.

Reel 9. The flash of disintegrating ankle is all right. Under no circumstance can the shot of his disintegrating face be seen. Very little if any of this disintegrating can be permitted."

That afternoon James Carreras and Tony Hinds met with the Board. The message was clear and Nicholls later made a file note under the above report: "Given to Col Carreras and Anthony Hinds at meeting." Reluctantly Carreras and Hinds agreed to more cuts and then to resubmit the film in colour and sound. Hinds sent it in on 3 April: "I have pleasure in re-submitting the above film in the glory of full colour. I am sure you will agree that it is far more innocuous now! I regret that neither the main titles nor the end titles are yet completed, but these are straightforward titles superimposed over a long shot of Dracula's castle. Should you wish to see these, however, I should be pleased to rush them round to you as soon as they are ready."

The Board watched it later that day and Nicholls replied to Hinds: "We have seen Dracula in colour today and are prepared to pass everything except:- Reel 8. The shot of Dracula's face approaching Mina as she lies on the bed, with her reactions, must go. There should be a cut from where he enters the room to the owl (and the sound of the scream) outside. Reel 9. The shot of the disintegrating hand, in close-up, must go. There should also be only one brief flash of the disintegrating face. Reel 8 should be resubmitted."

Hinds responded to Nicholls on 8 April with a healthy dose of emotional blackmail:

"Thank you for your letter of April 3rd. At our meeting some weeks ago, you warned me that certain shots, accepted in black and white, might have to be deleted when printed in colour. As a result of this meeting, I made certain alterations to the picture and then had it scored, dubbed, and the matrices made for the Technicolor print. I note now that the Board objects to the shot of Dracula's face approaching Mina in Reel 8, but I cannot see how his face looks more censorable in colour than it did in black and white: he is wearing no special make-up, there is no blood on his face, he is not wearing contact-lenses – in fact, the rather pink look he has makes him look, if anything, a little prettier than he did before!

"With regard to the Board's objections to Reel 9, I appreciate that the shot of the disintegrating hand looks different in colour from the way it did in black and white, but in my opinion it does not look worse but, if anything, less effective as the poor colouring exposes the trick much more than before. However, I am appealing against this cut not on the grounds of logic but on those of cost. As you know, the music has to be scored to fit exactly a sequence of this sort, and the cost of re-scoring, re-engaging an orchestra and scoring-theatre, and re-dubbing the reel, if we are forced to do this, will be fantastic. I know that you warned me that this might happen but I was so sure that you would agree with me that the shot looks far less effective in colour than it did in black and white that I took a chance. I am available to come and see you about this at any time to suit your own convenience. Hoping that you can see your way clear to modifying your decision."

Chief Examiner John Trevelyan made a note on this letter on 10 April: "Discussed with FNC/MCG/JC. All dislike this type of pressure. At the same time the general opinion is that neither of these is a 'life and death' cut. It was agreed that Mr Hinds should be seen. That pressure should be put on him at first – but that if he has a real case the objections should be dropped – with a warning that he should not do this kind of thing again."

On 14 April, Hinds was summoned before Trevelyan and Nicholls. Trevelyan made a file note: "Mr Hinds seen by JT and JN. R.8. The company was under the impression that at the interview on 14th February, they were told that this scene would be acceptable if it did not look worse in colour than in black and white. Despite our discussion on April 10th, we let him know that, although we did not like the scene, we would accept it in view of this misunderstanding. R.9. Mr. Hinds told that we would accept the disintegrating hand but not both shots of the

Syd Pearson disintegrates Christopher Lee at the climax of Dracula (1957).

disintegrating face. He agreed to cut the first shot, with the hand pulling down, which is much the worst of the two."

It would seem they had finally accepted Hinds' point of view and another compromise was struck. Nicholls put this agreement in writing the following day: "I am writing to confirm our conversation of 14th April, 1958, on the subject of the two reels of *Dracula*, resubmitted for further consideration. Reel 8. While we consider that, in the approach of Dracula to Mina the sex-element is still too prevalent, in view of the apparent misunderstanding over this and the technical difficulty of effecting further reductions, we are prepared to waive our objections to this scene. Reel 9. We are prepared to accept the disintegrating hand but not both shots of the disintegrating face. As agreed between us, the first shot of the face with the hand pulling down will therefore be cut. On receipt of your assurance that this cut has been made I shall be pleased to arrange for the issue of an 'X' certificate for this film."

Tony Hinds and James Needs made the final cuts and an 'X' was finally issued by the Board on 21 April. Hinds had dug his heels in deep for his concessions and the censor had taken note. Their worst battle was yet to come. While the finishing touches were being put to *Dracula* at Hammer House, the team at Bray were breathing life back into the Baron in *The Revenge of Frankenstein*.

While Universal's Frankenstein series had followed the continuing exploits of the monster, Hammer's series now concentrated on the doctor himself. This, of course, left Hammer temporarily embarrassed as they had already killed him off in the original. It was up to Jimmy Sangster to bring him back from the grave. *Revenge* therefore starts where *Curse* left off, but with the extra detail that Frankenstein had managed to find himself an accomplice (a crippled hunchback) within the prison, who agrees to save him from the guillotine in return for having his brain transplanted into a healthy body. The procedure goes wrong, however, and the 'new' man gradually degenerates into his former twisted self, with a taste for human flesh to boot. Sangster explains his cannibalistic angle so: "I wanted something that would really revolt me, because if it revolts me it probably revolts everybody else, so I thought of cannibalism."

Sangster was contracted to write his first draft on 24 July 1957, and his second draft on 15 October. Tony Hinds' secretary, Pamela Anderson, submitted the 'second draft screenplay' on his behalf to John Nicholls, Secretary of the BBFC, on 21 November. Reader Audrey Field sharpened her claws again when she reported on the script in an internal memo on the 25th:

"The end of this story shows that the Old Firm have their tongues even further in their cheeks than usual. The scenes between Frankenstein and the girls in the West End practice also indicate

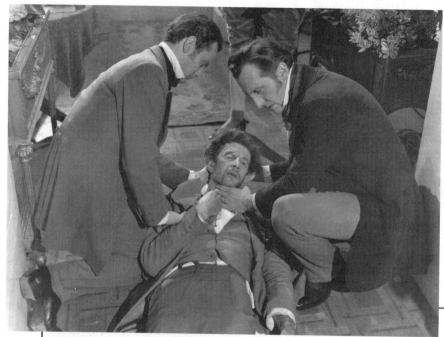

The new Karl (Michael Gwynn) collapses at the musical evening and is attended by Hans (Francis Matthews) and Frankenstein (Peter Cushing) in The Revenge of Frankenstein (1958).

THE REVENGE OF FRANKENSTEIN

PRINCIPAL PHOTOGRAPHY: 6 January to 4 March 1958
DISTRIBUTION:
  Columbia; 91 minutes; Technicolor. UK: certificate 'X'
UK RELEASE:
  PREMIÈRE: gala première on 27 August 1958, at the
  Plaza in Piccadilly Circus
  GENERAL RELEASE: 17 November 1958
US RELEASE:
  June 1958, with Curse of the Demon [ie, Night of the Demon]

DIRECTOR: Terence Fisher; PRODUCER: Anthony Hinds; ASSOCIATE PRODUCER: Anthony Nelson Keys; EXECUTIVE PRODUCER: Michael Carreras; SCREENPLAY: Jimmy Sangster with additional dialogue by H Hurford Janes; PRODUCTION DESIGNER: Bernard Robinson; DRAUGHTSMAN: Don Mingaye; DIRECTOR OF PHOTOGRAPHY: Jack Asher; CAMERA OPERATOR: Len Harris; FOCUS PULLER: Harry Oakes; ASSISTANT DIRECTOR: Robert Lynn; 2ND ASSISTANT DIRECTOR: Tom Walls; 3RD ASSISTANT DIRECTOR: Hugh Harlow; SUPERVISING EDITOR: James Needs; EDITOR/SOUND EDITOR: Alfred Cox; MUSIC: Leonard Salzedo; CONDUCTOR: Muir Mathieson; SOUND RECORDIST: Jock May; MAKE-UP: Phil Leakey;

HAIRSTYLIST: Henry Montsash; PRODUCTION MANAGER: Don Weeks; CONTINUITY: Doreen Dearnaley; WARDROBE: Rosemary Burrows; PROPERTY MASTER: Tommy Money; PROPERTY BUYER: Eric Hillier; CASHIER: Ken Gordon; STUDIO MANAGER: Arthur Kelly; CONSTRUCTION MANAGER: Mick Lyons; CHIEF ELECTRICIAN: Jack Curtis; MASTER PAINTER: Lawrence Wren; MASTER PLASTERER: Arthur Banks; MASTER CARPENTER: Charles Davis; CHIMP TRAINER: Molly Badham

Peter Cushing (Doctor Victor Stein); Francis Matthews (Doctor Hans Kleve); Eunice Gayson (Margaret); Michael Gwynn (Karl); John Welsh (Bergman); Lionel Jeffries (Fritz); Oscar Quitak (Dwarf); Richard Wordsworth (Up Patient); Charles Lloyd Pack (President); John Stuart (Inspector); Arnold Diamond (Molke); Margery Gresley (Countess Barscynska); Anna Walmsley (Vera Barscynska); George Woodbridge (Janitor); Michael Ripper (Kurt); Ian Whittaker (Boy); Avril Leslie (Girl) and Robert Brooks Turner (Groom); John Gayford (Footman); George Hirste (Dirty Old Patient); Raymond Hodge (Official); Eugene Leahy (Klein); Michael Mulcaster (Tattooed Man); Gordon Needham (Male Nurse); Julia Nelson (Inga); Gerald Lawson, Freddy Watts, Middleton Woods (Patients)

that part of the film is intended to be a howling jest. Nevertheless, a great deal of the script is much too gruesome and repulsive. Much as we should like to, I do not think we can very well refuse to allow any sequel to Frankenstein, but the makers will have to walk warily, in view of the reaction of many people to their first instalment. (Mary Shelley would turn in her grave if she could see her name on the title-page).

"There should be a very strong warning on treatment and on the avoidance of gruesome and repulsive details: and there is one thing, basic to the present story, which I do not think we can have – the cannibalism of the Monster. If it is asked why we should allow vampires (in moderation) in horror films, and not allow this, I have no logical answer, but I feel it to be too much, especially in this setting. I think they should make do with the usual tendency to turn dangerous and nasty-tempered. I have also a great number of comments on other details, amounting in sum to a considerable revision of the script."

She goes on to list her objections and concludes: "In conclusion, the more I look at this the less I like it. The policy to be adopted in regard to it is important at a time when sections of the trade are anxious about 'horror' films. I think the President should see the script notes, at any rate, after not less than two other readers have read the script."

The script was passed around as suggested. Frank Crofts remarked on 26 November, "It was inevitable that there should be a return of Frankenstein, but this goes too far ... I don't think we can refuse a second dosing, but there must be far less blood, no cannibalism and no mange." [Unlike the finished film, the draft script had the poor creature deteriorate as if with 'mange'.]

Newton Branch then commented on 29 November: "Before making his last film in England *The Judas Hole* [released as *Grip of the Strangler*], Boris Karloff made a broadcast over the BBC and, with great emphasis, made the point that 'horror' should never be disgusting. The true elements of the real horror film are terror, suspense, action, the unknown, the macabre. The very introduction of the 'mange business' in this script introduces a strong and quite unnecessary element of disgust: and puts one out of sympathy with the project. P.73 is one of the most disgusting I have read for a long while, and the writer should be ashamed of himself.

"His main problem here is the cannibalism. Again, I have a feeling of revulsion and disgust, since aversion to cannibalism is one of the strongest inhibitions of 'civilised' man. Yet, with discretion, cannibalism is fair enough in a 'horror' film provided the emphasis is on terror. In this script, the treatment of cannibalism is disgusting, especially since it's 'artificial' cannibalism and most particularly since it is associated with sex, eg, a) all the victims are women, b) Karl, after watching Margaret in some undress, lopes off to attack and devour a girl, Inga (P.65-66) who is obviously disappointed and piqued that her young man did not make love to her in some park.

"I agree in general with AOF's remarks. The rest of the details and the treatment largely depend on whether we allow the business of cannibalism or not. I would not mind the monster here attacking women only, if one felt that there was no sexual implication. And in defence of horror films proper, it might be pointed out that the most impressive and spine-chilling qualities of the original Frankenstein monster was its utter lack of 'human' feeling and discrimination in its attack on the human species." It's unclear here whether Branch is referring to the original Hammer monster or the Universal original from 1931; most likely the former.

A fourth reader on 5 October concurred: "I agree. We must draw the line at cannibalism." John Nicholls then replied to Tony Hinds on 6 December, incorporating his readers' comments:

"We have read the script entitled *The Revenge of Frankenstein*, which you sent us with your letter of 21st November, 1957. This script gives us considerable anxiety. It contains a good deal more in the way of nauseating and repulsive details than did your previous Frankenstein film, which itself went to the very limit of what we can allow in that respect. In particular, the cannibalism and the slow disintegration of the monster when he is attacked by a disease like mange are a good deal too repulsive, even for a 'horror' film, and I can hold out no hope that we should be able to pass these particular ingredients in your story. I would also draw your attention to the importance of discretion and restraint in the treatment throughout – in particular the avoidance of too many shots of blood.

Other details:
P.2. The sadistic delight shown at the execution has an unpleasant flavour and may well give trouble in the film. The shot of the blood seeping through the guillotine blade should be omitted.
P.6. The line "Fresh as a daisy – nice and fresh. They don't like offending the young ladies' noses" should be omitted.
P.7. The choice of the priest as the victim will give offence to many: someone else – perhaps the executioner? – should be substituted for Frankenstein at the execution. The shot of the headless body and of the head wrapped in a bloody sack may well prove too gruesome, and it would be wiser to establish the identity of the dead man by dialogue alone.
P.8. Fritz should not be buried alive. The shot of the cross on the grave should be left out.

P's. 15-18 & 39. Vera's provocativeness should not be overdone, and her repeated offers to undress, and shots of her in her underclothes should be omitted.

P.19. The shot of the woman in the workhouse being given pills, and the preceding dialogue "I tried to do what you told me, but the gentlemen get so impatient – you know how it is?" should be omitted.

P.20. The scenes in the hospital ward should be reasonably restrained and men and women should not be shown to be sharing the same ward.

P's 30-34 and elsewhere. The very greatest discretion will be needed, here and elsewhere, in all shots of parts of the human body being used for experiment or seen in the tank and in all shots of bodies which have been made up of pieces of different corpses. Details and close shots should be avoided. The experiment with the fire, the eyeballs and the hand, will need particular care if it is to be acceptable.

P.44. The shot of the dwarf's brain being dropped into the tank may pass if it is not a close shot, but discretion is called for. The shot of the dwarf's body being thrown into the furnace should be brief, and there should be no close or detailed shot.

P.44a. The 'new man' should not appear to be in agony as he comes to life.

P.44c. I would refer you to my remarks about cannibalism. There should be no suggestion that the chimp and the monster are subject to anything more sinister than fits of ungovernable rage.

P.57. A caution is needed on any shots of Karl's wounded head: there should not be too much blood.

P.59. The shot of the chimp rending meat, and Karl becoming bestial as he watches, should be omitted.

P.60. The killing of a victim out of frame is all right, provided that there is no suggestion, now or later, that the victim has been eaten. But there is an unpleasant flavour of sex sadism in the fact that all Karl's victims are women. Could you not substitute a male janitor here?

P.61. Great discretion should be used in shots of Karl after the murder: there should be few blood stains, and none on the mouth or face.

P's.63, 64. Margaret should be fully dressed, not in her underclothes, when Karl watches her, and his expression should not be lustful.

P.66. The scream when Inga is murdered out of frame should not be overdone.

P.67. Dialogue indicating that the girl was unrecognisable or mangled to pieces should be omitted (cf. "What a mess" and "As far as we can make out it was a human being.")

P.68. Karl's face and hands should not be bloodstained, and there should be little blood elsewhere on his body.

P.73. The 'terrible cry' from Karl outside the ballroom should not be too loud or horrible, and his appearance when he enters the ballroom "great patches of his face missing", and the rest "swollen" and "half blind", and shots of him moaning and crawling about are prohibitive.

P.76. The shots of the two bodies in the grave (one of them headless) may well be too repulsive.

P.81. The attempted lynching of 'Stein' in the hospital ward, the terrible noise, and the shot of him mauled nearly to death will all need considerable modification if they are to pass.

P's.82, 83. Equal discretion should be used in all later shots of Frankenstein, including the shot where he coughs blood, and the shot of him lying crumpled by the furnace door.

P.84. Discretion should be used in all shots of the composite body and face of the new man in the tank.

"I hope that the most careful attention will be paid to the points I have made in this letter; otherwise the cumulative effect of disgusting and nauseating details will make serious trouble inevitable when the film is submitted for censorship. I return the present script herewith, but we should like to see the revised script in due course."

This was probably the strongest condemnation by the censor yet on a Hammer film. Tony Hinds took the recommendations on board and replied to Nicholls on December, 9th:

"Thank you very much for your letter of December 6th. I quite agree that the script, as written, is too nauseating, and some of the details too repulsive. I have, therefore, instructed the writer to make the following alterations:

Frankenstein's office at the poor hospital and the graveyard at the beginning of The Revenge of Frankenstein (1958) were both revamps of the mausoleum in Dracula (1957)

P.2. Delete the shot of the blood seeping through the guillotine blade.

P.6. Delete and substitute 'Fresh as a daisy .....'

P.8. (a) Can Fritz actually die of fright, so that he is not buried alive? (b) Substitute a headstone for the cross.

P.19. Delete and substitute short scene between Stein and woman patient.

P.60. Substitute Male Janitor for Woman Concierge.

P.67. Amend dialogue, as instructed.

P.68. No blood on Karl's mouth or hands.

I have also instructed the director to watch the following points:

P.7. Watch that the headless body is not gruesome.

P.20. Watch that the workhouse ward scenes are reasonably restrained.

P.44. Watch that the shot of the dwarf's brain is not over-emphasised, also that the shot of the body's being thrown into the furnace is kept brief.

P.44a. The 'new man' should be in pain but not in agony when he is brought to life.

P.57. Not too much blood.

P.61. No blood stains on hands or mouth.

Pp.63/64. Karl must not look lustfully at Margaret

P.66. Inga's scream should not be overdone.

P.68. No blood on Karl's face and hands.

P.73. The 'terrible cry' from Karl should not be too loud or horrible.

P.81. Watch that the attempted lynching of Stein is not too brutal or gruesome.

Pp.82/83. Watch that the shots of Frankenstein after having been attacked are not too gruesome.

P.84. Use discretion with shots of the composite body and face of the 'new man' in the tank.

However I am appealing for a modification of your ruling regarding the disintegration of Karl and the cannibalism, because if I delete both these, I shall have no real picture at all.

May I make the following suggestions for a drastic modification?

1. The chimpanzee has turned cannibal (we never see this, it is only indicated in dialogue –

Karl (Michael Gwynn) attempts to burn his old body (Oscar Quitak) in The Revenge of Frankenstein (1958).

and we shall make sure that the meat he is given to eat could not possibly be mistaken for human or monkey flesh). Karl finds that he is going the same way, that he has a craving for human flesh. He is horrified by this (we establish earlier that he is basically a very normal, decent person), and we see him struggling with this strange, new emotion - and overcoming it (triumph of good over evil).

2. Instead of Karl's flesh peeling, etc., we see that his body begins to try to take on the original shape of the dwarf.

I, personally, much prefer this, as I think it is more dramatic: the picture becomes a tragedy instead of just a horror story. The scene of the dwarf struggling to overcome his terrible craving, and finally defeating it, can be very dramatic without being over-gruesome, and the idea that his new body begins to become like his old one is both ironic and, I feel, very moving.

There are a few other objections of yours which I should be very glad if you would reconsider:

P.7. The idea of using a priest was not, in any way, intended to be anti-religious, but was so that the body in the coffin could be immediately recognised without having to show its severed head (the priest's distinctive hat lying on top of the body would be enough).

Pp.15-18, 39. Vera will never be seen in her underclothes. She undresses behind a screen and comes virtually fully-clothed.

P.20. That men and women shared hospital wards is, I am assured, a historical fact for the period. However, if you feel strongly about this, I will make it a male ward only. Or perhaps have a curtain-partition.

Pp.63/64. The women's underclothing of the period (petticoat, corsets, crinoline, etc.)
revealed less than normal everyday wear today. It is dramatically better that Margaret should
have removed at least her top dress, so that she appears to be more defenceless.
I am sending this letter by hand and should be very pleased if you would treat the matter as urgent
because the picture is scheduled to start in eleven working days from now."

John Nicholls was quick to reply the following day:

"Thank you for your letter of 9th December, upon which we have the following observations:
P.6. We accept 'Fresh as a daisy', provided that the rest of the speech is omitted.
P.8. As long as it is established that Fritz is dead, we do not of course mind this incident.
P.19. We note that you will include a new scene (not yet scripted) between Stein and the
woman patient.
P.44a. We note that the 'new man' will be 'in pain but not in agony'. We hope that any such
shot will be brief and the indications of suffering very slight.
In regard to the suggestion that Karl should have cannibalistic leanings which he overcomes, we
do not quite see how you will establish this without his being supposed to have devoured part of
his victim's bodies, and without prohibitively ugly indications of greed for human flesh. But we
will of course look with an open mind at any sequences which you wish to send us.

We think that the proposal that Karl should begin to revert to his former appearance is a very good
one and, provided that the shots of the process are not in themselves too horrible, it should pass.

In regard to the other points you raise:
P.7. We wish you could think of some way round this difficulty. It does still strike us as a potential
source of trouble that a priest should be chosen, particularly after all the jubilation at the execution; and we should have thought that many audiences in the United States would like it even less.
Pp.15-18, 39. We think that shots of Vera in her Victorian underclothes may well be all right.
All we are concerned about is any danger of a horror film being too 'sexy': we often find that
the juxtaposition of sex and horror gives rise to unfavourable criticism.
P.20. Similarly, the nursing of male and female patients in the same ward has obvious sex
implications, and we should prefer the ward to be a male ward only.
Pp.63-64. Again, we do not mind Margaret appearing 'defenceless' and we are sure that the
shots of her would not be indecent: all we want is that a monster should not appear to be
lusting after her.
If there are any sequences about which you have doubts from the censorship point of view, we shall
be glad to help you by looking at 'rushes' in advance of the submission of the completed film for
censorship.

Thank you for your co-operation."

Tony Hinds replied to Nicholls on December 13th:

"Thank you for your letter of the 10th December and the promptness of your reply.

I note all your points and agree them.

1. Apparently this will not cause offence in the USA (copy of letter from Breen Office enclosed)

2. I note that you are not happy about the jubilation after the execution. Actually, I had already
intended to delete this.

Thank you for your co-operation."

Their differences settled, Hammer could continue. It is interesting, however, to compare the
BBFC's list of objections to those of the American censor board, the Motion Picture Association of
America (MPAA). Tony Hinds received a letter from Geoffrey M Shurlock of the MPAA on 4
December, after they had read the draft script:

"We have read the script for your proposed production, *The Revenge of Frankenstein*, and wish to
report that this property contains certain material which should be corrected before a finished
picture could be approved by this office.

Page 1. It will be necessary for you to obtain adequate technical advice regarding the portrayal
of the Priest.

Page 18. It will be unacceptable for the doctor to apply his ear to Vera's breast. The dissolve
should take place at the conclusion of Victor's line "If you'd rather my dear ... of course."

<u>Page 19</u>. The sequence between Victor and the Woman will be unacceptable if the impression is created that the pills that Victor gives her are for the purpose of curing a venereal disease or for the purpose of causing an abortion.

<u>Page 30</u>. There are several sequences in this story which could be nauseously gruesome in the finished picture. We urge that you exercise great restraint in filming these sequences. On this page, the business of the dwarf unwrapping the lower half of an arm should be established by flash footage.

<u>Page 32</u>. The description of the tank in which floats a pair of matching eyeballs seems excessively gruesome as written.

<u>Page 39</u>. We ask that you omit Vera's obvious frustration and the act of the doctor putting down the stethoscope in the dissolve on this page.

<u>Page 44</u>. The business of dropping the brain of the dwarf into the fluid seems excessively gruesome. The business of heaving the body into the furnace should be indicated out of frame.

<u>Page 60</u>. The concierge's expression "My gawd" is irreverent.

<u>Page 62</u>. Hans' expression "God" is unacceptable.

<u>Page 64</u>. Margaret should be attired in the equivalent of a full slip in the bedroom scene.

<u>Page 65</u>. The girl's line "They got on with it" and the boy's reply "On with what?" is offensively pointed and we ask that it be changed or eliminated.

<u>Page 83</u>. We ask that the camera not hold on the remains of Stein's body.

"We shall be happy to read any revisions you wish to submit correcting the above Code difficulties."

You could be forgiven for believing that the American censor board were reviewing an entirely different script. They seem more wrapped up with the anatomical details and any religious slurs in the dialogue; nowhere is there the moral objection to cannibalism which had dominated the British censor reports.

Shooting began at Bray on Monday 6 January 1958 using the same crew from *Dracula*, apart from a different editor (Alfred Cox) and Molly Arbuthnot taking a break from wardrobe supervisor to let her assistant, Rosemary Burrows, take over. Harry Oakes' diary notes several peculiarities during the shooting of the film: work on the trailer began on the same day the film itself began shooting; the next day (Tuesday 7 January), filming on the medical centre set was halted by an impromptu script conference; by the beginning of Week Five: "I've been off work for three days. Len has the bug. Gerald Moss operating"; on Thursday 6 February: "Eunice Gayson has a damaged nose"; and on Valentine's Day, "The glass water tank collapsed on Stage 1." Filming concluded on Tuesday 4 March with "Shots of the monkey, 'Harley St' and *Dracula* inserts," the artists having departed the day before. Oakes' diary on 4 March also adds, 'Bade farewell to Phil Leakey.' Unimpressed by their new venture into horror, Hammer's make-up artist was leaving the company.

Bernard Robinson's magnificent sets were largely recycled from *Dracula*. The existing library set on Stage 1 was reused with only minor changes for the interior of the Carlsbruck Medical Centre and was later modified to the ward at the poor hospital and finally to the interior of Frankenstein's laboratory; the hidden stairs were again revealed to become the entrance to the lab. Meanwhile, Dracula's crypt on Stage 1 (behind the library set) was now modified further into the graveyard where Frankenstein confronts the grave robbers, then to Frankenstein's office at the poor hospital and finally to the park. Van Helsing's hotel room on Stage 2 was converted to the waiting room of Dr Stein's surgery, while the remains of the morgue/Holmwood cellar set from *Dracula*, also on Stage 2, became the stables. Such modifications were necessary given that the film was being made back-to-back with *Dracula*. Meanwhile, the external castle set from *Dracula* on the back lot was reused as the exterior of Frankenstein's laboratory.

Fisher's direction concentrates on the tragedy of the story and brings out the pathos of Michael Gwynn's monster. Once more Fisher used the atmosphere on set to develop ideas, as he explained. "In *The Revenge of Frankenstein* there's a man in a hospital bed with no legs, because the Baron has cut them off to put them on his creature. So the man sits with his arm coiled round just where his legs were, as if he would have liked to rest his elbow on his knee but couldn't anymore. We only saw this on the floor. And did you notice the scene where Frankenstein lights the bunsen burner in front of the eyeballs in the tank? He wants to demonstrate the movement of the dismembered arm in the adjoining tank. The reflection of the flame in the glass seems to be touching the hand. And you feel the help-less fear of these dismembered parts. This sort of thing can hardly be visualised at the script stage." [4]

Peter Cushing was now able to develop his character much more and his performance is a joy to watch. So in demand was Cushing with the BBC that during shooting he had to find time to appear on their successful quiz show, *What's My Line?*, on 9 February and start rehearsals for another Rudolph Cartier teleplay, *The Winslow Boy*, on the 20th. [5] The 29-year-old Francis Matthews plays off Cushing well and would return to Hammer for *Dracula Prince of Darkness* and *Rasputin the Mad Monk* in 1965. Cushing and Matthews developed a lasting friendship on the film. During the long breaks while Jack Asher lit the sets, they amused themselves playing battleships and racing each other on the *Times* crossword. Matthews was always amazed at how quickly Cushing could resume his role after these diversions. "He was like a father to me – dear Peter Cushing. We had a great time," remembers Matthews. "We giggled and laughed and fell about all the time! I was always driving him home from the studio, because he didn't have a car. He didn't drive himself at all. He had the studio car, but some-times he'd say, 'Take me home with you, Francis, we'll go home together,' because I passed his place in Notting Hill on my way to Hampstead, where I lived at the time as a bachelor." [6] He also remembers being invited in to peruse Cushing's incredible collection of toy soldiers and to meet his wife Helen.

"We take a brain out of poor old Oscar Quitak's head and put it into the head of Michael Gwynn," Matthews continues. "We had a sheep's brain, which I gather is more or less the same size as a human brain. We had this sort of jelly stuff that they kept it in, to look as if it was formaldehyde or something, and it was going to stay alive in this stuff, but we didn't finish shooting the scene on the day we were using the brain and we had to pick it up the next morning. The technicians forgot to put the brain in the fridge and left it on the set. Well, sets get very warm during a day's shooting and they also get very warm when they are setting up the lights the next morning. There is a scene towards the end of the film in which I have to pour Peter Cushing's brain into the dish from this container and, when I opened it, it was actually alive and the smell was appalling. All the technicians were fainting! I said, 'I can't work with this. It's going to upstage me!' So we had to shoot on something else while they went to get another sheep's brain, but it's not that easy to get a sheep's brain. They ordered the one we had in advance, so they had to scour the countryside for a butchers that happened to have a sheep's brain in stock!" [6]

Oscar Quitak has vivid memories of playing Frankenstein's tragic assistant. "The deformed Karl was really agony, actually, because I had to have this one eye which they took about three hours to do in the make-up room. They covered one eye up with a sort of tissue and I found that the eye which I was using, which was not covered up, was actually agony after the day's shooting – it gave me terrible headaches. So that was more agonising than the actual deformity of the hump, which was actually just a thing stuck inside my coat, you know, nothing really complicated. But the eye was very painful. The role wasn't really a very great challenge except that I invented a walk for it, which I've managed to use quite a bit since – Feste in *Twelfth Night* and various other parts. I bring out this walk that I invent-ed for Frankenstein quite often. People seem to think it's quite good, so it's been quite useful." [7]

Cushing became very attached to his co-star, Lucy the chimpanzee. She was supplied courtesy of her trainer Molly Badham, who at the time ran the modest Hints Zoological Gardens before moving her operation to Twycross Zoo in 1963. Her zoo is famed for its primate-breeding programme and Molly supplied the chimps for a number of other movies, not to mention the popular series of PG Tips com-mercials on British television. Molly Badham explained, "She [Lucy] played an ape who turned savage. It was hilarious, because there was supposed to be a close-up of this monster ape eating raw meat with the blood running down her face and there was no way that any chimp would be persuaded to eat raw meat. In the end we had to fake it by dying a large pineapple blood red to get the right effect." [8]

Shooting ended on Tuesday 4 March (over schedule), having taken just over eight weeks.

Meanwhile, as the cameras rolled on the latest Frankenstein adventure, Michael Carreras was hard at work preparing Hammer's next production, *The Phoenix* (later retitled *Ten Seconds to Hell*), a prestige picture directed by Robert Aldrich, starring Jack Palance and Jeff Chandler, designed by Ken Adam (who would later create those incredible Bond sets) and to be filmed at Berlin's famed Ufa studios. The film was a tense thriller about six German POWs who return home to Berlin to defuse unexploded bombs. The plot comes to the boil when they decide to pool their pay and share

TEN SECONDS TO HELL

A Hammer-7 Arts production
PRINCIPAL PHOTOGRAPHY: 24 February 1958
DISTRIBUTION:
  United Artists; 93 minutes; b/w;
  UK: certificate 'A'
UK RELEASE:
  GENERAL RELEASE: 15 June 1959
US RELEASE: July 1959

OPERATOR: *Len Harris and Herbert Geier*; FOCUS PULLER: *Harry Oakes*; ASSISTANT DIRECTOR: *Rene Dupont and Frank Winterstein*; SUPERVISING EDITOR: *James Needs*; EDITOR: *Henry Richardson*; ASSISTANT EDITOR: *Chris Barnes*; MUSIC COMPOSER: *Kenneth V Jones*; MUSIC SUPERVISOR: *John Hollingsworth*; SOUND RECORDIST: *Heinz Garbowski*; SOUND EDITOR: *Roy Hyde*; PRODUCTION MANAGER: *Basil Keys and George Mohr*; CONTINUITY: *Phyllis Crocker*; WARDROBE: *Molly Arbuthnot*

DIRECTOR: *Robert Aldrich*; PRODUCER: *Michael Carreras*;
SCREENPLAY: *Robert Aldrich and Teddi Sherman based on the novel by Lawrence P Bachmann*; PRODUCTION DESIGNER: *Ken Adam*;
DIRECTOR OF PHOTOGRAPHY: *Ernest Lazlo*; CAMERA

Jack Palance (Eric Koertner); Jeff Chandler (Karl Wirtz), Martine Carol (Margot Hofer); Robert Cornthwaite (Loeffler); David Willock (Tillig); Wes Addy (Sulke); Virginia Baker (Frau Bauer); Jimmy Goodwin (Globke); Richard Wattis (Major Haven); Nancy Lee (Ruth Sulke)

Ten Seconds to Hell (1958) was Hammer's first credited collaboration with Seven Arts, although their association with the company dated back to The Curse of Frankenstein in 1956.

it out amongst whoever is still alive three months later. Unfortunately, the tension amongst the filmmakers would far outstrip the hoped-for tension in the story.

On Tuesday 7 January, Michael Carreras and Robert Aldrich flew to Berlin for pre-production purposes, and shooting began on Monday 24 February. Basil Keys joined the team as production manager. He explains: "My brother, who was Anthony Nelson Keys, called me up one day and said, 'There's a picture going. Do you want to do it?' The next day I caught the plane to Berlin. I can't remember if I'd met Michael Carreras before that. Robert Aldrich was the director. He was a very tough individual, but I got along splendidly with him. Jeff Chandler was starring in the film. I went up to say something to him one day and he was sewing a button on. I told him, 'You don't need to do that, the wardrobe will do it.' He said, 'You're not in the American Marines for nothing, you know!' Jack Palance is now a rather cosy figure when you see him on television but he was not cosy in those days. Then there was Martine Carol. She had rather large boobs and Michael and I had to go and see her one day because she was in bed with bronchitis. She noticed that our eyes were popping out of our heads, looking at her boobs under the covers, so she said, 'Ah!' – in French – and to our amazement brought out two hot water bottles which were lying on top of them!"

The film ran seriously over budget and over schedule as Aldrich wrested all control of the picture from Carreras, rewriting (with Teddi Sherman) Lawrence Bachmann's original screenplay and bringing in his own production manager (George Mohr), assistant director (Frank Winterstein) and camera operator (Herbert Geier), to the dismay of Hammer's own crew (Basil Keys, René Dupont and Len Harris respectively). The German technicians threw up their hands in horror at Aldrich's directing techniques. Carreras turned to Ray Stark for support, but Aldrich had Carreras removed from the production.

The horror continued into post-production. It was already a busy time for Hammer's editors. In January Bill Lenny was in the cutting rooms at Hammer House putting *Dracula* together. Meanwhile, Alfred Cox was at Bray piecing together *The Revenge of Frankenstein*. Supervising editor James Needs was overseeing both. It therefore fell upon Henry Richardson and his assistant Chris Barnes to take on the Aldrich project. The fun was just beginning, as Chris Barnes explains. "We edited it entirely at the Ufa studios in Berlin. Our cutting room had a 4/plate Steenbeck for editing and a flat-bed synching and rewind table, plus the usual bins and racks. Henry Richardson had asked for a moviola before leaving England, but Jim Needs said, 'Well, when in Rome, we should do as the Romans do', which was fair enough initially and we gave it a go.

"The Germans would expect 800 feet of action and sound a day – our first day's rushes were just under 5000 feet of action and sound. By the end of week one, we had about 20,000 feet of action and sound unnumbered, a frantic assistant not knowing what had hit her and me in the middle of it all, trying to sort it out. So I sent for help.

"Chris Greenham came out after a few weeks' shooting to prepare and shoot post-synch and Rusty Coppleman came out to assist him. Poor Rusty, on top of assisting Chris Greenham, finished up spending hours and hours numbering rushes for me on a very temperamental numbering machine. Jim Needs also came out after the first few weeks' shooting and he went into another room and cut a lot of sequences to help us catch up after so many delays at the start. The first cut was just over three hours. Jim Needs took it to America for screenings, returned to Berlin, and he and Henry did a lot of recutting. We were down to about two and a half hours I think by July time. We were told to send the cutting copy back to America and we packed the rest of the film trims and equipment, and sent it to England.

"Jim Needs asked me if I would like to assist Alfie Cox on *I Only Arsked*, as he would like me to be available to go back on *Ten Seconds to Hell* when it came back from America, and this I did. When it came back, I worked on it at Hammer House."

While *Dracula* was battling the censor and *The Revenge of Frankenstein* and *Ten Seconds to Hell* were being shot, work continued on the troubled pilot episode of *Tales of Frankenstein* for Screen Gems. Anton Diffring's agent, Rita Cave, wrote to Michael Carreras on 14 January:

"I am sorry to hear you are ill, as I was just on the point of coming round to finalise discussions on the above contract. As we seem to be missing each other, perhaps you would send it round and we will get it signed before Anton leaves. The terms, as agreed in your absence, are as follows:

Pilot

The Artist to leave London on 22nd January for two weeks' shooting in Hollywood for the sum of £500 payable at this end; you to pay First Class return transportation (he would like to return via New York), plus Hotel expenses, plus 25 dollars per day 'pocket money', and transport to and from the studio. I presume someone from your organisation will be seeing him off in order to pay for any excess baggage etc. Incidentally, he is rather concerned about taking the costumes with him as his own luggage as they are all rather 'odd', the Top Hat in particular! Perhaps someone will talk to me regarding this.

Option

You to have the option of making nine consecutive episodes, this option to be taken up within four weeks after the finish of the pilot; these episodes to be shot in England in mid-June, 1958; each episode to take five days; for the sum of £2,750. Also transportation to and from the studio in England as Anton does not drive.

Credit

On screen immediately after the title, 'With Anton Diffring', and no other Artist's name will be on screen until the end. His name also to appear, 'With Anton Diffring' on all paid publicity.

"Will you please send the contract round to my office as soon as possible, as time is getting short."

Disappointingly, we may never know how Hammer resolved the controversy over Diffring's top hat. The billing question was a more pressing one, in any case; on 19 January, Irving Briskin of Columbia wrote to Tony Hinds in an 'inter-office Columbia communication':

"I am in receipt of your memorandum concerning the Anton Diffring deal for *Frankenstein*. There are two points in it which bother me:

1) You talk about an option for nine additional episodes. It was my original understanding there would be a total of eight Baron Frankenstein episodes. Your memorandum now indicates 10 episodes. This will have to be corrected before you leave town.

2) The other point is the billing clause. Immediately following the title, you have a credit, 'with Anton Diffring as Baron Frankenstein'. We would prefer not to have this type of billing because the only thing that will come on will be the title, *Tales of Frankenstein*. All billing will appear at the end of the picture.

"Please get these points corrected."

Hinds replied in a memo the following day: "I am in receipt of your memo referring to the contract between Anton Diffring and Hammer Films, the contents of which I shall cable to my London office, who made the contract. However, before doing this, I should like to know exactly what billing can be given to Diffring. For instance, can the words: 'Starring Anton Diffring as Baron Frankenstein' appear in the credits at the end of the film?" Briskin replied, "That's okay." It would be enough to appease Diffring.

The pilot, called *The Face in the Tombstone Mirror*, was finally filmed in February but, like *Ten Seconds to Hell*, it wasn't really Hammer. Screen Gems had cunningly exploited the success of the Hammer series, but that's where it ended. Even Jimmy Sangster's original story was rejected in favour of one of their own by Henry Kuttner. For the record, the pilot was directed by Curt Siodmak, who had penned Universal's *The Wolfman* and *Frankenstein Meets the Wolfman* (as well as supplying the stories on which the scripts for *Son of Dracula* and *House of Frankenstein* were based). He had also written the novel *Donovan's Brain*.

On 28 February, Hinds wrote to Seymour Freedman of Screen Gems: "How goes the epic? Have you seen it? If so, what do you think?" Screen Gems' initial thoughts are unrecorded, but it would appear that Hammer were decidedly unimpressed. Plans for the projected series were eventually abandoned, although Tony Hinds would continue to commission story ideas until May 1958. The five story outlines would not be wasted. A R Rawlinson's story ('story no 1') of a soulless female creation would be echoed in Hinds' script for *Frankenstein Created Woman* in 1966, while Peter Bryan's tale ('story no 5'), submitted on 8 May, detailing Frankenstein's dirty dealings with a fairground hypnotist, would share similarities with Hinds' script for *The Evil of Frankenstein* (1963).

Michael Carreras later explained his frustration with the project and its inevitable failure, "The series was conceived here with the right talent. Jimmy Sangster wrote four pilot scripts. Tony Hinds went to America to Screen Gems and he ran into a lot of trouble ... they didn't understand the concept and they wanted to Americanise it. The Gothic genre isn't American, so that isn't possible, and you can't Anglicise it either – you have to present it as it is. Tony gave up, quite rightly. I went out and I ran into exactly the same problems. One of the funny stories is that they immediately wanted to rewrite everything. The other interesting thing is that the day I arrived, they played me the theme music and they didn't even know what the series would be about, just that it would be called *Frankenstein* ... They filmed a pilot. I came back to Screen Gems at Christmas and I agreed with Tony that it was a total conceptual cock-up. They wanted to do a series nothing like our films – so why would we be involved? The pilot was a dismal failure and, as far as I know, it's never been shown on television or even theatrically. I think they just threw it away!"[9] As far as UK television is concerned, Carreras was dead right.

Meanwhile, Hammer's publicity machine began to focus on the forthcoming release of *The Camp on Blood Island*. A feature article was run in the *Illustrated* supplement of the *Daily Cinema* on 29 March. Among the views canvased were comments by Leo Rawlings, an ex-gunner with the 137th Field Regiment, who had been a Japanese POW for three and a half years in 12 camps from Singapore to central Burma, including 18 months on Burma's infamous death railway. An ex-student of the Birmingham Central School of Art, as a POW he recorded his experiences on canvas, using primitive materials. He had this to say about the film: "It is the most accurate and sincere portrayal of a Japanese POW camp that I've ever seen. I sat through the film with a tremendous lump in my throat. That night, for the first time in eight years, my sleep was disturbed by nightmares." Lord Russell of Liverpool, the former assistant Judge Advocate-General, who was preparing a book on Japanese war crimes called *The Knights of Bushido*, agreed with Rawlings' interpretation of the film, adding later in the same article, "It is a sober and honest attempt to tell a terrible story." James Carreras then went on to say, "No one opposed the making of it and I believe these films should be made periodically to remind us. I agree with Lord Russell, whose words we are using on all our posters, 'We may forgive, but we should never forget.'"

The Camp on Blood Island was tradeshown at the Columbia Theatre, Wardour Street, on Thursday 10 April and had its world première at the London Pavilion on Friday the 18th. Among the dignitaries in attendance were James Carreras, Mike Frankovich, Tony Hinds, Val Guest and stars André Morell, Edward Underdown, Barbara Shelley, Liliane Sottane and Milton Reid. A group of ex-POWs were invited, including Leo Rawlings and Lord Russell of Liverpool. Many commentators said it should never have been made and condemned it for opening up old wounds. Nevertheless, the film was tremendously popular, proving to be one of Hammer's most successful films.

Behind the scenes at Hammer House, The Revenge of Frankenstein was now having its anticipated battle with the BBFC. A black-and-white copy was reviewed by examiners Audrey Field and Frank Crofts on 12 March and Board Secretary John Nicholls wrote to Tony Hinds the following day:

"The Revenge of Frankenstein was seen in black and white yesterday, 12th March. Before the film is viewed again in colour the following deletions must be made:
Reel 8. Shorten strangling of concierge [ie, janitor]. Remove all shots of Karl dribbling.
Reel 9. Remove all shots of Karl slobbering at the mouth, and with bloodstained face when he meets and kills Gerda.
Reel 11. Remove all shots of brain when it has been removed from Frankenstein's head.
"When the film is viewed in colour the following, in particular, may not be acceptable:
Shots involving blood.
Reel 4. Various isolated parts of the human body.
Reel 5. Shot of brain going into jar.
Reel 11. Frankenstein's face after he has been beaten up."

On 13 June, the new Secretary of the BBFC, John Trevelyan, wrote to H H Fullilove of Columbia Pictures in Britain: "I write to confirm my telephone message today, and to say that the Board is prepared to issue an 'X' certificate for The Revenge of Frankenstein subject to the following deletions being made:
Reel 2. Remove the shot of brain being dropped from the dish into the jar. It can be seen in the jar afterwards.
Reel 4. Delete the shot of Karl dribbling at the mouth after strangling the caretaker.
Since these are straight deletions it will not be necessary for us to view these reels again, and on receiving your written assurance that the above cuts have been made an 'X' certificate will be issued."

Tony Hinds wrote to Trevelyan on 20 June: "Your letter to Mr Fullilove of Columbia, dated June 13th, has been passed on to me as the Producer of the picture, and as far as reel 2 is concerned, as soon as my cutter returns from Berlin, I will have him attend to this shot according to your comment, although after the BBC's television programme, Your Life in Their Hands, I should have thought this was very tame stuff! Reel 4. Whilst appreciating your objections to this scene, I would respectfully point out that if we delete it, we are losing the only really moral scene in the whole picture. It is in this scene that 'the monster', Karl, looks to heaven appealing for God's help in overcoming the terrible desire which he is experiencing, and for the first time overcomes it. I should like permission to re-submit this reel, so that you can see what I am getting at."

Trevelyan replied to Hinds on 23 June: "As to the cut in reel 2, I think you will agree that colour makes quite a lot of difference in a shot of this kind. It looks pretty messy! I see your point about the scene in reel 4. We want to have it removed because this was one of the few places in the picture in which sexual impulse was evident. However, in view of the line that you take, we will have another look at this reel. Will you please arrange with Miss Barnes to have it sent in on a convenient day."

Tony Hinds was quick to respond to the bizarre reference to 'sexual impulse' and replied to Trevelyan on 24 June: "I really must be very innocent, but I honestly cannot see where any sexual impulse arises in the scene in question."

Trevelyan explained his mistake in his reply on 25 June: "We are to see reel 4 of The Revenge of Frankenstein tomorrow, but I must write now to apologise for a mistake on my part in referring to the scene in this reel. It was, of course, cannibal impulse that was bothering Karl, and not sexual

‘DRACULA’
PULLS IN
THE QUEUES

A Bank Holiday picture that tells its own story . . . The horror-sex blockbuster "Dracula," at the Gaumont, Haymarket, was pulling in queues. Business was "fantastic" and the film played to packed houses on each of the three days of the holiday. "Dracula"—a Hammer film, presented by U-I and released by RFD—stars Peter Cushing, Michael Gough, and Melissa Stribling, with Christopher Lee as the evil Count Dracula himself. It starts its London release on June 16 on the Gaumont circuit.

A cutting from
To-day's Cinema
on 28 May 1958
showing the
phenomenal
opening of
Dracula (1957).

impulse. This was entirely a mistake on my part so please accept it as such. I will let you know our decision as soon as we have seen the reel tomorrow."

A note on file at the BBFC reads: "Reel 4 was seen by the Secretary, IB, NKB and MCG on 26.6.58. It was agreed to waive the objection to Karl dribbling and to leave the reel as it stands." Supervising editor James Needs wrote to Trevelyan on 30 July: "This is to confirm that your objection in reel 2 of The Revenge of Frankenstein – the shot of a brain being dropped from the dish into the jar – has now been removed."

Personally, I'm a little confused here, because this sequence has been present in every print of the film I have watched. The scene was even included in the eight-minute digest Columbia subsequently issued on Super 8mm.

Meanwhile, throughout May and June, Hammer were busy promoting Dracula, which was now rushed into release ahead of The Snorkel (which had its première on board the Queen Elizabeth in May). Following a press screening in New York on Friday 2 May, Dracula had its world première at the Warner Theatre, Milwaukee, Wisconsin under its American title, Horror of Dracula, on Thursday the 8th. The picture grossed $1,682 on its first day and $10,600 in its first five days. On Wednesday 21 May Hammer put on a special trade press reception at the Hungaria restaurant in London. In attendance were James and Michael Carreras, Tony Hinds, Peter Cushing, Christopher Lee, Melissa Stribling, Carol Marsh, Harry Norris (Rank Film Distributors' managing director) and Universal International's Douglas Granville, with the atmosphere provided by Dracula's coffin, cobwebs, skulls and sinister subdued lighting.

On Thursday 22 May, the British première was held at the Gaumont Haymarket. The front of the cinema was adorned with a magnificent display. 'Dracula' was spelt out in giant neon letters together with a vivid proclamation, "Every night he rises from his coffin bed silently to seek the soft flesh, the warm blood he needs to keep himself alive!" A huge montage of Lee languishing over Melissa Stribling was erected for which, after weeks of experimentation, a mechanism had been rigged to make blood flow from Stribling's neck and drip continuously from her hair. In attendance were James and Michael Carreras, Terence Fisher, Peter Cushing, Christopher Lee, Melissa Stribling, Carol Marsh, Luciana Paluzzi, Hardy Kruger, Tony Wright, Michael Medwin, Jill Ireland, Delphi Lawrence, Barbara Lyon, Vera Day, April Olrich and Douglas Granville.

"I saw the first Dracula in a theatre then called the Gaumont, in London's Haymarket district," remembers Christopher Lee. "It was a big theatre, adorned with the most huge, lurid photographs of me outside and inside. I walked in in an absolute paroxysm of embarrassment. I don't think anybody recognised me. Nobody came up to me, nobody spoke to me. The only thing I do remember, and I've never said this before, is that Michael Carreras – the executive producer – was sitting next to me, and he turned to me afterwards and said, 'You know, you're one hell of an actor.'" [10]

The film broke all records for a first week take at the Gaumont since the theatre's opening in 1925. The Daily Cinema proudly proclaimed on 28 May, "A bank holiday picture that tells its own story ... the horror-sex blockbuster Dracula at the Gaumont Haymarket was pulling in queues. Business was 'fantastic' and the film played to packed houses on each of the three days of the holiday." Kinematograph Weekly explained further the next day: "... in its first four days [Dracula] has broken box-office records, realising the highest ever Bank Holiday Saturday and Monday figures at the theatre."

On Sunday 25 May, James Carreras, Tony Hinds, Christopher Lee and Peter Cushing left England to attend the New York première. While there, on Monday 26 May they celebrated Peter Cushing's 45th birthday at the top of the Empire State building. Christopher Lee celebrated his birthday the following day at a special press luncheon held by Universal. Al Daff (Universal's chief in America) presented the 36-year-old actor with a birthday cake at the reception. On Thursday 29 May, they attended the première at New York's Mayfair Theatre. Cushing and Lee were on hand in the lobby to sign autographs and each patron was given a complimentary pocketbook edition of the novel and soft drinks called 'courage cocktails'. The film played there for three weeks with The Thing That Couldn't Die, grossing $25000 in its first week, $17000 in its second and $14000 in its last.

Meanwhile, back in England a series of trade shows began across the country, beginning at the Newcastle Gaumont on Wednesday 28 May and leading to the film's general release on Monday 16 June in London on the Gaumont circuit. Kinematograph Weekly on 26 June judged "takings astronomical." The Daily Cinema on 13 August reported, "Jim Carreras was bursting to tell me that the Japanese version of Dracula ... has broken the all-time house record. The Japanese print of Hammer's horrifier has a much more emphatic shock content ... than its comparatively sedate British counterpart."

The film was a runaway success, surpassing even The Curse of Frankenstein. "I remember going with Peter Cushing, Jimmy Carreras and Anthony Hinds into the office of Al Daff, president of Universal in New York," remembers Christopher Lee, "and he said, 'Gentlemen, your film has just taken Universal out of bankruptcy.' I checked with Jim Carreras, I checked with Tony Hinds, I checked with Peter; I said, 'Am I wrong or did he say that?' He did."

Back in April, the Daily Cinema once more sang Hammer's praises in a supplement called 'Britain Presents'. "Skilful collective leadership (under James Carreras, Anthony Hinds and Michael Carreras) have [sic] put Hammer right on top. Leadership plus teamwork, know-how, a 'think big' approach to making and marketing films, and accurate anticipation of new entertainment trends. These are the factors behind Hammer's fabulous success story. 'But,' says managing director James Carreras, 'do not imagine our policy of exploiting a formula ties us to any one particular type of subject. Our job is to keep one jump ahead of public taste, to pioneer new tastes. We have built up a big story property reservoir. The moment audience reaction shows the slightest hint of staleness, the formula can be switched overnight. We have become famed for our horror films. But we can turn to comedy, social drama, historical pictures, or musicals at a moment's notice. That is the measure of our organisation's flexibility.'"

This flexibility was evident in Hammer's next two productions at Bray: Further Up the Creek, directed by Val Guest, and a film version of the popular TV comedy The Army Game – I Only Arsked.

Hammer and Val Guest must have felt confident about their maritime comedy co-production Up the Creek, because they set sail aboard the sequel even before it was released. Up the Creek premièred at London's Warner Theatre on Wednesday 7 May 1958, a mere 12 days before the sequel would roll at Bray, and by the time it went on general release on the ABC circuit on Monday 2 June, the sequel had already completed its first two weeks of shooting. The gamble seemed to pay off, though, as the response to Up the Creek was exremely enthusiastic.

Filming on Further Up the Creek began on Monday 19 May, ending on Friday 11 July after eight weeks. Cinematographer Gerald Gibbs returned, having previously photographed Hammer's sci-fi shockers X the Unknown and Quatermass 2 in 1956. George Provis gave Bernard Robinson a well-earned respite from set designing, though the bridge of the ship Aristotle was another revamp of the Castle Dracula set on the backlot, built up 40 feet high so the trees in the background would not be seen. Val Guest regular Bill Lenny was brought back to edit the film.

John Peverall now took over the regular post of first assistant director from Robert Lynn, with Tom Walls and Hugh Harlow remaining in their positions of 2nd and 3rd assistants respectively.

Filming Further up the Creek (1958) on the lot at Bray Studios. Picture shows Ken Goodman, Len Harris and director Val Guest.

FURTHER UP THE CREEK

A Hammer-Byron production
PRINCIPAL PHOTOGRAPHY: 19 May to 11 July 1958
UK DISTRIBUTION: Columbia; 91 minutes; b/w;
  Hammerscope; certificate 'U'
UK RELEASE:
  TRADE SHOW: 10 October at the Columbia Theatre
  PREMIÈRE: 20 October at the Metropole Victoria

DIRECTOR: Val Guest; PRODUCER: Henry Halstead; SCREENPLAY: Val Guest, John Warren and Len Heath; ART DIRECTOR: George Provis; DIRECTOR OF PHOTOGRAPHY: Gerry Gibbs; CAMERA OPERATOR: Len Harris; FOCUS PULLER: Harry Oakes; FIRST ASSISTANT DIRECTOR: John Peverall; 2ND ASSISTANT DIRECTOR: Tom Walls; 3RD ASSISTANT DIRECTOR: Hugh Harlow; SUPERVISING EDITOR: James Needs; EDITOR: Bill Lenny; MUSIC COMPOSER: Stanley Black; MUSIC SUPERVISOR: John Hollingsworth; SOUND RECORDIST: Jock May; MAKE-UP: Phil Leakey; HAIR STYLIST: Marjorie Whittie; PRODUCTION MANAGER: Pat Marsden; PRODUCTION SUPERVISOR: Fred Swann; CONTINUITY: Doreen Dearnaley; WARDROBE: Molly Arbuthnot; TECHNICAL ADVISOR: Commander Peter Peake; STUDIO MANAGER: Arthur Kelly

David Tomlinson (Fairweather); Frankie Howerd (Dibble); Shirley Eaton (Jane); Thora Hird (Mrs Galloway); Lionel Jeffries (Barker); Lionel Murton (Perkins); Sam Kydd (Bates); John Warren (Cooky); David Lodge (Scouse); Harry Landis (Webster); Ian Whittaker (Lofty); Howard Williams (Burns); Peter Collingwood (Chippy); Edwin Richfield (Bennett); Amy D'Alby (Edie); Esma Cannon (Maudie); Tom Gill (Phillippe); Jack Le White, Max Day (Kertoni Brothers); Mary Wilson (First Model); Katherine Byrne (Second Model); Eric Pohlmann (President); Stanley Unwin (Porter); Michael Goodliffe (Blackeney), Wolfe Morris (Algeroccan Major); John Singer (Dispatch Rider); Larry Nobel (Postman); Ballard Berkeley (Whacker); Judith Furse (Chief Wren); Michael Ripper (Ticket Collector); Joe Gibbon (Taxi Driver); Victor Brooke (Policeman); Cavan Malone (Signalman); Desmond Llewelyn (Yeoman); Basil Dignam (Flagship Commander); John Stuart (Admiral); Jess Conrad (Signalman); Patrick Holt (First Lt.); George Herbert (Officer); Charles Lloyd Pack (El Diablo); Walter Hudd (Consul); John Hall (Sea Scout)

Hugh Harlow recalls, "I can't remember what were the circumstances of Robert Lynn leaving. He had a lot of tummy trouble. I didn't get on too well with Robert; he was a very strict and stern man, if I remember. He was a major in the army and, when he came out, he went into the film industry. I don't remember him leaving Hammer, but I got on better with John than I did Robert, I remember that – a different working relationship, a closer one really." Robert Lynn went on to become an accomplished director on such diverse productions as *Dr Crippen* (1962) and the television series

Captain Scarlet and the Mysterons (1967), as well as producing Lionel Jeffries' acclaimed film The Railway Children in 1970. He died in 1982.

David Tomlinson reprised his role of Lt Fairweather but, unable to secure Peter Sellers, Val Guest hired Frankie Howerd for the chief comic support. Also returning in their original roles were Lionel Murton, John Warren (who co-wrote both voyages with Val Guest), Lionel Jeffries, Howard Williams, Peter Collingwood, Edwin Richfield, David Lodge and Sam Kydd. Bray receptionist Christine Stevens remembers, "When we did a film called Further Up the Creek, Frankie Howerd and David Tomlinson were in it and they were hysterical. Frankie had a dog that looked just like him. The top of Dracula's castle was the bridge of the ship, because I remember I had to deliver a telegram and had to walk up all these open steps to the top of the thing."

During filming on Friday 4 July, it was discovered, as noted by Harry Oakes in his diary, that "All the pay packets have been stolen. CID called in." Pauline Harlow remembers the details: "I was at that time in the office as Tony Keys' secretary and it was lunchtime. I was in the outer office, reading or something, and Ken Gordon, the accountant, came bursting through the door. He looked absolutely grey and said, 'Is he [Tony Keys] in?' I said, 'Yes, but he's having a little nap.' 'Oh, I have to wake him,' he said. 'The money's gone, the wages have gone.' So he burst into the inner office and then all panic was let loose. It seemed that the money had been stolen just as Ken Gordon slipped out for 20 minutes to have his lunch in the canteen. In those days we didn't have cheques, it was wage packets and cash. Anyway, the police came and he reckoned it was just over £2500. It doesn't sound much now, but it would have been a lot in those days. We never did find the culprit. They think it had to have been an inside job. I don't know how they got in, but it must have been lowered down out of the window to another person."

On 19 June 1957, ITV broadcast the first episode of a new Granada TV comedy show called The Army Game, starring William Hartnell, Alfie Bass, Bill Fraser and Charles Hawtrey. It became a huge hit and as, with so many successful TV shows, it soon fell under the scrutiny of Hammer. Darling of the show was the gormless Private 'Popeye' Popplewell, played by Bernard Bresslaw, and his catch phrase – 'I only arsked' – would give Hammer's spin-off its title. Bresslaw was a Hammer contract artist, having already appeared in The Men of Sherwood Forest and The Glass Cage and been considered for the Creature in The Curse of Frankenstein. He had also made a cameo appearance in the Baker and Berman production Blood of the Vampire, in 1957, scripted by Jimmy Sangster.

Filming began at Bray on Monday 21 July, a week after Further Up the Creek had ended and with much the same crew. The shoot finished on Friday 22 August after a modest five weeks. Hammer

I ONLY ARSKED

PRINCIPAL PHOTOGRAPHY: 21 July to 22 August 1958
UK DISTRIBUTION: Columbia; 82 minutes; b/w; certificate 'U'
UK RELEASE:
   TRADE SHOW: 1 November 1958
   PREMIÈRE: 7 November at the Plaza
   GENERAL RELEASE: 9 February 1959 on the ABC circuit

DIRECTOR: Montgomery Tully; PRODUCER: Anthony Hinds; ASSOCIATE PRODUCER: Anthony Nelson Keys; EXECUTIVE PRODUCER: Michael Carreras; SCREENPLAY: Sid Colin and Jack Davies based on Granada TV's 'The Army Game'; ART DIRECTOR: John Stoll; DIRECTOR OF PHOTOGRAPHY: Lionel Banes; CAMERA OPERATOR: Len Harris; FOCUS PULLER: Harry Oakes; ASSISTANT DIRECTOR: John Peverall; 2ND ASSISTANT DIRECTOR: Tom Walls; 3RD ASSISTANT DIRECTOR: Hugh Harlow; SUPERVISING EDITOR: James Needs; EDITOR: Alfred Cox; MUSIC COMPOSER: Benjamin Frankel; Song 'Alone Together' by Walter Ridley and Sid Colin; MUSIC SUPERVISOR:

John Hollingsworth; SOUND RECORDIST: Jock May; SOUND CAMERA: Peter Day; MAKE-UP: Phil Leakey; HAIR STYLIST: Henry Montsash; PRODUCTION MANAGER: Don Weeks; CONTINUITY: Doreen Dearnaley; WARDROBE: Molly Arbuthnot; SPECIAL EFFECTS: Syd Pearson; STUDIO MANAGER: Arthur Kelly

Bernard Bresslaw (Popeye); Michael Medwin (Cpl.Springer); Alfie Bass (Boots); Geoffrey Sumner (Maj. Upshot-Bagley); Charles Hawtrey (Professor); Norman Rossington (Cupcake); David Lodge (Potty Chambers); Arthur Howard (Sir Redvers), Marne Maitland (King Fazim); Francis Matthews (Mahmoud); Michael Bentine (Fred); Francis Matthews (Mahmoud); Michael Ripper (Azim); Wolfe Morris (Salesman); Ewen McDuff (Ferrers); Marie Devereux, Lizabeth Page, Claire Gordon, Barbara Pinney, Pamela Chamberlain, Jean Rainer, Clarissa Roberts, Gales Sheridan, Josephine Jay, Andrea Loren, Rebecca Wilson, Anna Griffiths, Pauline Chamberlain, Jennifer Mitchell, Julie Shearing, Maureen Moore, Anne Muller, Pamela Searle (Harem Girls)

I Only Arsked (1958) was based on the television sitcom The Army Game and featured a shambolic regiment of reluctant recruits: David Lodge, Geoffrey Sumner, Bernard Bresslaw, Alfie Bass, Norman Rossington, Charles Hawtrey and Michael Medwin.

cast busty glamour model Marie Devereux as one of the harem girls; she would figure memorably in some of the horrors to come. *The Revenge of Frankenstein*, meanwhile, had been released in the US in June (accompanied by Jacques Tourneur's classic *Curse of the Demon*, known in its native Britain as *Night of the Demon*). *The Snorkel* finally went on general release in England on the ABC circuit from 7 July.

A special gala première of *The Revenge of Frankenstein* was held on Wednesday 27 August at the Plaza, Piccadilly Circus, at the stroke of midnight. This was a celebrity preview for a predominantly showbiz audience, immediately prior to the British première the following day. Present were James Carreras, Tony Hinds, Tony Nelson Keys, Jimmy Sangster, Terence Fisher, Peter Cushing, Francis Matthews, Eunice Gayson, Oscar Quitak, Mike Frankovich, Valerie Hobson (over 20 years after her roles in *Bride of Frankenstein* and *WereWolf of London*) with her MP husband John Profumo (soon to hit the headlines himself), Donald Sinden, Princess Ingeborg Rhoesa and her escort Jon Pertwee. Also in attendance was a life-sized stuffed vulture called Frank N Stein. "I'll never forget the première in London," says Francis Matthews. "I nearly stopped the show and brought the house down! I said, staring at the bloodied body of Frankenstein, 'Pray God I have the skill to do this thing.' It got a great round of applause and Peter leaned over to me and said, 'My dear boy, what have you done?'" [11] The film went on general release around the rest of England from Monday 17 November.

As expected, the film did good business. Just as expected, the critics loathed it. "Films of this kind are the last refuge of unimaginative producers who have lost the art of communicating individually with human beings and have fallen back on the appeal to mass hysteria," wrote C A Lejeune in the *Observer* of 31 August.

Eliot Hyman's son Kenneth was working as sales officer at his father's AAP company, when he was introduced to Colonel James Carreras. "It was a trip that Jimmy and Mike (Carreras) were on to New York and, I think actually rather fliply, riding in a taxi one day, Jimmy said, 'Why don't you get out of this sales nonsense and come over to England and make movies?' And I said, 'That sounds wonderful,' and I started thinking, 'What could I do? I also realised that if I'm going to do anything, I better come with a bit of leverage. In other words, having a property. Now I'd never produced anything, I knew nothing about producing, but I acquired a literary property – I negotiated with the Conan Doyle estate and bought the rights to *The Hound of the Baskervilles* – which was a story I'd always liked. I went to Max Youngstein at United Artists – and I remember telling Max that I wanted to produce this movie and I thought that I could get Hammer as a partner and he said, 'What do you know about production?' And I said, 'Absolutely nothing, but I think I'm a good enough executive that I can hire the people who *do* know what they're doing, and I'll watch, learn and listen. I know there's a thing called a budget and a thing called a schedule – you have to stay on schedule and stay on budget – and I'll watch the store.' So he said, 'Okay. Today you are a producer.' So I called Jimmy and said, 'I'd like to take you up on your offer,' and I came over with partial financing from United Artists." [12]

James Carreras could hardly resist the offer; what better than the detective's most famous adventure and one that Hammer could easily dovetail into their new programme of horror films? While Kenneth Hyman got no producer credit in England, he did in America. He later went back to the States to move into his father's offices at Seven-Arts, but continued to bring the odd project to Hammer.

Tony Hinds commissioned ex-Hammer camera operator Peter Bryan to write the script: "Peter Bryan was my first camera operator and became a good friend. As a result of a car accident, he had to be replaced. He came back as a one-man operation making short 'interest' films for us, mainly in Ireland. I gave him the job of writing the screenplay of *The Hound of the Baskervilles* as his

Sherlock Holmes (Peter Cushing) calls on Bishop Frankland (Miles Malleson) regarding a missing spider in The Hound of the Baskervilles (1958).

THE HOUND OF THE BASKERVILLES

PRINCIPAL PHOTOGRAPHY: 8 September to 31 October 1958
DISTRIBUTION:
    United Artists; 87 minutes; Technicolor;
        UK: certificate 'A'
UK RELEASE:
    TRADE SHOW: 20 March 1959, at the Hammer Theatre,
        Hammer House
    PREMIÈRE: 28 March 1959, at the London Pavilion,
        Picadilly Circus
    GENERAL RELEASE: 4 May 1959
    US RELEASE: July 1959

EDITOR: Alfred Cox; MUSIC: James Bernard; MUSIC SUPERVISOR: John Hollingsworth; SOUND RECORDIST: Jock May; MAKE-UP: Roy Ashton; HAIRSTYLIST: Henry Montsash; PRODUCTION MANAGER: Don Weeks; CONTINUITY: Shirley Barnes; WARDROBE: Molly Arbuthnot; SPECIAL EFFECTS: Syd Pearson; PROPERTY MASTER: Tommy Money; PROPERTY BUYER: Eric Hillier; DOG MASK: Margaret Carter; MODEL DOG: Frank Pannicelli; CASHIER: Ken Gordon; STUDIO MANAGER: Arthur Kelly; CONSTRUCTION MANAGER: Mick Lyons; CHIEF ELECTRICIAN: Jack Curtis; MASTER PAINTER: Lawrence Wren; MASTER PLASTERER: Arthur Banks; MASTER CARPENTER: Charles Davis

DIRECTOR: Terence Fisher; PRODUCER: Anthony Hinds; ASSOCIATE PRODUCER: Anthony Nelson Keys; EXECUTIVE PRODUCER: Michael Carreras; SCREENPLAY: Peter Bryan; PRODUCTION DESIGNER: Bernard Robinson; ASSISTANT ART DIRECTOR: Don Mingaye; DIRECTOR OF PHOTOGRAPHY: Jack Asher; CAMERA OPERATOR: Len Harris; FOCUS PULLER: Harry Oakes; ASSISTANT DIRECTOR: John Peverall; 2ND ASSISTANT DIRECTOR: Tom Walls; 3RD ASSISTANT DIRECTOR: Hugh Harlow; SUPERVISING EDITOR: James Needs; EDITOR/SOUND

Peter Cushing (Sherlock Holmes); André Morell (Doctor Watson); Christopher Lee (Sir Henry); Marla Landi (Cecile); David Oxley (Sir Hugo); Francis De Wolff (Doctor Mortimer); Miles Malleson (Bishop); Ewen Solon (Stapleton); John Le Mesurier (Barrymore); Helen Goss (Mrs Barrymore); Sam Kydd (Perkins); Michael Hawkins (Lord Caphill); Judi Moyens (Servant Girl); Michael Mulcaster (Convict)

UNCREDITED: David Birks (Servant); Elizabeth Dott (Mrs Goodlippe); Ian Hewitson (Lord Kingsblood)

background was the theatre and I thought his camera knowledge plus his sense of drama would make him an ideal choice." [13]

Peter Cushing and Christopher Lee were back for their third Hammer adventure together. The pairing was now becoming as familiar as that of Karloff and Lugosi in the Universal horror films and they signed their contracts on 1 August. Who else could direct this latest remake but Terence Fisher? He signed his contract on the 7th. Tony Hinds brought back the same core team that had worked on his other three colour chillers: Jack Asher, Len Harris, Harry Oakes, Don Weeks, Jock

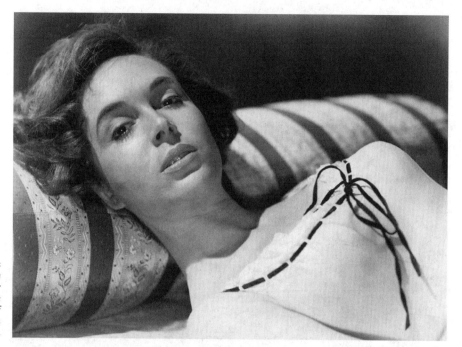

Marla Landi was discovered by Peter Cushing for the role of Cecile in The Hound of the Baskervilles (1958).

May, James Needs, and the stirling team of Bernard Robinson and Don Mingaye. John Peverall, Tom Walls and Hugh Harlow returned as 1st, 2nd and 3rd Assistant Directors, respectively.

For *The Hound of the Baskervilles*, Phil Leakey passed the make-up baton to Roy Ashton (born 17 April 1909). Leakey, who had grown disenchanted with Hammer after they had refused to continue his retainer, had been forced to go further afield for work and was unavailable. Anthony Nelson Keys inevitably turned to Ashton, who had previously assisted Leakey at Hammer. Ashton first cleared it with his friend, not wanting to intrude into his territory, but Leakey made it clear that, as far as he was concerned, he had finished with Hammer and urged his colleague to take the job. Ashton phoned Keys back and accepted. Phil Leakey would continue to work in films into the 1970s. He died at his home in Dorset on 26 November 1992, aged 84.

It would be the beginning of a tremendous association between Ashton and Hammer. Ashton had given up a promising career as a professional opera singer to concentrate on his vocation as a make-up artist, but this did not stop his many make-up chair duets with Christopher Lee. Lee remembers, "He was a professional singer, of course. A very good tenor and I did the baritone-tenor duets with him. We had a lot of fun – broadcast it through the studios. People were greeted by this and they must have thought it was rather weird, particularly the ones that weren't interested in opera, to hear this as they arrived for work. It's one way of passing the time."

The role of Holmes naturally went to Peter Cushing, an actor in whom Hammer now had complete confidence. The casting was as near perfect as Hammer could have dreamed. Cushing had been a staunch follower of Conan Doyle's detective since he was a boy and was the proud owner of a collection of the original *Strand* magazines. His preparation for Holmes proved to be even more exhaustive than usual due to his interest in the character. He based his appearance on the classic Sidney Paget illustrations and threw himself enthusiastically into the role. He was, as Hammer proudly proclaimed in their trailer, "a new and exciting Sherlock Holmes."

Cushing proved an invaluable asset to the film. In the scene where Dr Mortimer boasts of his generosity in remunerating the detective, Cushing, disliking his reply as scripted, was quick to drag in a passage straight out of Conan Doyle's The Mystery of Thor Bridge: "My professional charges are upon a fixed scale. I do not vary them, except when I remit them altogether." It was also Cushing who was responsible for the casting of Marla Landi as Cecile, having been impressed by her performance in the film version of Graham Greene's *Across the Bridge* in 1957: "I saw Marla on television before shooting began on *The Hound of the Baskervilles*. I knew that Tony Hinds was looking for a 'new face' to play the character who was the descendent of the slaughtered girl. I said to my dear Helen at the time, 'That's the girl for the part.' They accepted my recommendation and that's how she obtained that particular role." [14]

André Morell was cast as Dr Watson and was keen to avoid the dim-witted comic approach of Nigel Bruce, Basil Rathbone's Watson. "Terence Fisher and Anthony Hinds agreed not to do Watson as a comic character," Morell explained. "Conan Doyle, after all, felt that Watson was a doctor and a bit of an ass but not an idiot as he was often made out to be. Where the jokes came, fine. I deliberately avoided seeing Nigel Bruce, although he was very good – I just didn't want him to influence my acting of the part." [15]

On Wednesday 3 September, Whitbread and Co hosted a special press reception at the Sherlock Holmes pub in London's Northumberland Avenue. The pub stood on the site of the old Northumberland Hotel, where Holmes met Sir Henry in Conan Doyle's original novel. Present were the stars and production executives from Hammer's latest chiller. Guests included Peter Cushing, Christopher Lee, André Morell, Tony Hinds, Terence Fisher and Peter Bryan.

Shooting began at Bray the following Monday, 8 September, and continued over the next eight weeks, finishing on Friday 31 October. Bernard Robinson once more excelled with some wonderful sets. The interior of Baskerville Hall took pride of place on Stage 1. Outside, the standing castle set from *Dracula* was again put to use as the outside of Baskerville Hall. The moor scenes were a mixture of studio sets (the swamp and the abbey, again beautifully lit by Jack Asher) and location shots. The location work took place just outside London, around Chobham Common and Frensham Ponds. Of the latter, Terence Fisher recalled: "There are quite a few heights there and it closely resembled the dark barren emptiness of Dartmoor." [16] Despite this, focus puller Harry Oakes was taken off the filming of Hammer's next production, *The Man Who Could Cheat Death*, being sent instead to Dartmoor to capture some 2nd unit footage of the moors with cameraman Ted Catford and producer Tony Hinds. "We left studio at 9.30 in Tony Hinds' Bentley," he noted on 2 December. Having checked in at the Two Bridge Hotel, they "shot around Widdicombe and Hound Tor" the next day, taking in further shots at Mary Tavy on the morning of 4 December before getting back to the studio at 6.00 pm.

Harry recalls the trip: "We'd shot *The Hound of the Baskervilles* at Chobham Common, which is fairly nearby in Surrey, where there's an army training area for armoured vehicles. We got permission to shoot on that, but it didn't look very much like Dartmoor. In the end Tony Hinds told me to go down to Dartmoor to get shots of various peaks and also there was a day-for-night shot we still needed where there was a lantern glowing. It was just before Christmas and I set off with Teddy Catford, a retired cameraman who lived nearby at Maidenhead, and Tony Hinds in his Bentley. I was in the back and there was fog everywhere. I know Ted was very pleased and he said, 'I'll get a few days out of this.' You wouldn't believe it, but we got just beyond Okehampton to go towards Dartmoor and the weather suddenly cleared up: lovely sunny weather. I think we just had an overnight – we shot that day; certainly not more than two days there."

The original location work was dogged by poor weather. Assistant director John Peverall remembers: "We were out in Chobham Common and it was coming down in buckets. We were all sure there was no chance that we would shoot that day. Suddenly, Tony Hinds showed up in the doorway of one of the tents, asking, 'What the hell are you doing here? Get back into the studios.' By three in the afternoon, we started turning the cameras. In that sense, Tony taught me a great deal. The point was to 'never give up the day', you can always get a couple of shots." [17]

On 23 October, *Kinematograph Weekly* featured the following story:

SHERLOCK CUSHING AND THE CASE OF THE MISSING SUN

"Sherlock Holmes and Dr Watson have this week been investigating the Case of the Missing Sun. They were at Frensham Ponds, 40 miles from London, on location for Hammer's *The Hound of the Baskervilles*. And while it's true to say the sun has been shining more than somewhat on this particular company recently, it's also unfortunately true it has shone very little on this particular production. So much so that the unit has been unable to get in a full day's shooting for the important 'Dartmoor' scenes. This dispels the film-makers' fond belief that if you want sun on English location, the nearer you leave it to

Christmas, the better. 'It's all called for a certain amount of re-organisation,' explained producer Anthony Hinds, waiting gloomily for the sun to come out. 'We've split up into two units ... our director Terry Fisher is back at Bray doing the studio work and I'm here waiting to get in the establishing scenes we were unable to shoot last week. It means, despite the weather, we are able to keep fairly well on schedule.'"

Tony Hinds went on to add, "We believe our script is nearer to the novel than other versions, for one thing. That doesn't mean there haven't been changes. Anyone who has read the book will realise they are inevitable. There were several incidents in the book which were never satisfactorily explained. So we have had to write in explanations. Other incidents which took say three weeks to develop in the book have had to be compressed into a few days in our story. But we feel all the changes are in the spirit of the book. In fact if Conan Doyle had written the screenplay we are sure this is the way he would have done it!"

Brave words indeed from the Hammer publicity machine. In line with their successful horror pictures, Hammer chose to bring the horrific elements of Conan Doyle's story to the fore. The main problem with this approach was that so much emphasis was placed on the Hound from Hell that its eventual appearance could only be a disappointment. The 'ferocious' beast was a Great Dane called Colonel who was in fact the most placid creature you could hope to find. To make him look more terrifying, Bernard Robinson's future wife, Margaret Carter (born 31 January 1920), kitted the hound out with a monstrous mask made out of rabbit skin and rubber.

"I joined Theatre Zoo [a theatrical costumiers dealing in animal masks] in 1957," Margaret remembers, "and while I was working there, I was asked to make the mask for the hound in The Hound of the Baskervilles. I had tried to get into films without much success until then. Of course that was one of the jobs which was farmed out from Bray Studios, because once you worked there and had a union card, you couldn't have handled the variety of materials needed for the job. After making a cast of the dog's head, the mask was made of rubber and covered by rabbit skin – and that would have involved too many departments to be allowed to do it in the studio. After that I just kept my ear to the ground and Bernard actually tipped me off when there was nobody on the books at Bray for modelling and he needed someone to do modelling. So I got my union card and began to work as a modeller at Bray. Frank Pannicelli at Pinewood made the dead dog and I had to make the mask for that too. It was bigger than the real dog."

It was Bernard who rang her at Theatre Zoo. Since the dog was regarded, rather curiously, as a 'prop' rather than a performer, it fell to the art department to dress him. Margaret remembers fondly the Hound from Hell: "There were two dogs, Great Danes – one very tame, which actually belonged to dog trainer Barbara Woodhouse, and another more athletic one called Colonel, who was supposedly more ferocious. When I was asked to do the mask I was told I would be fitting the tame one. However, in the meantime they had discovered that Colonel was much better for the part and decided to use him instead without telling me! He turned out to be very affectionate and rather protective of me. He was a dog who, if he liked you, you were in; if he didn't like you, you had to watch out."

Christopher Lee for one was not impressed. "The Hound from Hell: poor thing. That's the one thing nobody's ever been able to do properly in The Hound of the Baskervilles. Now they probably could do it with CGI [and have], because it's the size of a small donkey according to Conan Doyle. The real dog was a very amiable Great Dane called Colonel. They had him on the set every day to get him used to it and, when the time came for him to go for me, they had to prod him and stick things into him to make him angry, whereupon of course he did. Then they put a mask on his face – oh, that was the weakness of the film. That was the one thing everybody was waiting to see, the Hound from Hell, and this was a very mild and cheerful animal that turned up."

Like an earlier scene in which Lee was threatened by a tarantula, the final assault on Sir Henry by the hound is a composite of a numerous shots and apparently took a lot of time and patience to film. As Lee describes it, "Everybody had been feeding him chocolate and looking after him and that meant the dog was not in a fierce frame of mind at all. So they had to infuriate him, which they then proceeded to do, so when he attacked me, he did in fact bite me, although not seriously." [18] For the close-up shots of the hound's head savaging Lee, they were forced to improvise, as Terence Fisher explained: "The dog was one of the kindest and loveliest dogs around. In fact, for a lot of the close cutting work we used an artificial head and kept on pushing it into the various actors' faces."[16] Indeed, as Lee remembered, "Close-ups were a dummy dog which was slammed into my face by the prop men and I got a throat full of false hair and quite a lot of bruises."[18]

Apparently, to make the scene more effective, a small crew headed by Alfred Cox, Len Harris and Harry Oakes were given an extra week to reshoot the scene using a boy dressed in Sir Henry's clothes on a scale set of the abbey to magnify the hound's dimensions. Art director Don Mingaye remembers setting up the scene: "Margaret used her callipers to measure the dog. We then had a reference and had to scale everything down to make the dog look bigger." According to Terence Fisher, the scene looked too contrived and was not used: "We tried that and it didn't work. It actually looked like a couple of kids and a very large dog ... It was a nice idea, though."[16]

Len Harris remembered further problems with the scene. "I did these shots 2nd unit. I showed the dog what to do; he was really quite intelligent, but he wouldn't do it. He'd just walk along the gantry, sit down and look at us. It took several days to get the shot. We had a studio cat at the time and he appears when they [Sir Henry and Cecile] go into the farmhouse. Anyway, he was watching us trying to film scenes with the dog and the boy. It got up finally, came around the back of the set, climbed over the rocks until he got in front of the boy and then he turned to the camera as much to say 'You can't expect a dog to do it!'"[19]

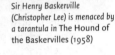

Sir Henry Baskerville (Christopher Lee) is menaced by a tarantula in The Hound of the Baskervilles (1958)

Alfred Cox remembers: "Fortunately, we had one standby props man whom the dog hated. I don't know why, but if Danny put in an appearance the dog would go spare. In this scene with the boy dressed up as Chris, the dog came out on the balcony and they said to me, 'It won't jump', because it was a Great Dane and they are notoriously weak on their front legs. The altar was pointing down, away from the balcony, and the dog came out and I prompted Danny to do his usual shouting at the dog. The dog jumped and came down on the altar stone and couldn't stop. Fortunately I got the boy to back out of shot before all this happened and the dog did stop eventually, with me underneath him!"

Camera operator Len Harris recalled problems filming the shock opening to the film immediately after the opening credits, when the servant girl's father is thrown out of the window. "We hold on the house for a long time, then gradually track up to this window. Obviously there are lights outside, but it is lit for night. We track up to this window, suddenly 'crash', he comes flying out of the window. What I hadn't anticipated was, although it was fairly low-key lighting inside, it was bright to my eye, and I was suddenly blinded by this light coming through. I knew this fellow had come through somewhere, but where I had no idea. The director asks how was it? And I said, 'Well, Terry, I wouldn't mind going again on this one.'

"They had anticipated this and had about three windows made up of this toffee glass stuff. It looks like stained glass. They put another one up and the same thing happened again, but I just saw enough of it to follow him in the water swimming. 'How was it?' Terry said. I thought I had him in there somewhere and I did a thing I would not have normally done. If you've missed a shot, it is best to say so, but I said, 'Yeah, I think it's all right, Terry.' So I was getting a bit worried to see the rushes. Tony Hinds always saw the rushes before we did. The next morning, he came up to me in the studio and said, 'Why did you want to go again on that shot? The first one was perfectly all right! It just took a long time doing another one, that's the only thing.' They used the first one in the film. I always prided myself on being able to follow people in falls and jumps and that sort of thing." [20]

As *Hound* entered post-production, editors Alfred Cox and James Needs took the editing over to Hammer House and music supervisor John Hollingsworth brought James Bernard back to score; his music had been sadly missing from *The Revenge of Frankenstein*. Bernard rustled up a particularly rousing score to enhance the pace and excitement. Reminiscent of the oft-recurring themes in the Universal monster movies of years before, the classic 'chase' music from *Dracula* was reprised in the scene where Sir Hugo pursues the servant girl across the moor. This came as quite a surprise to Bernard. "No, I didn't use it, they put that in. I was very cross. I'm sure it wasn't there when the film came out. I did a completely different section of music. I wouldn't have been so lazy as to use something I'd done in *Dracula*; I wouldn't have dreamt of it, I wouldn't have dared! I wrote a fast chase sequence, so, when I first saw the film after we had recorded the music, I'd have noticed if there had been *Dracula* music in it. It was only years later that somebody mentioned it to me. I was amazed."

On 20 October, Hammer consolidated their deal with Columbia when they announced plans for Columbia to buy a 49 per cent share of Bray Studios, adding to the roster of Hammer's company directors Mike Frankovich (Columbia's chief in Britain) and his associates Kenneth Maidment, Anthony Bray and L R Woolner. The same day saw the release of *Further Up the Creek*, which was rushed out quickly to capitalise on the success of the original. This probably explains, too, why *I Only Arsked* was rushed out behind it; the popularity of TV comedy shows can wane at any time. It premièred at the Plaza on Friday 7 November, a mere two months after shooting had been completed, and would go on general release on the ABC circuit from 9 February 1959. It did fairly well at the box-office, though reviews were mixed.

The impetus for Hammer's next horror movie is difficult to determine. By 1958 it was clear that Hammer was the new driving force in horror films and gradually the Hollywood majors started coming to them with the remake rights to their old projects in return for the exclusive and profitable distribution rights. Paramount was next, approaching Hammer with their rights to Barré Lyndon's play *The Man in Half Moon Street*, which they had filmed in 1944 with Nils Asther. What is not clear is the influence of ABC TV's version of the story, which formed part of their anthology series *Hour of Mystery*. The episode had gone out on ITV on Saturday 22 June 1957 (following part two of the Jimmy Sangster serial *Motive for Murder*) and starred Anton Diffring as Dr Thackeray (Dr Bonnet in Hammer's film) and Arnold Marle as his assistant. [21] Not only would they repeat their roles in the Hammer version, but Marle would retain the same character name: Dr Ludwig Weisz (though spelt slightly differently, as 'Weiss', in Hammer's script). Interestingly the female lead of the TV show was played by Melissa Stribling, heroine of *Dracula*. Hammer would replace her, ironically, with Hazel Court, heroine of *The Curse of Frankenstein*.

Jimmy Sangster was naturally called upon to add his slant to the story and he wrote his screenplay under the provisional title of *The Man in the Rue Noire*. With Tony Hinds distracted by the continuing negotiations with Columbia, Michael Carreras was called upon to steer Hammer's productions for a while. Indeed, not only was he handed *The Man in the Rue Noire*, but Carreras would go on to produce five of their eight productions of 1959, which would include their next two colour horrors, *The Mummy* and *The Two Faces of Dr Jekyll*.

Jimmy Sangster's adaptation of Lyndon's play tells of the 104-year-old Dr Bonnet, kept alive by a transplant of the uter-parathyroid gland (whatever that is; for the record, parathyroid glands have no prefix and are found in the neck, not the groin) every ten years. Towards the end of each cycle, he requires the use of a fluid to keep him alive, but it also instils in him unwelcome homicidal tendencies. Bonnet's assistant, Ludwig Weiss, refuses to lend a hand in the latest operation when Bonnet declares his intentions of turning his insane research on Janine, the lady in his life (well, the last few weeks of it, at any rate). Peter Cushing was offered the part of Bonnet on completing *The Hound of the Baskervilles* but turned it down. Instead, Anton Diffring was brought in to reprise his TV role, having previously filled Cushing's shoes in the ill-fated *Tales of Frankenstein*. Christopher Lee came in as the reserved Dr Pierre Gerrard, who is blackmailed into operating on Bonnet, as well as becoming embroiled with him in a desperate love triangle with Janine.

Bonnet (Anton Diffring) begins to age in front of the abducted Janine (Hazel Court) in The Man Who Could Cheat Death (1958).

THE MAN WHO COULD CHEAT DEATH

PRINCIPAL PHOTOGRAPHY: 17 November to 30 December 1958
DISTRIBUTION:
Paramount; 83 minutes; Technicolor;
UK: certificate 'X'
UK RELEASE:
TRADE SHOW: 4 June 1959
PREMIÈRE: November 30th, 1959, at the London Plaza
GENERAL RELEASE: On the ABC circuit with 'The Evil That is Eve'
US RELEASE: June 1959

DIRECTOR: Terence Fisher; PRODUCER: Michael Carreras; ASSOCIATE PRODUCER: Anthony Nelson Keys; SCREENPLAY: Jimmy Sangster, from a play by Barré Lyndon; PRODUCTION DESIGNER: Bernard Robinson; DIRECTOR OF PHOTOGRAPHY: Jack Asher; CAMERA OPERATOR: Len Harris; FOCUS PULLER: Harry Oakes; ASSISTANT DIRECTOR: John Peverall; 2ND ASSISTANT DIRECTOR: Tom Walls; 3RD ASSISTANT DIRECTOR: Hugh Harlow; SUPERVISING EDITOR: James Needs; EDITOR: John Dunsford; MUSIC: Richard Rodney Bennett; MUSIC SUPERVISOR: John Hollingsworth; SOUND

RECORDIST: Jock May; MAKE-UP: Roy Ashton; HAIRSTYLIST: Henry Montsash; PRODUCTION MANAGER: Don Weeks; CONTINUITY: Shirley Barnes; WARDROBE: Molly Arbuthnot; PROPERTY MASTER: Tommy Money; PROPERTY BUYER: Eric Hillier; CASHIER: Ken Gordon; STUDIO MANAGER: Arthur Kelly; CONSTRUCTION MANAGER: Mick Lyons; CHIEF ELECTRICIAN: Jack Curtis; MASTER PAINTER: Lawrence Wren; MASTER PLASTERER: Arthur Banks; MASTER CARPENTER: Charles Davis

Anton Diffring (Georges); Hazel Court (Janine); Christopher Lee (Pierre); Arnold Marle (Dr Ludwig Weiss); Delphi Lawrence (Margo); Francis De Wolff (Legris)

UNCREDITED: Gerda Larsen (Street girl), Middleton Woods (Little man), Denis Shaw (Tavern customer), Ian Hewitson (Roget), Frederick Rawlings (Footman), Marie Burke (Woman), Charles Lloyd Pack (Man), John Harrison (Servant), Lockwood West, Ronald Adam, Barry Shawzin (Doctors)

ALSO IN BRITISH PRESSBOOK BUT NOT IN FILM: Michael Ripper (morgue attendant)

Michael Carreras submitted the script to John Trevelyan, Secretary of the BBFC, on 29 October. Reader Audrey Field's comments weren't quite as scathing this time out. She reported on the next day:
  "A man who lights up like an electric-light bulb, so that his bones are seen in outline beneath the flesh, is a good horror gimmick, and this script has its moments of imaginative terror. The only serious difficulty is the end, where 'horror', properly so-called, gives way to a welter of hideous sadism. We had trouble enough over Frankenstein's poor monster blazing like a torch, and the decent sections of the public certainly would not stand for the slow death of a wizened old man of

104, however wicked, in this most painful way. The most that could happen would be for Margo to throw a lamp at him out of frame, after which, for the benefit of those without any imagination, there could be one scream. If this won't do, they should devise another ending to the film."

In the draft script, incidentally, Bonnet's character was called Bruner. John Trevelyan replied to Michael Carreras on 3 November:

"We have now read Jimmy Sangster's script entitled *The Man in the Rue Noir*, [sic] which I return herewith. In general this seems fair enough for an 'X' film, but there are various points of detail on which I would like to comment, as follows:

Pages 3-4. The throttling of the clerk should be discreet, and even more so the operation on him while he is still alive. I think that there should be no indication that the man is, or may be, conscious.

Pages 20-21. We would have no objection to Georges' face glowing luminously at times, but the result should not be too gruesome or macabre. We would want care taken, here and elsewhere, with people's flesh 'sizzling' when Georges touches them. There should certainly be no sound of 'sizzling', and care should be taken about resultant scars which should not look too unpleasant.

Page 23. Although the script generally uses the term 'busts' for Georges' sculptures, this scene, with Janine 'nude to the waist' (but back-view, of course) suggests that another meaning of the word 'bust' might come into it! When, later in the film, we see Georges' masterpieces in a warehouse, we would not want to see a whole lot of nudes 'to the waist' or further.

Page 50. If the 'inter-parathyroid gland' [as per the script] really looks like a 'pickled walnut' it should be all right, even if – as it appears – the film is to be shot in colour. Care should be taken with shots of bits and pieces of people in glass jars; a good many people are squeamish about such things.

Pages 58-59. The killing of Ludwig, as scripted, seems to be discreet enough, but care should be taken with burn scars.

The ageing Georges Bonnet (Anton Diffring) desperately tries to save the last of the life-giving potion he has spilt in The Man Who Could Cheat Death *(1958).*

Page 84. I must ask you to delete or alter the dialogue on this page which is reminiscent of [morgue attendant] Christie's perversion. The particular lines to which I refer are 'That all depends on what you'd be wanting it for...', and 'Female body indeed ... what does 'e think this place is.' The 'leers' of the attendant rubs this in.

Page 85. The murder of the girl seems to take place out of camera range, and we hope that there will be as little of this as possible, leaving it largely to the imagination.

Page 88 and following. Margo 'hideously scarred' and so mad that she giggles senselessly might easily present us with difficulties if not treated with care. We have always taken a strong line about nastily scarred faces and would have to do so again.

Page 97. Georges' transformation is legitimate, but his appearance should not be too ghastly. After all he is only 104 and centenarians do not as a rule look too bad.

Pages 98 and 99. This final scene, as scripted, presents us with difficulties. The burn on Janine's arm should not have 'sizzling', either visual or in sound. Margo should not hold the hot lamp against Georges' face, and there should not be 'a terrible sound of burning flesh', nor 'smoke'. We would not object to the place being on fire and to Georges and Margo perishing in the flames. The whole thing could easily be implied rather than seen without any loss of impact.

"I hope these comments will be helpful and avoid difficulties at later stages."

Audrey Field had also commented on page 98 in her report of 30 October:

"Janine gets a livid burn on the arm. Careful. And no sizzling. Margo should not hold the hot lamp to Bruner's face. Bruner seizes her and she sizzles. We really cannot have this sort of thing. (See opening remarks especially for preposterous shots of Bruner on fire.) I think the death of Margo herself under the pile of burning crates can be worked all right, as we can cut as the crates fall, and see nothing of her body. Why they think people on fire (in Westerns, gangster films, horror films etc, etc) are going to get back the lost cinema audiences, I really do not know."

Just two weeks after they had completed Hound, the same crew (now led by Michael Carreras) began work on The Man Who Could Cheat Death at Bray on Monday 17 November. Shooting continued for six weeks, running over the Christmas holidays and finishing on Tuesday 30 December. Filming took place under the provisional title of The Man in the Rue Noire, reverting to the more familiar title in post-production. As Alfred Cox was still at work on Hound at Hammer House, John Dunsford took over the cutting of The Man Who Could Cheat Death at Bray, while James Needs hovered over both productions in his capacity as supervising editor. Bernard Robinson and Don Mingaye returned to provide some splendid sets and, not surprisingly since the production was shot back-to-back with Hound, there was call for some urgent revamping. As a reminder of the proximity of the two productions, the decorative incense burner seen on the refectory table in Baskerville Hall reappears behind Hazel Court and Anton Diffring in Bonnet's studio in the scene where Weiss takes Gerrard away to discuss the operation. The set for Bonnet's secret hideaway is particularly splendid and packed with the sort of detail expected from Robinson.

To spice things up for the foreign market, Hammer turned from souped-up gore to a risqué nude shot of Hazel Court. "That was only for Europe," she protested, but added with a glint in her eye, "I got paid £2000. I always used to say, 'One [grand] for each bust!'" [22] Long has been the search by Hammer aficionados to find this missing scene, which is not in UK and US prints. Reportedly, the shot in question is pretty fleeting and involves Court exposing one of her breasts while modelling for Diffring, just before the arrival of Arnold Marle. John Peverall remembers shooting the scene: "She was on the set and called me over. She pointed out that the set was supposed to be closed, but that the gantry was full of electricians. It was very hard not to look down." [17] The censor's take on the nude scene was yet to come; in the meantime, a plaster bust of Hazel Court also had to be made. She recalls, "I remember doing the bust of me in the property shop, when they slapped plaster all over me to make it. I wasn't so keen on that."

The film called for Roy Ashton's first solo monster make-up at Hammer. However, though the story slowly builds to the inevitable climax when Bonnet reverts to 104, the elaborate and painstaking make-up – researched, tested and created by Roy Ashton – was condensed into mere seconds in the final film, to the chagrin of Ashton as well as the fans. "It used to take me four hours to make up Anton Diffring each day," remembered Ashton. "It was a difficult job, because I put it on piece by piece, but after a time experience teaches you all sorts of short cuts. Sometimes you can use the same appliances again on the following day if you don't damage them when you take them off." [23]

Being a monster maker was new to Ashton and called upon all his resourcefulness. "You know the string-like lumps of skin you find around the throats of very old people?" he explained. "I was rather vexed as to what to use to simulate this around Anton's neck. I would do it differently now, but at the time I thought of a window in the room next to mine at Bray. It had a fan light operated by thin cords, and I thought, 'Blow me! Those'll do!' I cut them up into small strips, treated them with latex and tissue, and that's what I used." [24] It was on this film that Ashton developed the technique of making veins from blue wool unravelled from his pullover. "For veins I would use blue wool, taking the strands and unravelling them. They are usually composed of three thin strands, and I used to take one, putting it down on the back of a hand, a face, what have you." [24]

On Friday 12 December, Hammer held a tenth anniversary party at the Hind's Head pub in Bray village (a favourite haunt for Hammer employees during lunch breaks). They later celebrated back at the studios with a screening of Dr Morelle – The Case of the Missing Heiress, the company's first official film back in 1948. As the year drew to a close, the Hammer personnel could reflect on their most productive year yet.

SEVEN

Terror from the Tomb

(1 9 5 9)

1959 started with editors John Dunsford and James Needs commencing post-production work on *The Man Who Could Cheat Death* while John Hollingsworth brought in Richard Rodney Bennett to compose the score. Then, following artists' tests on 1 and 7 January, Val Guest returned to Hammer on Monday the 12th to take his crew through the gruelling paces of another war picture. *Yesterday's Enemy*, based on the controversial BBC television play by Peter Newman, would take the action beyond the claustrophobic confines of *Blood Island*'s POW camp to the equally claustrophobic surroundings of the Malayan jungle. Guest assembled a very impressive cast for another harrowing widescreen drama, which proved that the British could give as 'good' as they got when it came to wartime barbarism.

The production began at Shepperton Studios (which accounts for the unfamiliar construction crew, led by Jack Bolam), where shooting continued for five weeks up to Saturday 14 February. The move to Shepperton had allowed Bernard Robinson to design a huge rotating jungle set. Val Guest remembers a particular incident on the stage: "There's a big scene in the film where the Japanese attack the village and blow up the huts with grenades; it was done with explosive charges set exactly where the grenades were expected to fall. The huts went up beautifully, but the heat from the blaze caught the studio roof. Luckily, the studio had its own fire brigade on hand to put it out." [1]

Assistant director John Peverall also recalled the incident. "The special effects man Bill Warrington worked on that. When the British came into the Japanese camp in their straw huts, they were throwing hand grenades. Bill had not wound the explosives tight enough. Instead of getting a big bang, there was too much flame and the straw huts started to burn down. I rushed to the stage and called the fire brigade. Two men came running in and saw the fire. They grabbed the hose on the wall and called for Fred to turn on the water. The water came out and sort of went, 'Neeeerrruuaawmnp' – no water pressure. The local fire brigade had to put that out." [2]

The crew returned to Bray on Monday 16 February for completion. Robinson now erected the swamp set, through which the soldiers have to wade. Harry Oakes recalls: "The swamp set was at Bray. It was quite a good set, that was, and it about filled Stage 1. If we had to go in there with waders on, we got an extra £2 a day, so I made every point of getting in there. When it was obvious the actors were 20 feet away, I still used to insist on measuring it!" Indeed, on the first day back at Bray, Harry recorded in his diary, "Hectic day on the swamp sequence. I got a soaking!"

Len Harris remembered an amusing incident involving the Japanese soldiers. "There were supposed to be Japanese soldiers looking for these two escaped prisoners. There weren't many Japanese extras in the guild – only one or two – so they found some chaps around a dock to be soldiers. They couldn't speak English at all and had to have an interpreter. Val Guest said to the interpreter, 'What I want them to do is just creep along the river looking around.' Just the one thing. So Val said, 'Let's try a take.' The leading one sort of trips up and falls spread eagle into the river – plop! All the rest of them got to that same point and they all went into the river one after the other!" [3]

Val Guest remembers his Japanese soldiers with affection, "Nearly all of those Japanese extras we had were Chinese waiters and, after we made that picture, every time I went to a Chinese restaurant, all the waiters would say, 'Hello Val!'" Switchboard operator Christine Stevens also remembers them. "Jimmy Vaughan used to bring all the Oriental crowd down. They used to sit and play cards all day. The money that used to change hands was amazing. Stanley Baker was a typical Welshman. He was lovely, but he didn't have a lot to do with anybody. He used to go and play cards with all these Chinese extras, then go on the set and do a scene and come back and play cards again."

James Needs and Alfred Cox then took the film into post-production. Guest, as always, followed the editing with keen interest, but had to fight to get his own way with the final soundtrack when he decided he did not want a conventional music score. As he explained, "I had a terrible battle. I orchestrated the jungle sounds to make a score and they thought I was out of my mind. They had a composer standing by, I think it was Jimmy Bernard, but they let me get away with it."

Meanwhile, *The Man Who Could Cheat Death* was being submitted to John Trevelyan, still under its working title of *The Man in the Rue Noire*. Examiner Audrey Field reported on 18 February: "Seen by President, Secretary, IB, JC, AOF. Story is on the papers, the script having been submitted. The present version is black and white with certain colour inserts, and any comments made at this stage cannot be considered final, as the film must be seen in colour."

Hammer Productions 1959

- ✦ YESTERDAY'S ENEMY
- ✦ THE MUMMY
- ✦ THE UGLY DUCKLING
- ✦ THE STRANGLERS OF BOMBAY
- ✦ DON'T PANIC CHAPS
- ✦ NEVER TAKE SWEETS FROM A STRANGER
- ✦ HELL IS A CITY
- ✦ THE TWO FACES OF DR JEKYLL

FEATURETTE
- ✦ TICKET TO HAPPINESS

OPPOSITE: *Kharis (Christopher Lee) rises from the swamp in* The Mummy *(1959).*

Colonel Yamazaki (Philip Ahn) turns the tables on Captain Langford (Stanley Baker) in Yesterday's Enemy (1959).

YESTERDAY'S ENEMY

PRINCIPAL PHOTOGRAPHY: 12 January to March 1959
DISTRIBUTION: Columbia; 95 minutes; b/w; Megascope;
UK: certificate 'A'
UK RELEASE:
  PREMIÈRE: 17 September 1959 at the Empire
  GENERAL RELEASE: 19 October 1959 on the ABC circuit

DIRECTOR: Val Guest; PRODUCER: Michael Carreras; SCREENPLAY: Peter Newman; PRODUCTION DESIGNER: Bernard Robinson; ASSISTANT ART DIRECTOR: Don Mingaye; DIRECTOR OF PHOTOGRAPHY: Arthur Grant; CAMERA OPERATOR: Len Harris; FOCUS PULLER: Harry Oakes; CLAPPER/LOADER: Alan McDonald; GRIPS: Albert Cowland; ASSISTANT DIRECTOR: John Peverall; 2ND ASSISTANT DIRECTOR: Tom Walls; 3RD ASSISTANT DIRECTOR: Hugh Harlow; SUPERVISING EDITOR: James Needs; EDITOR: Alfred Cox; SOUND RECORDIST: Buster Ambler; SOUND CAMERAMAN: Jimmy Dooley; BOOM: Peter Dukelaw; SOUND MAINTENANCE: Eric Vincent; MAKE-UP: Roy Ashton; HAIR STYLIST: Henry Montsash; PRODUCTION MANAGER: TS Lyndon Haynes; CONTINUITY:

Cheryl Booth; WARDROBE: Molly Arbuthnot; SPECIAL EFFECTS: Bill Warrington, Charles Willoughby; TECHNICAL ADVISOR: Peter Newman; STILLS: Tom Edwards; PUBLICIST: Colin Reid; PROPERTY MASTER: Frank Burden; FLOOR PROPS: T Frewer; PRODUCTION BUYER: Eric Hillier; CASTING DIRECTOR: Dorothy Holloway; CONSTRUCTION MANAGER: Jack Bolam; ELECTRICAL ENGINEER: SF Hillyer; MASTER PAINTER: S Taylor; MASTER PLASTERER: S Rodwel; MASTER CARPENTER: ED Wheatley; PRODUCTION SECRETARY: Doreen Jones

Stanley Baker (Captain Langford); Guy Rolfe (Padre); Leo McKern (Max); Gordon Jackson (Sgt. McKenzie), David Oxley (Doctor), Richard Pasco (Lt. Hastings); Russell Waters (Brigadier); Philip Ahn (Yamazaki); Bryan Forbes (Dawson); Wolfe Morris (Informer); Edwina Carroll (Suni); David Lodge (Perkins); Percy Herbert (Wilson); Barry Lowe (Turner); Alan Keith (Bendish); Howard Williams (Davies); Timothy Bateson (Simpson); Arthur Lovegrove (Patrick); Donald Churchill (Elliott); Nicholas Brady (Orderly); Barry Steele (Brown)

John Trevelyan wrote to Michael Carreras on the 19th:

"We saw your film *The Man in the Rue Noir* [sic] yesterday. I think that for the most part we should not have very much trouble, but there are certain scenes which are not acceptable to us in their present versions and there are other things on which we cannot make definite decisions until we have seen the colour version. Of course the film will be in the 'X' category. The following are the points which I must raise with you:

Reel 1. The murder by Bonner of the clerk in the park was almost invisible. From what we could see it appeared to be all right, but presumably there will be clear definition on the colour

print. We must therefore have a slight reservation about this scene until we can see it in colour.
Reel 2. We are worried about the burns on Margo's face. As I said in my letter on the script, 'There should certainly be no sound of sizzling, and care should be taken about resultant scars which should not look too unpleasant.' Here again we must reserve a decision until we see this scene in colour. I would like to have a confirmation that the sound-track will not include any sound of 'sizzling'.
Reel 3. As you expected, we shall not be able to accept the three front view shots of Janine posing in the nude. I am aware that there is dialogue over these shots but no doubt you can alter this without difficulty.
Reel 5. We think that the gland will look all right (I remember that in the script it was described as looking like a 'pickled walnut'!) but must reserve final judgment until we see it in colour.
Reel 6. The strangling of the old doctor [Weiss] seems to be all right except for the inter-cut close shot in the middle. We would like you to remove this. There was a brief flash in colour of the old man afterwards. This may be all right, but we would like to hold a final decision until a second viewing.
Reel 9. We would like you to reduce as much as possible of the shots of Margo in the cell. She is mad and badly scarred in the face, and the combination is really unpleasant. We would not expect you to remove everything, but do ask for a reduction.

"We are more worried about the final scenes in which Bonner is seen in flames. In my letter on your script I wrote about this scene as follows: 'This final scene, as scripted, presents us with difficulties. The burn on Janine's arm should not have 'sizzling', either visual or in sound. Margo should not hold the hot lamp against Georges' face, and there should not be 'a terrible sound of burning flesh', nor 'smoke'. We would not object to the place being on fire and to Georges and Margo perishing in the flames. The whole thing could easily be implied rather than seen without any loss of impact.' You have taken action on the first part of what I said, but there are several shots of Bonner staggering about in flames. We always dislike shots of people actually seen on fire, and I hope you will find some way of getting over this difficulty. If you have alternative takes it would be a great advantage. Failing this I must ask you to reduce the scene substantially so that the shots of Bonner in flames are cut to a minimum. This is the only scene in the picture which is going to present really serious difficulties for us and I hope that, in view of the warning that I gave, you will be able to produce an alternative version which we can accept.

"I think that the film was well made and convincing, and I think that it will be a success."

Michael Carreras replied to Trevelyan point-by-point on 24 February:

"Reel 1. The murder of the clerk in the park will, of course, be much clearer in the colour print, but I am sure that when you view this you will find nothing to trouble you here. This sequence has titles over.
Reel 2. The cuts of Margo's face showing the burn marks have been kept to the necessary minimum, and we have in no way tried to get special horror effects here. I assure you that the sound track will not include any sound of sizzling.
Reel 3. Naturally I am disappointed that we are not allowed to retain the shots of Janine in the nude. However, artistic as they may be I can see your point of view, but no doubt the foreign version will benefit greatly from their inclusion.
Reel 5. I am sure you will find nothing offensive in the gland.
Reel 6. We have removed as per your request the intercut shot of Ludwig.
Reel 9. In this reel, which we will be re-submitting to you in the next couple of days, you will find that we have reduced to what we consider the necessary minimum the shots of Margo in the cell, and we have also reduced substantially the shots of Bonner on fire, retaining only what we hope you will agree is the necessary minimum."

An internal note from Audrey Field on 25 February reads: "Reel 9 seen again by FNC/AOF. We think that the shots of Margo's face (though not heavily cut since the first viewing) may pass in the completed colour film, but that the shots of Georges on fire can, and should, be further reduced."

By April Hammer had again changed their position and were now seeking an 'A' certificate to widen their audience. An undated memo in the BBFC file explains, "Mr Bachmann (Paramount) is distributing *The Man in the Rue Noir* [sic] and wants you to see it again with a view to cutting for 'A' category." The BBFC re-viewed the film with this in mind on 2 April, now under the revised title of *The Man Who Could Cheat Death*, and an internal report was issued by Frank Crofts:

"We saw the whole film today. We do not think it is possible to cut it for 'A'. The general idea – a man murdering people in order to obtain parathyroid gland with which to keep himself alive – is much better left to 'X'. But in any case there are several scenes, apparently necessary for the story, which would have to be removed, eg. the attacks on Margo and Prof Weiss; shots of the victim's glands in jars; the mad and disfigured Margo in a cage or cell; and the whole of the final scene with Margo's face much in evidence, the transformation of Georges to a grotesquely old man and the burning of him and Margo. No doubt the film could end with the words 'He didn't perform the operation' (and possibly the rescue of Janine). It might be possible to keep certain shots of glands, but not that of the prostitute whom he kills – indeed the whole incident of her being picked up and killed should not remain. This is a reasonably competent film as an 'X' and would probably be quite successful: to cut out scenes unsuitable for 'A' would mutilate the film and leave it without a proper ending."

John Trevelyan wrote to Miss S White of Paramount Film Services on 3 April explaining the Board's findings. Paramount replied to Trevelyan on the 8th: "Replying to your letter of April 3rd it has been decided, as you foretold, to accept the 'X' certificate for *The Man Who Could Cheat Death*, and we would therefore be glad to have your certificate as soon as possible."

However, behind the scenes there were still problems. A further note of caution accompanied Crofts' report of 2 April: "We doubt whether the shots of Georges on fire in Reel 9 have been reduced since we saw the film on 25.2.59. We should like to see the reel again before we decide whether it will do even for 'X'." The reel was re-viewed the following day, and Crofts and Field reported: "We saw R.9 with the President, NKB and IB. It was agreed that the shots of Georges on fire must be considerably shortened and the reel be sent in again."

It is not clear from BBFC records how this was resolved, but the 'X' Certificate was finally issued on 8 April. While the deliberations over *The Man Who Could Cheat Death* went on, Hammer was busy on its next horror bonanza.

The *Daily Cinema* reported on Wednesday 20 August 1958: "Because of the fantastic business being done world-wide by Hammer's Technicolor version of *Dracula*, Universal-International, its distributors, have made over to Jimmy Carreras' organisation the remake rights to their entire library of classic horror films.

"This news, announced simultaneously today on both sides of the Atlantic – by Al Daff, U-I's chief in New York and by James Carreras, Hammer's managing director in London – adds up to one of the biggest co-production deals ever entered into between a major American company and a British producing organisation. Explaining Universal's decision to place their library of films at Hammer's disposal, Al Daff has stated that it is due entirely to the phenomenal business which *Dracula* is doing not only in the UK, the US and Canada, but in every country in the world. Wherever it has been shown, he points out, it has played in major theatres as a top feature in its own right. The result has been a global trail of broken box office records.

"In London, Jimmy Carreras describes the deal as 'one of the most exciting things that has ever happened to us.' He says: 'Universal have the greatest library of classic horror and shocker subjects of any company in the world. That they should have made this library of over a dozen famous titles available to us is a wonderful honour. Their decision is a measure of their delight at the box office success of *Dracula* and its quality as a production. Al Daff has told me personally that he knows of no company in the world that could have delivered a better job. Last night, when I spoke to him on the transatlantic telephone, I told him we have already chosen our first three subjects. They are *The Phantom of the Opera*, *The Invisible Man* and *The Mummy*.' All three will be filmed in Technicolor and will be made at Bray Studios by the same team responsible for *Dracula*, *The Revenge of Frankenstein* and *The Curse of Frankenstein*."

Hammer's choice was perhaps a little predictable and eventually they whittled the list down to that popular Universal monster, the Mummy. *The Phantom of the Opera* would follow in 1961, but *The Invisible Man* would never be realised. *The Mummy* again fell into the hands of Michael Carreras to produce. "This was my first Gothic. But it was the one Gothic that had that sort of 'pretty' element – this

Kharis (Christopher Lee) throttles John Banning (Peter Cushing) in The Mummy (1959).

THE MUMMY

PRINCIPAL PHOTOGRAPHY: 23 February to 16 April 1959
DISTRIBUTION:
  UK: Rank; certificate 'X'
  US: Universal-International.
88 minutes; Technicolor
UK RELEASE:
  TRADE SHOW: 20 August 1959 at the Hammer Theatre, Hammer House
  PREMIÈRE: 25 September 1959 at the London Pavilion, Picadilly Circus
  GENERAL RELEASE: 23 October 1959, on the ABC circuit with Bed Without Breakfast
US RELEASE: December 1959, with Curse of the Undead

DIRECTOR: Terence Fisher; PRODUCER: Michael Carreras; ASSOCIATE PRODUCER: Anthony Nelson Keys; SCREENPLAY: Jimmy Sangster; PRODUCTION DESIGNER: Bernard Robinson; ASSISTANT ART DIRECTOR: Don Mingaye; EGYPTIAN ADVISER: Andrew Low; MODELLER: Margaret Carter; DIRECTOR OF PHOTOGRAPHY: Jack Asher; CAMERA OPERATOR: Len Harris; FOCUS PULLER: Harry Oakes; CLAPPER: Alan MacDonald; ASSISTANT DIRECTOR: John Peverall; 2ND ASSISTANT DIRECTOR: Tom Walls; 3RD ASSISTANT DIRECTOR: Hugh Harlow; SUPERVISING EDITOR: James Needs; EDITOR: Alfred Cox; ASSISTANT EDITOR: Chris Barnes; MUSIC: Franz Reizenstein;

MUSIC SUPERVISOR: John Hollingsworth; SOUND RECORDIST: Jock May; BOOM OPERATOR: Jim Perry; SOUND CAMERA OPERATOR: Al Thorne; SOUND MAINTENANCE: Charles Bouvet; SOUND EDITOR: Roy Hyde; MAKE-UP: Roy Ashton; HAIRSTYLIST: Henry Montsash; PRODUCTION MANAGER: Don Weeks; CONTINUITY: Marjorie Lavelly; WARDROBE: Molly Arbuthnot; WARDROBE ASSISTANT: Rosemary Burrows; CASTING: Dorothy Holloway; SPECIAL EFFECTS: Bill Warrington; STUNTS: Eddie Powell; PROPERTY MASTER: Tommy Money; PROPERTY BUYER: Eric Hillier; CASHIER: Ken Gordon; STUDIO MANAGER: Arthur Kelly; CONSTRUCTION MANAGER: Mick Lyons; CHIEF ELECTRICIAN: Jack Curtis; MASTER PAINTER: Lawrence Wren; MASTER PLASTERER: Arthur Banks; MASTER CARPENTER: Charles Davis; STILLS CAMERAMAN: Tom Edwards; PUBLICIST: Colin Reid

Peter Cushing (John Banning); Christopher Lee (The Mummy/Kharis); Yvonne Furneaux (Isobel/Ananka); Eddie Byrne (Inspector Mulrooney); Felix Aylmer (Stephen Banning); Raymond Huntley (Joseph Whemple); George Pastell (Mehemet Bey); Michael Ripper (Poacher); George Woodbridge (Police Constable); Harold Goodwin (Pat); Denis Shaw (Mike); Gerald Lawson (Irish Customer); Willoughby Gray (Dr Reilly); John Stuart (Coroner); David Browning (Police Sergeant); Frank Sieman (Bill); Stanley Meadows (Attendant); Frank Singuineau (Head Porter)

Egyptian bit. I think I like that more than the horror aspect. I've never been into the Gothic; that was Tony ... but this was the one that fascinated me. I wanted to work with Terry, too – I liked Terry very much."[1] It's interesting that Carreras should have regarded The Mummy as his first 'Gothic'. Based in Egypt in 2000 BC and later in the little English hamlet of Engerfield in 1898, it seems no more deserving of the label of 'Gothic' than 'The Man Who Could Cheat Death' does, with its Paris backdrop of 1890.

Universal had produced several Mummy films, starting with the Karloff classic *The Mummy* in 1932 and progressing through a series of four 1940s programmers featuring another Mummy, Kharis (Karloff had played a largely unbandaged character called Imhotep), before trashing the Egyptian juggernaut in the inevitable *Abbott and Costello Meet the Mummy*. Jimmy Sangster plundered the series to come up with an amalgam of ideas that would provide the basis for another Hammer classic. From the original, Sangster took the Scroll of Life that had brought Im-Ho Tep back from the grave, rejecting the tiresome 'Tana leaves' routine of the Kharis cycle. From the latter, Sangster took several ideas to form the framework of his story, including the central characters of the High Priest Kharis and the Princess Ananka, the Banning family (who had desecrated Ananka's tomb and provoked the wrath of the Mummy) and the great God 'Karnak' (actually a place-name). In an inspired touch, Sangster took away the pronounced limp that had made the Mummy seem so unthreatening in the Universal series and gave it instead to Cushing's John Banning. The swamp from the climax of *The Mummy's Ghost* was used, but now to more spectacular effect, and the same film's idea of Ananka reincarnated (which had featured in the Karloff film, too) was modified so that Banning's wife merely bears an uncanny resemblance to her.

Michael Carreras submitted the script to the BBFC at the beginning of February and the Secretary, John Trevelyan, wrote back to him on the 5th:

"We have now read the script of *The Mummy*. In general this seems to be fair enough material for the 'X' category – a Sangster cocktail – but there are some comments that we should like to make as follows:

Pp. 15 & 29. Banning's mad screams should be tolerable.

Pp. 40-1. The killing of Banning by the Mummy should not be over-done. We would not want prolonged shots of throttling, close-ups of Banning's eyes turning up as he is throttled, or the 'cracking snap as Banning's neck breaks'.

P. 56. We hope that you will be reasonable about the screams when the Nubians are being slaughtered out of frame. The six maidens appear to be slaughtered in frame and I must give you a strong caution about this, and about any subsequent shots of the maidens weltering in their gore, eg. P. 58. If not shot with discretion these scenes [detailed above] might cause us a lot of trouble.

Pp. 60-1. While we would accept the tongue being cut out off screen we would not want the 'small piece of mangled, bloody flesh' held up afterwards for public view. Nor would we want shots of Kharis after the operation with blood coursing down his chin.

Pp. 66-7. The killing of Joseph needs the same kind of caution as that given for the killing of Stephen Banning. The throttling should not be too long, there should be no unpleasant close-ups and once again we should not like the 'brittle snap of the breaking neck'.

P.68. The shots of the Mummy with 'a great gaping hole in the bandages and what passed for flesh underneath, but which is in fact a dirty grey, mould like substance', should not be as unpleasant and gruesome as these words suggest that it might be.

P.86. The attempted throttling by John should not be too long.

P. 101. Here again the Mummy's appearance should not be too gruesome.

P. 102. As before throttling should be reasonably short.

P. 103. We would not like shots of the Mummy breaking Mehmet's arm and back, nor would we like cracks and crunches in the sound track.

P. 104. As a minor, but important, point, we would prefer a blow on the head to 'a wicked blow on the side of the neck' since these neck blows are imitable and dangerously effective.

Pp. 105-6. The final shots of the Mummy after both barrels are let off at close range into its face should not be gruesome or revolting. Sangster's vivid description makes us feel that they might be, eg. 'almost non-existent face' and 'practically nothing left, great holes having been torn in the bandages and in what passes for flesh underneath'.

"Although I made these detailed comments, you know our policy about these pictures so well now that I feel I can safely leave it to you to produce a picture made in such a way as to give us both the minimum of trouble."

Carreras submitted a revised script on 18 February: "I am sending you herewith a copy of the revised script of *The Mummy* for your comments. The alterations are all minor, with the exception of two sequences. The first consists of scenes 99 to 148, set in 2000 BC, which is a new sequence entirely. The second is a changed finale, commencing at scene 244."

Michael Carreras had employed Egyptian expert Andrew Low to supervise the production and together they had fleshed out the new flashback sequence to ancient Egypt, thereby allowing us the elaborate funeral procession. Margaret Robinson remembers Andrew Low: "Descended from Charles II on the wrong side of the blanket, fringe royalty, aristocracy, totally out of his century. He was looked upon as a snob and an intellectual; not one who dabbled in everything but one who was expert in everything – a bit of a modern Leonardo. He was compiling a Romany English dictionary and he was godfather to half the gypsy children in the West Drayton area, so he was an interesting one-off-type character."

Trevelyan replied to Carreras on Monday 23 February, the day filming was due to commence: "We have had a look at the revised script of The Mummy, and have the following comments to make: Scenes 99-148. There appear to be only two problems in these sequences:-
a) As scripted the Princess's costume is either transparent or non-existent, and I imagine that the same would apply to other maidens, including those slaughtered. I suggest that you take the precaution of having alternative takes for this scene in case, as I expect, they present difficulties as a result of the nudity.
b) The slaughter of the six maidens, as scripted, looks pretty unpleasant, and I must repeat the cautions given in my letter of 5th February.
Scenes 244-267. It is difficult to state whether this, from the angle of censorship, is a good exchange from the first script or not. It sounds rather unpleasant, particularly where 'great chunks of Kharis fly off in all directions' and where he is 'writhing about in blind agony'. If the scene were shot as scripted we would be unlikely to pass it."

"You seem to have made a few alterations as a result of my letter of 5th February, but some of the points that I made have not received attention, including sounds of bones snapping. As I told you, I am quite prepared to offer my advice over the processional and burial scenes when you reach that stage of production."

Throughout February, Andrew Low, with the sterling team of Bernard Robinson and Don Mingaye, drew up numerous designs of Egyptian artefacts, jewellery and furniture to recapture the tombs of the pharaohs and all things ancient Egyptian. Even Robinson's future wife, Margaret Carter, was re-employed to sculpt some of the props and masks.

Margaret Robinson remembers working on the film: "A lot of things were sent away to be made, because Andrew was very angry. In the procession there were bald-headed little priests carrying Ushabti, little vase things, and these had been made somewhere else and sent in. There were little Egyptian figures on the sides in slight relief and Andrew said, 'These will have to go back, Bernie, they've got the noses wrong. Those are Hittite, not Egyptian!' Bernard naturally didn't send them back, because who was going to notice – in a funeral procession with a sacred cow, a leopard and a lot of very nubile dancing girls – a Hittite nose on a small vase? Andrew Low was that sort of perfectionist. He was the advisory expert on Egyptology and he wanted everything to be exactly right. He waived some things, like the wax in the nose of the princess for the embalming scene, because it wasn't going to look pretty as well as not being very comfortable for the actress.

"I made the head of Hathor and the mask of Anubis, because I remember making that mask very large. I didn't know who was going to wear it, you see, and normally I do very careful measurements of whoever is wearing the mask. This I fitted over my landlord, who was a very big man, and I worked on top of layers of jersey so that it was a big mask. But when I was in Bernard's drawing office and the man came in to be fitted the day of the shooting, the doorway was filled with something a bit like Dave Prowse, the biggest Turk you ever saw or pictured, and he was naked from the waist up. Well, I had to put this mask on him and it was too small. I eased it out, but I made things strong – I always made things to last – and it was on a very strong piano-wire framework. I finally had to let him go off in it and I could see a little trickle of blood going down his back! A lot of the modelling, all the background stuff, was farmed out to Elstree. I think Arthur Healey made the full-length Anubis, but looked at closely, they weren't that wonderful, because they worked at speed."

Stephen Banning (Felix Aylmer) reads the scroll of life and unwittingly wakes the guardian of the tomb in The Mummy (1959).

The same production team was brought back from *The Man Who Could Cheat Death*, the main exceptions being Marjorie Lavelly on continuity, Alfred Cox as editor and Franz Reizenstein for the music. The film was again spearheaded by Peter Cushing and Christopher Lee under the direction of Terence Fisher. A fine support cast was assembled. Beautiful 30-year-old French actress Yvonne Furneaux played Banning's wife, while Felix Aylmer starred in the first of his two Hammer projects that year. Raymond Huntley was no stranger to horror: he had played Count Dracula on the London stage in the mid-1920s, later touring the US in the Hamilton Deane/John L Balderston adaptation while Bela Lugosi led a parallel company. And in the background was a host of Hammer 'rep' players: George Pastell, Michael Ripper, George Woodbridge, Harold Goodwin and Denis Shaw.

Shooting began at Bray on Monday 23 February with a projected budget of around £100,000. Principal photography took just under eight weeks, finishing on Thursday 16 April, including just over a week at Shepperton to film the archaeological sequence and the procession flashback on their more spacious stages. Harry Oakes' diary notes that Week One was devoted to the bog sequences, Week Two to Shepperton (finishing on Monday 9 March), that the coroner's office was sited on Stage 3 and the tomb interior on Stage 2. In the final week, he recorded a bit of typical Hammer camaraderie on Wednesday 15 April: "We had Peter Cushing's beer for lunch."

Harry Oakes recollects the crew's Shepperton stint: "All the big scenes with the tomb blowing up, the parade of all the courtesans and all the women parading around was shot at Shepperton, because we had to shoot that a couple of times. I'm pretty sure it was three times. We shot one where they were topless. I remember, too, the scene with Peter Cushing and Raymond Huntley when they blew up the tomb. This enormous bang went off and it was quite close to the artists. I remember weeks later, when I was in the production office looking for an inventory of some kind, I noticed on the desk there was an invoice from a Harley Street doctor saying it was so many guineas for examining Mr Peter Cushing's ears. I suppose it was an insurance thing."

Again, a lot of the success of the movie was down to Jack Asher's rich colour photography, highlighting Robinson's beautiful sets. "I did bring extra coloured gelatine lighting into play," observed Asher, "especially in the tomb scenes. I also introduced a form of air cleaning; because we were shooting on a large background, the back spotlights would immediately pick up any smoke or haze. The studio air plant was completely ineffective in clearing this. We had the painter take his high-pressure air-gun filled with water into the overhead catwalks. Immediately before each shot, he would spray the air at the top of the studio. The fine particles of water would descend, bringing the smoke particles with them, leaving the atmosphere crystal clear." [4]

Harry Oakes recalls an incident at Shepperton involving veteran actor Felix Aylmer. "He said to Len, 'These spectacles I have, are they going to be upsetting at all?' Of course, Jack Asher was nearby and he jumped in and said, 'Oh no, Felix. Not at all, but what you want to do is use your eyes and not your head. If you raise your head, then the lamps on the ground would reflect in the glass, so if you look up, try and just look up with your eyes.' And Felix said, 'Well, I only asked, because I'm only wearing the frames. I haven't any lenses in them.' I don't think Jack spoke to him for several days after that!"

The interior of Banning's house was erected on Bray's large Stage 1. The outside of ballroom Stage 3, with its arched French windows, doubled as its exterior and can be glimpsed briefly as the Mummy strides up to the house to attack John Banning. On the Bray external lot a sloping area of ground was constructed out of old railway sleepers and gravel and covered with grass, becoming known as 'The Mound'. This was first used in The Mummy as the bank down which the crate containing Kharis slides into the bog. It would be used regularly in Hammer's films at Bray up until they left in 1966 and was finally struck in 1969.

Pivotal to the production was a truly outstanding performance by Christopher Lee as Kharis, who, severely restricted by Roy Ashton's brilliant Mummy make-up, still manages to convey the full range of emotions from anger to overwhelming sadness with only his expressive movements and evocative eyes. This is exemplified in the scene where he stands helplessly before the image of his beloved princess in the shape of Isobel Banning. By bringing this element of sympathy to the role, Lee gives his characterisation an inner depth noticeably missing from Universal's Kharis cycle, where the Mummy was portrayed as a mindless automaton. Together with Lee's unprecedented dynamism, it makes for a much more exciting Mummy to watch. As Christopher Lee explains, "There was this contrast between this unstoppable machine, which is how I saw him, smashing glass and iron bars, killing people, like a robot out of control, and the fact that there was still a mind there and a memory and a gentleness, but only in one instance. I had a great sadness. That is the quality that I've tried to put into all these creatures."

Make-up artist Roy Ashton painstakingly researched the process of mummification, making countless sketches before he set to work on the final make-up. "I did a great deal of research first," he confirmed. "I consulted the usual books on Egyptology and also paid a visit to the British Museum, where they had a mummy in a great big case: you can examine the quality of the skin and everything really guided me. In those days there was a considerable interest in the subject, since there had been an exhibition of Egyptian works in London. I think they had discovered another pharaoh in some remote grave or something. Consequently, there was quite a bit of literature available about it, with many reproductions in colour. I always cut anything out of periodicals which I assume may possibly be of use to me in times to come.

"With that as a basis, I tried to recreate the effect on Chris Lee's face. I cast his head in plaster, so that whatever you made on it would fit because you invariably got the exact dimensions. I started off with a zip-fastener that I fixed on the model and built up from there onwards. I fabricated something I could pull into the zipper, like a sock covered up with strips of worn-out rag. An old handkerchief torn into shreds resembled the windings. I had to apply them one by one, until the whole head was clothed. Then, with rubber and plastic skin, I shaped the face. This operation lasted about one hour and a half." [5]

The make-up was not without its cost, though, as Ashton explained. "Unfortunately I didn't realise that this, my first attempt at Mummy make-up, would adhere so closely to his face. It was very uncomfortable for Chris, because there was nowhere really for him to breathe! Actually, the only place where the air could get into the make-up was around the eye holes, but in the later Mummy films, I realised that I could still suggest the appearance of a Mummy in a way that allowed for the presence of air-holes and all sorts of cavities that prevented pressure on the actor's face. The bandages, by the way, were done by the wardrobe department, but we worked together on that. The bandages were wound in such a way that they appeared as they originally did on actual Mummies, but of course they had to have built-in support, otherwise they would have fallen

Kharis (Christopher Lee) breaks into the lunatic asylum to kill Stephen Banning in The Mummy (1959).

straight down when he moved. They were reinforced with cotton wool and sewn together, so in effect they became a kind of uniform into which he could step. To make the join between the facial make-up and the bandages, I used some very old rags, which I made look hard with plaster."[6]

For Lee, this was to be another physically demanding role. At one stage he almost dislocated his shoulder when the prop door he was meant to burst through in order to kill Raymond Huntley had been left locked. The final sequence was also exhausting; because Yvonne Furneaux had to play unconscious, he had to carry her dead weight and it was an enormous strain on his neck, arms and back. Lee remembers, "The only way I could breathe was through the eyeholes and every time I breathed out it kind of fluttered. The only funny side was that, although I didn't speak when I was the Mummy, they could certainly hear me cursing: every single word I said. I had a very choice vocabulary during the making of that film and I used it most of the time, particularly in the swamp scenes where Yvonne Furneaux was whispering, 'Don't drop me, don't drop me!' And I'm crashing against all these pipes and things that are providing the bubbles in the tank. The language I was using trying to carry this girl, and smashing through windows and doors – well, they heard every word I said, which I suppose must have been very funny in some respects."

It was Roy Ashton who spotted the amazing likeness of stuntman Eddie Powell (born 9 March 1927) to Christopher Lee when working on The Death of Uncle George. He therefore suggested bringing him in as stunt double for Lee in The Mummy, an association which would take them through to Hammer's final horror in 1975, To the Devil a Daughter, and beyond, right up to the BBC production of Gormenghast in 1999, just before Powell's death in 2000. "Roy Ashton said, 'You'd be a very good double for Christopher Lee,'" Powell remembered. "I said, 'Who's Christopher Lee?' I'd never heard of him. At Hammer they used to get the heads of department around a table before the film started, so they could thrash out all the problems, and the next film that was made by Hammer with Chris in, they mentioned my name and that's when I actually started doubling for Chris."[7]

It's Eddie Powell we see as the Mummy takes the shot gun blasts in the chest from Peter Cushing. Christopher Lee recalls, "I did it in rehearsal with a much smaller charge. They didn't think it was very convincing, so they got Eddie to do it." Eddie remembered, "Yes, that was me. You can see the difference. You'll see that Chris has got a sharper nose than me, so if you look at the mask, you'll see it's sharper in outline. Chris actually smashed through the doors. It was all balsa wood and toffee glass and all that sort of thing, so really he shouldn't have hurt himself. Then for the shot blasts onto the chest, that was me. I had a breast plate underneath all the gear with a built-up section with explosive charge in, which was wired up to solenoid contacts on my finger tips, so when I pulled forward, I pressed one and one charge knocked me one way. Then I took another couple of steps and pressed the other one, which knocked me back on that one. Then I ended up being washed down by all these people from wardrobe, because all the black charge had got into the suit – that was the best part of it really!"[7]

It was also Eddie who emerged, and later submerged, in the swamp. "Funnily enough, they thought that was going to take a hell of a long time to do. I did it all in one take and Michael Carreras said, 'Whatever money you're paying him, double it!' I'd saved them so much time when they could be shooting other things, so it worked out very well."[8] It wasn't easy, as he explained. "It was a bit awkward because the suit itself was made up of something that floats and if you try to get down under the water with something that floats – it's impossible. I ended up with this huge weight in one hand and had to drag myself down to get to the point where I was sinking down with the Scroll of Life. And I had to hang on to this thing, waiting for all this crap on top to close up, so it wouldn't look like someone had just gone down."[7]

Assistant director John Peverall recalls the 2nd unit shooting the climax: "In the close shots for the shooting scene, we had a dummy of the Mummy that would turn and then all the guns would be fired at it. On Stage 2 of Bray we had a very small tank. Bill Warrington was the special effects man. Towards the end of the filming, we just had little shots like that to do. I asked Bill to explain to me how the shot was supposed to work. He had this piece of wood with a bunch of nails in it, with wires running to them. He said, 'You get the camera rolling. When you say 'Action,' the prop guys will turn the dummy, and then I'll get all the charges going.' I responded, saying, 'OK, let's do a rehearsal now, just so everyone knows what we are doing.' So I said, 'Action.' The prop men turned the dummy and he ran his key along the row of nails, forgetting it was a rehearsal. Of course, everything blew up, so we went to lunch!"[10]

The chemistry between Peter Cushing and Christopher Lee is nothing short of electrifying in this, their fourth team venture for Hammer. As with the climax of Dracula before it, Cushing again contributed to the action: "When I saw the posters advertising the film, I noticed that Christopher Lee, who was playing the name part, had a large hole in his diaphragm with a beam of light passing through it, which was never referred to in the script, so I inquired how it got there. 'Oh,' said the publicity man, 'that's just to help sell the picture.' 'Oh', I thought, 'that's just not on.' John Banning (my part) was attacked by Kharis, the Mummy, so I asked Terry if I could grab a harpoon hanging on the wall of Banning's study and, during the struggle for survival, drive it clear through my opponent's body. And that's what I did, thus giving some sort of logic to the illuminated gap depicted on the posters."[9] Again, his suggestion makes engaging viewing and livens up the melée.

Anthony Nelson Keys was promoted to General Manager of Bray Studios in April to accommodate Hammer's increasing production programme. Before this, on Saturday 28 March, Terence Fisher, Peter Cushing and Christopher Lee took time out from The Mummy to attend the British première of The Hound of the Baskervilles at the London Pavilion. On Tuesday 31 March, Tony Hinds left for America with James and Michael Carreras to deliver a print of the film to United Artists. The film went on general release in England from 4 May and in the States from July. Perhaps because it didn't have enough horror for the regular punters ("It's ten times the terror in Technicolor! The most horror-dripping tale ever written," the posters promised) – but too much horror for the Holmes purists – the film wasn't quite the box-office hit Hammer had anticipated.

The Mummy was now put into post-production with editors Alfred Cox and James Needs and sound editor Roy Hyde. John Hollingsworth brought in Franz Reizenstein to compose an excellent score to compliment the proceedings. Harry Oakes, meanwhile, was engaged on Monday 27 April in getting several pick-up shots ("Exteriors near Henley. Vistas of countryside," according to his diary), with further exterior long shots captured the next day.

On Monday 4 May, the same day The Hound of the Baskervilles went on general release, Hammer began its next film at Bray. The Ugly Duckling would be the first of Hammer's two 1959 adaptations of

Henry Jekyll (Bernard Bresslaw) tries to explain the stolen jewellery to his girlfriend (Jean Muir) and his father (Jon Pertwee) in The Ugly Duckling (1959).

THE UGLY DUCKLING

PRINCIPAL PHOTOGRAPHY: 4 May to 10 June 1959
DISTRIBUTION:
Columbia; 84 minutes; b/w; UK: certificate 'U'
UK RELEASE:
TRADE SHOW: 28 July 1959 at the Columbia Theatre
GENERAL RELEASE: 10 August 1959

MANAGER: Mick Lyons; CHIEF ELECTRICIAN: Jack Curtis; MASTER PAINTER: Lawrence Wren; MASTER PLASTERER: Arthur Banks; MASTER CARPENTER: Charles Davis; ELECTRICAL SUPERVISOR: George Robinson Cowlard; STILLS CAMERAMAN: Tom Edwards; PUBLICIST: Colin Reid; TRANSPORT DRIVERS: Coco Epps, Wilfred Faux, Sid Humphrey

DIRECTOR: Lance Comfort; PRODUCER: Tommy Lyndon-Haynes; EXECUTIVE PRODUCER: Michael Carreras; SCREENPLAY: Sid Colin and Jack Davies, from a story by Sid Colin; PRODUCTION DESIGNER: Bernard Robinson; ASSISTANT ART DIRECTOR: Don Mingaye; DIRECTOR OF PHOTOGRAPHY: Michael Reed; CAMERA OPERATOR: Len Harris; FOCUS PULLER: Harry Oakes; CLAPPER/LOADER: Alan MacDonald; ASSISTANT DIRECTOR: John Peverall; 2ND ASSISTANT DIRECTOR: Tom Walls; 3RD ASSISTANT DIRECTOR: Hugh Harlow; SUPERVISING EDITOR: James Needs; EDITOR: John Dunsford; ASSISTANT EDITORS: Peter Todd, Alan Corder; MUSIC: Douglas Gamley; MUSIC SUPERVISOR: John Hollingsworth; SOUND RECORDIST: Jock May; BOOM OPERATOR: Jim Perry; SOUND CAMERA OPERATORS: Al Thorne, Michael Sale; SOUND MAINTENANCE: Charles Bouvet; SOUND ASSISTANT: Maurice Smith; MAKE-UP: Roy Ashton; HAIRSTYLIST: Henry Montsash; PRODUCTION MANAGER: Don Weeks; CONTINUITY: Marjorie Lavelly; WARDROBE: Molly Arbuthnot; WARDROBE ASSISTANT: Rosemary Burrows; CASTING: Dorothy Holloway; PRODUCTION SECRETARY: Patricia Green; ASSOCIATE PRODUCER'S SECRETARY: Margot Wardle; PROPERTY MASTER: Tommy Money; PROPERTY BUYER: Eric Hillier; FLOOR PROPS: Peter Allchorne; CHIEF ACCOUNTANT: W H V Able; CASHIER: Peter Lancaster; STUDIO MANAGER: Arthur Kelly; CONSTRUCTION

Bernard Bresslaw (Henry Jekyll/Teddy Hide); Reginald Beckwith (Reginald); Jon Pertwee (Victor Jekyll); Maudie Edwards (Henrietta Jekyll); Jean Muir (Snout); Richard Wattis (Barclay); David Lodge (Peewee); Elwyn Brook-Jones (Dandy); Michael Ripper (Fish); Harold Goodwin (Benny); Norma Marla (Angel); Keith Smith (Figures); Michael Ward (Pasco); John Harvey (Det Sgt Barnes); Jess Conrad (Bimbo); Mary Wilson (Lizzie); Geremy Phillips (Tiger); Vicky Marshall (Kitten); Alan Coleshill (Willie); Jill Carson (Yum Yum); Jean Driant (M Blum); Nicholas Tanner (Commissionaire); Shelagh Dey (Miss Angers); Sheila Hammond (Receptionist); Verne Morgan (Barman); Ian Wilson (Small Man); Cyril Chamberlain (Police Sergeant); Ian Ainsley (Fraser); Reginald Marsh; Roger Avon; Richard Statman (Reporters); Robert Desmond (Dizzy); Alexander Dore (Chemist Shop Customer)

UNCREDITED: Malka Alamont (Fifi); Heather Downham (Margo); Lucy Griffiths (Cellist); Aldine Harvey (Jane); Ann Mayhew (Lucienne); Jacqueline Perrin (Ursula); Helen Pohlman (Amanda); Helga Wahlrow (Rosemary); Jack Armstrong, Jamie Barnes, Richard Dake, Stella Kemball, Aileen Lewis, Peter Mander, Lola Morice, Alecia St Leger (Old-Time Dancers)

with Joe Loss and his Orchestra

Robert Louis Stevenson's *Strange Case of Dr Jekyll and Mr Hyde*, and a strange case it was. Why Hammer took two stabs at the same story within the same year is perplexing, particularly with Universal's vaults still wide open to them. *The Ugly Duckling* was a comic reworking of the story; *The Two Faces of Dr Jekyll*, later in the year, would tell it straight but with a clever twist. As Michael Carreras explained in *Kinematograph Weekly* on Thursday 28 May (towards the end of the fourth week of shooting on *The Ugly Duckling*), "The two treatments are so far apart [as] to be [un]recognisable. *The Ugly Duckling* will do the straight version some good. It will reacquaint people with the names Jekyll and Hyde."

The film's star, Bernard Bresslaw, was big business at the time, thanks largely to the hit TV comedy show *The Army Game* (and Hammer's spin-off, *I Only Arsked*). In the autumn of 1958, Bresslaw had reached number six in the hit parade with a song called 'Mad Pashernate Love'. Hammer immediately commissioned Sid Colin, co-writer of *I Only Arsked*, to write a Bresslaw vehicle under the rather contrived rip-off title of, yes, *Mad Pashernate Love*. Somehow it became *The Ugly Duckling* and Tommy Lyndon-Haynes (who had previously worked as a production manager on *The Quatermass Xperiment*) was brought in to produce it. Michael Carreras confirmed in *Kinematograph Weekly* on Thursday 20 November 1958 that it was "a tailor-made subject for Bernard Bresslaw. We believe it will be one of the year's funniest comedies."

Irritating to fans and researchers alike is the fact that the film seems to have disappeared without trace. The basic story tells of the dim-witted Henry Jekyll who, after a laboratory explosion, finds his grandfather's long-lost secret formula. Experimenting, he produces a potion which transforms him into Teddy Hide (sic), who becomes the lion of the Palais dance hall. He also becomes involved with a gang of jewel thieves led by the hall's manager, Dandy. Another production for Columbia, it is interesting that the basic premise of the story would re-emerge in Paramount's 1963 Jerry Lewis vehicle *The Nutty Professor*. Both films share an inadequate bumbling scientist who unwittingly transforms himself into the local hipster: Teddy boy Teddy Hide and slick crooner Buddy Love respectively. The reference to Stevenson was clearer in Hammer's version, however, where the names Jekyll and Hyde were retained.

The crew of *The Mummy* returned after a two-week break, apart from a new lighting cameraman (Michael Reed, who had last worked for Hammer as focus puller in 1949) and a new editor (John Dunsford, who had last worked on *The Man Who Could Cheat Death*), brought in to allow Alfred Cox to finish *The Mummy* at Hammer House. Make-up man Roy Ashton's job was relatively simple this time, transforming Bresslaw into his alter ego by the use of sideburns, a moustache and a 'DA' flick to his hair. Like *The Two Faces of Dr Jekyll* to come, Hammer introduced evil as the more interesting and compelling alternative to the good in man.

Location shooting would take the crew to the Streatham Locarno for the nightclub scenes; Harry Oakes' diary notes that the cha-cha sequence was captured on Thursday 28 May. Continuity girl Marjorie Lavelly remembers working on the film: "I thought the script was very good – interesting. It was a happy film to work on with a lovely cast – Maudie Edwards, dear Dickie Wattis, Michael Ripper, Reginald Marsh, Harold Goodwin and, of course, Bernard Bresslaw, who I later knew from the Carry Ons (I did about four or five for Gerald Thomas). I seem to remember a lot of gags and laughter. The artists used to have their 'green room' near my desk and some of the anecdotes they told were superb. I know it was not a commercial success, which was a shame as a lot of hard work went into it, but that's life."

Principal photography closed on Wednesday 10 June, halfway through the sixth week. John Dunsford and James Needs then took the film into post-production. John Hollingsworth brought in Douglas Gamley to compose the score, though Hollingsworth curiously re-used James Bernard's classic three-note Dra-cu-la motif for when Jekyll first changes into Hyde.

Meanwhile, Michael Carreras submitted a black-and-white copy of *The Mummy* to the BBFC in May. The Board found the film remarkably tame by Hammer standards, as John Trevelyan's letter to Michael Carreras on 13 May shows: "This is to confirm, for the purposes of record, that we will defer the decision on category for *The Mummy* until we see the film again in colour. In black and white it looks as though it might well be considered for the 'A' category, but it is possible that the colour version, which is certain to have more impact, may make it more suitable for the 'X' category."

An 'A' certificate? After the difficulties he had experienced with the censor, Tony Hinds must have been astounded by the Board's leniency with his colleague's picture. Michael Carreras' reply to

Trevelyan on 14 May shows that the threatened 'A' was actually a pleasing prospect: "I have discussed the problem of the certificate on The Mummy with Jimmy, and he is delighted to think there is a possibility of our getting an 'A' for this subject. This, therefore, is the category we would like the picture to fall into. Can you, then, give us detailed 'do-s' and 'don't-s' before I start dubbing?"

Trevelyan replied the next day. "Many thanks for your letter about The Mummy. I had a word with Jimmy today and we have decided to leave the question of category open until we can see the complete colour version and until he has discussed the question of distribution with Jack Goodlatte. I have discussed details with our Examiners. I do not think that there are any points of detail that I need mention specifically, except that we might possibly want you to remove the close shot of John Banning being strangled, the shot in which his face is seen in close-up with that of Kharis. We might possibly accept this shot, but I mention it now in case we have to ask you for a cut later."

Not surprisingly, when the Board viewed the colour version on 17 June, they were forced to reconsider and the film was given an 'X' certificate. The censor's proposed leniency towards The Mummy would definitely not be extended to Hammer's next production.

Back in September 1958, Hammer had announced plans for The Horror of Thuggee, another Kenneth Hyman project, with a screenplay by David Z Goodman based on Sir William Sleeman's attempts to eliminate the Thuggee cult in India. Kenneth Hyman discusses the genesis of the project: "I had read the book by John Masters called The Deceivers, which was the story of Major Sleeman, who had infiltrated the Thuggees as a British officer. It was a wonderful novel and I found out that Rank owned the rights. Bob Benjamin was the official-quote-unofficial representative of Rank in America; he was one of the senior officers at United Artists. I went to Bob, who I was now friendly with, and he interceded on my behalf and set up an introduction with John Davis (Rank's managing director) and indicated to me that David would sell me the rights to The Deceivers for what they had paid for it, which he seemed to think was somewhere around $50,000.

"During this time, I had had some conversations with John Huston, who had indicated an enthusiasm to direct The Deceivers. When I finally got to see John Davis, it was at his offices on South Street in Mayfair, and he had this enormous office that you had to walk across – I think it was planned to intimidate you before you arrived at his desk. He proceeded to be totally honest with me and told me that his costs were something around $250,000, and I said 'Thank you very much Mr Davis' and walked out. I decided, 'What the hell, it's a true story, it's public domain and let's do it at Hammer' – and that's how The Stranglers of Bombay came into being." [11]

The film saw Hammer returning to a highly controversial, Blood Island-style subject, exploring the atrocities of the Kali-worshipping Thuggees, who strangled and mutilated thousands of victims, burying them in mass graves. Intended for Columbia and with plans to shoot it in colour mooted as late as December 1958, the project went through a name change to The Stranglers of Bengal before emerging as Hammer's next offering to start shooting at Bray Studios (on Monday 6 July) under the revised title The Stranglers of Bombay, in monochrome and so-called 'Strangloscope'.

Needless to say, with such a controversial subject, the original screenplay had to be toned down considerably. While the BBFC no longer has records of their correspondence on the film, Columbia passed on a copy of the script to the American censoring body, the Motion Picture Association of America (MPAA), for their comments. They replied to Columbia on Friday 10 July (the end of the film's first week of shooting):

"We have read the script dated May 29th, 1959, for your proposed production THE STRANGLERS, and wish to report that this story seems basically acceptable under the provisions of the Production Code. There are numerous scenes in this script which seem to contain an over-emphasis on gruesomeness. In order that we will be able to approve your finished picture, it will be essential for you to exercise careful restraint in the instances noted below:

Page 4: The cutting and cauterising could prove unacceptably gruesome.

Page 26: The mutilation of the prisoners seems to go too far.

Page 36: The alley scene indicates excessive brutality such as kicking and prolonged beating which could not be approved.

Page 41: Any undue featuring of the severed hand will be unacceptable.

Guy Rolfe is abducted by the children of Kali in The Stranglers of Bombay (1959).

THE STRANGLERS OF BOMBAY

PRINCIPAL PHOTOGRAPHY: 6 July to 27 August 1959
DISTRIBUTION:
  Columbia; 81 minutes; b/w; Megascope
  [Strangloscope]; UK: certificate 'A'
UK RELEASE:
  PREMIÈRE: 4 December 1959 at the London Pavilion,
  Piccadilly Circus
  GENERAL RELEASE: 18 January 1960, on the ABC circuit
  with *Kill Her Gently*
US RELEASE: May 1960

Chris Barnes; Music: James Bernard; Music Supervisor: John Hollingsworth; Sound Recordist: Jock May; Sound Editor: Arthur Cox; Make-up: Roy Ashton; Hairstylist: Henry Montsash; Production Manager: Don Weeks; Continuity: Tilly Day; Wardrobe: Molly Arbuthnot; Technical Adviser: Michael Edwards; Property Master: Tommy Money; Property Buyer: Eric Hillier; Studio Manager: Arthur Kelly; Construction Manager: Mick Lyons; Chief Electrician: Jack Curtis; Master Painter: Lawrence Wren; Master Plasterer: Arthur Banks; Master Carpenter: Charles Davis; Personnel Adviser: Jimmy Vaughn; Stills Cameraman: Tom Edwards; Publicist: Dennison Thornton

Director: Terence Fisher; Producer: Anthony Hinds; Associate Producer: Anthony Nelson Keys; Executive Producer: Michael Carreras; Screenplay: David Z Goodman; Art Director: Bernard Robinson; Assistant Art Director: Don Mingaye; Modeller: Margaret Carter; Director of Photography: Arthur Grant; Camera Operator: Len Harris; Focus Puller: Harry Oakes; Assistant Director: John Peverall; 2nd Assistant Director: Tom Walls; 3rd Assistant Director: Hugh Harlow; Supervising Editor: James Needs; Editor: Alfred Cox; Assistant Editor:

Guy Rolfe (Lewis); Allan Cuthbertson (Connaught-Smith); Andrew Cruickshank (Henderson); George Pastell (High Priest); Marne Maitland (Patel Shari); Jan Holden (Mary); Paul Stassino (Silver); Tutte Lemkow (Ram Das); David Spenser (Gopali); John Harvey (Burns); Roger Delgado (Bundar); Marie Devereux (Karim); Michael Nightingale (Flood); Margaret Gordon (Dorothy Flood); Steven Scot (Walters); Jack McNaughton (Corporal Roberts); Ewen Solon (camel vendor)

Page 48 and 53: Please reserve the use of the words 'hell' and 'damn' for dramatically valid occasions.
Page 68: The girl's reaction to the brutality should be minimised. The stomach slitting is unacceptable.
Page 72: We note more gruesomeness in connection with the murder of Flood.
Page 79: There seems to be an unacceptable amount of murders in this sequence.
Page 80: The abuse of the corpses is excessive.
Page 82: There is an unacceptable featuring of the mutilated corpses in this scene as presently described.

Page 83: The same applies to the corpses in this scene.

Page 84: The 'flaming' death of the priest should be handled by mere suggestion.

"You understand, of course, that our final judgment will be based on the finished picture."

With Tony Hinds back as producer, the man chosen to direct the atrocities was Terence Fisher. "I wasn't really appalled by it, but it was a fairly straight portrayal of what the Thuggees did at that particular time," he explained. "I didn't enjoy doing it a hell of a lot, because I didn't think there was the opportunity of developing enough the emotional relationships between the characters." [12] He continued: "The Stranglers of Bombay went wrong. It was too crude. The basic idea was the absolutely true story of Thuggee. The producers felt it was better in black and white, because it was a documentary story rather than a myth, but in the written word there was too much Frankenstein and Dracula, and I was still with the previous approach." [13]

Len Harris recalled: "A lot of the picture was shot on the lot at Bray and we had a heatwave. We had a lot of Indian extras on the set. Although we all felt the heat, the only ones passing out were the Indians." [14] According to Fisher, "In The Mummy, we had an animal procession – some gorgeous big oxen and camels. I think they popped up again in Stranglers. We were on location around London, shooting in some huge sand pits, and it was a sweltering hot day. I asked for the two camels for a specific shot and only one was brought on. 'Where's the other one?' I asked. Back came the reply, 'Sorry, it's got sunstroke.' Imagine it, camels and they got blooming sunstroke! Oh, that was a real calamity with those camels. They were probably born and bred in England." [15]

The same team from The Ugly Duckling returned, apart from a different lighting cameraman (Arthur Grant), editor (Alfred Cox) and continuity supervisor (Tilly Day). Tilly would now become Bray's regular on continuity, though she had previously worked on The Mystery of the Mary Celeste as far back as 1935. This was now the eighth film in a row since Further Up the Creek to feature the collective team of 1st assistant John Peverall, 2nd assistant Tom Walls and 3rd assistant Hugh Harlow. This would be their last call together, however, as Hugh would soon be promoted to 2nd assistant. The film also featured the final adaptation of Bernard Robinson's original exterior castle set from Dracula on the backlot; it was now transformed into an Indian village. The site would finally be cleared after shooting to make way for the erection of a new standing village square set, initially to see action in the first production of 1960, The Brides of Dracula.

The film's fine cast was headed by Guy Rolfe, in his second Hammer role that year (he had worked with Terence Fisher in Portrait from Life over ten years before), while busty Marie Devereux made a big impact as a sexy bird of ill omen, hovering over the most horrific scenes with an inner glow of twisted pleasure. Allan Cuthbertson is chillingly arrogant as the slimy Connaught-Smith and Hammer regulars George Pastell, Marne Maitland and Roger Delgado were on hand as the sadistic leaders of the 'Children Of Kali' cult.

Editor Alfred Cox remembers working with Terry Fisher: "He was great. He always knew where you were going. Terry would always threaten me, because anything to do with the animals that was not on principal photography, I got lumbered with. You know the feeling when you're doing something and suddenly become aware of somebody looking at you? I used to get that feeling, I remember, on The Stranglers of Bombay. I turned round one day in the cutting room down at Bray and there he was standing outside, looking in at me through the window. He'd got his arm bent at the elbow and at the wrist making like a cobra and I knew I was going to be in for it!" Cox was less impressed with the cobras themselves. "One escaped and the handler shouted, 'He's gone. Don't anybody leave the stage' – but he was too late, I'd gone! We also had a mongoose. It bit people. When the snake escaped, they lost the mongoose too. We never did find either of them!"

Camera operator Len Harris explained: "They had the snakes crawling around on the floor. The poison sacs had not been removed from these imported snakes because the snakes become sluggish and they wanted them to look lively. Guy Rolfe was 'tied' down. He could actually get right up very easily. There were snake handlers there from the zoo, too, with special gloves and equipment. To let the snake get close to Guy, a large sheet of glass was placed vertically between them. The snake was only an inch or so away from him, when it reared back and slammed into the glass. They come with some force, you know. Anyone with a snake bite would be half-knocked out anyway, because they're quite strong. We were afraid that the glass would break and come down all

DON'T PANIC CHAPS!

A Hammer-ACT production
PRINCIPAL PHOTOGRAPHY: July 1959
UK DISTRIBUTION: Columbia; 85 minutes; b/w;
certificate 'U'
UK RELEASE:
TRADE SHOW: 24 November 1959 at the Columbia
Theatre
GENERAL RELEASE: 21 December 1959 on the ABC circuit

DIRECTOR: George Pollock; PRODUCER: Teddy Baird; EXECUTIVE
PRODUCER: Ralph Bond; SCREENPLAY: Jack Davies based on the
radio play by Michael Corston and Ronald Holroyd; ART DIRECTOR:
Scott MacGregor; ASSISTANT ART DIRECTOR: Tom Goswell;

DIRECTOR OF PHOTOGRAPHY: Arthur Graham; CAMERA
OPERATOR: Eric Besche; ASSISTANT DIRECTOR: Douglas Hermes;
SUPERVISING EDITOR: James Needs; EDITOR: Harry Aldous; MUSIC
COMPOSER AND CONDUCTOR: Philip Green; SOUND RECORDIST:
Sid Wiles; SOUND CAMERA OPERATOR: Alan Hogben; MAKE-UP:
Peter Aramsten; PRODUCTION MANAGER: Clifford Parkes;

Dennis Price (Krisling); George Cole (Finch); Thorley Walters
(Brown); Harry Fowler (Ackroyd); Nadja Regin (Elsa); Nicholas
Phipps (Mortimer); Percy Herbert (Bolter); George Murcell
(Meister); Gerlan Klauber (Schmidt); Terence Alexander
(Babbington); Thomas Foulkes (Voss)

The crew of the wartime comedy
Don't Panic Chaps!: Percy
Herbert, Thorley Walters,
Terence Alexander, George Cole
and Nicholas Phipps.

over Guy. We had a doctor and nurse standing by any time the snakes were loose, which was the whole day. They had the serum ready. The RSPCA probably would not have allowed us to film a mongoose killing a snake, but Hammer was pretty good about that, anyway. We got the actual cobra-mongoose fight from an Indian documentary, which was also in black and white. If you look closely, our mongoose and the one in the fight are different shapes." [16]

Margaret Carter modelled the film's statue of Kali, which balanced precariously on one leg. "They never cast that," Margaret remembers. "They wheeled it on and off the set, but there she was with only one metal rod up and she wobbled terribly. But she survived to go into the foyer of the cinema for the première. She was there all week in Leicester Square.

"I remember watching them film a scene with the high priest," she continues. "I remember that, because I was holding the studio cat. She wanted to be on the altar and she was continually being retrieved from being in the picture, so I was holding her to keep her out of the way. The high priest was instructing all the little stranglers what to do to please Kali and his voice rose to a climax, and when he got to the climax of his speech, he said, 'And kill!' And they all chorused, 'Kill, kill, kill!' They all held their little strangler's scarves up high and the cat thought that they meant her and she dug her claws straight down my arm – it was summer and I was wearing a sleeveless dress. I wasn't seen for 3 days!"

Principal photography wrapped after just under eight weeks on Thursday 27 August.

Meanwhile in July, while *Stranglers* was filming at Bray, director George Pollock slipped in a £75,000 co-production between Hammer and ACT Films called *Don't Panic Chaps!* at Walton Studios and on location at Chobham Common. This was a World War II comedy about British and German soldiers fighting for control of an Adriatic island as an observation post. This was an adaptation of another radio play and starred Dennis Price, George Cole and Thorley Walters. James Carreras was heard to predict in the *Daily Cinema* on 21 October 1959 that "It's our funniest film yet!" However, many would consider this an inconsequential boast and the sun was soon to go down on Hammer's comedy sideline. The films had no real foothold in the States, after all.

After a trade show at the Columbia Theatre on Tuesday 28 July, *The Ugly Duckling* went on general release from Sunday 9 August to a very lukewarm reception. Not even Bernard Bresslaw's presence could save Hammer from the disastrous press response, and he would return to the company only briefly, for their space flick *Moon Zero Two*, a full ten years later.

The Stranglers of Bombay, meanwhile, went into post-production. A little confusing: this would see the collaboration of editor Alfred Cox with sound editor Arthur Cox. "My worst problem on *Stranglers* was the damned music with those drummers," remembers Alfred. "There were three native drummers and they couldn't converse together – one had to converse through another, because they didn't speak the same dialects. What's more, they couldn't sustain the beats, the rhythm, for the long periods needed in the film, so I had to make them all up out of loops. A bit of a nightmare." Music supervisor John Hollingsworth brought back James Bernard to compose a characteristically exciting score.

It's a shame the BBFC no longer hold their records on this film. It would have been fascinating to see how *Stranglers*, which is in many ways more sadistic than Hammer's Gothic horrors, managed to get away with a mere 'A' certificate!

With *Stranglers* well into post-production, Hammer's next project at Bray courted yet more controversy. *Never Take Sweets from a Stranger* was an adaptation of *The Pony Cart*, a stage play written by Roger Garis, which dealt candidly with the emotive subject of child molestation. Tony Hinds recalled, "It was based on a Canadian play called *The Pony Cart*. It had been sent to me for some reason and I read it on my routine train journey from Oxford to London (I was working in London at the time). I found it so absorbing that I nearly found myself on my way back to Oxford! The film was scripted by John Hunter, who was an agent who liked writing (and had an office above mine, which was handy), and directed by Cyril Frankel, who made a very good job of it, especially directing the children." [17]

Hammer was never a company to shy away from a controversial subject and Garis' play had already been headline news when staged in London's West End. Actress Janina Faye, who was then only 11 years old, still has vivid recollections: "The play was to be done as a one-off professional performance on a Sunday night at the Strand Theatre in London. In those days the licensing laws forbade children performing on stage or on television until they were 12 years old, although they could appear on film – don't ask me why. Because it was only a Sunday night performance, the people engaging me – I don't remember who they were now as my involvement was somewhat short-lived – thought they would be safe.

"Unfortunately, the then Lady Lewisham decided to object very strongly about a child appearing in a 'sex play' before the age of 12! She, of course, knew nothing about the context and message of the play before she raised such a fuss; it made all the newspapers and even got me my own 'Giles' cartoon in the *Daily Express*. The press reaction was quite remarkable, and my parents rightly decided to withdraw me from the production. I was devastated, as it would have been a very exciting experience for me, performing

Felix Aylmer as the lecherous Olderberry Senior in Never Take Sweets from a Stranger (1959).

on a West End stage for the first time. I knew enough about 'not talking to strange men' to know the difference between this play and a play about sex!"

Garis had written the play following an incident in 1953 involving his own daughter and intended it as a warning to parents everywhere. Lady Lewisham's 'one-woman crusade' filled all the tabloids, focusing on how the 'indecent' play was to expose 11-year-old Janina Faye to 'grave moral dangers'. A mildly facetious press release for Hammer's adaptation stated:

"A noted champion of causes, and fresh from her famous campaign against 'unwashed teacups' at London Airport, Lady Lewisham took the offensive with all barrels blazing. She declared that the production of *The Pony Cart* at the Strand Theatre must be suppressed. That its suppression would be an act of 'public service'. Nobody was more surprised – or disturbed – by all this brouhaha than Roger Garis, the play's American author. From his home in Massachusetts, Mr Garis, a distinguished and respected Professor of Law at Massachusetts University, and before that an equally

Jean (Janina Faye) is interrogated by Defense Counsel Niall MacGinnis in the troublesome court sequence of Never Take Sweets from a Stranger (1959).

NEVER TAKE SWEETS FROM A STRANGER

PRINCIPAL PHOTOGRAPHY: 14 September to 30 October 1959
DISTRIBUTION:
Columbia; 81 minutes; b/w; Hammerscope
UK: certificate 'X'
US TITLE: *Never Take Candy from a Stranger*
UK RELEASE:
TRADE SHOW: 26 February 1960 at the Columbia Theatre
PREMIÈRE: 4 March 1960 at the London Pavilion, Piccadilly Circus

DIRECTOR: *Cyril Frankel*; PRODUCER: *Tony Hinds*; EXECUTIVE PRODUCER: *Michael Carreras*; ASSOCIATE PRODUCER: *Anthony Nelson Keys*; SCREENPLAY: *John Hunter, from a play by Roger Garis*; PRODUCTION DESIGNER: *Bernard Robinson*; ASSISTANT ART DIRECTOR: *Don Mingaye*; DIRECTOR OF PHOTOGRAPHY: *Freddie Francis*; CAMERA OPERATOR: *Len Harris*; FOCUS PULLER: *Harry Oakes*; ASSISTANT DIRECTOR: *John Peverall*; 2ND ASSISTANT DIRECTOR: *Tom Walls*; SUPERVISING EDITOR: *James Needs*; EDITOR: *Alfred Cox*; MUSIC: *Elisabeth Lutyens*; MUSIC SUPERVISOR: *John Hollingsworth*; SOUND RECORDIST: *Jock May*;

MAKE-UP: *Roy Ashton*; HAIRSTYLIST: *Henry Montsash*; PRODUCTION MANAGER: *Clifford Parks*; CONTINUITY: *Tilly Day*; WARDROBE: *Molly Arbuthnot*; CASTING: *Dorothy Holloway*; PROPERTY MASTER: *Tommy Money*; PROPERTY BUYER: *Eric Hillier*; STUDIO MANAGER: *Arthur Kelly*; CHIEF ELECTRICIAN: *Jack Curtis*; MASTER PAINTER: *Lawrence Wren*; MASTER CARPENTER: *Charles Davis*; STILLS CAMERAMAN: *Tom Edwards*

Gwen Watford (Sally); Patrick Allen (Pete); Felix Aylmer (Olderberry Sr); Niall MacGinnis (Defense Counsel); Alison Leggatt (Martha); Bill Nagy (Olderberry Jr); Macdonald Parke (Judge); Michael Gwynn (Prosecutor); Bud Knapp (Hammond); Janina Faye (Jean); Frances Green (Lucille); James Dyrenforth (Dr Stephens); Estelle Brody (Eunice); Robert Arden (Tom); Vera Cook (Mrs Demarest); Cal McCord (Kalliduke); Gaylord Cavalaro (Phillips); Sheila Robins (Miss Jackson); Larry O'Connor (Sam); Helen Horton (Sylvia); Shirley Butler (Mrs Nash); Michael Hammond (Sammy Nash); Patricia Marks (nurse); Peter Carlisle (usher); Mark Baker (clerk); Sonia Fox (receptionist); John Bloomfield (foreman); Charles Maunsell (janitor); André Daker (chauffeur); Bill Sawyer (taxi driver); Jack Lynn (Dr Montfort); William Abney (trooper); Tom Bushby (policeman)

distinguished and respected journalist, was compelled in self-defence to issue a statement. He said he had written the play as a public service; that when it was produced in New York in 1954 he couldn't remember any of the morality folk bursting blood vessels over it. On the contrary, it had been highly praised by the critics as a serious, intelligent, thought-provoking work. 'I wrote the play,' Mr Garis added, 'to denounce a very serious social problem – one as prevalent in England as in America.'

"How, he wanted to know, could Lady Lewisham claim as a public service her call for suppression of a dramatic work written as a public service? It was obvious, he declared, that her attack had been made without proper knowledge of the facts. Mr Garis was right, for in the end *The Pony Cart*, not Lady Lewisham, won the day. The play was performed at the Strand and the London critics, without exception, hailed it as a first-class, absorbing, entertaining drama."

Cyril Frankel was appointed to direct Hammer's version and by chance, Janina Faye, the same little girl caught up in the West End controversy, was brought in to play the troubled Jean. "As far as I am aware," she recalls, "it was coincidental that I then got the part in the film. I was sent along with hundreds of others to audition for Cyril Frankel. We all auditioned several times at Hammer House in Wardour Street before final casting was made. Prior to the release of the film, I was told I would get no billing outside the cinema as my casting in the play had attracted so much adverse publicity." It looked, for once, as if Hammer were playing down the sensationalism to produce a well-meaning 'message' movie.

Despite the sensitive subject matter, Tony Hinds was late in sending a copy of the script to the BBFC. It was delivered by hand on 2 September. Audrey Field digested the draft screenplay the next day: "The important additions, from our point of view, are the trial scene (with the demand that Jean be medically examined to see whether she has been depraved by some past experience); Jean's scene with her mother in which she enlarges on the dancing episode; scenes of the children's escape and Olderberry's pursuit through the woods; and the shot of Olderberry standing over the dimly seen body of one of the children (the audience does not then know which)." She lists her objections, closing with: "I do not object in principle to old Richard Olderberry being fleetingly seen in frame with the two children, as long as he does not look too heavily lustful. I did think it would be helpful to keep him out of the picture altogether, but I can see that this would be cramping. The really important thing is that he should not be seen touching or about to touch them – or, of course, looking at them when they are naked. Does the title imply that we are to be asked to make the film 'A'?"

Another reader passed on his comments on 7 September: "I hope that this is intended to be an 'X' film. I think that with its teeth drawn for 'A' its essential horror (which is the horror of the child and the bogey man, as old as the hills) would be so much reduced as to be pedestrian. It is the loneliness of the children in the wooded countryside, the dark water, and the silent pursuer which could give an audience the willies, and I don't think I agree with AOF when she has misgivings about this. To my mind this would be legitimate 'X'. I don't like Jean's nightmare (p.28), but as this is the reason for Peter's subsequent action, and as the hint of the shadow in the cupboard (p.29) is very likely from a child with nightmare I would not object to it.

"For the rest I agree with AOF's comments. It wasn't, actually, attempted rape; it was something even worse to little girls, and it is a pity, I think, to mention rape. Then, in the trial scene, surely we would recoil from the idea of the child's being threatened with a medical examination, even if it were sound legally. AOF suggests that it is nonsensical, and I hope she is right: if she is it could spoil the picture, as well as upset us; but I have some misgiving about this, because the Judge's law point (p.88) sounds a little bit as if a legal mind has already offered some advice on this. If so, I believe our only argument could be that it is offensive as it stands. Incidentally, in the trial scene it seems to me a pity that Counsel uses the word 'naked' to the little girl. AOF does not object to this, but I wonder if 'without your clothes' or even 'without any clothes on at all' doesn't sound more suggestive and more the language one would use as a child.

"What a monster old Olderberry could be if rightly played, silence and all!

"PS. I was irritated by one thing which has nothing to do with censorship! Why must we have such silly things said in the title? It could be true ... it could happen here. But of course. It ought to be possible to say this of any good film of this type. What this may achieve, of course, and this is why it irritates me, is the mischief of arousing in the mind of the spectator a misgiving about neighbourly old men. It would be a pity if every old man became a DOM and a danger to little girls."

The latter comment referred to a title sequence after the credits (which Hammer were accustomed to having in a lot of their films), which effectively said that, while the events take place in Canada, they could occur anywhere. John Trevelyan summed up his reader's comments in a letter to Tony Hinds on 7 September:

"We have now read your script entitled *Never Take Sweets from a Stranger*. I think that this script has been well written and it should make a good and intelligent film. I have a few comments to make, as follows:

Jean (Janina Faye) awakens from a nightmare in Never Take Sweets from a Stranger (1959).

P.24 & 26. The words 'attempted rape' are used. We would like to avoid this if possible. The idea of indecent assault is bad enough but attempted rape is worse and there are in fact no grounds for this.

P.31. The reference to *Lolita* is not really necessary. Surely the dialogue could start with the line 'Just have a look at this Carlton guy's statement.'

P.42. Scenes 26 and 27 have not yet been scripted and we would like to see them in due course.

Pps.70 to 91. The trial is of course a scene which was not in the play at all. We would have no objection to it, although we would not be particularly happy about the effect on a child actress of playing this kind of part. On the other hand we would raise strong objection to the suggestion (Pps. 84-88) that the child should be medically examined. The case is unpleasant enough without this being added and it really seems offensive and unnecessary. On page 81 may I suggest that instead of the Defence Counsel saying, 'Was she naked?' he should say 'Had she taken her clothes off?' Somehow the word 'naked' has rather a shock impact in this setting and we would prefer that some other wording is used, such as I have suggested.

Pp.103-108. I hope that this scene will not be unduly prolonged. It might be very horrible if it were. Much will depend on how the old man looks. We would not want him to appear to be nastily lustful.

P.120. I think this scene should pass since it is to be shot in comparative darkness. We should not want any unpleasant picture of the dead child.

"You will appreciate that this film would have to be in the 'X' category because of its theme. Although it is not a point of censorship, I rather wish that you could omit the titles given in scene 1 on page 1. We do not want your audience looking suspiciously at kindly old men and regarding them as dangerous menaces to little girls. Surely the film does not really need a preliminary title of this kind."

Tony Hinds replied to Trevelyan on 10 September:

"Thank you for your prompt reply regarding the above, and I am glad that in general you approve. Re your detailed comments:

Page 31. If you really insist, I will delete the reference to *Lolita*.

Page 42. Scenes 26/27 will simply indicate the reactions of the town to the family. I will send them to you as soon as scripted.

Pp.103/108. I can assure you that old Olderberry will not appear to be too nastily lustful (I have cast Felix Aylmer for the part, which will ensure this).

Page 120. We will most certainly not show any unpleasant picture of the dead child.

Pp.24/26. Do you not think that an emotional mother would deliberately exaggerate the situation in order to emphasise her point? This is the reason why we have her say 'attempted rape'. It helps the playing of the scene, and I should like to be able to keep it in.

Pp.70/91. (a) We use the words 'take off her clothes' so often in the script that the word 'naked' comes as a refreshing change. Can we not keep it?

(b) There *was* a court scene in the play, in which Olderberry won his case by so flagrant a miscarriage of justice that we dared not use it. In our version, the unpleasant trick that Olderberry and his Counsel use to win their case is to make the whole trial so distasteful that the Father insists that the trial be stopped, by dropping the charge. For this reason, it is important to us that the trial should become, momentarily, very distasteful, otherwise we have no scene. (I have discussed the playing of this scene with the Director, who is arranging his camera set-ups so that the child actress need not be present during the more outspoken parts of this sequence).

"The reason for stating that the film, although set in Canada, could happen anywhere, is to avoid offending the Canadians, who might otherwise complain, 'Why pick on us?'"

A note in the BBFC files on 11 September by Audrey Field in response to this letter reads: "We do not really feel disposed to give them a free hand on any of these things, which we think are unnecessary turns of the screw. We feel *least* strongly about *Lolita* and the prologue, and *most* strongly about the request for a medical examination, which we think should be maintained at all costs."

John Trevelyan continued the debate in a letter to Hinds on Tuesday 15 September, now two days into the shooting: "I have discussed this fully with the Examiners who read your script and I have the following comments to make:

Page 31. We would not insist on the deletion of the reference to *Lolita*. We would just prefer not to have it.

Page 42. There appears to be no problem about scenes 26 and 27.

Pages 103-108. We are glad to hear that you have cast Felix Aylmer for the part of Olderberry Senior. This should certainly remove nastiness.

Page 120. I am glad to have your assurance that you will not show any unpleasant picture of the dead child.

Pages 24-26. It is true that an emotional mother might deliberately exaggerate the situation in order to emphasise her point but we feel that the words 'attempted rape' when relating to a child of this age give a particularly unpleasant thought. I admit that in some ways attempted rape of a child of this age would be less unpleasant than what Olderberry Senior actually did because he was clearly suffering from a sexual perversion. I think that perhaps it would be best for you to leave the words in the dialogue at present, but it might be helpful if you could have some alternative dialogue dubbed in case the words stand out and appear offensive.

Pages 70-91. a) We shall not insist on the alteration of the word 'naked'. Here again it will depend upon how it actually sounds and it might be as well if you had alternative wording in case we raise objection when the film is completed.

b) I had quite forgotten that there was a court scene in the play and I certainly cannot remember how Olderberry Senior won his case, but we feel very strongly that the scene as at

present scripted is most undesirable. The idea of a child being forced to have a medical examination to see whether or not she had been tampered with sexually is one that we would not be prepared to accept, and I must therefore ask you to find some other way in which you can reasonably get the father to drop the charge. I am sorry about this but we feel very strongly about it and feel that it is too distasteful even for the 'X' category.
"I note your reason for the subsidiary titles and we see that there is some point to them."

Hinds replied to Trevelyan on 23 September: "I have had a long session with the writer, and so far we have not come up with an acceptable alternative line that is strong enough to force the Father to demand that the trial be stopped. However, the writer has done a very much toned down version of this scene, in which the Defence Counsel is careful that the child does not understand what he is getting at, but the Father does. I enclose the relevant section of the scene for your consideration and, I should like to think, approval. It was nice seeing you the other day."

The new scene was submitted, but still contained a demand by the Defence Counsel for a medical examination. Examiner JC commented in an internal memo to Trevelyan: "I find that I cannot sufficiently remember the original of this scene; but my impression is that this new version does not entirely meet our objections. I would suggest that after the lines: 'Would you mind if we brought a doctor here to see you now?' the objection could come from Peter, and an immediate dissolve be made to the judge's room, where the judge could explain why he had invited all the parties concerned to meet. Even this, which would be enough in my view, waters down our original objection, which was that the whole idea of an examination might go and some other idea take its place."

Audrey Field added, "I agree. I don't like even the germ of the idea and the passage which JC mentioned is intolerable." Trevelyan relayed the feelings of his examiners in a letter on 24 September: "We are still worried about this. We suggest that you might consider a reduction of the scene. You could have the line 'Would you mind if we brought a doctor here to see you now?' If this were immediately followed by Pete's objection and the dissolve to the judge's room where the judge can explain why he had invited all the parties concerned to meet. In the revised version we would, I think, be worried about the lines given to Defence Counsel, such as 'I think we have a right to know whether this child is as innocent as she seems...' etc. As you will see from this we might accept the idea that a doctor should be brought in but we should definitely not want anything that would emphasise the reasons why this proposal was made. I think we are getting close to an acceptable version, so I suggest that you get the writer to revise his revision in light of my comments."

Back to the drawing board. Hinds submitted a further revision on 1 October but it was still not acceptable to the BBFC. Hinds submitted yet another draft on Monday 12 October, the start of the fifth week of shooting: "I enclose herewith a re-write of the section of the Courtroom scene to which you took exception, eliminating any suggestion of a medical examination. This is not very well written, but I have had to rush it through as we are shooting this scene tomorrow. If it is still not satisfactory, perhaps you will be so kind as to telephone me at the studios."

Trevelyan telephoned his acceptance on the scene later that day and confirmed it in writing: "Many thanks for your letter of today. I write to confirm my telephone message and to say that this new revision of the Court Scene in *Never Take Sweets from a Stranger* seems to be satisfactory. Thank you for your co-operation."

However, that was not the end of the incident. Filming of the courtroom sequence began as planned on Tuesday 13 October, but on the Thursday Hinds found himself writing to Trevelyan again: "When I presented my emaciated version of the climax in the Court scene to the director and actors, they were (not surprisingly) a little disappointed. The director asked me if we could work with them to increase the drama of the scene without re-introducing the idea of a medical examination, to which you had objected. I agreed provided he shot it in such a way that it could be re-edited if any further objection was made."

Trevelyan wearily replied the following day: "I think it is possible that the drama of the court scene could be increased without raising objections from us provided that there is no attempt made to reintroduce the idea of the medical examination. This is the one thing to which we are certain to object. I think it wise to shoot the scene, as you have suggested, in such a way that it could be re-edited if we have difficulties with it."

Meanwhile, on Monday 21 September, a week into production of *Never Take Sweets from a Stranger*, Val Guest took another Hammer team to the Associated British Studios at Elstree and on location in Manchester for the gritty crime drama, *Hell is a City* – spearheaded by Stanley Baker in his second Hammer/Guest collaboration that year.

The organisation required to run two prestige pictures side by side was challenging; Tony Hinds produced *Never Take Sweets from a Stranger* while Michael Carreras produced *Hell is a City*, and between them they had to share out their team of regulars. Arthur Grant shot the Carreras picture, while Hammer newcomer Freddie Francis shot the Hinds project. This was a coup for the company. Francis would become a two-time Oscar-winning cinematographer for his work, as well as reappearing at Hammer as a director. "Freddie Francis had been recommended to me as an up-and-coming cameraman," recalled Tony Hinds. "I told him he could have whatever equipment he wanted, but that we never stopped shooting, regardless of the weather. He told me later that was the main reason he took the job; he is a real pro and doesn't like hanging about wasting time." [17] Harry Oakes recalled: "It wasn't Freddie's usual lighting on that picture, not his style at all really, and afterwards we tackled him about it. He said, 'Well, it's Tony Hinds' idea. He wanted it to look like newsreel quality.' So it looked more authentic, not glossy."

Bray retained its usual team of Len Harris, Harry Oakes, John Peverall, Tom Walls, Bernard Robinson, Don Mingaye, Jock May and Tilly Day. Michael Carreras poached Bray's regular 3rd assistant Hugh Harlow and promoted him to 2nd assistant on *Hell is a City*. Bray's usual production manager Don Weeks was seconded to Val Guest's production, leaving Hinds with Clifford Parkes. Parkes would now effectively alternate productions with Weeks at Bray. Alfred Cox raced back from *Stranglers* to cut *Never Take Sweets from a Stranger*, while Hammer's other regular editor, John Dunsford, took over on *Hell is a City*. James Needs, of course, supervised both productions.

Harry Oakes' diary records details of shooting *Never Take Sweets from a Stranger*, noting Black Park locations in Weeks One, Three and Seven; exteriors at Burnham Beaches on 6 October and Oakley Court three days later; and, in a nod to a former denizen of Bray with whom he'd worked three years earlier, on Thursday 15 October: "Errol Flynn has died."

Never Take Sweets from a Stranger is an absorbing film, unfortunately rarely seen and often obscured by Hammer's mainstream horror pictures. Admirably, Hammer played down the sensationalism, allowing the drama to become more realistic via some fine acting from Gwen Watford, Patrick Allen, Felix Aylmer, Michael Gwynn, Niall MacGinnis – and, of course, Janina Faye and Frances Green as the two children.

Janina Faye remembers Cyril Frankel's novel approach to directing children: "Frankel always coached his children personally in their dialogue. The lines reach them from his own lips, not from the script. Cyril Frankel's approach to directing us was slightly unusual for me at the time as I had always been given film scripts in all my previous roles and asked to get the lines learnt and well-prepared before arriving on set. Rehearsals of the scenes took place in the small dressing room at Bray Studios and rehearsing the scenes without a script was much more scary than acting them on set. It would never be allowed now; two young girls and their male director alone in a closed room – what would Lady Lewisham have made of that?"

Frankel explained his approach in a press release for the film: "If a child has acted before, I break that down, make him or her forget it and start from scratch. Nor do I allow child artistes to learn their lines from a script. I don't even let them *see* a script. It's most important not to destroy the illusion that they are taking part in a story. It helps preserve their natural spirit of adventure and make-believe."

This explains why Janina wasn't allowed to meet Felix Aylmer prior to their scenes together. "Felix Aylmer was deliberately never introduced to us; this I now understand was to 'maintain our belief in the story.' For this reason I found him a rather sinister character, all dressed in white, and never speaking a word."

The now infamous courtroom sequence was also particularly gruelling since Frankel insisted on filming it, for the most part, in a single take. Janina Faye remembers, "The courtroom sequence threw up more difficulties for the technical staff than it ever did for me. I do remember my chaperone getting extremely irate at the close of shooting that day because Cyril Frankel insisted on going into overtime so that the scene could be finished. My chaperone thought that I had

Inspector Martineau (Stanley Baker) interrogates Gus Hawkins (Donald Pleasence) in Val Guest's gritty crime drama Hell is a City (1959).

HELL IS A CITY

PRINCIPAL PHOTOGRAPHY: 21 September to 5 November 1959
DISTRIBUTION:
UK: Associated British-Warner Pathe; 98 minutes; certificate 'A'
US: Columbia; 93 minutes
b/w; Hammerscope
UK RELEASE:
TRADE SHOW: 11 March 1960
PREMIÈRE: 10 April 1960 (northern première in Ardwick)
GENERAL RELEASE: 1 May 1960
US RELEASE: 18 January 1961

DIRECTOR: *Val Guest;* PRODUCER: *Michael Carreras;* SCREENPLAY: *Val Guest based on the novel by Maurice Procter;* ART DIRECTOR: *Robert Jones;* DIRECTOR OF PHOTOGRAPHY: *Arthur Grant;* CAMERA OPERATOR: *Moray Grant;* ASSISTANT DIRECTOR: *Philip Shipway;* 2ND ASSISTANT DIRECTOR: *Hugh Harlow;*

SUPERVISING EDITOR: *James Needs;* EDITOR: *John Dunsford;* MUSIC COMPOSER AND CONDUCTOR: *Stanley Black;* SOUND RECORDIST: *Leslie Hammond, Len Shilton;* RECORDING DIRECTOR: *AW Lumkin;* MAKE-UP: *Colin Garde;* HAIR STYLIST: *Pauline Trent;* PRODUCTION MANAGER: *Don Weeks;* CONTINUITY: *Doreen Dearnaley;* WARDROBE: *'Jacky' Jackson;* CASTING DIRECTOR: *Robert Lennard;* ASSISTANT CASTING DIRECTOR: *David Booth*

Stanley Baker (Inspector Martineau); John Crawford (Don Starling); Donald Pleasence (Gus Hawkins); Maxine Audley (Julia Martineau); Billie Whitelaw (Chloe Hawkins); Joseph Tomelty (Furnisher Steele); Vanda Godsell (Lucky Luske); Geoffrey Frederick (Constable Devery); Sarah Branch (Silver); George A Cooper (Doug Savage); Charles Houston (Clogger Roach); Joby Blanshard (Tawny Jakes); Charles Morgan (Laurie Lovett); Peter Madden (Bert Darwin); Dickie Owen (Bragg); Lois Dane (Cecily); Warren Mitchell (Comercial Traveller); Alastair Williamson (Sam); Russel Napier (Superintendent)

become genuinely hysterical and that the scene should be stopped there and then. Convincing stuff! Filming always meant time out from normal school work for many weeks," she added. "The film company provided a tutor and academic work was supposed to take place for four hours of every day. Achieving this was somewhat problematic and never happened consecutively. These hours were snatched here and there whenever filming allowed."

In stark contrast, *Hell is a City* is not a message movie. Michael Carreras had discovered the source novel by former Manchester policeman Maurice Procter and passed it on to Val Guest for scripting and directing. It is a hard-hitting crime drama following the exploits of Detective Inspector Martineau, played by Stanley Baker, and his search for the ruthless criminal, Don Starling (John Crawford), who has his own score to settle with Baker's brash policeman. Guest again directs tightly in his trademark documentary style, leading to a crashing finale atop

Manchester's Refuge Assurance Company building. Other Manchester locations permeate the production; Guest even used the regulars of The Fatted Calf pub that was standing in for The Lacy Arms, as well as enlisting the help of the local Manchester police force.

Of the supporting actors, Vanda Godsell and Sarah Branch would both return to Hammer the following year in Sword of Sherwood Forest. Donald Pleasence made his only Hammer appearance, in one of those twitchy roles he excelled at. Billie Whitelaw is also brilliant as Starling's ex-lover and provided Hammer's first (albeit brief) nude scene to find its way into a domestic print. Look out, too, for several faces that would crop up in future Hammer productions: Maxine Audley, George A Cooper, Charles Houston, Peter Madden, Dickie Owen, Lois Dane, Warren Mitchell and Alister Williamson.

Director Val Guest and actor Stanley Baker escaped the rigours of Hell is a City to attend the British première of Yesterday's Enemy on Thursday 17 September at the Empire Theatre, Leicester Square. This was a special gala performance held in honour of the Burma Star Association; the film had already had its world première in Tokyo in July. In attendance was Lord Mountbatten of Burma. Guest remembers, "Bernie Robinson built a jungle with various sections on a revolve, so that when you had walked through one section you could just revolve the section to get another part of the jungle. A brilliant idea. At the première I sat next to Lord Mountbatten of Burma and he thought he knew where it was. He kept saying, 'I know that place.' I hadn't the heart to tell him it was Shepperton!"

The press was very favourable. The Monthly Film Bulletin wrote: "This small-scale River Kwai, based on a well meaning but only partially successful television play, comes as something of a surprise for those who associate Hammer Films with horror and who recall that Val Guest's previous film on a related subject was The Camp on Blood Island ... We are made to realise that the whole business of total war, in spite of the individual acts of heroism, is a dirty, degrading, senseless waste of human life." Films and Filming added: "I applaud this piece of drama because it makes no attempt to pretend war can be fun, glamorous, heroic ... any of these overdone box-office clichés. Instead, it tries to probe the real meanings and qualities of courage ... after a progression of horror and war films in distressingly bad taste, it is good to see such a sincere piece of film making from Hammer." The film went on general release on the ABC circuit from Monday 19 October.

The Mummy was next, premiering at the London Pavilion on Friday 25 September, where it took more in its first four days than any other Universal/Rank release of the time. The Pavilion's huge cinema display can be seen briefly in the monster movie Gorgo, released the following year, as the dinosaur in question is driven through Piccadilly Circus. In the foyer at the première were actors playing Anubis and three Royal Egyptian hand maidens dressed in diaphanous gowns. The handmaidens presented guests with tablets of fresh bread impressed with the Royal cartouche of Ancient Egypt. The film went on general release from Friday 23 October, beating even the records set by Dracula the previous year. It was later released in the States in December, where it continued to break Dracula-set records.

Never Take Sweets from a Stranger finally wrapped on Friday 30 October after seven weeks and Hell is a City finished one week later on Thursday 5 November. As both films began post-production, Michael Carreras was preparing Hammer's next colour 'Gothic' at Bray.

Kinematograph Weekly on 12 March 1959 had warned the trade that The Ugly Duckling would "be followed later in the year by a 'straight' version." Although The Two Faces of Dr Jekyll was very much Michael Carreras' baby, it would seem he was heavily influenced by his friend Val Guest. Guest had been busy producing and directing a film version of Wolf Mankowitz' stage musical Expresso Bongo and had asked Mankowitz to write the screenplay, with music and lyrics by David Heneker and Monty Norman. The film was led by Laurence Harvey and Sylvia Syms, with Guest's wife Yolande Donlan and a young Cliff Richard in support. Around this time Guest introduced Mankowitz to Michael Carreras and they conceived a novel reworking of the Jekyll and Hyde tale, with Laurence Harvey in mind for the dual role. A further hangover from Guest's production was to ask Heneker and Norman to score the film, including a couple of songs. Harvey, however, was unavailable and the part eventually went to 27-year-old Canadian actor Paul Massie on the strength of his performance in Libel. Massie's debut in Orders to Kill the previous year had earned him the British Film Academy's Most Promising Actor award.

Mankowitz turned Stevenson's classic novel on its head, and his twist was in line with Hammer's classic depiction of what Fisher coined 'the charm of evil'. As Mankowitz himself

Hyde (Paul
Massie) transforms
at the inquest,
revealing his
terrible secret to
Litauer (David
Kossoff) and the
inspector (Francis
De Wolff, standing
in the background)
in The Two Faces
of Dr Jekyll
(1959).

THE TWO FACES OF DR JEKYLL

PRINCIPAL PHOTOGRAPHY: 23 November to 22 January
1959/60
DISTRIBUTION:
UK: Columbia; certificate 'X'
US: American International; US title: *House of Fright*
88 minutes; Technicolor; Megascope
UK RELEASE:
TRADE SHOW: 20 August 1960 at the Columbia Theatre
PREMIÈRE: 7 October 1960 at the London Pavilion,
Picadilly Circus
GENERAL RELEASE: 24 October 1960, on the ABC circuit
with *Hot Hours*
US RELEASE: May 1961 with *Terror in the Haunted House*

DIRECTOR: Terence Fisher; PRODUCER: Michael Carreras;
ASSOCIATE PRODUCER: Anthony Nelson Keys; SCREENPLAY: Wolf
Mankowitz; PRODUCTION DESIGNER: Bernard Robinson;
ASSISTANT ART DIRECTOR: Don Mingaye; MODELLER: Margaret
Carter; DIRECTOR OF PHOTOGRAPHY: Jack Asher; CAMERA
OPERATOR: Len Harris; FOCUS PULLER: Harry Oakes; ASSISTANT
DIRECTOR: John Peverall; 2ND ASSISTANT: Hugh Harlow;
SUPERVISING EDITOR: James Needs; EDITOR: Eric Boyd-Perkins;
ASSISTANT EDITOR: Chris Barnes; MUSIC AND SONGS: Monty
Norman and David Heneker; MUSIC SUPERVISOR: John
Hollingsworth; SOUND RECORDIST: Jock May; SOUND EDITOR:
Archie Ludski; MAKE-UP: Roy Ashton; HAIRSTYLIST: Ivy Emmerton;
PRODUCTION MANAGER: Clifford Parkes; CONTINUITY: Tilly Day;
WARDROBE: Molly Arbuthnot; COSTUME DESIGNER: Mayo;
DANCE DIRECTION: Julie Mendez; CASTING: Dorothy Holloway;

PROPERTY MASTER: Tommy Money; PROPERTY BUYER: Eric
Hillier; STUDIO MANAGER: Arthur Kelly; CHIEF ELECTRICIAN:
Jack Curtis; MASTER PAINTER: Lawrence Wren; MASTER
CARPENTER: Charles Davis; STILLS CAMERAMAN: Tom Edwards

Paul Massie (Jekyll/Hyde); Dawn Addams (Kitty); Christopher Lee
(Paul Allen); David Kossoff (Litauer); Norma Marla (Maria);
Francis De Wolff (Inspector); Joy Webster (First Brass)

UNCREDITED: Maria Andippa (Gypsy Girl); Frank Atkinson
(Groom); John Bonney (Renfrew); Percy Cartwright (Coroner); Dennis
Cleary (Waiter); Helen Goss (Nannie); Janine Faye (Jane); Felix Felton
(First Gambler); Walter Gotell (Second Gambler); Prudence Hyman,
Lucy Griffiths (Tavern Women); Doreen Ismail (Second Sphinx Girl);
Anthony Jacobs (Third Gambler); William Kendall (Clubman);
Roberta Kirkwood (Second Brass); Arthur Lovegrove (Cabby); Magda
Miller (Sphinx Girl); Oliver Reed (Tough); Joe Robinson (Corinthian);
Douglas Robinson (Boxer); Denis Shaw (Tavern Customer); Pauline
Shepherd (Tavern Girl); Donald Tandy (Plainclothes Man); Joan
Tyrill (Major Domo); Joyce Wren (Nurse); Archie Baker, Ralph
Broadbent, Alex Miller, Laurence Richardson (Singers); Anthony
Pendrell, Fred Stone (Cabinet ministers [Sphinx Customers]); Glenn
Beck, Alan Browning, Rodney Burke, Clifford Earl (Young bloods
[Sphinx Customers]); Roy Denton, Kenneth Firth, George McGrath,
Mackenzie Ward (Business men [Sphinx Customers]); John Moore, J
Trevor-Davis (Officers [Sphinx Customers]); Bandana Des Gupta,
Pauline Dukes, Hazel Graeme, Carole Haynes, Josephine Jay, Jean
Long, Marilyn Ridge, Gundel Sargent, Patricia Sayers, Shirli Scott-
James, Moyna Sharwin (Sphinx Girls)

explained, "Evil is attractive to all men, therefore, it is not illogical that the face of evil should be attractive. That is why I made Mr. Hyde handsome instead of repulsive. This is not a horror film; it is a comment on the two-facedness of respectable society." [18]

This is certainly the theme throughout. Few of the main characters have any redeeming features, from Jekyll's two-timing wife to his scheming, two-faced friend Paul Allen. Director Terence Fisher agreed. "There was not one redeeming character in *The Two Faces of Dr Jekyll*. Only one person had any semblance of good in him and that was Jekyll's friend who said, 'For God's sake be careful about what you're doing.' And he didn't do very much stopping. They were basically a shoddy lot, weren't they? Jekyll, who allowed himself to become shoddy. Chris Lee, who was shoddy. A wife who was no good anyway. God – raped by her reconstructed husband! It was an exercise, rightly or wrongly, badly done or well done, in evil. You didn't have a single character in that story who was worth tuppence ha'penny. I liked the script. I think Wolf Mankowitz wrote it partly from the point of view that Victorian England was corrupt. But it wasn't fundamentally a very deep script, was it? Its strength, I think, was that Wolf Mankowitz realised that evil wasn't a horrible thing crawling around the street. It's very charming and attractive and seductive. Temptation! That was the only strength of the script, and the only interesting thing too." [19]

Michael Carreras submitted a script to John Trevelyan towards the end of October. Trevelyan replied on the 29th: "I have now read through Wolf Mankowitz's revised script for *The Two Faces of Dr Jekyll*. This should make a powerful and gripping film. But, as I pointed out when we met, it raises censorship difficulties, some of which are important. The three ingredients of sex, violence and horror are here in full measure, and the combination produces a pretty deadly cocktail. I hope that you and Mankowitz will be able to weaken the mixture without spoiling the drink. The full strength mixture might be dangerous, particularly to some younger cinema-goers who are impressionable and see the relief from boredom and dull lives in what they would call kicks. They would not need chemical formulae to bring out their 'Hydes', and there is still a good deal of degradation to be found at comparatively small cost."

Philosophical stuff, as if Hammer really cared. Evidently Carreras and Mankowitz had planned a grandiose production. Mankowitz himself was a writer of some calibre and it perhaps didn't seem too ambitious at first to imagine Laurence Harvey in the role(s) of Jekyll and Hyde. Mankowitz's original treatment explored the corruptness of society more explicitly and looked set to run well over the usual 90 minutes – Carreras was definitely thinking big. Eventually, however, the script had to be pared down to fit a more realistic Hammer schedule. Add to that John Trevelyan's pound of flesh and Fisher's difficulty in warming to the project, and the final movie becomes a very diluted version of what might have been. Lost, for example, was the disturbing climax:

In the far distance ... we see a man on the gallows. We move in very fast till we are close to the face of Jekyll. The trap swings away, the body jerks as the rope tautens. Slowly the body revolves away. As the body again swings into camera we now see the dead face of Hyde.

Paul Massie signed his contract on Thursday 19 November, just four days before the film began rolling at Bray on Monday the 23rd. Interestingly, while the film was on the floor at Bray, the censor was still mulling over the script. Michael Carreras sent over some revisions to Trevelyan on 10 December: "I am looking forward to showing you some of the material already cut together on *The Two Faces of Dr Jekyll*. I understand this is being done on Tuesday of next week. In the meantime, I would like you to read the enclosed. You will undoubtedly remember that the major objection to our screenplay, and the one we were most reluctant to have to overcome, was the strangling of 'Paul' by the Python, simultaneously with the raping of 'Kitty' by 'Hyde'. The enclosed is our suggested amended version, separating the two incidents and I sincerely hope this will satisfy."

Trevelyan replied to Carreras on the 18th: "Since we have spoken over the telephone I have not previously acknowledged your letter of 10th December, but I do so now for [the] record. I was glad to receive the amended version of the scenes sent with your letter and think that the separation of the raping of Kitty and the killing of Paul is a definite improvement from our point of view. Provided that the visuals present no censorship trouble, the scenes should be acceptable."

After a break of three weeks, the same crew from *Never Take Sweets from a Stranger* was back, apart from a different lighting cameraman (the return of Jack Asher), editor (Eric Boyd-Perkins), hairstylist (Ivy Emmerton) and 2nd assistant (Hugh Harlow). "Michael Carreras was my mentor and he was the one that was kind of nurturing me to progress through the company," Hugh Harlow remembers. "When we did the half-hour featurettes, Michael was the one who took me with him to work on the floor as a runner and get my union ticket to become a 3rd. I got my first big break as 2nd on location in Alassio on *The Snorkel*, but I came back to do 3rd. My first full picture as 2nd was *Hell is a City* in Manchester and at ABPC as it was called then, Elstree Studios today. Michael kept me on as 2nd assistant for *The Two Faces of Dr Jekyll*. I seem to recall there being a union reaction to it, because it had put Tom Walls out of place. I was on permanent payroll, whereas Tom was not. He was on a picture-to-picture basis, more like a freelance."

After artists' tests on 12, 13 and 19 November, the picture began shooting on Monday the 23rd and moved into Elstree a week later, finishing there on 15 December. This allowed Bernard Robinson to erect his impressive lab and garden set on that studio's more spacious stages. Fisher tackled the production in Megascope – this was, after all, a Michael

Paul Massie as the bearded Jekyll in The Two Faces of Dr Jekyll (1959)

Carreras picture. Alas, Fisher found himself at odds with Mankowitz's characterisation of Jekyll and Hyde. "The initial idea of presenting evil as a young and seductive character was an exceptionally good one," he explained. "Maybe Hyde's character was not sufficiently compelling. Of course he represents evil, but he is also a living being and could have had a little more character and personality. Maybe he should have been written differently, but maybe my own direction might be mainly responsible for this lifelessness. You can't always blame the writers, you know. That's too easy! ... I must say that I don't really think I ever tried to love that film very much. It is one of those films out of which I never managed to get the maximum effect ... it isn't the ending that bothers me. It is just the Hyde character itself. I should have further emphasised his monstrous behaviour and at the same time made him more of a human being, torn between the duality of his personality. But, in spite of everything, the film does have some very good moments – Jekyll lying in the mud, for instance."[20]

Mankowitz's script seems, in any case, to have great difficulty in bringing out the evil side of Hyde. The best he can do to savour the heights of perversion is frequenting nightclubs, watching prizefights and smoking a bit of dope, antics which don't even come close to the depravity seen in the Fredric March and Spencer Tracy versions. The sexual tension which saturated those earlier films is also sadly lacking in Hammer's tale; it takes more than the graphic charms of a snake dancer, busty Sphinx hostesses and the promise of nudity to rival the unforgettable performances of Miriam Hopkins and Ingrid Bergman.

According to publicity releases at the time, Massie was initially chosen to play the part of Hyde only. Putting a strong case to Carreras, he persuaded him that he was capable of playing Jekyll also, with the aid of some simple make-up, and that having two different actors in the parts would only destroy the overall effect. For Jekyll, make-up artist Roy Ashton broadened the bridge of Massie's nose, added wrinkles under his eyes and gave him contact lenses, as well as a different wig and, of course, the token beard. Christopher Lee looked on in envy. He later admitted he would have loved to have had a stab at the part, but instead was offered only Jekyll's scheming friend Paul Allen, although it remains an excellent performance. He would later take the role of Jekyll and Hyde (renamed Marlowe and Blake) in Amicus' *I, Monster* (1970).

Continuity supervisor Tilly Day remembers the temperamental Paul Massie. "I think the one who lived his parts most was Paul Massie ... He kicked the make-up door in! He did that when they put

Henry Jekyll (Paul Massie) greets little Jane (Janina Faye) watched by his friend Litauer (David Kossoff) in The Two Faces of Dr Jekyll (1959).

the contact lenses in. In those days the use of contact lenses in film make-up was still quite new and could be really uncomfortable. When they fitted Massie with his, it hurt so much he'd kick the door really hard, on more than one occasion! One day Michael Carreras came on the set and heard that terrible noise from upstairs. When he asked what was going on, someone very nonchalantly replied, 'Oh, that's only Paul Massie kicking the door in again!'" [21]

In support were 29-year-old Dawn Addams as Jekyll's unfaithful wife Kitty (she flew into London from Paris to join the production on Thursday 26 November) and a Mankowitz regular, David Kossoff, as Jekyll's troubled friend and confidant, Ernst Litauer. Norma Marla had already appeared in the other Jekyll and Hyde caper, The Ugly Duckling, as well as putting in an appearance at the première of The Mummy. Of note in the background is a small appearance by up-and-coming young actor Oliver Reed. Hammer would have more substantial duties for him the following year, duties which would ultimately launch his international career, but for the time being it was a fitting introduction for the ex-nightclub bouncer to be involved in a nightclub brawl with Hyde. Also at the wrong end of a brawl was Janina Faye, fresh from Never Take Sweets from a Stranger, as one of the children allowed to play in Jekyll's garden.

One of the 'stars' of the film was the snake which kills Christopher Lee. Once more Hammer turned to Margaret Carter. "I had to go to the Raymond Revuebar where the snake dancer was appearing with the snake, and copy it so that there were two duplicates, a limp one made of foam rubber and painted for when it was dead – I think they used that – and an articulated one which was to fight Christopher Lee. You see, Christopher Lee couldn't fight with a real snake, that's why I had to make the articulated one. Then in the end they cut the fight scene. There was just him lying on the ground with the real snake crawling across him, so he'd obviously been talked into letting the snake be with him." She used the innards of her landlord's discarded piano to make the articulated snake, and points out that "It must have been good, because when the three were lying stretched out in a row, Michael Carreras picked up the real one by mistake! I was very put out when it wasn't used. I was paid for it but that was my prize snake. To pacify me, Michael Carreras assured me it would be used in a future production, The Indian Mutiny, based on a very good script by Tony Hinds. But would you believe it? The film was never made."

Bray's caretaker, Marje Hudd, also remembers how realistic Margaret's mock snake was. "I remember this rubber python was on the floor in our dressing room. Well, one of our cleaners was screaming 'Marje! Marje!' I said, 'Whatever's the matter?' She said, 'Come up here quick, I'm frightened to go in!' We all went rushing up there and there was this rubber snake. It was very lifelike!"

Marje also remembers the tragic story of the girl who came across to teach Norma Marla her snake dancing routine. "I remember they made Jekyll and Hyde and they had this little Peruvian girl. She was doing a play up at the Café de Paris in London. She wasn't much bigger than me and she had a python. She used to wind it around her. Peru was a very poor country; she was over here on a two-year working order to get money for her family. The studio hired her to teach the artist to hold this python long enough for the cameras to get it. Of course, we got chatting and she was ever such a nice little thing, who used to speak broken English, telling us how hard up they were. Well, the artist couldn't get on with it – she was terrified of this python. Eventually the little girl went back to the Café de Paris and they used a rubber python.

"But that little girl – it's a sad story really and I've always remembered it – she went back to the Café de Paris and, about three months later, Doreen on switchboard called me when I was going past in the corridor. She looked upset and I said, 'What's the matter?' She showed me a London paper and that python had killed her. A marksman shot it, but he wasn't quick enough and it killed her. The Café de Paris were very good. They sent the rest of the money that she would have earned home to Peru. We were very upset, because we had grown fond of her. We had all clubbed together and got her some money when she left and she was pleased as anything. It was a shame."

A newcomer to Hammer was Eric Boyd-Perkins, who took on the editing chores alongside James Needs. "Jimmy Needs rang me up actually and asked me if I was doing anything and would I like to take on the job," he recalls. "After that I did several for Hammer and we got on very well. I remember Jimmy Needs working at Pinewood in the early days when I was an assistant. He came to cut a film called *Boys in Brown* (1949), with Dirk Bogarde, so he was pretty experienced as an editor before he went to Exclusive. As supervising editor Jim was responsible to the management for the final result. I would do about 99 per cent of the editing and he would okay it. Occasionally he would sit down with me and we'd go through the material and see if we could find a better way to do it, but he was really what you would call a post-production supervisor. At music, post-synch and dubbing sessions I was on my own quite often as Jim would be checking on other projects. It was very good to be able to have somebody to talk to and to have influence with the producers and so forth."

Never Take Sweets from a Stranger was finally submitted to the BBFC on Thursday 19 November. No documentation survives as to how it was received, but it was clearly considered for the 'X' category. James Carreras was not satisfied; he'd been hoping for an 'A'. John Trevelyan wrote to Carreras on the 25th: "I have discussed the question of category for *Never Take Sweets from a Stranger* with our Examiners, several of whom saw the picture. They are absolutely definite in their view that the film should be in the 'X' category and that any attempt to get it into the 'A' category could only have the effect of spoiling a really good film. This kind of unhappy perversion which afflicts some old men is not the kind of thing that we want children to see, and we think that if there should be a warning it should be one for the parents rather than the children. I am afraid, therefore, that we must keep the category already chosen."

The debate would continue well into the coming year. Meanwhile, *The Man Who Could Cheat Death* was released on Monday 30 November on the ABC circuit. On 4 December, Terence Fisher escaped the grind of *The Two Faces of Dr Jekyll* to attend the British première of *The Stranglers of Bombay* at the London Pavilion. The film would go on general release on the ABC circuit from 18 January 1960. The critics were again repelled by the harsh and brutal storyline.

1959 had been an odd year for Hammer, with their side order of tough dramas (*Yesterday's Enemy*, *Never Take Sweets from a Stranger* and *Hell is a City*) proving to be just as interesting as their Gothic counterparts. Indeed, *Yesterday's Enemy* was nominated by the BFA (British Film Academy, now BAFTA) as 'Best Film' of 1959; the prize went to Basil Dearden's *Sapphire*. Also nominated by the BFA were Stanley Baker for 'Best Actor' and Gordon Jackson for 'Best Supporting Actor'. (These again went to *Sapphire* – Nigel Patrick and Michael Craig respectively). It's a shame that, within a year, Hammer would be forced to jettison similar projects, largely at the insistence of their main American backer, Columbia. In their place would spring a successful series of monochrome psychological thrillers, beginning with *Taste of Fear*.

EIGHT

The Werewolf and the Censor

(1 9 6 0)

In January 1960, Hammer were putting the finishing touches to *The Two Faces of Dr Jekyll*. Principal photography had been scheduled for the customary six weeks and was due to end on Wednesday 6 January. However, the production ran over schedule and over budget and finally finished on Friday 22 January at an inflated cost of £146,417 – astronomical by Hammer standards. James Carreras was not pleased.

Editors Eric Boyd-Perkins and James Needs, together with sound editor Archie Ludski, now took the film into post-production at Hammer House. Michael Carreras brought in Monty Norman and

David Heneker to compose the score and write the songs under the watchful eye of music supervisor John Hollingsworth. Norman, of course, would later become famous for his 'James Bond' theme. While all this was going on, Hammer's plans for the long-awaited sequel to *Dracula* were well underway.

Thousands had thrilled to the final death throes of Count Dracula in 1958. It was only a matter of time before Universal-International bent Hammer's arm for a sequel. Baron Frankenstein had already returned, courtesy Jimmy Sangster, and now Sangster was called upon to resurrect the Count. Sangster submitted his first draft in March 1959 under the title *Disciple of Dracula*. It told of the hero Latour's search for the Baron Meinster; at the end Latour conjures up the spirit of Count Dracula to destroy his unfaithful disciple. It was a start, but Tony Hinds was not entirely happy and in September he offered the project instead to his friend, ex-Hammer camera operator Peter Bryan, who had already penned *The Hound of the Baskervilles*. His remit – to remove Dracula altogether.

> ## Hammer Productions
> ### —— 1 9 6 0 ——
>
> + *THE BRIDES OF DRACULA*
> + *THE TERROR OF THE TONGS*
> + *THE FULL TREATMENT*
> + *SWORD OF SHERWOOD FOREST*
> + *VISA TO CANTON*
> + *THE CURSE OF THE WEREWOLF*
> + *A WEEKEND WITH LULU*
> + *TASTE OF FEAR*
> + *THE SHADOW OF THE CAT*

Bryan produced a new script, dated 19 November 1959, called *The Brides of Dracula*. Van Helsing was now added and Latour was relegated to a mysterious presence at the beginning. In diminishing the character, Bryan removed

OPPOSITE: *Oliver Reed as the lycanthropic Leon in* The Curse of the Werewolf *(1960).*

Sangster's opening, in which Latour kills a newly interred vampire by thrusting a spade through the coffin lid; the scene would be resurrected later by Tony Hinds for the opening of *The Kiss of the Vampire*. Sangster's two visiting English girls were replaced by French heroine Marianne Danielle and a horde of bats replaced the vengeful Dracula at the climax. As instructed, Dracula was omitted altogether and it was now clear that this was a vehicle for Peter Cushing's Dr Van Helsing.

What happened from this point on is not well documented and has always remained a source of contention among Hammer fans and historians alike. It appears that Tony Hinds submitted a copy of Bryan's revised script to Peter Cushing in November 1959 and that Cushing was unimpressed. "Peter Cushing would not agree to do it," recalled Tony Hinds. "I offered to employ another writer. I think he suggested Edward Percy, an elderly theatrical agent [actually a playwright] of the old school. We arranged to meet at the sombre, oak-panelled, oil-portraited Garrick Club in London. Tea and buttered toast were served by the blazing fire. Percy told me what ideas he had. I told him they were excellent (they were quite awful) and to get on with it as quickly as possible as we had a studio date. I left enough of his theatrical bits in to convince Peter it was a rewrite and that's what we used." [1]

According to Denis Meikle in his classic analysis of Hammer, *A History of Horrors*: "The 69-year-old Percy would add a touch of period colour but little else, though Cushing was to remain none the wiser." Meikle implies that the major changes which appeared in the final shooting script (dated January 1960 under the new title *Dracula II*, and containing no writer credit) were largely down to Hinds himself. It is interesting that Bernard Robinson's pre-production set designs for the film and Harry Oakes' diary also call the production *Dracula II*.

Hinds instituted two major changes. The first, and most significant, was the climax. As Bryan had realised it in his November 1959 draft, Van Helsing performs an ancient ritual to bring down a cloud of bats on Baron Meinster, afterwards casting the cruciform shadow of the windmill sails on him, as per the finished film. Accordingly, Bernard Robinson's future wife, Margaret Carter, was asked to fashion two prototype bats for the scene.

"I know that I had made two prototype bats, one of which was more detailed and well-made," she remembers. "Les Bowie lost the best bat and Bernard was very cross, because the second best bat was returned to us, but the best bat had vanished and nobody knew where it was. Though Bernard had the greatest regard for Les Bowie and he would not have suspected him, he felt very incensed that someone had got their thieving hands on the best bat and it hadn't come back from Les Bowie's studio. I was so amused, because it wasn't needed after all, but Bernard for some reason had got fond

Gina (Andrée Melly) rises from her coffin to terrorise Marianne (Yvonne Monlaur) in The Brides of Dracula (1960).

THE BRIDES OF DRACULA

PRINCIPAL PHOTOGRAPHY: 26 January to 18 March 1960
DISTRIBUTION:
  UK: Rank; certificate 'X'
  US: Universal-International
85 minutes; Technicolor
UK RELEASE:
  PREMIÈRE: 7 July 1960 at Odeon Marble Arch
  GENERAL RELEASE: 29 August 1960, on the Rank
    circuit with Teenage Lovers
US RELEASE: September 1960, with The Leech Woman

DIRECTOR: Terence Fisher; PRODUCER: Anthony Hinds; ASSOCIATE PRODUCER: Anthony Nelson Keys; EXECUTIVE PRODUCER: Michael Carreras; SCREENPLAY: Jimmy Sangster, Peter Bryan and Edward Percy; PRODUCTION DESIGNER: Bernard Robinson; ART DIRECTOR: Thomas Goswell; ASSISTANT ART DIRECTOR: Don Mingaye; DIRECTOR OF PHOTOGRAPHY: Jack Asher; CAMERA OPERATOR: Len Harris; FOCUS PULLER: Harry Oakes; GRIP: Albert Cowland; ASSISTANT DIRECTOR: John Peverall; 2ND ASSISTANT DIRECTOR:

Hugh Harlow; SUPERVISING EDITOR: James Needs; EDITOR: Alfred Cox; MUSIC: Malcolm Williamson; MUSIC SUPERVISOR: John Hollingsworth; SOUND RECORDIST: Jock May; SOUND EDITOR: James Groom; MAKE-UP: Roy Ashton; HAIRSTYLIST: Frieda Steiger; PRODUCTION MANAGER: Don Weeks; CONTINUITY: Tilly Day; WARDROBE: Molly Arbuthnot; SPECIAL EFFECTS: Sydney Pearson; STUDIO MANAGER: A F Kelly; CHIEF ELECTRICIAN: Jack Curtis; PROPS MASTER: Tommy Money; PROPS BUYER: Eric Hillier

Peter Cushing (Doctor Van Helsing); Martita Hunt (Baroness Meinster); Yvonne Monlaur (Marianne); Freda Jackson (Greta); David Peel (Baron Meinster); Miles Malleson (Dr Tobler); Henry Oscar (Herr Lang); Mona Washbourne (Frau Lang); Andrée Melly (Gina); Victor Brooks (Hans); Fred Johnson (Cure); Michael Ripper (Coachman); Norman Pierce (Landlord); Vera Cook (Landlord's Wife); Marie Devereux (Village Girl)

UNCREDITED: Susan Castle (Maid); Michael Mulcaster (Latour); Harry Pringle (Jacques); Harold Scott (Severin)

of that bat. I put a lot of work into it. The wings were a thin latex rubber and there was a very nice bit of velvety fur fabric on its back. It was quite a nice little bat and I'd used the face of the hog-nosed bat on it because, when I came to research bats, I found that the big bats and the fruit bats have quite pleasant faces, a bit like a mild fox, and the really grotesque one is the hog-nosed bat. I had done miniatures and when they wanted a large flying bat, I had wanted them to do an enlargement of the hog-nosed one, but they said, 'Oh no, we're using the biggest type of bat that is in existence'. They suddenly, in the midst of making a fantasy film, had to have the bat authentic!"

It's worth noting here in Margaret's defence that the highly unconvincing bat we see in the finished film, flapping lethargically on wires, was made by special effects man Syd Pearson.

While Bryan's version made for an exciting climax, Peter Cushing for one was far from impressed. "Well, I just thought it made no sense," commented Cushing, "that Van Helsing is brandishing crucifixes and Holy Water all through the film, and then, at the climax, he summons the forces of evil – a swarm of vampire bats – to destroy the vampire."[2] So Hinds removed the bats, replacing them with the simpler procedure of burning Meinster's face with Holy Water, which results in him kicking over a brazier and setting fire to the mill.

Hinds' second alteration would change the whole structure of the last third of the story. In Bryan's draft, when the Baron visits Marianne at the academy, he actually bites her and she is therefore left in his power. Hinds must have decided that there was no advantage in Meinster taking Marianne's blood, but with Marianne no longer under the influence of the Baron, her rather naïve decision to marry him becomes totally absurd. This change also meant that Hinds had to reshape the scene to come in the stables, when Gina rises from her coffin. Bryan's original script had the vampirised Marianne helping Gina get out of her locked coffin. Now Hinds cleverly changed the scene to the familiar one where the padlocks fall mysteriously from the casket, still locked, and Gina rises from within. To Hinds' credit, his rewrite this time is an improvement, adding a great deal of suspense, and the scene remains a memorable part of the movie.

With a projected budget of around £120,000, shooting began on Tuesday 26 January with Terence Fisher again at the helm. Harry Oakes' diary notes that filming started in Black Park in very foggy conditions and wound up on Friday 18 March with "burning sequence" on Stage 1. On Friday 19 February, he also noted that: "HM the Queen had a baby boy [Prince Andrew] 3.30 pm. We wet the baby's head at The Bells."

The team from *Jekyll* returned after less than a week's break, apart from a different production manager (Don Weeks, giving Clifford Parkes a rest to prepare Hammer's next production), editor (Alfred Cox, allowing Eric Boyd-Perkins to complete *Jekyll* at Hammer House) and two newcomers who would soon become regulars: hairstylist Frieda Steiger and sound editor James Groom. This was Hammer's eighth colour horror film and Terence Fisher, Jack Asher, Len Harris, Harry Oakes, Bernard Robinson, Don Mingaye, James Needs, Jock May, Rosemary Burrows, Hugh Harlow and John Hollingsworth had so far worked on all of them.

Tony Hinds respectfully remembers his team on *The Brides of Dracula*: "Bray was at its most efficient at the time of making *Brides* (although not the happiest time for me; I hadn't the confidence that I had later). Terry Fisher was at his happiest, I think, having found his real niche (he was also very tolerant of me putting him under pressure as he knew what pressure I was under). Jack Asher was lighting beautifully (albeit too slowly – I had to fire him later for this). Bernard Robinson was in his element (making bricks without straw)."[1]

However, times were changing. As indicated by Hinds, after *Brides* Hammer would jettison Jack Asher in favour of the more economical (ie, faster) Arthur Grant, who was doing some 2nd unit work on the film. Second assistant director Hugh Harlow compares Jack Asher to Arthur Grant: "They were both very experienced and very professional colour men. Jack, I suppose out of the two, was the more flamboyant in style and had a twinkle in his eye (and an eye for the girls), and was always smoking his pipe, whereas Arthur was incessantly puffing at a cigarette – as was Terry Fisher. Jack had this frozen shoulder, so when he turned his body to give directions for a lamp to be adjusted, his whole body would turn and he had this peculiar stance. He was one of these amusing characters that were nice to have around. Arthur was more staid, virtually humourless I thought, but a dear person though. Jack has been accused of being slow, but wrongly. Arthur was probably the faster, but I think Jack would experiment more."

The Brides of Dracula would become another Hammer classic. Lighting and camera work were as ever impeccable and Bernard Robinson's sets never looked better. Even the interior of the mill at the climax is crammed with detail. Margaret Robinson comments on her husband's critical eye for detail: "He had the reputation of being one of the few art directors who dressed his own sets. He liked things to be precisely where he wanted them, so, although he might have a set dresser, everything would be where Bernard wanted it. It might not be his hands that put it there, but he very much supervised that."

Cinematographer Jack Asher concurred. "Bernard Robinson was an art director par excellence. His genius in designing those wonderful sets was that, economically, they were also worthwhile.

They would be reused or revamped time and time again ... Bernard was also able to ring the changes on the smaller sets, too. This economic usage must have slotted ideally into Tony Hinds' time and cost studies. Bernard's attention to detail was amazing. The objets d'art that dotted the sets were always first class. He must have saved Hammer a great deal of money while providing them with period sets that still exuded grace and style. We worked closely together and, when we talked at production meetings, he had my complete attention and he would reciprocate. I would later find some small suggestion I had made, long after I had forgotten, just where it should have been. He was undoubtedly a great, great man." [3]

Robinson used the four stages and external lot at Bray to the full. On Stage 1, he built the impressive hall and staircase; one can even spot the same triangular candelabra and twisting stone pillars that had adorned the hall and stairs of Castle Dracula itself. This was later revamped into the Baron's quarters and the exterior graveyard set, where the twisted Greta calls forth the vampire woman. For the latter, the hall's ornate fireplace was modified into the crypt behind the vampire woman's grave. The set for the Baron's quarters consisted of two sections divided by a wall of arches, forming the interior of his room and its outside balcony (complemented in the film by a tremendous Les Bowie matte painting). Brick Stage 2 was used to construct the lower section of the windmill and to contain the blazing finale. The rectangular Stage 3 was again used to house the token village inn, as well as Van Helsing's room, the stables, and the upper section of the mill.

Meanwhile, on the external lot, the original *Dracula* castle set had been struck after *The Stranglers of Bombay* and a village square erected in its stead. *Brides* saw it used for the first time. At the outset it consisted of a short tunnel archway leading to a courtyard containing several houses and an inn. Like the *Dracula* set before it, in order to save time and money, instead of being struck it was expanded and disguised over subsequent years to become two village square complexes and thus re-used in a number of films, until it was finally torn down in 1964.

This was the first of three films in which draughtsman Thomas Goswell received billing as art director (the others being *The Terror of the Tongs* and *Visa to Canton*). Then assistant art director Don Mingaye remembers: "He'd been a draughtsman in the industry from quite a young man and he was a fairly elderly man when he worked at Hammer. He'd worked for British National and Associated British Pictures in the art department. Then he joined Hammer as senior draughtsman. If I remember, Bernard had to have some leave, because his wife was not a very well lady, and Thomas Goswell came in to run the picture that Bernard had already set up." Robinson's wife died and he later married Margaret Carter. Margaret remembered Goswell too: "He was a shy, lovely person. I was surprised when Bernard told me he was over 70. He didn't go around the workshops much. The men for some reason didn't relate to Tommy, so he stayed in the drawing office and did the drawings while Bernard buzzed around the workshops."

Margaret was herself employed to model the griffins that decorate Bernard Robinson's ornate staircase. The largest pair stood 17 feet high. Margaret explains her craft: "If the model was freestanding it would need a wooden armature. If it was up to nine feet, I made the armature and did the lot. If it was over nine and up to 12 feet, the plasterers made it, because they were able to use wood to a certain extent to build armatures. If it was more than 12 feet, such as the 17-foot griffins on the stairs in *The Brides of Dracula*, the carpenters had to make it, because you were in the area of danger. A weak structure could have collapsed and killed somebody. Once the armature is made, chicken wire netting is put over it with staples. I usually did that and then I modelled it in clay. For that 17-foot statue I was allowed a labourer to carry the clay up, but he wasn't allowed to touch the actual clay, just put it on the tray and carry it up to me. I had to put it on the model. If he had put a bit of it on the model, there would have been a strike! In fact I saw him watching me put the staples into the wire netting and he was longing to take the hammer from me and do it, because I was a little inept standing up a ladder bashing staples in. Then the plasterers would cast it, because I wasn't allowed to handle plaster."

Len Harris remembered details of the film's powerful branding sequence: "In *The Brides of Dracula* the scene where Peter Cushing burns out the vampire's bite was well done. We started out with a long shot of Peter pumping up the fire. He put a real poker into the fire and stirred up real sparks. We tracked into a close-up for a reaction from him. Meanwhile, the property man crawled in under

LEFT: *Van Helsing (Peter Cushing) clashes with vampire Baron Meinster (David Peel) in* The Brides of Dracula *(1960).*

BELOW: *Van Helsing (Peter Cushing) dodges the vampire bat in* The Brides of Dracula *(1960).*

the camera. While Peter's arm was moving as if stirring the fire, he dropped the real poker and picked up the wooden one from the property man. The prop man moves back and so does the camera. Peter holds up the prop toward the camera to show that it is 'hot' (a special effects trick), and then puts the prop on his neck and reacts as you would expect the character to. The strength in the shot is Peter Cushing's acting, because when he puts the poker on his neck, you really feel it." [4]

In support, David Peel revelled in the role of the sardonic Baron, Hammer's blonde vampire. It is hard to believe that he was almost 40 when he played the part. The 20-year-old beauty Yvonne Monlaur, dubbed 'France's latest sex-kitten' by Hammer publicity, played the fetching Marianne Danielle. She recalls, "Hammer saw me in *Circus of Horrors* and with joy and pride I got the part of Marianne in *The Brides of Dracula*. It was a great chance to meet the splendid Hammer team. Although I spoke little English, it wasn't too difficult, because they were very understanding. I didn't have a dialogue coach, I just had to work hard on my French accent. Terence Fisher was a charming, courteous person, directing coolly but firmly. Often strong sequences would be shot in a relaxed atmosphere with jokes and nice cups of tea. All my English co-stars were so helpful but Peter Cushing was the cherry on the cake. He was a real gentleman, a great actor and,

Baroness Meinster (Martita Hunt) conceals her fangs from vampire-hunter Peter Cushing in The Brides of Dracula (1960). The censor would curtail her subsequent staking.

off the set, interested in everything. I remember we had fun when I taught him a little Russian. He talked about books, his work and his wife, whom he loved so much. I have always kept carefully the pink scarf he offered me at the end of the picture. It is still a sort of talisman for me. David Peel was a lovely man. I was amazed by his diction and his wonderful voice."

Martita Hunt played the sinister Baroness. Continuity girl Tilly Day fondly remembered her: "At eight o'clock in the morning she would sit at the head of the table and while I'd be doing something or other she'd say to me, 'Would you like a glass of warm wine, dear?' She was a sort of female Bela Lugosi! But she was good-looking and dignified. Very tall too! I also remember that she wouldn't wear the fangs. She was too vain. She told Terry, 'I really don't need those. I'll just cover my mouth with my shawl.'" [5]

Harry Oakes continued: "There was this big long table. Martita was at one end and Yvonne Monlaur was at the other. They had this dialogue going and of course we had to shoot it several times, long shot, medium shot, over-shot and so on. I think it was after lunch, because she liked a gin or two, you see, and Yvonne said something like, 'It's a wonderful place you have here, do you entertain here?' Martita answered, 'Oh yes, we have dances and parties and banquets...' And then she forgot her lines and said 'Balls!' Oh, we fell about laughing. Anyway, it was all quietened down, but she was rather pleased with this and she said, 'Terry dear, I want to keep this in.' And he had to acquiesce to this, but I had to leave the floor, it was so funny, because we had to listen to this so many times. It was fixed focus and I had to leave the set and as soon as the red valve was on, I'd come back on the set. It was still funny in the rushes the next day!" Sure enough, Hunt's reference to "balls" was not present in the final shooting script.

Second assistant director Hugh Harlow remembered her also, "The assistant director, John Peverall, asked me to go and collect Martita Hunt from her dressing room. I knocked at the door but there was no answer. I knocked again ... still nothing. I tried the door knob, but the room was locked, so I went downstairs and into the front courtyard. Now the female star dressing room was the top right window as you faced the house, so I crawled up the drainpipe to call her from her window and I got such a shock. She was sitting on the floor stark naked with her legs crossed in a trance doing her yoga! I went back to John on the set and I told him she wasn't ready and was in a trance. 'What do you mean, in a trance?' he said. So I showed him. He followed me up the drainpipe and I've never forgotten his comment: 'Have you ever seen two fried eggs nailed to a wall?'"

The film is permeated with strong characterisations which enhance it greatly. Freda Jackson is superb as the cackling Greta; 25-year-old Andrée Melly, sister of jazz musician George Melly, is outstanding as the wide-eyed bloodsucker Gina; busty Marie Devereux is back as Meinster's other bride; Miles Malleson, Henry Oscar and Mona Washbourne are all priceless. While the film is sometimes inconsistent in plot (just who is the mysterious man at the beginning and who did bring in Marianne's bags?), it is littered with memorable and moody scenes: Terence Fisher at his considerable best.

Principal photography ended on Friday 18 March after eight weeks. Location work had taken the team to Black Park, just outside Pinewood Studios near Slough, for the forest scenes, while the entrance to Oakley Court became the entrance to Chateau Meinster.

As Alfred Cox took his cutting of Brides to Hammer House, Malcolm Williamson was brought in to compose a very pleasing and appropriate score for the movie. Williamson was quite an acquisition for Hammer; he would be appointed Master of the Queen's Musick in 1976. "I guess it was John Hollingsworth, Hammer's music director, who recommended me to Anthony Hinds," remembers Williamson, "and he gave me my first major assignment – the scoring of The Brides of Dracula. It had the organ music in it as well as the orchestra. I can play the organ and the piano, but I did not do so for this score. The organ music was taped at a school in London; it wasn't done in sync – it was not done [in time] to the film, in other words. I wasn't interested in horror films at that time; much later I became interested ... Hammer did send me off to see some of Jimmy Bernard's pictures to study his scores. I thought of him as faultless; I only wish I could write horror scores of that quality."[6]

Meanwhile, it was time to submit Dr Jekyll to the BBFC. Michael Carreras diplomatically wrote to John Trevelyan on 3 February: "Tomorrow, Thursday, you are viewing the fine cut of the above picture. As this film, in its early stages, presented certain problems, I am taking this opportunity in advance of your seeing the film to let you know how we tackled various criticisms contained in your letter of October 29th. Basically, I think you will find that the whole subject has been handled tastefully and discreetly (not too much so, I hope), as we believe that in this subject implication will be more successful ... than going deliberately for the shock horror treatment. As for your detailed comments, they have been handled as follows:

1. The clientele and atmosphere of the Sphinx has been very controlled. We will go mainly for very atmospheric crowd sound track noises to give the whole place an open atmosphere of jollity, and not, as you might imagine on seeing these sequences, by any more sinister effects.
2. Maria's python dance will probably present two problems. Firstly, the close shot of the python entwined around her body, on which we have left our full footage a) for your enjoyment and b) for your guidance on how much of this material we may finally use. Secondly, the finale of the dance; at the present moment the music track ends before the finale. This will naturally be extended to cover her last actions. I want you to know that there is far less in the dance as performed in the film than in the dance as it is performed (by the same girl) in public. We have not dreamed anything up, or embellished anything – only toned it down.
3. The conversation between Paul and the two whores in the Sphinx – 'we are glad for the rest' etc – has been left in, but played with humour (and we therefore hope you will not find anything objectionable here), as has the remainder of the whore's dialogue throughout the scene.
4. Paul and the whores exhausted: this scene has been deleted from the script.
5. The mixture of sex and violence (original pages 50/52): this has undergone complete changes. We have deleted Hyde taking his booster shot after leaving Maria's bed, and we no longer return to the Sphinx from here, but go straight to his scene at Kitty's house.
6. The line 'They've got everything already except for certain organs for which usurers don't have any use' has been deleted.
7. The montage: Again I think you will find that great discretion has been used (almost too much, I fear). The Black Mass, cock fighting, dwarf and bull-mastiff have all been deleted.
8. The second python dance: deleted.
9. Maria 'gives him the lot', which bores him, etc: this scene has been deleted.
10. The word 'pressure': This we have left, as no alternative containing the meaning required was found as a suitable replacement, but I hope that in the context of the scene you will not find this offensive.
11. The scene where Hyde returned to the illegal sporting club and took combat with the Corinthian has been deleted.
12. Hyde's violence to the child. Physically this has been played down to nothing. Naturally we will wish to heighten the scene by the change of theme music, indicating that something of Hyde remains within him.
13. The phrase 'last supper': this has been deleted.
14. The association between the python killing Paul and Hyde raping Kitty has undergone a complete change along the lines of my previous letter to you [in] reference [to] this matter.

The sequences are now completely divorced from one another – the killing of Paul taking place prior to the rape of Kitty.

15. Hyde's killing of Maria: This does take place in Kitty's bed, but they are not in bed together. "In general, I hope you will find that we have either deleted or handled discreetly anything that was liable to have become horror comic stuff! I hope you will enjoy the film, and I will interestedly await your comments. My only fear, which I hope is not justified, is that we have all been a little over-cautious, after the various warnings we received, in translating the script to film, and that our 'by implication' treatment has not proved as successful as our earlier horror treatments."

Carreras' reference to leaving in the complete snake dance "for [Trevelyan's] enjoyment", while knowing perfectly well that Trevelyan would prevent impressionable cinemagoers from sampling it for themselves, was a smart nod to the essential hypocrisy of censorship. Whether Trevelyan got this or not, he was obviously impressed with Carreras's candidness elsewhere and replied on 8 February:

"I enclose the Exception Slip for The Two Faces of Dr Jekyll. The cuts in reel 4 are those which you expected. I do not think there need be much trouble about the other three cuts. You might, however, want to discuss these with me. If so give me a ring and we can arrange a time. I would like to say how very much we have appreciated your co-operation over this picture. Your letter of 3rd February was most helpful, and showed how much you have taken into account what I had advised.

R.4. Shorten Maria's snake-dance; shots that must be removed are (a) those where the snake is between her legs (b) those where she puts the snake in her mouth.

R.5. In the love making between Hyde and Maria stop the first scene before he removes her cloak. In the second scene remove shots where her bare breast is seen and the shots of her naked when she gets out of bed.

R. 8. Shorten the scene in which Hyde rapes Kitty; remove particularly as many as possible of the shots of his tearing off her clothes.

R.9. Shorten the strangling of Maria. Resubmit these reels."

A note on the letter dated 12 February, following discussions with editor James Needs, suggests that the cut they had most difficulty with was reel 4 part b, involving the snake-in-mouth routine. And it's interesting to hear Trevelyan's reference to another Hammer nude scene. Once more the censor prevailed and Norma Marla's brief nudity followed Hazel Court's in The Man Who Could Cheat Death and the legendary topless maidens from The Mummy straight onto the cutting room floor. Unfortunately, the cut is painfully noticeable in the release print of Jekyll.

Meanwhile, the debate over the certificate for Never Take Sweets from a Stranger was still raging. On 29 February, James Carreras wrote to John Trevelyan: "The press show is tomorrow, but almost every society interested in the welfare of children have seen the film, every leading crime reporter in Fleet Street saw the film last Friday and in almost every case they all said what a pity John Trevelyan did not give the picture an 'A' certificate. I have read Jack Lewis's article in Sunday's Reynold News and it seems that you refer to the picture as a borderline case... isn't it possible for you to change your mind and give the picture an 'A' certificate? It is because the dialogue is so clean and the action so inoffensive that I ask this and the fact that older children will never see the film seems to me a great pity. I wonder whether you could reconsider your decision."

Carreras sent a further message to the BBFC the following day: "In answer to your questions re the film Never Take Sweets from a Stranger. The Rev Arthur Morton of the NSPCC is enthralled by the film and wants to contact you and have a talk with you. At the press show today it was sensational – Jympson Harman said that every child should see it and that it should be shown at children's matinées as a warning. Thomas Wiseman said that it was sensational and mad to give it an 'X'. The general feeling was that it should be left to the parents' discretion as to whether a child should see it but most parents would appreciate it as a warning. The Daily Herald, see attached, voices the general opinion. In USA, France and Germany Welfare Authorities have the same opinion and urge for all children to see it."

Trevelyan's response was clear: "After careful consideration it was decided that the film should remain in the 'X' category. The Board felt that the warning given in this film was important but that, in view of the way in which it was given, it was more suitable as a warning to parents than to children direct. It is believed that children tend to identify themselves with child characters on the screen, and in this film two little girls are shown in a desperate situation and thoroughly

Janina Faye and
Frances Green hide
from the sinister
Olderberry in
Black Park in
Never Take
Sweets from a
Stranger (1959)

frightened. Young children seeing the film might themselves be frightened and might not
understand the exact nature of the danger. They would be aware that the old man was the source of
the fear and some might even think that they should be afraid of old men. There are other scenes
in the film which might disturb and worry some young children. For instance, the little girl has a
nightmare after the first incident, and in the court scene she is seriously upset after being handled
roughly by the Defence Counsel. The theme of the story is an unpleasant one and the film is full of
powerful tension. In the opinion of the Board, all these things made it desirable that the film
should be in the 'X' category so that it could not be seen by young children. It should be appreciated
that if it had been placed in the 'A' category it could have been seen by children as young as five if
they were accompanied by an adult."

Never Take Sweets from a Stranger finally premièred at the London Pavilion on Friday 4 March. Of
course, since the film was an 'X' certificate, its star, 12-year-old Janina Faye, was not allowed in to
see it. She recalls, "My mother took me up to Leicester Square to see my life-sized picture on the
poster outside the London Pavilion. To a 12-year-old girl that was big stuff and very exciting."

The film, while generally acclaimed by critics and many relevant organisations, still had its
detractors, accusing Hammer of exploiting an important and sensitive subject. For some, the
company seemed inseparable from the lurid horror movies it was renowned for. Michael Carreras
recollected: "We approached it absolutely seriously from our point of view, but the moment the film
came out the critics said, 'Oh, here we go – look at Hammer taking a social problem about people
interfering with little children and capitalising on it.' I don't honestly know how they could have
thought that of that film because it was beautifully made and finely acted and there was never any
attempt to exploit the subject. We were most careful about the stills, we were most careful about the
advertising with the distributor, so I think the critics did a lot of harm to that picture."[7]

Indeed, the fall-out from Never Take Sweets from a Stranger would creep into 1961, with further
claims that the way the little girl was treated in the courtroom scene could make parents in future
very reluctant to report similar cases. Trevelyan wrote to James Carreras on 28 April 1960: "You will
remember that I asked you to add a foreword to the film Never Take Sweets from a Stranger so that
parents should not be discouraged by the court scenes from taking action if their children are
assaulted. The point was raised with me by Mrs Frankenburg of the National Council of Women."

In a further letter to Carreras on 23 June, Trevelyan suggested an appropriate foreword: "This story is set in another country but it could happen here. Parents should realise that in this country the magistrates would not allow child witnesses to be treated in the way shown in the film and would send the public out of the court while they gave evidence."

Carreras agreed, but Columbia were not informed and the film was distributed without the foreword, giving rise to more clashes with Mrs Frankenburg over the months to come.

Tony Hinds had never been as diplomatic as Michael Carreras when it came to the BBFC. Neglecting to send in a script for *The Brides of Dracula* before shooting, Hinds sent in a copy of the final shooting script after the film had been shot. The readers' reports are quite amusing, particularly the one from Newton Branch on 21 March:

"Obviously written by an insane, but very precocious schoolboy. Two new elements here (new to me):

P. 55. 'By taking the blood of his own mother, he has broken the laws even of the Damned.' ie. our handsome Dracula seems to have had a slight Oedipus complex, in the already complex Dracula complex.

P.77. Gina (a village girl, turned vampire) seems to have become a weensy bit of a lesbian. She says to the heroine (a real ninny): 'My darling. You haven't forgotten your little Gina. Put your arms around me please. Hug me. I want to kiss you. Please be kind to me. Say you'll forgive me for letting HIM love me.' Girlish talk, perhaps? (They have burnt toast in their dorm together.) But what next? Dracula, the Homosexual vampire?

"Otherwise, this seems to me to be the sort of 'ghoul-ash' which would be screamingly funny if done and really well cooked up by the Goons."

The report from Audrey Field on 22 March had this to say: "This film has already been shot, but at least we shall have the benefit of the script to refer to when it comes in for censorship this week ... Quite the stupidest vampire film so far, but no nastier than the others on the whole. If there were time to say anything to the company, I would say:

P.30. A caution on the Baron's bloody fangs in close up.

Pp. 48-49. A strong caution on all shots of the village girl breaking out of the grave (potentially very disgusting and horrible).

P.52. Caution on shot of dead Baroness' face.

P.62. Caution on shot of Baron moving towards Gina, teeth bared, blood-red eyes. (The actors' oculists would not like these red contact-lenses at all, I feel sure.)

P. 62. There must be no shot of the stake actually being driven into the Baroness' chest. A strong caution on any sounds.

P.76. Caution on Gina's fangs.

P.77. Caution on mutilated body of Severin. All this loving talk between the lady vampires is dangerous, and the line 'We can both love him, my darling' very steep indeed and not likely to pass.

P. 81, foll. A caution needed on the whole fraças in the mill, c.s.'s [close shots] vampires' faces, struggle with Van Helsing, ghastly cry when Greta hits millstone. P. 82. Chain in fight, body of Greta, grinning vampire woman watching the blood-sucking. P. 83. Shot of the Baron with his teeth wet with fresh blood after he has bitten Van Helsing. P.84. Shots of cauterising, hissing of burning flesh. P.86. Strong caution on Baron's scar, shots of his smouldering clothes, etc.

P.87. Caution on spasms when Baron dies in shadow of cross."

Strangely enough, the following day a black-and-white cut of the film was reviewed. A scribbled file note reads: "R.7. Remove the shot of HELSING driving a stake into the Baroness' body and of blood welling up from the wound. Before we can decide about R.9 we wish to see it in colour: cuts in it may be needed."

Perhaps unsurprisingly, the film was rejected. Tony Hinds wrote to Trevelyan on 28 March: "I have just returned from a short holiday to find, to my surprise, your rejection slip for the above. I say 'to my surprise' because I felt certain that there was nothing in *Brides* which was even as horrifying as our original *Dracula*. I refer in particular to the shot of Van Helsing driving – with one clean blow – a rather discreet stake into an elderly and silent Martita Hunt, compared with the two blows (with two inserts of the stake) driven into an attractive and noisy young girl which you allowed us in the first

Dracula. Can I persuade you to reconsider?"

Trevelyan remarked in a note on 1 April: "Agreed that [we] would consider a reduced version of this scene – without prejudice."

On 21 April, the Board viewed the latest offering. Newton Branch commented: "Reel 9 seen again in colour by JT, JC, NKB and is all right. Reel 7 (stake in woman's heart) sent in in black and white. It should be resubmitted in colour and marked up."

Hammer sent in the colour reel and Frank Crofts reported on 26 April: "We saw R.7 with the President; it is now in colour. It appears that the stake incident has been shortened. FNC did not feel very strongly about it in this form, but AOF thought it disgusting and would cut the shots of welling blood out … It was decided to try to get the shot of the welling blood out. The rest of the scene, including two later shots of the stake in the dead woman, will pass."

To cover themselves, Crofts consulted the Board's files on *Dracula* the same day to remind himself of their rulings on a similar scene: "As the company has referred to a similar incident in the first *Dracula* of theirs, I have looked at the file. Originally we said 'R.7 the whole episode of a stake being driven into Lucy, together with her screams, writhing and agonised face. The scene can retain only shots of Dr. Van Helsing taking up the stake and mallet, possibly one blow on the mallet as seen from outside the coffin, followed by him and Arthur looking at Lucy's peaceful face.' This was written in a report after Hammer said 'All shots of the stake being driven into the girl's heart have been removed entirely!' Finally we said 'We are prepared to pass everything (including the staking of Lucy as reduced and without screams) …' There was apparently no shot of welling blood."

David Peel as the charismatic Baron Meinster in The Brides of Dracula (1960).

The adjudication over, the film was finally granted its 'X' certificate. Meanwhile, Hammer continued their 1960 programme. Ever keen to cut production costs, they now started down a path they would subsequently follow time and time again – they planned two Chinese projects, one to follow on from the other, to save money on set design. Ken Hyman spearheaded the first, commissioning Jimmy Sangster to write a script on 1 February. Initially announced as *Terror of the Hatchet Men*, the film eventually became *The Terror of the Tongs*. The other project, *Visa to Canton*, was intended as the pilot for an aborted television series. Still smarting from *Tales of Frankenstein*, Hammer aimed for a theatrical release.

"Hong Kong, 1910. A bustling, growing city – but hidden deep amongst its teeming thousands was an organisation that thrived on vice, terror and corruption – the Red Dragon Tong." So began Hammer's latest offering. *The Terror of the Tongs* tells of Captain Jackson's struggle against the Red Dragon Tong, a murderous secret society presided over by the evil Chung King, which terrorises the Hong Kong waterfront and is responsible for the murder of Jackson's daughter. Kenneth Hyman submitted Sangster's draft screenplay to the BBFC in late March. Audrey Field read the script on 25 March and passed on the following comments:

"It will be seen that this is basically *Boy's Own Paper* stuff, transformed into criminal Lunatic's Own Paper stuff by the addition of some recherché brutalities. I have searched in the Westminster Reference Library for reliable information about the Tong, but can find none. I suspect that the fertile imagination of Jimmy Sangster has been at work in details of how they carried on, though I am told that they really did carry and use hatchets for their killings. This is a very difficult story from our point of view. It is the obvious descendant of *Stranglers of Bombay*, which I am told was a pretty weak film on

The doctor (Charles Lloyd Pack) reports back to Chung King (Christopher Lee), watched by Wang How (Roger Delgado) in The Terror of the Tongs (1960).

THE TERROR OF THE TONGS

PRINCIPAL PHOTOGRAPHY: 19 April to 30 May 1960
DISTRIBUTION:
  UK: BLC; certificate 'X'
  US: Columbia
79 minutes; Technicolor
UK RELEASE:
  TRADE SHOW: 12 September 1961 at the Columbia
    Theatre
  PREMIÈRE: 29 September 1961 at the London Pavilion,
    Piccadilly Circus with Homicidal
  GENERAL RELEASE: 20 November 1961, on the ABC
    circuit with Homicidal
  US RELEASE: October 1961 with Homicidal

DIRECTOR: Anthony Bushell; PRODUCER: Kenneth Hyman;
ASSOCIATE PRODUCER: Anthony Nelson Keys; EXECUTIVE
PRODUCER: Michael Carreras; SCREENPLAY: Jimmy Sangster;
PRODUCTION DESIGNER: Bernard Robinson; ART DIRECTOR:
Thomas Goswell; ASSISTANT ART DIRECTOR: Don Mingaye;
DIRECTOR OF PHOTOGRAPHY: Arthur Grant; CAMERA
OPERATOR: Len Harris; FOCUS PULLER: Harry Oakes; GRIP:
Albert Cowland; CLAPPER: Alan MacDonald; SOUND CAMERA
OPERATOR: Michael Sale; ASSISTANT DIRECTOR: John Peverall;
2ND ASSISTANT DIRECTOR: Hugh Harlow/Joe Levy; 3RD
ASSISTANT DIRECTOR: Dominic Fulford; SUPERVISING EDITOR:
James Needs; EDITOR: Eric Boyd-Perkins; ASSISTANT EDITOR: Chris
Barnes; MUSIC: James Bernard; MUSIC SUPERVISOR: John
Hollingsworth; SOUND RECORDIST: Jock May; BOOM: Jim Perry;
SOUND EDITOR: Albert Streeter; MAKE-UP: Roy Ashton and Colin

Guard; HAIRSTYLIST: Frieda Steiger; PRODUCTION MANAGER:
Clifford Parkes; CONTINUITY: Tilly Day; WARDROBE: Molly
Arbuthnot; WARDROBE ASSISTANT: Rosemary Burrows;
CONSTRUCTION MANAGER: Arthur Banks; MASTER PLASTERER:
Stan Banks; MASTER CARPENTER: Charles Davis; MASTER
PAINTER: Lawrence Wrenn; MASTER ELECTRICIAN: Jack Curtis;
MASTER RIGGER: Ronald Lenoir; PROPS BUYER: Eric Hillier;
PROPS MASTER: Tommy Money, FLOOR PROPS: Peter Allchorne;
STUDIO MANAGER: A F Kelly; PRODUCTION SECRETARY: Ann
Skinner; CASTING: Dorothy Holloway; ACCOUNTANT: W H V Able;
BRAY ACCOUNTANT: Ken Gordon; CASHIER: Peter Lancaster

Christopher Lee (Chung King); Geoffrey Toone (Jackson); Yvonne
Monlaur (Lee); Brian Worth (Harcourt); Richard Leech (Inspector
Dean); Marne Maitland (Beggar); Tom Gill (Beamish); Barbara
Brown (Helena); Marie Burke (Maya); Bandana Das Gupta (Anna);
Burt Kwouk (Ming); Roger Delgado (Wang How); Milton Reed
(Guardian); Charles Lloyd Pack (Doctor); Eric Young (Confucius);
Michael Hawkins (Priest); Johnny Arlan (Executioner)

UNCREDITED: Ewen Solon (Tang How); Santos Wong (Sergeant);
Andy Ho (Lee Chung); Arnold Lee (Spokesman); Julie Alexander,
Harold Goodwin, Peter Gray, Ronald Ing, Jules Ki-Ki, Su Lin,
Michael Peake, Walter Randall, Poing Ping Sam, Ann Scott, Steven
Scott, Cyril Shaps, Vincent Wong (other roles); June Barry, Mary
Rose Barry, Audrey Burton, Ruth Calvert, Marialla Capes, Katie
Cashfield, Patty Dalton, Louise Dickson, Pauline Dukes, Hazel
Gardner, Valerie Holman, Julie Shearing, Valerie Shevaloff, Barbara
Smith (Tong Room Girls)

the whole, but which nevertheless occasioned some angry comment, and some criticism of the 'A'
Certificate, because of the brutality. This film would be no ornament to the 'X' category, but even with
necessary toning down of details it might be unsafe to guarantee it any other certificate, because it

could turn out to be the sort of film from which younger children would have to be protected. From what we know of this company, they will want as much lurid savagery as we will let them have!

"The main trouble is the lopping off of fingers – a sickeningly nasty idea, quite apart from any censorable visuals. I think the makers of the film should be required to invent some other 'trade-mark' of the killings, such as an emblem left near, or on, the body. A secondary trouble is the shots of the hatchet wounds (such as gaping cut throats) and, worse, shots of hatchets sticking in the victims' bodies. Most of this sort of thing would be intolerable as scripted. We probably could not say that hatchets could not be used; but the blows, and their effects, would have to be left mainly to the imagination. I have noted with a good deal of revulsion the following details..."

She goes on to list her objections, which would later be summarised in a letter by Trevelyan, and closes with: "P.97 Hatchet is seen sweeping towards Harcourt's neck. He is seen in a later shot decapitated. However much this may serve him right, it does not serve *us* right. Or at any rate, there may be many members of the audience who have done nothing to deserve it."

Newton Branch also commented on the draft script on 26 March: "This is an 'A' film, though much of it is 'U'. There are a few scenes and certain gruesome shots which are 'X'. These must be removed or done with discretion especially if the film is to be in colour. Hammer will certainly remember the criticism we had over *Stranglers of Bombay* over the few horror scenes in that dull, slow moving film. I think it was because the film was so dreary that we allowed those scenes. Here, by contrast there is plenty of action and some spiffing fights. So the accent in this film must be on 'mystery and adventure' rather than emphasis on gruesome mutilation and hatchet work generally ... There will obviously be alternative shots for export. But the director should aim for an 'A' for the home market. Whereas the theme of *Stranglers* was far more chilling, there is something very nasty about mutilation – especially, I think, of the hands."

John Trevelyan summarised the details in a letter to Kenneth Hyman on 30 March: "We have now read your script *The Terror of the Tongs*. I always like, if possible, at the script stage to give some indication of the category in which the film is likely to be placed. In this case I find some difficulty. Basically it should be acceptable for the 'A' category, but there are a few scenes and some rather gruesome shots which would not be suitable for this category. I think it will depend on treatment as to whether we can give it an 'A' certificate or whether we must put it in the 'X' category. We gave an 'A' certificate to the film *The Stranglers of Bombay* and there were some criticisms about our decision on the grounds that the film contained too much nastiness and gruesomeness. We shall therefore want to be careful in our judgment of this new film. The main trouble, as you anticipated, is with the Tong trade-mark – the lopping off of fingers, together with shots of hatchet wounds and shots of hatchets sticking in victims' bodies. We do not say that hatchets must not be used, but we would ask you to use them with discretion and we would like you to think up a less unpleasant alternative for the Tong 'trade-mark'. For instance, could there be a primitive drawing of a hatchet cut into a man's arm leaving permanent scars, or something of this kind? I have a fair number of comments on points of detail as follows:

Page 2 Scene 2. We would much prefer not to have the lopping off of the fingers, the screams of agony and the subsequent shots.

Page 6 Scene 5. For an 'A' film we would not like the line 'Your body has become satiated....'

Page 10 Scene 6. Some fairly nasty shots here, the worst being that of Ming's body being split by a hatchet which leaves 'a great gaping wound'. Anything of this kind should be treated with great care.

Page 11 Scene 6. The killing of the Executioner by the Doctor should be discreet and without emphasis on the knife.

Page 17-8 Scene 10. There is a bit too much of an orgy about this. We would not mind a lively party but the semi-nudity and mauling of women would be more than we would accept in a picture of this kind.

Page 23-4 Scene 12. The dialogue referring to the fate of the First Officer, although somewhat obscure, does suggest sexual mutilation. We would want to avoid this. Once again we have the Tong 'trade-mark'.

Page 25 Scene 13. This scene as scripted would be quite impossible and should be very greatly

Yvonne Monlaur interrupts Geoffrey Toone's execution in The Terror of the Tongs (1960).

modified. Similar modifications should be made to the subsequent scenes in which Helena's body is found.
Page 29 Scene 17. The words '...and God knows what else before' suggests rape prior to the murder. This seems unnecessary. We do not want it.
Page 33 Scene 21. The 'trade mark' again.
Page 36 Scene 23. For an 'A' film we would want to avoid obvious reference to brothels and prostitutes.
Page 41-2 Scene 25. Jackson's violence to Tang How should not be excessive.
Page 50 Scene 29. The strangling of the victim should not be excessive.
Page 60 Scene 37. In Lee's description of life, the words '...and most times worse than that.' might be a bit much for the 'A' category.
Page 62 Scene 38. See my comments on the party scene (Pages 17-18).
Page 64 Scene 38. Harcourt is offered "three new girls from the mainland without 'experience'." This brothel stuff would not be suitable for the 'A' category.
Page 68-9 Scene 42. The beating up of Jackson, as scripted, is much too vicious and nasty.
Page 70 Scene 43. The shot of the hatchet in the Guardian should not be gruesome.
Page 75-6 Scene 48. This is pretty nasty and we do not like too much emphasis on the hatchet or the knife or on the Doctor's death agonies.
Page 79-80 Scene 50. There is more knife work here. We would like it kept to a minimum.
Page 81 Scene 53. We would not accept even for the 'X' category the shots of the hatchet man with his hands cut off at the wrists and his throat cut.
Page 82 Scene 54. Here is more talk about 'You will satiate your body with desires of the flesh', and 'lust and impurity....' For the 'A' category we would not want this type of thing.
Page 84 Scene 55. Lee caresses Jackson's chest. This should be treated carefully. We do not want much sex in this picture.
Page 89 Scene 57. Harcourt hits Lee hard on the side of her head with a stick and fells her. We do not like this kind of thing.
Page 93 Scene 62. This is a nasty scene when the hatchet missing Jackson hits Lee and she is covered in blood. This should be treated with great care.
Page 94 Scene 62. This 'free-for-all' should not be full of brutality and nastiness and we do not like seeing implements sticking in victims.
Page 97 Scene 68. We see the hatchet aimed at Harcourt's neck and a few moments later we see him decapitated. This just will not do."
On the Board's copy of this letter, Trevelyan has scribbled a note dated 1 April, "Discussed with Mr Ken Hyman. He said that it had been decided that this film should be made with the 'X' category in mind. I discussed detail with him." As a result it would seem probable that Hyman had Sangster soup up some of the more lurid elements to justify the 'X' slant. One notable inclusion was the infamous bone-scraping scene which was absent in the submitted draft. Reader Audrey Field, in her synopsis of the script accompanying her report of 25 March, described the original scene as: "Jackson makes the girl Lee tell him where Tang How's contacts are, and hurries to the place – Lee Chung's, an ante-room to the Tong headquarters. Here he is drugged and taken to the Tong room, where he is told that he must die: but first, he is beaten up. A beggar whom we have seen before – one of the Good Chinese in opposition to the Tong – releases him." Now Sangster would have Jackson considerably more than just 'beaten up', subjecting him instead to the kind of torture that could only find its place in an 'X' film. It was clear that *The Terror of the Tongs* was not designed to be a *Boy's Own* adventure story after all. It was another Hammer horror.

EIGHT · **The Werewolf and the Censor** (1960)

The team of Bernard Robinson, Thomas Goswell, and Don Mingaye now designed the Chinese sets to accommodate *The Terror of the Tongs* and *Visa to Canton*. Bray's master plasterer Arthur Banks now took over as Construction Manager from Micky Lyons, who had to retire due to a health problem. Banks took charge of a hard-working team of very competent labourers, headed by master plasterer Stan Banks (taking over the job vacated by his brother), master carpenter Charles Davis, master painter Lawrence Wrenn, master electrician Jack Curtis and master rigger Ronald Lenoir.

Assistant art director, Don Mingaye, remembers the regular construction team at the time. "They were all 100 per cent craftsmen and they knew their stuff. Construction manager Arthur Banks was in charge and he was a very nice guy. He was very efficient. Very conscious of his team and what they were able to achieve in the time allotted. His brother, master plasterer Stan Banks, was also extremely efficient. On average he had about four plasterers under him. I think the most we ever had was six. Master carpenter Charles Davis worked originally for Gainsborough Studios and I think he was a foreman carpenter at Bray at one point and then gradually worked his way up. I think he took over from Micky Lyons when he became Construction Manager. He was an excellent man, somebody you could really talk to. If you had a problem he'd help. He'd sometimes solve it himself or help you to. He had a team of eight carpenters under him.

"Then we had a rigging department for scaffolding, which Ronnie Lenoir was in charge of. He was an excellent fellow. Quite often the riggers came from the Navy, from dockyards and things, so they were a pretty tough bunch and knew their stuff. Lawrie Wrenn was master painter at Hammer. Very often they only had three or four painters at most in his department. He would be asked to do all sorts of things, apart from literally wallpapering and painting a set. If we needed, as sometimes we did, a stained glass window, he would do it. If we had to produce a teak door or a teak bar or marble work, he would do it. If he marbled a fireplace, you would have an awful job just looking at it to say it wasn't marble.

"When we were filming anywhere, we always had one member from each department attached to the film unit, ie. a carpenter, a plasterer, a painter, etc, because in those days it wasn't one multi-skilled person as it is today, there were lines of demarcation. We worked with and through the Construction Manager, but I used to individually go to the different departments. For instance, I would go to the carpenters – one chap there was very good and I would lay out the stuff and go through with him what was required and the best way of achieving it, and he would advise me sometimes. He would say, 'Look, it would be better if we did this or that,' and in conjunction with him you would work out a scheme to produce whatever's required – generally very successfully, because they were a pretty good team."

In charge of props were the sterling team of props buyer Eric Hillier and props master Tommy Money. Don Mingaye recalls: "When I first met Eric Hillier, he was already the buyer. I think he worked in the property department as a younger man and he decided that he'd rather go looking, because you had to have a very good knowledge of period furniture and what is correct in certain climates. So he became a production buyer and the industry had a series of suppliers in and around the London area, where he would know instantly where to go if he needed a 17th century bureau, for example. Eric was a very nice guy and a very good buyer. We would provide him with a list of action props that were needed, together with set dressing props, and he would usually provide them." Margaret Robinson adds, "Bernard was very fond of Eric and he was in fact our son Peter's godfather. He knew exactly what Bernard would want, they'd worked together so much, and in an outfit like Hammer, time is of the essence. He would give him a prop list, but if there was any choice between different bits of furniture, he would know which piece of furniture Bernard would choose himself."

Tommy Money was Hammer's long-serving props master. Don Mingaye remembers: "Tommy Money was a prop man in the theatre originally and then he came to Hammer and became their property master, and it was quite a responsibility. He would be responsible for seeing all the stuff in, making sure it wasn't damaged, and making sure it wasn't damaged when it was sent back, and he would have a team of men under him, who would literally carry the furniture in from the prop store and at my direction, or Bernard's direction, would set the furniture out on the set. They were like furniture removers and they would be on the unit when we were shooting, under what you call floor props."

The Terror of the Tongs began filming at Bray on Tuesday 19 April. Christopher Lee's scenes, which were all filmed on the same set, were scheduled for the first two weeks, finishing on Friday 29 April[8]; this gave him a breathing space prior to his next film, The Hands of Orlac, which was due to start on the French Riviera on 16 May[9]. At the helm was director Anthony Bushell, once right-hand man to Sir Laurence Olivier and remembered by fantasy fans for his portrayal of Colonel Breen in the original TV version of Quatermass and the Pit. He warmed to the atmosphere and professionalism at Bray. "There's a feeling here which you don't get at many studios. Everyone, from top to bottom, seems to know exactly what's going on. The terrific enthusiasm and one-mindedness toward film-making here is the nearest thing to working in a French studio."[10]

Christopher Lee now got his first top billing at Hammer as Chung King, a forerunner to his successful Fu Manchu series. "I was playing the conventional Chinese Tong leader with the rather unlikely name of Chung King and Roger Delgado was my right-hand man," he recalls. "He was a most sweet man, killed in a car crash on location in Turkey. There was Geoffrey Toone, a well-known leading man, and Brian Worth, whom I knew very well. Sadly he's no longer with us. He more or less retired from acting and opened a wonderful restaurant in London called La Parra, which means The Vine. He was bilingual in Spanish and married a Spanish woman and, in fact, during the war he was head of the Spanish section in the Special Operations Executive.

"The eye make-up was murder. It was the most uncomfortable make-up I've ever had to wear – the Oriental eye, the epicanthic fold as they call it. They have to take a mould of your eyelids and the shape of your eye and the make-up starts by the nose, goes right underneath the eyebrow, covers the eyelid and goes on beyond it. You have to be terribly careful that you don't see the edges, which in some cases did happen. Not on that film I don't think, but in the first Fu Manchu it certainly did. The problem with it is that it takes two hours to put on, and, in those days, because of what it was made of, although they put make-up on it to match with the rest of your colouring, it used to go white when you were in front of the lights. So they had to keep rushing forward putting more make-up on with a brush. It used to drive me crazy and it was murderously difficult to wear. The problem is, when you're shooting you cannot look up, or all you see is a white eyeball, and you cannot look down or your own eyelid comes down from underneath, which is why you have to play the whole thing with your head horizontally."

Geoffrey Toone played the square-jawed hero, Captain Jackson Sale. "I was interviewed by the producer, Kenneth Hyman, who was an American," remembers Toone. "I went and talked to him and he was very agreeable and I thought no more about it. I'd been living in Hollywood for about four years and was now living back in England. Suddenly an agent I had in Hollywood got through to me and said that they were doing a pilot for a new series out there. They asked if I could roughen up the accent and I did takes for them on the telephone. They sent for me and I shot across. However, the series was never made. I thought I'd cash in my first class ticket, go home later and just hang around for a bit. I did several televisions, including one for the fiendish Sam Peckinpah and one with Ray Milland. I thought I don't really want to live here again, because I didn't really like Hollywood, but I was sort of falling into it, because the work was coming in. I was staying with a friend when, all of a sudden, through the post came this great heavy script for The Terror of the Tongs and I thought, 'Thank God. I've got the job. I can go home and I haven't got to stay here!' So I came back and did it."

Fresh from The Brides of Dracula was French starlet Yvonne Monlaur. Hiding behind Roy Ashton and Colin Guard's Oriental make-up were a number of Hammer regulars: Marne Maitland, Roger Delgado, Charles Lloyd Pack, Ewen Solon, Milton Reid, Harold Goodwin. Character actor Goodwin, who played a brief cameo as a mutilated Chinaman, remembers how Bushell coaxed the genial Yorkshireman into this unlikely role: "The first time I met him was at St James' Theatre in 1950, when I had to go and have an interview with Laurence Olivier and I found out that he was his right-hand man. Some time later, Michael Rennie was doing The Third Man series and Tony Bushell rang me up to do an Irish part. Then I got a script for The Terror of the Tongs. John Redway was casting, and I said, 'It's a Chinaman!' He said, 'Yes, and it's very interesting, isn't it?' I said, 'I can't do a Chinaman.' He said, 'Well, that's it, and it's about four days.' I said, 'No, I can't do it. This is ridiculous.'

"So I put the phone down and it rang again about ten minutes later. 'Are you turning down work for me?' I said, 'You what?' Then the voice said, 'Bushell here!' I said, 'Hello, Tony.' And he said,

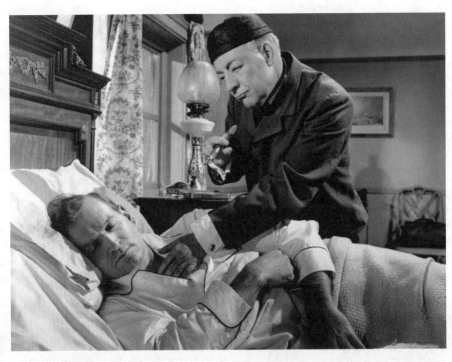

A Tong doctor (Charles Lloyd Pack) attempts to kill the sleeping Captain Sale (Geoffrey Toone) in The Terror of the Tongs (1960).

'Are you turning work down? Come immediately. It's four days and it's only on a week.' I said, 'But it's a Chinaman.' He said, 'You'll be very good as a Chinaman. A North Country Chinaman!' So I turned up and all he'd do was come into the make-up room and fall about laughing while they plastered me up as a Chinaman. It was unbelievable. It took an hour and a half to two hours and I had to get up at a damn awful time."

Geoffrey Toone also felt it was odd that all the Chinese were played by British character actors. "I always thought it was funny that the film opened with me as the captain of the ship having an interview with Burt Kwouk. He was a darling man and I was very fond of him. We had a serious little talk in my cabin about how I was going to support him against the Tongs. Anyway, we said our goodbyes and he walked down the gangplank and was promptly killed. So there they were having killed the only real Chinaman and the only person who looked Chinese in the whole thing. They even had a lovely Indian character actor, Marne Maitland, as a Chinaman, who by no stretch of the imagination was Chinese. Nobody was Chinese!"

The team from *The Brides of Dracula* was back sans Jack Asher, Don Weeks (it was Clifford Parkes' turn to be production manager again; he had been preparing *Tongs* while Weeks was filming *Brides*), Alfred Cox and James Groom. First assistant director John Peverall was enthused by the project,: "I knew Anthony Bushell when he was an actor. I worked as a fourth assistant on *Hamlet* with Laurence Olivier at Denham Studios. Anthony was in that, along with Peter Cushing. What was so lovely about both of these gentlemen was that, 14 years later, they both remembered me from *Hamlet*." [11] Second assistant director Hugh Harlow had to leave the production to start his National Service and Joe Levy took over for him. "I was working on *The Terror of the Tongs*," Hugh remembers. "I was the 2nd and I was in line to get my first break as 1st for Michael on *Visa to Canton*. Then my call-up papers came through and I had to leave. I think it was literally the first week of shooting *Tongs*, so I never did do *Visa to Canton*." Dominic Fulford joined the team as 3rd assistant.

The film lacked the cold, stark realism and almost documentary style of Fisher's *The Stranglers of Bombay*, which was shot in black-and-white. With the benefit of glorious Technicolor, the film seems more akin to Hammer's mainstream Gothic horrors, its rich and colourful interiors capably lit by Arthur Grant in his first colour film for Hammer. The film also has its fair share of grisly torture and brutal ritualistic murders, including the much talked-about bone-scraping sequence. Geoffrey Toone remembers his torment in vivid detail. "Christopher says to me, 'Have you ever had your bones scraped, Captain Sale?' I always wanted to say, 'Oh no. I must remember to make an appointment!' It sounded like it was something you went to Harley Street for. I do remember Milton Reid, who always played executioners. He drove about in a huge open Cadillac all the time. He did the bone scraping for Mr Lee, you see, and in order to make it look like these needles were sticking out of my chest, they put flesh-coloured wax over me and stuck them into that. I asked them what it was and they said it was morticians' wax, which they use to make-up corpses. I also remember making the soundtrack for when I was being tortured. It sounded exactly as though you were having an orgasm the whole time."

Toone also remembers the quaint routine on the backlot for continuity purposes. "The set of the docks with the side of the ship was built for another film and they re-used it. I always remember, being England it could rain at any time and so, for continuity, the whole thing had to be wet all the time. Every morning they had to hose down the ship and hose down the quay and hose down everything in case it rained, because otherwise you wouldn't get continuity, but of course it never did rain! That was fairly cunning. It was a wonderful set. Working at Bray Studios was very pleasant. It had a sort of family atmosphere. It was very relaxed and very agreeable really. Some of the time I came back to London and some of the time I stayed in a hotel, the Hinds Head at Bray."

Following its gala première on 10 April at the Apollo Theatre in Manchester, Val Guest's gritty police drama *Hell is a City* went on general release on Sunday 1 May to rave reviews. The following day, with *Tongs* still on the floor at Bray, Guest's next production, *The Full Treatment*, started shooting in Cannes during the film

Val Guest directs Françoise Rosay and Claude Dauphin in The Full Treatment (1960).

festival, returning to the Associated British Studios at Elstree by the end of the month. Guest had bought the rights to Ronald Scott Thorn's novel while he was directing *Hell is a City*. He produced and directed the movie under the nominal aegis of Falcon Films, the Hammer subsidiary that operated Bray. It was an elaborate psychological thriller akin to the series of suspense thrillers Jimmy Sangster would soon spawn. The plot revolves around the sinister psychiatrist Dr Prade (played by Claude Dauphin) who tries to convince his patient (Ronald Lewis) that he has murdered his wife (Diane Cilento). Guest wanted Stanley Baker for the lead, whom he had directed twice before for Hammer. However, Baker was

THE FULL TREATMENT

A Falcon Film production
PRINCIPAL PHOTOGRAPHY: 2 May to July 1960
DISTRIBUTION:
  UK: Columbia; 109 minutes; certificate 'A'
  US: Columbia; 93 minutes; US title: *Stop Me Before I Kill*
  b/w; Megascope
UK RELEASE:
  GENERAL RELEASE: 20 February 1961
  US RELEASE: 17 May 1961

DIRECTOR: Val Guest; PRODUCER: Val Guest; ASSOCIATE PRODUCER: Victor Lyndon; SCREENPLAY: Val Guest and Ronald Scott Thorn based on Thorn's novel 'The Full Treatment'; ART DIRECTOR: Tony Masters; ASSISTANT ART DIRECTOR: Geoff Tozar; DIRECTOR

OF PHOTOGRAPHY: Gilbert Taylor; CAMERA OPERATOR: Moray Grant; ASSISTANT DIRECTOR: Kips Gowans; SUPERVISING EDITOR: James Needs; EDITOR: Bill Lenny; MUSIC COMPOSER: Stanley Black; MUSIC SUPERVISOR: John Hollingsworth; SOUND RECORDIST: Bert Ross; MAKE-UP: Tony Sforzini; HAIR STYLIST: Ivy Emmerton; PRODUCTION MANAGER: Clifton Brandon; CONTINUITY: Doreen Dearnaley; WARDROBE: Muriel Dickson; COSTUMES: Beatrice Dawson; SET DECORATOR: Scott Slimon

Claude Dauphin (Doctor David Prade); Diane Cilento (Denise Colby); Ronald Lewis (Alan Colby); Françoise Rosay (Madame Prade); Bernard Braden (Harry Stonehouse); Katya Douglas (Connie Stonehouse); Barbara Chilcott (Baroness de la Vaillon); Ann Tirard (Nicole); Edwin Styles (Doctor Roberts); George Merritt (Doctor Manfield) unavailable so Hammer contract artist Ronald Lewis deputised. It would be Guest's last association with Hammer for some time. He would become heavily involved with his pet project *The Day the Earth Caught Fire* in 1961, but would return to Hammer to write and direct *When Dinosaurs Ruled the Earth* seven years later.

Principal photography on *Tongs* finally ended on Monday 30 May, after six weeks. To celebrate the filming of *Tongs*, on Wednesday 18 May Hammer held a garden party beside the river on the lawn outside Stage 3 – and what better way than with a Chinese barbecue. Christopher Lee, not yet required for *The Hands of Orlac*, was in attendance alongside several cast members from the West End hit, *The World of Suzie Wong* (none of whom, regrettably, were actually cast in *Tongs*, being passed over, as noted, in favour of Harold Goodwin and co in unconvincing Chinese make-ups). Now *Tongs* entered post-production under editors James Needs and Eric Boyd-Perkins and sound editor Alban Streeter. John Hollingsworth brought back his friend, James Bernard, to compose the score.

Meanwhile, as *Tongs* entered its last week of shooting at Bray, *Sword of Sherwood Forest* started on Monday 23 May at Ardmore Studios in County Wicklow, Ireland. This meant that the expanding company had three films on the floor at the same time, spreading the available Hammer team far and wide. Indeed, as the Val Guest and *Sherwood Forest* units continued to toil at Elstree and Ardmore, *Visa to Canton* would start at Bray on Thursday 19 June.

From 1955 to 1959, ITC's *The Adventures of Robin Hood* ran to 143 episodes and confirmed Richard Greene as TV's favourite Lincoln Green outlaw. Hammer were familiar with the subject matter after their 1953 production *The Men of Sherwood Forest*, directed by Val Guest, but the first move had not been theirs. Greene had seen the potential of a big screen version and, to that end, formed his own production company, Yeoman Films, with his television producer, Sidney Cole. Yeoman approached Hammer and they agreed to co-produce another Robin Hood feature, which became *Sword of Sherwood Forest*, Greene naturally taking on his usual role as Robin Hood.

Terence Fisher was brought in to direct a subject he too was familiar with, having already directed eleven TV episodes during the show's earliest years. Fisher had an impressive cast at his disposal (together with some splendid locations tailor-made for Megascope), the film promised to be a sensational production. However, it's let down by a rather leaden script and the ill-advised decision to kill off Peter Cushing's brilliant Sheriff of Nottingham far too early in the proceedings. According to Terence Fisher's wife Morag, "Peter Cushing and his wife were staying at the same hotel and Peter went out painting when he wasn't shooting. He does lovely watercolours."[12] There was strong support from Richard Pasco as the conniving Earl of Newark, Niall MacGinnis as a pleasing Friar Tuck and the dependable Nigel Green as Little John, while Sarah Branch made a charming Maid Marian.

Stuntman Jackie Cooper made his first contribution to a Hammer film on *Sherwood Forest*. An expert archer as well as diver, he became their Hammer's Master of Archery. Continuity supervisor Dot Foreman was replaced by Pauline Wise – her first screen credit for Hammer. "I would probably have stayed on as Tony Keys' secretary," she remembers, "but there was a shortage of script supervisors, or continuity girls as they were then called. Tilly Day was the resident continuity, but they seemed to be doing two films at the same time. Very often Tilly had to prep and I know they couldn't get other people down. It was a long way and the M4 wasn't built then. It was a problem for them to get good ones, so they asked me, as I lived locally, if I would like to train to do continuity under Tilly for a whole year. I said yes, I wouldn't mind that. I did *The Stranglers of Bombay* with her on the floor, then I went into the cutting rooms, to see it from that angle. I remember the film in the cutting room was *Never Take Sweets from a Stranger* with Alfred Cox and Jimmy Needs, and they were teaching me the cutting side of it. After that I did a few more films with Tilly such as *The Two Faces of Dr Jekyll*, *The Brides of Dracula* and *The Terror of the Tongs*. Tilly was very kind to me and she was a great teacher. I did all the typing of her notes, while she was teaching me how to do the job. She would dictate the notes and I would type them up for the editors. I have fond memories of her."

Pauline recalls the difficulties she encountered in finally going solo. "Tilly was at Bray and they needed someone for *Sword of Sherwood Forest*, which they were making at Ardmore Studios in Ireland. They did have somebody start on it, but Richard Greene had her replaced. They sent me over there, very nervous, reading the script going out on the plane. I was picked up in Dublin and

Robin Hood (Richard Greene) demonstrates his prowess with the bow to Friar Tuck (Niall MacGinnis) and the Earl of Newark (Richard Pasco) in Sword of Sherwood Forest (1960).

SWORD OF SHERWOOD FOREST

PRINCIPAL PHOTOGRAPHY: 23 May to 8 July 1960
UK DISTRIBUTION: Columbia; 80 minutes; Technicolor; Megascope; certificate 'U'
UK RELEASE:
  TRADE SHOW: November 1960
  GENERAL RELEASE: 26 December 1960, on the ABC circuit
US RELEASE: January 1961

DIRECTOR: Terence Fisher; PRODUCERS: Richard Greene and Sidney Cole; EXECUTIVE PRODUCER: Michael Carreras; SCREENPLAY: Alan Hackney; ART DIRECTOR: John Stoll; DIRECTOR OF PHOTOGRAPHY: Ken Hodges; CAMERA OPERATOR: Richard Gayley; ASSISTANT DIRECTOR: Bob Porter; SUPERVISING EDITOR: James Needs; EDITOR: Lee Doig; MUSIC: Alan Huddinott; MUSIC SUPERVISOR: John Hollingsworth; ORIGINAL SONGS: Stanley Black; SONG BY Denis Lotis; SOUND RECORDISTS: John Mitchell and Harry Tate; SOUND EDITOR: Alban Streeter; MAKE-UP: Gerald Fletcher; HAIRSTYLIST: Hilda Fox; PRODUCTION MANAGER:

Ronald Liles and Don Weeks; CONTINUITY: Pauline Wise and Dot Foreman; COSTUME SUPERVISOR: John McCorry; WARDROBE MISTRESS: Rachel Austin; CASTING: Stuart Lyons; MASTER OF ARCHERY: Jack Cooper; MASTER AT ARMS: Patrick Crean; MASTER OF HORSE: Ivor Collin; MAIN TITLES: Chambers & Partners

Richard Greene (Robin Hood); Peter Cushing (Sheriff of Nottingham); Richard Pasco (Earl of Newark); Sarah Branch (Maid Marian); Niall MacGinnis (Friar Tuck); Edwin Richfield (Sheriff's lieutenant); Vanda Godsell (Prioress); Nigel Green (Little John); Denis Lotis (Alan A'Dale); Brian Rawlinson (1st falconer); Patrick Crean (Ollerton); Derren Nesbitt (Martin); Reginald Hearne (1st man at arms); Oliver Reed (Melton); Jack Cooper (Master of Archery); Jack Gwillim (Hubert Walter); Adam Kean (Retford); Charles Lamb (Old Bowyer); Aiden Grennell (1st veteran outlaw); James Neylin (Roger); Barry De Boulay (officer); John Hoey (Old Jack); Anew McMaster (Judge); John Franklyn (Walter's secretary); Maureen Halligan (portress); Desmond Llewellyn (traveller)

they never told Richard Greene that I'd not done it before. They told me that one of the big problems he'd had was with the arrows in his quiver. He'd either be sent into battle without any, or he'd have spent them in fighting and would then ride into a clearing where he'd have a quiverful of arrows and that's what mostly annoyed him. So I made sure he always had arrows! But I do remember one of the very first scenes, where I was absolutely scared stiff. It was a sort of rape and pillage scene in a monastery, where Oliver Reed and Richard Pasco were attacking the nuns and fighting. In comes Richard Greene as Robin Hood and there was this free-for-all and, really, I hadn't got anything written down in my pad. I didn't know who was who, I didn't know who to watch. It was scary, but that was just an early experience. Anyway I seem to have got through that film all right and they told Richard Greene on the last day that I was a new girl – well-trained, but new all the same. Terry Fisher was the director and he was lovely."

Shooting ended on Friday 8 July after seven weeks. The crew returned to London for post-production and, on 17 August, Harry Oakes commented in his diary: "Worked on inserts for the 'Irish Robin Hood' picture."

Meanwhile, Bray was busy polishing off its two back-to-back productions. *The Terror of the Tongs* had finished shooting on Monday 30 May and the same crew (apart from Eric Beche, who replaced Len Harris as camera operator, Alfred Cox, who took over editing, and a change-over of assistant directors necessitated by Hugh Harlow's call-up) returned less than two weeks later to start filming *Visa to Canton* on Thursday 9 June, re-using Bernard Robinson's Chinese sets.

Tongs, meanwhile, was offered up to the BBFC. Examiner Newton Branch commented on a black-and-white edit on 7 June:

"Reel 3. Remove shot of First Officer's mutilated hand. Remove shots of Helena's hand being held down by Tong men on a table and her reactions as her fingers are struck by axe.

Reel 7. There must be a considerable reduction in the torturing of Sale: in particular remove all shots of the needles in contact with his flesh.

Reel 8. Remove shot of the torturer lying on ground with axe in his body and blood all around it.

Reel 9. Remove close shot of man's bloody body after it has been repeatedly stabbed and shots of his mutilated hand.

"These are minimum cuts. We shall want to see the missing scenes in Reels 1 and 10. The film should be submitted in full colour and with full sound."

A colour print was submitted to the Board in August and Trevelyan wrote to Kenneth Hyman on the 19th: "We have now had a look at the whole of *Terror of the Tongs* in colour. Some of the cuts that we asked for before have been made, but some have not been made. After seeing the colour version we have made the following decisions:

Jimmy Sangster, Michael Carreras and Val Guest on the set of *Visa to Canton* (1960).

D. Reel 2. The mutilated hand of the first officer can still be seen. The shot must be removed. The shots of Helena's hand being held down on a table and her reactions as her fingers are struck by the axe are still in the scene. These shots must also be removed. We feel that the scene can be revised in such a way as to give the impression that she faints from the shock of the man rushing into the room rather than from the severing of her fingers by the axe.

VISA TO CANTON

running time 75 minutes
RELEASE: [UK] 1960; BLC [US] 1961; Columbia; US title: *Passport to China*
UK: Technicolor; US: b/w
PRINCIPAL PHOTOGRAPHY: 9 June to 1 July 1960
DISTRIBUTION: Columbia; 75 minutes; b/w;
  UK: Technicolor; certificate 'U';
  US: b/w US TITLE: *Passport To China*
UK RELEASE:
  TRADE SHOW: 20 November 1960
  GENERAL RELEASE: 26 December 1960
  US RELEASE: February 1961

DIRECTOR: Michael Carreras; PRODUCER: Michael Carreras; ASSOCIATE PRODUCER: Anthony Nelson Keys; SCREENPLAY: Gordon Wellesley; PRODUCTION DESIGNER: Bernard Robinson; ART DIRECTOR: Thomas Goswell; ASSISTANT ART

DIRECTOR: Don Mingaye; DIRECTOR OF PHOTOGRAPHY: Arthur Grant; CAMERA OPERATOR: Eric Beche; ASSISTANT DIRECTOR: Arthur Mann; SUPERVISING EDITOR: James Needs; EDITOR: Alfred Cox; MUSIC COMPOSER: Edwin Astley; MUSIC SUPERVISOR: John Hollingsworth; SOUND RECORDIST: Jock May; MAKE-UP: Roy Ashton; HAIR STYLIST: Frieda Steiger; PRODUCTION MANAGER: Clifford Parkes; CONTINUITY: Tilly Day; WARDROBE: Molly Arbuthnot

Richard Basehart (Don Benton); Lisa Gastoni (Lola); Athene Seyler (Mao Tai Tai); Eric Pohlmann (Ivano); Allan Gifford (Mr. Orme); Bernard Cribbins (Pereira); Burt Kwouk (Jimmy); Hedgar Wallace (Inspector Taylor); Marne Maitland (Han Po); Milton Reid (Bodyguard); Yvonne Shima (Liang Ti); Robert Lee (Officer); Zoreem Ismail (Sweekim); Paula Lee Shiu (Croupier); Soraya Rafat (Hostess); Gerry Lee Yen (Room Boy); Ronald Ing (Sentry)

D. Reel 3. The torture of Sale is still too long. There must be no shot of the needle in contact with his chest. We can accept only one of the torture scenes.

"I shall be glad if you will confirm in writing that the cuts that we require in Reel 2 have been made. When you have made the reduction in D. Reel 3 we would like to see it again. It would save time if the scenes were marked up."

Michael Carreras wrote to Trevelyan on 31 August: "This is to confirm that we have complied with your request, that the scenes of 'the first officer's hand' and 'Helena having her fingers chopped off by the Tong men' in Reel 3 of *The Terror of the Tongs* have been deleted." The film was duly granted its 'X' certificate.

On Thursday 7 July, the Marble Arch Odeon hosted a spectacular première for *The Brides of Dracula*. Yvonne Monlaur arrived in a horse-drawn carriage (the Baroness' coach from the film itself, no less) to be greeted by Peter Cushing at the entrance. Also present for the festivities were Henry Oscar, Mona Washbourne, Michael Carreras, Tony Hinds, Anthony Nelson Keys, Val Guest, Hazel Court and her husband Don Taylor. Alas, Terence Fisher could not make it. He was still at work on *Sword of Sherwood Forest* in Ireland. Hammer once more had a winner on their hands and the success continued with the film's general release from Monday 29 August.

Inspecting Universal's monster properties, Hammer had taken no immediate interest in the company's lycanthropic subjects (*WereWolf of London* plus *The Wolf Man* and sequels). However, Universal did own Guy Endore's 1933 novel, *The Werewolf of Paris*, and early in 1960 they sub-contracted the rights to Hammer. At the same time, Michael Carreras was making plans for a movie based on the Spanish Inquisition, which at various times went under the proposed titles of *The Rape of Sabena* and *The Inquisitor*, and now Hammer decided to schedule both productions back-to-back, changing the location of their werewolf project from France to Spain, so as to make two films with Spanish locations in order to economise in the same way they had done with *The Terror of the Tongs* and *Visa to Canton*.

1960 was proving to be a busy year and Tony Hinds knew that funds were at a premium. He therefore decided to adapt Endore's novel himself, explaining: "I wrote it because the budget I was given as a producer wasn't enough to include a writer." [13] Hinds was already well-versed in rewriting parts of other people's scripts. "I worked as a co-writer without credit on one or two shows, notably *X the Unknown* and the first *Frankenstein*," he once said, adding: "I am not trying to take anything away from Jimmy Sangster, who did all, or most, of the actual writing." [14] Indeed, we have already seen how he rescued *The Brides of Dracula* as uncredited *fourth* writer.

The Curse of the Werewolf would be Hinds' first solo Hammer screenplay, for which he cheekily assumed the pen-name John Elder. "When I was a boy, I edited a magazine for a group attached to my school," Hinds remembers. "And when you're editing those things, you usually end up writing a lot. The chap who was typing it for me rang me up and said, 'Look, I can't give you the by-line on everything, so for the serial story, can you give me a different name?' There was a man working for my father at the time – my father was very slightly involved in films – called Jim Elder Wills. So I said, 'Oh, how about Jim Elder?' And the typist got it wrong and typed it John Elder. And that's how John Elder was born." [15]

In June 1960 Hinds put together a 'synopsis for consideration' called *The Werewolf* [16]. This original draft was considerably different from his final shooting script which followed in August, now under the more familiar title *The Curse of the Werewolf*. It started by introducing the aged Professor Don Carido (sic), who is lecturing to a group of zoology students about wolves. He becomes sidetracked by the subject of werewolves and starts his narration. Like the final script and film to come, the story again tells of the Castle Siniestro, the evil Marquis, the beggar and the girl. She is found in the woods by Don Alfredo, where she is now looked after by him, his wife Isobella and their servant Maria (in the final script he would have no wife and his servant would be called Teresa). The girl dies in childbirth, but Hinds' original treatment had them christen the boy Bernardo (renamed Leon in the final script). The story then continues as in the final film (except for more name changes – the plucky girlfriend Christina was originally called Teresa), up to the point where the werewolf kills the prostitute Vera and his friend José in the brothel. In the original synopsis, Bernardo returns to the Carido home, but is followed by the madame of the brothel, Senora Zumara, who, knowing he is the killer, blackmails Don Alfredo. She is bought off, but Don Alfredo whips Bernado in a fit of rage and

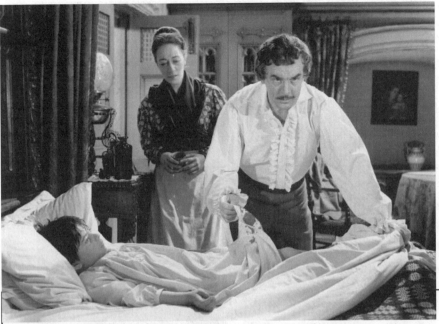

Don Alfredo
(Clifford Evans)
and Teresa (Hira
Talfrey) learn the
awful truth about
young Leon (Justin
Walters) in The
Curse of the
Werewolf (1960).

THE CURSE OF THE WEREWOLF

PRINCIPAL PHOTOGRAPHY: 12 September to 2 November
1960
DISTRIBUTION:
UK: Rank; certificate 'X'
US: Universal-International
88 minutes; Technicolor
UK RELEASE:
PREMIÈRE: 12 April 1961, with The Shadow of the Cat
GENERAL RELEASE: May 1st, 1961, with The Shadow of
the Cat
US RELEASE: 7 June 1961, with The Shadow of the Cat

DIRECTOR: Terence Fisher; PRODUCER: Anthony Hinds; Associate
Producer: Anthony Nelson Keys; EXECUTIVE PRODUCER: Michael
Carreras; SCREENPLAY: John Elder, based on the novel The
Werewolf of Paris by Guy Endore; PRODUCTION DESIGNER:
Bernard Robinson; ART DIRECTOR: Don Mingaye; DIRECTOR OF
PHOTOGRAPHY: Arthur Grant; CAMERA OPERATOR: Len Harris;
FOCUS PULLER: Harry Oakes; CAMERA ASSISTANT: Alan
MacDonald; GRIP: Albert Cowland; ASSISTANT DIRECTOR: John
Peverall; 2ND ASSISTANT DIRECTOR: Dominic Fulford;
SUPERVISING EDITOR: James Needs; EDITOR: Alfred Cox; MUSIC:
Benjamin Frankel; SOUND RECORDIST: Jock May; BOOM
OPERATOR: Jim Perry; SOUND EDITOR: Alban Streeter; MAKE-UP:
Roy Ashton; MAKE-UP ASSISTANT: Colin Guard; HAIRSTYLIST:
Frieda Steiger; PRODUCTION MANAGER: Clifford Parkes;
CONTINUITY: Tilly Day; WARDROBE: Molly Arbuthnot; SPECIAL

EFFECTS: Les Bowie; CASTING: Stuart Lyons; CONSTRUCTION
MANAGER: Arthur Banks; MASTER PLASTERER: Stan Banks;
MASTER CARPENTER: Charles Davis; MASTER PAINTER: Lawrence
Wrenn; MASTER ELECTRICIAN: Jack Curtis; MASTER RIGGER:
Ronald Lenoir; PROPS BUYER: Eric Hillier; PROPS MASTER:
Tommy Money; STILLS PHOTOGRAPHER: Tom Edwards

Clifford Evans (Don Alfredo Carido); Oliver Reed (Leon); Yvonne
Romain (Servant Girl); Catherine Feller (Christina); Anthony
Dawson (The Marques Siniestro); Josephine Llewellyn (The
Marquesa); Richard Wordsworth (The Beggar); Hira Talfrey
(Teresa); Justin Walters (Young Leon); John Gabriel (The Priest);
Warren Mitchell (Pepe Valiente); Anne Blake (Rosa Valiente);
George Woodbridge (Dominique); Michael Ripper (old soak); Ewen
Solon (Don Fernando); Peter Sallis (Don Enrique); Martin Matthews
(José); David Conville (Rico Gomez); Denis Shaw (gaoler); Charles
Lamb (chef); Serafina Di Leo (Senora Zumara); Sheila Brennan
(Vera); Joy Webster (Isobel); Renny Lister (Yvonne)

UNCREDITED: Francis De Wolff (man in bar); John Bennett, Alister
Williamson (policeman); Desmond Llewellyn (1st footman); Gordon
Whiting (2nd footman); Hamlyn Benson (landlord); Kitty Atwood
(midwife); Stephen W Scott (irate farmer); Ray Browne (official);
Frank Sieman (gardener); Max Butterfield (cheeky farmer); Michael
Peake, Howard Lang (farmers); Rodney Burke (1st customer); Alan
Page (2nd customer); Richard Golding (3rd customer); Michael
Lewis (page); Lorraine Caruana (servant girl when young)

tells him the truth. Then, as in the final version, Bernardo runs back to the vineyard, where Don
Fernando has him arrested when he attempts to run away with his daughter.

Here the treatment diverts from the final film once more. Bernado is thrown into a cell with
Pepe (not the so-called 'Old Soak'), who has been arrested for the murders. Bernardo is tried,

Wolfman Oliver Reed lurks behind his mother (Yvonne Romain) in this publicity still for The Curse of the Werewolf (1960).

found guilty and sentenced to be burnt at the stake. However, on the evening before his execution, he kills the gaoler and escapes into the forest, where he changes into the werewolf. Don Alfredo tracks him down and Bernardo, 'his voice half human, half animal', begs him not to let Teresa see him in this state. His eyes filled with tears, Don Alfredo shoots him dead with a silver bullet and Bernardo reverts to his human form. Thankfully Hinds decided to change this rather anti-climactic ending in his final shooting script to the more exciting one we are now familiar with, where the werewolf is chased through the streets and ascends the belltower. Hinds re-used his idea of a talking lycanthrope for the climax of *The Legend of the Werewolf*, which he scripted for Tyburn in 1974.

Meanwhile, Hammer finally scheduled the two productions. *The Rape of Sabena* was due to go before the cameras on Monday 29 August and *The Curse of the Werewolf* on Monday 17 October. Peter R Newman had written the script for *Sabena*, John Gilling was slated to direct and Philip Latham and Kieron Moore to star. All seemed well on the surface and Bernard Robinson was given the go-ahead to design his Spanish sets. All was not well, however, at Hammer House.

Hammer's association with Columbia was flagging. They knew what Hammer were good at – horror pictures – and began to get cold feet about any ventures outside the genre. Hammer's future schedule for Columbia, which was announced that August, had displeased them due to its lack of horror-related subjects: *The Rape of Sabena, Hell Hath No Fury, One More River* (a dramatic story about a mutiny aboard a tramp-ship on the West African coast, with a huge cast of international names to be directed by Val Guest), *The Brutal Land* (a Western also penned by Peter R Newman), and *The Man with Two Shadows*.

On 12 August, Hammer submitted the scripts for their two Spanish-based productions to the BBFC. John Trevelyan sent a word of warning to James Carreras on 22 August: "Over the weekend I read the two scripts from Hammer – *The Rape of Sabena* and *Curse of the Werewolf*. Each of these is liable to run into serious censorship trouble; this may not surprise you. I am, however, more worried about the effect of these two pictures on your company's growing reputation. I know this kind of thing makes money, and I do not for the moment blame you for wanting to do so, but I do feel that the reputation of your company is important both here and abroad."

James Carreras replied to Trevelyan the same day: "I must say that I agree with your comments entirely and have recently had a meeting with Michael and Tony when we decided to be very careful as to the type of subjects which we will be making during the end of 1960/61, and I think you will find that subjects, as per the two above, will have been deleted from our programme."

Enough was enough. Columbia was never going to swallow the project which, as Carreras pointed out to Trevelyan, was now called *The Inquisitor*. Too much money had already been poured into its pre-production, and now major rewrites were needed close to its proposed starting date. James Carreras had no choice; he phoned his son and told him to pull the plug on the project. In its stead, James brought forward the werewolf picture to 12 September, for Universal. The decision would cause a serious rift between father and son. Michael would leave the company, licking his wounds, and form his own company, Capricorn Productions, in December 1960, taking with him the jettisoned project, *The Brutal Land*, which he would now make as *The Savage Guns* in October 1961.

Not that *The Curse of the Werewolf* was having an easier ride. Not since *The Revenge of Frankenstein* or the aborted *I Am Legend* had Hammer incurred so much disgust with the reader/examiners at the BBFC, thanks to Tony Hind's no-holds-barred foray into lycanthropy: a buxom servant girl is raped by a fanged unkempt beggar, who is being kept as a pet in cage by a wicked Marques, and then hides in the woods for months, where she lives like an animal, only to die giving birth to the titular werewolf on Christmas Eve. Quite a change in direction from the heady days of Universal, when a bite from Bela Lugosi was sufficient to do the trick! Reader Audrey Field passed her usual sharp comments to John Trevelyan on 15 August:

"There is some imaginative writing in the first few pages and I had high hopes that this would be a superior werewolf story, for those who like these things. When we came to the taunting and brutalising of the beggar, his life in chains and the rape of the dumb serving-wench, I thought we had a candidate for rejection. When we got into the darkest forests of Gothic horror again, I was on familiar ground, following the well-beaten track of the 'Hammer X'.

"I conclude that the main story will do (subject to the usual cautions on details), but the introductory subsidiary story of the bestial beggar and the dumb serving-wench is intolerable. This is not the legitimate thrill of horror, but caters for very debased and perverted sexual tastes. Tinkering with details will not suffice: the concept of a man being chained up and deliberately turned into a beast is not likely to prove acceptable in a sensational film of this kind (if at all); and the idea of the dumb girl being deliberately given to another man to be raped because she defied the Marques is also surely prohibitive. The Marques could turn her out into the forest because she rejected him, and she could then have the misfortune to meet a 'wild man of the woods', provided we did not see details of the rape; but this leaves them with a new beginning to devise, and I think they must do so."

She went on to list her objections. Newton Branch's comments on 18 August were just as unflattering:

"In the old days werewolves and vampires were supernatural creatures so one could discount some of their goings-on. But here, man becomes dog and rapes dumb girl watched by a poor man's Marquis de Sade. The first 18 pages come to a climax not of horror but of sheer bestiality. I'm not even much in favour of AOF's idea of a hairy chap in the forest producing a werewolf. It's still a beastly idea. I know Carreras says that when he makes an honourable film, he loses money, but he should feel a bit ashamed of this obscene muck."

John Trevelyan summarised his readers' comments in a letter to Tony Hinds on 22 August: "We have now read your script entitled *The Curse of the Werewolf*. The critics will say 'Hammer at it again' or something like this! There are certain themes in this script of a bestial nastiness which we would want you to change. These are:

1. The harmless old beggar being kept as a pet in a cage and becoming a wild beast and
2. The deaf and dumb girl being pushed into the cage and raped by what was once a harmless old beggar.

"In our view these two incidents are deplorable and go beyond what is legitimate in a horror film. Surely you can devise alternatives which will be acceptable and which will be equally good from the point of view of the story. Such scenes could only run into serious censorship trouble. I would like to make the following comments on points of detail:

Page 6. We want to avoid sadism in the treatment of the chef by the Marques.

Page 12-14. These scenes as previously indicated would <u>not</u> be acceptable.

Page 18-19. These scenes as previously indicated would <u>not</u> be acceptable.

Page 19. We do not like the shot of the metal sconce being plunged deep into the Marques' back, with fresh blood welling from the wound, especially if the film is in colour.

Page 27. The labour pains should not be excessive. They are described as 'great discomfort' which suggests that they may be reasonable.

Page 30. We would not like to see any close-up of the lamb's torn throat.

Page 35. Here we see trails of blood. We do not want a great deal of blood in this film.

Page 37. I must issue a general caution about Leon's wound.

Page 46. The 'animal screams' may be quite unpleasant as they come from a child, but should not be so unpleasant as to be censorable.

Page 57-9. I must issue a general caution about the 'bordel' [sic] scenes. This is not the sort of film which should include nudity or too much eroticism.

Page 61-2. We do not want 'brutal love-making' combined with a sadistic treatment of the girl as the script suggests. The whole thing can be implied and not shown.

Page 63. The shot of Vera with blood on her neck sounds as though that might be really nasty. There is no reason to convey the impression 'that she may be naked'. We might accept, as we have accepted before, blood sucking, but we would be unhappy about it if it were combined with the suggestion that it followed sexual relations.

Page 63. The murder of José, as described, would be censorable. We would certainly not want 'awful crunching' when Leon makes a meal of him!

Page 65. Here we get crunching of bones again. We would dislike this.

Pages 80, 82 and 83. Shots of Leon as a 'werewolf' should not be too unpleasant or terrifying."

Tony Hinds replied to Trevelyan on 24 August: "Thank you very much for your letter. I absolutely agree with what you say in connection with this script, and will make alterations accordingly."

Hinds made a rudimentary stab at toning down the script based on the Board's comments, before going on holiday and leaving it to his secretary, Pamela Anderson, to send his corrections to the Board on Tuesday 30 August: "Mr Hinds re-wrote the sequence about the prisoner in the 'kennel', before departing to the South of France. He is interrupting his holiday to come back to England tomorrow and Thursday, and I wondered if you would be kind enough to glance through the enclosed revision pages so that I can tell him they are acceptable before we <u>both</u> go away on holiday, on Friday."

John Trevelyan was not to be hoodwinked that easily; he was used to Hammer's tactics. Reader Audrey Field commented on the 'replacement pages' on 30 August: "They do not seem to have rewritten the very offensive scene at the wedding-breakfast when the Marques makes the beggar behave like a dog – I did not like this. The beggar is no longer kept in the kennels (or so it seems, but we have not seen any replacement scenes for the bit where the Marques gave orders for him to be flung into the kennels?). However, he still seems to have turned into an ape-like creature covered with hair and having 'vampire' teeth. This is very ugly and retains the suggestion of bestiality to which we previously objected. The suggested changes do not reach the heart of the problem. I do not see how the nastiness of this story can be removed (or rather, brought within bounds) without a really drastic change in the account of how little Leon came to be born with werewolfish tendencies. People who have not read the original script will be even more disgusted than we are by the new (and admittedly slightly less nasty) version."

Trevelyan wrote back promptly to Miss Anderson the same day: "We are by no means happy about these revisions as they do not seem to have got to the root of the problem. The fact is, that we must ask for a drastic change in the story of how little Leon came to be born with werewolf tendencies. The present story is perhaps a little less nasty than the original but it is still not acceptable. We would like you to get the old beggar out completely. I hope Mr Hinds can find some satisfactory alternative."

Desperately, Hinds and the film's appointed director, Terence Fisher, met with Trevelyan and Field on Thursday 1 September to discuss the script. Trevelyan's own hand-written notes on the Board's records confirm the compromise: "In view of special production problems the early scenes cannot be entirely omitted.

On location for The Curse of the Werewolf (1960). Director Terence Fisher looks through the viewfinder; camera operator Len Harris is at his side.

We agreed that the best solution would be to have the girl sent to look after the prisoner – and being kind to the beggar, whom she knows before his incarceration. The prisoners were forgotten by the Marques and left indefinitely. One day she makes a mistake and opens the door of the beggar's cell and that causes the trouble. We discussed the other points in my letter of 27th August and emphasised that we do not accept a mixture of sex and blood sucking."

While Hinds would choose to disregard the full ramifications of this compromise (he still has his Marques shut the servant girl in with the beggar to teach her a lesson), it did at least give him the green light for the production, less than two weeks before shooting was due to commence.

Meanwhile, the construction crew at Bray worked on erecting Bernard Robinson and Don Mingaye's Spanish sets. The Curse of the Werewolf gave Mingaye his first credit as art director. Of his working relationship with Bernard Robinson, he says: "We had set responsibilities basically, but there were occasions when things overlapped. Bernard as production designer would be responsible for the overall concept of the production and produce sketches and I, as art director, would have to take them and consider them for budgeting and draughting up in the office, when I would have either Ken Ryan or Tommy Goswell draughting up the stuff. That's how we would work in conjunction with each other. When Bernard handed me a sketch, I might say, 'Well, this is fine, but because it's got to go here, it won't fit. We need to rethink this.' And he would make one or two adjustments in his designs and I would carry them out in practice and be responsible for all the work going through the workshops. Then having constructed a set, for example an interior, and this is where we overlapped, we would consult each other and choose the type of furniture required together. I worked closely with Bernard, so closely in fact that it was said at one time that the company couldn't tell who'd done what!"

The exterior Spanish sets expanded the village square on the backlot even further. A flight of steps was added to the tunnel archway and the square now included the impressive church and gaol. Another archway was built to represent the entrance to the village, which later doubled as the entrance to the vineyard. The stone gargoyle reflected in the font at Leon's christening was modelled by Margaret Carter. "It was just a head that came out of the wall above the pulpit," she remembers. "It was constructed in a different way to the griffins in The Brides of Dracula, because it didn't need an armature. You just had a wooden board and started building it straight onto the board with clay, because it didn't need support."

Another important job that was necessary before shooting could commence was to decide on the actual werewolf design. This onerous task befell Hammer's chief make-up artist Roy Ashton, who leapt at the challenge. Once more his research was scrupulous and with good reason, as he explained. "*The Curse of the Werewolf* was another film I researched painstakingly. I went to the Natural History Museum to draw and photograph the exhibits, since a basis of correct anatomy was very important. You see, if something like that is not right anatomically, it doesn't work well, destroying the whole illusion. Even the layman with no knowledge of anatomical construction can tell if you have not done the job properly." [17]

Ashton discussed his werewolf research further in another interview. "First I read the script and talked it over with Tony Hinds and Terence Fisher at the pre-production conference. We agreed that to start with we had to have a good idea of a real wolf. So I went to the Natural History Museum, where they have a big stuffed wolf in a showcase. I took my camera along and photographed it. When my film was processed the pictures turned out to be very good and they provided the basis from which I started to work. Then it was a question of having a good face to adapt to the werewolf make-up or vice versa. I suggested Oliver Reed to Tony Keys because he looked exactly right, especially in the structure of his bones. He already looked like half a wolf when he was getting angry anyway." [18]

Accordingly, the role of Leon, the unlucky lycanthrope, was given to Oliver Reed. He had already featured in two cameo roles for Hammer (in *The Two Faces of Dr Jekyll* and *Sword of Sherwood Forest*), and this was to be his first starring role. According to director Terence Fisher, Reed's broody performance as Leon was his best ever. Indeed, in the British pressbook for the film, Fisher is quoted as saying: "Were I invited to predict sure stardom for an unknown young actor of today, and asked to back that prediction with a heavy bet, the youngster I'd pick would be 22-year-old Mr Reed."

"The werewolf design took me several weeks of study and experiment," Ashton continued. "Oliver Reed had to submit to a number of tests, but he was splendidly co-operative and patient. The make-up basically was a false cranium which fitted over his own and came down to tuck into his eye sockets. The ears took some adjusting in the design before they looked acceptable. The neck and chin was a complex arrangement of hair somewhat in the manner that sheaves are organised in thatched roofing, as the head movement demanded that the layers had the freedom to move around one another. The body was a leotard covered with yak hair." [19] Ashton cunningly dilated Reed's nostrils, using sections from a candle with the wick removed to enable him to breathe. Jagged canines were put over his real teeth and contact lenses used for close-ups. In total the make-up took about two hours.

Jackie Cooper would stand in for Reed as the werewolf climbs the buildings in the village square. While Roy Ashton designed the prosthetics, his assistant Colin Guard applied them to Cooper for these exciting climactic scenes. "I had to have the full make-up," remembered Cooper. "I didn't have to wear the contact lenses, because they never saw my face that close – they'd have known it wasn't Oliver! The hair was all laid on a piece at a time. It took about an hour and a half to two hours' work in the morning putting it on. I never got to do really close-up shots, except when I come off the tower. When they're making it up and want it to stay on, like hair, they put it on with a latex. It's not a glue, you can smile and open your mouth and things like that. In those days it was put on with a sort of rubber solution." Cooper recalls that a photograph was taken of him standing next to Reed, both wearing their werewolf make-ups.

Shooting started at Bray on Monday 12 September, wrapping seven and a half weeks later on Wednesday 2 November. As we have seen, the rape sequence had to be moderated for the censor, although Terence Fisher defended it: "It was an integral part of the story. It was one of the few times that John Trevelyan really dug his heels in. It really wasn't that he objected to anything that I shot, he objected to the fact in principle of mixing sex with horror, because he had a strong feeling about that. We argued and argued and said this was an integral part of the film. Finally he decided that the audience must guess what had happened or what was implied had happened." [20]

In 1978, Fisher explained his passion for the film in the foreword to *Fandom's Film Gallery # 3*, an in-depth review of the picture by Jan Van Genechten. "The main reason why, of the films I have directed in the so-called horror genre, I have a particular regard for *The Curse of the Werewolf* is that I consider it to be a tragic love story and not fundamentally a 'horror' story. Admittedly it is set within the legend of the werewolf, but the basic theme is the love of two young people for each other, which ends in tragedy. I feel strongly that the character involvement and the interplay of emotions is greater in this film than any of the others I have directed; they are more important than the situations that the characters are placed in." On another occasion, he remarked that "I liked that [film] because of the

LEFT: *Teresa (Hira Talfrey) comforts Leon (Oliver Reed) when he learns of his terrible legacy in* The Curse of the Werewolf *(1960).*

BELOW: *Prostitute Sheila Brennan is brutally murdered in* The Curse of the Werewolf *(1960). The BBFC voiced their oft-expressed concern about mixing sex with horror.*

tremendous inter-relation between the characters, between Reed and the girl. Hell, anyone can turn into a werewolf, can't they? But it was his situation that made it exciting. The horror of him knowing that this was happening to him and the conflict between this and his love for the girl. An audience, I think, will respond to this because they can understand the emotional pull between people rather than the fact of someone turning into a werewolf." [21]

The film marked the first of a number of Hammer appearances for the 22-year-old Yvonne Romain. Her genre debut came in *Corridors of Blood* in 1958, a medical-horror drama starring Boris Karloff, Christopher Lee and Francis Matthews, in which she was billed as Yvonne Warren. Married to composer/lyricist Leslie Bricusse, she changed her name to Romain and went on to star in *Circus of Horrors* in December 1959 alongside Anton Diffring and Yvonne Monlaur. Her cousin Loraine Caruana played her younger self, when we are first introduced to her in the dungeon. In contrast, this would be 21-year-old Catherine Feller's first major film role after theatre and television work. "I remember during the night location," she recalls, "we were given food at three in the morning, because sometimes you would work all night. In big tents, they had big tables with the food. I didn't want to sit with Oliver Reed because he was made-up as the werewolf, with blood and hair and things on his face. He had such a terrible face that I refused to sit and have supper with him, and I think he never forgave me." [22]

The picture was cinematographer Arthur Grant's first real colour Gothic (ignoring his work on *Tongs*), and he proved just as capable as Jack Asher in bringing out the right atmosphere; the scene in the prison cell when Leon waits for the moon to rise is testament to this. Focus puller Harry Oakes remembers the difficulties presented by another scene: "I think it was the scene where Oliver Reed first realised he is the werewolf and he had to cry during the sequence. Terry wanted a loose shoulder shot and then a very slow and dramatic track into his eyes. It would have been a doddle with a zoom lens, but we didn't have them then and I don't think we were using the Vinten camera, so there was no way that Len could be sure that it was sharp all the way. I thought I had a brilliant idea by suggesting that we shot in reverse, so I said, 'Why don't we start with a close-up of the eyes, run it in reverse and then track back?' Well, they thought this was brilliant. I got brownie points for that, but I lost them the next day because, when I saw the rushes, the tears were going up into his eyes!"

Bray caretaker Marje Hudd remembered Oliver Reed: "He was a lovely man. I remember on *The Curse of the Werewolf*, he went to the little pub at the top of the lane for his lunch in his make-up.

They used to take the head part off, but they couldn't take all the rest off, because it would take too long to dress him again. So he put a white robe around him to cover his hairy skin and off he went to the local. There was a girl behind the bar. She was only about 19, a little country girl, and she didn't see anything until he came to pay. Of course he held his hand out and it was all long hairs and these black talons. The poor kid fainted and Oliver was so upset."

On 9 October, Southern England was hit by its worst flooding for seven years and, as Harry Oakes' diary testifies ("Still it rains!"), the downpours would take take their toll on the production, necessitating considerable rescheduling.

Hammer were still flush with projects. While *The Curse of the Werewolf* was on the floor at Bray, they had to begin their next two productions elsewhere. *A Weekend with Lulu* started at Shepperton on Monday 3 October and *Taste of Fear* started shooting in France on the 24th, moving to Elstree (to make room for Bray's next production, *The Shadow of the Cat*) on 14 November. *A Weekend with Lulu* was another low-budget comedy, telling of the misfortunes of a bunch of holidaymakers in a caravan (the 'Lulu' of the title), who get stranded in France. It was directed by John Paddy Carstairs, Anthony Nelson Keys' brother. Down the pecking order, the voluptuous Marie Devereux was back as one of the 'Lulubelles' who add to the confusion. Obviously, while the team of regulars were still at Bray, Hammer had to rustle up different crews for their new productions at Shepperton and Elstree.

Chaos in a caravan – Shirley Eaton, Bob Monhouse, Irene Handl and Leslie Phillips in A Weekend with Lulu (1960).

Terence Fisher took time out from *The Curse of the Werewolf* to attend the London première of *The Two Faces of Dr Jekyll* on Friday 7 October at the London Pavilion. Bernard Robinson's future wife, Margaret, was none too pleased when she spotted some familiar sitting room wallpaper in Norma Marla's bedroom. She explains, "Bernard would order extra rolls of wallpaper for himself. I know the wallpapers in our front and back sitting rooms were the ones used in *The Two Faces of Dr Jekyll*. He said if you bought the paper in a shop, it would be £7 a roll, which was a lot for wallpaper then. So he ordered extra, knowing that he would like it in his house, and then bought it cheaply through the firm at £2 a roll." The film went on general release on the ABC circuit from 24 October but fared poorly

A WEEKEND WITH LULU

PRINCIPAL PHOTOGRAPHY: 6 October to 10 December 1960
DISTRIBUTION:
 UK: Columbia; 89 minutes; certificate 'A'
 US: Columbia; 91 minutes
b/w
UK RELEASE:
 GENERAL RELEASE: 10 April 1961 in Halifax
US RELEASE: 1 November 1961

DIRECTOR: John Paddy Carstairs; PRODUCER: Ted Lloyd; EXECUTIVE PRODUCER: Michael Carreras; SCREENPLAY: Ted Lloyd based on an original story by Ted Lloyd and Val Valentine; ART DIRECTOR: John Howell; ART DEPARTMENT ASSISTANT: Helen Thomas; DIRECTOR OF PHOTOGRAPHY: Ken Hodges; CAMERA OPERATOR: Brian Wert; CLAPPER: Bob Stillwell; GRIP: M Walters; Assistant Director: Chris Sutton; 2ND ASSISTANT DIRECTOR: Patrick

Hayes; 3RD ASSISTANT DIRECTOR: Michael Klaw; Supervising EDITOR: James Needs; EDITOR: Tom Simpson; MUSIC COMPOSER: Trevor H Sanford; MUSIC CONDUCTOR: Tony Osborne; SOUND RECORDIST: Bill Salter; BOOM OPERATOR: Tom Buchanan; DUBBING EDITOR: Alan Morrison; MAKE-UP: Dick Bonner-Morris; HAIR STYLIST: Bill Griffiths; PRODUCTION MANAGER: Jacques De Lanc Lea; CONTINUITY: Splinters Deason; WARDROBE: Maude Churchill; CASTING: Stuart Lyons; STILLS CAMERAMAN: Robert Penn; PRODUCTION BUYER: Charless Townsend; PUBLICITY: Dennison Thornton; ACCOUNTANT: W. Able; CONSTRUCTION MANAGER: Jack Bolam; TRANSPORTATION: L.C. Wenman, Peter Willetts

Shirley Eaton (Diedre); Leslie Phillips (Tim); Bob Monkhouse (Fred); Alfred Marks (Count de Grenable); Irene Handl (Florence); Heidi Erich, Sally Douglas, Marie Devereux, Eve Eden, Janette Rowsell (The Lulubelles)

at the box-office. It wouldn't get a US release until May 1961, when American International Pictures put it out under the revised title *House of Fright*.

The Curse of the Werewolf finished filming on Wednesday 2 November and editors Alfred Cox and James Needs, with sound editor James Groom, took it into post-production at Hammer House. Benjamin Frankel was brought in to compose and supervise his own score. On Saturday the 5th, Bernard Robinson married Margaret Carter. Soon after she would become pregnant with their son Peter and left Hammer's employ. She mused, "I made a Kuan Lin, which is a fertility goddess, for *Visa to Canton*. I knew I was getting married when I was making her and, being 40, I thought maybe I wouldn't have any children. I'd left it a bit late and as I was making the goddess and thinking of the women who pray to the Kuan Lin for a baby, I thought, I wonder if she'll work for me? Well, *something* worked for me!"

By 1960 Sangster was growing weary of writing Gothic horrors and was afraid that he was becoming typecast in this capacity. He therefore turned to writing psychological thrillers, the first of which was *Taste of Fear*, which he both wrote and produced. "I wrote it as an original screenplay," he remembers. "I didn't even show it to Hammer. I wrote it for Sydney Box and I was going to produce it as part of a three-picture deal I had with him. I'd been writing for two to three years and I wanted to get back on the floor again. However, Sydney had a heart attack and he had to get out of the movie business. Peter Rogers took over his business at that moment and all he wanted to do was get rid of it. He was busy making Carry On pictures. He wanted to get rid of all Sydney's obligations, so I said, 'Maybe I'll buy the script back from you.' He said, 'Yes, please.'

"So I took it back and I didn't even take it to Hammer then. I took it to Monty Berman and Bob Baker at Tempean. They said, 'Yes, fine.' I said, 'But I want to produce it.' They said, 'No, no, you can't do that.' So I finally took it to Michael at Hammer. Michael liked it and said 'Yes.' I said, 'But I want to produce it.' So Michael went to the head of Columbia, Mike Frankovich, and said, 'We want to do this picture. We've got the script, but there's one problem. Sangster wants to produce it.' Frankovich said, 'What do you want to do that for? What about you and Tony?' Michael said, 'Either he produces it or we don't get the script.' So Frankovich said, 'All right, but you'll be supporting him the entire time, won't you?' Michael said 'Yes.' So that's how I came to produce it, but only because Michael Carreras was sitting on my back the whole time as executive producer.

"As producer I was told who was going to be the star – Susan Strasberg. She came as part of a package. I chose the director. Well, I say I chose the director. Michael said, 'There's this guy, Seth Holt. Do you want to see what he can do?' We looked at his work and we liked what we saw. Michael let me be producer as long as I didn't do anything to upset him. If I'd said I wanted to sack the director after week one or I was ferociously over schedule, or anything like that, then he would have stepped in, but I was line producer basically."

Sangster's tale is a twisting, convoluted one. Though some changes would occur between this first draft and the final shooting script, the basic plot remained the same. A young wheelchair-bound girl, Penny Appleby, is being driven insane by her stepmother, who uses the corpse of Penny's father as part of a scheme to nullify the girl's inheritance in his will.

Sangster submitted the script under its working title of *See No Evil* to John Trevelyan on 14 July. Reader Frank Crofts read it the next day, commenting: "The foreword shows that two changes are to be made in the film as compared with the script. a) The recovery of a girl's body at the beginning is to take place in England not France, and the main action of the film is to be in France, not England. b) The chauffeur, Bob, is a friend and hanger-on of Appleby and an enemy of the latter's second wife, Doris [Jane in the film; Bob's role as her enemy seems to have been taken on by Dr Gerrard in the final version]. This is a fairly good thriller, something on the lines of two French films we had about 2-3 years ago, but I don't know what category the company has in mind. Much of this is suitable for 'A', but there are several scenes which will need considerable care if they are not to be too strong for that category. These are:

a) The recovery of the girl's corpse at the beginning (this is the real Penny) This is described on p.3: 'her face was finely drawn, the face of a delicate person ... But this was in life. In death with wide open eyes, it is a mask, a set cut like a hideous China wall plaque.' [sic]

b) Penny's discovery of her father in the summer-house (pp.23-5). This scene ends with her screaming in terror, as a spider runs across his open eye.

Susan Strasberg, Christopher Lee and Ann Todd keep the audience guessing in Taste of Fear (1960).

TASTE OF FEAR

PRINCIPAL PHOTOGRAPHY: 24 October to 7 December 1960
DISTRIBUTION:
  UK: BLC; certificate 'X'
  US: Columbia; US TITLE: Scream of Fear
82 minutes; b/w
UK RELEASE: April 1961
US RELEASE: August 1961

DIRECTOR: Seth Holt; PRODUCER: Jimmy Sangster; EXECUTIVE PRODUCER: Michael Carreras; SCREENPLAY: Jimmy Sangster; PRODUCTION DESIGNER: Bernard Robinson; ART DIRECTOR: Thomas Goswell; ASSISTANT ART DIRECTOR: Bill Constable; DIRECTOR OF PHOTOGRAPHY: Douglas Slocombe; CAMERA OPERATOR: Desmond Davies; 2ND UNIT CAMERA: Len Harris, Harry Oakes; ASSISTANT DIRECTOR: David Tomblin; 2ND ASSISTANT DIRECTOR: Terry Lens; SUPERVISING EDITOR: James Needs; EDITOR: Eric Boyd-Perkins; MUSIC: Clifton Parker; MUSIC SUPERVISOR: John Hollingsworth; SOUND RECORDIST: Leslie

Hammond, E Mason and Len Shilton; SOUND EDITOR: James Groom; MAKE-UP: Basil Newall; HAIRSTYLIST: Eileen Bates; PRODUCTION MANAGER: Bill Hill; Continuity: Pamela Mann; WARDROBE: Dora Lloyd; SPECIAL EFFECTS: Les Bowie; SPECIAL EFFECTS ASSISTANT: Ian Scoones; CASTING: Stuart Lyons; STILLS PHOTOGRAPHER: George Higgins; PUBLICITY DIRECTOR: Dennison Thornton; UNIT PUBLICIST: Colin Reid

Susan Strasberg (Penny Appleby); Ronald Lewis (Bob); Ann Todd (Jane Appleby); Christopher Lee (Dr Gerrard); John Serret (Inspector Legrand); Leonard Sachs (Spratt); Anne Blake (Marie); Fred Johnson (Father)

UNCREDITED: Bernard Brown (Gendarme); Mme Lobegue (Swissair Hostess); Richard Klee (Plainclothes Sergeant); Fred Rawlings (Plainclothes Sergeant); Rodney Burke, Gordon Sterne (Uniformed men); Heinz Bernard, Brian Jackson, Frederick Schrecker (Plainclothes men)

c) Her discovery of her father in her room (pp.59-60). He moves his arm, which is presumably manipulated by a string. More screams.

d) Bob finds the corpse in the swimming pool (p.82). 'There is a rope tied under the arms of the body, which keeps it suspended in a parody of a standing position. The head is hanging forward, and the hair is streaming outwards from the head, and moving gently in the water ... Indeed the whole body seems possessed of some form of life as it sways gently, undulating at the end of its rope ... for one moment the glassy eyes are staring full into camera.'

e) Penny sees her father's body in the car. 'Buckled half on the floor, half on the seat is her father's body. Freshly dragged out of the water it is still soaking, with particles of weed

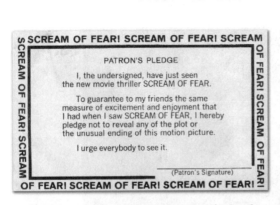

SCREAM OF FEAR! SCREAM OF FEAR! SCREAM OF FEAR! SCREAM OF FEAR! SCREAM OF FEAR! SCREAM OF FEAR!

PATRON'S PLEDGE

I, the undersigned, have just seen the new movie thriller SCREAM OF FEAR.

To guarantee to my friends the same measure of excitement and enjoyment that I had when I saw SCREAM OF FEAR, I hereby pledge not to reveal any of the plot or the unusual ending of this motion picture.

I urge everybody to see it.

(Patron's Signature)

adhering to the face. The eyes are turned up and glassy. The head flops grotesquely at the motion of the car.' (p.88) She screams once (p.89).

f) Doris falls screaming to her death (p.108).

g) She is seen lying on her back, 'her eyes are open in death and the sea is lapping gently across her upturned face." (p.110)

TOP LEFT: *A promotional gimmick handed out to American cinema audiences. In the US* Taste of Fear *was retitled* Scream of Fear.

"Only b) and c) should cause difficulty: as in *The Fiends* [ie, *Les Diaboliques*] two lovers are trying to drive a supposedly nervous person mad with a corpse kept usually in a swimming pool. This suggests something more than merely frightening: and this idea of the macabre is reinforced by the unnecessary shots of staring eyes and grotesque postures in some of the other scenes. A warning may be enough."

ABOVE: *Director Seth Holt made his Hammer debut with* Taste of Fear *(1960).*

Audrey Field passed her comments on 19 July: "I agree with FNC that the only potentially 'X' scenes, as far as visuals go, are the ones which he has listed. But it seems to me that those scenes are the essence of the story, that it would be the aim of this particular company to make them as macabre as possible, and that, even if they toned them down, there is something most horrific in the very idea of attempting to frighten a girl out of her mind by repeatedly showing her, in very gruesome circumstances, the corpse of her own father (in fact, he is *not* her father, since she is only impersonating Penny, but neither the conspirators nor the audience know this at the time the corpse appears). The 'feel' of the story is like *Les Diaboliques*, and I have never seen a more 'X' film than that."

John Trevelyan replied to Sangster on 25 July: "We have now read your script of *See No Evil*. This is a good and exciting macabre thriller, rather on the lines of *Les Diaboliques*. I should think it would certainly be in the 'X' category if it has any real impact, which it should have. For this category there is nothing in the present script which we would not accept."

As *The Two Faces of Dr Jekyll* went on general release, *Taste of Fear* began shooting in the South of France on Monday 24 October. There the unit toiled until Thursday 3 November, taking in such locations as Nice (including the airport), the Villa de la Garoupe, Cap d'Antibes and its adjoining cliffs, and roads at Villefranche. Then it was back to Elstree for the interiors, where shooting continued until Wednesday 7 December.

Seth Holt (1923-1971) had been an editor and associate producer at Ealing prior to making his directorial debut with *Nowhere to Go* (1958). In *Taste of Fear*, he gives maximum impact to the several shock appearances of Penny's deceased father, particularly in an underwater scene shot by Egil Woxholt and John Jordan.

The Shadow Of The Cat is a bona fide Hammer film, despite going out as a BHP production. BHP was formed in February 1960 by writer George Baxt, theatrical agent Richard Hatton and producer Jon Pennington. Baxt wrote a script and they took the project to Hammer, who in turn secured backing from Universal on 17 August. The film would eventually be shot by Hammer's regular crew at Bray and production stills bare reference to it being Hammer's 73rd production.

The villainous Walter Venable (André Morell) in The Shadow of the Cat (1960).

THE SHADOW OF THE CAT

PRINCIPLE PHOTOGRAPHY: 14 November to 22 December
DISTRIBUTION:
  UK: Rank; certificate 'X'
  US: Universal-International
79 minutes; b/w
UK RELEASE:
  PREMIÈRE: 12 April 1961, with *The Curse of the Werewolf*
  GENERAL RELEASE: 1 May 1961, with *The Curse of the Werewolf*
  US RELEASE: 7 June 1961, with *The Curse of the Werewolf*

DIRECTOR: John Gilling; PRODUCER: Jon Pennington; SCREENPLAY: *George Baxt*; PRODUCTION DESIGNER: *Bernard Robinson*; ART DIRECTOR: *Don Mingaye*; DIRECTOR OF PHOTOGRAPHY: *Arthur Grant*; CAMERA OPERATOR: *Len Harris*; FOCUS PULLER: *Harry Oakes*; ASSISTANT DIRECTOR: *John Peverall*; 2ND ASSISTANT DIRECTOR: *Dominic Fulford*; SUPERVISING EDITOR: *James Needs*; EDITOR: *John Pomeroy*; MUSIC: *Mikis Theodorakis*; SOUND RECORDISTS: *Jock May, Ken Cameron*; SOUND EDITOR: *Alban Streeter*; MAKE-UP: *Roy Ashton*;

HAIRSTYLIST: *Frieda Steiger*; PRODUCTION MANAGER: *Don Weeks*; CONTINUITY: *Tilly Day*; WARDROBE: *Molly Arbuthnot*; SPECIAL EFFECTS: *Les Bowie*; SPECIAL EFFECTS ASSISTANT: *Ian Scoones*; CASTING: *Stuart Lyons*; CAT TRAINER: *John Holmes*; CONSTRUCTION MANAGER: *Arthur Banks*; MASTER PLASTERER: *Stan Banks*; MASTER CARPENTER: *Charles Davis*; MASTER PAINTER: *Lawrence Wrenn*; MASTER ELECTRICIAN: *Jack Curtis*; MASTER RIGGER: *Ronald Lenoir*; PROPS BUYER: *Eric Hillier*; PROPS MASTER: *Tommy Money*; STILLS PHOTOGRAPHER: *Tom Edwards*

André Morell (Walter Venable); Barbara Shelley (Beth Venable); William Lucas (Jacob); Freda Jackson (Clara); Conrad Phillips (Michael Latimer); Richard Warner (Edgar); Vanda Godsell (Louise); Alan Wheatley (Inspector Rowles); Andrew Crawford (Andrew); Kynaston Reeves (Grandfather); Catherine Lacey (Ella); Tabatha (Cat)

UNCREDITED: *Rodney Burke (Workman); Vera Cook (Mother); Angela Crow (Daughter); John Dearth (Constable Hamer); George Doonan (2nd Ambulance Man); Howard Knight (Boy); Charles Stanley (Dobbins); Fred Stone (1st Ambulance Man); Kevin Stoney (Father)*

The film saw the welcome return of John Gilling to Hammer. Since his unceremonious departure in 1951 after falling out with James Carreras on *Whispering Smith Hits London*, Gilling had broken into directing, including *Mother Riley Meets the Vampire* with Bela Lugosi (1952), *The Gamma People* (1955) and *The Flesh and the Fiends* (1959). The latter was an impressive piece, which Gilling wrote and directed, relating the story of Burke and Hare and their association with the infamous Dr Knox, impeccably played by Peter Cushing.

Gilling immediately decided to change the thrust of George Baxt's screenplay for *Cat*. In Baxt's version, the cat was never seen. In classic Val Lewton style, the wrongdoers were to be plagued by their own consciences, merely imagining they could see or hear it. Certainly this sounds more plausible than the final plot created by Gilling, in which the villains embark on a pointless vendetta to trap the poor moggie as if it was going to run to the police and spill the beans. Silly or not, this uncredited rewrite earned Gilling an extra £150 above his director's fee.[23]

Shooting started at Bray on Monday 14 November, less than two weeks after completion of *The Curse of the Werewolf*, and ended six weeks later on Thursday 22 December. The same team were back from *Werewolf*, noticeable exceptions being Don Weeks replacing Clifford Parkes as production manager (Parkes was already planning Bray's next project, *Watch It Sailor!*) and John Pomeroy replacing Alfred Cox as editor, to allow Cox to finish editing (and complying with the censor) on *Werewolf* at Hammer House. Stuntman Jackie Cooper was brought back to disappear into the bog and hang from the roof at the climax. However, the film remains a rather lacklustre thriller. Gilling failed to bring any tension to the story and even Arthur Grant's anamorphic lens to simulate the vision of the cat couldn't infuse any interest.

Though a good director, Gilling had questionable 'people skills' and his bad temper was legendary. Assistant director John Peverall remembers: "John Gilling was terrible. There's a scene where the young couple come into the house and there's something going on upstairs. There had to be some plaster falling, or something to make them look up. We had set up a tracking shot coming in through the door and down the hallway. There were a couple of prop men up above the set with some boards and plaster and some Fuller's Earth for dust and other bits of stuff to drop down. We did the first take, and they didn't drop enough. Gilling started to rant and rave at these two guys.

"We set up another take. Now, the guys say they slipped, but I know they just dropped the whole lot of material. There was a big mess with huge clouds of Fuller's Earth filling the set. Gilling started screaming, 'Cut, cut!' There were literally pyramids of this dust on top of the actors' heads and shoulders where it had fallen. I started to laugh. I couldn't help myself. I thought I was going to die. I was howling and tears were coming out of my eyes. Gilling started screaming, 'Get Tony Keys on the set! Get Tony Keys on the set! You're fired.' And he started pointing at people. 'You're fired! And you're fired!' Tony came running on the set, asking, 'What happened? What happened?' I started to tell him the story, while I was still laughing. I put my arm around Tony, and he started to laugh, too. Anyway, Gilling was a real pain."[24]

Meanwhile, Hammer's battle with the censor over *The Curse of the Werewolf* began in earnest. Hammer submitted a black-and-white cut of the film to the BBFC at the end of November and immediately incurred the Board's wrath for their blatant disregard of the readers' original warnings. Newton Branch commented on 21 November: "The scenes of Leon in the belfry must be drastically reduced (particularly when one thinks of possible full sound effects). We are very dubious about the shot of the bullet hitting Leon's chest and the blood spurting out of his fur. We do not want to see any shots of the werewolf after he has died. <u>Note</u>, this film, we take it, will be in colour and the sound track is very incomplete at the moment. When the film is complete, it will probably be a good deal more horrid than it is now. We should like the President and other members of the Board to see this film."

A note dated 23 November reads: "Seen with the President and JT. The President would have liked to reject it, but it was agreed that a list of heavy cuts should be made without a promise for eventually passing it. The only possible category is 'X'."

Another from the same date: "There is a good case for rejecting this film. The theme is horrible enough and it has been made, despite all our warnings, in a morbid and disgusting fashion – a very good example of classic horror comic ... We are not (reels 2 and 3) committed to anything more than the establishment of the werewolf's paternity, i.e. we are not committed to the Marques' attack on the girl (when she bites him), her being taken down to the dungeons, thrown into the beggar's cell, the rape and the subsequent scenes in the dungeon. We are agreed that we should allow no more than the Marques ordering his servants to take the girl to the dungeons. We would also remove close shots of the Marques' disease ridden face (peculiarly disgusting). The killing of the Marques is revolting and we should like to see it gone. In any case it will have to be cut, along with the earlier shots of the Marques picking at the pimples on his face. We do not want to see his footman removing the girl from the dungeons or hear his, 'You know where you've got to go now.'

REEL 4. Remove the whole baptism sequence. In any event we would not have any reflections seen in the water of the font.

REEL 5. Remove shot of boy's arm which has werewolf hair on it.

REEL 7. Remove the whole sequence which takes place in prostitute's bedroom (beginning with the couple going into the bedroom and ending with the murder).

REEL 8. Reduce the scene in which werewolf kills José and in particular remove close shot of José's face when he is being choked.

REEL 10. The transformation of Leon into werewolf in the cell should be shortened and the killing of Leon's fellow prisoner should be removed."

Tony Hinds defiantly defended his position in a letter dated 28 November: "You will appreciate that the Board's long list of exceptions to the above has come as a terrible shock to me. Unfortunately, our American partners have already submitted the script to the MPAA, who have passed it without any cuts, so I shall have to score, dub and cut the negative of the full version for them. When I have done this and have a colour print of the complete picture, I should like to re-submit it for reviewing by the Board. However, for the first time, I feel that the Board has been very unfair. Many of the cuts asked for were either in the original script and passed by you, or the revisions were talked out in your office so as to make them acceptable to the Board. For instance:

REEL 3. The scene in which Teresa tells Alfredo it is a superstition in her village that it is unlucky for an illegitimate child to be born on Christmas Day. This scene was in the original script, and was passed by the Board.

REEL 4. The scene in which little Leon is baptised and, for a moment, it looks as if the devil has appeared. This was shot exactly as described in the script, which was passed by the Board.

REEL 5. The shot of Leon's hairy hand. This scene was also in the script, and no objection or warning was given.

REEL 10. The killing of the Beggar was in the script, although I admit it was shot differently – but not, I would have thought, any more 'horrificly'.

"In REEL 2, the original line (passed by the Board) was from the Marques to a servant: 'Send her to my room tonight.' In the rewriting which we did as a result of our discussions, the scene became one between the Marques and the Girl, so we changed the line to: 'You come here tonight and show me' (referring to the fact that she is high-spirited). Surely this is no better nor worse than the original line?

"In REEL 7, you warned me that you did not want to see any 'brutal love making combined with sadistic treatment'. Leon's kiss could hardly be described as that, surely? I agree that we took a chance with the shot of the Girl with her neck torn, but we were very careful not to suggest that there had been any sexual relations between them.

"I also agree that, in REEL 3, you did warn us about the stabbing. But after seeing a recent 'X' film set in contemporary America, in which a young pervert dressed as a woman stabs a naked girl to death in the bath to satisfy some queer lust of his own [Hinds is referring to Psycho here], I felt we were reasonably safe, in a story set in Spain 200 years ago, in showing a normal healthy girl protecting her honour by stabbing her would-be seducer.

"With regard to the shots of the werewolf's dead face, with the tear trickling from the eye... it was only because I was once told by the psychiatrist, Dr David Stafford-Clarke, that horror films were only dangerous if there was a complete lack of sympathy for the 'monster', that we put into the picture this shot and the shot of Alfredo looking down at him with compassion.

"Finally, you may remember that I came to see you before we started shooting, to see if we could find a different way of showing the girl seduced by the Beggar and thereby fathering the child that later becomes the werewolf. It was agreed that the script should be re-written so that the Marques did not watch her being attacked; indeed, that he should not even remember that the Beggar was still in the dungeons when he has her sent there. This is what we did.

"PS. In spite of the above, and in case I don't see you before, I wish you a happy Christmas."

Trevelyan wrote back to Hinds on 30 November: "Your reaction did not come as a surprise to me. I think that, in view of the American position, you should score, dub and cut the negative of the full version for them and re-submit the complete picture in colour for further consideration here. In the meantime, it might help if you and I had a talk about the cuts our Examiners want. I

LEFT: Inspector Rowles (Alan Wheatley) tries to unravel the case with Elizabeth (Barbara Shelley) and Michael (Conrad Phillips) in The Shadow of the Cat (1960).

BELOW: Barbara Shelley with feline friend on the set of The Shadow of the Cat (1960).

think that we might find a way in which to deal with some of the objections by re-editing."

The ironic feature of this debate was that, not only did the film escape the scissors of America's censor board, but over there Hammer's films were often showed at matinées where kids could attend. However, in England it seemed that concessions were necessary for it even to secure an Adults Only 'X' certificate. Hinds met with Trevelyan on 5 December and Trevelyan made a note in his files: "Discussed with Mr Hinds. He will make cuts where possible and resubmit the film in colour."

Editors James Needs and Alfred Cox began paring down some of the offending scenes. Exorcised at this stage was the shot of the werewolf being shot, with a very contrived jet of blood spurting from his chest. "The final scenes were quite a laugh," remembered Roy Ashton. "This chap, the werewolf, had to be put out of his misery by being shot with a bullet, molten from a silver crucifix. Tony Hinds said to us there had to be a lot of blood spurting out of him when he was shot. I mentioned to him that if you would shoot him from the front, the bullet would come out of his back and that is where the blood would flow. But Tony insisted on a tremendous spurt from the front, where the bullet would enter. So we rigged up a bicycle pump with a tube to a reservoir, concealed within the werewolf's chest. When the shot was fired, with a strong push on the pump, we forced a terrific spurt of blood from the front, all over the focus puller and the legs of the camera." [25]

The editorial headaches for Needs and Cox would continue into the early part of 1961. Now, as the year drew to an end, Hammer pushed out a double-bill of Sword of Sherwood Forest and Visa to Canton on 26 December. It had been an exhausting year.

NINE

Murder at the Opera

(1 9 6 1)

First thing in 1961, Hammer were finishing off *A Weekend with Lulu* with exterior shooting at Shepperton on 6 and 13 January. Harry Oakes' diary on Tuesday the 10th records an important date for Hammer: "Exteriors at Black Park for *Taste of Fear*. Rained all day. Fire wrecked Stage 3 during the night." Len Harris also remembered the incident: "I was doing some 2nd unit work at Black Park, a woodland not far from Bray. It was early morning and we were waiting for our equipment to arrive from Bray. It didn't turn up. Finally we got a phone call that there had been a fire and the equipment had been pulled out and was lying all over the Bray grounds. When we got back later, I saw that it was the old ballroom studio. They patched it up and repaired it eventually." [1]

According to caretaker Marje Hudd, "It started up in the crowd rooms above Stage 3, just through an electrical fault. It was an old building and the wiring was very old. When the cleaners had gone, the night watchman came up to our flat, which was upstairs looking onto the backyard (wardrobe was above us), for a cup of tea. His hours were from 10.00 pm to 6.00 am. He left our flat at 9.45 and, as he opened the door, the whole of the studio was covered in smoke. I rang the fire brigade and then my husband had to go down the stairs and turn right through Stage 3 to get out into the yard to open the bottom gates. As he opened the door to Stage 3, the air caused the lot to go up in flames and he had to go through the flames. The night watchman went down the back to open the back door. I managed to get down the stairs and along the corridor to reception. I couldn't see or hear anything of the fire engine, so, knowing what Maidenhead was like (they only had one engine, would you believe?), since the switchboard at that time wasn't affected, I nipped in there and rang them again and I've never forgotten what she said: 'The engine's on its way!' I said, 'The engine? Half the studio's alight!' 'Oh well,' she said, 'when it gets there, they will assess the damage and if he wants any help, he can call.' I thought, 'Oh my God!' Anyway, I phoned Mr Kelly and Jack Curtis from there and they got on their way.

"It was hair-raising. I just about got into the yard when the ceilings began to fall. We just had to get out into the yard and stay there. The problem was, it was going towards Mrs Davies' house next door and the firemen had to concentrate on that more than anything else, to try and stop it spreading there. The fire went on till 4.30 in the morning, with 40 firemen attending and well over half the studio was destroyed. There was a meeting with the fire chiefs, Mr Kelly, Jack Curtis and myself and it was agreed that the fault was a faulty electrical wire. Then we had a conference with the insurance people, which was a bit dicey. Jack saved the day, I think, because they weren't going to pay out if it was caused by old wires that had never been checked, but Jack blinded them with science. I think Jack knew what he was doing and we got away with it."

Despite the disaster, Harry Oakes' diary for the next day reads: "Black Park but sunny this time. Finished the schedule." This was presumably the opening pre-credits sequence in which a body is retrieved from a 'Swiss' lake. Les Bowie added to the magic with a wonderful matte painting of the Alps, to offset the trees at Slough. He was assisted by newcomer Ian Scoones: "Les took me on as a trainee matte artist and the first glass that I did was in Kit West's flat, not in the studio, for *Taste of Fear*. We painted in the mountains to go above the lake at Black Park. I painted the right-hand side and Les did the other. He then used his airbrush to bring the two together with a little bit of mist."

It was Peter Cushing who arranged for the young Scoones to visit Bray (just after the fire), initially to meet Bernard Robinson with a view to working in the art department. "Just as Bernard Robinson told me he had no positions available," remembers Scoones, "suddenly a foot came through the plaster of the ceiling above and Bernard said, 'Just a minute, there's somebody you should meet.' That was the owner of the leg, special effects man Les Bowie. Les had been clearing up the attic after a fire. He had taken a lot of his stuff from ABPC Elstree and put it in the attic, including all his storyboarding for *The Dam Busters*, and Les had brought these charred storyboards down into the art department, apologising for the hole he'd made in the ceiling. Les looked through my portfolio of drawings and he said, 'Right, when can you start?' I said, 'Tomorrow, Mr Bowie.' He said, 'Nobody calls anybody mister in the film business, it's Les.' That was the Friday and on the Monday I started down in Barnes on *The Day the Earth Caught Fire*, which was not a Hammer picture, and lived with Kit West, who at the time worked with Les. He had a flat there and the studio that we used for a lot of the effects was a converted squash court called Prospect Studios and that was my first introduction."

Hammer Productions 1961

- WATCH IT, SAILOR!
- CASH ON DEMAND
- THE DAMNED
- THE PIRATES OF BLOOD RIVER
- CAPTAIN CLEGG
- THE PHANTOM OF THE OPERA

FEATURETTE
- HIGHWAY HOLIDAY

OPPOSITE: Herbert Lom looks suitably menacing as The Phantom of the Opera (1961).

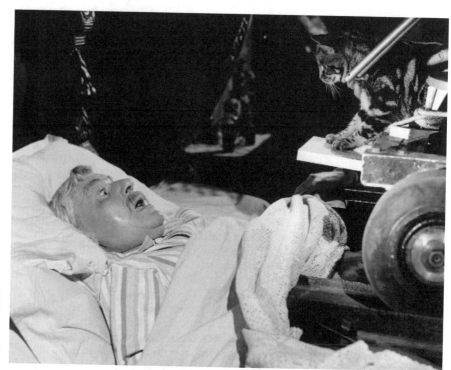

André Morell shrinks back as the camera crew wheels Tabatha on for a close-up in The Shadow of the Cat (1960).

Scoones was also involved with post-production work on *Shadow of the Cat*. "Les Bowie had this problem with trying to get a cat to jump from one set to another and so it was decided that instead of wasting the time of the whole crew, it would be done as an insert. This is where Kit West would always come in as lighting cameraman to match the lighting with Arthur Grant's. They look at their key lights and then can shoot it anywhere at any time. As long as the key lights match, it will match when the editor cuts it in. Les had got the idea to electrify this cat. He told me to connect these two electrodes to a car battery. He would hold the cat above his head, I would touch it with these two electrodes, causing a spark (which you can't do nowadays because of the animal protection league), and the cat would leap up in the air and obviously go to the nearest thing to land on, which was the piece of wall we wanted. What actually happened was that Les held on too long, the cat got electrified and shat all over him and he smelt for three weeks afterwards. Dreadful diarrhoea. He had this green duffel coat and it absolutely stank even after three or four washes. Nobody would go near him in the pub in the evenings – dreadful! What was worse, the original cat (supplied from a proper animal training school for films) was too costly to re-hire for this insert, so Les had borrowed a moggie from the Duke of Edinburgh in Windsor. Not the Duke himself, I hasten to add, but a pub we used to stop off at on the way to Slough. Needless to say – an electrified cat is not going to come back in the night when you cry, 'Here, Kitty Kitty!' We never saw it again, so in order to appease the landlady when she wondered where her pussy was, Les had me take one of the stray tabbies who lurked under the plasterer's shop at Bray, spray it with a bit of hairspray and deliver it to the Duke of Edinburgh at a time when we knew the owner, who luckily liked her tipple, would be totally inebriated!!"

On Monday 30 January, Hammer began their next production on Stage 1 at Bray, a comedy called *Watch It, Sailor!*.

Watch It, Sailor! was another service comedy, this time based on a successful stage play, itself a sequel to the money-spinning *Sailor Beware!* The part of Ma Hornett, previously immortalised by Peggy Mount, was taken by Marjorie Rhodes, with Vera Day (returning after *Quatermass 2*) and Australian actor John Meillon as the prospective bride and groom around whom the fun revolves. Frankie Howerd made a Hammer comeback, though further down the pecking order, and casting director Stuart Lyons would take note of Miriam Karlin and Renée Houston, using them again later in the year in *The Phantom of the*

WATCH IT, SAILOR!

PRINCIPAL PHOTOGRAPHY: January to 1 March 1961
UK DISTRIBUTION: Columbia/BLC; 89 minutes; b/w;
  certificate 'U'
UK RELEASE: 14 August 1961

COMPOSER: Douglas Gamley; MUSIC SUPERVISOR: John
Hollingsworth; SOUND RECORDIST: Jock May; MAKE-UP: Roy
Ashton; HAIR STYLIST: Frieda Steiger; PRODUCTION MANAGER:
Clifford Parkes; CONTINUITY: Tilly Day; WARDROBE: Rosemary
Burrows; CASTING: Stuart Lyons; STILLS: Tom Edwards

DIRECTOR: Wolf Rilla; PRODUCER: Maurice Cowan; ASSOCIATE
PRODUCER: Anthony Nelson Keys; EXECUTIVE PRODUCER:
Michael Carreras; SCREENPLAY: Falkland Carey and Philip King
based on their stage play; PRODUCTION DESIGNER: Bernard
Robinson; ART DIRECTOR: Don Mingaye; DIRECTOR OF
PHOTOGRAPHY: Arthur Grant; CAMERA OPERATOR: Len Harris;
FOCUS PULLER: Harry Oakes; ASSISTANT DIRECTOR: John
Peverall; SECOND ASSISTANT DIRECTOR: Dominic Fulford;
SUPERVISING EDITOR: James Needs; EDITOR: Alfred Cox; MUSIC

Dennis Price (Lt. Cmdr. Hardcastle); Liz Fraser (Daphne); Irene
Handl (Edie Hardcastle); Graham Stark (Bligh); Vera Day (Shirley);
Marjorie Rhodes (Ma Hornett); Cyril Smith (Mr. Hornett); John
Meillon (Tufnell); Frankie Howerd (Organist); Miriam Karlin (Mrs.
Lack); Arthur Howard (Vicar); Renee Houston (Mrs. Motram); Brian
Reece (Solicitor); Bobby Howes (Drunk); Harry Locke (Ticket
Collector); William Mervyn (Captain); Marianne Stone (Woman);
Diane Aubrey (Barmaid)

Opera. Also back was Brian Reece, who had played the title role in Hammer's two PC 49 adventures in 1949 and 1951.

The same crew from *The Shadow of the Cat* were back, apart from Clifford Parkes, who returned as production manager, Alfred Cox as editor, escaping from the horrors of *The Curse of the Werewolf* (leaving James Needs to pick up the pieces there), and Rosemary Burrows getting the wardrobe credit instead of Molly Arbuthnot. In fact, apart from the absence of Molly Arbuthnot, this was the same crew that had shot the werewolf picture. Speaking of which, 30 January was also the day that Hammer sent in a full colour print of the film to the BBFC. Tony Hinds' covering letter to Trevelyan explained:

"Re: *The Curse of the Werewolf.* I am resubmitting the above, as instructed. The following cuts have already been made:

REEL 2. We have re-cut to avoid the big close-up of the Marques's diseased face. We have trimmed two shots of the old Beggar. We have trimmed the shot of the dead Beggar to the very minimum, to allow us to pick up the Servant Girl at the barred door in the next cut. The shot of the Servant Girl being thrown into the gaol has been trimmed.

REEL 5. We have trimmed the shot of Leon's hairy hand.

REEL 8. The throttling of the boy, José, has been drastically trimmed.

"At the moment, the Baptism Scene and the shot of the dead 'tart' are still in, but the former can be deleted completely if you still wish it, and we have a replacement shot of the latter which I am having printed up in colour."

The examiners watched the film on 1 February and John Trevelyan wrote to Tony Hinds the following day:

"This is the first time that we had seen this film in colour and, while the colour greatly improved the picture, it does in certain scenes add to our censorship problems. We gave this film most

Vera Day in a provocative
publicity shot for Watch It
Sailor! (1961).

careful consideration and made the following decisions:

REEL 2: We are now prepared to accept the scene between the Marques and the girl, since you have removed the close-up shot of the Marques's diseased face. We are now prepared to accept the line of dialogue 'You come here tonight and show me.' The scene in the dungeon must stop as soon as the girl is thrown into the cell and looks up fearfully, and the scene can only resume with the shot of her being released from the cell. We cannot accept any shots of the beggar, alive or dead, or any shots of her lying after the rape in a corner with lacerations on her face and chest. (Incidentally, these lacerations were not visible in the black and white version.)

REEL 3: We must insist on you removing the whole scene in which the Marques waits for the girl, attacks her and is killed by her. This will mean that from the girl's release from the cell you must move immediately to the shot of her running through the wood. We are prepared to waive our objection to the dialogue about illegitimate children born on Christmas Day.

REEL 4: We are prepared to waive our objection to the baptism scene. (This is less offensive in colour than it was in black and white.)

REEL 5: We must ask you to remove any shot which shows hair on Leon's hands. This seems to us most offensive with so young a child. (This is worse in the colour version than it is in black and white.)

REEL 7: We must maintain in full our previous objection to the scene in the prostitute's bedroom. We do not want the scene to convey the impression that Leon has had sexual relations with the prostitute before strangling her, but equally, we do not want to show that he has bitten her for blood-sucking. We would certainly not want the line which the girl says, 'If you want that kind of thing you can go elsewhere.' We can therefore allow the first part of the scene up to the point just before he pushes her down on the bed, and we will accept the shot of his throttling her. I hope this will convey the impression that there has been no love-making or blood-sucking and that he has just attacked her and throttled her. We will consider your substitute shot of the dead tart but if it is anything approaching the present shot, it will be quite impossible.

REEL 8: We will accept the scene in which José is murdered as now submitted since your cuts are satisfactory. Since we last saw the picture the sound track of the murder of Dominic [sic] seems to have been altered and it now contains loud groans and growls. These must be considerably reduced.

REEL 10: We will accept the transformation of Leon into a werewolf, both in hands and face, but the most we might allow of the murder of the beggar would be the shots of the beggar's frightened face, the shot of the werewolf's eyes in large close-up and the zoom of the werewolf's face towards the camera. We would not accept shots of the werewolf's face covered with blood. Immediately after the zoom shot you should go straight to the werewolf's escape from the cell and attack on the jailer, thus avoiding shot of his bloodstained face. In the final scene in the belfry, you should remove all close shots of the werewolf's dead face and body. We will then see this scene again and consider whether with these deletions it will be acceptable.

"I know you are disappointed in these decisions, and I think that I must justify them by some general explanation. There are two serious points which arise. The first is that, unlike your previous horror films, there is a good deal in this film which provides a combination of horror and sex. We have always taken the line that this is a dangerous cocktail and we feel this strongly. This is the kind of thing that runs into so much public criticism. A few years ago the horror comics imported from America were the subject of press comment. You will remember from past experience with us that we have always taken this line. Admittedly you can quote against us certain pictures which we have passed, but I think that in most cases at least I would be able to put up a reasonable justification for our action. In any case, this kind of thing is much more open to criticism in a horror film of the kind that you have now sent to us than it is in certain other types of pictures. You may not be ready to accept this argument so I will leave this for discussion when we next meet.

"The other point is that since we last had a horror picture from your company there has grown up a quite considerable criticism of this Board for passing such pictures at all. Admittedly this criticism sometimes comes from people who do not go to the cinema and who do not see such films, but I can assure you that it would be most unwise at the present time to provide these people

The BBFC objected to Yvonne Romain stabbing Anthony Dawson in The Curse of the Werewolf (1960). Tony Hinds pointed out that the scene was no worse than Hitchcock's shower stabbing in Psycho (1960).

with ammunition which they can use not only to criticise us but to harm the industry. If you had heard the points of view expressed to me recently when I met the Magistrates in Glasgow and similar expressions of opinion at other meetings, you would realise that this is a significant and important point. If then you think that we are treating your picture more roughly than we would have treated a similar picture two years ago, you may have some justification, but you must realise that we stand between the industry and such pressures and that it is a part of our job to assess the potential danger of pressures at any given time. Frankly, I am reluctant to pass a picture of this kind at all at the present moment, even in a heavily censored version, but I will not go so far as this since I have no wish to take such a drastic course. But I must emphasise that without the cuts that I have set out in this letter, I cannot at the present time take the risk of passing this picture."

Tony Hinds was still not happy and replied to Trevelyan on 6 February: "Thank you for your letter of February 2nd. In particular, there is only one cut against which I should like to appeal, and that is the shot of the werewolf's face with a tear trickling down his nose, which is the last shot in the picture. We have a bad enough ending as it is, but without this shot we have no ending at all. May I leave it in for your next viewing, to see if you re-consider? It really is quite inoffensive (if not slightly comical!). In general, I do not think it is quite fair to level at us the accusation that this is a horror/sex picture. Indeed, we were very careful to make sure that, after the boy had changed into a werewolf, his attacks were only against men (José, Dominique, the old prisoner, and the gaoler)."

Trevelyan replied to Hinds the following day: "We will certainly reconsider our final objection. I seem to recollect that you had two close-up shots of the werewolf's face. Can you reduce this to one? If you will send in the reel again marked up just before the belfry scene we will have another look at it. I did not mean to make any specific accusation about this picture, but it does I think open up the possibility of criticism that it contains 'horror comic' material. I think that our cuts will eliminate most of this, but in the original form I think it would have been tricky. I realise, however, that it is extremely difficult to make this kind of picture without including some material of this kind."

The Board viewed the film again with the new cuts on the 15th and Trevelyan replied to Tony Hinds the following day: "Our Examiners saw Reels 2, 3, 5, 7 and 10 of *The Curse of the Werewolf* yesterday. Reels 2, 3, 5 and 7 as submitted are satisfactory in view of the assurance that I have had this morning from Mr Needs by telephone – (a) that the shots of the hair on the child's hands have been entirely eliminated and (b) that there is to be no substitute shot of the dead prostitute. Our Examiners considered the appeal for the retention of the close shot of the dying werewolf in Reel 10 but felt that they could not accept this shot. I think you will find that the scene ends satisfactorily with the turning over of the body and without the large close shot of the face. Before finally clearing the film we would like to see Reel 10 again in colour and without the close shot."

Over a month went by before Hinds tried a different approach. His letter to Trevelyan dated 22 March reads: "Douglas Granville of Universal has just been on to me, in near tears, saying that CMA have viewed the emaciated version and state that they do not want to book it because it is so tame they can't understand why it has not got a 'U' certificate. Actually, I have kept Douglas Granville informed of every stage of our battle, but apparently he did not realise how ruthless your cuts were. He has beseeched me to get on to you to appeal for at least something to go back into the film. I told him the chances were slender, but that I would try. Is there not anything that we can put back?"

Trevelyan replied the next day: "I cannot say that the attitude of CMA surprises me. At the same time I think that they are extremely foolish at present to want more horror than we are prepared to allow in your film. There have been a good many complaints about 'X' films, and in particular horror films, and I am convinced that it would be most unwise for us to go further than we are going at present. Douglas Granville is unlikely to be able to see this, but if I have an opportunity I will try to explain the position to him."

Finally, in notes written on 4 April, Trevelyan conceded on the final cut of the close-up of the dying werewolf and granted Hammer their certificate: "I viewed the scene privately. I then discussed the position with FNC and NKB. We agreed that we could not justifiably insist on this short shot being removed, especially when we had been tough with this film elsewhere with more censurable material. So I later informed Mr Hinds that we would accept it. The film is now cleared for the 'X' category."

The BBFC had indeed been ruthless, imposing painfully visible cuts enhanced by tell-tale jumps in the soundtrack. The film has since been restored and premièred on BBC TV in 1994. Among the many restitutions, the werewolf's dead face finally came into close-up, a single tear escaping from his eye before it is finally covered over. Tony Hinds had been right: it restored some of the emotion that was the driving force of the movie.

Watch It, Sailor! finished shooting at Bray on 1 March, leaving Hammer more than a month (luxurious by their standards) to prepare for their next production, *Cash on Demand*, due to start on Tuesday 4 April. Based on Jacques Gillies' television play, *The Gold Inside* (first transmitted on ITV on Saturday 24 September 1960, and the shooting title of the movie), *Cash on Demand* features André Morell as a smooth military type and Peter Cushing as the uptight bank manager he relieves of £93,000. The film is essentially a psychological drama, the clever Gore Hepburn feeding off the negative emotions of the prissy Fordyce, taunting him with the threat of harm to his family and exposing his human failings into the bargain.

Director Quentin Lawrence piles on the suspense with the help of Arthur Grant's bleak black-and-white photography. Cushing gives his usual polished performance, coming at a time in his career when he had temporarily disappeared from the horror scene. Between *The Brides of Dracula* early in 1960 and *The Evil of Frankenstein* late in 1963, Cushing starred in nine films, none of which were horror. They included three for Hammer, *Sword of Sherwood Forest*, *Cash on Demand* and *Captain Clegg* (though clearly

Hepburn (André Morell) torments the hapless Fordyce (Peter Cushing) in Cash on Demand (1961).

CASH ON DEMAND

PRINCIPAL PHOTOGRAPHY: 4 to 27 April 1961
DISTRIBUTION:
  UK: BLC; 66 minutes; certificate 'A'
  US: Columbia; 84 minutes
b/w
UK RELEASE: 15 December 1963
US RELEASE: 20 December 1961

DIRECTOR: Quentin Lawrence; ASSOCIATE PRODUCER: Anthony Nelson Keys; EXECUTIVE PRODUCER: Michael Carreras; SCREENPLAY: David T Chantler and Lewis Greifer, from a play by Jacques Gillies; PRODUCTION DESIGNER: Bernard Robinson; ART DIRECTOR: Don Mingaye; DIRECTOR OF PHOTOGRAPHY: Arthur Grant; CAMERA OPERATOR: Len Harris; FOCUS PULLER: Harry Oakes; ASSISTANT DIRECTOR: John Peverall; SUPERVISING EDITOR: James Needs; EDITOR: Eric Boyd-Perkins; MUSIC: Wilfred Josephs; MUSIC SUPERVISOR: John Hollingsworth;

SOUND RECORDIST: Jock May; Sound EDITOR: Alban Streeter; MAKE-UP: Roy Ashton; HAIRSTYLIST: Frieda Steiger; PRODUCTION MANAGER: Clifford Parkes; CONTINUITY: Tilly Day; WARDROBE SUPERVISOR: Molly Arbuthnot; WARDROBE MISTRESS: Rosemary Burrows; CASTING: Stuart Lyons; CONSTRUCTION MANAGER: Arthur Banks; MASTER PLASTERER: Stan Banks; MASTER CARPENTER: Charles Davis; MASTER PAINTER: Lawrence Wrenn; MASTER ELECTRICIAN: Jack Curtis; Master Rigger: Ronald Lenoir; PROPS BUYER: Eric Hillier; PROPS MASTER: Tommy Money

Peter Cushing (Harry Fordyce); André Morell (Colonel Gore Hepburn); Richard Vernon (Pearson); Barry Lowe (Harvill); Norman Bird (Sanderson); Edith Sharpe (Miss Pringle); Charles Morgan (Collins); Kevin Stoney (Det Inspector Mason); Alan Hatwood (Kane); Lois Daine (Sally); Vera Cook (Mrs Fordyce); Gareth Tandy (Tommy); Fred Stone (window cleaner)

the Gothic trappings of the latter traded off his notoriety as a horror star). André Morell, no stranger to Hammer, is also terrific as the dapper yet ruthless bank robber. Reunited after their Holmes and Watson partnership in The Hound of the Baskervilles (as well as the classic BBC adaptation of Nineteen Eighty-Four), Cushing and Morell made a formidable team, but, sadly, the only other time Hammer were to use it was very briefly and ineffectively in She (1964). The crew from Watch It, Sailor! returned, with the exception of Eric Boyd-Perkins as editor and Molly Arbuthnot as wardrobe supervisor.

With a lightning shooting schedule, filming finished on Thursday 27 April after just over three weeks. Harry Oakes' diary records that a full 11 minutes' footage was obtained on Wednesday the 5th alone, and that the last day of shooting saw the film going over schedule: "Jack Asher couldn't stay. Len Harris lit. I operated. 19 set-ups." The film would be released in America on 20 December, but Britain would have to wait another two years to see a version trimmed by a massive 22 minutes.

Jimmy Sangster delivered a print of *Taste of Fear* to Columbia's New York office on 15 March. It was released in Britain during Easter week in April 1961 and the reception was good, making it one of Columbia's top money earners that year. The film would be released in the States in August, where the MPAA International Film Relations Committee voted the poster the best of the year. It would pave the way for a whole cycle of Hammer suspense thrillers under the watchful eye of Jimmy Sangster.

Meanwhile, on Wednesday 12 April, *The Curse of the Werewolf* and *The Shadow of the Cat* premièred as a double-bill and went on general release from Monday 1 May. It's strange that, for all the *Werewolf* fraças with the BBFC, in the States it emerged in June with fewer cuts, just in time for the school holidays! Indeed, Roy Ashton commented: "What particularly amused me at the pre-production conferences was the producer saying: 'Look, lads, I think we have a jolly good picture here, but we've got to have it finished in six weeks, because by April the 12th we have to deliver it to America to release it for the children's holidays.'" [2] The box-office returns were adequate, but not enough to interest any distributors in another werewolf project.

As the chapter closed on *The Curse of the Werewolf*, another struggle was about to begin with Hammer's next fantasy offering, *The Damned*, for Columbia. Throughout February Tony Hinds was completing a script called *The Children of Light*, based on the novel by H L Lawrence, which was then handed over to Ben Barzman to tidy up in April. Columbia were happy with the result and Tony Hinds submitted the script to the BBFC on 21 April: "Please find enclosed the script of *The Children of Light* (tentative title), which we start on location on May 8th. I realise that this is a completely adult subject and is in the 'X' certificate category."

The story was a chilling tale revolving around a ruthless Teddy Boy motorcycle gang and a dark experiment involving innocent radioactive children. John Trevelyan was on holiday and examiner Audrey Field had cause to lead the assessment, given that the date for shooting was already looming. Her internal report on 24 April reads:

"It seems that the people behind this project are against Teddy Boys, 'The Establishment' and the nuclear deterrent. What they are in favour of is less easy to guess, though it seems likely that they are ardent fellow travellers or fully paid up members of the Communist party and would look with a less jaundiced eye on repression and regimentation from the Left. Anyway, we cannot concern ourselves with the ideas, which in any case may escape the sort of 'X' film patrons we want to protect! The worry here is the unhappy Mr King and friends with the bicycle chains (and one or two other bits of nasty violence). The makers of the film are doubtless right in saying that it ought to be 'X', though the reason they give (ie, that it is a 'very adult subject') is perhaps not very sound: the bits that would appeal to morons of violent inclinations are much more undesirable for children. I think myself that the story is a lot of symbolic claptrap, though I don't deny that some of the radioactive cavern stuff may have a weird force and power (it is certainly not much more incredible than the behaviour of the characters in the outside world!)."

Field's comment about the film's intellectual content being likely to be lost on "the sort of 'X' film patrons we want to protect" is staggering stuff. Newton Branch's response on 26 April is less elitist: "This is described as a shooting script but we are warned that there may be dialogue improvements and some simplification of action, especially at the end. Despite a very arty description of what the cameramen are to do – one expects a BFI sort of script from reading it – the story is a mixture of cliché themes and not a very savoury kettle of fish. However, I don't think we can go far wrong on AOF's suggestions. Any serious changes in dialogue might be conveyed to us?"

Frank Crofts added the same day: "It snips at the explanations – why did the children survive? What has given Bernard and co this power of life and death? What is all this talk about radio-activity everywhere when nobody in the everyday world of the film has suffered from it? It looks to me as if this is the work, originally, of some ban-the-bomb fanatic and Hammer have grafted onto it King, his gang and his weapons on one hand and nudity on the other. Perhaps we cannot do much about the propaganda but we should certainly make it clear to Hammer that the nudity, the baited chain and the general beastliness of the gang will have to go: I suppose they think that much of this will creep in under cover of an 'X'."

This draft script, it should be noted, opens very differently to the final film. In the movie, the central character of Simon Wells is introduced walking through the streets of Weymouth, where he

The children are intrigued by the warm bodies of Shirley Ann Field and MacDonald Carey in The Damned (1961).

THE DAMNED

PRINCIPAL PHOTOGRAPHY: 8 May to 22 June 1961
DISTRIBUTION:
UK: BLC; 87 minutes; certificate 'X'
US: Columbia; 77 minutes; US title: These Are the Damned
b/w; Hammerscope
UK RELEASE: 20 May 1963, with Maniac
US RELEASE: 7 July 1965

DIRECTOR: Joseph Losey; PRODUCER: Anthony Hinds; ASSOCIATE PRODUCER: Anthony Nelson Keys; EXECUTIVE PRODUCER: Michael Carreras; SCREENPLAY: Evan Jones, based on the novel The Children of Light by H L Lawrence; PRODUCTION DESIGNER: Bernard Robinson; ART DIRECTOR: Don Mingaye; DIRECTOR OF PHOTOGRAPHY: Arthur Grant; CAMERA OPERATOR: Anthony Heller; FOCUS PULLER: Harry Oakes; ASSISTANT DIRECTOR: John Peverall; 2ND ASSISTANT DIRECTOR: Dominic Fulford; SUPERVISING EDITOR: James Needs; EDITOR: Reginald Mills; MUSIC: James Bernard; MUSIC SUPERVISOR: John Hollingsworth; SONG 'Black Leather Rock' by Evan Jones and James Bernard; SOUND RECORDIST: Jock May; SOUND EDITOR: Malcolm Cooke; MAKE-UP: Roy Ashton; HAIRSTYLIST: Frieda Steiger; PRODUCTION MANAGER: Don Weeks; PRODUCTION ASSISTANT: Richard

MacDonald; CONTINUITY: Pamela Davies; WARDROBE: Molly Arbuthnot; SPECIAL EFFECTS: Les Bowie; SPECIAL EFFECTS ASSISTANTS: Ian Scoones, Kit West; CASTING: Stuart Lyons, CONSTRUCTION MANAGER: Arthur Banks; MASTER PLASTERER: Stan Banks; MASTER CARPENTER: Charles Davis; MASTER PAINTER: Lawrence Wrenn; MASTER ELECTRICIAN: Jack Curtis; MASTER RIGGER: Ronald Lenoir; PROPS BUYER: Eric Hillier; PROPS MASTER: Tommy Money; SCULPTURES: Elizabeth Frink

MacDonald Carey (Simon Wells); Shirley Ann Field (Joan); Viveca Lindfors (Freya); Alexander Knox (Bernard); Oliver Reed (King); Walter Gotell (Major Holland); James Villiers (Captain Gregory); Thomas Kempinski (Ted); Kenneth Cope (Sid); Brian Oulton (Mr Dingle); Barbara Everest (Miss Lamont); Alan McClelland (Mr Stuart); James Maxwell (Mr Talbot); Rachel Clay (Victoria); Caroline Sheldon (Elizabeth); Rebecca Dignam (Anne); Siobhan Taylor (Mary); Nicolas Clay (Richard); Kit Williams (Henry); Christopher Witty (William); David Palmer (George); John Thompson (Charles)

UNCREDITED: David Gregory, Anthony Valentine, Larry Martyn, Leon Garcia, Jeremy Phillips (Teddy Boys); Fiona Duncan (Control Room Guard); Edward Harvey (Doctor); Neil Wilson (Guard)

is attacked by King's gang. He later meets King's sister, who decides to take off with him in his boat but is chased by King and his crew. In the first draft script, Simon and King are introduced in a much more disturbing fashion. As Audrey Field described it in her synopsis of the script:

"Simon Wells arrives home to find his wife with her lover. She tries to stab him with a pair of scissors, but in the ensuing struggle she is stabbed herself. Simon runs away. She dies, but first accuses Simon of murder, in the hearing of the porter of the block of flats, who repeats it to Abbas, the police

Oliver Reed and gang menace Shirley Ann Field in this publicity shot for The Damned (1961).

officer in charge of the case, so that in the ensuing hue and cry everyone is sure Simon is guilty. Simon hastens to Portland, where he has a boat; he meets a friend who tries to help him, but, still sure he has no chance of refuting the charge against him, he drives away in his friend's Bentley. A sinister gang of 'Teds' follow, rob and kidnap him. He is taken to the house of their leader, King, who is larger than life in his evil depravity and plans to torture him for fun. King has a sister, Joan, whom he calls 'Princess': he is determined that she shall keep herself unspotted from the world, so he knocks her about if she uses scent or so much as glances at a man. When King goes off to sell the stolen Bentley, leaving one of his gang called Sid in charge of Simon, Joan, who has understandably had enough of King, appears with a gun and frees Simon, leaving a message with Sid for King, to the effect that she has gone off to spend the night with a wife-murderer and serve King right. Simon and Joan take refuge in a mysterious and remote house in the neighbourhood, called the Bird House because it is supposed to belong to a Henry Moore-ish type of sculptor and is full of weird models of birds. When they have satisfied their hunger for food, Simon rapes Joan (he would have been a little more subtle in his approach if he had known she was a virgin, but he didn't think King's sister could be)."

On 27 April, Field replied formally to Tony Hinds: "I am sorry Mr Trevelyan has been unable to have a look at your script entitled The Children of Light, but he is away on leave, and in view of the early shooting date we expect that you would like to have a report without delay. We agree that this is an 'X' subject, but even for an 'X' there are high spots of violence and savagery which are likely to be troublesome in the completed film, and one or two other points to which we ought to draw your attention at this stage:

Pp. 3-4 (5). It is not clear from the directions here what Sally and her lover will be wearing; but Sally is said later on to have been naked: if she is, we do not think you will be able to shoot this scene in a way which would be acceptable to us. And the scissors incident is nasty. Could not some other weapon be chosen? In any case, we would not want too much blood, or any close shot of the blood-stained scissors or of the weapon being pulled out of the wound.

On P. 5 (8 and 17). Also we would not want too much blood.

P.18 (54). There should not be a shot of Simon's exposed neck held for the cosh-blow.

P.20 (58). We are not happy about the references to Sally having been 'all naked' (which she should not have been in any event – see above). (These scenes, and the whole of the episodes with the 'Teds', are designedly ugly, and will need to be handled with restraint).

Pp. 21-22 (59). We would not want the slapping and beating-up of Joan, or the other boys' reactions to it. The most we could allow would be a couple of slaps, and they should not be too violent. The flick-knife work should be kept to a minimum, and close shots avoided.

P.24 (59). We are not happy about the idea of hanging Simon just 'for the hell of it'. This is the sort of violence for which the 'X' certificate is not much help, because the main appeal is to youths who would see it anyway.

P.26 (66). We are very much worried about the chain (apparently barbed – see later descriptions) which King uses as a weapon: we think it is likely to make necessary a number of cuts in the film, and we feel you should do well to substitute something less horrible. (Cf.83 (157), 105 (226), 114 (249), 116 (252).

P.38 (84). We hope that Simon's sexual onslaught on Joan will not be shown at length or in too much detail.

P.83 (157), 84 (157). The accumulation of violence here may be troublesome, even if something less horrible is substituted for the barbed chain, and we do not like the lines about 'ripping' Abbas' face, 'to see his flesh rip, the blood spurt'. The Judo-blow, and the shots of the assorted weapons, are also troublesome from our point of view.

Pp. 101-2 (224). If the children look like adolescents, we will not want full-length front- or side-view shots of the girls, at any rate, in this sort of context.

"I hope the foregoing comments will be helpful to you. If you would like to discuss them with Mr Trevelyan on his return to the office, I am sure he will be pleased to see you."

James Carreras wrote to Trevelyan on 2 June: "I understand from Tony Hinds that the script of On the Brink which you refer to was submitted to you under the title of Children of Light. I also understand from Tony Hinds that there are no objections to it whatsoever. What about lunch in the near future?" This prompted a terse reply from Trevelyan's staff. Frank Crofts wrote back on 6 June: "As Mr Trevelyan is away on holiday I am acknowledging your letter of June 2nd. I will show it to him on his return. About the script Children of Light – I am afraid it is not correct that there are no objections. Our letter of April 27th to Mr Hinds had quite a lot to say about it."

To direct, Hammer brought in Joseph Losey, the spectre of McCarthyism (which had terminated his involvement with X the Unknown five years before) now no longer an issue. However, this association was to prove far from ideal. Two weeks before principal photography was due to begin (on 8 May on location in Weymouth), Losey told Michael Carreras that he would not shoot the film unless he could make his own version of the script. Consequently, he brought in Evan Jones for a complete rewrite. "I very arrogantly said I could do better than that in two weeks," recalled Jones. "He said: 'You're on,' and so I did it, revising it as we went along, which was always the way with Joe. All that was left of [Ben] Barzman was the story slant." [3]

With Hammer engaging an American lead, reminiscent of their Exclusive procedures, Losey was reunited with MacDonald Carey, whom he had previously directed in The Lawless (1950). Alexander Knox had also worked with Losey before, on The Sleeping Tiger. "There was no money again, so Joe was pushed, as usual," remembered Knox. "Evan did his best, but it still fell between two stools: a bang-bang thriller and a serious message. Viveca [Lindfors] tried to introduce even a third element with all this psychological carry-on. I remember a scene that should have taken

25 minutes to do took three hours, and here we were going against the clock and the budget."[4]

According to Harry Oakes' diary, he arrived at Weymouth's Gloucester Hotel at 2.00 pm on Saturday 6 May and promptly settled down to watch the Cup Final. The following day, title background shots were taken at Portland Bill. Principal photography began at 7.00 am on Monday 8 May with "interior Gloucester Hotel". There was another early call the next day for "Shots of motorcycles on causeway. Then re-take monument." The quayside supervened on Wednesday and Thursday, with "exteriors in back streets of Portland" on Friday and, on Sunday the 14th: "At the Bird House. Lovely day but only three shots." Week Two involved evening calls at the Bird House for night exteriors and, after a long weekend back home, Week Three began after lunch on Tuesday the 23rd. The next day, the crew "worked until 10.00 pm outside Gloucester Hotel." Thursday necessitated "three cameras on car crash," cave interiors occupied Friday, and Sunday was singled out as a "Lovely day shooting in the Bird House," concluding with "A party in the Casa Mia!"

Having left Weymouth at 12 noon the following day, shooting began on Bray's Stage 2 on Tuesday the 30th. Friday 2 June bears the cryptic message: "A hectic afternoon finishing VL", which presumably means that Viveca Lindfors' contracted commitment was up and it was a struggle to complete her scenes in time. Finally, after several late nights in Week Six and travelling matte work in Week Seven, Harry concludes on Thursday 22 June with "Worked until 10.00 pm and finished the picture."

"Joe Losey was a difficult chap," Harry reflects. "I remember when we were shooting at Portland Bill. It was a Scope picture and behind the gate we had to use an 85 filter for shooting colour in daylight. It had to be an orange filter, because that film was incandescent, so I kept it in the camera. It was in June and we'd shot all day with this. It went on a bit in the evening and we broke for supper, came back and went to shoot this big scene, and it was only when I went to check the gate that I found I hadn't taken the filter out, so we had to shoot it again. But, funnily enough, they were very nice about it. I said sorry to Tony Hinds, but he was just relieved that we'd seen it. I remember Joe, too; he was also very nice about it. I was expecting to get a right bollocking, but they were just pleased that I'd noticed it."

Assistant director John Peverall vividly remembers Losey. "Losey had a thing about a sculptress named [Elizabeth] Frink. We were out shooting on the cliffs when they started to deliver all these pieces of art. The film's shooting title was On the Brink. We were actually 'on the brink' with Frink. At one point MacDonald Carey and Shirley Ann Field had this very intense scene. During rehearsal, they were giving their all and Joe just walked between them to move one of the statues a tad to one side. He returned to his chair and they just stopped and looked at each other, wondering what that was all about.

"Another time we had to wait for an hour for the arrival of another piece by Miss Frink. It was called 'Reclining Figure' and it was being delivered to the set by ambulance. A plasterer on the set, named Mickey, was standing next to Joe and I was standing next to Mickey. We were all waiting for this new sculpture to arrive. Finally it gets there, and they brought it out of the ambulance on a stretcher covered with a muslin drop-cloth. Joe bends over reverently and uncovers the 'Reclining Figure'. It's basically a bunch of plastery sticks sticking up. It looks vaguely like a person. Joe stands up and steps back to look it over. Mickey turns to him and says, 'Gawd, fuck me, Guv. If you'd told me what you wanted, I could have made that in about five minutes!'"[5]

Mickey's down-to-earth attitude to a world-famous sculptress aside, Harry Oakes recalls the incident for a different reason. "I remember we had to shoot one Sunday. We used some lovely spots on Portland Bill, where there were these huge quarries that looked like natural coves, and it involved a sculptress in this scene. Apparently they were waiting especially for this sculptress to come down from London with some figures and we were hanging around all this Sunday morning for her. She didn't turn up till about half past eleven and Joe wouldn't shoot without these figures. Then, as soon as he put it down, he draped it in sack cloth. So we said, 'What are you doing? We've been waiting all morning for this!' And Joe said, 'Well, sculptors wouldn't leave their sculptures in the sunlight. They always cover them up!' I found that quite strange. We'd been waiting all morning for this and he draped it over with sack cloth!"

As noted, on Thursday 25 May, the unit filmed the scene in which Oliver Reed's character drives his Jaguar over a bridge. The plucky driver was stuntman Jackie Cooper, risking life and limb in a stunt that nearly went dreadfully wrong. "I had rigged the whole thing near enough myself." remembers Cooper. "The car belonged to Roy Ashton's assistant Colin Guard. He was banned from driving so he sold it to Hammer to use for this stunt. I put a hundred weight of sand in a sack in the boot, thinking that would weigh it down at the back. It was open top, so I didn't have much protection, and I wound the windows down and took the near side seat out, so that when I hit the water I could duck down, because I thought the windscreen was going to come in on me. I never got time to do that, though, because it was over so quickly.

"They cut the iron rails on the bridge and put wooden rails in their place, so I had to hit just between where they'd replaced them. So I turned the car into it and put my foot down, because it had to go up a slight curve which we'd filled in to make more or less a ramp with sand. When I put my foot down, it jumped forward. I made sure I was in a low gear and then you're in the lap of the gods. I didn't put a seatbelt on. There weren't any seatbelts in the car in those days anyway. I didn't have any straps around me, because I didn't want to be clamped in. I thought if I didn't have them, I had a better chance of getting out but, as it happened, it trapped my feet underneath anyway. I can't believe it

Freya (Viveca Lindfors) with one of Elizabeth Frink's striking sculptures from The Damned (1961).

went in so quick and it seemed to hit the bottom straight away. I thought it was still going down to the bottom but the water rushing past me caused it to fall over on its back. I think the windscreen, just before it collapsed, saved me. I got out, but I felt the boot of the car, as I went clear, push my feet into the sand at the bottom. I also hit the top of the windscreen with my face and had a couple of stitches, but it came off all right."

Jackie continues: "They pulled the car out and an electrician gave them £20 for it. He had it drained and cleaned out and had it back on the road in about three days! The funny story was about the guy who owned the pub on the bridge at Weymouth. I had to go and look round underneath the bridge with diving equipment on first to make sure that there was no old rubbish down there. We used the pub because the downstairs had a platform, which we could dive off. I was with a few people, because you don't do these jobs on your own, and when I came out, the pub owner asked me what I was doing. I said, 'I'm going to drive a car off there tomorrow.' He said, 'I'd do that for nothing.' I said, 'You can't, because I'm getting paid for it.' He didn't think I was going to do such a thing, but the funny thing was, when I came up after the stunt and they dragged me to the side, the speed boat came up and I said, 'I've taken a bit of a whack.' I was bleeding from the face where I had hit the windscreen. So they towed me over slowly to the landing stage and got me out. Eventually I was standing up and thought I was all right and this man, who 'would do it for nothing', pushed through the crowd with a bottle of brandy and a glass in his hand, and he was shaking so much he couldn't pour the drink! I got hold of his wrist and said, 'Here, let me help you.' They took me away to the hospital for a check-up, but I was all right."

On the unit's return to Bray, there was a modification of the regular Bray team. Losey had brought with him editor Reginald Mills, sound editor Malcolm Cooke and continuity supervisor Pamela Davies. Alternating with Clifford Parkes, it was Don Weeks' turn to be production manager; Parkes was now busy breaking down the script for Hammer's next production at Bray, *The Pirates of Blood River*. Principal photography finished on 22 June but Hammer weren't satisfied with the final film and pick-up shots were done on 11 and 12 September. Meanwhile, the budget escalated to £170,155.[6] In particular, Hinds ordered Losey to shoot an extra scene to clarify the relationship between King and his sister and an alternate climax was filmed where Freya is shot by one of the passing helicopters

THE PIRATES OF BLOOD RIVER

PRINCIPAL PHOTOGRAPHY: 3 July to 31 August 1961
DISTRIBUTION:
UK: BLC; certificate 'U'
US: Columbia
84 minutes; Technicolor; Hammerscope
UK RELEASE:
TRADE SHOW: 5 May 1962 at the Columbia Theatre
PREMIÈRE: 13 July 1962, at the London Pavilion with
Mysterious Island
GENERAL RELEASE: 13 August 1962, on the ABC circuit
with Mysterious Island
US RELEASE: July 1962

DIRECTOR: John Gilling; PRODUCER: Anthony Nelson Keys;
EXECUTIVE PRODUCER: Michael Carreras; SCREENPLAY: John
Hunter and John Gilling, from a story by Jimmy Sangster;
PRODUCTION DESIGNER: Bernard Robinson; ART DIRECTOR: Don
Mingaye; DIRECTOR OF PHOTOGRAPHY: Arthur Grant; CAMERA
OPERATOR: Len Harris; FOCUS PULLER: Harry Oakes; ASSISTANT
DIRECTOR: John Peverall; 2ND ASSISTANT DIRECTOR: Peter
Medak; SUPERVISING EDITOR: James Needs; EDITOR: Eric Boyd-
Perkins; MUSIC: Gary Hughes; MUSIC SUPERVISOR: John
Hollingsworth; SOUND RECORDIST: Jock May; SOUND EDITOR:

Alfred Cox; MAKE-UP: Roy Ashton; HAIRSTYLIST: Frieda Steiger;
PRODUCTION MANAGER: Clifford Parkes; CONTINUITY: Tilly Day;
WARDROBE SUPERVISOR: Molly Arbuthnot; SPECIAL EFFECTS: Les
Bowie; SPECIAL EFFECTS ASSISTANTS: Kit West, Ian Scoones, Brian
Johncock; CASTING: Stuart Lyons; HORSE MASTER AND MASTER
AT ARMS: Bob Simmons; CONSTRUCTION MANAGER: Arthur
Banks; MASTER PLASTERER: Stan Banks; MASTER CARPENTER:
Charles Davis; MASTER PAINTER: Lawrence Wrenn; MASTER
ELECTRICIAN: Jack Curtis; MASTER RIGGER: Ronald Lenoir;
PROPS BUYER: Eric Hillier; PROPS MASTER: Tommy Money

Kerwin Mathews (Jonathon Standing); Glenn Corbett (Henry);
Christopher Lee (Captain LaRoche); Marla Landi (Bess); Oliver
Reed (Brocaire); Andrew Keir (Jason Standing); Peter Arne (Hench);
Michael Ripper (Mac); Jack Stuart (George Mason); David Lodge
(Smith); Marie Devereux (Maggie Mason); Diane Aubrey (Margaret
Blackthorne); Jerold Wells (Commandant); Dennis Waterman
(Timothy Blackthorne); Lorraine Clewes (Martha Blackthorne);
Desmond Llewellyn (Blackthorne); Keith Pyott (Silas); Richard
Bennett (Seymour); Michael Mulcaster (William Martin); Denis
Shaw (Silver); Michael Peake (Kemp); John Colin (Lance); Don Levy
(Carlos); John Bennett (guard); Ronald Blackman (Pugh); John
Roden (settler)

instead of by Bernard. Losey appealed to Columbia and Hammer were forced, reluctantly, to back off.

The Damned starts unpromisingly, with the unconvincing tug-of-war contest between Simon, King and Joan, but the second half of the film becomes genuinely disturbing as we meet the unfortunate children who are ignorant of their unique predicament. As Bernard so eloquently puts it to Freya, "To survive the destruction that is inevitably coming, we need a new breed of man. An accident gave us these nine precious children, the only human beings who have a chance to live in the conditions which must inevitably exist when the time comes ... When that time comes the thing itself will open the door and my children will go out to inherit the earth." It is a chilling premise.

The Damned headed into post-production under editors James Needs and Reginald Mills with sound editor Malcolm Cooke. John Hollingsworth brought in James Bernard to compose the sombre score. The irritatingly catchy song, 'Black Leather Rock', which is used to compliment King's irresponsible gang, was written by Bernard with lyrics by Evan Jones. After the soul-destroying battle with the censor over The Curse of the Werewolf, it must have been with some trepidation that Tony Hinds approached them with Losey's latest. This time, the process was equally frustrating but for different reasons, as Hinds also had to take Losey's wishes into account. The debates continued throughout the year, Hammer finally losing enthusiasm and interest. The film would not get a screening in England until 1963, and even later in the USA. More of this later, however – it was summer 1961 and Hammer were about to swash their buckle.

"I remember I wrote the story outline for The Pirates of Blood River," recalls Jimmy Sangster. "Michael Carreras said he wanted to make a pirate picture. Our families were all sitting around a swimming pool one Sunday and he said, 'I'd like to make a pirate picture. Do you want to write one?' I said, 'Yes, I'd like to give it a try.' He said, 'But I can't afford a boat.' It was like asking someone to do a Robin Hood picture without bows and arrows. So I wrote a 12- or 15-page treatment."

John Gilling returned to Hammer to complete the screenplay and assume the director's chair, while associate producer Anthony Nelson Keys would get his first call as producer for Hammer on the film. "Michael was in the London clinic at the time and I went to see him," Keys recalled. "We were preparing this picture and I was talking to Michael about it. Jimmy Carreras came in to see his son and Jimmy turned around – 'By the by, Michael, who is going to produce the picture?' And Michael said, 'Oh, Tony is.' 'Good, great, right, I'm off to a meeting and I'll be back later.' And out

LEFT: *Kerwin Mathews escapes from the penal colony in* The Pirates of Blood River *(1961).*

BELOW: *Colony leaders Andrew Keir, Michael Mulcaster and Jack Stuart watch as the piranhas devour the hapless girl in* The Pirates of Blood River *(1961). The BBFC wanted to limit the Piranha attack.*

strode Jimmy. And I said, 'Thank you very much.' And that was it."[7]

Gilling's screenplay tells of a Huguenot colony threatened by a bunch of vicious pirates, led by Christopher Lee's LaRoche. Shooting started on location at Egham on Monday 3 July, just one week after principal photography on *The Damned* had ended, with further location work at trusty Black Park and the Shepperton lot. Casting was inspirational. In the lead, Hammer brought in Kerwin Mathews, who had buckled his swash so well in Ray Harryhausen's fantasy epic *The Seventh Voyage of Sinbad*. And who better to play the dastardly Captain LaRoche than Christopher Lee, who had just returned from Rome's Cinecittà Studios and Mario Bava's *Ercole al centro della terra* [Hercules in the Centre of the Earth].[17]

Called, rather prosaically, Captain Doom in earlier drafts of the script, he was described thus: "DOOM is a strange and fascinating creature – but the fascination is evil. At first glance, he might be called handsome. The bone structure of his face is good. But there is a strange emptiness about it – for it is the face of a man without a heart. DOOM has wit, intelligence, energy – even a sense of humour. But where his heart should be, there is a piece of ice – or nothing." Yet the captain has a flaw: "DOOM's whole appearance and the way he moves is so elegant that it is some moments before we notice that he is a cripple. His left arm is badly withered, bent at the elbow and held close against his body. His hand, with its fingers crooked upwards, is like an upturned claw."

Lee gives a sensitive performance, bringing to the character unusual depth, as well as showing off his skill with a blade. In fact, the colony's leader, Jason Standing (played by Andrew Keir in a welcome return to Hammer, having made his film debut for them in 1950's *The Lady Craved Excitement*), is the real villain of the piece. He is exactly as the original shooting script so aptly describes him: "the crumbling shell of a man consumed by the inward fires of religious mania." The pirate entourage is full of familiar faces, headed by Michael Ripper and Oliver Reed is back (whose character, Brocaire, was rendered as Brooker in the original script). For femme interest, we have Marie (*Stranglers / Brides*) Devereux and Marla (*Baskervilles*) Landi. Michael Mulcaster is lurking in the shadows, as usual, and 13-year-old Dennis Waterman plays young Timothy Blackthorne, described as 17 in the script. Waterman would go on to fame the following year as TV's *Just William*. In his autobiography, Waterman explains unforgivingly how John Gilling made him charge around like a Method actor so that he would be breathless enough to play the scene where he races to alert the villagers. (Unfortunately, he calls Gilling John Guillermin, which would no doubt come as a shock to the director of *The Towering Inferno*.) It was an energetic movie all round; disaster struck when actor Glenn Corbett (a Columbia appointee) fell from his horse and was hospitalised, taking him out of the picture.

Christopher Lee recalls how he drove pirates Oliver Reed and Denis Shaw to the studios: "I used to give them a lift every day. Oliver sat in the back seat: thin, nervous and worried, muttering about leaving the industry and how he wasn't cut out to be an actor. Denis Shaw sat in the front. There was just about enough room for him; chain-smoking, he nearly set fire to the car once. It was my first car, a second-hand Merc. I used to pick them up in Cromwell Road, opposite what is now Sainsburys and was BEA in those days. They would get there somehow, having been through Soho the night before. Denis was the one that got Oliver into all the fights, including the one where he got cut up. He'd start the trouble, then push Ollie in."

The usual Bray team were back. It was Clifford Parkes' turn for production manager, while Don Weeks prepared for the next production, *Captain Clegg*. Arthur Grant shot the production in Technicolor and the full glory of Hammerscope. A new second assistant, Peter Medak, joined Hammer, and Eric Boyd-Perkins with his assistant, Chris Barnes, cut the film under the usual guidance of James Needs. Bernard Robinson and Don Mingaye built the grand hall of the Huguenots on Stage 1 at Bray and the front façade of the stockade was erected on the back lot. Robinson also designed the plan of the Huguenot settlement, which was adapted by Les Bowie into an impressive matte painting and incorporated into the opening of the film, over which the introductory voice-over runs. From *The Pirates of Blood River* on, Hammer would now make a point of including both wardrobe supervisor (usually Molly Arbuthnot) and wardrobe mistress (usually Rosemary Burrows) in the credits. Before then, Rosemary's endeavours had gone uncredited in the background, in much the same way as Don Mingaye's had as 'assistant art director' before *The Curse of the Werewolf*.

The woods and lake of Black Park now stood in for the Caribbean island retreat of the Huguenots. The lake, in particular, caused problems for some actors. Michael Ripper, for one, remembered: "We had a God-awful scene in that one. It was a location shoot in Black Park near Pinewood, by now a familiar haunt to Hammer Films. It was a swamp scene we were filming. Hell, it was dreadful. Well, this swamp was actually a lake, but Christ, the stink, the smell from it was hideous. It was pollution at its worst, the water was just heavily stagnant. But the worst of it was that me and about 20 other actors, including Christopher Lee and Ollie Reed, had to go into this lake from hell. It was appalling, dreadful. I was most unhappy about this and so, I think, was Christopher. He was the first one to go in as he was the leader of our pirate band. When you got into this lake, as well as the smell you had underwater horrors to deal with, branches and suchlike. You literally sank into the thick mud that was under your feet. I must admit I was in fear of drowning. Dear old Christopher was almost up to his chin in it and he's a big chap. A very kind actor called Kerwin Mathews dragged his way with me through this horror and actually held onto me. Ollie Reed had a fight scene in the muck, and I got splashed in the face quite heavily. Believe me, I was glad to get back onto dry land, but it did leave one or two actors feeling quite ill, me included." [8]

The memory remains indelible to Christopher Lee as well: "It was agonising, because one's boots filled with water and there was God knows how much mud and broken glass in this lake, which we found out later was condemned. It was almost impossible to move. Finally we got through, with people disappearing under the water. Michael Ripper, of course, had to be carried and his language was something to be heard, which doesn't surprise me; I don't blame him. The stuntmen refused to do it again. They said it was too dangerous and most of them were Jock Easton's crew. Also Peter Arne, who is no longer with us, and Oliver Reed, who started a fight. One of the stuntmen pushed him under the water and kept him there and he had to go to hospital – infection in the eyes. They lied to us. They said that one of the stuntmen had been across the lake and it wasn't too deep and it was perfectly all right, but that was the other end of the lake. We went over the other side and I said, 'Follow me.' I walked in and went straight up to my chin and I'll never forget the expressions on the faces of my bold buccaneers when I turned around and saw them, particularly Michael, just paralysed. But we did it. And Gilling thought it was very funny; I could see him laughing and that's why I really let him have it. No, in that particular case, my memories are not pleasant ones. I couldn't walk upstairs properly for months afterwards. The strain had been so terrible on my legs and on my back. You can't imagine what it was like. It was like coming out of cement."

Christopher Lee shows Hammer enthusiast Sammy Davis Jr around the set of The Pirates of Blood River (1961).

During the shoot, self-confessed Hammer fan Sammy Davis Jr visited the set. Christopher Lee remembers: "We were shooting an interior. He was, of course, our biggest fan. I used to see him a lot when we later lived in the States. He was absolutely blown away by it all. He couldn't believe that we created these pictures on such a small stage. The swords were real, you know. I think he thought we were doing it with rubber swords."

Shooting ended on Thursday 31 August, after a luxurious nine weeks. Meanwhile, *Watch It, Sailor!* Had been released on the 14th. Its dire box-office and negative reviews would convince Hammer to put a hold on comedies – a resolve which would last ten years, until *On the Buses* screeched onto the nation's screens in 1971.

After shooting, Eric Boyd-Perkins and Chris Barnes took *Pirates* to Hammer House, where they were joined by Alfred Cox as sound editor. John Hollingsworth brought in Gary Hughes to compose the score. Hughes would become a favourite for Hammer's costume adventures. Next it was time to face the BBFC. John Trevelyan nominated the movie as "the only film I can remember that started as an 'X' film and went out as a 'U' film ... In the early part of the film a young girl, escaping from a villain, plunged into a river and set out to swim to the other bank. In the 'X' version a shoal of Piranha fish rushed through the water and attacked the girl, who struggled and was apparently dragged under the water which then became tinged with blood; in the 'A' version the Piranha fish rushed through the water, but the scene stopped as they reached the girl; in the 'U' version the Piranha fish never appeared at all." [9]

Piranha fish or no Piranha fish – it still fell upon Les Bowie's special effects unit to provide them in case the censor felt indulgent. Assistant special effects man Ian Scoones recalls Bowie's ingenuity: "I remember Les telling me, 'Everybody has all these American-type capsule guns for bullets in the water.' He showed me a very simple little trick. He said, 'What I've always used is a brass tube, the same diameter as Woolworths' marbles, and if you fill it up with marbles and throw them over your head, they go bup, bup, bup in the water and they look just like bullet shots.' And that's what he used. That was Black Park and Les always used to say, 'It's not a proper lake this, the septic tanks of Pinewood run into it [which explains the actors' horrors, quoted above] and it's bottomless. It just goes into darkness.' He knew this because he was a diver. Where we were it was just thick, black mud, which you sank into. There's no glamour in effects work at all!"

Another of Les Bowie's young assistants was Brian Johncock (now Johnson), who had just returned from National Service. He also remembers Bowie's Piranha fish, which sadly never made it into the final edit to ensure the 'U' certificate: "When you see films of Piranhas, all you see are these flashes of silver bodies and very little else. So what Les did was to get loads of bits of silver foil tied on black string with little bits of cork and then lots of air lines with little bubbles coming out of them, and we carried it and laid the rig into the lake at Black Park. Then, when we pressed the button, not only did the bubbles of water come up in a big area and blood around where the artist was standing, but you had these little flashes of silver from the bubbles carrying up these little bits of silver foil on the cork. They were wiggling around with the bubbles going by them and jets of water. It was so good. He was just magic about things like that."

While Hammer's partnership with Columbia continued, they were still allowed the occasional feature outside of the deal. Now, as 1961 was nearing its end, Hammer slipped in a neat little double-bill for Universal: another adventure yarn, *Captain Clegg*, and the long-anticipated reinterpretation of *The Phantom of the Opera*.

Captain Clegg was Hammer's screen adaptation of Russell Thorndike's popular *Dr Syn* novels. The books relate the story of Christopher Syn, the vicar of Dymchurch-under-the-Wall, who turns to a life of piracy as the ruthless Captain Clegg. Years later Syn returns to Dymchurch as vicar, now using the alias 'The Scarecrow' and leading a band of smugglers, the Night Riders, against the King's revenue men. The story was first brought to the big screen by Gainsborough Pictures in 1937 as *Doctor Syn*, starring George Arliss as the nefarious priest-cum-pirate.

The project was first brought to Hammer's attention by producer John Temple Smith and his company, Major Films. Originally planned as *Dr Syn – The Curse of Captain Clegg*, Hammer were dismayed when they discovered that Walt Disney was also preparing a version of the story, called *Dr Syn – Alias the Scarecrow*. On looking into the matter further, Hammer were distressed not only to find that Disney's preparations were well in advance of their own but that Disney had already copyrighted the name *Dr Syn*. Embarrassingly for Hammer, it appeared that the rights Temple Smith had brought them from Rank were only those for a remake of the original film and next to useless if Disney now owned the rights to the books. However, Hammer were not giving up that easily, particularly when they found out that Disney had not copyrighted any of Thorndike's other characters in the series. So all Hammer had to do was change the name of the central character from Dr Syn to Dr Blyss and shorten the title to *Captain Clegg*.

Surprisingly, when Disney's film was produced (after Hammer's, as it turned out), it was based not on the original *Dr Syn* novel but on the eighth and last book in the series, which had been finished by William Buchanan on the death of Thorndike. Thus, *Dr Syn – Alias the Scarecrow* made no reference to his past life as Captain Clegg and instead moulded the Scarecrow character into a latterday Robin Hood figure. Hammer's film revolved around the original novel and was more or less a straight remake of Gainsborough's original, with a few minor changes.

While Clegg sails away with his followers at the end of the original film, in Hammer's version he falls victim to the Mulatto. The villainous Mr Rash becomes the innkeeper instead of a school-teacher and the squire's son, whom Clegg marries to his daughter Imogene, was changed from Denis to Harry. Tony Hinds' final screenplay was delivered on 18 September and the film went into production a week later, on Monday the 25th. Hinds gave the story the usual Hammer treatment, infusing into it the expected amount of adventure and shock horror. Hence the film concentrates on Thorndike's Night Riders, roaming the Romney marshes under cover of darkness and under a spookier name, the Marsh Phantoms.

In the director's chair was Peter Graham Scott, who had already directed three features for Temple Smith's Major Films, *The Hide Out* (1956), *Account Rendered* (1957) and *The Big Chance* (1957). Heading the cast was Peter Cushing, who could switch from Blyss to Clegg practically by just taking off his glasses. Cushing had encountered Scott when they worked together in television in the 1950s and collaborated with him on polishing the screenplay. Again, the film is testament to how meticulously Cushing prepared a role; he even consulted Bray's parish priest, the Reverend Sidney Doran, to coach

Peter Cushing, Derek Francis, David Lodge and Patrick Allen survey the grave of the infamous Captain Clegg (1961).

CAPTAIN CLEGG

PRINCIPAL PHOTOGRAPHY: 25 September to 6 November 1961
DISTRIBUTION:
UK: Rank; certificate 'A'
US: Universal-International; US TITLE: Night Creatures
82 minutes; Technicolor
UK RELEASE:
PREMIÈRE: 7 June 1962, at the Leicester Square Odeon with The Phantom of the Opera
GENERAL RELEASE: 25 June, on the ABC circuit with The Phantom of the Opera
US RELEASE: 13 June 1962

DIRECTOR: Peter Graham Scott; PRODUCER: John Temple Smith; SCREENPLAY: John Elder with additional dialogue by Barbara S Harper [from the novel by Russell Thorndike]; PRODUCTION DESIGNER: Bernard Robinson; ART DIRECTOR: Don Mingaye; DIRECTOR OF PHOTOGRAPHY: Arthur Grant; CAMERA OPERATOR: Len Harris; FOCUS PULLER: Harry Oakes; GRIP: Albert Cowland; ASSISTANT DIRECTOR: John Peverall; 2ND ASSISTANT DIRECTOR: Peter Medak; SUPERVISING EDITOR: James Needs; EDITOR: Eric Boyd-Perkins; MUSIC: Don Banks; MUSIC

SUPERVISOR: Philip Martell; SOUND RECORDIST: Jock May; SOUND EDITOR: Terry Poulton; MAKE-UP: Roy Ashton; HAIRSTYLIST: Frieda Steiger; PRODUCTION MANAGER: Don Weeks; CONTINUITY: Tilly Day; WARDROBE SUPERVISOR: Molly Arbuthnot; WARDROBE MISTRESS: Rosemary Burrows; SPECIAL EFFECTS: Les Bowie; SPECIAL EFFECTS ASSISTANTS: Ian Scoones, Ray Caple, Brian Johncock; CONSTRUCTION MANAGER: Arthur Banks; MASTER PLASTERER: Stan Banks; MASTER CARPENTER: Charles Davis; MASTER PAINTER: Lawrence Wrenn; MASTER ELECTRICIAN: Jack Curtis; MASTER RIGGER: Ronald Lenoir; PROPS BUYER: Eric Hillier; PROPS MASTER: Tommy Money

Peter Cushing (Dr Blyss); Yvonne Romain (Imogene); Patrick Allen (Captain Collier); Oliver Reed (Harry); Michael Ripper (Mipps); Martin Benson (Rash); David Lodge (Bosun); Derek Francis (Squire); Daphne Anderson (Mrs Rash); Milton Reid (Mulatto); Jack MacGowran (Frightened Man); Peter Halliday (1st Sailor); Terry Scully (2nd Sailor); Sydney Bromley (Tom Ketch); Rupert Osborn (Gerry); Gordon Rollings (Wurzel); Bob Head (Peg-Leg); Colin Douglas (Pirate Bosun)

UNCREDITED Bowles Bevin's 'Men of Song' (Choir); Gerry Crampton (Tatooed Sailor); Harold Gee (Fiddler); Kate O'Mara (Girl at inn)

him in the marriage service. And Cushing was ably supported by another cast of regulars. Back from *Blood River* were Oliver Reed, Michael Ripper and David Lodge. This was Oliver Reed's third film for Hammer that year, reuniting him with Yvonne Romain, who had played his mother in *The Curse of the Werewolf*, though in truth they'd only met for a series of publicity photos on that occasion.

Special effects assistant Ian Scoones remembers Sydney Bromley racing through the marshes at the beginning of the film: "Sydney Bromley gets chased and falls into a swamp. As an actor, he

can't just fall into a swamp, we have to make it comfortable for him, so we had to put a mattress under the water and make sure it was waterlogged, so it wouldn't rise up and he could fall onto it backwards. Would you believe, like so many actors, he missed his mark totally and had to be carted off complaining bitterly that he had broken his spine. But he managed to walk into the bar OK!"

Michael Ripper is again on scene-stealing form, this time with the touching climax in which Mr Mipps carries Clegg's dead body to his bogus grave. Strangely enough, this is the only Hammer film in which Ripper had on-screen time with Cushing. Peter Graham Scott fondly remembers Ripper: "I had seen Michael many times in small parts in films (some of them for Hammer), but when I was asked to direct *Captain Clegg*, he was suggested for the important part of Mipps, a former member of Clegg's pirate crew, now the village carpenter, and I was sure he would show up well. Michael has a likeable comedian's face and twinkling eyes, which I used in close-up to good effect on his reactions to the 'vicar's' interrogation by a suspicious naval officer (Patrick Allen). Without further dialogue, the bond of loyalty and mutual respect between the two men was economically demonstrated.

"In the end, Doctor Blyss (Clegg) is murdered by a vengeful Mulatto and a sorrowful Mipps has to carry his dead skipper to his grave. In reality, small Michael had no hope of supporting six-foot Peter Cushing in a long slow walk, so we arranged for him to lift a lighter costumed dummy in the long shot and I cut as soon as possible to a close-up of him 'carrying' the real Peter, who was actually supported under the shoulders and knees by two off-screen, slowly walking prop men. Despite the mechanics, Michael's face bore a memorable and truthful grief, which was remarked on by several critics."

The same crew that had worked on *Blood River* returned three weeks later to shoot *Captain Clegg*, apart from the return of production manager Don Weeks, allowing Clifford Parkes to begin preparations for Hammer's next production, *The Phantom of the Opera*. Editor Eric Boyd-Perkins and his assistant Chris Barnes had only just finished post-production on *Blood River* at Hammer House when they launched into the new one at the Bray cutting rooms. Continuity supervisor Tilly Day celebrated her 300th film and was presented with a cake on the set by Tony Hinds. Coincidentally, assistant director John Peverall would leave Hammer after the next production, *The Phantom of the Opera*, and go to work on Disney's *Dr Syn – Alias the Scarecrow* at Pinewood, also as assistant director.

Peverall recalls, "One time, Jackie Cooper, the stuntman, was giving Oliver Reed a ride to the studio, and they were late. Jackie rolled the car over and broke Ollie's shoulder. We didn't know this had happened. That day, we were shooting a scene where Ollie was being arrested and there was supposed to be a bit of a punch-up. One of the other actors grabbed Ollie's arm and he let out a huge scream. That's when he found out he had broken his shoulder. He was turning white with the pain. We said we could shoot around him and do other scenes, but Ollie insisted on doing his scheduled scenes. When we finished shooting with him at 4.30 pm, he went to Staines Hospital." [5]

The film was again lensed on Hammer's stages at Bray. Hammer's Dymchurch was a combination of location work at the village of Denham in Buckinghamshire and Bray's trusty village square complex on the back lot. Houses now appeared on the other side of the original tunnel archway to form a second square. The interior and exterior church scenes were shot at the condemned Braywood Church. In 1958, the parish of Braywood was reunited with Bray and it was decided to demolish the old church. Still standing in 1961, Hammer took over the disused church and the team of Bernard Robinson and Don Mingaye dressed the interior. Braywood graveyard was also used, as was Copstone Mill on Turville Heath in Fingest, Buckinghamshire. Other location work took place at Chobham in Surrey (the marshes and hill sequences) and Bray gravel pits (tropical island and the rest of the marsh sequences). The marsh scenes were further enhanced by Les Bowie's magnificent background matte paintings. In fact, much of the eerie atmosphere of these scenes – the fog-enshrouded marshes with a full moon peeping out from a sombre Hammer skyline – is down to Bowie's team. His phantoms when they are seen are justly terrifying: fluorescent skeletons on horseback, gliding through the night, scaring anyone to death foolish to be out and about.

Captain Clegg was the first film on which Ian Scoones was allowed to assist Les Bowie with the special effects proper. "There was a lot of extra glass painting and models," he recalls. "I say models... Les painted on glass and I put some moss in front with a little bit of dry ice, under his direction of course. But Peter Graham Scott got his director's line confused. Basically that means he put the camera in the wrong place, so when he had someone following somebody, it looked like they were running the wrong way. When we saw the sailors who were supposed to be chasing the Marsh Phantoms, it looked as if one lot were going one way and another lot were going another way. Normally you'd say 'Cut to Seagull', which means you distract the eye of the viewer by cutting to something else quickly and then, by the time you come back, it looks as though they've turned a corner. Peter got this a little wrong and the only way around this was cutting to the Scarecrow.

"However, the whole film had been finished by then, so instead of making use of the whole day we had with the Scarecrow that Ollie Reed was in, Les said we would paint the Scarecrow and give him a better marsh atmosphere. Les did these wonderful paintings on hardboard and Kit West panned across them. One was the village of Dymchurch, which I think Les painted in a phenomenal 48 hours non-stop. The other one was for the pan across right at the beginning with the narration, and I said 'Why don't we put in a little figure here?' Because we cut to Sydney Bromley. Les said, 'That's a good idea.' We had done the same with a boat for *The Day the Earth Caught Fire*. We drilled two holes and made a tiny cut-out figure, put it on nylon and just pulled it from the back so it appeared to be moving, but you hardly see this at all in the film, because of the lettering that was superimposed on the top. These paintings were eight to twelve feet and involved a lot of detailed work.

"The glowing Marsh Phantoms were again a Bowie trick. Reflective Codit paint, which is made by the Minnesota Mining Company and is basically the same paint you see on road signs, which when you are in your car glare back at you. You are basically looking down an axis of your headlights, reflecting these millions of little beads, and you only lose about two per cent of the light that is put on to them. Les' idea was to put a Brute, one of the big lamps, one on each side of the camera lens, and shoot the real horses with real stuntmen on them. Bob Simmons was in charge of the horses on that film. He was already a stuntman but he was later very well known for all the early Bond pictures. We did an experiment in the garden at Bray down by the river and it worked. Then we did it for real and again it worked, with a little bit of help from the laboratory. The only thing that registered was the Codit paint, which we painted onto Hessian canvas, made with the help of the wardrobe department, for both the horses and the actors. Nowadays it's manufactured in plastic form and used on traffic police uniforms and roadworkers' protective clothing – even ship's lifebelts. Easy to think of materials that give a reflective effect nowadays, but *Captain Clegg* was made 40 years ago!"

Also on the Bowie team was Kit West (later to win an Oscar for *Raiders of the Lost Ark* and a BAFTA for *Return of the Jedi*), who shot the miniatures; Ray Caple (later to do mattes on *Alien*, *Superman* and *Highlander*), who helped Scoones make the fibreglass Scarecrow mask worn by Oliver Reed; and Brian Johnson (later to supervise effects on *Alien* and *Return of the Jedi*, among others), who assisted Scoones in dressing the models. Johnson recalls, "I went and got all the moss and dressed the set with Les for the marshes and we just dribbled dry ice and a little bit of hot water in it. I do remember driving to Burnham Beaches and Stoke Common and picking up tiny bits of moss from trees and things to get the right scale for the landscapes."

Scoones was responsible for finishing off Peter Cushing: "Peter got me a job with Hammer and the first film we work together on, I kill him off! This was the first effect I really did on the floor. After Les had rehearsed it with me, he let me do it: Peter with a harness and a wire, being pulled out of camera range but as close to the lens as we could. Then the harpoon was just literally me with a hollow harpoon which we had made, throwing it down and hoping to God that it would go into the cork and polystyrene block that was on Peter's back. Peter was told to keep the strain up and lean forward, and he was very patient. I did a similar job on Martin Benson. Les was watching and said, 'The only way to do it is to do it and then you've got the experience.'

"I was meeting all sorts of people and sometimes I'm afraid I spoke out of turn," Scoones continues. "Peter Graham Scott talked a lot about what he wanted for the opening and he said he wanted to cut to trees bending. Les said, 'Right, we'll have a wind machine and we'll put wires on a tree.' Now, I had done a project on *Great Expectations* at college and I said, 'But if you get a little bit of library film from the opening of *Great Expectations*, it's already there. David Lean cut to waving trees.' Les said, 'For God's sake!' But Peter Graham Scott said, 'That's a good idea!' And that's what we used! Of course, the reason Les was upset with me was that it did him out of work. I got the original clip of little Pip, Anthony Wager, kneeling at the graveyard just before you cut to the trees, which of course went to Jimmy Needs, the editor. If you look at *Clegg*, you will see those trees, so David Lean had a hand in *Captain Clegg*! Of course, Les, remember, had actually worked on *Great Expectations* at Pinewood."

Lightning never strikes twice, apparently, but it did for camera operator Len Harris. "Strangely enough I had worked on *Doctor Syn* for Gainsborough Pictures just before the war," he explained. "George Arliss was the star and he wouldn't work after 4.30 in the afternoon, because he was a big star then and quite an elderly man, so he made his own rules. Well, in those days we used to work until any old time at night, so when we finished at 4.30 we had to find something else to do. We'd probably do another scene, but usually those were fairly early nights. The only time we worked late on *Doctor Syn*, until about seven or eight, was in the scene where the harpoon is thrown into the back of the chair where they think Dr Syn is. When we did *Captain Clegg* years later, the rules were you had to finish at 5.30. If you wanted to work later then it was a special do, so Hammer made this arrangement for this one particular scene, and strangely enough it was the harpoon scene again, when we worked until about 7.00 pm!" [10] Another *Clegg* contributor had also worked on the Gainsborough version, incidentally – make-up man Roy Ashton.

Principal photography ended on Monday 6 November after six weeks. After a trade show on 12 September, *The Terror of the Tongs* finally premièred at the London Pavilion on the 29th with William Castle's *Homicidal*, going on general release on the ABC circuit from 20 November. From now on, the films produced for the on-going Columbia deal would be released in Britain by British Lion Columbia (BLC), while parent company Columbia maintained distribution rights for the rest of the world.

Now *Captain Clegg* began post-production under the editorial team of Needs, Boyd-Perkins and Barnes, aided and abetted by sound editor Terry Poulton. John Hollingsworth brought in Australian Don Banks to compose his first Hammer score. The end result was a pleasing adventure thriller, with horror trimmings, and the BBFC was content to give it an 'A' certificate.

"Cary Grant came to us and said he wanted to make a horror film," remembers Tony Hinds. "The only thing we could think of was *The Phantom of the Opera*. I knew he'd never make it, but he was

THE PHANTOM OF THE OPERA

PRINCIPAL PHOTOGRAPHY: 21 November to 26 January
1961/62
DISTRIBUTION:
UK: Rank; certificate 'A'
US: Universal-International
84 minutes; Technicolor
UK RELEASE:
PREMIÈRE: 7 June 1962, at the Leicester Square Odeon
with *Captain Clegg*
GENERAL RELEASE: 25 June 1962, on the ABC circuit with
Captain Clegg
US RELEASE: 15 August 1962

DIRECTOR: *Terence Fisher*; PRODUCER: *Anthony Hinds*; ASSOCIATE
PRODUCER: *Basil Keys*; SCREENPLAY: *John Elder, from the
composition by Gaston Leroux*; PRODUCTION DESIGNER: *Bernard
Robinson*; ART DIRECTOR: *Don Mingaye*; DIRECTOR OF
PHOTOGRAPHY: *Arthur Grant*; CAMERA OPERATOR: *Len Harris*;
FOCUS PULLER: *Harry Oakes*; GRIP: *Albert Cowland*; ASSISTANT
DIRECTOR: *John Peverall*; 2ND ASSISTANT DIRECTOR: *Peter Medak*;
SUPERVISING EDITOR: *James Needs*; EDITOR: *Alfred Cox*; MUSIC:
Edwin Astley; SOUND RECORDIST: *Jock May*; SOUND EDITOR:

James Groom; MAKE-UP: *Roy Ashton*; MAKE-UP ASSISTANT: *Colin
Guard*; HAIRSTYLIST: *Frieda Steiger*; PRODUCTION MANAGER:
Clifford Parkes; CONTINUITY: *Tilly Day*; WARDROBE MISTRESS:
Rosemary Burrows; WARDROBE SUPERVISOR: *Molly Arbuthnot*;
SPECIAL EFFECTS: *Les Bowie*; SPECIAL EFFECTS ASSISTANTS: *Ian
Scoones, Brian Johncock, Pat Moore*; OPERA SCENES STAGED BY:
Denis Maunder; CONSTRUCTION MANAGER: *Arthur Banks*;
MASTER PLASTERER: *Stan Banks*; MASTER CARPENTER: *Charles
Davis*; MASTER PAINTER: *Lawrence Wrenn*; MASTER
ELECTRICIAN: *Jack Curtis*; MASTER RIGGER: *Ronald Lenoir*;
PROPS BUYER: *Eric Hillier*; PROPS MASTER: *Tommy Money*

Herbert Lom (The Phantom/Professor Petrie); *Heather Sears*
(Christine Charles); *Edward De Souza* (Harry); *Thorley Walters*
(Lattimer); *Michael Gough* (Ambrose); *Harold Goodwin* (Bill);
Martin Miller (Rossi); *Liane Aukin* (Maria); *Sonya Cordeau*
(Yvonne); *Marne Maitland* (Xavier); *Miriam Karlin* (charwoman);
Patrick Troughton (Ratcatcher); *Renée Houston* (Mrs Tucker); *Keith
Pyott* (Weaver); *John Harvey* (Sergeant Vickers); *Michael Ripper* (1st
Cabby); *Miles Malleson* (2nd Cabby); *Ian Wilson* (the Dwarf)

UNCREDITED: *Leila Forde* (Teresa); *Geoff L'Cise* (Frenchman in Tavern)

insistent, so I wrote the thing for him. He was
on vacation, and I knew that once he got back to
the States his agent would tell him he couldn't
make it. And that's what happened." [11] With
Grant in mind, Tony Hinds set about furnishing
a script. To moderate the Phantom's dirty
doings, he introduced the murderous dwarf,
who saves the scarred Professor Petrie from his
watery grave beneath the London Opera house.
The Phantom avenges himself on the wicked
entrepreneur, Ambrose D'Arcy, and in the
climax sacrifices his own life to save Christine,
when the dwarf accidentally sends the
chandelier crashing down upon her. Hammer's
approach would be more in line with Universal's
remake of 1943 starring Claude Rains than the
original classic of 1925 starring Lon Chaney.

Hinds acted early this time, no doubt still
influenced by the film's potential star, and sent
in a copy of his draft script to John Trevelyan on
11 July. Audrey Field's comments were as follows: "I am told that we have had 'The Phantom'
about four times before. The last time seems to
have been in 1943, when it was 'A'. It has probably always been 'A' but Hammer have not made
it before, and there is a good deal of potentially
'X' stuff here. I understand that the book, which I have not read, did not have the
dwarf, and that the phantom, far from being tamed, deliberately brought the
chandelier down on the audience. But all this is change for a shilling, except that
the dwarf increases the opportunities for shots that could easily be 'X'. I think the

Herbert Lom as The Phantom
of the Opera (1961).

makers should be told that they could make it in an 'A' way if they liked, but that the script as it stands has quite a bit of 'X' stuff. Probably they want this category anyway."

Trevelyan replied to Hinds on 19 July: "This must be about the fifth time this story has come to the screen, but the last time appears to have been in 1943 when there was no 'X' category. We imagine that in this version you will be thinking of the 'X' category rather than the 'A', and the script certainly gives this impression. On the basis of the 'X' category, I have the following comments to make:

Page 17 Scene 65. The shot of the scene-shifter's 'horribly dead' body hanging up-side down should not be too gruesome. We do not, for instance, want to see blood pouring from his mouth or any nasty mutilations.

Page 36 Scene 101. We should not be prepared to accept the old woman's joke 'And so I says to 'im – if you can't raise the money, it's no good tryin' to raise anything else!'

Page 44 Scene 118. Care will be needed in treatment of this shot. Presumably it will be a reverse shot of the dagger seen from the rat-catcher's eye-line. Anything else might well be too nasty for us to accept.

Page 44 Scene 119. We do not want a lot of blood in this scene, or anywhere else.

Page 45 Scene 121. We much dislike the shots of rats squealing and running around after their death. I hope you will omit them.

Page 45 Scene 125. This might well be all right, but it could be too horrific.

Page 63 Scene 167-8. In these scenes in which Christine is dragged by the dwarf into the subterranean stream, we would not want nasty violence, nor would we want the dwarf to look too horrific.

Page 65 Scene 180. We do not much like the idea of the hideous mask filling the screen. These extremely close shots are often objectionable.

Page 71 & 74 Scenes 193, 195 & 202. In these scenes Christine has some pretty rough treatment. This should be kept to a minimum. We do not like this kind of violence to a woman.

Page 81 Scene 227. It seems unnecessary that the vicious blow that Ambrose gives the Professor should be across his face. This really only adds to the element of brutality.

Page 82-3 Scene 237. In the flashback we see the flames engulf the Professor's face and hear his screams of pain. This should be very discreetly done and should not be over gruesome or too unpleasant. We do not like shots of people on fire.

Page 92 Scene 302. Here we see the Professor's 'hideously scarred face.' This could be too unpleasant to be acceptable and if you intend to go to town on the shot you would be advised to have an alternative.

Page 92 Scene 307. The shot of the chandelier squashing the Professor could be very nasty.

Page 93 Scene 312. Here we have the face of the Phantom again and the previous comments apply. "As I have told you, criticism of the 'X' category horror films has increased in the last two years and we have to react to more criticism than we used to get. In the circumstances I must ask you to take special care in the shooting of all shock sequences."

Hinds cast 44-year-old Herbert Lom as the tragic Professor Petrie, scarred by acid when he attempts to burn the plates of his music stolen by the unscrupulous Lord Ambrose D'Arcy. Lom was no stranger to Hammer, having starred in their 1951 production, *Whispering Smith Hits London*. Lom recalls, "I was enjoying a well-earned rest from filming when Hammer contacted me and asked if I would like to play the title role. I said I was neither interested or disinterested, so they sent me a script. When I read the script I jumped straight out of my chair, grabbed the telephone and told producer Anthony Hinds it was a deal ... I suggested to Terence Fisher, who was to direct the film, that it might be a good thing if I saw the two previous versions of the story, but Mr Fisher was firmly against this. He felt it would be to the advantage of our production if I created the role my own way." [12]

26-year-old Heather Sears played Christine Charles. Sears had won a British Academy Award and the New York Critics' Award for her role in *The Story of Esther Costello*, going on to star in the British classics *Room at the Top* and *Sons and Lovers*. Brian Johnson worked as special effects assistant and recalls, "Heather Sears was in it. I think her and Tony Masters the production designer had just got married. He used to drive over in his Bentley and collect Heather. That was the first time I met him. Years later I worked for him on a number of things including *2001: A Space Odyssey*."

No surprise to Hinds, Cary Grant had second thoughts and his intended role instead went to Edward De Souza. "I was cast by Terence Fisher," De Souza explains. "That was quite a jolly story, because he'd seen me in a play at the Mermaid Theatre. He'd actually come to see somebody else. He'd come to see David Kay for the part of the dwarf, but David Kay didn't like playing the dwarf. It was a coincidence that I happened to be in that play, so I got an interview with Terence Fisher. I'd just been in a play on television called *So Long at the Fair*. There were clips in it from one of Terence Fisher's films. [From, in fact, Fisher's 1949 film version of the same story.] He was astonished. The thing was, there I was in a television play set at the turn of the century – and, of course, *The Phantom of the Opera* was set at the turn of the century – it was the most extraordinary piece of good fortune, and that's how I got the part." [13]

Ian Wilson, though merely diminutive, was finally picked to play the malicious dwarf. And who better to play D'Arcy than Michael Gough, who relished the part. Search the background and you'll find the usual Hammer regulars, this time Harold Goodwin, Marne Maitland, Patrick Troughton and John Harvey. Michael Ripper and Miles Malleson turn up in memorable cameos as cab drivers. It would be Malleson's final film for Hammer; he died in 1969.

Shooting started on Tuesday 21 November. The same crew from *Captain Clegg* were back after a two-week rest, except for the addition of Clifford Parkes, whose turn it was as Production Manager, and Alfred Cox as editor, allowing Eric Boyd-Perkins to finish *Clegg* at Hammer House. A fortnight's respite meant a hectic time for Hammer's art department and construction crew, although one imagines the considerable location work on *Clegg* and the scheduling of location work first on *Phantom* would have given them some extra breathing space. In pride of place was the Phantom's subterranean lair on Stage 1. Don Mingaye remembers, "It was quite a task. Again, we were able to bring in the plastering department and we made a fibreglass base to take the water." Brian Johnson recalls, "I really enjoyed working on *The Phantom of the Opera*. The sets were wonderful. I used to go onto the stage at lunchtime and sit there, and just look at the set of the sewers with all the water. The way Bernie Robinson had done them, and how much production value they got out of those sets, was amazing."

The exterior scene in which Ambrose D'Arcy knocks the Professor to the ground beside his carriage took place in Oakley Court carpark on 22 January, while the new village square on the Bray lot can be glimpsed when the acid-scarred Lom runs into the street from the printers. An opera house was required too, of course, and Tony Hinds finally settled for the rather modest Wimbledon Theatre. Here Fisher would utilise the auditorium, wings and overhead flies, the latter for the scenes in which a stagehand chases the dwarf. Len Harris explained, "The theatre was much smaller than you'd think, and Terence Fisher was at his wits' end to give it some size. We only used a few extras in costume to fill the seats and kept moving them around, changing hats and coats, to make it look like an army." [14]

Hinds had his opera house; now all he needed was an opera and, with that in mind, he brought in 35-year-old Edwin Astley to reportedly write an original five-act act opera based on George Bernard Shaw's *Saint Joan*. The crew moved into the Wimbledon Theatre on Monday 27 November and shot the opera scenes over the next two weeks, finishing on 12 December. Bernard Robinson was of course brought in for the stage designs and Denis Maunder assisted Fisher in staging the operatic scenes. Singer Patricia Clark was later brought in to dub Heather Sears. Liane Aukin played the diva, Maria, and 24-year-old Sonya Cordeau, a professional singer/actress, played Yvonne, Christine's plucky would-be replacement.

Hinds' next challenge: what should his Phantom look like? Bernard Robinson's wife Margaret was originally asked to design the mask for the Phantom, no doubt due to her previous experience at Theatre Zoo, which specialised in animal masks: "At the time I had just had my son Peter and had become a full-time mum. I said I would do it if he [Herbert Lom] could come to the house for measuring, but Bernard said, 'Don't be silly, they'll say that he'll come to the house, but he won't be able to. You'll find that you'll be waiting in draughty dressing rooms to measure him as he comes off stage.' Peter was a baby at that time and I couldn't leave him for any length of time, so I turned it down. I did suggest someone else to do it, but they didn't like his designs and got rid of him, so Roy Ashton did it instead. I don't know what I'd have done, something very classical and beautiful, I suppose, to contrast with his ugliness. I don't think Roy was very happy with it in the end; it was a very spur-of-the-moment mask."

Filming The Phantom of the Opera (1961) on the Bray village set. Len Harris and Harry Oakes sit with the camera, while Terence Fisher, Edward De Souza and Heather Sears lean on the wall.

Roy Ashton described his frustration: "About six weeks before the picture was due to go into production, the question of the mask arose. At the recommendation of the art department, Tony Hinds had called upon a mask-maker to come up with something suitable for the Phantom to wear. He was responsible for a number of designs, some of which I saw, that were beautiful. Nevertheless, they were not what was requested and the make-up section had to fill in some ideas as usual. My suggestion was that the Phantom almost certainly would have picked up some masks from the theatre properties to conceal his features. Something readily available, because he wouldn't be going into shops or anything like that: it wouldn't matter very much what it was, it only had to be distinctive and immediately recognisable. I thought about old Japanese masks as they were pictured in a sumptuous publication entitled *Masks of the World*, which I found in the Victoria and Albert Museum. I invited Tony Hinds to come and have a look, but he told me he couldn't spare the time. So I made a few drawings and showed them to him, but it was not exactly what he hoped for.

"I next appeared with a book of Japanese kabuki masks. 'That is not bad,' he uttered when seeing one of them, and he tore the page out, pushing a hole through one of the eyes. 'He's got to look out of one of these, hasn't he?' He waved away my objection that this was not a way to treat literature. Still he couldn't make up his mind, even when they began shooting the film. Three weeks later we were in the theatre where they had to photograph Herbert Lom with his mask on, and no decision had been taken yet. 'Look,' I said, 'give me five minutes and I will make you one.' I got an old piece of rag, tied it round his face, cut a hole in it, stuck a bit of mesh over one of the eyes, two bits of string around it, and tried it. 'Great!' they cried out, 'that is just what we want! Phantom of the Opera.' I often laugh when I think back on that; only a piece of nothing, having had a professional artist there for six weeks, books, and God knows what!" [15] It was this imaginative quick thinking and ability to improvise that made Roy Ashton so indispensable on Hammer's tight schedules; the final result was simple, but extremely effective.

Terence Fisher admitted that the film had its faults and that, as with The Two Faces of Dr Jekyll, he was not entirely satisfied with it. "The main weakness of Phantom is the fact that [the] realism wasn't really justified. The Phantom wasn't sufficiently motivated for his deeds. He remains somewhat vague to us. How, for instance, can he love a girl he doesn't know and has hardly ever seen at all? What he loves is her voice. He respects her for her voice and she understands that, but that's hardly true love, eh? In any case, this would never have made a [Frank] Borzage film. I mention him because I love his work, especially the pre-war films. Here the amorous sentiments do not play a decisive part ... I think a great deal of the film's relative failure is due to the editing, which could have been better. I also think the film lacked a certain punch. And for that, we're all responsible." [16]

One weakness of Fisher's film is that the unmasking scenes (two of them) lack impact. In the first, D'Arcy rips the mask off the Phantom, who is standing with his back to us. We therefore never see his face, only D'Arcy's horrified reaction. While this is not a particularly powerful sequence, the unseen is always more frightening and Fisher cleverly leaves things to our imagination, which works well. However, this has only succeeded in priming us, raising our expectations, so much so that when the Phantom finally removes his mask at the climax to leap onto the stage and save Christine, we are left bitterly disappointed, given Roy Ashton's rather modest make-up job. Fisher has prepared us for a hideous monstrosity and all we get are a few scabs and scars that from a distance look like a port wine stain.

Admittedly, this was not entirely Ashton's fault. The film was being geared up for an 'A' certificate, which meant that his more radical ideas could never be realised. Again, Ashton experimented through a series of drawings – all variations on an acid-scarred face – which again had to be shown to the producers for their approval. However, as with the mask, they could not make up their minds. Interestingly, one of Ashton's drawings is annotated 'Hiroshima type burns molten flesh,' indicating that Ashton was obviously prepared for a truly horrific make-up. One such design drawing is dated 2 December (the end of the second week), indicating that Hammer still hadn't decided what their Phantom should look like well into production. Gradually Ashton was forced to moderate his ideas, and make-up tests were made on stuntman Jackie Cooper, who was to double for Lom in the film. Roy explained, "The make-up for the Phantom wasn't very complicated. A great deal of pieces, with the wrinkled flesh and everything, had been manufactured beforehand. The final application required nothing more than some adjustment, the trimming of edges etc. That was all." [15]

Herbert Lom discussed his difficulties with the role: "You try acting in a one-eyed, mouthless mask for hours on end and you'll see what I mean. Acting with a mask or a heavy, horrific make-up is as much an ordeal as it is a test of an actor's capabilities. There is no 'direct visible' communication with the audience, because your face is hidden, so whatever effects you wish to create you have to depend largely on mime." [16]

Lom's stunt double, Jackie Cooper, recalls: "They put scar tissue over one side of my face. It's like a gum that goes on and then shrinks and pulls your skin up." He also remembers the climactic leap from the box at Wimbledon Theatre. "The jump was not very dangerous at all. The box was quite close to the stage. I don't suppose it was more than ten or 12 feet high. They shot it from a distance, so it only looked like I had one eye. I needed both eyes open for the jump." He also had to double for Lom for the scene in which the Phantom floats into the sewer following his accident: "I ended going through a sluice gate for him on location somewhere. I had a rubber suit on and was buoyant."

Les Bowie was again in charge of special effects. Assisting him were Ian Scoones, Pat Moore and Brian Johnson. Scoones remembers, "Les had a number of assistants at this time. He got nick-named 'Bowie and his boy scouts'. He had a young protégé, Pat Moore, who was far, far more talented on the 'floor effects' side of things. He was an Australian working as a petrol pump attendant

Ian Wilson as the crazed dwarf watches as he sends his master to his death in The Phantom of the Opera (1961).

at the garage opposite Pinewood. Les was such a wonderful man; he picked up all these odd people, including myself, from nowhere. None of us came from the usual route. Les was working on *Lancelot and Guinevere* and here was Pat Moore, petrol pump attendant, who said yes, he could sword fight and so on. He always did everything he said he could, but he'd never done it before. Pat Moore and I did a lot of preparation on *Phantom*, rigging everything, then Les would come, because he was working on other films at the same time. We had to rig the fire in the printing room set. We had prop effects such as a small gas jet in a stove, which was made of wood, as scenery. I remember Les got these chunks of glass, which had come from a kiln, and if you put light underneath them, they looked like burning coals when you flickered the light. So we had this fire to make and get it all ready for when they were hoping to film it at two o'clock, after lunch. Later, for the big effect, the actual fire, obviously Les had more experienced people in as well as us and himself.

"Then there were the rats. I've still got a scar on my index finger. We couldn't get the rats to come out of Pat Troughton's sack. Ian Wilson played a dwarf who jumps on Troughton's back and knocks the sack onto the ground; the camera then cuts to the sack and out come the rats. That's what the script says. Everything was fine until trying to get the rats out of the sack and so it was decided that we'd do it again as an insert. We put chicken wire on artificial cobbles on one of the sets and everybody was there, including many of the actors, and we dropped the sack but nothing happened, cameras rolling. I think we had two cameras. Les said, 'We'll try it with some smoke.' That didn't work, it just looked wrong. Then we tried clapping hands. That didn't work, because rats like the darkness, they don't like the bright lights, and they were quite happy in the warm of the sack and wouldn't come out. In the end he made up a little charge with a det [detonator] and put that in the sack; that did actually make them jump so much they came streaming out. We got the shot but what we didn't realise was that one of the legs of the catwalk above us goes up to the lighting rail, and all the rats went straight up the chicken wire into the Kapok, which is used in the walls to soundproof the stage. They were never seen again. Luckily, we had many wild cats that the plasterers used to feed, and presumably all the rats were chased away by the cats."

Brian Johnson remembers the fun they had on the movie. "We had this big rain rig. The director was Terence Fisher and the assistant director was John Peverall. John Peverall was very pushy and he later went on to become line producer in one of the big production companies. They had a camera crane and these are counterbalanced so that, when everybody is on the crane, lead weights are put on the other end to balance it. And in those days nobody got off until they got the say-so from the grip, otherwise the crane would be completely out of balance and might go shooting up in the air or crash heavily to the ground. So Peverall was standing on this thing and we had all this rain on the set outside. Buckets of rain; Terence had said to me, 'I want lots of rain, dear boy.' So we had lots of rain and I had this directional thing that I could really let rip by the camera.

"After we had done a few takes and Terence was quite happy, he set John Peverall up, because he wanted to play a trick on him. Peverall was standing on the crane with his loud hailer and said, 'Let's roll the camera.' The crew were in on it and knew we weren't rolling and Terence had said to me, 'Just get Peverall with everything you've got!' So I had to aim all these jets at John and once the track had started, John couldn't get off, he was part of it. He was just standing there and he was absolutely bucketed with this water. When we got to the end-of-picture party, Terence came up to me and gave me a huge bottle of whiskey and said, 'Dear boy, that was absolutely the best thing I've ever seen!' And I got a Christmas card from him thanking me for my 'assistance'."

"I can remember there were two funny things about *Phantom*," says Edward De Souza. "The diving into the water toward the end of the film – when my character hears the singing from the sewers and dives in. Well, that was me. I had to do that. They rather cynically left that for practically the last shot in the film in case I succumbed to the cold waters. It was made in the winter. They didn't want to have a dead actor to play in the rest of the film. The other thing about *Phantom* – when I first kissed Heather Sears we were on the lot. They arranged that very sensitively, I thought. We had an evening shoot and there was funny old Miles Malleson, the cabbie, on the top and Heather and me in the carriage. It was all very cosy, wonderfully romantic. Absolutely irresistible. And there we were, we had a couple of glasses of wine and felt very romantic. So the kissing was really no trouble at all. In fact, we both felt quite warm and happy about that. But on the lot that evening, it was drizzling and in fact that take had to be thrown out, because there was a certain amount of spoiling from the rain. The result was that we had to do it the following morning as the very first shot, eight o'clock in the morning. And we felt absolutely nothing at all. Absolutely nothing. None of that stirring was taking place. But in fact, when I looked at that particular scene, I thought it looked pretty romantic. So it really gives the lie to the idea that you've got to feel these things in order to be convincing." [13]

Thorley Walters looks pensive as Lattimer in The Phantom of the Opera (1961).

Shooting would continue into the new year. Meanwhile, Hammer were still trying to get *The Damned* past the BBFC. On 21 November, Tony Hinds wrote to John Trevelyan: "I understand that *The Damned* has been rejected for an 'X' certificate because of the shot of KING striking out of frame with his umbrella. To eliminate this would necessitate re-recording the whole reel. Surely, as the action is out of frame, this should be acceptable for the 'X' certificate (even though made in England!)?"

For once communications seemed to falter. The next missive is dated 11 December, with Trevelyan asking Hinds: "Will you please let me know for my records what you decided to do about the umbrella shot in *The Damned*?" Hinds responded two days later: "I am sorry I have not advised you before, but as you know, there are other people involved in any decisions and I am still waiting for someone to make up his mind. As soon as I am able to do so, I will write again." That 'someone' was almost certainly Joseph Losey and, to cut a long story short, it took until 21 August 1962 before Hinds could put Trevelyan's mind at rest: "I am sorry that this has been outstanding for so long, and I now confirm that we shall make the cut required by you (the 'umbrella' shot) in order to qualify for the 'X' certificate." Then more problems arose when the 100-minute film was deemed too long by its distributor and had to be chopped down to a more manageable 87 minutes.

As 1961 wound down, another turning point in Hammer's history was just around the corner. When *The Phantom of the Opera* finished shooting early in 1962, many changes would take place. The Bray rep company would be finally disbanded, bringing to an end what many people consider to be the golden age of Hammer horror.

TEN

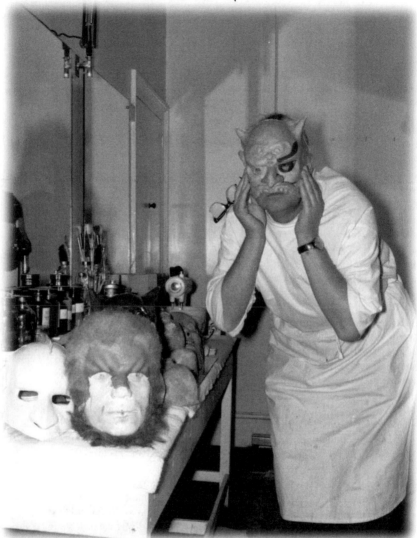

The Kiss of Death

(1 9 6 2)

1962 would be a year of change. *The Phantom of the Opera* finished shooting on Friday 26 January after a luxurious ten weeks (coming in at around £171,000) and then went into post-production under editors Alfred Cox, James Needs and assistant Chris Barnes, with sound editor James Groom. Edwin Astley, who had composed the opera, stayed on to complete the rest of the score.

There was crushing news for the crew that cold January, however. As Len Harris explained, "There were rumours floating around for a couple of days and then we were all called together in the theatre. They told us we were going to cease production, because there wouldn't be any more money coming from American sources. They hoped to resume production in the near future, but they had nothing confirmed for us. We finished up *Phantom* probably by the end of that week. Tony Nelson Keys might have made the announcement or the studio production manager. I had my contract which ran out at the end of 1961, so I stayed on for a little bit in 1962, but I didn't have another contract. A lot of people seemed surprised that they let me go. I wasn't, since I knew they didn't have any production going on. A few maintenance people were kept on. The sound maintenance man looked after the sound equipment. He also kept an eye on the camera equipment, but he didn't do any maintenance on it. They kept some heads of departments like the chief electrician, the chief engineer, the construction manager and the master of props. If they planned to rent out the studio for other productions, they would need these people to run things." [1]

Hammer Productions 1962

+ THE OLD DARK HOUSE
+ MANIAC
+ PARANOIAC
+ THE KISS OF THE VAMPIRE
+ NIGHTMARE

OPPOSITE: Make-up artist Roy Ashton clowns around in his office with a mask from The Kiss of the Vampire (1962). Note the appliance for werewolf make-up over a cast of Oliver Reed's head.

The exact reasons behind this hiatus remain a mystery – Hammer's relationship with American distributors Columbia and Universal would continue for some time yet. It is known, however, that James Carreras was starting to become disenchanted with Bray, which he considered expensive to maintain inbetween productions. In 1962 he made the first of many attempts to sell the studio, appointing estate agents Harris and Gillow to find a buyer. Initial interest was expressed by the BBC and the Rodwell Group, but the mothballed studio would stay under Hammer's control for some time to come.

The crew had mouths to feed and, relieved of their Bray commitment, the team dispersed. Left behind were studio manager Arthur Kelly and the construction team under construction manager Arthur Banks: master plasterer Stan Banks, master carpenter Charles Davis, chief electrician Jack Curtis and master painter Lawrence Wrenn. Also retained were props master Tommy Money and props buyer Eric Hillier. When Hammer eventually pulled themselves together later in the year, some of the old guard would return, but the core would now be employed elsewhere. Gone was Len Harris, camera operator par excellence, and his focus puller Harry Oakes. Gone were continuity girl Tilly Day, editor Alfred Cox, assistant director John Peverall and 2nd assistant director Peter Medak. Sound recordist Jock May would be available for the next production, *The Old Dark House*, but then would be gone too.

Some would make it back. Fortunately, Bernard Robinson and his right-hand man Don Mingaye returned, as did make-up man Roy Ashton, production manager Don Weeks, supervising editor James Needs, music supervisor John Hollingsworth, wardrobe ladies Molly Arbuthnot and Rosemary Burrows, and hairstylist Frieda Steiger. Pauline Wise would take over the continuity chores vacated by Tilly Day and her husband-to-be, Hugh Harlow, would become the regular 2nd assistant once he returned from National Service. While the continuity of a regular camera operator and assistant director would now be lost, Ken Rawkins would step into sound recordist Jock May's shoes and James Groom, later followed by Roy Hyde and Roy Baker, would provide some continuity as sound editor. A new team for a tougher future.

Len Harris would return to Hammer for some 2nd unit work on *The Gorgon*, *The Reptile*, *Quatermass and the Pit*, *A Challenge for Robin Hood* and *Frankenstein Must Be Destroyed*. He recalled, "Hammer later contacted me and said they were starting up production again and wanted to know if I'd like to come back. Their plan, however, was to only do one picture. I had a bunch of work lined up on films at Shepperton by then. I'd liked to have gone back, because I liked working there. If I went back for one picture, I would have put myself out of work for a long time. Sometimes when I had a break at Shepperton, I'd get contracted and offered a few days of second unit work for Hammer. I did some stuff on *The Gorgon*, a *Dracula* and a *Frankenstein* at Elstree. Then they offered me 2nd unit work on *The Devil Rides Out*. Terry Fisher had asked me to do that. I knew the story and it fit into my Shepperton schedule. Then a series of delays came along on starting the 2nd unit work. Finally the film's production manager called with a definite start date and said they were happy to have me back. But I couldn't do it because of other commitments. Then he said I was letting them down!" [1]

Harris had given Hammer ten years of good service since he started with them on a proposed one-picture deal on *Mantrap* in 1952. He died, a month after attending Peter Cushing's memorial service and being reunited with Christopher Lee, on Tuesday 14 February 1995. According to friend and colleague Harry Oakes, "I first worked with Len at Hammer on *The Saint Returns* in January 1953 and then worked with him for the following nine years. He was marvellous to work with, almost too tolerant. Looking back, I am surprised he tolerated me for so long!" [2]

Harry Oakes' diary of his final Hammer film concludes on an ambivalent note; on Friday 26 January 1962 he notes: "My last day at Bray. Have mixed feelings – should have left long ago. Drinks on Stage 1 and at The Queen's Head."

"I left because at that time there was no continuity," he says now. "One of the first jobs I did afterwards was to operate on a series for the BBC and then I worked for Granada Television. Then I had a call from the Gerry Anderson outfit to work on *Thunderbirds*. I think they chose me because I lived near Slough and I stayed with them a long time. I was also 2nd unit cameraman on their live action adventures, *UFO* and *Space: 1999*. My first big break was getting on 2nd unit on *Superman*. Since then I've done *Superman 3* and *4*, *Flash Gordon*, *Dracula* [Langella] and *Aliens*. The last picture I worked on as special effects cameraman was *Memphis Belle*. Gerry Anderson got me back working again a few years ago on *Space Precinct*. I'd worked on the pilot some years earlier, but I didn't enjoy it, and after 12 episodes I left." Harry Oakes did return briefly to Hammer for some 2nd unit work on *The Brigand of Kandahar* in 1965.

Also gone was assistant director John Peverall. He remembers, "About six months later, I got a call from Tony Keys inviting me back to AD on another picture, but I had to turn him down ... I think my four years at Hammer were extremely good years to me. They showed me how films could be made – and could still be made without spending all those huge amounts of money." [3] In 1978, along with fellow producers Barry Spikings, Michael Deeley and Michael Cimino, Peverall picked up the Oscar for best film – *The Deer Hunter*.

What had caused Hammer to release its staff? Certainly 1961 had not been kind. They had scored with *Taste of Fear* but their distributors can't have been impressed with the lukewarm box-office figures for their other releases that year. *The Curse of the Werewolf* had failed to draw the usual horror crowds and two of their Columbia films, *Cash on Demand* and *The Damned*, were gathering duat awaiting a British release. It was perhaps an inauspicious time, then, to mount an ambitious picture like *The Phantom of the Opera*, with its long schedule and expanding budget.

What had 1961 taught the company? Comedies were out. Gothics were so-so, provided you chose your subject carefully, but psychological thrillers were definitely in. *Psycho* had confirmed the fact and Jimmy Sangster had proved he had a talent for them with *Taste of Fear*. Of Hammer's five films in 1962, three would be Sangster suspense thrillers. And to help the Gothic revival, they needed a no-risk approach – it was time, therefore, for *Dracula 3*. Gradually Hammer began to find their feet again, although their first impending project, *The Old Dark House*, could hardly be considered safe ground.

In the meantime, Hammer set about getting *The Phantom of the Opera* to the BBFC. This was one film they had to get out, particularly since they had plans to release it alongside *Captain Clegg* for a Universal/Rank 'A' certificate double-bill. James Carreras submitted the film to the BBFC on Monday 2 May. Examiner Newton Branch noted: "Request for an 'A' for the film. This is a very restrained 'X' and much of it is 'A'. At times the atmosphere may spook younger children and there are certain scenes which are definitely 'X' ... I talked to JC about category again after our discussion with JT. I think she feels more strongly about 'X' on the grounds of the film's general atmosphere. I can therefore only suggest other examiners have a look at it and be told that Hammer want an 'A'."

Frank Crofts and Audrey Field saw the film on the 7th and John Trevelyan replied to James Carreras later the same day: "Our Examiners had a look today at *The Phantom of the Opera* with a view to seeing whether we could by cutting make the film suitable for the 'A' category. As you anticipated, some cuts would be required. The question is whether these can be done in a way that will not damage your picture. I can only tell you what cuts will be required and leave it to your people to see what they can make of them. The cuts required would be as follows:

Reel 1. Shorten the incident of the man hanging above the stage. The scene should be cut before the man is seen swinging backwards and forwards, and only enough should be left to show that there is a corpse.

*The end of an era:
Len Harris and
Harry Oakes' final
collaboration for
Hammer was on
The Phantom of
the Opera (1961).*

Reel 2. You should remove the shot of the dwarf stabbing the rat catcher in the face and the shot of his bleeding face immediately afterwards. Remove the big close-up of the masked man where the details of the mask are not clearly seen. This is followed by a similar shot in brighter lighting which may be acceptable.

REEL 3. When the dwarf appears at the girl's window the scene should be cut before the window is opened and the dwarf thrusts his head forward.

REEL 5. Shorten the shots and sounds of the Professor's agony after the acid has spurted into his face. Remove if possible all shots of the Professor's face without the mask. The shots immediately following the removal of the mask must be removed, but, if it is impossible to remove all the other shots for reasons of continuity, we will consider retaining one or more of them. We would like out as many as possible of the shots.

"After cuts have been made, we would like to see Reels 1, 3 and 5 again in order that we may decide whether they are sufficiently cut."

Carreras submitted the next cut on 15 May. Trevelyan replied to him on the 17th: "*The Phantom of the Opera* was seen again on Tuesday 15th May with cuts made in order to make the film suitable for the 'A' category. The position is now as follows:

REEL 1. The incident of the man hanging above the stage is still more than we can accept. It should be reduced to an absolute minimum.

REEL 2. The shot of the rat catcher's bleeding face has not been deleted. It must be removed. The big close shot of the man in the mask is still seen in the reel and should be removed.
REEL 3. This scene in which the dwarf appears at the girl's window is acceptable.
REEL 5. Some further reduction is necessary. The shots of the Professor hitting his head against the wall after the accident are too harrowing and should be reduced to an absolute minimum. We would also like to have some further reduction of the shots of the Professor's face without the mask. These shots are really rather strong for the 'A' category.

"On seeing this film again we felt that one further cut should be made in addition to those given in my letter of 7th May. At the opening of the film in the pre-credit sequence, there is a shock shot of the masked face with a gleaming eye. This, coming at the very beginning of the film, intensifies the shock element and we would like this removed. It becomes acceptable when partially covered by titles. I think we are getting near to the 'A' category, but we shall really have to do rather more to the scenes that I have mentioned in this letter. I do not think that further cutting will seriously damage the film. When the further cuts have been made, we shall want to see reels 1, 2 and 5 again. P.S. Since Rank Film Distributors are now directly concerned with the film, I am sending a copy of this letter to Mr Toms for his information."

It isn't clear why Rank were now getting directly involved or why Tony Hinds was absent from the negotiations. However, scribbled notes by the Board's Examiners on 23 May suggest that further cuts were made and Mr J Toms at Rank was notified:

"Seen by AOF, JT and IB. Pre-credit cut made. Reel 1. Hanging man not cut. This should be cut, we think, as follows: only a brief flash of man as he swings forward and then have him swinging back. Reel 2. Rat catcher cut made. The close up face not cut but cut waived. Reel 5. Cut not made but accepted as it stands by majority. Re-submit reel 1. Discussed on telephone with Mr Toms. Only the scene in Reel 1 still to be cleared." Further cuts were apparently made and Reel 1 resubmitted the following day: "Seen by FNC and IB. Only a brief flash of the hanging man's swing forward has been cut. We want reverse. This must be done and only brief flash of the swing forward left."

A note the same day reads, "Explained this to Mr Toms." He was not a happy man and replied to Trevelyan on 25 May: "I have now re-cut the hanging scene and reduced the shot to the absolute minimum consistent with continuity of sound. Actually, this shot is now only a length of some 20 frames in which the man can be clearly seen. I do hope this now meets with your approval, particularly as we have a trade show arranged for early next week." The film was reviewed the same day: "Seen again by JT, AOF and FNC. The corpse swings to and fro but the sight of it has been further reduced. It will now just pass. Film now cleared."

And so *The Phantom of the Opera* finally got its 'A' certificate.

Out of the frying pan into the fire. As if Hammer didn't have troubles enough, their next production would also become a problem picture regarding distribution. *The Old Dark House* was a co-production with US producer William Castle, who was of course no stranger to horror movies having spearheaded a series of 'gimmick' horror pictures in America. Hammer's remake of *The Old Dark House* would contain none of Castle's trademark promotional wheezes, however; they presumably believed that the teaming of Castle and Hammer was a sufficient 'gimmick' in itself.

Roderick (Robert Morley) shows Penderel (Tom Poston) his gun collection in The Old Dark House (1962).

The film was a (very loose) remake of Universal's 1932 classic based on J B Priestley's novel *Benighted*. Like *Captain Clegg* before it, Hammer's tentative plans to remake this film for Universal in 1961 were quashed when they discovered that Castle was preparing his own version in the States. This time, though, as

Tom Penderel (Tom Poston) is caught between the sinister Morgan (Danny Green) and his daughter Morgana (Fenella Fielding) in The Old Dark House (1962).

THE OLD DARK HOUSE

PRINCIPAL PHOTOGRAPHY: 14 May to 22 June 1962
DISTRIBUTION:
 UK: BLC; 77 minutes; Technicolor; certificate 'A'
 US: Columbia; 86 minutes; b/w
UK RELEASE: 16 September 1966, on the ABC circuit with
 Big Deal at Dodge City
US RELEASE: 31 October 1963 with Maniac

DIRECTOR: William Castle; PRODUCERS: William Castle and
Anthony Hinds; ASSOCIATE PRODUCER: Donna Holloway;
SCREENPLAY: Robert Dillon, based on the novel Benighted by J B
Priestley; PRODUCTION DESIGNER: Bernard Robinson; DIRECTOR
OF PHOTOGRAPHY: Arthur Grant; CAMERA OPERATOR: Moray
Grant; GRIP: Albert Cowland; ASSISTANT DIRECTOR: Douglas
Hermes; 2ND ASSISTANT DIRECTOR: Dominic Fulford; 3RD
ASSISTANT DIRECTOR: Hugh Harlow; SUPERVISING EDITOR:
James Needs; MUSIC: Benjamin Frankel; SOUND RECORDIST: Jock
May; SOUND EDITOR: James Groom; MAKE-UP: Roy Ashton;

HAIRSTYLIST: Frieda Steiger; PRODUCTION MANAGER: John
Draper; CONTINUITY: Pauline Wise; WARDROBE SUPERVISOR:
Molly Arbuthnot; WARDROBE MISTRESS: Rosemary Burrows;
SPECIAL EFFECTS: Les Bowie; SPECIAL EFFECTS ASSISTANTS: Kit
West, Ian Scoones; TITLE BACKGROUNDS DRAWN BY: Charles
Addams; CONSTRUCTION MANAGER: Arthur Banks; MASTER
PLASTERER: Stan Banks; MASTER CARPENTER: Charles Davis;
MASTER PAINTER: Lawrence Wrenn; Master ELECTRICIAN: Jack
Curtis; MASTER RIGGER: Ronald Lenoir; PROPS BUYER: Eric
Hillier; PROPS MASTER: Tommy Money

Tom Poston (Tom Penderel); Robert Morley (Roderick Femm);
Janette Scott (Cecily Femm); Joyce Grenfell (Agatha Femm); Mervyn
Johns (Potiphar Femm); Fenella Fielding (Morgana Femm); Peter
Bull (Casper & Jasper Femm); Danny Green (Morgan Femm); John
Harvey (Club receptionist)

UNCREDITED: Amy Dalby (Woman Gambler)

Castle's preparations were still very much in their infancy, they decided to collaborate. Castle had
already visited Bray in the summer of 1961 during filming of The Pirates of Blood River and later, in
March 1962, Tony Hinds flew out to New York to discuss the project with him. As both parties were
at the time contracted to Columbia (indeed, The Terror of the Tongs had gone out alongside Castle's
Homicidal), it seemed appropriate to approach them for financing. Hammer sent a copy of the script
to the BBFC in April and John Trevelyan replied to Tony Nelson Keys on the 16th, explaining that the
material was too much for a 'U' but would be suitable for an 'A' certificate. This did not stop
Hammer's quest for a 'U' when the film was later sent in for certification. William Castle arrived in
England on Tuesday 17 April to direct the picture.

Shooting began at Bray on Monday 14 May. It was time to develop a new team. Moray Grant slipped into the camera operator position (by chance, Len Harris had taken over from him in 1952), with Douglas Hermes stepping in as assistant director. Hermes was no stranger to the fantastic; in 1959 he had been 1st assistant on *Gorgo*. Pauline Wise, who had been trained by Tilly Day, would now take on continuity regularly at Bray. Her husband-to-be, Hugh Harlow, had just returned from National Service. Though the deal was that your employer had to keep your job open, the former 2nd assistant would revert to 3rd for now on *The Old Dark House*. The production benefited from wonderful sets by Bernard Robinson and Don Mingaye, including the interior of the decaying Femm household and the in-construction Ark on the backlot. Oakley Court was used for the exterior shots of the house. The production was lit by the dependable Arthur Grant and supervising editor James Needs took sole charge of the editing with assistant Chris Barnes. Shooting was interrupted at Bray by an electricians' strike and the production went over schedule, ending on Friday 22 June.

While not exactly a rib-tickling comedy, the result is amusing in places and Castle manages to instil enough creepiness to get you at least partially on the edge of your seats. There are sumptuous cameos from several British character stars, while US import Tom Poston had come fresh from another Castle genre film, *Zotz!*. "William Castle was a very funny man," recalls heroine/villainess Janette Scott. "A strange sense of humour that I very quickly got used to. I enjoyed watching people meet him for the first time and being taken aback by him. He would say, 'I'm William Castle. You can call me Mister Castle.' A funny man, a nice man. *The Old Dark House* came along at a time when I was getting absolutely sugary-sweet in the parts I was playing. I absolutely loved it. Even though I was sweet and charming again, in the end, everyone was going to find out that I did it! To all of them!" [4]

In charge of special effects was Les Bowie again, assisted this time by Ian Scoones and Kit West. "I worked very closely with Kit on *The Old Dark House*," recalls Scoones. "It was a black comedy and, apart from the usual floor effects, special props etc, we also had the usual insert shots to shoot as a separate second unit, with Kit 'operating' the camera and lighting. One memorable shot which comes to mind was the 'pushing off' of a statue from a pillar at the gates of the old house. We had rain and lightning as the statue starts to rumble, shake, and eventually fall – plus the fact that we were shooting at night added to the costs. All was OK until we saw the rushes the next day – there was my hand and arm in the position where the statue had originally been! We couldn't cut this, as the statue was still falling in slow motion!

"Les went mad and I was in big trouble – thinking he would have to shoot it again out of his own pocket! He was dreading showing it to William Castle, who was already not very happy working at Bray Studios on the main unit, as there had been a series of strikes by the electricians. Anyhow, fate was shining on me that day – for as Castle viewed the rushes and saw our Bowie insert, he roared with laughter and said, "Gee, that's great Les! It's a joke and there's supposed to be somebody pushing it. Wish I'd thought of it, Les. Keep the arm in – I'll buy it – well done, guys!' So that's how I came to have my first 'bit' part. Kit bought me a double that night!"

Two weeks after *The Old Dark House* started filming at Bray, producer Jimmy Sangster started Hammer's next production, *Maniac*, in the Camargue region of Southern France on Monday 28 May. The last three weeks of interiors were scheduled for Bray but, when *The Old Dark House* ran over schedule at Bray, the scenes were relocated to MGM Studios, Borehamwood. *Maniac* was the second in Jimmy Sangster's series of psychological thrillers and the first of three he would write for Hammer in 1962. In the producer's seat once more, Sangster brought back Michael Carreras as director. This was Carreras' first return to Hammer since he had left to form Capricorn Films in December 1960. He had just completed his first film, *The Savage Guns*, which was shot over October and November 1961 on location in Almería.

Sangster had his *Maniac* script in preparation as early as 16 June 1961. Like *Taste of Fear* before it, the story was full of Sangster's usual twists and turns, detailing the committal to a lunatic asylum of Georges Beynat after viciously killing the man who raped his daughter, Annette. Later, a young American painter, Geoff Farrell, falls in love with Beynat's wife. They plan to help Beynat escape from the asylum in return for a divorce, but Farrell is being tricked and they are releasing her real lover, a deranged male nurse who plans to murder Farrell with an oxyacetylene torch. The climax of the film differs from Sangster's original script, where Geoff saves Annette from the clutches of

The maniacal
Donald Houston
threatens Kerwin
Mathews with his
oxyacetylene torch
in Maniac (1962).

MANIAC

PRINCIPAL PHOTOGRAPHY: 28 May to July 1962
DISTRIBUTION:
  UK: BLC; certificate 'X'
  US: Columbia
86 minutes; b/w; Megascope
UK RELEASE: 20 May 1963, with *The Damned*
US RELEASE: 31 October 1963, with *The Old Dark House*

DIRECTOR: Michael Carreras; PRODUCER: Jimmy Sangster;
SCREENPLAY: Jimmy Sangster; ART DIRECTOR: Edward Carrick;
ASSISTANT ART DIRECTOR: Jean Peyre; DRAUGHTSMAN: Fred
Carter; SCENIC ARTIST: Felix Sergejak; DIRECTOR OF
PHOTOGRAPHY: Wilkie Cooper; CAMERA OPERATOR: Harry
Gillam; FOCUS PULLER: Tommy Fletcher, Trevor Wrenn;
CAMERA GRIP: L Kelly; CLAPPER/LOADER: Ray Andrew; ASSISTANT
DIRECTOR: Ross MacKenzie; 2ND ASSISTANT DIRECTOR: Terry Lens;
SUPERVISING EDITOR: James Needs; EDITOR: Tom Simpson; MUSIC:
Stanley Black; MUSIC SUPERVISOR: John Hollingsworth; SOUND
RECORDIST: Cyril Swern; BOOM OPERATOR: Bill Baldwin; SOUND

CAMERA OPERATOR: Ron Matthews; SOUND MAINTENANCE: Peter
Martingell; SOUND EDITOR: Roy Baker; MAKE-UP: Basil Newall;
ASSISTANT MAKE-UP: Stella Morris; HAIRSTYLIST: Pat McDermott;
PRODUCTION MANAGER: Bill Hill; CONTINUITY: Kay Rawlings;
WARDROBE SUPERVISOR: Molly Arbuthnot; WARDROBE
MISTRESS: Jean Fairlie; ASSISTANT TO PRODUCER: Ian Lewis;
MAIN TITLES: Chambers & Partners; PRODUCTION SECRETARY:
Marguerite Green; PROP BUYER: Margery Whittington; STILLS
PHOTOGRAPHER: James Swarbrick; CARPENTER: Tommy
Westbrook; PAINTER: A Smith; STAGEHAND: E Power; RIGGER:
V Bailey; ELECTRICAL SUPERVISOR: Bert Chapple; ELECTRICAL
CHARGEHAND: Geoff Hughes; PROP CHARGEHAND: Tommy
Ibbetson; PROPERTY STAND-BY: M Lord; DRIVER: Ron Warr

Kerwin Mathews (Geoff Farrell); Nadia Gray (Eve Baynat); Donald
Houston (Georges Beynat); Liliane Brousse (Annette Baynat);
Norman Bird (Salon [gendarme]); George Pastell (Inspector
Etienne); Jerold Wells (Giles); Arnold Diamond (Janiello); Leon Peers
(Blanchard); Juistine Lord (Grace)

the bogus Beynat, who is duly arrested and led off by the police. Hammer must have thought this an anti-climax and in the end decided to finish Beynat off, when Annette pushes him off a ledge after he loses his footing.

Unfortunately, Michael Carreras was let loose with his widescreen lens and the first half of the film almost turns into a travelogue of the French Camargue. Locations used included Arles and its arena; Bac du Sauvage (for the exterior of the café), Les Baux (countryside and caves), Stes Maries de la Mer, Plaine de la Crau and Alberon. While beautiful to watch, the film does not evoke the creepy mood and unnerving tension that Seth Holt had mustered throughout *Taste of Fear*.

It was just like Hammer, after an impromptu break, to suddenly kick off two productions at the same time. Again, this meant finding a second crew, with the core team employed on the Bray feature. The second team comprised Ray Harryhausen's favourite DP, Wilkie Cooper; highly respected art director Edward Carrick, and Bill Hill, Sangster's production manager from *Taste of Fear*. Molly Arbuthnot supervised wardrobe on both productions; Rosemary Burrows assisted on *The Old Dark House*, Jean Fairlie on *Maniac*.

The casting was also good. Kerwin Mathews returned after his *Blood River* (he had been replaced by Don Taylor at the last minute on Carreras' *The Savage Guns*). He recalls, "This was my first extended stay in France, particularly in the South. I've lived there occasionally since then. I'm a blatant Francophile because of *Maniac*! Michael Carreras was just breaking through my shield of insecurities on *Maniac* and I always wished we could have had another chance on another film, as he found his way as a director and I matured as an actor." [5] Berlin-born Nadia Gray, remembered for her role as the stripteasing Countess in Fellini's *La dolce vita* (1960), asked during shooting if a friend could visit the set. Sangster reluctantly agreed, provided he kept well out of the way. Imagine his surprise when the friend turned out to be none other than Orson Welles... Donald Houston, according to the British pressbook, "found his role so frightening that it kept him awake at nights." Hammer veteran George Pastell looks a little out of place as the inspector, while poor Norman Bird is all too obviously dubbed by André Maranne, the clerk in the *Pink Panther* films.

Maniac finished shooting in mid-July, with earlier Hammer products finally being let loose in the nation's cinemas. First up was the double-bill of *Captain Clegg* and *The Phantom of the Opera*, which premièred at the Leicester Square Theatre on 7 June and went on general release from the 25th. To live up to its Gothic partner, Hammer bolstered *Clegg*'s more sinister undertones, the poster concentrating on the Marsh Phantoms with the impressive declaration, "Their oath was ... terror! Their cry ... blood!" Even Universal tried to capitalise on this by releasing it as *Night Creatures* in the US on 13 June. The film remained a favourite of Peter Cushing and in 1972 he even wrote a 22-page draft outline for a further remake called *Waiting Revenge*. Sadly, this was never realised. However, while *Clegg*'s reviews were favourable by and large, *Phantom*, in which Hammer had invested so many hopes, came under harsh attack and box-office takings were correspondingly unimpressive.

Luckily, Christopher Lee's pirate team came to the rescue. *The Pirates of Blood River* was paired up with Ray Harryhausen's *Mysterious Island* and premièred at the London Pavilion on 13 July, the pair going on general release on the ABC circuit from 13 August and forming Britain's top-grossing double-bill of 1962. The success of *Blood River* could not have come at a better time. It would at least ensure the survival of Hammer's colourful swashbuckling adventures, which would make up half their output the following year.

Paranoiac was the third in Sangster's suspense thriller series. This time it was not based on an original story by Sangster but on a Josephine Tey novel, *Brat Farrar*, which Hammer had acquired the rights to in 1954. They first advertised the film in their 1955 schedule but nothing materialised. The project next appeared as part of Hammer's 11-film production programme for 1958-9. The *Daily Cinema* had reported it as part of a programme of "four big international co-productions" on Monday 16 June 1958, and that it would "be made in Technicolor for Columbia release." Once more the project was cancelled. It would seem that after the success of *Taste of Fear*, the script was taken off the shelf again and given to Jimmy Sangster to rewrite.

An impostor claiming to be the dead Tony Ashby presents himself to his brother, unstable lout Simon, his fragile sister Eleanor, and his weak aunt Harriet. Eleanor is due her half share of the Ashby fortune and it seems that Simon is trying to drive her insane to cheat her of it. The bogus Tony eventually falls for Eleanor and they find the mummified body of the real Tony, bricked up in the family chapel, murdered by his brother when he was a boy. Sangster's screenplay retains the essence of Tey's tale with some changes, notably the removal of the novel's central showjumping theme. Sangster twisted the character of Simon into a fiery pub-brawling lunatic and the convenient fire at the end was also Hammer's conception, Patrick [ie, Simon] having toppled the murderous Tony over the edge of a quarry in the book.

This was Anthony Nelson Keys' second film as producer, this time assisted by his brother Basil in the associate producer's chair. Tony Keys submitted the scripts for *Paranoiac* and Hammer's next production, *The Kiss of the Vampire*, to John Trevelyan on 5 July. Reader Newton Branch was not impressed with the former, reporting on 9 July:

Happy families – Oliver Reed, Sheila Burrell, Alexander Davion and Janette Scott in Paranoiac (1962).

PARANOIAC

PRINCIPAL PHOTOGRAPHY: 23 July to 31 August 1962
DISTRIBUTION:
  UK: Rank; certificate 'X'
  US: Universal
82 minutes; b/w
UK RELEASE:
  TRADE SHOW: 7 September 1963, at the Hammer
    Theatre, Hammer House
  GENERAL RELEASE: 26 January 1964, with The Kiss of the
    Vampire
US RELEASE: 15 May 1963

DIRECTOR: Freddie Francis; PRODUCER: Anthony Nelson Keys;
ASSOCIATE PRODUCER: Basil Keys; SCREENPLAY: Jimmy Sangster;
PRODUCTION DESIGNER: Bernard Robinson; ART DIRECTOR: Don
Mingaye; ASSISTANT ART DIRECTOR: Ken Ryan; DIRECTOR OF
PHOTOGRAPHY: Arthur Grant; CAMERA OPERATOR: Moray
Grant; FOCUS PULLERS: David Osborne and Robin Higginson;
CAMERA GRIP: Albert Cowland; CLAPPER/LOADER: Bob Jordan;
CAMERA MAINTENANCE: John Kerley; ASSISTANT DIRECTOR:
Ross MacKenzie; 2ND ASSISTANT DIRECTOR: Hugh Harlow; 3RD
ASSISTANT DIRECTOR: Ray Corbett; SUPERVISING EDITOR: James
Needs; ASSISTANT EDITOR: Chris Barnes; MUSIC: Elisabeth Lutyens;
MUSIC SUPERVISOR: John Hollingsworth; SOUND RECORDIST: Ken

Rawkins; BOOM: Ken Nightingale; BOOM ASSISTANT: R A Mingaye;
SOUND MAINTENANCE: Charles Bouvet; SOUND EDITOR: James
Groom; SOUND TRANSFER OPERATOR: Al Thorne; MAKE-UP: Roy
Ashton; MAKE-UP ASSISTANT: Richard Mills; HAIRSTYLIST: Frieda
Steiger; PRODUCTION MANAGER: John Draper; CONTINUITY:
Pauline Wise; WARDROBE SUPERVISOR: Molly Arbuthnot;
WARDROBE MISTRESS: Rosemary Burrows; SPECIAL EFFECTS:
Les Bowie; SPECIAL EFFECTS ASSISTANTS: Kit West, Ian Scoones;
CONSTRUCTION MANAGER: Arthur Banks; MASTER PLASTERER:
Stan Banks; MASTER CARPENTER: Charles Davis; MASTER
PAINTER: Lawrence Wrenn; MASTER ELECTRICIAN: Jack Curtis;
MASTER RIGGER: Ronald Lenoir; PROPS BUYER: Eric Hillier;
PROPS MASTER: Tommy Money; PRODUCTION SECRETARY:
Maureen White; STILLS PHOTOGRAPHER: Curtis Reeks; STUDIO
MANAGER: A F Kelly; PUBLICIST: Brian Boyle; FLOOR PROPS
CHARGEHAND: W. Smith; ELECTRICAL CHARGEHANDS: George
Robinson, Vic Hemmings; DRIVERS: 'Coco' Epps, Laurie Martin

Janette Scott (Eleanor Ashby); Oliver Reed (Simon Ashby); Liliane
Brousse (Françoise); Alexander Davion (Tony); Sheila Burrell
(Harriet); Maurice Denham (John Kossett); John Bonney (Keith
Kossett); John Stuart (Williams); Colin Tapley (Vicar); Harold Lang
(RAF type); Laurie Leigh (first woman); Marianne Stone (second
woman); Sydney Bromley (tramp); Jack Taylor (sailor)

"This is atrocious rubbish, obviously aimed at the 'X' category and a nasty audience. The
problems are:

The suggestions of incestuous love
P.8. Simon touches aunt Harriet's cheek with his hand. She lets it stay there, then pulls away
and he says unpleasantly, 'There, we could have the whole house to ourselves.'
P.23. Simon says to Harriet 'What are you upset about aunty? The fact that I sneak up to see that

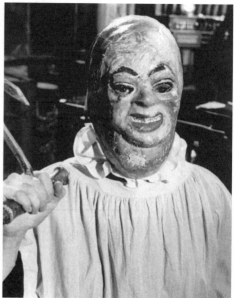

LEFT: *The crazed Oliver Reed in Paranoiac (1962).*

ABOVE: *The grotesque figure strikes in Paranoiac (1962).*

'poor girl' (ie, Marjorie) ... or the fact that I don't sneak up here?' (ie, to Harriet's bedroom). "Though we have been told that the real Tony had been a choir boy in the church (in the opening sequence), I still cannot understand why aunt Harriet has to dress up as a choir boy while Simon has his bizarre sessions at the chapel organ and a gramophone plays a choir boy's song. Is there meant to be something about all this that this foolish examiner has missed? Why does Simon plunge into the burning chapel at the end shouting, 'I'm coming ... Tony?' and then, suicide? In the case of Tony and Brad-Tony and Eleanor, the incestuous feelings are very clear. Though his sister may not be conscious of them, the audience will be left in no doubt about these peculiar relationships.

Pp.12-13. In a conversation between Marjorie and Eleanor, I got the first hint of something slightly abnormal between brother and sister.

P.75. Brad-Tony says uneasily, 'Perhaps I'm not this brother you remember?' She answers, 'Yes you are. And having you near me makes me feel safe ... Remember how I used to get into bed with you when I was frightened, and how you used to put your arms around me and talk till everything was all right?' At this, 'a shadow of embarrassment' flicks across Brad-Tony's face.

P.79. After their escape from the sabotaged car, Eleanor embraces Tony. He registers 'depression and doubt.'

Pp.90-91. Eleanor gives Tony a lingering kiss. Suddenly the penny drops. She derives that this Tony is an impostor. He admits it. 'Thank God,' she says.

"Incest is becoming fashionable in films these days, but we should discourage it as a gimmick in rubbish of this sort. Enough that Eleanor has a deep sisterly love for her brother which turns to womanly love when she knows that the 'prodigal brother' is an impostor.

Straight Sex   ·

Pp.20-22. It is very obvious that Marjorie is the mistress of Simon. This bedroom scene, with a dress that comes unbuttoned twice, should be all right for 'X'.

P.80. But 'Marjorie, presumably with nothing on, is lying on the bed, covered with a sheet' (while shirt sleeved Simon is looking out of the window etc...) needs caution.

Horror and Sacrilege

Pp.46, 85-86, 101. My dictionary defines the latter as 'the sin or act of violating or profaning anything sacred, including sacramental vows.' Though the private chapel may have been disused for a number of years, the horrid goings-on in the Ashby chapel cannot but give offence to a great many people for religious reasons, quite apart from the bad taste of Mr Sangster run amok on consecrated grounds. It is the mixture of horror and sacrilege which makes these sequences so peculiarly cheap, ghoulish and nasty.

"The horror can easily be clipped, but the general idea can't be, without radical changes. If these can't be made, I think we should menace Hammer with rejection. I can only suggest that the chapel be turned into a family vault (cf, *Premature Burial*, where skeletons fall out of cupboards, etc). This is the more acceptable guise of the Grand Guignol horror film. There Simon can play the organ and have hidden away his murdered brother and so on to his heart's content. But surely we do not want an altar as a centrepiece behind which a boy has been murdered by his 15 year old brother, on which a gramophone keeps playing choir boy songs, on which Simon finally perishes and by which the hero has been strung up as if crucified etc, etc. We have had cowboys shooting it out in a belfry and a werewolf, with 'the curse', being shot in a belfry, but never before have we had such ludicrous goings-on in a church or chapel.

Violence

P.93. Perhaps there is a misprint when Marjorie is knocked for a loop '20 feet into the air' by Simon's car. Two feet might do – or, as a flight of fancy, 200 feet. But not 20 feet. Nor do we want to see anything unduly nasty of her after this final experience."

Frank Crofts added on 11 July: "A few years ago neither the Board nor the public would have had to worry with this sort of stuff. I agree with NKB that we do not want incest between apparent brother and sister or between aunt and nephew: the later suggestion is Sangster's and Simon's idea of light relief – at least Simon had the excuse that he was insane. Also there should be no goings-on in a chapel. Most of these changes are quite simple, because the author has put them in only to dress up a ridiculously weak story. I agree about the car, murder and bed scene. Add P.10 Eleanor's night-dress (visible up to P.16) should not be too 'diaphanous'.

"Even on its own level, this story is weak. What is the point of Harriet's masquerading as a choirboy, armed and with a horror mask on? (of course we can guess why the author put the mask in). The author doesn't even bother to be consistent – P.85: 'Standing close to the organ, back to the camera, is a small figure, dressed in a choir boy's surplice ... then the boy stands up, disclosing a full-grown person who up until now has been kneeling.' Can we believe that if Simon was a homicidal maniac he would not have committed a murder or assault between the ages of 15 (murder of Tony) and 23 (attempts on Tony and Eleanor; murder of Marjorie) or that in any case no one except Harriet would have known about his madness? Would Marjorie, a trained nurse, have had an affair with him or wanted to go off with him? How did Keith embezzle money from the family property, when it was in the charge of his upright father? Who would risk imprisonment for impersonation – or indeed the difficulties and embarrassments inherent in such an impersonation for the sake of only £100? (p.64) How did a 15 year old boy murder his elder brother [and] inter him in the family chapel without anyone knowing? How could Keith have got Brad into knowing (a) where the various rooms in the house were (b) what presents he received from everyone on each birthday (Pp.60-61)? As though anyone, however genuine, could remember such things."

Unsurprisingly, Sangster was forced to make 'some revisions' and Anthony Nelson Keys forwarded the 'final' screenplay on the 16th. The new script fell to Audrey Field, who wrote on 19 July: "JT. I have not passed revised script to a second reader, as Newton and Frank both read the first and IB is away. If you would like anyone to read it, will you please pass it on yourself? I have not read (and don't think I need read) the previous script. The story seems to be basically unchanged, except that Simon's mistress (now called Frieda) is held under water till she drowns, instead of being knocked 20 feet into the air by a motor car.

"This seems to be the garbled remains of a good, tense mystery story by (I think) Josephine Tey, called *Brat Farrar*. I don't remember the story very well, but I don't think there was any incestuous feeling between the murderer and the aunt; there was a painful time for the sister when she found herself falling for the impostor, whom she still believed to be her brother. There was certainly none of the macabre denouement in the chapel: I believe the brother's body was found by Brat when he fell into a disused quarry.

"I fully agree with the readers of the first script about incest needlessly dragged into this type of thriller: the idea of Eleanor falling for 'Tony' when she still thinks he is her brother is not without precedent in thrillers and I think it will pass, except that it is needlessly rubbed in here. But there is no need for the 'aunt' incest idea, or for any overt suggestion that Eleanor was nearly in love with her real brother (however, I think that this latter element is no more than discreetly hinted at, and it might pass for 'X'). I also fully agree that the body ought not to be discovered anywhere in a chapel; nor should the final destruction by fire take place there. They must I fear be allowed some sort of disgusting exhibition of the long-dead brother, on the lines of *Psycho*, but it ought to be less horrible than *Psycho*, because the film does not display the Hitchcock expertise and I am afraid disgust will get the better of surprise."

She went on to list her objections which were summarised in a letter from John Trevelyan to Tony Hinds on the 25th: "In general the film should be suitable for the 'X' category, but there are two general points about which we have some concern.

1. There is a clear suggestion of incestuous relations between Simon and Aunt Harriet. This should be avoided and their relations shown solely as one in which the aunt spoils him to an absurd extent. With this in view, I suggest that you should avoid the hints of incest on pages 8-9 ... and you should certainly alter [the scene] where the aunt is undressing Simon after he has got wet. Such a line as 'Enjoying yourself, Aunty?' would be impossible. There is also a possible hint of incest in the past between Eleanor and the real Tony. I do not think that this was intended but it might be so interpreted ... This should be avoided.

2. We are concerned about the scenes in the chapel. We have found from experience that a lot of people object to what seems to them to be sacrilege, and I think this would fall into that category. I think that you can get over the difficulty quite easily by making it a family vault with an organ in it, and avoid showing an altar, crucifix or any such obvious Christian symbols. You pointed out that the film opens with a family grave out of doors. This is clearly shown to be a recent grave and one can indicate that the family vault used by ancestors of earlier centuries was now full up. In any case it seems a more appropriate place than a chapel to bury the corpse of the brother.

"Apart from these two general comments I have comments on points of detail as follows:

<u>Page 12 Scene 26.</u> See my general comments. Frieda's talk about drowned bodies is really rather nasty and macabre in the circumstances, and I hope that you can either modify it or make it possible to cut if necessary.

<u>Page 19-22 Scene 51-4.</u> While it can be clear that Frieda does not mind Simon coming into her room when she is not dressed, we do not want her stripped down or any shots of her bare breasts or titillating semi-nudity. Aunt Harriet's participation in this scene would be all right provided that the suggestion of incest was removed.

<u>Page 69-70 Scene 123.</u> I hope you can find some way of avoiding the use of a broken bottle, which is a dangerous and easily obtainable weapon.

<u>Page 74 Scene 182.</u> See my general comments. We think that Aunt Harriet will have to have maternal feelings for Simon if she behaves in the way that she apparently does.

<u>Page 76 Scene 130.</u> Eleanor's reference to Tony having being in the habit of getting into bed with her when she had nightmares and the false Tony's reactions are tricky, and should be done in such a way as to avoid any suggestion of an incestuous relationship.

<u>Page 80 Scene 156.</u> The script direction describes Frieda as seen presumably with nothing on lying in the bed covered with a sheet. Sexual titillation should be avoided.

<u>Page 81 Scene 156.</u> We do not care for Simon's suggestion that Frieda enjoyed his cruelty. This is nasty sex sadism.

<u>Page 89-90 Scene 172-7.</u> This may well be a tricky scene. I suggest that in this scene the 'light kiss' should not turn into a passionate one and that she should not keep on about being 'dirty'. The line which causes us most concern is 'You're my brother and I'm in love with you.' Surely the situation could be made clear without being so explicit.

<u>Page 94 Scene 179-80.</u> The drowning of Frieda as scripted is much too long and unpleasant. It is made worse by the previous embrace, and I hope you can avoid this.

Two contact-sheet pictures from Paranoiac (1962), showing the crew preparing to film Oliver Reed, and the scene where the car falls over the cliff.

Page 102-9 Scene 188-198. See my general comments about the alteration of the setting from a chapel to a family vault. Blasphemy must be avoided. Surely you can find something other than an altar to move to get to the wall. The visuals of the dead body may well be very macabre, and if they come out in a way that we regard as disgusting we shall have to cut them. You should avoid having Tony tied to the cross-beam in a way that makes it appear to be a parody of the crucifixion. I suppose we must have Aunt Harriet dressed in a surplice: this may be acceptable if it is clearly not a place of worship. I think you should avoid the vicious kick aimed at Tony's head, Page 104 [scene] 188."

Tony Hinds replied to Trevelyan the same day: "I have made careful note of all the advice you have given me regarding *Paranoiac*, and I am sure we can protect ourselves in every instance so that the final result for the UK market will be quite acceptable. For various reasons with which I will not bore you, it is not very convenient for us to change the chapel to a vault. However, my Art Director has suggested that we can make the chapel into a completely ruined chapel, as we did in *The Hound of the Baskervilles* (where it was apparently entirely acceptable). We will remove the altar, or any suggestion of an altar, and the organ will be the only part of the chapel in really good repair. I think you will agree that this covers your concern about this point. Wherever possible, we will refer to it in the dialogue as 'the ruined chapel'."

Trevelyan replied to Hinds on 27 July: "While we would prefer a family vault to a ruined chapel, I think that we would accept the latter provided that it was roughly similar to that in *The Hound of the Baskervilles*. The important thing is for you to avoid any recognisable Christian symbols, eg: altar, crucifix, etc."

Shooting began at Bray on Monday 23 July. At the helm was Academy Award-winning cinematographer Freddie Francis. He was now branching out into direction, having previously lit Hammer's *Never Take Sweets from a Stranger*. Arthur Grant returned as lighting cameraman, though under the more than watchful eye of Francis himself. "I was very fond of Arthur," remembers Francis, "and I knew he had it in him to do better stuff than he did normally, so it was a very friendly relationship, because I liked him very much. And I used to sort of encourage him, because I knew he was sort of thirsting for encouragement." [6] Returning from *The Old Dark House* were production manager John Draper and camera operator Moray Grant. Assistant director Ross MacKenzie joined the production fresh from *Maniac*. Hugh Harlow now got his regular spot back as 2nd assistant, while Ray Corbett stepped into 3rd. Ken Rawkins joined the team as Hammer's regular sound recordist. Bernard Robinson and Don Mingaye revamped the interior sets of Femm Hall from *The Old Dark House* for the grand Ashby household. (There must have been a touch of déjà vu for Janette Scott as she descended the hall's Y-shaped staircase.) Ken Ryan now joined the team as assistant art director.

Roy Ashton had two challenges on *Paranoiac*. The first was designing the garish mask that Aunt Harriet wears to protect her nephew. The second was in creating the decomposing body of Tony Ashby. "First of all I obtained a medical skeleton and rubberised the face and hands, to which I added layers of tissue paper," remembered Ashton. "I took great pains over the face, though it came out looking like thin concrete in the finished film because of the way it was lit. I prided myself on the subtlety of the decaying features as I flaked the skin and gave the poor chap a few hairs, warts, bumps, and made sure the colouring was right. When the body was finished, I used to keep him in my workshop, locking him out of harm's way at night in a cupboard. One evening I forgot to do this and the next morning the cleaning woman came in, only to rush straight out shouting that there was a dead man in the make-up room!" [7] Unfortunately, we see the corpse only fleetingly in the finished film (courtesy the BBFC) and it seems Roy's hard work was in vain – particularly when one consults publicity photographs of it, confirming Roy's incredible eye for detail.

Shooting ended on Friday 31 August after six weeks. Editors Needs and Barnes and sound editor James Groom now took *Paranoiac* to Hammer House for post-production and Freddie Francis brought in Elisabeth Lutyens to score the movie. "I asked Elisabeth Lutyens to do the film because she did the music for *Never Take Sweets from a Stranger*, which I thought was very good," explains Francis. "That's why I wanted her to do it, not that normally one had much choice. I probably got her because she was cheap. I sort of showed her the film, told her I'd like that music and told her the way I felt about it. And then they had John Hollingsworth, the music director, who also spoke to her. So she went away and did it. And this is one of the terrible things about films. Even a big budget film's music is a terrible risk, because you try to explain to the composer what you want and you really don't know until the day comes to record the music if he's seen it right. If he's seen it wrong, then we're in trouble. But her score was, I thought, terrific." [8] So much so that Lutyens was retained for several of Francis' films for rival outfit, Amicus.

After the success of *The Brides of Dracula*, Hammer were quick to make plans for their third film in the series. James Carreras had written to Tony Hinds on 11 July 1960: "*Brides of Dracula* is taking a packet in the USA. It has opened at that graveyard, the Odeon Marble Arch, to really fantastic business, which makes me think that we can start another one for Universal sometime in 1962. Would you please put the wheels in motion so that well before that time we can have a script which has been approved by Universal." Indeed, Carreras then wrote to Universal on 4 August 1960: "I have seen your letter of August 1st to Dennison Thornton and am very happy to see that *Brides of Dracula* continues to do very well at the box office. Tony Hinds has already started an outline on *Dracula 3* and would appreciate your OK on this subject as soon as possible. I have no doubt that there is room for another one."

Michael Carreras first declared the production to the press in December 1960 and *Dracula 3* duly appeared on Hammer's schedules on 2 January 1961. Tony Hinds set himself to write it under his nom de plume, John Elder. Though the project started out as *Dracula 3*, this time the action was even further removed from Stoker and became a plain old vampire story, with no reference to the Count or Van Helsing, under the revised title of *The Kiss of the Vampire*. The opening and closing scenes were lifted from discarded segments of old *Brides* scripts. Hinds borrowed the opening

Dr Ravna (Noel Willman) with disciples (Isobel Black, Barry Warren and Jacquie Wallis) in The Kiss of the Vampire (1962).

THE KISS OF THE VAMPIRE

PRINCIPAL PHOTOGRAPHY: 7 September to 25 October 1962
DISTRIBUTION:
  UK: Rank; certificate 'X'
  US: Universal; US TITLE: The Kiss of Evil
87 minutes; Eastman Colour
UK RELEASE:
  PREMIÈRE: 5 January 1964, at the New Victoria
  GENERAL RELEASE: 26 January 1964, with Paranoiac
US RELEASE: 11 September 1963

DIRECTOR: Don Sharp; PRODUCER: Anthony Hinds; SCREENPLAY: John Elder; PRODUCTION DESIGNER: Bernard Robinson; ART DIRECTOR: Don Mingaye; ASSISTANT ART DIRECTOR: Ken Ryan; DIRECTOR OF PHOTOGRAPHY: Alan Hume; CAMERA OPERATOR: Moray Grant; FOCUS PULLER: David Osborne; CAMERA GRIP: Albert Cowland; CLAPPER/LOADER: Bob Jordan; CAMERA MAINTENANCE: John Kerley; ASSISTANT DIRECTOR: Douglas Hermes; 2ND ASSISTANT DIRECTOR: Hugh Harlow; SUPERVISING EDITOR: James Needs; MUSIC: James Bernard; MUSIC SUPERVISOR: John Hollingsworth; PIANO SOLOIST: Douglas Gamley; SOUND RECORDIST: Ken Rawkins; BOOM OPERATOR: Ken Nightingale; BOOM ASSISTANT: R A Mingaye; SOUND MAINTENANCE: Charles Bouvet; SOUND CAMERA OPERATOR: Al Thorne; SOUND EDITOR: James Groom; SOUND TRANSFER OPERATOR: H C Allan; MAKE-UP:

Roy Ashton; MAKE-UP ASSISTANT: Reginald Mills; PRODUCTION MANAGER: Don Weeks; CONTINUITY: Pauline Wise; WARDROBE SUPERVISOR: Molly Arbuthnot; WARDROBE MISTRESS: Rosemary Burrows; SPECIAL EFFECTS: Les Bowie; SPECIAL EFFECTS ASSISTANTS: Kit West, Ian Scoones, Brian Johncock, Ray Caple; CONSTRUCTION MANAGER: Arthur Banks; MASTER PLASTERER: Stan Banks; MASTER CARPENTER: Charles Davis; MASTER PAINTER: Lawrence Wrenn; MASTER ELECTRICIAN: Jack Curtis; ELECTRICAL CHARGEHANDS: George Robinson, Vic Hemmings; MASTER RIGGER: Ronald Lenoir; PROPS BUYER: Eric Hillier; PROPS MASTER: Tommy Money; FLOOR PROPS CHARGEHAND: Peter Day; DRIVERS: 'Coco' Epps, Laurie Martin; PRODUCTION SECRETARY: Maureen White; STILLS PHOTOGRAPHER: Curtis Reeks; PUBLICIST: Brian Doyle; CHIEF ACCOUNTANT: W H V Able; STUDIO MANAGER: A F Kelly; CASTING DIRECTOR: Irene Lamb; CHOREOGRAPHER: Leslie Edwards

Clifford Evans (Professor Zimmer); Noel Willman (Ravna); Edward De Souza (Gerald Harcourt); Jennifer Daniel (Marianne); Barry Warren (Carl); Jacquie Wallis (Sabena); Isobel Black (Tania); Peter Madden (Bruno); Vera Cook (Anna); Noel Howlett (Father Xavier); Brian Oulton (First Disciple); John Harvey (Police Sergeant); Stan Simmons (Servant); Olga Dickie (First Woman at Graveyard); Margaret Read (First Girl Disciple); Elizabeth Valentine (Second Girl Disciple)

sequence from Sangster's first draft screenplay, called Disciple of Dracula, where the hero, Latour, kills a vampire woman by slamming a spade through her coffin lid. Hinds was also impressed by the climax of Peter Bryan's November 1959 draft script, where Van Helsing calls forth a horde of bats in a satanic ritual to dispose of the vampire. Peter Cushing had objected to the scene and it was dropped, but Hinds eagerly resurrected it for his climax, where now it is Professor Zimmer who performs the ceremony to destroy Dr Ravna and his coven of vampires.

Anthony Nelson Keys submitted a script to John Trevelyan in July 1961. Trevelyan replied to him on the 27th: "We have now read the script entitled *The Kiss of the Vampire*. We note that this is a first draft screenplay, and this suggests that there is to be at least another draft which, from the notes on page 1, would seem to be longer. The best thing that I can do therefore is to give you general guidance. The theme is somewhat familiar, and we think that it would be acceptable for the 'X' category, provided that you succeed in avoiding disgusting detail. With the 'X' category in mind I have the following comments to make:

Page 2-3 Scene 1. This burial scene might be extremely nasty. As you know, we have had trouble with stakes going into vampires before, and we have always wanted you to avoid shots of the stakes going in and shots of blood welling out. Here a spade is used, which is a variant, but the blood is still there. We would want as little as possible of this, and as much as possible of what is happening should be inferred rather than shown.

Page 50 Scene 62. Care will have to be taken with the shot of Ravna with a thin trickle of blood appearing at the corner of his mouth and staining the bed. This is rather nauseating stuff.

Page 52-3 Scene 65. As you will know from the past, we are always worried about scenes which are a mixture of vampirism and sex. This scene falls into this category. The script direction says 'His eyes blaze with lust, his lips draw back in an animal smile...' I think that we must permit him to enfold her in a not too lustful embrace and then get on with the blood-sucking, but this should all be kept to an absolute minimum.

Page 67 Scene 77. Although Zimmer is here condemning vampirism, his phrases are perhaps a bit unfortunate in places. In particular we do not care for '...he can persuade himself that his filthy perversion is really some new and wonderful experience, to be experienced only by the favoured few ...' 'Filthy perversion' implies a sexual implication. I suggest that this is modified.

Page 74 Scene 91. In this scene again the sex should be kept down. We would prefer 'I will obey only you' to 'I love only you', with the appropriate modifications where necessary.

Page 75 Scene 91. We would not care to see a shot of Tania ripping open Gerald's shirt and giving him a vampire bite. Surely the scene could be shot in a discreet and less disgusting way, just enough to establish what happens and to provide blood for Gerald's subsequent action. Here again we would not want too much blood about.

Page 76 Scene 91. Here there is a bit of violence, and the servant's face is seen bleeding. In this film the less blood the better.

Page 77 Scene 97. We would want no nasty shots resulting from the gargoyle landing on the servant's head.

Page 83-4 Scene 106-13. Although we appreciate that this is not black magic or a parody of Christian rituals, discretion should be used in these scenes.

Page 84-5 Scene 114-6. The bats attack the vampires and overcome Ravna; he is last seen covered by their pulsating bodies. This all sounds very nasty and I must ask you to use great discretion. Surely you could have a kind of nightmare sequence of surrealist bats, without our seeing them fasten on anyone or sucking them dry. I must just tell you that we have our doubts about this scene and leave it to your good sense to find something that is acceptable. "I note that the author suggests that black paper bats should be released in the auditorium during this final scene. Although this is not really my business, I do not think that it would be a good idea and I have no doubt that it would produce criticism, so I hope you will discourage anything of the kind."

Throughout July and August, Terence Fisher had sought refuge in East Germany and Ireland with *Sherlock Holmes und das Halsband des Todes* (aka *Sherlock Holmes and the Deadly Necklace*), starring Christopher Lee and Fisher favourite Thorley Walters as Holmes and Watson. It is possible that this made Fisher unavailable for the scheduled September start of *The Kiss of the Vampire*. But was the Hammer/Fisher relationship cooling off somewhat after the poor box-office returns from *The Two Faces of Dr Jekyll*, *The Curse of the Werewolf* and *The Phantom of the Opera*? Whatever the situation, Tony Hinds approached Australian director Don Sharp instead. Born in Hobarth, Tasmania in 1922, Sharp remembers: "I met with Tony Hinds and told him that I'd never seen a horror picture. He said

*Edward De Souza
awakes to find his
wife missing –
Noel Howlett and
Peter Madden
maintain a
suspicious silence
in The Kiss of the
Vampire (1962).*

to me, 'Well, from what I've seen of your work I think you'd be able to handle it, but why don't I run a few for you?' So over the next few days I saw *The Curse of Frankenstein*, *Dracula* and *The Stranglers of Bombay* at Hammer House in Wardour Street. What intrigued me about them was that after about 20 minutes I was totally hooked despite a totally absurd situation. I thought it was wonderful – here was a genre with its own ground rules and self-contained world, and you could be theatrical but treat it realistically to grab the audience and make them believe something absurd." [9]

Attempting to break the Cushing/Lee mould, Sharp, no doubt influenced by his own theatrical background, decided to bring in a number of classical actors. Clifford Evans, of course, had played Don Alfredo in *The Curse of the Werewolf*, while Edward de Souza was also no stranger to Hammer, having starred in the previous year's *The Phantom of the Opera*. Isobel Black, cast as fascinating teen vampire Tania, had come to Hammer's attention via the TV drama *Emergency Ward 10*.

"My recollection is of coming in to work knowing that I was going to have a good time," says Edward de Souza. "It was really a wonderfully friendly place. You see, the thing was that, whatever film you were making at Bray, it was the only piece of work that was being done, so everything was focused onto what you were doing and so you felt very important without feeling self-important; you knew that you were involved in the only piece of work. Whereas if you went to Elstree, there would be all sorts of things going on and you never felt the same sort of specialness. Somehow or other I think that the fact there was only one movie being made at a time at this studio, that specialness rubbed off – everybody felt special, the films felt special – everybody – and that was part of the friendliness and part of the way in which those films weren't turned out like sausages. Each one had its own particular story to tell and each one was done with a special devotion."

Shooting started at Bray on Friday 7 September. Don Sharp recalls that "I thought it [the script] was a bit too bloody and a bit too gruesome. I always felt it was better to tease an audience with suspense than to show them everything. It's what they don't know that they fear. The less often you show a particular horror, the better. You can hit an audience quite hard in the beginning, then tease them along and go for a big climax. He agreed. He was marvellous, and so we did some changes. Tony Hinds is just about the best producer I ever worked with." [10]

The rich colour photography was this time the work of Alan Hume, highlighting yet more exquisite sets by Bernard Robinson. The lavish interiors of Chateau Ravna conjure up memories of

The secret of the bats revealed. The rubber bats are suspended on their wire frame outside Bernard Robinson's impressive stained glass window for the climax of The Kiss of the Vampire (1962).

Castle Dracula and Chateau Meinster. Indeed, the twisted pillars and triangular candelabra in Ravna's house are the same ones that adorned the stairs and dining room set of *Dracula*. The large composite set comprising the exterior entrance to the chateau, the interior hall and drawing room was erected on Bray's Stage 1, with the Y-shaped staircase (with stained glass window behind) from *The Old Dark House* and *Paranoiac* putting in yet another appearance. "Bernie was marvellous," recalls Don Sharp. "He would do sketches of the sets and, if you had ideas about how you wanted to shoot scenes that wouldn't work with the sketches, you would talk it out with him. Sometimes he would do a grand set for you and you knew it was something you wanted to be close in on; that what was happening between two people was far more important than what was happening on the set. One would discuss it with him. You would get his feelings of what he was trying to get over, with contrasting styles and different characters and all the rest of it. Sometimes he would ask if I could revise the way I was going to shoot it. It was very amicable and very good. Usually if one found that you didn't need as big a set as the one he was sketching, he was delighted because he could take the money saved and put it onto another set and make it more splendid than he thought he was going to be able to do. We always worked very well together." [10]

A new 'Gothic structure' was constructed on the lot between the two village squares and the mound, which would effectively form the entrance to the squares. This was first seen in the opening burial sequence and was re-used later in the film for the lodge entrance to Ravna's chateau. This, like the village square set, was to be re-used over many pictures up to and including the 1963 production of *The Gorgon*. The hotel façade was erected in the original village square. "It was a little more difficult, sometimes, working things out on the lot," Sharp remembers, "because there were standing sets there which were modified from one picture to another, with all the scaffolding there permanently. Bernard was obviously restricted on how much cover he could give you there. That was one area where we had to compromise and where one wasn't able to do what one wanted." [10]

Les Bowie's special effects team built the model chateau that we see in long shot, shrouded in the Bavarian forest. Special effects assistant Ian Scoones remembers: "We had a wonderful freelance carpenter called George, and George, when you could get him out of the pub, was great. Les had 'borrowed' him from Bill Warrington. He'd made this super model boat for the Richard Widmark Yugoslavian-shot film *The Long Ships*. He'd got no teeth and he was a character, the sort of guy you don't find nowadays. George made the castle, which was basically Bernie Robinson's design. I think Bill [Warrington] was doing something at the studio at that time and he gave the little tip of using fibreboard and, if you use a blow lamp on it, you get a wonderful stone effect once you've painted it. I built the background set with Les. Les painted it, I dressed it, to Kit West's camera and we did a number of shots on it from different angles – static and tracking for inserts."

Some stability was returning to the Hammer team. Moray Grant had now worked as camera operator on all three of Bray's films since their hiatus. He would take a break from the company after *Kiss*, returning in 1965. Don Weeks was back as production manager and Douglas Hermes returned as first assistant director after his spell on *The Old Dark House*. Roy Ashton was on hand for the modest make-up jobs required, as well as designing the gorgeously grotesque masks for the masquerade ball.

Composer James Bernard had to get involved at an earlier stage than usual. He explained, "That was another of the occasions where I asked John Hollingsworth for an orchestrator, because that was another film where I had a hectic rush and I had to write the waltzes quite early so that they could use them, playing them on a piano when they were filming the actual sequence. Leslie Edwards from the Royal Ballet was the senior dancer and did the choreography for that scene. Of course, John Hollingsworth was one of the chief conductors of the Royal Ballet in those days. I'd written the tunes for the waltzes, then as I was doing the rest of the score, I realised I had very little time to get everything finished on schedule. They were meant to be like Viennese waltzes and so didn't need any kind of peculiar orchestration and I asked John if we could get someone in to orchestrate them. He said, 'Oh yes, Douglas Gamley will do it brilliantly', so it was Douglas who orchestrated the waltzes."

Gamley also doubled for Ravna's son Carl at the piano, playing James Bernard's 'Tooth Concerto'. "That was John's and my silly name for it," laughed Bernard. " I think John called it 'The Tooth Concerto'. As you know, in that film Dr Ravna, played by Noel Willman, who was a dear friend of mine – a very gentle person who played evil people on screen – had a son who played the piano and sent Jennifer Daniel into a trance. I had to write the bit of music he played. I've always been a great admirer of the work of Liszt, a wonderful composer, and I thought I would try and do a sort of Liszt rhapsody and I simply took it from there. Douglas Gamley was a brilliant orchestrator and I know he used to orchestrate for Henry Mancini. He was also a very good pianist and composer; he wrote a number of film scores, including some for Amicus." Gamley, of course, had already scored Hammer's *The Ugly Duckling*. It is interesting to note that the piece Carl plays as the Harcourts arrive at Ravna's chateau is the same as the one played on the gramophone when Oliver Reed arrives home drunk at the beginning of *Paranoiac*.

Of course, the most memorable sequence in the film is the climax, when Professor Zimmer conjures up the horde of bats to attack Ravna's minions. This task befell Les Bowie and his team of special effects wizards. The scene opens with an animated swarm of bats descending on the castle. Among initial ideas to capture this scene was to film burning paper as its black wisps spiralled up into the air. In the end they settled for cartoon animation. Ian Scoones remembers, "The job was farmed out to a guy called Pearce. Alan Tavner, who ran an optical company in Slough, suggested it to Les." Then inside, on an interior set, they had to conceive the scene where the bats swarm over Ravna and his disciples. "First of all Les and I went to Woolworths," recalls Scoones. "He said, 'When in doubt, that's the best prop shop in the world.' We went to Woolworths in Windsor and at the time they had little rubber bats. We just used them as they were, strung up with nylon line on a big frame made out of chicken wire, which we suspended from the 'gods' and swung for a shadow effect."

For the main attack on the actors, the special effects crew constructed purpose-built bats. Scoones recalls, "I was going out with a girl that was an old art college friend of mine, called Eileen, and she was good at sculpting and Les put us to work on these bats. Eileen and I made 20 bats in plasticene, but we only needed one for making a mould and this is where Ray Caple came in. He made the mould and then we poured three or four in one go with latex, and one of the girls managed to get some mole pelts for the furry bit. Bill Warrington was around at the time and he said, 'The teeth will fall out, unless you keep them both together. Why not just use an ordinary farm-type wooden staple?' So that's what the teeth were and the eyes were those little red pins that you use for maps, so everybody had a hand in it. Then I finished up painting them with Eileen. We made them in Les' little shed at Bray.

"Then we had to rig the bats to attack the actors. That was again a Les trick. If you put a staple on the set behind the actor's head and you put a nylon line through the staple and the bat has a little hollow brass tube running along its belly, you can catapult it down the nylon line or wire line (we used both) and then it's up to the actor to react to it as though it's attacking him. Then we also had them on sticks. One was very rude; it was Noel Willman, who happened to be gay anyway, so he enjoyed every minute of it. I had to have my hand between his legs with this stick with a bat on the end, coming through a hole in his costume as if it was attacking his neck. At rushes the next day, Tony Keys said, 'Christ, we can't use that, it looks as though he's being wanked off!'"

Isobel Black remembers the ordeal: "The mechanical bats were wonderful reproductions, but we had to lie there for ages while they wired them all over us. And then, of course, once the camera started to roll, they became animated. It wasn't so much that it was frightening, but the wires cut into your clothes and you got very sore. I think a lot of the screaming was quite for real." [11]

Special effects assistant Kit West had the dual role of helping out with the physical effects and photographing the effects scenes. He explains, "The bats coming in through windows and flying through the set and past camera were shot by me. I actually went onto the floor after they had finished shooting on the same set. We had all our guys up in the gantry puppeteering them all, and I photographed all that. So, having spent five weeks on the physical effects, I put my other hat on. I remember the bats at the end. I can't think of the name of the actress, but we made her cry. She was crying because we covered her in all these bats and stuck them on her with wires around the back and we had some on her bosoms and she was absolutely petrified at these rubber bats that Les had concocted."

Another effect the team had to contend with is the sequence where Zimmer scorches the vampire's bite from his arm. Scoones remembers, "Bungie Toys was near Shepperton and Les had this arm made by them. By putting in staples and having wires fitted underneath the fingers and pulling it at the back, he said we'd use this for the branding and it would just move a little in a quick cut, but the director did not like it. That was Don Sharp. He never liked effects anyway, even years later when I worked with him on an episode of the *Hammer House of Horror* TV series, *Guardian of the Abyss*. Anyway, he wasn't satisfied, he didn't like it, and Les said, 'Right, I'll use my own arm!' There was a chemical that had just come out in those days used in welding, that when you braze-weld anything that is delicate, or near to something that's very delicate, it acts for a short time as a barrier. So he put this cream on and did it for real, but he did burn himself a little! With all effects such as that, things can change literally by the moment by the director's whim, and it's a battle to always be one step ahead. It's like all conjurors. If one trick doesn't work one way, then you make sure it works the next way."

Shooting ended on Thursday 25 October after seven weeks, leaving James Needs and James Groom to see the film through post-production. As Hammer began to prepare their next film, another Sangster suspenser, it was time to see what the BBFC thought of their earlier one, the 'incest' thriller *Paranoiac*. Audrey Field passed comment on 12 December:

"Reel 3 – Remove shot of Harriet caressing Simon's chest.

Reel 4 – Reduce Eleanor's hysteria and remove her words: 'I am dirty.' Remove shot in which nurse's head is held under water.

Reel 5 – Reduce scene so that there are fewer shots of the mummy, in particular close shots. Resubmit these reels – marked up."

Tony Hinds objected in a letter to Trevelyan on the 14th: "In Reel 3 it is quite possible for us to remove the shot of Harriet caressing Simon's chest – in fact, I think we shall adopt the rather drastic solution of deleting the scene entirely. In Reel 4, to remove Eleanor's words 'I'm dirty!' would mean re-scoring and re-dubbing a complete section. Obviously, we would rather not be involved in

Gerald (Edward De Souza) is held back by servant Stan Simmons, watched by Ravna's son Carl (Barry Warren) in The Kiss of the Vampire (1962)

this expense, and I should like to ask you if you would reconsider this – bearing in mind the 'X' certificate. (Actually, I quite honestly cannot see the objection to this line: the situation is a girl who thinks she is going out of her mind and has become physically attracted to her brother, but *we* know – and so, shortly, will she – that this is not the case.) Reel 4: Surely we can show a shot of a girl being murdered by drowning in a picture of this type? She is only held under for a second before we cut away to the ducks flying away. (I know it is only a second, because she could not hold her breath any longer!) Perhaps you would reconsider this. Reel 5: None of the shots of the mummy seems very terrifying to me (I wish they were more so!), and eliminating a couple of them might do us more good than harm. However, if you will let me know which of the shots in particular you do not like, I will set about eliminating them."

Hinds' comments about Reel 5 were perhaps a form of reverse psychology, since Roy Ashton's 'mummy' was actually an excellent piece of work, though used ineffectively. Hammer made some cuts and resubmitted the reels, which were seen by Trevelyan and Crofts on 27 December. Trevelyan wrote to Hinds the following day: "The position is now as follows: Reel 3. The cut has been made satisfactorily and this reel is now acceptable. Reel 4. We are prepared to waive the first objection in this reel, and will accept the shots of Eleanor's hysteria and her dialogue line 'I'm dirty!' The scene in which the girl is embraced and then drowned is still rather worrying for us. It is primarily the association of a rather passionate embrace with an almost immediate killing. We agree that the shot of the girl held under water is very short and we wonder whether our objection could be met in another way by shortening the previous embrace. We never like any scenes which involve a combination of sex and killing. Perhaps you will let me know if there is anything you can do in this way. Reel 5. We agree that the shots of the mummy are not particularly terrifying, but it is a rather nasty idea to have the mummified corpse of Simon's brother dressed in a surplice. The nastiest shots are of the corpse being dragged along in long shot near the flames with its skeleton hips and legs visible and the one of Simon and the mummy seen side by side as the flames devour them. We would like you to make some reduction in these scenes removing as much as possible without destroying continuity completely. When you have done these cuts we would like to have a further look at the scenes in Reels 4 and 5 again."

NIGHTMARE

PRINCIPAL PHOTOGRAPHY: 17 December to 31 January 1962/63
DISTRIBUTION:
UK: Rank; certificate 'X'
US: Universal
82 minutes; b/w; Hammerscope
UK RELEASE:
PREMIÈRE: 19 April 1964, at the New Victoria with *The Evil of Frankenstein*
GENERAL RELEASE: 31 May 1964, on the ABC circuit

DIRECTOR: *Freddie Francis*; PRODUCER: *Jimmy Sangster*; SCREENPLAY: *Jimmy Sangster*; PRODUCTION DESIGNER: *Bernard Robinson*; ART DIRECTOR: *Don Mingaye*; DIRECTOR OF PHOTOGRAPHY: *John Wilcox*; CAMERA OPERATOR: *Ronnie Maasz*; CAMERA GRIP: *Albert Cowland*; CAMERA MAINTENANCE: *John Kerley*; ASSISTANT DIRECTOR: *Douglas Hermes*; 2ND ASSISTANT DIRECTOR: *Hugh Harlow*; SUPERVISING EDITOR: *James Needs*; MUSIC: *Don Banks*; MUSIC SUPERVISOR: *John Hollingsworth*; SOUND RECORDIST: *Ken Rawkins*; SOUND

CAMERA OPERATOR: *Al Thorne*; SOUND EDITOR: *James Groom*; MAKE-UP: *Roy Ashton*; Assistant MAKE-UP: *Reginald Mills*; HAIRSTYLIST: *Frieda Steiger*; PRODUCTION MANAGER: *Don Weeks*; CONTINUITY: *Pauline Wise*; WARDROBE SUPERVISOR: *Molly Arbuthnot*; WARDROBE MISTRESS: *Rosemary Burrows*; SPECIAL EFFECTS: *Les Bowie*; SPECIAL EFFECTS ASSISTANTS: *Kit West, Ian Scoones, Ray Caple*; CONSTRUCTION MANAGER: *Arthur Banks*; MASTER PLASTERER: *Stan Banks*; MASTER CARPENTER: *Charles Davis*; MASTER PAINTER: *Lawrence Wrenn*; MASTER ELECTRICIAN: *Jack Curtis*; MASTER RIGGER: *Ronald Lenoir*; PROPS BUYER: *Eric Hillier*; PROPS MASTER: *Tommy Money*; STILLS PHOTOGRAPHER: *Tom Edwards*; STUDIO MANAGER: *A F Kelly*

David Knight (Henry Baxter); *Moira Redmond* (Grace Maddox); *Brenda Bruce* (Mary Lewis); *Jennie Linden* (Janet); *George A Cooper* (John); *Irene Richmond* (Mrs Gibbs); *John Welsh* (Doctor); *Timothy Bateson* (barman); *Clytie Jessop* (woman in white); *Hedger Wallace* (Sir Dudley); *Julie Samuel* (maid); *Elizabeth Dear* (Janet [as a child]); *Isla Cameron* (Janet's mother)

The sequences were resubmitted and passed by Frank Crofts and Newton Branch on 7 January: "We saw single reels 8, 9 today. In R.8. the embrace has been shortened and we think that the incident will now pass. In R.9. there has been some cutting, especially of the corpse being dragged about, and this too will pass."

Nightmare was another complex, convoluted thriller from the pen of Jimmy Sangster, with enough plot twists to keep you guessing to the end. Sangster had just cause to question the film's original title, *Here's the Knife Dear – Now Use It*, for, as he would explain in *Kinematograph Weekly* on 3 January 1963: "The only trouble about the title is that it more than tells you something – it tells you everything."

Sangster was back in the driving seat as producer and he again brought in Freddie Francis to direct. For the central role of Janet, Hammer initially cast a young Julie Christie. However, when she was suddenly offered the lead part in John Schlesinger's *Billy Liar*, Hammer reluctantly released her from her contract after much cajoling from her agent.

"I remember Jimmy Sangster and I motoring down during the winter," recalls

Brenda Bruce comforts Jennie Linden in Nightmare (1962).

Freddie Francis. "During the snow we motored down to Worthing, where we heard a little girl was in the rep theatre there. And that's where we found Jennie Linden. In those days with Hammer one had a lot of freedom in casting, except when you're doing a Dracula film."[6] Satisfied with what they saw, they cast Linden in the Janet role.

Shooting began on Monday 17 December at Bray. Snow covered the ground, as caretaker Marje Hudd remembers: "On *Nightmare* I had to get the cleaners to come in and help with the snow, but as they tried to sweep it up, it just came back and the inside of the studio was just like Christmas!" The exterior of the boarding school was good old Oakley Court and the lovely model asylum, eerily set against a Ray

Clytie Jessop as the mysterious woman in white in Freddie Francis' Nightmare (1962).

Caple painted background, was put together by Ian Scoones and photographed by Kit West at Les Bowie's studio. The exterior of Janet's home was also a Les Bowie matte painting.

Bernard Robinson's sets were sombrely lit by John Wilcox. "Arthur Grant must not have been available, or must have been ill or something," Freddie Francis points out. "John would have been my choice anyway ... because I thought John was a fine cameraman. John was not as fast as Arthur Grant. He was a better cameraman, but he wasn't as fast as Arthur." [13] The film was again deftly handled by Francis. "I think my interest in these films was not necessarily the basic premise of each story," he says, "but I used to take great delight in my choice of set-ups and possibly mood, cheating the audience. And I used to have this sort of game with the audience, which was my biggest enjoyment out of those films, I think." [12] Rehearsals at Hammer were a luxury, as Francis explains: "You don't have a rehearsing period. You can't afford to get the artists in before you start the movie. You'd rehearse on the floor, but I like not to give the artists any ideas. I just let them do it. And then you go from there, because I believe in letting an artist do what they like, but it's got to fit in with my overall picture anyway." [6]

1962 ended in the grip of another bitter winter. It had been a year of change, but the company had seen it through and was settling down again. And 1963 would be intriguing, with two more costume capers and two new colour Gothics, including the long-awaited return of Baron Frankenstein...

ELEVEN

The Devil-Ship Disaster

(1 9 6 3)

A s 1963 opened, Hammer continued shooting *Nightmare* at Bray. Filming finally wrapped on Thursday 31 January. James Needs and James Groom once more took the film through post-production and John Hollingsworth brought back Don Banks to score.

The success of *The Pirates of Blood River* prompted Hammer to open 1963 with two further widescreen costume adventures for Columbia. First off would be *The Scarlet Blade*, which Hammer would rush through for a summer release to capitalise on the school holidays. Hammer's other releases that year would be three overdue productions, finally dusted off: *Cash on Demand* and *The*

Damned from 1961 and *Maniac* from 1962; big things were presumably expected of the latter since Hammer had already shot the next two in the Sangster series. There would still be no sign, however, of *The Old Dark House*.

The *Scarlet Blade*, a Civil War adventure, was once again the brainchild of writer/producer John Gilling, who would go on to claim it as his favourite action film. The story tells of Edward Beverley, who fights the Royalist cause under the name of the Scarlet Blade, his chief adversary being Colonel Judd, a former Royalist turned Ironside, appointed by Cromwell to hang Royalist traitors. An interesting cast included Lionel Jeffries and (in a much bigger part than his previous Hammer swashbucklers) Oliver Reed, plus debut Hammer roles for Suzan Farmer and Duncan Lamont, both of whom would become familiar faces over the next few years.

Hammer Productions
— 1963 —

✦ THE SCARLET BLADE
✦ THE DEVIL-SHIP PIRATES
✦ THE EVIL OF FRANKENSTEIN
✦ THE GORGON

OPPOSITE: Prudence Hyman as The Gorgon (1963).

Shooting began at Bray on Friday 1 March. Cinematographer Jack Asher made a welcome return to Hammer, his luscious colour photography later being nominated for a British Film Academy award. "Tony Keys and Michael Carreras, feeling most proud, had booked a table on the night in question at the hotel for my wife, my daughter and myself," Asher remembered. "I seem to remember that John Gilling was present as director of the film. We were also graced by the presence of Prince Philip, Duke of Edinburgh and president of the Academy, at the next table. Audrey Hepburn, looking most regal and beautiful, was distributing the prizes and chatting to the winners. I recalled that I had photographed her first film test in a studio." [1]

The village square complex and Gothic structure on the backlot would be used extensively in 1963. First off, the houses were dressed Tudor-style for *The Scarlet Blade* and *The Devil-Ship Pirates*. The Gothic structure had now effectively become the entrance to the village square site, leading to a path separating both squares. Another path lay in front of it, bordered by low walls. This would become the entrance to Beverly Manor, which stood in the second village square. Black Park was also extensively used for location scenes, and the climactic pitched battle took place on the grassy area referred to as 'the clearing'.

Of course, you can't make a costume adventure without costumes and *The Scarlet Blade* was a very challenging production for the Molly Arbuthnot/Rosemary Burrows team. The costumes for Hammer's productions would usually be hired from Bermans costumiers, or sometimes made specially, and would be chosen in consultation with the director and art director. Fittings were arranged before shooting began and the wardrobe people would be on hand during shooting for little repairs or even to help the actors get into the more elaborate costumes. Hammer's wardrobe department also had to work within a very tight budget and, given the company's characteristically bloody style, quite often duplicate costumes had to be provided. This was due to the fact that sequences were not shot consecutively; a scene where a costume is blood-stained or torn may have been shot before another scene which requires the costume to be intact. For *The Scarlet Blade*, wardrobe mistress Rosemary Burrows researched the costumes at the British Museum before getting them from Bermans. Because the costumes were so complicated and some items had to be put on before others, she found herself practically having to dress the main stars. For Cromwell's army, as a matter of

Lionel Jeffries as Colonel Judd in *The Scarlet Blade* (1963).

Clare (June Thorburn) enters into a dangerous alliance with Captain Sylvester (Oliver Reed) in The Scarlet Blade (1963).

THE SCARLET BLADE

PRINCIPAL PHOTOGRAPHY: 1 March to 17 April 1963
DISTRIBUTION:
UK: Warner-Pathe; certificate 'U'
US: Columbia; US TITLE: The Crimson Blade
82 minutes; Technicolor; Hammerscope
UK RELEASE: 11 August 1963, on the ABC circuit with The Son of Captain Blood
US RELEASE: May 1964 with The Devil-Ship Pirates

DIRECTOR: John Gilling; PRODUCER: Anthony Nelson Keys; SCREENPLAY: John Gilling; PRODUCTION DESIGNER: Bernard Robinson; ART DIRECTOR: Don Mingaye; DIRECTOR OF PHOTOGRAPHY: Jack Asher; CAMERA OPERATOR: Cece Cooney; FOCUS PULLER: Mike Sarafian; GRIP: Albert Cowland; CLAPPER/LOADER: David Kelly; CAMERA MAINTENANCE: John Kerley; ASSISTANT DIRECTOR: Douglas Hermes; 2ND ASSISTANT DIRECTOR: Hugh Harlow; 3RD ASSISTANT DIRECTOR: Stephen Victor; SUPERVISING EDITOR: James Needs; EDITOR: John Dunsford; MUSIC: Gary Hughes; MUSIC SUPERVISOR: John Hollingsworth; SOUND RECORDIST: Ken Rawkins; BOOM: Peter Pardoe; SOUND CAMERA OPERATOR: Al Thorne; SOUND EDITOR: James Groom; MAKE-UP: Roy Ashton; MAKE-UP ASSISTANT: Richard Mills; HAIRSTYLIST: Frieda Steiger; PRODUCTION MANAGER: Clifford Parkes; CONTINUITY: Pauline Wise; WARDROBE: Rosemary Burrows; SPECIAL EFFECTS: Les Bowie; SPECIAL EFFECTS ASSISTANTS: Bill Warrington, Kit West, Ian Scoones; CONSTRUCTION MANAGER: Arthur Banks; MASTER PLASTERER: Stan Banks; MASTER CARPENTER: Charles Davis; MASTER PAINTER: Lawrence Wrenn; MASTER ELECTRICIAN: Jack Curtis; MASTER RIGGER: Ronald Lenoir; PROPS BUYER: Eric Hillier; PROPS MASTER: Tommy Money; FLOOR PROPS: John Goddard; PRODUCTION SECRETARY: Pauline Wise; STILLS PHOTOGRAPHER: Tom Edwards; PUBLICITY: Brian Doyle; STUDIO MANAGER: A F Kelly; DRIVER: Coco Epps

Lionel Jeffries (Colonel Judd); Oliver Reed (Captain Sylvester); Jack Hedley (Edward Beverley); June Thorburn (Clare Judd); Duncan Lamont (Major Bell); Suzan Farmer (Constance); Michael Ripper (Pablo); Charles Houston (Drury); Harold Goldblatt (Jacob); Clifford Elkin (Philip); Michael Byrne (Lt Hawke); John Harvey (Sgt Grey); John Stuart (Beverley); Harry Towb (Cobb); Robert Rietty (King Charles I); John H Watson (Fitzroy); Douglas Blackwell (Blake); Leslie Glazer (Gonzales); John Woodnutt (Lt Wyatt); Eric Corrie (Duncannon); Denis Holmes (Chaplain)

UNCREDITED: George Woodbridge (Town Crier)

convenience she drew up a chart listing the correct order in which to get dressed: rust jacket, buff coat, thigh boots, breast- and back-plate, baldric, armour waist-belt and red sash. With such attention to detail, the film had again the feel of a big-budget production.

Cece Cooney made his first appearance for Hammer as camera operator and Clifford Parkes was back as production manager. This was Douglas Hermes' third Bray film in a row as assistant director, but John Gilling's rantings would keep him away from Hammer till 1966. Hugh Harlow, the 2nd assistant, explains: "I had to take over as 1st assistant director. John Gilling was the director. That was a very unhappy film and I didn't enjoy it. Dougie Hermes was the 1st, but he left the film over an incident in Black Park, which was our location for several weeks. We were setting up a scene where the Roundheads had captured a man who was sympathetic to the Cavaliers. The actor was being brought on an open cart – pulled by a horse, his hands behind his back – to a noose hanging from the bough of a tree. Gilling wanted the cart to come in and the actor to put his head into the noose in one shot. Dougie refused and said that anything could happen, the horse could bolt and we'd have a terrible problem on our hands. He suggested that we did the shot of the head going into the noose as a separate shot, as a close-up, and the man would now be standing on a box, but not standing in a cart pulled by a horse.

"It was a relevant point and they had a row about it. John was a very difficult person to work with, a very difficult man, always shouting and barking, and Dougie said, 'You're not doing it; over my dead body.' And John said, 'I'm going to shoot it my way.' Dougie walked off and he never came back. I was the 2nd and was asked to take over. I very reluctantly took over the rest of the day's work and this was the first shot after lunch. In the end, John brought him to the noose but didn't put his head in the noose in the same shot. But in the course of shooting the scene, the horse bolted and he went straight over Jack Asher and Cece Cooney, the operator. It caused quite a controversy that day, because Dougie was proved right. It happened in the early stages of the film and I carried on as 1st." Stephen Victor joined the team as 3rd assistant.

Continuity girl Pauline Wise had become engaged to Hugh Harlow that February and they would marry just before the next production, *The Devil-Ship Pirates*. Pauline remembers: "*The Scarlet Blade* was directed by John Gilling. I was afraid of John because he swore a lot and shouted and screamed. You couldn't relax very much with him. It was quite a busy film, with crowds, and I remember in one of the skirmishes with the horses, it was a period film and someone had forgotten that his cigarette was still in his mouth as he was fighting. We'd turned over and were filming and I thought, 'My goodness, I can see that man's got a cigarette hanging out of his mouth.' Anyway, John was so furious he had him fired there and then, so that poor ageing stuntman lost his job. The other thing that happened was that there was some dialogue between these actors on horseback. When we finished, John said, 'Cut. That was all right, wasn't it?' Well, one of the horses had farted all over this crucial dialogue and you couldn't hear it properly, so I told John Gilling and we had to shoot it again."

Les Bowie brought in Bill Warrington to assist with the physical effects for the battle scenes. Ian Scoones explains: "That was an odd one, because Les at that time was not terribly experienced with battle scenes. We brought in an amazing character, an ex-major from the army, to do all this and then eventually Bill Warrington came in, because he was a pyrotechnic expert. He had already got an Oscar for *The Guns of Navarone*, the first British effects man to win an Oscar. We did most of that at Black Park. It was a good film to work on. The hanging tree used a hanging rig and that was the first time I knew how to hang a man without hurting him. It was a Troll harness, which takes the weight of the body, and then you have a wire that goes out of shot but holds the weight. You put a dummy rope around and the noose is loose on the other piece of rope. I did have one personal problem on that. I had a slight reputation for being late on set. Black Park is very popular for filming and it's a very small world, the film game, you get to meet the same canteen people, everybody. For once I was early and I thought I would get a hot roll at the chuck wagon. I was standing there and somebody said, 'How are you doing? What effects have we got on this? We haven't got any effects!' I said, 'Yes we have, you've got this blowing-up in this battle scene.' All the actors and extras were out of sight, because I was so early and they were still being fitted with costume and make-up, but I had to be early for Les. Then I realised to my horror that I was on the wrong set. Our canteen wagon was another mile into the Black Park forest. So as usual I turned up late!"

Co-ordinating the action was stunt supervisor Peter Diamond. "I was working with Roger Moore on the *Ivanhoe* series in 1957," he recalls, "and about four years later he got *The Saint* and he very kindly suggested that I co-ordinate it for him. John Gilling was directing one of the episodes and it was the first time I had met him. I doubled an actor called Charles Houston on a backwards stair fall and I know, without being facetious, that I did a blinding stair fall and John said, 'That's terrific, Peter, thanks very much.' Now I lived in Elstree in those days and I was shooting at Elstree and I'd only been home about an hour when the phone rang. 'It's John Gilling here. I'd just like to say thank you very much for today. I've just been speaking to Roger, I didn't know you were a swordsman. I'm doing this picture called The Scarlet Blade. Will you ring Hammer and tell them I want you to do the sword fights?' And that's how it happened. Roger was instrumental, with John Gilling, in getting me into Hammer. Tony Keys thought the sun shone out of my backside. I saved them a lot of money, you see, which is important, because I know how to cut corners and get the effect. And nobody gets seriously hurt, which is very important."

Diamond discusses how he staged the huge battle scene. "That battle scene was shot in half a day in Black Park, so considering what was on the screen I think we did well. I was in there myself. In fact, I was all over the place. I also had to co-ordinate the horse sequences. If you remember, a lot of explosions were going on at that time and the horses had to be pulled down. You have to prepare a bed for the horses to fall on. You can't just pull the horses down, it has to be a trained horse and you have to make sure no animal gets hurt. You don't do it so much like that nowadays, because of the different EU legislation, but that's how we did it in the old days. We also have to work together with special effects. They advise us, we advise them, because where explosions are concerned, you only need one mistake and somebody can get seriously hurt.

"There was also a big fight between Jack Hedley and a trooper in the inn. I played the trooper and we actually shot the fight in two hours, using about four cameras, and we just went hell for leather. It had all been rehearsed, obviously, and we saved them a lot of shooting time. Jack and I had worked on that about a week inbetween other things. He didn't have a double, he did it all himself, because he had the confidence that I was fighting him. For one thing, he was an ex-army man. Very fit and to me he was great to work with, because he co-ordinated well and he listened. John Gilling had said the responsibility was mine. He said, 'You come in, there's a couple of lines of dialogue, the fight starts, then I leave it entirely to you.' And that's how it worked."

Shooting finished on Wednesday 17 April after just under seven weeks. Editors James Needs and John Dunsford, with sound editor James Groom, then rushed the film into post-production for its summer release date. John Hollingsworth again brought in his action favourite, Gary Hughes, to score.

On Sunday 19 May, Hammer's double-bill of Maniac and the long-delayed The Damned was released on the ABC circuit by British Lion. Maniac would be released in the States on 30 October with The Old Dark House as another double-bill for Columbia. Britain had to wait until 1966 to see the latter. As the top half of the UK double-bill, Maniac was given mixed reviews, but there was some excitement over The Damned in the wake of Losey's success with The Servant. As the Times put it on 30 May, "Mr Joseph Losey is one of the most intelligent, ambitious and consistently exciting filmmakers now working in the country. It would be a thousand pities were his latest film, after 18 months on the shelf, to go out unremarked as the lower half of a 'double X' all-horror programme." Films and Filming went further: "This is undoubtedly one of the most important British films of the year, even, perhaps, of the 60s."

The Damned had an even more difficult launch in America, being consigned to Columbia's vaults and apparently forgotten, possibly thanks to lingering ill-feeling towards Losey. In 1964, however, the film won the Golden Asteroid at the second Trieste Science Fiction Film Festival and finally appeared in the US on 7 July 1965, but only after a further ten minutes had been extracted so that it could support Genghis Khan.

Unlike the rush-released The Scarlet Blade, The Kiss of the Vampire was still going through hoops at the BBFC some nine months after shooting had finished. Tony Hinds submitted a cut of the film in July, and the examiner's comments on the 3rd read:

"Reel 3. Remove scene in which Ravna puts surplice over Marianne.
Reel 4. Remove Professor's remark to Gerald: '...She was riddled with disease.' Remove Marianne's line to Ravna, 'I love only you ... I want only you.' Shorten to a glimpse only of Tania advancing towards Gerald with her mouth open to give him the 'Vampire's Kiss'.
Reel 5. Considerably reduce sequence in which bats attack vampire people. In particular, remove shots of the bats sucking women's necks, bosoms and legs and guzzling blood generally: and also shot in which woman's thigh and buttock are visible."

Anthony Nelson Keys, Oliver Reed and Jack Hedley take a break during the filming of The Scarlet Blade (1963).

Hinds wrote to John Trevelyan on 11 July: "I have received your rejection slip for The Kiss of the Vampire and noted the contents (some of which were not unexpected). With reference to Reel 3, we can do this without much difficulty. (Funnily enough, we expected an objection from the Breen office [in the USA] on this, but not from you: as it turns out, however, they have not objected.) Reel 4. I can't quite see the objection to the fact that the girl was a diseased vampire. We can easily take out 'I want only you', but may we keep 'I love only you' – otherwise the re-cutting becomes a bit messy? Surely when the audience goes in to see The Kiss of the Vampire, they expect to see a few bites? May I ask you please to re-consider this one – it really is pretty tame. Reel 5. We expected an objection to some of these!"

Trevelyan replied to Hinds on the 17th: "Our comments are as follows: Reel 4. The word 'diseased' implies VD, which in turn implies that the vampire had had sexual intercourse with the girl. This does not give us any pleasure. We think that 'I love only you' will be acceptable if you will remove 'I want only you.' We think that there should be a shortening of the scene in which Tania advances towards Gerald with her mouth open. Here again we do not mind vampire biting, but we do want to get rid of the suggestion that sex is involved also. I hope you will find some way of doing this."

Hammer resubmitted the reels, which were seen by Audrey Field and Frank Crofts on 22 July: "We saw reels 4 and 5 today. R.4. (a) Cut not made (b) No cut made (c) Nothing seems to have been done. R.5. Very little, if indeed anything, has been done to this scene. When the scenes have been cut as asked for, they should be sent in again. A letter is needed about R.3."

Hammer paid lip service to the promised cuts and resubmitted the reels. A note from Audrey Field on 29 July says: "Reel 4 is all right: the words 'She was riddled with disease' and 'I want only you' have gone, and we accept the shots of Tania advancing toward Gerald, which seem to have been slightly shortened. Reel 5 has not been adequately cut. There are a number of shots of girls' bare thighs, some with vampire bats fastening on them, and bats pulsing as they suck human blood. Almost all of these shots should go. JT will speak to the company. Resubmit Reel 5 when cut."

A further note the following day reads, 'Went through Reel 5 scenes with Mr Needs and pointed out the shots that we do not like. He will make further cuts and resubmit this reel.' The examiners reviewed the latest cut to Reel 5 on 8 August but were still concerned about the vampire bat sequence. Trevelyan wrote to Hinds the next day: "I am writing to confirm my telephone message about The Kiss of the Vampire. In Reel 5 we need a few further cuts in the bat sequence. You should remove all shots of the girls with their dresses up to their waists, showing their thighs (these have remained as flash shots), and the shot of the girl lying down with bats at her throat and blood all over her. The reel should be resubmitted when these further cuts have been made."

A note scribbled on 12 August by an examiner reads, "Seen again by FNC and NKB. There is still one very brief shot of girl with thighs showing but other cuts have been made and sequence will now pass." Interestingly, although allegedly cut as the examiners' comments suggest, the final print would still contain Zimmer's line stating that his daughter was "riddled with disease" and Marianne's line to Ravna stating "I want only you." Audiences would also see Ravna putting a surplice around Marianne. The extended bat sequence can still be seen on some American prints and even found its way into the *World of Hammer* compilation series.

The Scarlet Blade was released in England on Sunday 11 August on the ABC circuit to a favourable response, supported by *The Son of Captain Blood*. In fact, the pair constituted the second highest-grossing double-bill for ABC that year. Hammer accordingly set to work on their next swashbuck-ler, which would see the welcome return of Christopher Lee.

Jimmy Sangster's cunning tale based around the Spanish Armada has Captain Robeles steering the damaged Diablo to the British coast and convincing the out-of-touch locals that England has lost. The villagers smell a rat, however, and prepare to stand their ground against Robeles' men – who are actually ruthless pirates. Producer Anthony Nelson Keys brought Don Sharp back as director. Though Sharp had been a newcomer to horror, he admitted to finding *The Kiss of the Vampire* an easier film to handle than *The Devil-Ship Pirates*, given Hammer's straitened budget. Sharp recalls: "It was a very difficult one. We had a ship that was part of the Armada which had to be burned. It had a lot of physical action in it, which I loved, but it was difficult to do on a tight schedule. Action has to look dangerous, and it is dangerous unless it is well rehearsed and lots of precautions are taken. That takes time. The demands of the producer to keep going mean that you can't do as well as you want to." [2]

Shooting began at Bray on Monday 19 August. Michael Reed returned to Hammer as cinematog-rapher after lighting Hammer's so-called 'lost' film, *The Ugly Duckling*. Don Weeks returned as production manager. Alan Hall took over as camera operator for his only Hammer engagement and back from *The Scarlet Blade* were Ken Rawkins, Roy Ashton, Frieda Steiger, Molly Arbuthnot, Rosemary Burrows, Hugh Harlow, Stephen Victor and Pauline Harlow. On 3 August, two weeks before shooting began, Hugh Harlow had married Pauline Wise. "We had some joke telegrams," Hugh remembers. "Tony Hinds sent one: 'May the continuity of your togetherness be fruitful.'"

The film brought in Bert Batt as 1st assistant; he would continue to work on and off with Hammer, even writing their 1969 extravaganza, *Frankenstein Must Be Destroyed*. "My previous film had been *Zulu*," Batt recalls, "and its production manager was Basil Keys. He recommended me to his brother Tony Keys." According to Hugh Harlow, "Bert is one of the front line, first division 1sts – he's a tremendous assistant director. He's just retired now, but we worked together very recently on *Rasputin* in Russia with Alan Rickman. I learned an awful lot from Bert. I was his 2nd on a number of films. He was like a sergeant major, very strict on the floor and very much in control. He was the best 1st Hammer ever had."

"Terry Fisher and John Gilling always knew what they wanted to do," Batt states, "but they would spend a while exploring the various possibilities of a scene, how best to put it together, with the actors and the sharp end of their crew. It never took long. Don was quite different. He came to work with a rigid shot list and to an inch knew where the camera would be for every set-up. I much preferred the former way of working. However, each director to his own way of working and you give them your full support."

The casting was superb, Christopher Lee giving great presence to his Captain Robeles, who has fewer redeeming features even than his LaRoche in *The Pirates of Blood River*. The film marked the beginning of a successful association between Sharp and Lee, which would soon include *The Face of Fu Manchu* and, for Hammer, *Rasputin the Mad Monk*. A splendid cast of Hammer regulars was in full support: fresh from *The Scarlet Blade* came Suzan Farmer, Duncan Lamont, Michael Ripper and Charles Houston, while Barry Warren had previously appeared in Sharp's *The Kiss of the Vampire*. Andrew Keir was back, too, this time playing a sympathetic hero.

Barry Warren challenges the crew when they declare their intention to return to a life of piracy in The Devil-Ship Pirates (1963).

THE DEVIL-SHIP PIRATES

PRINCIPAL PHOTOGRAPHY: 19 August to 4 October 1963
DISTRIBUTION:
UK: Associated British Pathe; certificate 'U'
US: Columbia
86 minutes; Technicolor; Hammerscope
UK RELEASE:
TRADE SHOW: 29 May 1964, at the Columbia Theatre with The Invincible Seven
GENERAL RELEASE: 9 August 1964, on the ABC circuit with The Invincible Seven
US RELEASE: May 1964, with The Crimson Blade [ie, The Scarlet Blade]

ASSISTANT: Ron A Mingaye; SOUND EDITOR: Roy Hyde; MAKE-UP: Roy Ashton; MAKE-UP ASSISTANT: Richard Mills; HAIRSTYLIST: Frieda Steiger; PRODUCTION MANAGER: Don Weeks; CONTINUITY: Pauline Harlow; WARDROBE: Rosemary Burrows; SPECIAL EFFECTS: Les Bowie; SPECIAL EFFECTS ASSISTANTS: Kit West, Ian Scoones; FIGHT ARRANGER: Peter Diamond; SAILING MASTER: Capt R C S Garwood; CONSTRUCTION MANAGER: Arthur Banks; MASTER PLASTERER: Stan Banks; MASTER CARPENTER: Charles Davis; MASTER PAINTER: Lawrence Wrenn; MASTER ELECTRICIAN: Jack Curtis; MASTER RIGGER: Ronald Lenoir; PROPS BUYER: Eric Hillier; PROPS MASTER: Tommy Money; STUDIO MANAGER: A F Kelly; DRIVER: Coco Epps; STILLS PHOTOGRAPHER: Tom Edwards

DIRECTOR: Don Sharp; PRODUCER: Anthony Nelson Keys; SCREENPLAY: Jimmy Sangster; PRODUCTION DESIGNER: Bernard Robinson; ART DIRECTOR: Don Mingaye; DIRECTOR OF PHOTOGRAPHY: Michael Reed; CAMERA OPERATOR: Alan Hall; GRIP: Albert Cowland; SOUND CAMERA OPERATOR: Al Thorne; ASSISTANT DIRECTOR: Bert Batt; 2ND ASSISTANT DIRECTOR: Hugh Harlow; 3RD ASSISTANT DIRECTOR: Stephen Victor; SUPERVISING EDITOR: James Needs; MUSIC: Gary Hughes; MUSIC SUPERVISOR: John Hollingsworth; SOUND RECORDIST: Ken Rawkins; BOOM

Christopher Lee (Captain Robeles); Andrew Keir (Tom); John Cairney (Harry); Duncan Lamont (the Bosun); Michael Ripper (Pepe); Ernest Clark (Sir Basil); Barry Warren (Manuel); Suzan Farmer (Angela); Natasha Pyne (Jane); Annette Whiteley (Meg); Charles Houston (Antonio); Philip Latham (Miller); Harry Locke (Bragg); Leonard Fenton (Quintana); Jack Rodney (Mandrake); Barry Lineham (Gustavo); Bruce Beeby (Pedro); Michael Peake (Grande); Johnny Briggs (Pablo); Michael Newport (Smiler); Peter Howell (the Vicar); June Ellis (Mrs Blake)

The village square was again prominent and was practically the same as it had been in The Scarlet Blade, only with a different inn sign to put us off the scent. Hammer's construction manager, Arthur Banks, excelled himself and built a full-size replica of the Diablo, based on Bernard Robinson's designs, at a cost of £17,000. The result was set afloat on the flooded Bray gravel pits (now Bray Marina). "I was heavily involved in that," remembers Don Mingaye. "It was supposed to be a replica of the Golden Hind. So I went down to the Maritime Museum, poking around there, seeing what I could come up with. Chatting to the chief model-maker, within a couple of days I

The doomed
Diablo on the
flooded Bray
gravel pits in The
Devil-Ship
Pirates (1963).

found myself at his house and workshop in Leatherhead. He came up with a draft of the Golden
Hind, which he loaned me. At that stage we weren't sure whether we could build the thing in its
entirety, so lots of meetings took place and it was decided to build it on a raft made of oil drums,
which were like ballast tanks; they were all rigged together. I believe Lloyds of London actually
insured it in the end. So we actually built that rib by rib at the studio in three sections and it was
then loaded down to the quarry near Maidenhead. Anyway, to cut a long story sideways, this lovely
man from the museum, whose name escapes me, was engaged by the company as technical
adviser, but he became very frustrated because we thought, 'We don't think that's necessary, we
want to do it our way.' And that would make him sulk."

Even the best intentions can go awry, however, as Bert Batt explains. "One day during my two
weeks' pre-production preparation, I went down to the flooded gravel pit to see how the Diablo was
coming along. It was being constructed on the bank. Ronnie Lenoir, the chief rigger, and his men
had erected a long tubular structure, upon and around which the carpenters laid the deck and clad
the sides with about six feet of hull. Ronnie pulled me aside to tell me that we were in trouble. Bernie
[Robinson] had told him to put the buoyancy tanks at the bottom of the rig and Ronnie could not
dissuade him from this. He said that they should be higher up, at a very precise point, but Bernie
said that marine advice had been taken and would Ronnie kindly install them where he was told.

"Come the day of the launching, it was a big day for Hammer: publicity, cameras, some of the
stars, the executives. Two cranes fore and aft took the strain. The weight had been underestimated
and the ship didn't budge an inch. So we all toddled off for a nice publicity lunch. A few days later,
appropriate cranes placed it on the water and we faced two problems. Ronnie Lenoir had been
right; give or take a few inches, the entire thing was floating on the surface. The buoyancy tanks
were almost entirely above the water and a mass of tubular above them disappeared behind the six
or so feet of hull cladding. It was like a pea on a drum and if one person too many stood on one
side of the ship, it keeled over. This meant that we couldn't work on it. The second problem was
how were people going to get on and off? Whereas we should have been able to open the gate in
the gunwale and help people up or down a few steps of a rope ladder, we were looking at the
equivalent of a two-storey house. Four pontoons tied together solved both problems. Ronnie
Lenoir wrapped them around with tubular and erected a tubular tower that reached up to deck

level. It was planked over and a ladder went down to the pontoons that were also planked over. It was then tied to the side of the ship, which was then towed out to the centre of the lake and moored. All the camera angles had to take account of the fact that we were surrounded by land and the masts were eight feet high stumps. There were no sails and as a ship in the open sea gives no sense of forward movement, it was not necessary for it to move."

Ian Scoones recalls, "By law if you have a boat that is a boat, you have to have a captain for it, so they brought in some retired captain who was a gin-swigger. Now no director or assistant director wants to be told by a layman what to do and what not to do, so they used to give him a bottle of gin and by ten o'clock in the morning he was totally pie-eyed. But he kept saying, 'This boat will sink. We're all doomed. We'll all drown!' They used to tell him to shut up, but he had this plumbline with an arrow swinging by the side of the ship's bridge and it was already about 20 degrees out, but nobody noticed. He was totally right, but no one would listen to him."

It was, as they say, an accident waiting to happen. Bert Batt explains, "On the appointed day, we began work on the ship, which was stabilised by the pontoon platform, and all went well. One of the electricians, old Alf – very rotund, bald and toothless – knew with absolute certainty that the ship would sink and he refused to set foot on it even if it meant getting the sack. The gaffer looked kindly on him and gave him the task of sitting on the bank surrounded by electrical gear and his own row-boat. There was little space on the deck and anything not needed for a shot was either on the pontoon's two platforms or on the bank. There was no below deck. One afternoon, the caterers arrived at the bank with the crew's afternoon tea and old Alf was always their first customer, but he wasn't there so they loaded their boat with tea urns and trays of cakes and set off to the ship.

"Old Alf returned to see his tea and bun being rowed away. He got into his boat and took up the oars. This coincided with the shooting of a scene in which there were six very heavy stuntmen. We got the shot, I called for a workboat to come over and take them off and, leaving the deck, they stepped onto the top pontoon platform just as old Alf was stepping out of his boat onto the lower platform – where stood two caterers, two tea urns and trays of cakes on a table. What no one had noticed was that the pontoons had begun to take on water and this sudden accumulation of weight pushed them down and under the surface. Poor old Alf had the distinction of being the first to go under. This now rapidly sinking structure was tied to the side of the ship and as it went down it pulled the ship over. How the nine people on that pontoon escaped injury is a miracle.

"On deck it was equally so. Thirty-five or 40 people were on the ship. Eight cannons shot from one side to the other and slammed into the gunwale, smashing holes in it. A mast toppled over. Camera boxes, sound equipment, props, reflectors and lamps on stands were all over the place. People were thrown over the side; quite a few of them jumped and some of us clung on to whatever was fixed and at hand. One of the actors was playing the part of a Spanish officer and his face was a study. And then there was Sammy. Sammy was a jovial-faced Jamaican electrician who had never come to terms with the British climate. Even in the height of summer, and this was a warm day, he wore a trilby hat and a long overcoat. Thus attired, he rocketed down the acute incline and shot straight through the open gunwale gate and into the water, where he went down like a stone. And he couldn't swim. Somehow he clawed his way back to the surface and people grabbed him. Apart from a few odd cuts and bruises, no one was hurt and the workboats were quickly on the scene and had us all ashore."

"When people talk about disaster movies, that was one of the worst!" laughs special effects assistant Ian Scoones. The tale of the doomed Diablo would remain a Hammer legend. Many have their own stories to tell of that fateful day. First, Hugh Harlow. "I was there when that happened. I was part of the rescue team! Nobody, fortunately, was drowned, but there was a very near one. Third assistant Stephen Victor dived down and managed to cut some guide-lines that were trailing around one of the unit members and freed that person, who managed to swim up to the surface. It wasn't terribly deep, but it was deep enough to cause a nasty accident. Anyway, boats were rowing backwards and forwards. I was in one, bringing members of the crew back to the shore."

Christopher Lee recalls, " I remember I was up near the bows, as were the camera crew and other members of the cast. All of a sudden the ship started tilting. People started sliding off, others were jumping off. The camera went in the water. Almost everyone went off the ship. I stayed on the ship...

as the Captain should of course! I stayed on the bridge holding onto something, and I rescued the continuity girl's typewriter, which was my act of heroism for the day, which she's never forgotten, bless her. Tony Nelson Keys, who was the producer, was out on some sort of flat raft when this happened; of course, his craft started tilting down towards the water as well, and I remember vividly this picture of him – thumbs in line with the seams of his trousers, feet together, as an officer and gentleman should – slowly sliding into the water and shouting at the top of his voice, 'Don't panic, don't panic!' A lot of people did panic and a stunt man dived down and retrieved the camera.

"It's amazing nobody was killed, because they could have been trapped between the side of the ship and the mud and muck underneath the ship. There was a photograph taken and I think it was in the paper. Another thing that stands out vividly in my memory is Duncan Lamont, who played the Bosun. All of these people were in the water screaming at the tops of their voices: 'Save the camera', 'Save me', or whatever, and somebody shouted out: 'Help, help! Throw us a rope!' And Duncan Lamont said, 'Here y'are,' and threw down his rope's end, which he used as Bosun to bash pirates with when they got out of hand. It was only two or three feet long, if not shorter!"

Pauline Harlow remembers, "Lots of people were thrown off. I remember sliding down the deck into a corner and being engulfed in rigging and nets. And that's where I stayed for a long time, not knowing if the ship was going down. Christopher Lee was the only person I could see. He'd climbed up onto the aft deck. You could hear screams and everything and for about half an hour, until I was rescued, Christopher gave me a running commentary on what was happening. Fortunately, nobody was lost at all, but we had to have a roll-call on the bank and Tony Keys took charge. Everybody had to be accounted for. It was pretty scary, but we were all rescued."

Bert Batt discusses the inevitable post-mortem. "With Don Sharp and Tony Keys, who happened to be there, I went back to the studio for a meeting with Don Weeks, our production manager, and Bernie Robinson. Together we re-arranged the schedule to keep us going until the ship was put right, but there could be no shooting the next day. The fact that Bernie's buoyancy tanks had necessitated the pontoons that nearly sank the ship and brought the production to a standstill was studiously avoided. The next day I went back to the wreckage with a stuntman/frogman, who would dive and bring up equipment that was on the bottom. In his rubber suit and with his heavy air-tank strapped to his back, he stepped off the side of the boat, legs astride. Six inches below the surface his testicles collided with one of the dislodged bars of the pontoon's tubular rig. I wouldn't be surprised if his scream was still echoing around the gravel pit to this day!"

The camera equipment was naturally lost. "It went straight to the bottom," explains Peter Diamond. "They sent divers down for it, but all the lenses and Panavision cameras had been damaged and weren't much use. It was a big insurance claim." Stuntman Jackie Cooper remembers, "I didn't work on the film but, when the film was packed up, I got a call to go down with diving equipment and get a generator that had sunk to the bottom. They asked me to get them out of trouble there, because they either had to pay for the generator or send it back. It was cold and my hands were freezing, but I dived in and brought it up for them."

Pauline Harlow laughs when she remembers the insurance claims that followed. "If we lost anything, we all had to fill in insurance claims. I only had a few little work pieces; I lost a polaroid camera and a stopwatch. But apparently all the people that went in the water, which was the majority of people – all the electricians, riggers, stuntmen – everyone seemed to have had a Parker pen on them that day, or really expensive watches and wallets full of money. There was no proof that they didn't have them. Tony Keys, I remember, said, 'What are electricians doing with Parker pens and gold watches?'"

The show, of course, had to go on. "It was decided to shoot the remaining scenes with the ship on dry land," Bert Batt explains, "and, while we were shooting other things, it was hauled ashore and repaired. However, the boat was now almost surrounded by trees that we could not cut down, so all the remaining scenes were shot to the roaring accompaniment of half a dozen fog machines that blanked out all that should not be seen."

And not just trees, according to Don Sharp. "One of the reasons there was so much battle smoke," he points out, "was that on the other side of the lake they were starting to build the M4 motorway and we didn't want all the trucks in the background." [3] This only led to more problems, as Ian Scoones explains. "My own disaster day came when, having employed two army smoke machines called 'Bezzlers' from Pinewood to blot out the new M4 in the background, the wind suddenly changed and my thick cloud of dense smoke drifted onto the AA and RAC organisations, not to mention irate drivers who complained in the local paper! Luckily, no one crashed. Add to this the fact that one night, after filming was over for the day, one of my heavy Bezzler machines carrying a 45-gallon drum of smoke oil wasn't secured to the shoreline and overturned on its punt and sank! I had to get divers in to locate and retrieve it! And of course, in the meantime, oil had seeped out all over the surface of the water!"

A further mishap occurred during the filming of Christopher Lee's climactic duel with Barry Warren. As Lee explains, "At the end I was shot and went back into the flames. I actually did slip in one of the rehearsals and my wig caught fire, or started to smoulder anyway. I was a fast mover in those days. Something always happened on every

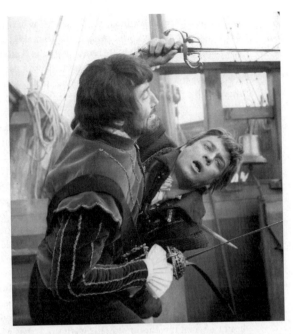

Christopher Lee fights Barry Warren at the climax of The Devil-Ship Pirates (1963).

Hammer movie, or even every movie, come to that. I don't think I've ever done a sword fight with an actor where I haven't been injured. Never with a stuntman; always with another actor." Bert Batt agrees: "I can still see Christopher struggling manfully through the sword fight. He was quite deft with a sword, but his actor opponent, I cannot remember who, was not. His accuracy at finding Christopher's knuckles with his blade was first class, however. Mr Lee left the studio that evening in not a particularly good mood, with his right hand smothered with sticking plasters."

Once more Peter Diamond had to co-ordinate the sword play. "There was John Cairney fighting with one hand with the oar and Christopher, of course, had that final fight on board ship with Barry Warren and I co-ordinated the whole thing for that. And, of course, lovely Michael Ripper. Strangely enough, he didn't do a sword fight, though Michael was a very good swordsman. Small people are better swordsmen than tall swordsmen. He'd actually done some fencing but he didn't tell anybody. I spotted this straightaway and I talked to him and said, 'Where did you do this?' And he said at so-and-so, it was just one of his hidden talents. Christopher Lee obviously had a lot of experience, so he was easy to adapt. He moved well and he looked good in the film, which is the important thing. The last fight with Christopher and Barry took a week to rehearse actually. Also, it's not like a stage fight, it's broken up, so you can cut and pick it up again and, if there's a mistake, say, 'Right, cut, let's do it again.' It's a ballet. It's choreography, completely. First of all you have to find out the capabilities of the actor, whether he's left- or right-handed, whether he co-ordinates, what he's going to look like. Nine times out of ten I teach them parrot fashion. I can't possibly teach them technically, because they're never going to remember the terminology or anything."

Oddly enough, the damage done to the Diablo had a beneficial effect where the realism of the film's ending was concerned. "Hammer had intended to hire the boat out later on to other studios as a permanent pirate ship if anybody wanted one," claims Ian Scoones. Consequently, Hammer's special effects team had prepared a model of the ship for the fiery climax. "The model was intended for burning only," Scoones points out. "It was quite a large model. George the carpenter made it and it was about 12 feet long." Some model shots were actually filmed; "I did a lot of the photography of the model galleon in the mist," Kit West points out. But the full-size ship was so damaged by the end of filming that Hammer decided to torch it for real at the climax. "It was the first film that Les let me supervise without him being there," says Scoones. "He said, 'I'll come in for the big fire at the end, but you've learnt to do all the other stuff now' – cannons blowing holes in balsa wood parts of the boat, etc. So there I was with two experienced other guys, one of whom didn't like me anyway. So if I was going to make a mistake, he'd let me make a mistake..."

Scoones shudders when he remembers the dangerous finale. "That was the worst day of my life ever and Les should have known better. He was panicking a bit on that one. We had these large metal trays that we put in the scaffolding underneath the duckboards and the decking, and we filled these with a mixture of petrol and paraffin. Around the gunwales we had these fish-tails, which had to be lit from the boat before we got off – this is gas burning, although it's turned down – knowing that the fumes were building up all the time from the petrol inside it. If it had gone up, Les and I would have gone. Nobody else would do it with him. They all said, 'This is madness, Les!'

"We'd already got a lot of what we call B4s and Y4s (one's black smoke, the other's white smoke) and a few other blackbursters to explode as if it were gunpowder going off. They were all wired up electrically and that was okay – those wires went to the mainland. We also had these gas hoses from the mainland, from large propane bottles, wired to the inside of the ship, knowing that we would lose the rubber tubing. Les and I had to literally scramble about in semi-darkness until we saw daylight and knew there was a fish-tail to be lit, then call out to the mainland, 'Turn it on, Charlie!' Then there was a whoosh of air and a little flame and we had to shout, 'Turn it down!' – so that we just had it smouldering. But all the time that we were playing with this fire, we knew that behind us were these trays of diesel fuel mixed with petrol and paraffin. And it was very hairy, because it was like a timebomb ready to explode. In hindsight, because I didn't see the danger, I didn't understand the chemistry. We had the fire brigade there. We had about four cameras on that and one of the cameras was fine, but it caught an over-zealous fireman running in with his hose, because when it went up, it really went up. It was a fantastic, wonderful blaze, which was great, but he'd never seen anything like this and he thought it was time to put it out. He ran right in front of the main camera's lens, after being told not to."

Don Mingaye also remembers the blaze: "They fired it at the end, set fire to the whole thing. When they fired it, it tilted and capsized. We had some riggers standing by and one of the oars broke. One of the rigger chaps got caught by this and was injured, but I don't think that ever reached the papers."

Filming ended on Friday 4 October after seven weeks. Post-production was a more relaxed affair this time, as the film wasn't due for release until the following summer. James Needs again edited with assistant Chris Barnes. Roy Hyde returned as sound editor, having previously worked on The Mummy, and would now stay on in this capacity for the year. John Hollingsworth again got Gary Hughes to score the film. During filming, in August, Hammer's business manager, Brian Lawrence, joined the Board of Directors.

On 14 February, surgeons at Leeds General Infirmary in Britain had revealed that, two months previously, they had successfully transplanted a kidney from a dead man, with the consent of relatives, into a living patient. Renal transplantation is today a matter of routine but in 1963 it was a revelation. The medical world was fast catching up on the exploits of Mary Shelley's infamous creation, but, for the moment, the Baron still had a trick or two up his sleeve. Indeed, he was about to burst onto the screen again in Hammer's latest instalment.

The Evil of Frankenstein was the third film in Hammer's Frankenstein series, but it wasn't a sequel – or, for that matter, related in any way – to the previous two movies. Instead, Tony Hinds started the story from scratch, retelling, quite differently, the Baron's early experiments. Hinds' script had certain similarities with a script Peter Bryan had submitted on 8 May 1958 ('story no 5') for the aborted Tales of Frankenstein TV series. Sadly, no documents remain at the BBFC to gauge their reaction to Hinds' script. For whatever reason, Terence Fisher was not available to direct and Freddie Francis was brought in to fill the gap in what was to be his first colour film as director (apart from the lighthouse sequences he had contributed to Steve Sekely's The Day of the Triffids).

This was Hammer's first and only Frankenstein to be financed by Universal, which meant that the copyright restrictions on their original Jack Pierce make-up were lifted. Not that that made the search for the right 'look' any easier, as once more, as in The Phantom of the Opera, Roy Ashton found himself at the whim of indecisive producers. Ashton must have been under considerable pressure to emulate Pierce's original masterpiece, since all his pre-production sketch designs for the creature,

THE EVIL OF FRANKENSTEIN

PRINCIPAL PHOTOGRAPHY: 14 October to 16 November 1963
DISTRIBUTION:
 UK: Rank; certificate 'X'
 US: Universal
84 minutes; Eastmancolor
UK RELEASE:
 PREMIÈRE: 19 April 1964, at the New Victoria
 GENERAL RELEASE: 31 May 1964, on the ABC circuit
  with *Nightmare*
US RELEASE: 8 May 1964

DIRECTOR: Freddie Francis; PRODUCER: Anthony Hinds;
SCREENPLAY: John Elder; DIRECTOR OF PHOTOGRAPHY: John
Wilcox; CAMERA OPERATOR: Ronnie Maasz; FOCUS PULLER:
G Glover; CLAPPER/LOADER: Tony Richmond; CAMERA GRIP: Albert
Cowland; CAMERA MAINTENANCE: John Kerley; ASSISTANT
DIRECTOR: Bill Cartlidge; 2ND ASSISTANT: Hugh Harlow;
3RD ASSISTANT: Stephen Victor; ART DIRECTOR: Don Mingaye;
DRAUGHTSMAN: Fred Carter; SUPERVISING EDITOR: James Needs;
ASSISTANT EDITOR: Chris Barnes; MUSIC: Don Banks; MUSIC
SUPERVISORS: John Hollingsworth/Philip Martell; SOUND
RECORDIST: Ken Rawkins; BOOM OPERATOR: T Buchanan; BOOM
ASSISTANT: Roy Mingaye; SOUND TRANSFER OPERATOR: Michael
Sale; SOUND MAINTENANCE: Charles Bouvet; SOUND CAMERA
OPERATOR: A Thorne; SOUND EDITOR: Roy Hyde; MAKE-UP: Roy

Ashton; MAKE-UP ASSISTANT: Richard Mills; HAIRSTYLIST: Frieda
Steiger; ASSISTANT HAIRDRESSER: Daisy Bais; PRODUCTION
MANAGER: Don Weeks; CONTINUITY: Pauline Harlow; WARDROBE:
Rosemary Burrows; ASSISTANT WARDROBE: Maggie Lewin; SPECIAL
EFFECTS: Les Bowie; SPECIAL EFFECTS ASSISTANTS: Ray Caple, Ian
Scoones, Kit West; STUDIO MANAGER: Arthur Kelly; PRODUCTION
SECRETARY: Maureen White; CHIEF ACCOUNTANT: W H V Able;
BRAY STUDIOS ACCOUNTANT: Ken Gordon; CONSTRUCTION
MANAGER: Arthur Banks; CHIEF ELECTRICIAN: Jack Curtis;
MASTER CARPENTER: Charles Davies; MASTER PAINTER: Lawrence
Wrenn; MASTER PLASTERER: Stan Banks; PROPERTY MASTER:
Tommy Money; PROPERTY BUYER: Eric Hillier; FLOOR PROPS
CHARGEHAND: Danny Skundric; ELECTRICAL SUPERVISOR:
George Robinson; ELECTRICAL CHARGEHAND: Vic Hemmings;
STILLS: Tom Edwards; DRIVERS: Coco Epps, Laurie Martin

Peter Cushing (Frankenstein); Peter Woodthorpe (Zoltan); Duncan
Lamont (Chief of Police); Sandor Eles (Hans); Katy Wild (Beggar
Girl); David Hutcheson (Burgomaster); James Maxwell (Priest);
Howard Goorney (Drunk); Anthony Blackshaw; David Conville
(Policemen); Caron Gardner (Burgomaster's Wife); Kiwi Kingston
(The Creature)

UNCREDITED: Tony Arpino (Body Snatcher); Frank Forsyth
(Manservant); Robert Flynn, Derek Martin (Roustabouts)

which totalled 120 by the end, were subtle variations on Pierce's Monster.
Eventually, after much deliberation and soul-searching, the powers that
were finally decided they liked design number 112. "For *The Evil of
Frankenstein* I did hundreds of different drawings before the producers
could fix their ideas on what they wanted. When they eventually decided
on the design, I set it up full-size in clay, then photographed it. They said
it was okay and gave me the go-ahead to go on with it. The design had
some resemblance to the original American *Frankenstein* with Boris
Karloff, but was different in several ways. I had the idea of the cranium
being opened across the top of the forehead and rather clumsily sewn
together with large thongs [in actual fact boot-laces], to suggest the crude
surgical procedures of the time. I think I put the electrodes on the temple
whereas, in the Karloff one, they put them on the neck. A wrestler called
Kiwi Kingston played the monster. I had him wear divers' boots which I
thought would suggest a great lumbering creature." [4]

Further conflict arose, as Ashton explained. "*The Evil of Frankenstein* was
really Tony Hinds' and Freddie Francis' picture. I only executed their
ideas and it was already good enough for me if I could get them to
agree to something. In fact, I had been modelling on a project for the
monster's head, which is a very time-consuming business, and coming
back I found a very large gouge right across the top of the forehead, half
an inch deep. I was furious. Well, a little later on, the two of then simply
stepped in and said, 'We are sorry we did that, but we wondered what the
effect would be if we had a great big groove there.' 'Thanks very much,'
I replied, 'it only took me about three days to get this one ready.' Now,
as they had approved the basic structure, which was very square, I had
actually made the foundation and I had cast and moulded it. And then

*The Creature wakes. Kiwi Kingston in The
Evil of Frankenstein (1963).*

Baron Frankenstein (Peter Cushing) tries in vain to prevent the Creature (Kiwi Kingston) from drinking a bottle of chloroform in The Evil of Frankenstein (1963).

they asked, 'Do you think you could round it off a bit?' Another few days of hard labour to do! They just didn't realise how long such a process is." 5

Shooting began on Monday 14 October. In total Universal contributed £160,000 to the production. Surviving The Devil-Ship Pirates were Don Weeks, Hugh Harlow, Stephen Victor, Don Mingaye (in charge of the art department while Bernard Robinson took a break), James Needs, Chris Barnes, Ken Rawkins, Roy Ashton, Frieda Steiger, Pauline Harlow and Rosemary Burrows (taking over the wardrobe department while Molly Arbuthnot likewise had a rest). Freddie Francis favourite John Wilcox was brought in to light the picture and Ronnie Maasz returned to Hammer to operate after working on Francis' Nightmare. Halfway through production, accountant Roy Skeggs joined the company after completing Zulu. Skeggs would become production supervisor in the seventies, then producer, and would eventually take over the company.

Though an excellent DP and a more than capable director of Hammer's psychological thrillers, Freddie Francis had difficulty in relating to the Gothic genre (which he openly admits) and, indeed, couldn't elicit any of the Gothic atmosphere that had so enriched Terence Fisher's films. The film nevertheless saw the very welcome return of Peter Cushing to the Frankenstein role, with Hungarian actor Sandor Elès (in a poorly motivated 'assistant' role), Peter Woodthorpe and Katy Wild in support. Duncan Lamont returned after appearing in Hammer's last two adventures, The Scarlet Blade and The Devil-Ship Pirates.

At 6'5" and 238 pounds, New Zealand wrestler Kiwi Kingston was called upon to play the monster. Unfortunately, the end result of Roy Ashton's painstaking make-up research resembled little more than an inanimate papier-mâché mask, allowing no facial movements and thus losing all trace of humanity. Coupled with Kingston's limited repertoire of stomping around in his heavy diving boots, the upshot was a robotic, stumbling brute which, to all intents and purposes, was little more than an expensive prop.

In compensation, the visuals are colourful to watch, thanks to John Wilcox's stunning colour photography, particularly in the lab scenes. Francis explains, "I did persuade Hammer to spend quite a large share of our rather low budget on the laboratory set, which I think was pretty good. We had managed to get a wonderful guy with the name of Frank Humphries, who, of all things, did the most fantastic drawings for kids' comics – you know, cowboys and Indians type of things. He drew some wonderful way-out sketches for the laboratory. I was hoping to make it quite effective. And obviously there was no actor around of the calibre of Boris Karloff so I thought I'd take a chance on somebody like Kiwi Kingston, who was a wrestler and a very nice, gentle soul … [I wanted] two ingredients in the film which I thought were completely right – which was sort of a good-looking, interesting and exciting type of laboratory, and a gentle giant who one really felt sort of sorry for. But Karloff was so wonderful in the part, it's jolly hard to compete … mine was just a pale imitation." [6]

Don Mingaye led the art department with some fine sets, including the wonderfully dilapidated chateau on Stage 1. The watermill at the beginning was based on a working mill Mingaye visited. The village square on the backlot was used to good effect, particularly during the carnival scenes, and the Gothic structure, previously seen as the entrance to Beverly Manor in *The Scarlet Blade*, now became the entrance to Chateau Frankenstein. Location shooting took the crew to Monkey Island Lane, the road which today leads to Bray Marina, for the scene where Frankenstein's carriage happens upon the beggar girl escaping from the youths.

Make-up man Roy Ashton had a field day kitting out the masks for the carnival scenes. Some of them were left-overs from the ball sequence in *The Kiss of the Vampire*. Ashton's ingenuity was also called for in another scene, as he explained: "Freddie often got last-minute ideas. On one occasion he wanted the Frankenstein Monster to bash his hand through a glass panel and, since this was not in the script, no sugar glass had been prepared. 'Roy,' he accosted me, 'I apologise for springing it on you, but can you help us there?' As they were shooting already, everybody was waiting for me to produce a brilliant brainwave, so I had to gallop around somewhat." [5] He continued, "I knew there was a piece of tin in the make-up department. I ran up the stairs into one of the workshops and borrowed a pair of tin-snips. I made an enclosure which resembled a clenched hand out of this metal and packed it with sponge plastic and so on, so that it would not injure [Kiwi's] knuckles, and then on the outside of the metal piece I fashioned other knuckles out of rubber and so on, which resembled a hand, a clenched fist. They were holding up the film until I could do it – I was running from one place to another." [7]

The film contains an excellent matte painting of the valley as the graverobber carries the body to Frankenstein's shack in the pre-credits sequence. Ian Scoones remembers, "Ray Caple painted that and he animated the water by stop-frame. Ray was solely taught by Les and is sadly no longer with us. He was an untrained artist that just listened to the way Les taught him. Always the quick gimmicks, such as holding two or three brushes at once, one with yellow, one with green, one lighter green, and just twisting the wrists and doing a whole tree in seconds."

Just after the credits we witness Frankenstein animating a freshly extracted heart. Scoones explains the effect: "The heart was modelled out of plasticene to start with, then a mould was made in plaster, which was then filled up with latex. We put in a balloon connected to a compressed-air rig, which was literally an air bottle, an aqualung. Aqualungs are very useful in special effects. By just twisting it on and off, because the seal wasn't complete, you'd inflate the balloon, which made the rubber heart expand. And then you'd turn the gas off, the pressure goes down and the heart would deflate. So by turning it on and off again, but only very slightly, you got the illusion of the heart beating. It was as crude as that."

The film ends with one of Hammer's blazing spectaculars on brick Stage 2. Scoones remembers the blowing up of the chateau at the end: "The chateau was half-3D model and half-painting. The background part was on hardboard and the wing with the tower was built using little toy builders' bricks. The whole of the turret, which had to blow up with miniature pyrotechnics, was shot at high

A publicity shot from The Evil of Frankenstein (1963) showing Creature Kiwi Kingston with Katy Wild and Nightmare star Jennie Linden.

speed to give it the right scale. Les was used to blowing up paintings. Since the movie is shot in two dimensions, the eye is fooled."

Shooting ended on Saturday 16 November, after a lightning five weeks. A special dinner party was held in the Lancaster Room of the Savoy Hotel on Wednesday 13 November to celebrate the completion of Anthony Hinds' 50th film as producer (though *The Evil of Frankenstein* was actually his 51st). Over 60 guests were present, including James Carreras, Brian Lawrence, Peter Cushing, John Trevelyan, Terence Fisher, Arthur Banks, Arthur Grant, Freddie Francis, Oliver Reed, Heather Sears and Michael Carreras. The atmosphere was enhanced by large posters on the walls depicting the Hammer classics, place-names held aloft by little skeletons and a table centrepiece consisting of a monster labelled 'The Pit Of Doom', with the caption, 'Do not feed ... you will be his dinner'. The guests entered into the spirit of things by wearing scarlet-lined cloaks.

Following this, Hinds' name would only appear once more as producer (on *Fanatic* in 1964); with Michael Carreras gone, he had to fulfil more of an executive role, although he still remained the guiding light behind the scenes, assisting the various producers. He took the change in tempo surprisingly well: "You know, I thought I would miss being on the floor terribly (actually physically acting as producer) but, in the event (the event being that Michael Carreras had decided to go it alone and I had to work from Wardour Street), I found I quite enjoyed my brief stint as an executive. It was very cloistered. I used to train up from the country every morning and train back in the evening, never leaving my office, not even for lunch, and not seeing anyone other than those who dropped by to see me. You get a lot of work done that way." [8]

As *The Evil of Frankenstein* went into post-production with editors Needs and Barnes and sound editor Roy Hyde, music supervisor John Hollingsworth brought in Don Banks to score the picture. Alas, Hollingsworth died at his Hammersmith flat on 29 December 1963, at the age of 47, from tuberculosis. Hammer asked Philip Martell to step in and complete *The Evil of Frankenstein*; he would soon stay on as Hollingsworth's successor. While Hollingsworth's name appears on most of Hammer's fantasy films up to that time, in truth a lot of his work had to be completed by other conductors and directors in his declining years. Hollingsworth had been suffering from tuberculosis for a long time and his doctor had instructed him to convalesce for a few months a year in Switzerland. It was during these convalescent periods that other conductors had to step in to help. For now, Marcus Dods would step in to cover the next production, which was already in preparation.

In 1963, Canadian writer John Lewellyn Devine approached Hammer with a story synopsis called *The Gorgon*, which was eventually expanded into a script and submitted on 1 May. It would appear that Hammer felt this script was too 'cumbersome' and so commissioned John Gilling to simplify the story (including the names) and to convert it into a working screenplay in line with the film we know today. Thus, the village of Villandondorf and the Castle Barsikoff in the Devine script were changed to the less troublesome Vandorf and Borski respectively. It would also appear that Hammer were purging all English references in the script, transforming it into another mid-European Gothic horror; hence Gilling got rid of Bannister and his nephew Richard Chapter, replacing them with the doomed Heitz family. While Gilling retained Professor Masterson of London, the character would eventually change in the film to Professor Meister of Leipzig.

Another important change was in the concept of the Gorgon, who was transformed from the beautiful temptress of the original story to the hideous creature we see at the end of the film. The major change between the two scripts, however, lies in the climax. In Devine's story Masterson and

Richard Pasco turns to stone, the final victim of The Gorgon (1963).

THE GORGON

PRINCIPAL PHOTOGRAPHY: 9 December to 16 January 1963/4
DISTRIBUTION:
  UK: BLC; certificate 'X'
  US: Columbia
84 minutes; Eastmancolor
UK RELEASE:
  TRADE SHOW: 19 August 1964, at the Columbia Theatre with *The Curse of the Mummy's Tomb*
  GENERAL RELEASE: 18 October 1964, on the ABC circuit with *The Curse of the Mummy's Tomb*
US RELEASE: 31 December 1964, with *The Curse of the Mummy's Tomb*

DIRECTOR: Terence Fisher; PRODUCER: Anthony Nelson Keys; SCREENPLAY: John Gilling, based on an original story by J Llewellyn Devine; PRODUCTION DESIGNER: Bernard Robinson; ART DIRECTOR: Don Mingaye; DIRECTOR OF PHOTOGRAPHY: Michael Reed; CAMERA OPERATOR: Cece Cooney; CAMERA GRIP: Albert Cowland; ASSISTANT DIRECTOR: Bert Batt; 2ND ASSISTANT DIRECTOR: Hugh Harlow; 3RD ASSISTANT DIRECTOR: Stephen Victor; SUPERVISING EDITOR: James Needs; EDITOR: Eric Boyd-Perkins; MUSIC: James Bernard; MUSIC SUPERVISOR: Marcus

Dods; SOUND RECORDIST: Ken Rawkins; SOUND EDITOR: Roy Hyde; MAKE-UP: Roy Ashton; MAKE-UP ASSISTANT: Richard Mills; HAIRSTYLIST: Frieda Steiger; PRODUCTION MANAGER: Don Weeks; CONTINUITY: Pauline Harlow; WARDROBE SUPERVISOR: Molly Arbuthnot; WARDROBE MISTRESS: Rosemary Burrows; SPECIAL EFFECTS: Syd Pearson; SPECIAL EFFECTS ASSISTANT: Ray Caple; FIGHT ARRANGER: Peter Diamond; STUDIO MANAGER: Arthur Kelly; CHIEF ACCOUNTANT: W H V Able; BRAY STUDIOS ACCOUNTANT: Ken Gordon; CONSTRUCTION MANAGER: Arthur Banks; CHIEF ELECTRICIAN: Jack Curtis; MASTER CARPENTER: Charles Davies; MASTER PAINTER: Lawrence Wrenn; MASTER PLASTERER: Stan Banks; PROPERTY MASTER: Tommy Money; PROPERTY BUYER: Eric Hillier; STILLS: Tom Edwards

Peter Cushing (Doctor Namaroff); Christopher Lee (Professor Meister); Richard Pasco (Paul Heitz); Barbara Shelley (Carla Hoffmann); Michael Goodliffe (Professor Heitz); Patrick Troughton (Inspector Kanof); Joseph O'Conor (Coroner); Prudence Hyman (Chatelaine); Jack Watson (Ratoff); Redmond Phillips (Hans); Jeremy Longhurst (Bruno Heitz); Toni Gilpin (Sascha Cass); Joyce Hemson (Martha); Alister Williamson (Janus Cass); Michael Peake (Policeman)

UNCREDITED: Sally Nesbit (Nurse)

Namaroff arrive at Bannister's house to find the Gorgon already dead, killed off screen by Richard, whose body is found clutching a shield and bloodied sword. Gilling added Paul's exciting fight with Namaroff in the more fitting surroundings of the castle, Namaroff's death scene that followed and Meister's on-screen beheading of the Gorgon. Again, no paperwork survives at the BBFC to see what their reaction was when the script was originally submitted.

Namaroff (Peter Cushing) hides Carla's (Barbara Shelley) secret in The Gorgon (1963).

Back were Anthony Nelson Keys in the producer's chair and Gothic favourite Terence Fisher. It was Fisher's first film for Hammer in the nearly two years since the disappointing Phantom and, despite doing his best with the subject matter, it would almost be another two years before his Gothic touch was fully reinstated in Dracula Prince of Darkness. The subject appealed to Fisher, who loved to centre the drama around one key family he had with The Curse of the Werewolf, which remained a personal favourite of his. Fisher recalled, "I am unashamedly, and totally without modesty, very proud of The Gorgon. It is a film that emphasises the poetics of the fantastic, rather than the horror. I am very pleased with the characters in that film; they're a lot more complex than usually is the case and there's more mystery lurking around them too, which can be pretty rare in this type of film, where far too often only the spectacle counts, rather than the psychological motivation leading up to that event. The script was written by John Gilling, and it is one of the best scripts I've ever worked on." [9]

Shooting started at Bray on Monday 9 December, just three weeks after principal photography on The Evil of Frankenstein had ended. That film's core team returned, but they were now joined by lighting cameraman Michael Reed, production designer Bernard Robinson, assistant director Bert Batt (all of whom were last involved with The Devil-Ship Pirates), camera operator Cece Cooney (last seen on The Scarlet Blade), wardrobe supervisor Molly Arbuthnot (last seen: Nightmare) and editor Eric Boyd-Perkins (last seen: Captain Clegg). Bert Batt remembers working with Terence Fisher: "As a first assistant director, working with and for Terry Fisher was pure joy and that went for all his crews and actors. He was a real gentleman who knew his craft backwards and was never averse to an idea that was better than his. He would say 'Well done' and use it. However, he was so on the ball that that didn't happen very often and his actors had total trust in him in not letting them go over the top, which is easy to do in a horror movie. He was a little fellow with a big sense of humour and he loved to laugh. He would throw his head back and guffaw, shaking from head to foot. He is remembered with respect and affection by everyone who knew him."

The film reunited the successful trio of Peter Cushing, Christopher Lee and Terence Fisher for their fifth film together after a break of almost five years since The Mummy. The previous four films were now considered classics of the genre, but The Gorgon would struggle to get there, due not to

Fisher but a rather poor Gorgon, which we'll come to later. The casting was first rate, providing leads Cushing and Lee with some very interesting role reversals – Cushing cold and villainous, Lee brusque but avuncular. Lee recalls: "I had a vague idea of Professor Meister being an Einstein-like figure, which is why I wore a wild wig and a bushy moustache. That didn't please Jimmy Carreras very much. He said, 'I don't know why they've made you look like that.' I said, 'Well, they've made me look different.' He said, 'Yes, but it's just Christopher Lee made up!' I said, 'What about some of the other things I've done?' He said, 'Ah – but they didn't look like you!' Peter Cushing played Dr Namaroff and I kept on calling him 'Dr. Nasty-cough', because he did have a cough at that time. We found it very difficult on occasions to keep a straight face, extremely difficult.

"The Gorgon was a good idea, but they got the name wrong. Megaera was not a Gorgon, she was a Fury. Medusa, Euryale and Stheno were the Gorgons." Nor was Lee impressed by the Gorgon's appearance. "The make-up, I have to say, was extremely unconvincing and I think everybody was aware of it. The whole film built up to the climax when you see the Gorgon and it really was a let-down. It built up to an anti-climax."

So what went wrong with the Gorgon? A clash of ideas and too many cooks. The Gorgon's head was a collaborative effort between Roy Ashton, doing the facial make-up, and special effects man Syd Pearson doing the snakes in her hair. Unfortunately, both men had different concepts of the snakes. The producers settled for Pearson's idea, which had half a dozen large mechanical snakes darting in and out of her head rather unconvincingly. "That really wasn't to my taste," Ashton lamented. "I felt that the snakes were too big. If you remember, it was Cellini who had this sculpture of a warrior holding the severed head of Medusa. And the snakes were smaller, in clusters rather than two or three big serpents as in the film. Really, each lock of hair should be a serpent. That would have been my approach to it. I suggested that they should get these little rubbery snakes which they use in these imported children's toys. These were the toys which if held in the hand would writhe about in a most lifelike way. I thought if they went about it in that way they could have an appearance of constant movement. They finally agreed to having the snakes and lights controlled by a remote control unit." [10]

Prudence Hyman took over when Barbara Shelley's Carla Hoffman transformed into the Gorgon. Shelley explains, "If I was needed on the set as Carla, the nurse who turned into the Gorgon at the full moon, it would take one to two hours to switch from the Gorgon to Carla, or even longer the other way. As I said to Anthony Nelson Keys, the producer of the film and a great friend of mine, there was no need at all for make-up since I am not afraid of snakes and they could have just threaded a hundred grass snakes through the headpiece. Half the audience wouldn't have even seen the face with all the snakes whipping around. They would see the snakes and dive under the seats and we would have had the classic Gothic horror film of all time." [11] It's interesting to note that Shelley's concept also conjures up Cellini's work, although the RSPCA might have had a word or two to say about it.

Syd Pearson's idea was different and unfortunately the producers agreed. Pearson explains, "There were quite a few problems in making this picture. The greatest of course was the Gorgon's head, with the snakes writhing in the hair ... After giving it a considerable amount of thought we decided to make the snakes out of rubber. I sought the services of a sculptor and he designed and made for me the necessary plaster moulds in which I was able to cast latex rubber snakes. I made a dozen of these and we had about a foot of snake's body as well as the head. The tongues were articulated so that we could move them, flash them around, and the body of the snake itself was again articulated so that we could make them writhe, withdraw them, extend them, and all this was placed in what I would call a skull cap, because we had an actress [Prudence Hyman] wearing this black long-haired wig containing the snakes. She wore this, bless her heart, throughout the whole of the sequences dealing with Megaera – the Gorgon. And although she had lots of cables and pipes trailing behind her, I don't think anyone ever realised it. She walked with an air and grace of some-body out of this world, and we were able to execute these shots by means of a small, what I call, an organ, which I personally played, which caused the snakes to writhe, as many as were required, one, two – up to a dozen at any one time. As she walked forward down the stairs, we were able to trail all these cables and electronic pieces of equipment without them being noticed by anyone." [12]

Bert Batt remembers Megaera's 'air and grace' rather differently. "During preparation of *The Gorgon*, Tony and Terry decided that the Gorgon should appear to be floating as she moved across the floor or negotiated a staircase. They wanted her clothed in diaphanous materials, their effect to be enhanced by a gentle wind machine. Who better then than a ballet dancer to double for Barbara Shelley in the wide and long shots? A woman totally trained in graceful movement. They hired Pru Hyman, a charming lady who was very excited at the prospect of being a Gorgon. This was not to last. Having had this very good idea, Tony and Terry unwittingly wrecked it.

"A special effects man presented them with the Gorgon's head, Pru some time previously having had her head measured. Mounted on a plastic skullcap was a marvellous wig from which protruded nine utterly realistic snakes. They were of course thin rubber tubes with coiled springs inside. As the head moved the snakes swayed about. 'Very nice,' said Tony and Terry, 'but there is no menace there. The snakes should dart back and forth as when they attack. Their mouths should be open and their tongues should flicker and their eyes should be pulsing green pea bulbs.' Unfortunately, they omitted to tell [Pearson] that the Gorgon was required to float about. Had they done so, the SPFX man would have told them that they needed a weightlifter and not a ballet dancer.

"By the time the new specification head was ready, the commencement of shooting was close. Pru was called to the studio to try it on. Each snake now had three sections of articulated metal tube inside it. To motivate them a steel cable was inserted plus an electric wire to power the eyes and a thin rubber air-tube to activate the tongue. Hanging from the back of the skullcap were now nine cables, nine electric wires and nine rubber tubes. They trailed back 15 or 20 feet. The cables went through nine holes in a wooden box and were attached to nine eccentric wheels. Protruding from the box was a winding handle. The electric cables were hooked up to a dimmer and the nine air tubes were inserted into a large black rubber bulb. When set to work it looked great.

"Pru was called down again. We placed the contraption on her head; she staggered under the weight and winced as the nine nuts securing the snakes to the cap ground into her skull, and the weight of the trailing cables and tubes pulled it off her head and she fell over. So we picked her up and sent her home pending adjustments. A wide belt was made and stitched to the back of it were leather tubes through which the cables, wires and rubber tubes were threaded. With the belt around her waist and all the wires and cables going down her back and trailing from her middle section, the snakes stayed put. But as for elegant movement, she may as well have been wearing an old deep-sea diver's helmet and his massive boots. As with the Diablo of *The Devil-Ship Pirates*, shooting was upon us and it was too late to do anything about it.

"Shooting had its problems. Three men were required to be behind Pru as she struggled to float along; they had to be one behind the other and crouch when walking, the first man winding the handle on the eccentric wheel box, the second working the dimmer slide, and the third squeezing and releasing the rubber bulb. Bodies make shadows and on the floor it looked as though the Gorgon was trailing a rope to which were clinging three rather large chimpanzees. The cameraman had the job of sorting that out. On the days that Pru worked, she didn't eat much. Her stomach was full of aspirins. Barbara Shelley had her problems too. Actors like to perform on a quiet stage, sound mixers are fond of that too, but all the time there was the sound of a dimmer slide moving back and forth like someone grinding coffee. It was great fun!"

For the decapitation sequence, Pearson set up a replica head made of latex rubber, which Lee then knocked off a dummy body. The scene could have turned nasty, according to Roy Ashton. "The decapitation was rather phoney. Actually, it was nearly a real head that whistled down there. Prudence Hyman was supposed to duck when Christopher Lee swung his massive sword in her direction. However, we rehearsed the scene and everything was fine. Then came the actual thing; Chris Lee had to wield this six-foot sword and Prudence Hyman had to duck, but she forgot to – luckily for her Bert Batt, the assistant director, could somehow sense this and yanked her off the stairs while Chris' sword whistled through the air, just where her neck had been!" [10]

The rolling of the dummy head down the stairs had to be filmed a number of times until it came to rest in a suitable position to show its transformation back to Carla. Pearson then took still photographs of its position for reference and the rest was done in his small studio. For the first stage he took the script literally; reasoning that the snakes were meant to represent extensions of

Megaera's hellish brain, he pulled back the snakes to give the impression that they were retracting inside her head. For the next phase, the transmogrification back to Carla, Pearson used stop-motion animation.

Pearson explained, "I had plaster casts made of the actress who played the Gorgon – her face – and we made wax casts of the face, which were made up by the make-up man exactly as he had made up the actress as the Gorgon. Now this very thin wax face was placed over the head and hair of the latex cast of Barbara Shelley, which had been made up to look like Barbara Shelley lying asleep. When this was done, we then locked off our camera, and made sure that nothing moved – the set-up remained absolutely stable – the stage doors were virtually kept locked. The atmosphere was kept as near as we could at a constant temperature, because you can imagine how many hours a day we worked ... working as we were with a stop-motion camera, we didn't know what our results were and we had to rely on the fact that everything was exactly the same the following morning as it was the previous evening when we left ... and then very slowly, as you can well imagine on a stop-motion camera, we removed tiny particles off the face to reveal that of Barbara Shelley underneath ... This scene, though only running some 15 seconds on the screen, took us four and a half weeks to shoot, frame by frame, working solidly, with breaks of course, for approximately 10-12 hours a day. And, as you may well know, using the stop-motion camera you cannot go and see the rushes on the morrow, you have to wait, and I consider it to be my most frustrating period in motion pictures, waiting that five weeks approximately to see the results of my transformation." [12]

Meister (Christopher Lee) prepares to slay The Gorgon (1963).

Bernard Robinson revamped a number of Don Mingaye's standing sets, both external and internal, from the previous Frankenstein production. Robinson transformed Mingaye's interior set of the dilapidated Chateau Frankenstein on Stage 1 into the suitably decaying interiors of Castle Borski, which Fisher used superbly to pile on the tension. Peter Cushing faced a further touch of déjà vu when Frankenstein's laboratory was revamped into Namaroff's. Meanwhile, on the Bray lot, the Gothic structure, which had formed the outside entrance to Chateau Frankenstein, now became the entrance to Castle Borski, and the pub from The Evil of Frankenstein now became the outside of Heitz's house. In addition, Ray Caple's superb matte painting of the mountain, valley and cottage, seen in the pre-credits sequence of the previous film, was re-used in The Gorgon, just after the credits, to introduce Heitz's house.

During production, James Carreras brought a party of Columbia executives down to Bray to watch filming. The delegation consisted of Anthony Bray (Secretary of Columbia Pictures and Director of British Lion Columbia), Kenneth Maidment (Joint Managing Director of Columbia Pictures) and Bill Graf (Vice President of Columbia Pictures). Also during filming, on Sunday 15 December, Cash on Demand was finally released in England. As the year drew to its close, filming continued on The Gorgon. 1964 was to be another year of change for the company.

TWELVE

Elstree Calling

(1964)

As 1964 began, Hammer were still hard at work on *The Gorgon*. Principal photography ended on Thursday 16 January after six weeks. On Thursday the 5th, *The Kiss of the Vampire* finally premièred with *Paranoiac* at the New Victoria Theatre, going on general release on the ABC circuit from the 26th. The double-bill was well received critically but *Kiss* would later be severely butchered for transmission on American television. Not only were most of the violent scenes extracted, including the bat attack at the end (leaving only the long shot of the bats swooping down on the chateau), but, in order to pad the film out for its two-hour running time on commercial TV, Universal took it upon themselves to shoot and insert extra scenes using American actors. These naturally had to be isolated from the rest of the film and told the riveting story of the family who sew Dr Ravna's ceremonial gowns! (Those surplices that caused so much angst at the BBFC.) To add insult to injury, Universal then changed the title of the film to the more ambiguous *Kiss of Evil*.

As *The Gorgon* went into post-production under editors James Needs and Eric Boyd-Perkins and sound editor Roy Hyde at Hammer House, Marcus Dods took over from John Hollingsworth as music supervisor and James Bernard composed another haunting score. "Marcus Dods was a rather shy, retiring man and I never got to know him well," remembered Bernard. "He also died comparatively young (in his sixties I think). He never really wanted to butt in on the two scores I did with him. I think he felt he was only filling in and didn't want to become fully involved with Hammer. We'd have the music sessions like we always did and do a music breakdown and decide where we needed the music. *The Gorgon* was most interesting and it was Marcus who had the idea for the voice of the Gorgon. We wanted to have a semi-human sound of the Gorgon calling from the depths of the forest and he said, 'What about if we put a soprano voice in unison with an electronic instrument?'

> **Hammer Productions**
> —— 1 9 6 4 ——
>
> + HYSTERIA
> + THE CURSE OF THE MUMMY'S TOMB
> + THE SECRET OF BLOOD ISLAND
> + SHE
> + FANATIC
> + THE BRIGAND OF KANDAHAR
>
> SHORT FEATURES:
> + THE RUNAWAY
> + DELAYED FLIGHT

OPPOSITE: Ronald Lewis and Yvonne Romain in the costume adventure The Brigand of Kandahar (1964).

"Of course this was early days, not like now when everybody has synthesisers, and I asked what we could use. He said, 'There's a very good thing called a Novachord', which was really like an electric piano. And he knew someone who had one and performed on it, so he got this man to come down. I'd written the part and there was a very good singer called Patricia Clarke, who had one of those very pure voices, which she could make completely asexual. She sang absolutely in unison with the Novachord and you got a rather strange sound: is it human or is it not? I thought that was a clever idea of Marcus' and I thought it worked quite well."

Meanwhile, major changes were afoot at Hammer House that would leave the future of Bray Studios in jeopardy. James Carreras was a good friend of CJ Latta, managing director of the Associated British Picture Corporation (ABPC), through their mutual association with the Variety Club of Great Britain (Latta was one of the twelve founding members). In 1963 ABPC decided to buy into Bray studios, and from 1964 became part-owners alongside Hammer and Columbia (although Hammer would retain the controlling interest). ABPC's influence on Hammer was growing, just as Hammer's relationship with US distributors Columbia and Universal began to collapse. The prospect of a new distribution deal (which would finally crystallise through a joint arrangement which saw Hammer carve up territories between ABPC, 20th Century-Fox and Seven Arts) could not have come at a better time. However, it would come at a price. ABPC owned Elstree Studios and now they insisted that if they were to engage in any such deal, Hammer would have to move their operation to Elstree. This did not worry James Carreras particularly; whilst many saw the advantages of the house studio, in truth Bray was becoming an expensive burden to the Hammer chief. Consequently, after *The Gorgon* Hammer were forced to decant their ABPC pictures to Elstree, using Bray only when the larger studio was unable to accommodate them.

As Hammer moved out of Bray they initially sub-let the studio to producer Bill Luckwell for two low-budget Hammer co-productions: *The Runaway* and *Delayed Flight*. *The Runaway* was a 62-minute black-and-white film about a Polish industrial chemist who gets mixed up in espionage. It starred Greta Gynt, Alex Gallier (who had starred in *The Curse of Frankenstein*) and Paul Williamson and was directed by Tony Young. Not much is known about *The Runaway*, but even less is know about its back-to-back production, *Delayed Flight*. The film starred Helen Cherry, Hugh McDermott and Paul Williamson and was again directed by Tony Young.

Amnesiac Robert
Webber is almost
knocked down by
a car in Hysteria
(1964).

HYSTERIA

PRINCIPAL PHOTOGRAPHY: 10 February to 23 March 1964
DISTRIBUTION:
 MGM; 85 minutes; b/w; UK: certificate 'X'
UK RELEASE:
 TRADE SHOW: 21 May 1965
 GENERAL RELEASE: 27 June 1965
US RELEASE: April 1965

DIRECTOR: Freddie Francis; PRODUCER: Jimmy Sangster;
SCREENPLAY: Jimmy Sangster; PRODUCTION DESIGNER: Edward
Carrick; DIRECTOR OF PHOTOGRAPHY: John Wilcox; CAMERA
OPERATOR: David Harcourt; ASSISTANT DIRECTOR: Basil

Rayburn; SUPERVISING EDITOR: James Needs; MUSIC:
Don Banks; MUSIC SUPERVISOR: Philip Martell; SOUND
RECORDIST: Cyril Swern; SOUND EDITOR: Roy Hyde; MAKE-UP:
Alec Garfath; HAIRSTYLIST: Alice Holmes; PRODUCTION
MANAGER: Don Weeks; CONTINUITY: Yvonne Axworthy;
WARDROBE: Maude Churchill; TITLES: Chambers and Partners

Robert Webber ('Mr Smith'); Lelia Goldoni (Denise); Anthony
Newlands (Doctor Keller); Jennifer Jayne (Gina); Maurice Denham
(Hemmings); Peter Woodthorpe (Marcus Allan); Sandra Boize (English
girl); Sue Lloyd (French girl); Marianne Stone (Allan's secretary); Kiwi
Kingston (French husband); with John Arnatt, Irene Richmond

The vacated Bray Studios would continue to prove a headache for James Carreras. In June 1964 the company's accountant reported that the gross running costs of the mothballed Bray totalled £260 a week. That summer the back lot was cleared and the village square complex that had stood there since 1960 was torn down. With it went the Gothic structure erected in 1962. They would be replaced the following year by the sets for the four back-to-back horror pictures that Elstree would be unable to accommodate and which would be part of the new deal with 20th Century-Fox and Seven Arts.

The choice of projects in 1964 reflected the current climate; two more psychological thrillers, a war film, a costume adventure, a big-budget fantasy adventure and one rather lonely horror picture. However, the move from Bray had caused the Hammer team to fragment once again just as it was becoming re-established. On 10 February, they set sail on another psychological thriller, Hysteria, at the MGM Elstree Studios, while on 24 February they would start work on The Curse of the Mummy's Tomb at the nearby ABPC Elstree studios.

Hysteria was the fifth in Jimmy Sangster's tangled series of psychological thrillers and the third to be directed by Freddie Francis. American 'Chris Smith', found tossed from a crashed and burned-out car four months previously, still suffers from amnesia, unable to even remember his real name. The only thing found on him at the time of the crash was a torn photograph of a beautiful girl... So begins Sangster's latest elaborate and twisting tale of murder and neurosis.

By now the storylines were becoming somewhat familiar, with the usual confusing plot and counterplot where someone is being driven insane for the benefit of others. In fact, the plot bears many close similarities to *Taste of Fear* and *Nightmare*, the only significant difference being that this time it's the male of the species who is being driven off his rocker.

Shooting began on Monday 10 February with a completely new team. Most of the regulars would be employed on Michael Carreras' Mummy vehicle; the only familiar faces that made it out of *The Gorgon* were Don Weeks, James Needs and Roy Hyde. In saying that, poor Don Weeks was employed on both productions, which must have been a colossal headache. Freddie Francis brought back his favourite lighting cameraman, John Wilcox. Sound recordist Cyril Swern had last worked for Hammer on *Maniac*. Edward Carrick took over the art direction as Bernard Robinson was engaged on the other project, which was a satisfactory arrangement for a contemporary story. Of interest were the two portraits in the apartment, which were painted by Sangster's wife (and Hammer's former hairstylist), Monica.

"My heart just wasn't in it," Francis admits. "Too many problems ... I enjoyed working with Robert Webber as little as I've ever enjoyed working with anybody. He was impossible, and he decided to make life as difficult as possible for the little girl we had in the movie, Lelia Goldoni." [1] Jimmy Sangster concurs: "The male lead in *Hysteria* was played by an American actor, Robert Webber. He was a very good actor indeed. He'd never become a 'star' but he was always working. You might not remember the name, but you'd recognise the face straight away. The female lead was an actress named Lelia Goldoni, who was relatively new in the business. For some reason Webber took an instant dislike to her and proceeded to put her down whenever he could. This destroyed whatever confidence she might have had, which affected her performance. It wasn't her fault and Freddie and I did everything we could to set things right. But Webber was a mean-minded guy. Whenever the two of them were on the set at the same time, it cast a pall of gloom. I'm sure we had some light moments, but the overall memory is of an unhappy movie." [2]

Both Peter Woodthorpe and Kiwi Kingston returned after their roles in *The Evil of Frankenstein*, and it's interesting to see the man behind the monster, although his appearance as the fuming Sue Lloyd's husband is very brief. Principal photography ended on Monday 23 March after a painful six weeks. James Needs and Roy Hyde took the film into post-production and Philip Martell returned as music supervisor, bringing back Don Banks to score the film.

Meanwhile, two weeks later on Monday 24 February, the cameras rolled on *The Curse of the Mummy's Tomb* on Elstree's large Stage 3. The *Daily Cinema* tribute to Tony Hinds on his 50th production described Hammer's second Mummy adventure thus: "*The Curse of the Mummy's Tomb* concerns a group of archaeologists on a routine expedition into the Sahara desert who discover an ancient tomb containing the mummy of a pharaoh. Dabbling in things they don't understand, they bring to life a monstrous 20-foot giant which goes on a murder rampage in Cairo. When the gigantic creature escapes into the desert, aircraft and parachute troops go in pursuit. All hell breaks loose in a shattering climax." A little fanciful perhaps? Particularly when what actually followed was a rather dull entry in the developing series.

Although he had long since become frustrated with horror films, Michael Carreras had retained a strong desire to produce another Mummy movie. Now Hammer finally fulfilled his wish, and not only was he allowed to produce and direct it, he was also given the opportunity to write the film as well, which he did in association with director Alvin Rakoff. As an in-joke for his friend Tony Hinds, who had set off on a successful writing career under the pseudonym of John Elder, Carreras chose Henry Younger as his pen name. Though Carreras' story contained an ingenious twist, with the Mummy's brother alive and well and living in London, it nevertheless degenerated into a rather repetitive and over-familiar story of a rampaging mummy intent on wiping out the desecrators of its tomb.

Hammer's Pamela Anderson submitted the script to John Trevelyan on 28 January. Audrey Field commented two days later: "I don't know what they mean by 'original story': it is [reminiscent of] another Hammer film, to say nothing of sundry other effusions, and even a dash of real life, in the background of 'mysterious deaths.' However, it does rather out-Herod Herod in parts, and there are things which are likely to be disgusting. General: There should be a warning on the appearance of the mummy. I do not expect this to be any worse than the other Hammer mummy or mummies.

King (Fred Clark) and Achmed (Michael Ripper) reflect on the curse of the pharaohs in The Curse of the Mummy's Tomb (1964).

THE CURSE OF THE MUMMY'S TOMB

PRINCIPAL PHOTOGRAPHY: 24 February to 27 March 1964
DISTRIBUTION:
  UK: BLC; certificate 'X'
  US: Columbia
80 minutes; Technicolor; Techniscope
UK RELEASE:
  TRADE SHOW: 19 August 1964, at the Columbia Theatre
    with *The Gorgon*
  GENERAL RELEASE: 18 October 1964, on the ABC circuit
    with *The Gorgon*
  US RELEASE: 31 December 1964, with *The Gorgon*

DIRECTOR/PRODUCER: Michael Carreras; ASSOCIATE
PRODUCER: Bill Hill; SCREENPLAY: Henry Younger [ie, Michael
Carreras]; PRODUCTION DESIGNER: Bernard Robinson; ART
DIRECTOR: Don Mingaye; DIRECTOR OF PHOTOGRAPHY: Otto
Heller; CAMERA OPERATOR: Bob Thompson; ASSISTANT
DIRECTOR: Bert Batt; 2ND ASSISTANT DIRECTOR: Hugh Harlow;

SUPERVISING EDITOR: James Needs; EDITOR: Eric Boyd-Perkins;
MUSIC: Carlo Martelli; MUSIC SUPERVISOR: Philip Martell;
SOUND RECORDIST: Claude Hitchcock; SOUND EDITOR: James
Groom; PRODUCTION MANAGER: Don Weeks, MAKE-UP: Roy
Ashton; HAIRSTYLIST: Iris Tilley; CONTINUITY: Eileen Head;
WARDROBE: Betty Adamson and John Briggs; CASTING: David
Booth; TECHNICAL ADVISER: Andrew Low

Terence Morgan (Adam Beauchamp); Ronald Howard (John Bray);
Fred Clark (Alexander King); Jeanne Roland (Annette Dubois);
George Pastell (Hashmi Bey); Jack Gwillim (Sir Giles Dalrymple);
John Paul (Inspector Mackenzie); Dickie Owen (The Mummy); Jill
Mai Meredith (Jenny); Michael Ripper (Nightwatchman); Harold
Goodwin (Fred); Jimmy Gardner (Bert); Vernon Smythe (Jessop);
Marianne Stone (Landlady)

UNCREDITED: Olga Dickie (Housekeeper); Michael McStay (Ra);
Bernard Rebel (Professor Dubois)

We don't want anything too crumbly and worm-eaten in appearance, particularly in close shot. There should also be a *very strong caution* on all shots of severed hands. There is a lot of severed-handiwork in this script and it is going to be fairly disgusting however it is treated. Certain shots are mentioned below as, in my opinion, prohibitive." Reader Newton Branch added on 2 February: "I did not, thank Allah, see the twin mummy of this cursed script, but obviously AOF's general comments follow precedents on the first film and I agree with her detailed comments. This is not 'horror-comic' stuff but there are strong elements of 'horror-disgust'. We should, in the script letter, be detailed and firm, I think."

Trevelyan then summarised Audrey Field's 'detailed comments' in a letter to Pamela Anderson: "This should be basically acceptable for the 'X' category provided that it is in line with previous Hammer productions of this kind, but there is one thing which worries us a good deal. An important point in the story is that at various points people's hands are cut off, and, according to the script, we are to see this. This is not at all a nice idea, and the most that we would accept would be the cutting off of the hands by suggestion or implication; we would not want to see trick shots which convey the impression that the hands are actually cut off, or shots of the results. My comments on points of detail are as follows:

Page 3. Scene 17: Here we have Dubois killed with a knife to the stomach. This may be all right provided that we do not see the knife going in. The script suggests that we are to see blood coming from his mouth. We would not like this.

Page 3. Scene 19: Here we have the first occasion on which we are apparently to see the hand cut off. The script direction reads, 'suddenly the leader's knife enters frame with a mighty blow and severs the hand from the wrist. Blood spurts from the wrist as the dismembered hand topples to the sand. Camera pans with the dismembered hand as the leader raises it and holds it before him. He slowly and painstakingly begins to pry the clenched fingers open, one by one'. This does not appeal to us at all. Could you do this scene in some other way which is less unpleasant and nauseating?

Page 4. Scene 21 & 22: Here we still have trouble with the severed hand. My previous comments apply. We appreciate that in scene 22 the shot will be under titles, but it may well be troublesome.

Page 4. Scene 23: The shot of the beetle on the roast pig sounds a bit disgusting. It may pass, but it seems unnecessary for the incident to appear at all.

Page 9. Scene 34: We would not want any nasty shot of Dubois' body. The script direction says 'It is not a pretty sight. The severed arm is visible.' We would not want the arm to be visible unless it was something that nobody would object to.

Page 12. Scene 46: Here we have 'the bloody stump of Professor Dubois' hand, its fingers crooked upwards.' My previous comments apply. We do not like this idea. If we have to have it, it should be in long shot and very brief.

Page 21. Scene 63: The costume of the Arab dancer is not described. This should not be censorable.

Page 25. Scene 68. In this scene we are apparently to see 'the twisted body of the night watchman lying across an opened packing case. From the position of his head it is apparent that his neck has been broken.' This suggests that we may have a very unpleasant shot. Great care should be taken.

Page 30. Scene 78. The description of this scene suggests that we may have a violent low blow. This should be avoided.

Page 36. Scene 93. Care should be taken with shots of the body being pulled aboard, when 'a sudden mixture of water and blood spreads out from the body.' This could be very unpleasant and macabre. The shot of the body itself in scene 94 should be reasonable.

Page 46. Scene 114. In this scene we have another hand being cut off in flashback. My previous comments apply. We would not want to see it done, or to see shots of spurting blood or the unpleasant results.

Page 78. Scene 182. If the Mummy is no worse than its predecessors we should have no trouble with it, but care should be taken not to make it too unpleasant.

Page 79. Scene 189-190. We never like close shots of people being throttled. The script direction reads 'his eyes bulge, his tongue protrudes ...' etc. This is the kind of thing that worries us. Care should be taken with this. Would it not be possible for the Mummy to hurl King down the steps and kill him in this way, without throttling coming into it?

Page 79. Scene 191. It seems unnecessary for the man to hit the child as described, and I think you could get rid of it.

Pages 84-5. Scene 112. We would not want a really unpleasant shot of the mummified flesh sealing itself 'as if it were oozing mud.' This seems a bit nauseating. Nor would we want Sir Giles killed in this way. The breaking of his back, with the effects on the soundtrack, would be more unpleasant than we would like. Surely there is some more conventional way in which these scenes can be shot?

Page 85. Scene 213. Not too much screaming please!

Page 90. Scene 232 and following. Annette is to be seen wearing a negligée which is described as 'disarranged'. Since she has been subjected to violence by the Mummy we would not want any shot which suggested that there had been some sexual impulse in the violence.

Pages 95-96. Scenes 258-260. We would not want to see Hashmi's head being squashed under the Mummy's foot. Nor would we want to hear any nasty reactions from him, or to see much of the reactions from the bystanders.

Pages 103-4. Scenes 275-278: These scenes, as described, are very unpleasant. We would not want a close shot of Adam's hand trapped in the door, nor of him writhing in agony; nor would we want to see the hand falling to the floor 'bleeding profusely and jerking spasmodically as the nerves play out their final convulsions.' This goes far beyond what we would expect. Adam wrenches the remains of his crushed arm from the crack and falls backwards screaming into the whirling waters of the sewers. I hope you will find some other way of dealing with Adam in this situation, in a way that is more acceptable for the cinema screen. We could have an indication of what happens with some groans, but we really do not want to see hands coming off, bleeding stumps, etc. In this kind of scene horror film material goes into disgust.

Pages 106-107. Scenes 288-292. Again these scenes are very nasty. We would not want any shots of the torn arm waving about during the drowning. Surely the wretched man could be tipped in and left to drown. The script direction suggests that we are to see the corpse floating about among a lot of floating debris. I would think that most cinema audiences would object to this, but would accept the sort of sewer we had in *Les Misérables*.

Page 108. Scene 297. We would not expect any great trouble with the Mummy's hand, but reasonable care should be taken."

Carreras shared the day-to-day producer's work with Bill Hill. As Carreras put it, "The budget was so small. Bill Hill was a friend of mine, but a good producer. I said, 'Bill, I want to direct it, I don't want to have the production chores. But it's got to come in on schedule, so you have to push me hard as far as the schedule is concerned. But I don't want to hear a figure, I don't want to know anything about cost.' Once we'd cast it and put it to bed, ten per cent of everything saved under the budget was his [Hill's]. And if it's more than ten per cent, he got a case of champagne as well." [3] Of interest is a file note in the BBFC records, written by Frank Crofts on 16 March following a query by Hill: "Mr Hill rang up and asked if we were likely to object to a belly-dance by a girl whose navel was bare. I said that it would depend on the way it was done, but I did not think that we should object as long as discretion was used. I suggested that, if he was worried, he should have some cover shots (where her navel was covered). He said he expected an 'A' or even an 'X' for the film."

It was a Michael Carreras film, so naturally it was shot in the glory of widescreen (Techniscope on this occasion). More of the regular team moved across to join the production from *The Gorgon*: production manager Don Weeks (working on *Hysteria* too), assistant director Bert Batt, second assistant Hugh Harlow, production designer Bernard Robinson and his art director Don Mingaye, editors James Needs and Eric Boyd-Perkins, and make-up artist Roy Ashton. Otto Heller was brought in to light the film and Claude Hitchcock joined the team as sound recordist. He had been boom operator on *Quatermass 2* and would continue working on and off with Hammer into the 1970s. He was also sound recordist on *Zulu* and *Born Free*. James Groom returned as sound editor, having last worked on *The Scarlet Blade* before Roy Hyde took over.

The cast is somewhat middle-of-the-road. Burmese-born Jeanne Roland is an obviously dubbed female lead, while the ageless pharaoh Terence Morgan is uninspiring. There's good support from Fred Clark, Ronald Howard, Jack Gwillim and George Pastell. (Poor George Pastell. He didn't fare too well in these mummy films; after having his back broken in the first one, he now gets his head trodden on in this one.) But even delightful cameos from Michael Ripper and Harold Goodwin can't save the show. As for Dickie Owen, the pot-bellied Mummy, his conception takes us right back to Universal's 1940s series, in which the mummy is a lumbering brute. Hammer had no need for such retrograde steps; their success had come by virtue of their originality in depicting the

LEFT: *The Mummy (Dickie Owen) bursts onto the ballroom stage in* The Curse of the Mummy's Tomb *(1964).*

BELOW: *Michael Carreras directs Ronald Howard and Jeanne Roland in* The Curse of the Mummy's Tomb *(1964).*

classic movie monsters as all-new, dynamic and colourful creations. Christopher Lee's mummy had been testament to this.

The make-up, however, was impeccable and Roy Ashton remembered vital lessons learnt from *The Mummy* in order to make it more user-friendly. "In the second one, I had learned from the previous experience and cut breathing holes into the wrappings, in order not to make it too much of a trial for the actor involved. In one of the scenes this chap, Dickie Owen, had to walk around through an underground sewer and a whole lot of debris had to fall on his head. I warned the first assistant that they had to be aware of the extreme danger of letting that man flounder in

water that was fairly deep: he could lose his footing and drown. 'That will be all right,' he said. However, I stood quite close there with a pair of scissors in my hand. And sure enough, when all the stuff came bashing down, he couldn't keep his balance and fell over. I leapt straight in and removed everything so that he could breathe freely again. He already had water in his throat. One cannot be too careful about these situations."[4]

With a projected budget of £103,000, the final picture was evidence of Hammer's sliding production values when away from Bray. The film opens on completely the wrong foot by using an in-studio desert set that looks totally unconvincing; in fact, there were no exteriors or location shooting in the film at all. Not even the obsessive detail of Egyptian adviser, Andrew Low, could save the project. A stickler for accuracy, Low painstakingly drew scale diagrams of all the artefacts, furniture and jewellery that were constructed for the opening of the tomb and consequently this remains the only uplifting moment in a rather dreary movie.

Filming ended on Good Friday, 27 March, after five weeks. Along with *Hysteria*, the film went into post-production under the watchful eye of editors James Needs and Eric Boyd-Perkins and sound editor James Groom. Philip Martell brought in Carlo Martelli to compose the score, throwing in a snatch of Franz Reizenstein's original score from *The Mummy* during the Ancient Egyptian flashback. Bert Batt recalled, "My outstanding recollection of that film is the end-of-picture party in a Turkish restaurant somewhere in the City. The belly-dancer was great but the food was bloody awful!"

It was certainly a busy time for Hammer's editors. As the latest two films entered post-production, they were still complying with the BBFC over *The Evil of Frankenstein* and *The Gorgon*. Sadly, only a few BBFC notes remain regarding these two productions. In fact, the only documentation on *The Evil of Frankenstein* is a fading handwritten note made on 25 March, which gives us a brief glimpse of the scenes causing most problems: "<u>Reel 1</u>. Remove all shots in close-up and medium close-up of the heart in and out of the tank, being placed in the tank, and when seen with Baron Frankenstein's bloody hand on the heart. <u>Reel 4.</u> Reduce monster's beating up of Burgomaster. Re-submit both reels. Please mark up reel 4."

A little more survives on *The Gorgon*. John Trevelyan wrote to Anthony Nelson Keys on 5 March: "We think that the film will be acceptable for the 'X' category, but we must reserve final judgment until we see certain scenes again in colour and with full sound. It is possible that at this stage we may ask you for more cuts, but we may find the completed film acceptable. The scenes that we shall wish to see again are as follows:

<u>Reel 1.</u> The opening scenes and the scene in which a man is seen hanging from a tree.
<u>Reel 4.</u> The reflections of the Gorgon.
<u>Reel 6.</u> The scene in which the doctor removes the girl's brain and puts it in a jar; incidentally we would not want unpleasant noises on the soundtrack during the operation.
<u>Reel 9.</u> The fighting and the decapitation of the Gorgon. I think it possible that we may ask you to remove the shot of the decapitated head rolling into frame.
"We were impressed with the standard of acting in this film, and we think it should turn out well."

Audrey Field and Frank Crofts viewed the film on 29 April: "<u>Reel 3b.</u> Remove shots of brain being placed in and lying in glass jar. <u>Reel 5a.</u> Remove both shots of severed head with blood-stained neck." Trevelyan then made a handwritten note on 12 May: "Mr Keys appeals against the two cuts asked for. I agreed that we would see the scenes again and reconsider."

On 20 March, the *Daily Cinema* announced Hammer's forthcoming projects: *Blood of the Foreign Legion*, *The Devil Rides Out*, *Brainstorm*, *Hammerhead*, *Horror of the Zombie*, *Curse of the Reptiles*, *Dracula III* and *The Mutation*. Meanwhile, *The Evil of Frankenstein* premièred at the New Victoria on 19 April and went on general release on the ABC circuit from 31 May as a double-bill with *Nightmare*. Unfortunately, *Evil* got the same treatment as *The Kiss of the Vampire* when Universal adapted it for American commercial TV. Once more they elected to shoot extra, meaningless scenes with US actors (which they did on 14 January 1966) to fill out its two-hour television slot.

As post-production work continued behind the scenes, Hammer gave themselves a well-earned break from filming for a few months before launching themselves in July into an equally hectic second half of the year, with no fewer than four overlapping productions. *She* started filming in Israel while *The Secret of Blood Island* was on the floor at Pinewood. As soon as the latter ended, *Fanatic* began at Elstree, joining *She*, which was still on the floor. As soon as *She* ended, *The Brigand of Kandahar* started, with *Fanatic* still on the floor. This meant that on 7 September and 16 October, they had three productions on the go at once.

The Camp on Blood Island had been one of Hammer's biggest money-spinners so it came as no great surprise when they decided to revisit it. This was not a direct sequel, since the first film chronicled the events leading to the closure of the camp at the end of the war. For *The Secret of Blood Island*, John Gilling wrote a completely new and unrelated saga revolving around the desperate attempts of the prisoners to hide a female British agent who has bailed out of a crashing plane nearby.

Quentin Lawrence was brought in to direct; he had already directed the charming *Cash on Demand* for Hammer. The film also saw the welcome return of lighting cameraman Jack Asher, but the end result proved no match for Val Guest's original. Shooting began on 23 July at Pinewood Studios for

Major Jacomo
(Patrick Wymark)
interrogates Major
Dryden (Charles
Tingwell) watched
by Lieutenant
Tojoko (Michael
Ripper) in The
Secret of Blood
Island (1964).

THE SECRET OF BLOOD ISLAND

PRINCIPAL PHOTOGRAPHY: 23 July to 7 September 1964
DISTRIBUTION:
  UK: Rank; certificate 'X'
  US: Universal
84 minutes; Eastmancolor
UK RELEASE:
  TRADE SHOW: 13 May 1965, at the Rank Theatre
  GENERAL RELEASE: 14 June 1965, on the ABC circuit
    with The Night Walker

DIRECTOR: Quentin Lawrence; PRODUCER: Anthony Nelson Keys;
SCREENPLAY: John Gilling; PRODUCTION DESIGNER: Bernard
Robinson; DIRECTOR OF PHOTOGRAPHY: Jack Asher; CAMERA
OPERATOR: Harry Gillam; ASSISTANT DIRECTOR: Peter Price; 2ND
ASSISTANT DIRECTOR: Hugh Harlow, SUPERVISING EDITOR:

James Needs; EDITOR: Tom Simpson; MUSIC: James Bernard;
MUSIC SUPERVISOR: Marcus Dods; SOUND RECORDIST: Ken
Rawkins; SOUND EDITOR: James Groom; MAKE-UP: Roy Ashton;
HAIRSTYLIST: Frieda Steiger; PRODUCTION MANAGER: Don Weeks;
CONTINUITY: Pauline Harlow; WARDROBE: Jean Fairlie; SPECIAL
EFFECTS: Sydney Pearson; STILLS: Tom Edwards; TECHNICAL
ADVISER: Freddy Bradshaw

Barbara Shelley (Elaine); Jack Hedley (Sgt Crewe); Charles Tingwell
(Major Dryden); Bill Owen (Bludgin); Peter Welch (Richardson); Lee
Montague (Levy); Edwin Richfield (O'Reilly); Michael Ripper (Lt
Tojoko); Patrick Wymark (Major Jacomo); Philip Latham (Capt
Drake); Glyn Houston (Berry); Ian Whittaker (Mills); John
Southworth (Leonard); David Saire (Secret Police Chief); Peter Craze
(Red); Henry Davies (Taffy)

two weeks, followed by location work in neighbouring Black Park. Here the camp was erected
under Bernard Robinson's supervision. Jack Asher remembered his frustration with the huts:
"The sets, all bamboo huts, were the real thing and caused me many problems. Because half the
dialogue scenes were interiors, I resorted to the use of small incandescent lamps with an
incandescent negative, rather than using huge unwieldly carbon arcs. This also meant using a
fairly wide open lens aperture. But this meant that exteriors, seen through windows and doorways,
would be completely overexposed and the wrong colour. We actually used large gelatines that
coupled a neutral density change with colour correction. These were stationed outside every
opening, to correct the light in theory. But in actual practice high winds would ripple and tear the
materials, while clouds and alternating sunlight were a source of despair to my carpenters,
electricians and myself. Can you imagine the anguish of replacing these huge gels many times,
sometimes during a scene while the camera was panned away to a different angle?" [5]

Jack Hedley relaxes with director Quentin Lawrence on the set of The Secret of Blood Island (1964).

Alas, this would be Asher's last film for Hammer. In recent years he had been dropped from the regular production team in favour of the more economical approach of Arthur Grant. This was shown clearly in a report Michael Carreras requested from Tony Hinds on Asher's suitability: "I think his lighting to be excellent, never better. I also think the acting of Sir Laurence Olivier to be excellent and the music of Sir Arthur Bliss to be excellent, but we cannot afford either of them. In the same way, and especially in view of our future production policy, I do not think we can afford Jack Asher." [6] This was an undignified end for someone who had given so much to the company. He died in July 1991.

Back from the original film came Barbara Shelley, Lee Montague, Edwin Richfield and Michael Ripper. Jack Hedley, who had played the dashing hero of The Scarlet Blade, returned to Hammer as the determined Sergeant Crewe and Bill Owen played the likeable and tragic George Bludgin, who is savagely beaten to death while concealing the prisoners' secret. He affectionately remembered his co-star Michael Ripper: "Michael was cast as a Japanese commander of a Japanese prisoner of war camp. Not exactly typecasting, but he frightened the life out of we other 'principals' playing the 'inmates'. Now the extras engaged as the other POWs were perfect, emaciated, bent and bony, a sorry lot, but not the principal actors, however. We had not received orders to starve. On the first day of shooting Michael appeared, the personification of a wicked camp commandant with a suitable North Finchley Japanese accent. Turning to the director, he inquired, 'Please, what is my attitude towards these fat prisoners of war?'" [7]

Stunt co-ordinator Peter Diamond recalls that "We had a special effects guy called Gordon Baber, and they had a sequence where they meant to blow up the actual camp. All the British prisoners were paraded outside and Quentin Lawrence was directing it. The place was supposed to catch alight slowly, but it didn't catch alight slowly, the gas never ignited, and when the gas had all built up, there were suddenly explosions. The actors ran like mad away from the set!" Jack Asher concurred: "Towards the end of the film, the whole camp goes up in flames. This was of course saved to the end of the shoot. Somehow the effects men got too enthusiastic and the whole set was in flames in a matter of seconds. We could feel the heat from some distance off. My operative cameraman was dutifully completing a long and difficult tracking shot. Instead of jumping off and running away as we all did, he bravely stayed with the camera and completed the shot. We later found that his eyebrows and hair had been singed." [5]

Filming ended on 7 September, the film heading into post-production with editors James Needs and Tom Simpson, while Ken Rawkins returned as sound editor. Marcus Dods returned as music supervisor after his stint on *The Gorgon*, again bringing in the dependable James Bernard to score. Bernard recalled, "I do remember on *The Secret of Blood Island*, because it was so brutal, I wrote a rather repetitive score to try to give the feeling of the brutal monotony of life in the prison camp and I remember Marcus saying to me afterwards, 'I did rather wonder about the repetitiveness of some of the material, but I think you were right; it worked very well with the film.'"

The Secret of Blood Island brought Hammer's generally fruitful association with Universal to an ignominious end. The distributor reportedly had difficulty selling the film in certain far eastern territories, and – already disillusioned by its relationship with Hammer – never collaborated with the company again.

Kenneth Hyman, vice-president in charge of European production of his father's company Seven Arts, had approached Hammer with the idea of adapting Rider Haggard's *She* back in 1962. Hyman explains, "I had been a house guest in the New Forest and found an old paperback which I read in one evening. On the Monday after that, I walked into Tony Hinds' office with it and said, 'I think I've found another Hammer movie', which he agreed with and we acquired the rights and it came into being." [8] Haggard's sometimes horrific and harrowing novel, written in 1887, tells of the journey of Ludwig Horace Holly, his adopted son Leo, their manservant Job, and an Arab called Mohammed across unexplored regions of Central Africa to find the lost city of Kor, where presides the immortal Ayesha, 'She-Who-Must-Be Obeyed'. One lurid passage describes how a ceremony is lit by perfectly preserved Kor corpses: "We were surrounded on all three sides by a great ring of bodies flaring furiously, the material with which they were preserved having rendered them so inflammable that the flames would literally sprout out of the ears and mouths in tongues of fire a foot or more in length." No wonder Hyman saw this as the perfect story for Hammer.

While Seven Arts and the ABPC agreed to co-finance the film, *She* had a long and complicated pre-production history with countless script rejections. Tony Hinds first commissioned John Temple Smith (originator of *Captain Clegg*) to write a screenplay in late 1962 for Universal-International, which he redrafted in February 1963. Temple Smith prefixed the script with a startling catalogue of its lurid highlights:

"Straightforward research shows that the book of *She* has been making money ever since it was first published. This script is derived from Rider Haggard's classic story tailored to appeal to the

SHE

PRINCIPAL PHOTOGRAPHY: 24 August to 17 October 1964
DISTRIBUTION:
  UK: Warner-Pathe; certificate 'A'
  US: MGM
104 minutes; Metrocolor; Hammerscope
UK RELEASE:
  TRADE SHOW: 12 March 1965, at Studio One
  GENERAL RELEASE: 18 April 1965, on the ABC circuit
    with *Pop Gear*
US RELEASE: 1 September 1965

DIRECTOR: Robert Day; PRODUCER: Michael Carreras; ASSOCIATE PRODUCER: Aida Young; ASSISTANT TO PRODUCER: Ian Lewis; SCREENPLAY: David T Chantler, based on the famous novel by H Rider Haggard; ART DIRECTOR: Robert Jones; ASSISTANT ART DIRECTOR: Don Mingaye; DIRECTOR OF PHOTOGRAPHY: Harry Waxman; CAMERA OPERATOR: Ernest Day; ASSISTANT DIRECTOR: Bruce Sharman; SUPERVISING EDITOR: James Needs; EDITOR: Eric Boyd-Perkins; MUSIC: James Bernard; MUSIC SUPERVISOR: Philip Martell; SOUND RECORDIST: Claude Hitchcock; SOUND EDITORS: James Groom, Vernon Messanger and Roy Hyde; RECORDING DIRECTOR: A W Lumkin; MAKE-UP: John O'Gorman; SPECIAL EFFECTS MAKE-UP: Roy Ashton; HAIRSTYLIST: Eileen Warwick; PRODUCTION MANAGER: R L M Davidson; CONTINUITY: Eileen Head; WARDROBE: Jackie Cummins; COSTUMES FOR MISS ANDRESS: Carl Toms; SPECIAL EFFECTS: Bowie Films Ltd; SPECIAL PROCESSES: George Blackwell; SPECIAL EFFECTS ASSISTANTS: Kit West, Ian Scoones; RESEARCH: Andrew Low; CHOREOGRAPHY: Cristyne Lawson; CONSTRUCTION MANAGER: Arthur Banks; LOCATION MANAGER: Yoski Hausdorf

Ursula Andress (Ayesha); Peter Cushing (Holly); Bernard Cribbins (Job); John Richardson (Leo); Rosenda Monteros (Ustaine); Christopher Lee (Billali); André Morell (Haumeid); Soraya, Julie Mendez, Lisa Peake (nightclub dancers); John Maxim (guard captain); Cherry Lamen, Bula Coleman (handmaidens); Oo-La-Da Dancers (native dancers)

UNCREDITED: Eddie Powell (stranger in bar)

Ursula Andress and John Richardson relax during the shooting of She *(1964).*

young audiences of today. For this reason, whilst it retains the theme of suspense and mystique in the searching for SHE, it highlights many moments of physical danger and violence which are box office today. As for example:

(1) The cobra attacking Job and its decapitated body writhing on the ground.

(2) The vultures scrabbling over the bodies in the boat and picking the flesh away just to leave skeletons.

(3) Native killed by crocodile during the fight in boat.

(4) The shattering of the red hot vessel after it has been held over Job's head, and the red hot fragments falling in amongst screaming women.

(5) Ogono falling back on to the spears during the fight with the Amahagger.

(6) Holly smashing skulls together.

(7) Prisoners driven forward by man with a whip on the journey to Kor.

(8) SHE knifing Lumpala in the belly.

(9) SHE plunging the dagger into Kallikrates (flashback)

(10) Body of Kallikrates destroyed by acid.

(11) Ustane, half-naked, flogged by the guards.

(12) The guards of SHE are silently overwhelmed at the foot of the mountain. Their throats are cut.

(13) Job collapsing with a spear through his throat.

(14) Slaughter of the Amahagger.

"At the same time, the part of SHE is always presented in 1963 terms of glamour and appeal, and the scenes of high passion in the original story have been developed in this script so that the unique settings at all times contribute to their intensity. But none of these ingredients can top the final climax of SHE's bodily disintegration which must be without equal in the history of storytelling. The word-of-mouth potential of an audience exposed to this shattering climax must be enormous. NOTE: Although the picture will have many beautiful and exotic girls in it, it is not felt that Universal-International need go to the considerable expense of bringing in 'handmaidens' from all over the world."

Meanwhile, Seven Arts brought in Ursula Andress to play Ayesha early in 1963, following her success in the first James Bond outing, Dr. No (1962). However, Universal soon pulled out and, unhappy with their current script, Hammer engaged Berkeley Mather (who had co-written Dr. No) to refashion the screenplay over the summer, submitting a second draft on 8 September 1963.

However, in January 1964, Hammer were rehashing the screenplay yet again, with director Robert Day submitting a rewrite of the earlier John Temple Smith script. Interestingly, as the scripts progressed, the horrific elements were damped down to pave the way for a straightforward action movie. Ayesha's wickedness, in particular, is considerably muted as the scripts develop. In the initial scene of the Temple Smith version, where Ayesha meets Holly, the Amahagger prisoners are dragged before her and she stabs the ringleader, Lumpala, in the belly. In the same scene in Day's rewrite, this sequence is removed. Also, Day excised a scene in which Ayesha shows Holly a rotting charnel pit filled with thousands of gleaming skeletons. "With my own hands I threw them down there – black and stinking as they were," 'She' gloats.

Meanwhile, Hammer were still searching for a major distributor. When both Joe Levine and American International Pictures turned them down in January 1964, Hammer brought back Michael Carreras to salvage the project, who in turn commissioned David T Chantler (co-writer of Cash on Demand) to finalise the script. Chantler drew elements from the earlier scripts by Temple Smith, Mather and Day, dropping the Cambridge opening common to all three and inexplicably changing Haggard's lost city of Kor to Kuma. He also divorced Billali from Ustane (they were brother and sister in the early drafts) to make Billali the unscrupulous, power-mad High Priest, thereby introducing the character of Haumeid, Ustane's father and chief of the Amahagger. Chantler also fashioned a more exciting climax. In the earlier scripts, Ayesha steps into the flames alone and disintegrates, thus denying us Billali's fight with Leo and Leo's final dilemma. Chantler's characterisations were also different from Temple Smith's and Day's; in these early drafts, Billali was more humble, quaking before the majesty of 'She', Holly was far more arrogant and Leo was more protective of Ustane, particularly in the scene where Ayesha threatens to kill her. At last the script was shaping up and eventually, in June, Hammer secured the backing of MGM, putting the picture on line.

Robert Day was brought in to direct, but most of the Hammer regulars were already working on The Secret of Blood Island. While production manager Don Weeks supervised the Japanese atrocities at Pinewood, new face R L M Davidson took over on She. Bernard Robinson was also employed on Blood Island, allowing Robert Jones to take over Ayesha's art direction. Back from The Curse of the Mummy's Tomb were editor Eric Boyd-Perkins, sound recordist Claude Hitchcock and continuity girl Eileen Head. Another face returning to Hammer was associate producer Aida Young, who had last worked for them as second assistant director on The Quatermass Xperiment. She had recently worked with Michael Carreras as associate producer of his Capricorn production What a Crazy World; he now employed her in the same capacity on She.

Young recalls, "Michael was highly amused by me, having a woman there, but we got on terribly well and we were friends socially as well. So I learnt a lot from him, but he really didn't want to be a producer, you know. He really only wanted to be a director and writer. He hated being a producer so he left a lot to me. As associate producer I would mainly stand in for Michael, who sometimes wasn't there, and make sure that everything went smoothly, and I was the liaison between the director and he. I tried to stop things from happening before they happened. In a way I was a superior production manager but had more responsibility. You had the responsibility of the cast and you were in at the script meetings and so on."

The cast is first rate. This was Cushing and Lee's sixth venture for Hammer – they had just finished shooting Amicus' first anthology picture, Dr Terror's House of Horrors – and again they demonstrate remarkable chemistry in their few scenes together. As Ayesha, Ursula Andress is as statuesque as could be desired, while Rosenda Monteros, romantic lead in John Sturges' The Magnificent Seven, is good value too. There's also a welcome return from André Morell, although it's distracting to hear him dubbed by George Pastell.

Shooting started on location in southern Israel on Monday 24 August, where a small unit, including stars Peter Cushing, John Richardson, Bernard Cribbins and Ursula Andress, braved the desert heat. It is ironic that Hammer's 'mountains of the moon' were in fact the mountains of the legendary King Solomon's mines, which had formed the subject of another Rider Haggard story. The crew stayed at a small town on the coast called Eilat. By 6.00 am the unit would be on their rugged 90-minute journey into the desert in an armada of army trucks loaded with equipment. By eight, everything was ready and director Robert Day could begin rehearsals. It was an arduous shoot for all in the baking heat of the Negev desert. It was so hot the artists didn't visibly perspire, so make-up had to apply a fine spray of moisture to their faces to simulate it. Miss Andress was mainly on hand to keep the press and photographers happy.

"We were in Israel, during a very heavy political climate" recalled Peter Cushing. "We had to start very early in the morning, starting at 4.00 am, and work was impossible in the afternoon, as the heat was unbearable. While we were in the Danago desert the Arab sector was quite near and they just sat there with their machine-guns in their laps. In the meantime we were popping off our prop guns hoping we would not be attacked. We were lucky they seemed to be enjoying us; it was quite an exciting period." 9

The shoot was not without incident. John Richardson caught dysentery and filming was delayed. Then there was a nasty accident in the desert, as Aida Young explains. "That was terrible, it was the last location shot on the picture. They were over the hill, doing the last shot of the battle, and I was sitting down with the Israeli production manager, who was called Yoski, and a couple of other people and I said to him, 'Well, Yoski, it's all over.' At that minute there was somebody on the skyline waving madly at us and I said to Yoski, 'What do they want? You go out and see what they want.' He took the four-wheel drive up there and the next thing I knew I was summoned up there also. I went up to the crew and what had happened was that the chap we got from the Israeli army to do the special effects had been holding a grenade – he had taken the pin out and had forgotten – and it went off in his hand and it blew two fingers off. He calmly knelt down on the sand and picked the two fingers up in his fist so that they could put them back on again. Blood was flowing and everybody was so horrified and the first assistant went berserk. It was terribly hot and he couldn't stand the sight of the blood and somebody had to knock him out.

"Then, because of all the things that were going on, Bernie Cribbins walked where he shouldn't have walked and tripped on a wire and this buckshot went up his bum and he was yelling and screaming and jumping around because it was very painful. So there we were with an ambulance taking the three of them, the special effects man, the first assistant and Bernie Cribbins, to the nearby hospital. Poor Bernie, he was very nice about it all and very funny. It was just one of those things, but they sewed the fingers onto the special effects man and he went back into the army, so he was all right in the end. The first assistant went on to be a director, so he was all right in the end too, and the film itself turned out to be a great success."

Editor Eric Boyd-Perkins remembers the arrangements for editing while the crew were on location. "We stayed back at Elstree. As far as I remember they sent over the film each day and we would run the dailies and they would see it when they got back. We would look at it and send out reports of how it was and if anything extra was needed. These days it's different; they have bigger budgets and people order double prints and you keep one print back and send one print away, whereas with Hammer, that wouldn't be in their budget to do that. We would start cutting it while they were away."

It was a busy time for make-up artist Roy Ashton as he was employed on both *The Secret of Blood Island* and *She*, though John O'Gorman attended to the conventional make-ups on the latter. The climax of *She* provided Ashton with another frustrating job, in which, just as in *The Gorgon*, he was not allowed to have his own way. Ashton had planned the disintegration of Ayesha using a series of progressively older women, and seven drawings were prepared which followed this logical sequence of events. Ashton explained, "You see, the problem with most sequences of this sort is that during the process of ageing the face wastes away. The skin becomes very fine, the bones become pronounced and the hair thins extensively. Instead of diminishing the features, the make-up artist has to build upon what is already there, fattening and rounding the face to such a degree that the result is often, I think, implausible. If you ever have the misfortune to actually see a real corpse in an advanced state of decomposition, you'll see that it is just putrescent skin and bone.

"I suggested four or five women of successive ages," Ashton continued, "ending up with an old woman without any teeth. Unfortunately, when the time came they only provided me with *one* old dear, upon whom I had to apply the pieces needed to make her look far in excess of her already

LEFT: *Billali (Christopher Lee) conspires with guard John Maxim in* She *(1964).*

BELOW: *Bernard Cribbins and friend in* She *(1964).*

advanced years, but she had a prominent nose and features totally dissimilar to Ursula's." [10] Once more Ashton's work was compromised by circumstances beyond his control. Aida Young recalled of the scene, "All I remember was that I had decided to do a Saturday shoot for the ageing of Ayesha and just call in the people necessary, because I knew it would be a long job. I mean it's not as it is now, you could do it in half an hour on the computer. There were about seven shots we had to do that Saturday morning and I was called into the make-up room where they were making Ursula up for the second shot, where she is really ageing, and she couldn't bear the sight

of herself. She burst into tears and all her make-up was ruined. I was called in because she wouldn't have it done, but finally she did."

Kit West assisted Les Bowie with the special effects. He remembers, "A lot of slaves had to be pushed down a fiery pit. That was at ABPC and I photographed all the original exposures from the roof of the stage. Then we added the flames and there were little model black slaves going down into the pit." To create the flame of eternal youth, West adds, "We had to change the colour of the flames. The colour had to change from normal to blue. To do that, we tried a lot of things like putting various crystals into the source, but we eventually did it optically through using the blue register and mixing through from normal. We shot the flames against black in the right place so that when overlaid on the original scene they sat around this plinth where Ursula Andress was standing. It was a straight overlay, but they married it up together in the bi-pack camera. There was a cameraman whose name was Paul DeBurg, who would marry it up in the dark room with bi-pack cameras, scenes that these days would be done by CGI, but in those days it was all done in camera in an optical printing process."

Philip Martell returned as music supervisor with composer James Bernard. This was their first full collaboration and they would prove to be a successful team. As with *The Kiss of the Vampire*, Bernard's expertise was required earlier than usual. "There were several sections that were needed for use during the actual shooting," Bernard remembered. "First came the trumpet fanfares associated with the imperious Ayesha. For these, Phil Martell had the excellent idea of getting trumpeters from the Royal School of Military Music. They were recorded in a separate session under their own director of music. There were 12 trumpets, which gave the fanfares an impressive (and indeed imperious) power." [11]

Bernard had also prepared a religious chant in conjunction with Christopher Lee. Bernard explained: "Christopher played the wicked High Priest Billalli and it was planned that there would be a scene in which the assembled populace of the Kingdom of She would be lined up in front of She and Billalli and he would sing a religious chant. I wrote a simple tune for it, which was based on the 'She who must be obeyed' theme. Christopher wrote some wonderful words in an unknown language and we actually rehearsed it at the piano with Phil Martell. Unfortunately, they got behind schedule and it just had to be cut out." Christopher Lee concurs. "Michael Carreras, who knew I could sing – he'd heard it often enough – thought it a great idea to hear a voice chanting, though not necessarily the character I played, and they got some sort of music together. I can't remember what it was, some kind of chant, it was more sounds than words. I did do it and they did record it, but it was never used."

Principal photography ended at Elstree on Saturday 17 October. Now *She* entered post-production with editors James Needs and Eric Boyd-Perkins and sound editor James Groom. Eric Boyd-Perkins remembers, "Robert Day used to view the scenes as I completed them, but he didn't get involved an awful lot. On those sort of schedules, the directors, apart from Seth Holt, wouldn't be able to have too much influence, because there wasn't time on the schedule. If you produced something good that was acceptable, you didn't have time to play around with it." During dubbing André Morell's voice wasn't the only casualty; Ursula Andress was dubbed by Monica Van Der Syl, who had previously dubbed her in *Dr. No*.

While *She* was still shooting at the ABPC Elstree studios, *Fanatic* began directly after *The Secret of Blood Island*, also at Elstree.

Fanatic was different to Hammer's other psychological thrillers for two reasons. For a start, it was the first of the series to be shot in colour and, secondly, Jimmy Sangster had nothing to do with it. Instead, Richard Matheson was brought in to write the script based on Anne Blaisdell's novel, *Nightmare*. Matheson's first association with Hammer had not been a successful one; they were forced to drop plans to shoot a film based on his book *I Am Legend* for censorship reasons.

Legendary Hollywood actress Tallulah Bankhead was brought in to play the fanatical Mrs Trefoile. Matheson's original script was about a reclusive Welsh woman. When Bankhead was cast, the central character became a fanatical convert (and former actress) who had previously married a Welsh seaman. The plot revolves around a young American girl, Patricia Carroll, who pays a courtesy visit to Mrs Trefoile, the mother of her dead fiancé. Unfortunately, Trefoile is a religious fanatic and announces that she intends to cleanse Patricia so that she can marry her son in the after-life.

Bankhead arrived in London on Thursday 20 August to begin shooting on Monday 7 September. It was her first visit to England in 30 years but the only time she ever left her suite at the Ritz Hotel was to be taken to the closed set in a black Rolls-Royce provided by Hammer, bearing the appropriate registration HEL 777. 21-year-old Stefanie Powers played the likeable heroine, Patricia. Powers was an Olympic swimmer and got a chance to show off her expertise in the scene where she tries to escape via the lake. It is reported that it was her athleticism in *Fanatic* that later won her a TV series of her own, *The Girl from UNCLE*. Also in the cast was a virtually unknown Canadian actor called Donald Sutherland, who played the simple gardener, Joseph. He too had played in *Dr Terror's House of Horrors* during the summer. Cast as Patricia's new fiancé was Maurice Kaufmann

Tallulah Bankhead
as the Fanatic
(1964).

FANATIC

PRINCIPAL PHOTOGRAPHY: 7 September to 27 October 1964
DISTRIBUTION:
  UK: BLC; 96 minutes; Technicolor, certificate 'X'
  US: Columbia; 105 minutes; Eastmancolor;
    US TITLE: Die! Die! My Darling!
  UK RELEASE: 21 March 1965, on the ABC circuit with
  The Killers

DIRECTOR: Silvio Narizzano; PRODUCER: Anthony Hinds;
EXECUTIVE PRODUCER: Michael Carreras; SCREENPLAY: Richard
Matheson, based on the novel Nightmare by Ann Blaisdell;
PRODUCTION DESIGNER: Peter Proud; DIRECTOR OF
PHOTOGRAPHY: Arthur Ibbetson; CAMERA OPERATOR: Paul
Wilson; ASSISTANT DIRECTOR: Claude Watson; 2ND ASSISTANT:

Hugh Harlow; SUPERVISING EDITOR: James Needs; EDITOR: John
Dunsford; MUSIC: Wilfred Josephs; MUSIC SUPERVISOR: Philip
Martell; SOUND RECORDIST: Ken Rawkins; SOUND EDITOR: Roy
Hyde; MAKE-UP: Roy Ashton; MAKE-UP ASSISTANT: Richard
Mills; HAIRSTYLIST: Olga Angelinetta; PRODUCTION MANAGER:
George Fowler; CONTINUITY: Renée Glynne; WARDROBE: Mary
Gibson; STILLS: Tom Edwards; SPECIAL EFFECTS: Syd Pearson;
FIGHT ARRANGER: Peter Diamond

Tallulah Bankhead (Mrs Trefoile); Stefanie Powers (Patricia Carroll);
Peter Vaughan (Harry); Maurice Kaufmann (Alan Glentower); Yootha
Joyce (Anna); Donald Sutherland (Joseph); Gwendoline Watts (Gloria);
Robert Dorning (Ormsby); Philip Gilbert (Oscar); Winifred Denis
(shopkeeper); Diana King (woman shopper); Henry McGee (Vicar)

(then married to actress Honor Blackman), who had last appeared for Hammer ten years before in
The Quatermass Xperiment.

Tony Hinds was back as producer, bringing in Canadian-born Silvio Narizzano to direct his first
feature film after an award-winning career in British and American television. Second assistant
Hugh Harlow and sound recordist Ken Rawkins joined the production from The Secret of Blood Island
while John Dunsford returned to edit after last working on The Scarlet Blade. Peter Proud took over
as production designer and the film saw the welcome return of continuity supervisor Renée
Glynne, her first continuity work for Hammer since The Steel Bayonet in 1956. She had left to bring
up her family, but did continue to work for Hammer on and off, preparing release scripts for The
Curse of the Werewolf among others. Roy Ashton was still flitting from production to production, this
time assisted by Richard Mills.

Tallulah Bankhead was not an easy actress to work with. For the climactic cellar scenes where
Trefoile is surrounded by memorabilia of her past life, production designer Peter Proud decked out

RIGHT: Tallulah Bankhead is led onto the set of Fanatic (1964). Note her Rolls-Royce in background with the registration plate HEL 777.

BELOW: Ex-Olympic swimmer Stefanie Powers during the filming of Fanatic (1964).

the set with old Bankhead memorabilia. However, she threw a tantrum, accusing Hammer of invading her privacy. During shooting, she threw further tantrums and is reputed to have walked off set at least three times. Despite this, director Narizzano didn't find her quite the tyrant he had expected. "I thought she was going to be, but she was not formidable. She liked to be shown everything. I remember getting mad at her one day and saying, 'I don't know how to do it – you're the actress!' And she said, 'I'm *not* an actress, dahling ... I'm a star!' And she literally wanted me to show her everything. I'd put the lipstick on and everything and she'd watch and then she would do it. She thought the whole thing was kinda dumb. Each morning she'd say, 'What dumb thing are we gonna do today, dahling?' We had a lot of fun doing it. She'd go off in a great big Rolls-Royce back to the Ritz and I would get driven home and take a bath and then go over to the Ritz and play poker with her every night. She was very lonely when she was over here." [12]

Make-up artist Roy Ashton also had his problems, as Narizzano explains. "She was very miserable about having to take all the curl out of her hair and knot it back. The make-up man, Roy Ashton, had an awful time. He just couldn't get Tallulah's lipstick off. He said, 'Those are redheads. She's so dirty that she hasn't developed blackheads or whiteheads – she's developed redheads under all that smear lipstick." Narizzano also explains the effect used for the scene in which Peter Vaughan's character is shot in the head. "How to shoot Peter Vaughan in the head with bullets? No one seemed to know how to do that. Tallulah was supposed to shoot him three times. It was my idea to keep the camera rolling. A make-up man stepped in three times and made a black hole in Peter's forehead. After each time, Peter made a violent movement with his head. And what we simply did was cut out the make-up man. Peter had to put his back against a pillow so basically he would keep his position and it was just his head that moved. I think that worked quite simply and effectively." [12]

The success of *Fanatic* is all Narrizano's. Overall it is an extremely tense thriller, though Narrizano himself felt that with greater care it could have been another *Whatever Happened to Baby Jane?* But he found Bankhead's performance a little too camp and would have preferred someone like Flora Robson in the role.

Renée Glynne also remembers Bankhead. "She was wonderful. There are lots of stories about that shoot. One was about the runner, Nigel Wooll, who became a producer. He was very young at the time, polite and public school. He was chosen as the special assistant to escort Tallulah from her dressing room down the iron staircase and onto the set. On this occasion he knocked on her dressing room door, was told to enter and, when confronted with her nakedness, she said, 'Don't worry, you'll only see that I'm a natural blonde!' She defied me on continuity on one occasion – 'No, I had my legs crossed this way and my glass in this hand.' 'Oh, Tallulah, you had them that way.' 'Oh, no I didn't' – and she was quite nasty to me. However, later that day, she tottered across the set with her companion, bringing me a glass of whiskey as a peace offering. And another story. For a scene with a long threatening speech to Stefanie Powers, she had to have her glasses, Bible and gun, and sit on a large basket armchair, her little legs dangling. She cried out that she couldn't do the dialogue holding all these props and seated on this chair. Silvio Narizzano screamed at her, 'Give me the f**king glasses and I'll show you how to do it!' At which point she rose up, practically falling off the chair, and said, 'Don't ever use that word 'glasses' to me again!' She stormed off the set and sent a message to say that she wasn't coming back unless he publicly apologised to her and kissed her full on the mouth. It was appalling for him to have to do it, but he did it. I've never forgotten that, because it was so beautifully handled.

"After the film finished, Tallulah gave us presents. She gave me a silver hip flask from Aspreys, engraved 'To Renée with love from Tallulah'; regrettably it has since been stolen. In return I bought her a gift and passed by the Ritz Hotel to drop it off on a Sunday afternoon, my two young sons with me. The porter suggested she might like to receive us. She did. We went up to her suite where she was reclining on her bed, curtains drawn, hair flowing, fully lipsticked, and most welcoming. She ordered the Ritz's trolley of sumptuous afternoon tea and allowed, even encouraged, the two boys to scramble all over and under her bed and play hide and seek among her gowns in the wardrobes. Prompted by my telling her that, as a youth, my brother-in-law had worshipped her, she reminisced about her days on the London stage. She also told my sons to 'always take care of your mother.' This is my lasting memory of her."

While the film was being shot, *The Gorgon* and *The Curse of the Mummy's Tomb* went on release as a Hammer double-bill on the ABC circuit from Sunday 18 October. The pairing proved a great success, making *Kinematograph Weekly*'s 'Top Money-Makers' list. They later went out in America on 31 December. Hammer horror was still a highly lucrative business and the double-bill would help secure the deal with 20th Century-Fox the following year.

Principal photography on *Fanatic* ended on Tuesday 27 October after seven weeks. It then went into post-production with editors James Needs and John Dunsford and sound editor Roy Hyde, who had last worked on *Hysteria*. Music supervisor Philip Martell brought in Wilfred Josephs to compose the score. Narizzano remembers, "Wilfred liked the idea of a harpsichord. He thought it had a quaint Victorian feel – which suited the Tallulah character because she was living in this backwater. Everybody thought it was a cute idea. I disliked the music intensely." [13]

The Brigand of Kandahar brought the year to a sad and sorry close. The project originated in a 1956 Columbia/Warwick Victor Mature vehicle called *Zarak*, about an Afghan outlaw who saves the life of a British officer but loses his own in the process. Some of the action sequences were cut from the finished movie and Columbia suggested to the film's second unit director, John Gilling, that he pen another project to incorporate these cut scenes. The project was taken on by Hammer and Gilling directed the film also. The story is about Lieutenant Case, a mixed race officer in the Bengal Lancers who returns to Fort Kandahar to be accused of abandoning his colleague in battle. Faced with a

Ronald Lewis duels
Oliver Reed in
The Brigand of
Kandahar (1964).

THE BRIGAND OF KANDAHAR

PRINCIPAL PHOTOGRAPHY: 16 October to 26 November 1964
DISTRIBUTION:
UK: Warner-Pathe; certificate 'U'
USA: Columbia
81 minutes; Technicolor; Hammerscope
UK RELEASE: 8 August 1965, on the ABC circuit

RECORDIST: Simon Kaye; SOUND EDITOR: Roy Hyde; RECORDING
DIRECTOR: A W Lumkin; MAKE-UP: Roy Ashton, Richard Mills;
HAIRSTYLIST: Frieda Steiger; PRODUCTION MANAGER: Don Weeks;
CONTINUITY: Pauline Harlow; WARDROBE: Rosemary Burrows;
SPECIAL EFFECTS: Syd Pearson; FIGHT ARRANGER: Peter Diamond

DIRECTOR: John Gilling; PRODUCER: Anthony Nelson Keys;
SCREENPLAY: John Gilling; Production DESIGNER: Bernard
Robinson; ART DIRECTOR: Don Mingaye; DIRECTOR OF
PHOTOGRAPHY: Reg Wyer; CAMERA OPERATOR: Harry Gillam;
ASSISTANT DIRECTOR: Frank Nesbitt; 2ND ASSISTANT: Hugh
Harlow; SUPERVISING EDITOR: James Needs; EDITOR: Tom Simpson;
MUSIC: Don Banks; MUSIC SUPERVISOR: Philip Martell; SOUND

Ronald Lewis (Lieutenant Case); Oliver Reed (Eli Khan); Duncan
Lamont (Colonel Drewe); Yvonne Romain (Ratina); Catherine
Woodville (Elsa); Glyn Houston (Marriott); Inigo Jackson (Captain
Boyd); Sean Lynch (Rattu); Walter Brown (Hitala); Jeremy
Burnham (Connelly); Caron Gardner (serving maid); Henry Davies
(Crowe); John Southworth (Barlowe); Jo Powell (Colour Sergeant)

UNCREDITED: John Maxim (prison guard)

court-martial for cowardice, he escapes into the clutches of the ruthless Gilzhai leader, Eli Khan, and his scheming sister, Ratina, who enlist him to train their warriors to attack the British. It's a tale of revenge, deceit and racial discrimination in the usual Hammer tradition.

Shooting began at the ABPC Studios Elstree on Friday 16 October, directly after She had finished and while Fanatic was still on the floor. The cast was serviceable: contract artist Ronald Lewis was back after Taste of Fear and Oliver Reed played his usual unhinged villain as well as being reunited with the luscious Yvonne Romain, his co-star from The Curse of the Werewolf and Captain Clegg. Duncan Lamont's in there too and Caron Gardner returns after The Evil of Frankenstein. Even Jo Powell, stuntman brother of Eddie Powell, joins in as the Colour Sergeant. Jo had founded Britain's first stunt agency with Jock Easton.

The film was a milestone. It was Oliver Reed's last movie for Hammer. Ex-Hammer wardrobe mistress Rosemary Burrows remembers her rapturous greeting from him when they were reunited in 1998 on *Gladiator* and how he warmly recalled their Hammer days. The film turned out to be his last.

Like *The Curse of the Mummy's Tomb*, *The Brigand of Kandahar* seems to lack the normal Hammer polish. In fact, it looks decidedly cheap. It seemed that Hammer were having difficulty with their mainstream low-budget pictures at the larger studios. Again like the Mummy picture, there was no exterior or location work; the whole thing was shot in the studio. Consequently, the action scenes (apart from those inserted from *Zarak*) look claustrophobic and, if this were not enough, the final battle scene is betrayed by some lousy back-projections of Lewis and Lamont on horseback.

"I doubled Ronald Lewis," recalled stunt co-ordinator Peter Diamond. "We never left the studio. We shot the whole thing at the old ABC studios. They built a desert there, all in perspective, so it looked miniature in the background. We did the complete battle sequence in the studio, all the horses being pulled down, the fighting and everything else. We spent a day getting the horses used to the battle. John Gilling was directing and he just shot anything that moved. He just put his camera down and said, 'Shoot it!' There wasn't any planning, we just shot it. 'Do this, do that.' That's how we got through it. I think we were on stage number 3. It was one of the largest then, but it worked. Ollie, of course, was in it and I had him using two swords, to give him a different kind of fight. He was very heavy, but was such an excellent motivated guy and powerful. He just went hell for leather for it. Ronnie Lewis was marvellous. I was so sad when he later committed suicide. He was the easiest-going guy you could think of."

Shooting finished on Thursday 26 November after six weeks. James Needs and Tom Simpson took the film to the next stage with sound editor Roy Hyde. Philip Martell brought back Don Banks for the score. Banks wrote another of his characteristically rousing scores, but it was too late to save the picture. It was the last film made as part of Hammer's regular and long-standing association with Columbia.

The Brigand of Kandahar came at a time of crisis for Hammer, during which they lost the support of two major US distributors and their production values seemed to slip somewhat. Their 1965 schedule would soon put them back on course as the leading light in horror pictures with four back-to-back productions at Bray Studios. First, however, came a horror of a different kind in the form of Bette Davis...

Camera operator Harry Gillam shoots a scene from The Brigand of Kandahar *(1964) with a hand-held camera on the stage at Elstree.*

THIRTEEN

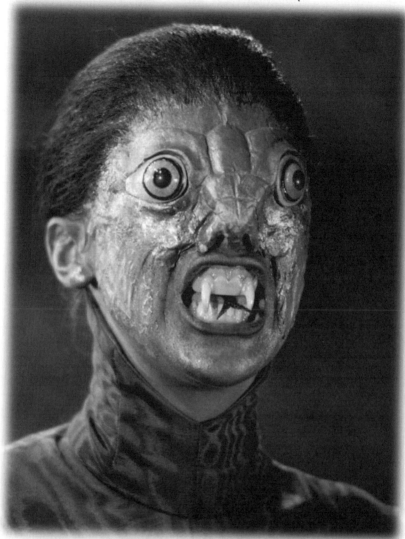

Back-to-back at Bray

(1 9 6 5)

In 1965, Hammer's relationship with Eliot Hyman's Seven Arts organisation continued to flourish. Since first becoming involved with Hammer in the late 1950s, Seven Arts had set up offices in London and producing such notable films as *Lolita* (1962) and *The Hill* (1965). In December 1961, they signed a deal with Sir Michael Balcon's Bryanston Films and, in July 1962, a 20-picture agreement with MGM. When Seven Arts' Kenneth Hyman approached Hammer with the idea of adapting H Rider Haggard's *She*, the film became the latest in a long line of co-productions. The film would benfit from the casting of contract artist Ursula Andress, already an international star following her appearance in Dr. No (1962). She was released by MGM in America as the last film of their existing deal with Seven Arts, while Warner Pathe (formed in September 1959 by a merger between Associated British-Pathe Distributors and Warner Bros UK Ltd) released the film in Britain.

In 1964, Hammer's episodic association with Universal had come to an end with The Secret of Blood Island; their association with Columbia concluded later in the year with The Brigand of Kandahar. During this time they maintained their links with Seven Arts, who co-financed Fanatic as well as reissuing The Curse of Frankenstein and Horror of Dracula as a US double-bill on 16 December 1964. However, bigger plans were afoot and in June 1965, in the wake of the British success of She (it remained unreleased Stateside until September), James Carreras, Tony Hinds and Brian Lawrence flew to New York to sign an 11-picture deal with Seven Arts and 20th Century-Fox. Seven Arts and ABPC would co-finance the pictures, which would then be distributed by Warner Pathe on the ABC circuit in England (and the Commonwealth) and by 20th Century-Fox in the US and the rest of the world.

Obviously the deal had been under negotiation for some time, because by the time it was finalised and signed the first two films of the package, The Nanny and Dracula Prince of Darkness, were already in post-production and the third, Rasputin the Mad Monk, was on the floor. The 11 films would comprise Hammer's total output for 1965 and 1966. In advance of the deal, Hammer had originally announced the following films as part of the package: The Nanny, The Horror of the Zombie, The Curse of the Reptiles, Rasputin the Mad Monk, Dracula III, One Million Years B.C., Ayesha – Daughter of She, Prehistoric Women and Fear of Frankenstein.

More importantly, the deal would be the kiss of death for Bray.

It was a slow start to the year for Hammer production-wise, due no doubt to the new deal that was forming. Meanwhile, Fanatic was released on the ABC circuit on 21 March, paired with The Killers. To capitalise on Tallulah Bankhead's catchphrase, 'Dah-ling', and the Bette Davis shocker Hush, Hush, Sweet Charlotte (1964), the title was changed in America to the quirky Die! Die! My Darling! Allegedly, she was not amused. The American print was also nine minutes longer than the British one.

On 6 April, Julie Andrews won an Oscar for her role as the magical nanny, Mary Poppins. The day before, Hammer had started work on a film which would tell of a very different nanny...

The Nanny was the first film of the new 11-picture deal. Hammer had bought the rights to Evelyn Piper's novel of the same name and commissioned Jimmy Sangster to write a script. After two years of psychiatric treatment, 10-year-old Joey Fane returns home to his parents, who believe he is suffering from a massive guilt complex due to the accidental killing of his sister Susy. He is terrified of his nanny, who turns out to have been the killer, albeit an inadvertent one. Sangster recalls: "We tried to get Greer Garson for it. I even went over to her ranch in Sante Fe, New Mexico to see her, but she decided she didn't want to do it. Bette Davis said she wanted to do it and she was much better than Greer Garson would have been." Seth Holt was appointed to direct and Sangster had to fly him out to meet Davis in Los Angeles, since she insisted on 'director approval' before starting on a film.

Sangster explains, "She didn't like Seth. She called him a 'Mountain of Evil', but she respected him enormously as a director. We'd already hired him and I had to ship him over to LA for her to audition him. She accepted him and he really was a very good director." Sangster continues in his autobiography, "She arrived in England two weeks before shooting started. She came in on one of the ocean-going Queens. Seth and I drove down to Southampton to meet her. We had rented for her a huge house in Elstree quite close to the studios and she was accompanied by her son, around ten years old, and a rather strange lady companion/gofer-type person named Viola Rubber."[1]

Shooting began at Elstree on Monday 5 April. It was again a patchwork quilt of a team, as Hammer's regulars would be joining the crew of Dracula Prince of Darkness, shooting simultaneously at Bray. In fact, the only regular faces were editors James Needs (also working on DPOD) and Tom Simpson (who had just finished The Brigand of Kandahar) and continuity supervisor Renée Glynne.

Hammer Productions 1965

+ THE NANNY
+ DRACULA PRINCE OF DARKNESS
+ RASPUTIN THE MAD MONK
+ THE PLAGUE OF THE ZOMBIES
+ THE REPTILE
+ ONE MILLION YEARS B.C.

OPPOSITE: Jacqueline Pearce as The Reptile (1965).

William Dix is suspicious of The Nanny (1965), played by Bette Davis. His mother (Wendy Craig) maintains her faith in Nanny.

THE NANNY

PRINCIPAL PHOTOGRAPHY: 5 April to 21 May 1965
DISTRIBUTION:
  UK: Warner-Pathe; certificate 'X'
  US: 20th Century-Fox
93 minutes; b/w
UK RELEASE:
  TRADE SHOW: 1 October 1965
  PREMIÈRE: 7 October 1965, at the Carlton Haymarket
  GENERAL RELEASE: 7 November 1965, on the ABC circuit
US RELEASE: 27 October 1965

DIRECTOR: Seth Holt; PRODUCER: Jimmy Sangster; EXECUTIVE PRODUCER: Anthony Hinds; SCREENPLAY: Jimmy Sangster, based on the novel The Nanny by Evelyn Piper; PRODUCTION DESIGNER: Edward Carrick; DIRECTOR OF PHOTOGRAPHY: Harry Waxman;

CAMERA OPERATOR: Kelvin Pike; ASSISTANT DIRECTOR: Christopher Dryhurst; SUPERVISING EDITOR: James Needs; EDITOR: Tom Simpson; MUSIC: Richard Rodney Bennett; MUSIC SUPERVISOR: Philip Martell; SOUND RECORDIST: Norman Coggs; SOUND EDITOR: Charles Crayford; RECORDING SUPERVISOR: A W Lumkin; MAKE-UP: Tom Smith; HAIRSTYLIST: A G Scott; PRODUCTION MANAGER: George Fowler; CONTINUITY: Renée Glynne; WARDROBE CONSULTANT: Rosemary Burrows; WARDROBE MISTRESS: Mary Gibson

Bette Davis (Nanny); Wendy Craig (Virgie Fane); Jill Bennett (Penelope); James Villiers (Bill Fane); William Dix (Joey); Pamela Franklin (Bobby); Jack Watling (Dr Medman); Maurice Denham (Dr Beamaster); Alfred Burke (Dr Wills); Harry Fowler (Milkman); Angharad Aubrey (Susy); Nora Gordon (Mrs Griggs); Sandra Power (Sarah)

Lighting cameraman Harry Waxman was back after last working on She, but this time photographing in spooky monochrome. George Fowler was back as production manager after last working on Fanatic; what an introduction to Hammer that must have been, having to work with Tallulah Bankhead and Bette Davis in his first two movies! Edward Carrick was back as production designer after last working on Hysteria; Bernard Robinson and Don Mingaye would be planning Hammer's next four productions at Bray. Rosemary Burrows acted as wardrobe consultant to Mary Gibson (who had previously worked on Fanatic), though she would also be employed on the productions at Bray.

Bette Davis was at her best as the deranged nanny. Sangster remembers, "She really wanted it done her way, but only if she thought her way was best for the movie. She wouldn't say, 'I don't want to do this shot because I don't want to.' She would say, 'I don't want to do this shot because it's not right for the movie.' A lot of the time she was right, but some of the time she was wrong and if you could convince her that it was right for the movie, she would say, 'Fine, you're right.' She was the most professional person I have ever worked with – but a difficult bitch. I mean, you can't believe how difficult she was trying to get her own way. She would always begin, 'I've starred in however many films and...' How could you argue with that? Time-keeping was very important to her. If the call sheet said she was to be on the set at a certain time she would be there and there'd be hell to pay if we weren't ready for her and she had to hang around. Another thing that bugged her was the fact that we could get a drink at lunchtime in England, because the American studios were dry."

Sangster recalls his horror of entertaining her: "She was a lonely and not a very happy woman. It was essential for her to be the centre of attention in any social gathering. If you behave badly enough, shout loudly enough, this isn't too hard. Monica decided she'd like to give a dinner party for her at our house, where Bette behaved so badly that Denise, our au pair girl (who was doubling as maid that evening), got so scared she dropped the coffee tray. One Friday night Monica and I managed to put together a small group and, with Bette, we went to Danny La Rue's nightclub. Just before the cabaret started, a couple of the Beatles arrived. Bette said she was going to get their autographs for her daughter. She returned to our table a couple of minutes later almost apoplectic. 'Little bastards didn't know who I was,' she said. And she bitched about it loudly all through the cabaret, which she hated." [2]

Renée Glynne also remembers Bette Davis: "She listened to everything regarding continuity. She used to rehearse, even for a walk-through at the beginning or end of the day, wearing all her padding, so that she was in character. I remember at the end-of-picture party at The Old Barn in Elstree, she looked petite and most elegant. She gave a speech and said it had been the happiest film she'd ever been on where she didn't have to fire the director or cameraman."

"The day I put Bette on the plane home the Sangster household breathed a vast sigh of relief," Sangster adds. "Monica also said that if I ever did another movie with Bette, she was going to leave the country the day Bette arrived and not come back until I put her on the plane back to America. Not to worry, I told her. No way on God's green earth will I ever put myself through that again." [3] Of course, two years later she was brought back for Hammer's The Anniversary, which Sangster also produced. As promised, Monica Sangster left the country the day she arrived and returned the day she flew home.

In support of la Davis, Hammer assembled a top-notch cast, comprising Jill Bennett, Wendy Craig, James Villiers, Maurice Denham, Alfred Burke and three remarkable child actors: William Dix, Angharad Aubrey and Pamela Franklin (already a veteran of The Innocents and others). In the tradition of his earlier Taste of Fear, Seth Holt created an atmosphere of unnerving tension, assisted by Harry Waxman's moody black-and-white photography. The film has several moments of pure horror, notably the sequence in which Jill Bennett's Aunt Pen succumbs to a heart attack and Nanny sweetly withholds her medication. Holt also orchestrates the death of Susy in flashback, and her discovery by Nanny, with considerable sensitivity.

Filming ended on Friday 21 May, on schedule, after seven weeks. During shooting, She went on release on 18 April on the ABC circuit, paired with Pop Gear to become one of the year's biggest money-spinners. To help the promotion, Andress even posed nude for the June 1965 issue of Playboy. The Nanny then went into post-production with editors James Needs and Tom Simpson and sound editor Charles Crayford. The film had just been cut when Seymour Poe, head of Fox's worldwide distribution, demanded to see a print. The first cut ended just after Nanny had recovered her wits and saved Joey from a watery death. Pathetically, she goes off and packs her bags and the film ends. Poe was outraged by this rather downbeat climax and demanded that the film be given a happy ending. Sangster had to pen an extra scene, rent studio space, build a new set and recall Wendy Craig and William Dix. The final act of the movie, where Joey makes amends with his mother, was then shot over two days. Philip Martell then brought in Richard Rodney Bennett to compose the score.

Thrift was in the air again. Tony Hinds and Anthony Nelson Keys, in their wisdom, decided to shoot the next four productions back-to-back in order to re-use the sets and release them as two double-bills. This had first been announced in the Daily Cinema in January 1965 by James Carreras: "We shall make four horror pictures. The titles have not yet been decided, but the pictures will be made back-to-back, in pairs, and released as two of the greatest all-horror programmes seen in years!" More money would be spent on the first two productions, Dracula Prince of Darkness and Rasputin the Mad Monk, which would be the two main features and would both star Christopher Lee. The two support features, both set in Cornwall – The Plague of the Zombies and The Reptile – would be shot back-to-back next.

Many commentators have gone to great lengths to explain the significance of this arrangement, as if it were an innovation for Hammer. However, as we have seen, the concept was all too familiar to the canny company. They had already shot a number of films 'back-to-back', the classic examples being *Dracula* and *The Revenge of Frankenstein*. Hammer were also well versed in deliberately planning two similar productions in order to re-use standing sets, such as *The Terror of the Tongs* and *Visa to Canton*. And Hammer's distributors were certainly familiar with the concept of the double-bill, which had started with *The Curse of the Werewolf* and *The Shadow of the Cat* in 1961 and continued with *The Phantom of the Opera*/*Captain Clegg*, *Maniac*/*The Damned*, *The Kiss of the Vampire*/*Paranoiac*, *The Evil of Frankenstein*/*Nightmare* and *The Gorgon*/*The Curse of the Mummy's Tomb*.

The huge success of the latter double-bill towards the end of 1964 certainly showed that this approach was still big money. (One must remember that the main feature of a double-bill would get the lion's share of the programme receipts and that Hammer's films were often only support features – *The Old Dark House*, for instance, got only 25 per cent of the house when it supported *Big Deal at Dodge City*). So, with all this in mind, Hammer now decided to bring these two money-saving ideas together, shooting two custom-made packages that would save even more money. It was a tall order: both packages were set for an early 1966 release. But Hammer were confident they could do it.

All four pictures would take Hammer back to Bray, as Elstree was too busy to accommodate them. It would also take them back to Transylvania, and the return of Christopher Lee, after seven long years, to the role that had made him famous – Count Dracula.

By 1965, Hammer's Count Dracula had returned from his Swiss tax exile and all that was needed was a suitable script. Jimmy Sangster had since divorced himself from the Gothics, however, finding a nice little niche writing thrillers. He therefore wrote the screenplay under his nom de plume, John Sansom. (He had first used this name on screen for the 1963 production *To Have and To Hold*, but he'd used it years earlier for the UK edition of his *The Man Who Could Cheat Death* novelisation.) The genesis of the script lay in *The Revenge of Dracula*, which Sangster wrote back in 1958 as a direct sequel but discarded.

Sangster's shooting script was drawn up on 4 March and Anthony Nelson Keys submitted it to the BBFC on the 11th: "Herewith *Dracula Prince of Darkness* script which I am starting at Bray on April 26th. I want an 'X' certificate but I think that I have borne in mind all your past comments about our scripts. I have made a point of keeping out any sex and violence. You will notice that the shots of Dracula's cellar have all been arranged rather subtly."

Frank Crofts read the script on 16 March and commented: "A silly piece of cack, with a glaring inconstancy at the outset. Vampirology has always insisted that a vampire is either revivable or destroyed. Once destroyed he cannot be revived. Here Dracula has been reduced to ashes and there-fore was not revivable. Again Karl had been a hopeless idiot for years but he sheds his idiocy on the very night that Dracula plans to invade the monastery." A little unfair to challenge Hammer on the fantastical elements of their story, and it seems obvious that Karl (later Ludwig in the finished film) has remained under the influence of Dracula during his 'absence', hence the reason he apparently loses his 'idiocy' when the Count reappears. Crofts went on to list his objections, closing sarcastically with, "Don't miss *Dracula Bites Again*." The next day, Audrey Field commented: "I thought it was going to be above average when the driverless coach came along, but I was soon disillusioned!"

John Trevelyan summarised the objections in a letter to Anthony Nelson Keys on 19 March: "I am now in a position to send you our comments about *Dracula Prince of Darkness*. The film will, of course, be one for the 'X' category. For this category I have the following comments to make: Pages 49-51. Scenes 97-113. It looks as though these scenes will run into trouble, if shot as described, on the grounds of disgust. Klove repeatedly stabs Alan, hoists him up with a pulley until he hangs head downwards over Dracula's coffin; he then cuts off his head and throws it away. We feel that there should not be frequent stabbing; that the decapitation should be removed; and that the body should not be hung upside down. It appears that there will be a great deal of blood about (see scene 112). This should not be excessive. Page 52. Scenes 114-118. These scenes should not give us trouble on grounds of disgust. Care should be taken. Page 54. Scene 123. Screams should not be extensive.

Suzan Farmer and vampiric Barbara Shelley recoil at the sight of Dracula Prince of Darkness (1965).

DRACULA PRINCE OF DARKNESS

PRINCIPAL PHOTOGRAPHY: 26 April to 4 June 1965
DISTRIBUTION:
  UK: Warner-Pathe; Technicolor; certificate 'X'
  US: 20th Century-Fox; Deluxe Color
90 minutes; Techniscope
UK RELEASE:
  TRADE SHOW: 17 December 1965, with The Plague of the Zombies
  GENERAL RELEASE: 9 January 1966, on the ABC circuit with The Plague of the Zombies
  US RELEASE: 12 January 1966, with The Plague of the Zombies

DIRECTOR: Terence Fisher; PRODUCER: Anthony Nelson Keys; SCREENPLAY: John Sansom [Jimmy Sangster], from an idea by John Elder; PRODUCTION DESIGNER: Bernard Robinson; ART DIRECTOR: Don Mingaye; DIRECTOR OF PHOTOGRAPHY: Michael Reed; CAMERA OPERATOR: Cece Cooney; GRIP: Albert Cowland; ASSISTANT DIRECTOR: Bert Batt; 2ND ASSISTANT DIRECTOR: Hugh Harlow; SUPERVISING EDITOR: James Needs; EDITOR: Chris Barnes; MUSIC: James Bernard; MUSIC SUPERVISOR: Philip Martell; SOUND RECORDIST: Ken Rawkins; SOUND EDITOR: Roy Baker; MAKE-UP: Roy Ashton; HAIRSTYLIST: Frieda Steiger; PRODUCTION MANAGER: Ross MacKenzie; CONTINUITY: Lorna Selwyn; WARDROBE: Rosemary Burrows; SPECIAL EFFECTS: Bowie Films Ltd; STILLS: Tom Edwards; PUBLICITY OFFICER: Tony Tweedale; FIGHT ARRANGER: Peter Diamond; STUNTMAN: Eddie Powell

Christopher Lee (Dracula); Barbara Shelley (Helen); Andrew Keir (Father Sandor); Francis Matthews (Charles); Suzan Farmer (Diana); Charles Tingwell (Alan); Thorley Walters (Ludwig); Philip Latham (Klove); Walter Brown (Brother Mark); George Woodbridge (Landlord); Jack Lambert (Brother Peter); Philip Ray (Priest); Joyce Hemson (Mother); John Maxim (Coach Driver)

Page 63. Scene 147. In view of the alteration that I have proposed to scene 111, removing the decapitation, Scene 147 would have to be altered also. In any case we would not want any disgust shot here, or a shot that is really gruesome.

Page 67. Scene 157. I take it that the 'terrifying thud' here is no more than a conventional bang on the soundtrack.

Page 68. scene 162. Not too much blood or nastiness please.

Page 69. Scene 166. Not too much should be made of the throttling, or of Dracula's enjoyment of it. His enjoyment increases the sadistic element.

Pages 84-86. scenes 191-198. We think that the eating of live flies is a gratuitous piece of nastiness. We appreciate that in scene 198 he does it as a blind, but would prefer you to find some other way of his doing this.

Father Sandor (Andrew Keir) admires the craftsmanship of Ludwig (Thorley Walters) while Charles (Francis Matthews) looks on in Dracula Prince of Darkness (1965).

Page 89. Scene 204. The biting of Diana's wrist could be unpleasant. Care should be taken.
Page 90. Scene 204-207. The same applies to the cauterising and her screams.
Page 95. Scene 222. We have always taken the line that we should not see stakes actually going into vampires. Here in scene 222 we see it in silhouette. We do not mind stakes being hammered providing that the point cannot be seen going into the body, and this applies as much to silhouette as to a straight shot. Her 'unearthly scream' may give trouble if not handled with care.
Pages 99-100. Scenes 242-243. These scenes [Dracula alone with Diana] are sadistic and quite disgusting and should be entirely removed.
Page 100. Scene 245. It seems unnecessary to have Dracula hit Diana and knock her senseless. We do not like brutality to women.
Page 108. Scene 277. Care should be taken with the soundtrack when Dracula's wrist breaks. we would not want to hear nasty cracking noises."

Nelson Keys replied to Trevelyan on 14 April: "You will be pleased to know that Dracula doesn't throttle Charles and get sadistic pleasure out of it. We have noted your remarks regarding the fly eater and have decided to play this strictly for comedy. I must admit that I didn't think you would take objection as this character was in the original book and in the play, but as we are now playing it for comedy, I do not think this will give offence. We are not decapitating Alan, which I am sure you will be pleased to hear, so I hope you will have no objection to him hanging upside down. I have deleted the scene where Dracula pulls Diana to his chest and her face is covered with blood. Instead, he starts to pull her towards him, but is interrupted by bangs on the door. Also, we are not breaking Dracula's wrist in the end scene. Many thanks for you guidance."

Trevelyan replied on the 21st: "It certainly looks as though you are meeting our objections in a most satisfactory way. The only reason why I write again is to suggest that you might have an alternative take in which Alan is hung the right way up so that if we should take objection to his hanging upside down you would have a suitable alternative."

Dracula Prince of Darkness began shooting at Bray on Monday 26 April and was the first film to be shot there since The Runaway and Delayed Flight shorts of spring 1964. Terence Fisher was back and supported by a loyal band of Hammer regulars. In fact, apart from a new production manager (Ross Mackenzie), editor (Chris Barnes), sound editor (Roy Baker) and continuity girl (Lorna Selwyn), it was the same team that had worked on The Gorgon. Michael Reed was back on lighting, with Cece Cooney behind the camera. Bert Batt was back as assistant director with Hugh Harlow as second. The stability of the team is further shown by Bernard Robinson, Don Mingaye, James Needs, Roy Baker, Roy Ashton, Frieda Steiger, Lorna Selwyn and Rosemary Burrows, who would work on all four films in the back-to-back package. In addition, Bert Batt, Hugh Harlow and Ken Rawkins would work on the first three. Michael Reed, Cece Cooney and Ross Mackenzie would work on the first two main features.

Bernard Robinson and Don Mingaye were back in full control at Bray Studios. The village square set and Gothic structure had been cleared after *The Gorgon* and in their stead was erected the front façade of Castle Dracula, complete with ice-covered moat. A bridge straddled the moat, connecting the castle to The Mound, which was still standing after its inauguration on *The Mummy* in 1959. The door through which Christopher Lee exits at the climax, carrying Suzan Farmer in his arms, was the main entrance to Down Place in the front courtyard leading to the reception area. The long shot of the castle was the same Les Bowie model used for Chateau Ravna in *The Kiss of the Vampire*. Ray Caple's superb glass painting of the valley from *The Evil of Frankenstein* and *The Gorgon* was re-used for the inn at the beginning. The shooting schedule shows where the various sets were erected and the order in which they were used, thus demonstrating how the art department revamped the sets:

DRACULA PRINCE OF DARKNESS SHOOTING SCHEDULE

Mon 26 April	INT. INN	Stage 3
Tue 27 April	INT. INN	Stage 3
Wed 28 April	INT. SANDOR'S STUDY	Stage 2
Thurs 29 April	INT. SANDOR'S STUDY	Stage 2
Fri 30 April	INT. LUDWIG'S CELL	Stage 4
Mon 3 May	INT. LUDWIG'S CELL	Stage 4
Tue 4 May	EXT. MONASTERY COURTYARD & GATES	Stage 2
Wed 5 May	INT. HALL & STAIRS, CASTLE DRACULA	Stage 1
Thurs 6 May	INT. HALL & STAIRS, CASTLE DRACULA	Stage 1
Fri 7 May	INT. HALL & STAIRS, CASTLE DRACULA	Stage 1
Mon 10 May	INT. HALL & STAIRS, CASTLE DRACULA	Stage 1
	INT. DIANA'S ROOM/CORRIDOR, MONASTERY	Stage 4
Tues 11 May	INT. DIANA'S ROOM/CORRIDOR, MONASTERY	Stage 4
Wed 12 May	EXT. CASTLE DRACULA	Lot
Thurs 13 May	EXT. CASTLE DRACULA	Lot
Fri 14 May	EXT. CASTLE DRACULA	Lot
Mon 17 May	EXT. CASTLE DRACULA	Lot

[Weather cover for these three days: 1st & 2nd BEDROOM/CORRIDOR, CASTLE INTERIOR STAIRS & CELLAR, CASTLE]

Tue 18 May	1st & 2nd BEDROOM/CORRIDOR, CASTLE	Stage 1
Wed 19 May	1st & 2nd BEDROOM/CORRIDOR, CASTLE	Stage 1
	INT. STAIRS & CELLAR, CASTLE	Stage 2
Thurs 20 May	INT. STAIRS & CELLAR, CASTLE	Stage 2
Fri 21 May	INT. STAIRS & CELLAR, CASTLE	Stage 2

Mon 24 May to Fri 4 June: LOCATION WORK

Christopher Lee returns as the definitive Count in Dracula Prince of Darkness (1965).

Both main features were shot in a widescreen process. This posed a slight problem when Hammer decided to use the finale of *Dracula* for the opening pre-credits sequence, with an Andrew Keir voice-over to remind audiences of what had gone on before. To blend this standard format with the Techniscope process, the outer edges of the frame were shrouded in billowing mist, which conveniently also gives this flashback sequence a dreamlike, surreal quality of its own. The reason for adding this sequence was reputedly due to the fact that the film was considered too short to be a main feature. This turned out to be quite an expensive idea as Hammer had to buy back the rights to their original film from Universal, necessitating the use of production money set aside for *Rasputin the Mad Monk*. Tony Hinds even paid for the repair of Peter Cushing's roof in acknowledgment of his part in the sequence.

LEFT TO RIGHT:
Jack Goodlatte
(managing director
of Associated
British Cinemas),
James Carreras,
Barbara Shelley,
Tony Hinds and
Brian Lawrence at
Bray during the
filming of Dracula
Prince of
Darkness (1965).

BELOW: Roy
Ashton applies the
vampire bite to
Barbara Shelley
for Dracula
Prince of
Darkness (1965).

One thing in particular drew the attention of both audiences and critics alike and that was the fact that, in the whole picture, Dracula doesn't utter a single word. Why this created such a stir isn't clear; after all, this approach is not inconsistent with the previous movie, where dialogue was only used by Dracula at the beginning of the film and then only by way of introducing himself *before* his vampiric side had been revealed. In the new film, from the moment he is reincarnated Dracula is simply played as the same silent embodiment of evil that had dominated the latter three quarters of the original. Certainly it's difficult to write convincing lines for the character and all the drab one-liners in the later films bear witness to this. Silent, he is more sinister and spectre-like, not needing to belittle himself with such small talk. Christopher Lee at various times has claimed that, in the original shooting script, lines were written for Dracula which he considered 'unspeakable' and therefore deleted. However, no such lines are present in Sangster's original shooting script of 4 March, which is how Sangster remembers it in his memoir Inside Hammer.

Key features of the script contradicted the original film. One was the appearance of Klove, Dracula's servant. Nowhere in Dracula are we led to believe that Dracula had such a devoted servant, apart from a line he delivers to Jonathan Harker as he carries his bags up the stairs: "My servants are away... a family bereavement you understand," a line which is little more than a convenient ruse to quell Harker's suspicions. Hammer's castle, in stark contrast to Lugosi's, was immaculately well-kept, however, and, though Stoker's Count is spotted doing the housework in the novel, it's hard to imagine Christopher Lee's Dracula walking around with a feather duster in his hand. In any case, the art directors now changed the external and internal appearance of the castle as well as relocating Dracula's crypt. It was no longer located outside the main building but inside, in a cellar concealed by a wall tapestry.

Inconsistencies, scenes culled from the original book, new characters and innovative ideas – the script had them all and an impressive cast and crew had been assembled to do it justice. Terence Fisher focuses once more on the sexual bond between Dracula and his victims: first the dependent Helen, craving his attention, and then Diana, whom he is intent on seducing after she is snatched away from him. In a daring sex act lifted from the pages of Stoker himself, Dracula invites Diana to lick the blood from his chest, which takes the bondage-by-blood angle to kinky extremes. (Though censorship objections at the script stage, noted above, permitted only the invitation, not the licking itself.) Surprisingly, this proved to be Fisher's last vampire film; he was slated to direct the next sequel, *Dracula Has Risen from the Grave*, but Freddie Francis had to take over when Fisher was injured in a road accident.

Fisher smoothly orchestrates the scene the BBFC were most concerned with, as he explained: "When Klove ... cuts Alan's throat to obtain blood to pour upon Dracula's ashes, to resurrect him, the scene could have been played in quite different ways. Klove could have played it with speed and triumph – he cannot wait to see Dracula again – or he could have played it almost weeping and overcome with emotion, causing perhaps bungling and uncertain movements. I chose to play it slowly and ritualistically, in the same way a priest would administer the Sacrament; an anti-Christ ceremony. There was no indication in the script of how this sequence was to be treated." [4]

Barbara Shelley had some trouble speaking with her fangs in. "I hadn't realised there would be any difficulty," she remembers. "I had to walk towards Suzan Farmer, who was out of shot, and I had to walk into a big close-up and look at her and say the line, 'You don't need Charles.' The fangs were a tremendous impediment and so it came out like, 'Hew gon't gleed Kharlz', at which, of course, everybody just roared with laughter, and I had to go into my dressing room for about 20 minutes and practice very carefully speaking around the fangs." [5]

The fangs caused more problems in the scene where she is staked by Andrew Keir's Father Sandor. "I struggled very violently, and when the scene was over, I went to the assistant director, a marvellous man called Bert Batt, and said to him, 'Bert, I don't want to worry Terry, but in the middle of that scene, I swallowed one of my fangs.' Now the fangs were made to fit very closely and in the course of the scene I had, in fact, swallowed one. Bert went to Terry and I heard him say, 'Terry, Barbara has swallowed one of her fangs,' to which Terry replied, 'What was the angle, did we see it in the camera?' And Bert said, 'No, it was the side of her face away from camera.' Terry replied that that was fine and started to get ready for the next set-up, but Bert said, 'We can't get ready for the next set-up because there's only one set of fangs and she'll have a fang missing', to which Terry replied, 'Well, that's all right. We'll wait until tomorrow.' Well, I wasn't going to wait for the fang to make that sort of exit, so I went and drank some salted water and we got the fang back and we were able to continue shooting." [6]

The film's memorable climax was set on the icy moat beneath Dracula's castle. Les Bowie recalled: "I've lost count of the times I've killed Christopher Lee. Syd Pearson finished him off in the first Hammer *Dracula*, but I handled the falling through the ice sequence in the second one, *Dracula Prince of Darkness*. We utilised a number of methods to get these scenes ... sometimes we used real blocks of ice in a swimming pool for a few of the close shots ... for other shots we used wax ... if you pour wax on water it forms a coating on the surface. For the final shots of Dracula sliding under the 'ice' we used a circular section of plaster mounted on pivots." [7] At least one of those pivots is plainly visible in the finished film, unfortunately. To depict the cracks in the ice caused by Sandor's shotgun, Bowie used irregularly shaped pieces of plastic, which looked like the real thing in long shot.

The scene gave rise to a series of mishaps. Francis Matthews, making his first Hammer appearance since I *Only Arsked*, threw himself enthusiastically into the fight sequences and injured his back in a rehearsal of the climactic battle on the ice, when he fell backwards onto the mallet he had dropped. The makeshift ice also caused a painful moment for Christopher Lee, when Roy Ashton dropped one of his contact lenses onto the salt-covered wax and unthinkingly put it straight back into the actor's eye without cleaning it.

Furthermore, stuntman Eddie Powell almost drowned as he doubled for Lee in his climactic death plunge. "Things go wrong when you think you've covered everything," remembered Powell.

"Of course the ice ... was on a swivel thing and ... the water underneath came right up to the underside. It was all on scaffolding and, being supported, Chris did his bit, then I came in. I had arranged it so that I had an air bottle on the bottom – it was only about ten feet deep – because when it closed, you need some air, because they were shooting from a distance. So I worked everything out, I knew where everything was. I thought 'Terrific,' and on 'Action', tipped up, went down and this bloody thing closed behind me, which it was supposed to do, but of course it was pitch black. I hadn't thought of that. Now I'm looking for this bloody thing down below to get an airline and thinking, 'Christ, I've had it,' because the water's up to the underside of this sort of ice and there's no air up there. Eventually I found it, lungs bursting, and they came along and picked me up. But it's silly little things like that that cause these sort of accidents."[8]

The cracks in the ice seen in long shot at the climax of Dracula Prince of Darkness (1965) were in fact bits of plastic stuck on the wax floor.

Principal photography ended on Friday 4 June after six weeks. Location shooting had been arranged for the final fortnight to allow last-minute revamping of sets necessary for *Rasputin the Mad Monk*, which was due to start the following Tuesday. *Dracula Prince of Darkness* now went into post-production. James Needs and Chris Barnes took the editing to Hammer House to allow Hammer's ex-sound editor Roy Hyde to begin work on *Rasputin*. With the company's regular sound editor now turning his hand to film editing, Roy Baker joined the team in his place and would work on all four back-to-back productions. Barbara Shelley's deep voice made screaming difficult so her screams had to be dubbed (interestingly, however, Shelley's own scream remains on the soundtrack of the trailer). Philip Martell brought in James Bernard to compose the score, who successfully reprised his three-note Dracula theme last heard in, of all things, *The Ugly Duckling*. On 25 June, sound effects were recorded at the Anvil Theatre in Beaconsfield.

For Hammer, there was no respite. It was a case of one down, three to go. As soon as the cameras stopped rolling on DPOD, it was full steam ahead on *Rasputin*.

Rasputin already had a long cinematic history, starting with *The Fall of the Romanoffs* in 1917 – only a year after his death. When Hammer came to produce their version of the story, they did not want any of the legal problems that had befallen the 1932 MGM production *Rasputin and the Empress*. Tony Hinds had allegedly prepared a script painstakingly based on accounts by Rasputin's chief assassin, Prince Yusupov himself, but rewrote it radically when Hammer received a letter from the representatives of the still-living Prince, warning them of possible repercussions.

Hinds' final shooting script was entitled *The Mad Monk* (under which title the film was actually shot) and on the title page he wrote: "This is an entertainment, not a documentary. No attempt has been made at historical accuracy ... all the characters and incidents may be regarded as fictitious." To cover themselves, Hammer had Yusupov sign all the script pages as an indemnity against a lawsuit. As Hammer were accustomed to doing, they heightened the horrific elements of the story and added some graphic touches of their own, including a severed hand and a victim scarred by acid.

Tony Nelson Keys submitted the script to John Trevelyan on 18 May. Frank Crofts read it on the 21st and commented: "In a note at the beginning, the script writer disclaims any attempt at accuracy and well he might (Rasputin certainly did not die in this way). It is the usual nasty Hammer stuff with the emphasis on bleeding stumps. Even Hammer won't try to turn this into 'A' or 'U'." Reader Newton Branch commented the following day: "I agree with FNC. The Rasputin story is a 'natural', full of strangeness, sex and horror, and it's a pity that Hammer plays the fool with it in this squalid fashion. We should not be lenient."

John Trevelyan summarised their recommendations in a letter to Tony Nelson Keys on 24 May: "We have now had a look at your script of *The Mad Monk*. This is, of course, basically suitable only for the 'X' category, which is what you want. Even for this category there must be limits to the degree of nastiness. My comments on points of detail are as follows:

Rasputin the Mad Monk (1965) was shot back-to-back with Dracula Prince of Darkness. Suzan Farmer, Francis Matthews and Barbara Shelley all joined Rasputin after Dracula. Here, they're joined by Dinsdale Landen.

RASPUTIN THE MAD MONK

PRINCIPAL PHOTOGRAPHY: 8 June to 20 July 1965
DISTRIBUTION:
  UK: Warner-Pathe; Technicolor; certificate 'X'
  US: 20th Century-Fox; Deluxe Color
91 minutes; Cinemascope
UK RELEASE:
  TRADE SHOW: 14 February 1966, at Studio One with The Reptile
  GENERAL RELEASE: 6 March 1966, on the ABC circuit with The Reptile
US RELEASE: 6 April 1966, with The Reptile

DIRECTOR: Don Sharp; PRODUCER: Anthony Nelson Keys; SCREENPLAY: John Elder; PRODUCTION DESIGNER: Bernard Robinson; ART DIRECTOR: Don Mingaye; DIRECTOR OF PHOTOGRAPHY: Michael Reed; CAMERA OPERATOR: Cece Cooney; ASSISTANT DIRECTOR: Bert Batt; 2ND ASSISTANT DIRECTOR: Hugh Harlow; SUPERVISING EDITOR: James Needs; EDITOR: Roy Hyde; MUSIC: Don Banks; MUSIC SUPERVISOR: Philip Martell; SOUND RECORDIST: Ken Rawkins; SOUND EDITOR: Roy Baker;

MAKE-UP: Roy Ashton; HAIRSTYLIST: Frieda Steiger; PRODUCTION MANAGER: Ross MacKenzie; CONTINUITY: Lorna Selwyn; WARDROBE: Rosemary Burrows; DANCE DIRECTOR: Alan Beall; Fight Arranger: Peter Diamond

Christopher Lee (Rasputin); Barbara Shelley (Sonia); Richard Pasco (Dr Zargo); Francis Matthews (Ivan); Suzan Farmer (Vanessa); Dinsdale Landen (Peter); Renee Asherson (Tsarina); Derek Francis (Innkeeper); Joss Ackland (The Bishop); Robert Duncan (Tsarevitch); Alan Tilvern (Patron); John Welsh (The Abbot); John Bailey (Court Physician)

UNCREDITED: Mary Barclay (Superior Lady); Michael Cadman (Son); Lucy Fleming (Wide Eyes); Michael Godfrey (Doctor); Fiona Hartford (Daughter); Prudence Hyman (Chatty Woman); Bryan Marshall (Young Tough); Bridget McConnel (Gossip); Bartlett Mullins (Waggoner); Veronica Nicholson (Young Girl); Mary Quinn (Innkeeper's Wife); Celia Ryder (Fat Lady); Cyril Shaps (Foxy Face); Leslie White (Cheeky Man); Brian Wilde (Burly Brute); Jeremy Young (Court Messenger); Helen Christie; Maggie Wright (Tarts); Jay McGrath, Robert McLennan (Dancers)

Pages 10-11. Scene 10. This scene will need care and discretion both in its sex and its violence. We do not like script directions such as 'equally suddenly, she gives in and thrusts her whole body to him, searching for his lips with open mouth.' The violence produces the gimmick of the apparent cutting off of the boy's hand. We would not want this, so I suggest that you find something less troublesome. Surely a more normal wound would be enough, without too much blood about.

Page 13. Scene 15. Here we have the severed hand on the Abbot's table. Since I want you to alter the original scene in which the hand is severed, it would appear that you will have to alter this also. I suppose that you can do the whole thing by suggestion.

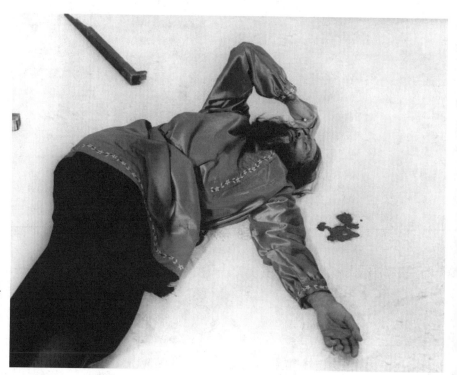

A scene cut from the end of Rasputin the Mad Monk (1965). Rasputin lies dead on the ice, his hand held up in benediction.

Page 39. Scene 36. This is a sadistic scene, and it may be too sadistic for our liking. We do not like Rasputin's vicious blow on Sonia.

Page 41. Scenes 36-37. Great discretion will be needed in shooting these scenes. We would not want to see Sonia stripping in front of Rasputin, or to hear a 'sharp cry of pain'. In the subsequent scene on the bed the girl should be adequately covered; and the same applies to her in the tattered bathrobe.

Page 52. Scene 42. We would not be likely to accept the shot of Rasputin forcing the prostitute to eat a mangled fish. This is quite disgustingly sadistic.

Page 84. Scene 63. Here Sonia is humiliated again, to the point where she attacks Rasputin, 'scratching, biting, kicking.' Discretion should be used if this is to pass. Even Zargo is 'disgusted by it all.'

Page 84. Scene 64. Here we have more sadism with Rasputin threatening Sonia with acid, and a nasty shot of Zargo in pain as acid falls on his hand. I wish you could get this sadism down much further; it seems to us much overdone in the present script.

Page 88. Scene 65. We would not want too much blood when Sonia cuts her wrist with the glass, especially if the film is to be in colour.

Page 94. Scene 68. The same applies to the blood coming under the door and the 'pool of wet blood' on the floor.

Page 96. Scene 69. It seems quite unnecessary to have Rasputin cutting off Peter's fingers. Once again we have unnecessary sadism, and something more conventional should be used. We would certainly not want to see a shot of Peter's hand with blood pouring from the stumps of his fingers.

Page 97. Scene 70. We would not want more than the suggestion of Peter's agony when the acid burns his face; certainly not a nasty shot of the results.

Page 105. Scene 80. Discretion should be used in this scene in which Rasputin is killed. We would not want close or nasty shots.

Page 106. Scene 81. Discretion should also be used with this scene. We would not want too much agony or any close or prolonged shots of Peter's face.

"As I said earlier, there is some nasty stuff in this script, and there are limits to what we would accept even in the 'X' category. So I urge you to use discretion throughout and, if it seems desirable, to have alternative material for submission to this Board."

Tony Nelson Keys replied on Friday 4 June. Time was at a premium; this was the last day of shooting on *Dracula Prince of Darkness* and they were due to start shooting *Rasputin* on the Tuesday: "Many thanks for your letter of 24th May regarding *The Mad Monk*. With reference to your comments on the following:

Scene 10: Rest assured that this scene will be played with the utmost discretion, and the cutting off of the boy's hand will be done by implication and will not actually be seen.

Scene 15: With reference to the severed hand on the Abbot's table, I would like to point out that there was a similar scene in *The Curse of the Mummy's Tomb*, *The Curse of Frankenstein* and, if my memory serves me right, in two other Hammer productions. I am sure you will find that this is played with great discretion.

Scene 36: Rasputin will not give her a vicious blow, but will smack her across the face.

Scenes 36&37: You will not see Sonia stripping in front of Rasputin, and there will be no 'sharp cry of pain'. This of course will be done by implication, and the girl on the bed will be adequately covered.

Scene 42: Rasputin will not force the prostitute to eat a mangled piece of fish. It was a habit of Rasputin to dive into bowls of fish and pick out the best pieces, one of which he will offer the prostitute.

Scene 63: I can assure you that Sonia's attack on Rasputin will be handled with great delicacy.

Scene 64: This scene with Sonia is not played for sadism, and there will be no more or less than in *The Phantom of the Opera*.

Scene 65: We do not actually see Sonia cutting her wrists.

Scene 68: We will certainly be very discreet about the pool of wet blood on the floor.

Scene 69: You will be pleased to hear that Rasputin does not cut off Peter's fingers.

Scene 70: Here again this will be no more or less than in *The Phantom of the Opera*.

Scene 80: The death of Rasputin will be handled with delicacy.

Scene 81: Here again this will be no more than allowed in *The Phantom of the Opera*.

"I can assure you that all the above points will be watched most carefully."

Don Sharp was appointed director (his third Hammer movie) and the same crew from *Dracula Prince of Darkness* (apart from a new editor, Roy Hyde) started shooting *Rasputin* on Tuesday 8 June. The film started with location shooting at Black Park to allow revamping and completion of the internal sets, which had already begun during the location shooting at the end of DPOD. Castle Dracula on the backlot would now become the front of Ivan's house and Christopher Lee would again meet his demise on the mock ice surrounding it. Dracula's cellar on Stage 2 became the interior of the Café Tzigane. The St Petersburg marketplace replaced the monastery courtyard outside Stage 2.

Rejoining Christopher Lee after the Dracula adventure were co-stars Francis Matthews, Barbara Shelley and Suzan Farmer. While their parts were vastly different, they nevertheless followed similar patterns: Lee is the hypnotic bad guy who violates Shelley, Matthews and Farmer are the romantic leads (though brother and sister this time), Matthews kills Lee at the end on the very same ice, etc. Offering fine support were Richard Pasco (last seen in *The Gorgon*) as the drunken Dr Zargo and Renée Asherson as a Tsarina conspicuously unaccompanied by a Tsar.

Lee is something of an authority on Rasputin and was not impressed with the script. "I've been to the Yusupov Palace in St Petersburg and I've been to the room. I also knew Rasputin's daughter and I met Yusopov and the Grand Duke Dmitri when I was a small boy. So I knew a good deal about him and I took the trouble, of course, to read as much as I could – which didn't help me at all, because he was a great enigma. I tried to represent the character of Rasputin as well as I could with the material at hand. Hammer's version lacked two very important things. First of all, the ending was totally incorrect, but Yusupov wouldn't let us do what really happened. Part of it was correct: poisoning the cakes, the convulsions. We didn't use the name Yusupov, because we weren't allowed to; the Grand Duke Dmitri didn't even come into it, nor did Dr Lazovert, the doctor who poisoned everything, nor did the deputy Purishkevich or Sukhotin the army officer. None of the conspirators came into it. We had a sort of mixed-up character played by Francis Matthews and a drunken doctor played by Richard

Pasco. So we were constrained, and so was I, by Yusupov's conditions. That was the first major problem. The second major problem was that you didn't see the Tsar and the Tsarina hardly appeared. It was through her neurotic worship of Rasputin that he was able to do what he did, to order the army around and get rid of the chief politicians. He did it through her, so there was so much missing."

Don Sharp recalls: "Tony Hinds came to me and said we were running over budget and asked for my input on scenes that had to be cut to compensate. So we ended up losing a whole ballroom set and cutting scenes involving the Tsar's court. Originally the part for Renée Asherson as the Tsarina was intended to be bigger, which is why we were able to get her. She ended up being wasted and was very uncomfortable. I had had two very happy associations with Hammer previously but that regime had ended and Tony Keys had taken over. He had this idea of doing four films back-to-back, with no gap in between, and it all became like a factory line. You could talk about a number of things to do with a picture with Tony Hinds, but Tony Keys didn't know what the hell you were talking about. He really didn't seem to care – he was only interested in getting things done on budget and schedule.

"There was total trust between Christopher and I. We worked out on an empty set how exactly to play the hypnotism routine and he used to be quite exhausted after filming some of those sequences. Everybody knew this was a terrific performance, even the people who thought 'Not Chris Lee again' Chris always did a lot of research on his roles and he talked quite a lot about aspects of Rasputin that weren't in the script but just interested him. He'd bring up little anecdotes from his readings and I'd either say 'We can't show that' or 'That's a good idea, we can use an element of that.' But he was very good in that he'd always put up ideas and you'd talk it out and there'd be an agreement. Some of Rasputin's dance was a bit freewheeling, and what I did with the poisoning was to tell him to sketch out how he wanted it to start and where we wanted it to end and then just do a half-pace rehearsal of what he might do in between. We then lit for that and did it following him with hand-held cameras." [9]

It was Barbara Shelley's turn to be injured this time. "During the first week, when I had a fight scene in the laboratory, I had a bad accident with some breakaway curtains. Chris was supposed to catch me as I swung back into the lab on these curtains after he had pushed me out, and I fell and struck my head. The director, Don Sharp, wanted to go again because of technical problems and I fell again and this time displaced my coccyx. I felt it go and it was really quite frightening. So I spent the rest of the picture in great pain. It was difficult to sit and walk and, after the film was over, I had to go and have a lot of osteopathy and treatment." [10]

Principal photography ended on Tuesday 20 July after six weeks. The original budget had been set at £99,862 but finished at £111,617. During filming, The Secret of Blood Island went on release on the ABC circuit on 14 June, paired with another William Castle shocker, The Night Walker, while Hysteria was put out on 27 June. The Damned was finally released in America as These Are the Damned on 7 July. Also that month, Hammer announced that Ursula Andress would star in the sequel to She, Ayesha – Daughter of She.

Now Rasputin was rushed into post-production under editors James Needs and Roy Hyde and sound editor Roy Baker. Philip Martell brought in Hammer regular Don Banks to compose the score. The editing of the film featured some apparently overzealous and unnecessary cuts to the climax. Although it was filmed, for reasons known only to themselves Hammer decided to abbreviate the exciting fight sequence between Ivan and Rasputin at the end. As it was originally scripted:

INT. COACH HOUSE
84.   OUTSIDE DOOR
IVAN *appears at the top of the steps just as the door flies open to reveal the terrified ZARGO.*
ZARGO *(screams out)* He won't die! He is the Devil … I've killed him but he won't die!
IVAN *hesitates only for a moment, then he strides in.*
INSIDE ROOM
85.   IVAN *bursts in. The room is empty.*
IVAN *takes a couple of paces into the room, then turns back to ZARGO, bewildered.*
It is ZARGO who sees RASPUTIN, who has crawled behind a screen, and who now has his ornate knife poised ready to throw.
ZARGO Look out!

And he throws himself at IVAN, knocking him
sideways.
And rolls over, the knife deep in his back.
IVAN has not time to get up before RASPUTIN
pounces.
The two men struggle, crashing about the room,
smashing the furniture, the screens, the decanter,
as they sway.
ZARGO tries to get to his knees, but cannot.
RASPUTIN finally forces IVAN against the
window. There is a screech of protesting wood
work, and the casement gives way, sending the
frame and shattered glass to the ice below.
RASPUTIN sees his advantage, forces IVAN
further and further back.
Just when it looks as if the boy must fall,
ZARGO reaches out and grabs him by the ankle.
RASPUTIN looks down, sees what is happening, and kicks ZARGO away.
But this is just enough to give IVAN the advantage. He twists his body and, with a jerk,
topples RASPUTIN so that he hangs for a moment at the point of balance, then with a
blood-chilling scream, he:

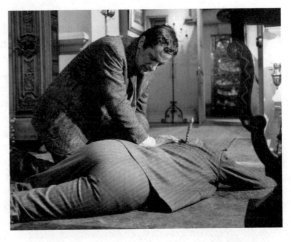

Ivan (Francis Matthews)
inspects the body of Zargo
(Richard Pasco) in Rasputin
the Mad Monk (1965). Note
the blood on Francis Matthews'
face – the middle section of the
fight was cut and these injuries
are unexplained in the final cut.

EXT. IVAN'S HOUSE
86.   hurtles to the parapet below.

Despite the fact that this sequence took three days to shoot, Hammer pruned it down so that, when
Zargo is impaled, we cut immediately to Rasputin and Ivan at the window. Ivan has only been
pushed to safety by Zargo yet, when we next see him, he is lying dazed under the window, his
clothes dishevelled and his face cut and bleeding. Without the full fight his appearance is totally
inexplicable and gives the impression of a careless continuity error.

Francis Matthews remembers filming the scene: "It was a huge fight, took us three days. Nearly
a day to set the fight up and for the double to teach me what to do ... It was the big climax to the
film. and I did an awful lot of fairly dangerous things. I had to smash into a huge glass cabinet and
go over the back of it and then we had a lot of fist fighting."[11] Christopher Lee adds, "They even
filmed a sequence where, after I've fallen from the window, I'm lying on the ice with my arm held
out as if in benediction. I have a still to prove it, but they didn't use it. I can't explain why they cut
it." Don Sharp muses, "I was there for the first cut, but because I had to go on to Morocco [to film
Our Man in Marrakesh], it was one of the only films I did where I wasn't present all the way through.
So Tony Keys probably just got impatient in thinking the fight scene went on too long and had it
cut. Had it been Tony Hinds, he would've found a better way."[9]

While Rasputin was being shot at Bray, the editing team at Hammer House were in the process of
submitting Dracula Prince of Darkness to the BBFC. Examiners Frank Crofts and Newton Branch
watched a black-and-white cut on 30 June and commented:

"R.9. Remove the whole incident in which Dracula bares his chest, scratches it and tries to get
Diane to suck the wound. Before we give a final opinion about the rest of the film we wish to see in
colour Reel 5 (episodes in which Alan is hung upside down, stabbed and drained of blood and in
which Dracula revives) and Reel 9 (episode in which the monks struggle with Helen, put her on a table
and drive a stake into her, including shot of her corpse). Also we should like to hear what the missing
scene in R.10 is. Please mark up reels 5,9." A note on file from 9 July says: "Mr Needs is worried about
removing the entire episode and will try reduction." A further cut was made and the reels resubmitted.
Frank Crofts commented on the 13th: "We saw R.9 in black and white. The 'scratch-and-kiss' scene
has been cut at the point where Dracula, having scratched his chest, advances on Diana and puts his
hand on her shoulders. This will do. Reels 5 and 9 to be seen in colour for other episodes."

Hammer finally submitted the offending reels in colour and Frank Crofts and Audrey Field watched it on 8 September. Crofts wrote to Tony Nelson Keys later that day:
"We saw the resubmitted reels 5, 9, 10 in colour today and have the following comments to make:
Reel 5. There must be no shot of Alan being slashed (when he is hanging up), no shot of blood pouring from him and no shot of blood flowing into or congealing in the sarcophagus.
Reel 9. The struggle of Helen and her guards should be shortened and there must be no shot of the stake being driven into her and of blood spouting from the wound.
Reel 10. The missing scene is all right.
"We shall want to see reels 5 and 9 again when the cuts have been made."
Trevelyan made a handwritten note on 16 September: "Discussed on the telephone with Mr Keys. I agreed that he could try reduction in the R.5 scene since there is continuity difficulty and a reduction in the scene in R.9. I must see these scenes when resubmitted." Audrey Field closed the innings with a note on 22 September: "Reels 5 and 9, with the relevant scenes shortened, seen by NKB/AOF with JT (reel 9 not in colour). We agreed that the shortened versions were acceptable. An 'X' certificate may now be issued."

Meanwhile, as *Rasputin* wound up on Tuesday 20 July, Hammer were making ready to plunge into *The Plague of the Zombies* on Wednesday the 28th.

The origins of *The Plague of the Zombies* dated back to 1962, when Peter Bryan put forward a story synopsis called *The Zombie*. Tony Hinds developed the story further in September 1963 and the film was announced as part of Hammer's schedule in the *Daily Cinema*'s tribute to him in November of that year: "What promises to be one of the most terrifying and exciting films ever made by Hammer is *The Zombie* from an original story by Peter Bryan." The project next appeared in Hammer's 1964 programme under the new title *Horror of the Zombies*, and was later announced as part of Hammer's new 11-picture deal as *The Horror of the Zombie*.

Peter Bryan was now brought back in and he completed his first draft screenplay in June 64 under the more familiar title *The Plague of the Zombies*. The story told of mysterious goings-on in deepest Cornwall, where the evil Squire Hamilton, au fait with voodoo after a spell in Haiti, is killing and then reviving numerous villagers to work his tin mine as zombies. Hammer secretary, Pamela Anderson, submitted the script to John Trevelyan on 30 June, on behalf of Tony Nelson Keys. Reader Newton Branch was not impressed: "This insane rubbish can be cut down to 'X' standards. But the horror-comic elements must go and there should be a general warning about gore and female terror. As noted, this is a (short 100-page) first draft. We should see the final edition if, God forbid, there should be one."

John Trevelyan wrote back to Miss Anderson on 14 July, listing the objections: "We have now read the draft screenplay of *The Plague of the Zombies*. This seems rather familiar material, and most of it should be acceptable in the 'X' category, but there are some things which we do not like. Our comments on points of detail are as follows:
Pages 2-3. Scenes 8-10. This spitting blood all over the place is pretty nauseating, and is made more so by 'the blood-sodden effigy' filling the screen as the titles come up. Could he just not pour the blood from the phial on to the doll?
Page 9. Scene 22. When the coffin breaks open we are to see its 'macabre contents'. We would not want to see anything really unpleasant.
Pages 30-32. Scenes 46-48. Violence to Sylvia should not be excessive, and we would not want any suggestion that the Bloods are drawing cards with a view to choosing the one who should rape her. We do not at all like the idea of Denver, with his hunting crop, apparently about to rip off her clothes, just before Hamilton comes in and deals with the situation. All this should be toned down.
Pages 37-38. Scene 53. This scene looks as though it might be acceptable but it should not go too far. The final directions suggest that the end of the scene might be very unpleasant. If the film is to be shown in colour there should certainly not be too much blood about.
Page 46. Scene 57. Care should be taken with the shot of the dead body of Alice, which is described as 'huddled grotesquely.'
Pages 46-48. Scene 58. Discretion should be used with this scene, which could be quite nauseating to people who do not like operations or blood.

Stunt arranger-cum-zombie Peter Diamond in The Plague of the Zombies (1965).

THE PLAGUE OF THE ZOMBIES

PRINCIPAL PHOTOGRAPHY: 28 July to 6 September 1965
DISTRIBUTION:
   UK: Warner-Pathe; Technicolor; certificate 'X'
   US: 20th Century-Fox; Deluxe Color
91 Minutes
UK RELEASE:
   TRADE SHOW: 17 December 1965, with Dracula Prince of Darkness
   GENERAL RELEASE: 9 January 1966, on the ABC circuit with Dracula Prince of Darkness
   US RELEASE: 12 January 1966, with Dracula Prince of Darkness

DIRECTOR: John Gilling; PRODUCER: Anthony Nelson Keys; SCREENPLAY: Peter Bryan; PRODUCTION DESIGNER: Bernard Robinson; ART DIRECTOR: Don Mingaye; DIRECTOR OF PHOTOGRAPHY: Arthur Grant; CAMERA OPERATOR: Moray Grant; ASSISTANT DIRECTOR: Bert Batt; 2ND ASSISTANT DIRECTOR: Hugh Harlow; SUPERVISING EDITOR: James Needs;

EDITOR: Chris Barnes; MUSIC: James Bernard; MUSIC SUPERVISOR: Philip Martell; SOUND RECORDIST: Ken Rawkins; SOUND EDITOR: Roy Baker; MAKE-UP: Roy Ashton; MAKE-UP ASSISTANT: Richard Mills; HAIRSTYLIST: Frieda Steiger; PRODUCTION MANAGER: George Fowler; CONTINUITY: Lorna Selwyn; WARDROBE: Rosemary Burrows; SPECIAL EFFECTS: Bowie Films Ltd

André Morell (Sir James Forbes); Diane Clare (Sylvia);, Brook Williams (Dr Peter Tompson); Jacqueline Pearce (Alice); John Carson (Clive Hamilton); Alex Davion (Denver); Michael Ripper (Sergeant Swift); Marcus Hammond (Martinus); Dennis Chinnery (Constable Christian); Louis Mahoney (Coloured Servant); Roy Royston (Vicar); Ben Aris (John Martinus); Tim Condron, Bernard Egan, Norman Mann, Francis Willey (The Young Bloods)

UNCREDITED: Jolyon Booth (Coachman); Jerry Verno (Landlord); Peter Diamond, Del Watson, Keith Peacock, Reg Harding (zombies)

Pages 64-65. Scenes 72-74. Here we have the spitting of the blood again. See my previous comment. It seems even more unpleasant in this context.

Pages 75-78. Scenes 83-87. A lot of the material in these scenes would be unacceptable. First we get what may be a nasty shot of Alice's body in the coffin, with the following description 'All her beauty has gone – instead a lecherous bloated mask of death – a parody of her former self.' Great care must be used if this is to be acceptable. Alice then begins to crawl out of her coffin 'like some giant, obscene insect' and Sir James smashes her with a spade, severing her head. We would certainly not accept this if shot in anything like the way it is described. Nor would we want to see the severed head of Alice in the trick sequence that follows. We get nasty shots of the dead rising from their graves and the headless torso with severed head smiling. This is horror-comic material which simply would not do, it must be rewritten.

Page 93. Scene 114. We would not want any close shot of the blood-caked dolls especially if the film is in colour.

Page 95. Scene 116. We would not like a shot described as '… his first blow thuds into the man's neck, cutting a deep gash from which the blood spurts.'

Page 99. Scene 135. We would not want to see even a zombie apparently in flames.

Page 100. Scene 135. We would not want any shot of smouldering zombies and dead Bloods. "If the script is modified on these lines the film should not present any serious trouble."

The decapitation of Alice (scene 85) had also touched a nerve with the American Censor Board (MPAA), Geoffrey Shurlock objecting in a letter dated 7 July: "In the action where Sir James decapitates Alice, the business of bringing the spade down on her must be done out of frame … Sir James is described as striking a second and third blow with the spade and starting to strike a fourth. Peter is described as 'stumbling, gagging' at this as a result, and we urge that you omit the second and third blows lest the audience likewise gag."

Anthony Nelson Keys got Peter Bryan to attend to the recommendations and Bryan submitted his 'revised final script' to Hammer on 20 July. Keys then replied to Trevelyan point-by-point on the 23rd:

"Scenes 8-10. This will be taken care of. We will shoot this in a way which will not be offensive.

Scene 22. There will not be any macabre contents – just a body in a shroud.

Scenes 46-48. Rest assured, this will all be toned down as you suggest.

Scene 53. Every care will be taken to conform with your remarks.

Scene 58. Rest assured, that this will not be shot in an offensive way, bearing in mind that this is the wife of the young doctor.

Scenes 72-74. We have noted this, and will be getting around it.

Scenes 83-87. Your contents are noted and we will handle this with great delicacy. Regarding the severed head, we would treat this in the same manner as you allowed us to show in The Gorgon.

Scene 114. When you see this, I am sure you will have no cause for concern.

Scene 116. We will exercise our usual discretion on your behalf.

Scene 135. The zombies in flames will be no more than you allowed us to see in The Curse of Frankenstein."

Director John Gilling recalled that "The Plague of the Zombies and The Reptile were offered to me on a 'back-to-back' basis … One of my tasks was to shoot these two subjects so that the dual use of the sets emerged reasonably undetected. This involved more than usual liaison with the art director, careful re-vamping, re-dressing and so on. The fact that, in spite of such handicaps as this, the films have rated such critical acclaim is very rewarding. The scripts were written by John Elder and Peter Bryan and they each contained a good idea which attracted me. I agreed to undertake the job on condition that I had full control of the scripts, which I re-wrote more or less as I went along. I think the films succeeded because for those days they were considered somewhat 'way-out'. Like so many successful thrillers, the dramas unfolded against tranquil, soothing backgrounds like Cornwall, thus heightening the foreground action that was concerned with thrills and horror." [12]

Most of the core team from Rasputin returned, apart from lighting cameraman Arthur Grant, returning to Hammer for the first time since Paranoiac in 1962; camera operator Moray Grant, last employed on The Kiss of the Vampire, also in 1962; and production manager George Fowler, late of The Nanny. While Roy Hyde was busy editing Rasputin, Chris Barnes returned after his Dracula duties to cut Plague under James Needs' supervision. Needs would also be supervising the editing of Rasputin as well as dealing with the censor's final demands on Dracula Prince of Darkness.

The external set on the lot that had doubled as Dracula's castle and Ivan's country house was now revamped into a Cornish village. The frozen moat below was converted into a sunken churchyard and the bridge was retained as an entrance into the village. The large wheel of the tin mine was built on the external Bray lot just behind the village set and the old buildings seen behind it were in fact the carpenter's shop, the plasterer's property store and the paint shop. The impressive manor house exterior with fountain and ornamental dolphins was the neighbouring Oakley Court. Further location work took place at Chobham Common (the fox hunting scenes) and Black Park (the woodland scenes). Again all four stages at Bray were used. The following shooting schedule for the film again shows how the stages were deployed:

THE PLAGUE OF THE ZOMBIES SHOOTING SCHEDULE

Wed 28th July	INT. SIR JAMES STUDY	Stage 3
	INT. MANOR HOUSE/HALL	Stage 1
Thurs 29th July	INT. MANOR HOUSE/HALL	Stage 1
Fri 30th July	INT. MANOR HOUSE/HALL	Stage 1
Mon 2nd August	EXT. COUNTRYSIDE , LOCATION: CHOBHAM	
Tue 3rd August	EXT. WOODLAND, LOCATION: BLACK PARK	
Wed 4th August	INT. MANOR HOUSE/DEN	Stage 2
Thurs 5th August	INT. MANOR HOUSE/DEN	Stage 2
	INT. POLICE STATION	Stage 4
Fri 6th August	INT. POLICE STATION	Stage 4
Mon 9th August	INT. INN	Stage 3
	EXT. MANOR HOUSE, LOCATION: OAKLEY COURT	
Tue 10th August	INT. TOMPSON PARLOUR	Stage 1
Wed 11th August	INT. TOMPSON PARLOUR	Stage 1
Thurs 12th August	INT. TOMPSON PARLOUR	Stage 1
Fri 13th August	INT. TOMPSON PARLOUR	Stage 1
Mon 16th August	INT. TOMPSON PARLOUR	Stage 1
Tue 17th August	INT. TOMPSON KITCHEN	Stage 1
	INT. COTTAGE SURGERY	Stage 1
Wed 18th August	EXT. VILLAGE SQUARE	Lot
Thurs 19th August	EXT. VILLAGE SQUARE	Lot
Fri 20th August	EXT. VILLAGE SQUARE	Lot
Mon 23rd August	EXT. VILLAGE SQUARE-GRAVEYARD	Lot
Tue 24th August	EXT. VILLAGE SQAURE-GRAVEYARD	Lot
Wed 25th August	EXT. VILLAGE SQUARE-GRAVEYARD	Lot
Thurs 26th August	EXT. VILLAGE SQUARE-GRAVEYARD	Lot
Fri 27th August	INT. MINESHAFT-ALTAR AREA	Stage 2
Mon 30th August	BANK HOLIDAY	
Tue 31st August	INT. MINESHAFT	Stage 3
Wed 1st September	EXT. MINESHEAD	Lot
Thurs 2nd September	EXT. MINESHEAD	Lot
Fri 3rd September	INT. SYLVIA'S BEDROOM & CORRIDOR	Stage 1
Mon 6th September	INT. SYLVIA'S BEDROOM & CORRIDOR	Stage 1
	INT. TOMPSON BEDROOM	Stage 1
	INT. CARRIAGE	Stage 1

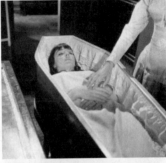
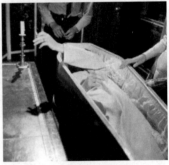

A series of contact-sheet pictures of Jacqueline Pearce lying in her coffin in The Plague of the Zombies (1965). At top she is joined by director John Gilling and co-star Diane Clare. Middle, the scene as filmed. Below, a quick cigarette!

The cast, led by André Morell and John Carson, is excellent as usual, with a particularly haunting performance from Jacqueline Pearce as Alice. The most memorable sequence in the movie remains the decapitation of Alice and the subsequent nightmare 'rising of the dead'. Alice's metamorphosis into a zombie is chilling to watch, as is her relentless advance towards the heroes. Roy Ashton padded out Pearce's cheeks to give her a bloated, corpse-like appearance and the decapitation is well staged, even if Ashton's dummy head isn't overly convincing. Jacqueline Pearce remembers, "Roy Ashton made a plaster-cast of my face for the sequence where my head was chopped off. It was dreadful. I had to stop halfway through because, at that time, I was very claustrophobic. Suddenly I was having this plaster of Paris all over me with just slight holes left for the nose and it's very, very heavy and at one point, I just said, 'I can't take it any more! You've got to take it off!' And then we just had to start all over again. It was very unpleasant. I suppose it must have taken about half an hour for it to set." [1]

Her claustrophobia also caused problems, unsurprisingly, when she was enclosed in her coffin. "It's a very strange feeling, being in a coffin, six feet under, with the lid on. I used to get very claustrophobic, but we had a very good crew and a wonderful first assistant called Bert Batt. He was in charge of all that and made sure that it was never on for too long and that I had a communication system

RIGHT: *Moray Grant films Diane Clare running through Black Park on location for* The Plague of the Zombies *(1965). Walking at the side are Bert Batt and John Gilling.*

BELOW: *Brook Williams and André Morell discuss the prospect of graverobbing over the dishes in* The Plague of the Zombies *(1965).*

whereby I could scream and they'd let me out!" [13] Batt concurs: "Jackie's claustrophobia was easily taken care of. Someone went down with her under the coffin that had a hole cut in the bottom so that hands could be held."

The surrealistic dream sequence that follows has been acclaimed by many critics alike, even those who do not usually warm to Hammer's horrors. Stunt co-ordinator, Peter Diamond, reveals that "I was one of the zombies coming up from the grave, from the earth. Del Watson strangled Brook Williams. The other zombies were Keith Peacock, Reg Harding and Ben Aris." It was Roy Ashton's job to create the film's living dead, assisted by Richard Mills. For their faces, Ashton used crumpled tissue paper covered with liquid latex. Ashton recalled their contact lenses: "The zombies wore, on my suggestion, ones that were entirely white, except for a little dot at the centre which enabled the actors to see." [14] Diamond recalls, "Roy Ashton and his assistant Dickie Mills glued pieces of thin latex to our faces and hands – then applied make-up – each make-up took about two hours and was touched up by Roy and Dickie throughout the shooting day." It was a hot summer and publicity shots exist of Diamond in make-up reading a newspaper and sucking on an ice lolly!

Still, it was not all fun for a zombie, as Bert Batt recollects. "They were all stuntmen. They were covered in filth and rags, buried alive, beaten to work in a mine, and some of them set fire to. They never had a comfortable day but, pros that they were, they suffered it all with humour and certainly earned their pay." Indeed, Peter Diamond remembers the climax vividly: "There were four of five of us alight in one particular scene and it wasn't like nowadays, when you have big fire suits and everything. You just tied a bit of asbestos around you, put the gel on and set yourself alight. I had taken my elder son, who was five, to the studio because my wife was tied up having another baby,

The dead rise in the dream sequence of The Plague of the Zombies (1965).

and I said to him, so he wouldn't worry about it, 'Now, what you're going to see today is your dad alight, but not to worry, it's quite funny really.' So he was sitting on the set watching this and I was going to have a full burn and Keith Peacock was going to have his arm alight. We put the gel on and this special effects guy lit Keith's arm and was trying to strike a match to set me alight. In the meantime, Keith was saying, 'Come on, get a move on!' The match wouldn't light and in the end I just threw myself on Keith, the gel went up and I ran into the shot. That was the kind of thing we were up against."

Ashton also had to create John Carson's mask. "The mask John Carson wore was the result of both documentation and imagination. I scratched my head a good deal about ideas for that one, investigating voodoo ceremonies on the Caribbean islands. For instance, there was a certain symbolism in the letters 'BS' which were appearing on the forehead: an abbreviation of 'Baron Samedi', a colourful story in itself. I was very puzzled as well about choosing the substance to make it. After pondering on the matter I went home, where I unearthed an old polished cloth that I had been using on the motor car for years and which by that time looked pretty disgusting. I cut the voodoo mask out of it while the little leather thongs on it were actually my boot laces." [15]

Principal photography ended on Monday 6 September. The film then went into post-production with editors James Needs and Roy Hyde and sound editor Roy Baker. Philip Martell brought back James Bernard to compose a thunderous score, fresh from *Dracula Prince of Darkness*. While the film was still on the floor, a black-and-white print of *Rasputin the Mad Monk* was submitted to John Trevelyan and viewed on 19 August by Frank Crofts. Trevelyan summarised his observations in a letter to Tony Nelson Keys later the same day:

"We saw *Rasputin* today. As you will know this was mostly in black and white. As a result of our viewing I have the following points to raise with you.

Reel 2. We want you to remove the shot of the severed hand falling onto the straw.

Reel 3. We think that the shot of the hand lying on the table before the Abbot will probably be acceptable, but before making a decision about it we would like to see this scene in colour.

Reel 4. We want you to remove the shots of Rasputin embracing Sonia when she is half undressed, and finish this scene where the clothes drop to the ground and her petticoat is seen.

Reel 7. We want you to make very considerable reductions in the scene in which Sonia becomes hysterical and attacks Rasputin. We want as little as possible of this struggle. We certainly want you to remove all shots in which the flask of acid is near her face when she is bent backwards over the bench. Before making a decision about the shot of Sonia after she has slashed her wrists we would like to see it in colour.

Reel 8. We want you to reduce to an absolute minimum Rasputin's attack on Peter with acid, and remove all shots of his face after the attack. We may want you to cut after his first scream to the back view shots of his leaving the house, but we might possibly accept a little material if his face is not clearly seen and if his agonised screams are kept down.

Reel 9. We do not like the retching sounds that Rasputin makes after being poisoned by the chocolates. Could you not replace this by moans and groans? We do not like the shots of Peter's face showing acid burns. We realise that what he says to Ivan provides a motive for him joining in the attack on Rasputin. This could be removed without essential loss of continuity, but before insisting on your removing all the shots of him we are prepared for a further look at them in colour; you would be wise to have the print dark enough to hide the detail of the make-up.

"When you have made the further cuts we would like to see Reels 3, 4, 7, 8 and 9 again in colour appropriately marked up. The difficulty presented by this film is that it is a sadistic piece. For this reason both normally acceptable horror material and normally acceptable sex are more troublesome to us than usual."

Anthony Nelson Keys was not amused and replied to Trevelyan on 24 August:

"I am in receipt of your letter of the 19th, which, I must say, surprised me enormously.

Reel 2. You want us to remove the shot of the severed hand. I did not expect you to object to this, especially as you passed this in The Stranglers of Bombay and more recently The Curse of the Mummy's Tomb.

Reel 3. The hand lying on the Abbot's table. I am sure that you will accept this when you see it in colour.

Reel 4. The shots of Rasputin embracing Sonia when she is half undressed we would like to keep in. I have seen more than this in 'A' pictures.

Reel 7. Scene where Sonia becomes hysterical and attacks Rasputin: we will certainly make reductions to this. You will appreciate that it is vital we see the acid for continuity reasons.

Reel 8. When shooting Rasputin's attack on Peter with the acid, we were most careful. We have shown much less than the shots in The Phantom of the Opera. When you have seen this in colour, I am sure you will feel happier.

Reel 9. Rasputin's retching sounds after eating the poisoned chocolate will be toned down.

"I shall be grateful if you will let me have your further observations, as I am recording music on September 2nd."

Keys followed this up with a phone call to Trevelyan the following day. The negotiations would continue throughout the shooting of The Reptile and a further cut was seen by the Board on 6 October: "The reels seen again by AOF, JT and NKB. Reels 1b, 4a and 5a were all right. But the dissolve in 2b should start before Rasputin undoes Sonia's shirt and reveals her naked to the waist and there must be a considerable reduction of shots of Peter's face after the acid has been thrown. Please resubmit and mark up Reel 8." Keys replied to Trevelyan on the 20th: "This is to confirm that we have shortened the dissolve in Reel 4 (Rasputin and Sonia – where she is half undressed), as requested."

However, a note by the Board the following day suggests there were still problems with reel 8: "Seen again by FNC, JC with JT. We think that the second shot of Peter's face should go altogether (cut back to Rasputin, watching), and that one of the shots by the wall, as he staggers away, should go or be shortened."

Trevelyan wrote to Keys about this on the 25th:

"On seeing Reel 8 again last week we decided that some further reduction would be needed in the scene in which Peter has acid thrown in his face. As suggested by telephone I think that the best way of dealing with this would be as follows: First Cut: Leave as at present. Second Cut: Entirely remove. Third Cut: Retain, but remove final shots where Peter removes his hands from his

Jacqueline Pearce
attacks Noel
Willman in The
Reptile (1965).

THE REPTILE

PRINCIPAL PHOTOGRAPHY: 13 September to 14 October 1965
DISTRIBUTION:
  UK: Warner-Pathe; Technicolor; certificate 'X'
  US: 20th Century-Fox; Deluxe Color
91 Minutes
UK RELEASE:
  TRADE SHOW: 14 February 1966, at Studio One with
  Rasputin the Mad Monk
  GENERAL RELEASE: 6 March 1966, on the ABC circuit
  with Rasputin the Mad Monk
US RELEASE: 6 April 1966, with Rasputin the Mad Monk

DIRECTOR: John Gilling; PRODUCER: Anthony Nelson Keys;
SCREENPLAY: John Elder; PRODUCTION DESIGNER: Bernard
Robinson; ART DIRECTOR: Don Mingaye; DIRECTOR OF

PHOTOGRAPHY: Arthur Grant; CAMERA OPERATOR: Moray
Grant; ASSISTANT DIRECTOR: Bill Cartlidge; SUPERVISING
EDITOR: James Needs; EDITOR: Roy Hyde; MUSIC: Don Banks;
MUSIC SUPERVISOR: Philip Martell; SOUND RECORDIST:
William Bulkley; SOUND EDITOR: Roy Baker; MAKE-UP: Roy
Ashton; HAIRSTYLIST: Frieda Steiger; PRODUCTION MANAGER:
George Fowler; CONTINUITY: Lorna Selwyn; WARDROBE:
Rosemary Burrows; SPECIAL EFFECTS: Bowie Films Ltd

Noel Willman (Dr Franklyn); Jennifer Daniel (Valerie); Ray Barrett
(Harry Spalding); Jacqueline Pearce (Anna); Michael Ripper (Tom
Bailey); John Laurie (Mad Peter); Marne Maitland (Malay); David
Baron (Charles Spalding); Charles Lloyd Pack (Vicar); Harold
Goldblatt (solicitor); George Woodbridge (Old Garnsey)

face and the face is clearly visible. Since there are intercuts of Rasputin watching the effects of the acid attack the cuts should not be difficult to make. We would like to see the scene again when you have re-edited it."

Rasputin finally achieved closure with a file note on 28 October: "Reel seen again by JT, JC, NKB. Cuts made as requested." Of course, by that time *The Reptile* would be in post-production. For the moment, it was still waiting to be shot.

Hammer's next production was also announced in the *Daily Cinema*'s tribute to Tony Hinds in November 1963, under the title *The Reptiles*. The project was rejected by Universal, but the following year it reappeared in Hammer's schedule under the new title *The Curse of the Reptiles* (*Daily Cinema*, 20 March 1964). The film was finally dusted off to complete Hammer's back-to-back package in 1965 under its original title of *The Reptiles*. Hinds, under his pen name of John Elder, delivered his draft screenplay on 18 August. The tale, again set in Cornwall, tells of the unfortunate Anna

Jacqueline Pearce
as the fearsome
snake woman in
The Reptile
(1965).

Franklyn, who has become a victim of an obscure Malayan sect, the Ourang Sancto, periodically transforming into a venomous snakewoman.

Pamela Anderson submitted the script to John Trevelyan on the 23rd. Reader Newton Branch commented four days later: "Obviously this nasty rubbish will be an 'X' if we allow it. I am in doubt about this horrid and repulsive story. We are used to and indeed addicted to vampire women with their 'goofy' canines. But this goes much too far into the realms of the horror-comic. I suppose we could allow the theme but I do feel that it should be re-scripted so that the horror comes far more by implication. It would be easy enough to deal with the agony, convulsions, foamings at the mouth of Anna's victims (indeed, a man bit [sic] by a cobra is paralysed in a matter of seconds and collapses without all this business). But unless Anna's appearance and behaviour is toned right down – I would say almost merely suggested – we should discourage this project. It's morbid and disgusting in its present form."

"I agree," observed Frank Crofts. "I suppose that digging up corpses will be all right but not the nudity." On behalf of Trevelyan, he wrote back to Miss Anderson on 1 September: "As the Secretary is on holiday I am writing to you about this script which we have now read. We think that the theme would be all right for the 'X' category, but we are worried about some of the details. It is not clear how far Anna is turned into a snake, but some of the descriptions of her suggest that there might be trouble when the film finally reaches us and we would suggest that these parts of the script which deal with her as a snake should be rewritten and sent to us. We should not be happy with her if some of the descriptions now in the script were carried into the film itself. Would it not be possible to do more by suggestion and less by actual shots of her? One incident which should certainly be removed is that on page 75 where her father discovers on her bed what he thinks is her naked body but which is in fact her skin which she has sloughed. In this kind of film nudity would be, from our point of view, out of place.

"The other details which cause us concern are those of the various victims, especially the shots of the dying Peter on page 32 when he appears at the window of the cottage with his blackened and distorted face in the middle of the night. I believe that the victims of cobra bites do not in fact turn black or suffer convulsions, and these shots may easily be too strong, even for an 'X'. I am returning this script to you and shall look forward to hearing from you later about any changes that you propose to make."

The *Reptile* followed *Plague* into production, with only a week's break, on Monday 13 September. Once more John Gilling was slated to direct and he was joined by his *Plague* team, apart from a new assistant director (Bill Cartlidge), a new 2nd assistant director (following the departure of Hugh Harlow; he would later return to Hammer as production manager), a new editor (Roy Hyde returning to allow Chris Barnes to finish editing *Plague*), and a new sound recordist (William Bulkley). The Cornish village and churchyard on the backlot were re-used, as were Bray's four stages. Again the shooting schedule shows their deployment:

THE REPTILE SHOOTING SCHEDULE

Mon 13th Sept	INT. SOLICITOR'S OFFICE	Stage 1
	INT. CELLAR AND PASSAGE	Stage 1
Tues 14th Sept	EXT. COTTAGE, LOCATION: GRAINGERS FARM, WOKING IN SURREY	
Wed 15th Sept	EXT. MOORS, LOCATION: FRENSHAM PONDS	
Thurs 16th Sept	EXT. WELL HOUSE, LOCATION: OAKLEY COURT	
	INT. PUB	Stage 3
Fri 17th Sept	INT. PUB	Stage 3
Mon 20th Sept	INT. PUB PARLOUR	Stage 4
Tues 21st Sept	INT. CAVERN	Stage 2
Wed 22nd Sept	EXT. VILLAGE AND GRAVEYARD	Lot
Thurs 23rd Sept	EXT. VILLAGE AND GRAVEYARD	Lot
Fri 24th September	EXT. VILLAGE AND GRAVEYARD	Lot
Mon 27th Sept	INT. DOWNSTAIRS PASSAGE	Stage 1
	INT. CAGE ROOM	Stage 1
	INT. SANCTUM	Stage 1
Tues 28th Sept	INT. SANCTUM	Stage 1
Wed 29th Sept	INT. COTTAGE SITTING ROOM	Stage 4
Thurs 30th Sept	INT. COTTAGE SITTING ROOM	Stage 4
Friday 1st October	INT. COTTAGE SITTING ROOM	Stage 4
Mon 4th October	INT. COTTAGE SITTING ROOM	Stage 4
Tues 5th October	INT. COTTAGE SITTING ROOM	Stage 4
Wed 6th October	INT. COTTAGE KITCHEN	Stage 4
	INT. UPSTAIRS CORRIDOR	Stage 1
Thurs 7th October	INT. ANNA'S BEDROOM	Stage 1
Fri 8th October	INT. COTTAGE BEDROOM	Stage 2
Mon 11th October	INT. WELL HOUSE HALL	Stage 1
Tues 12th October	INT. WELL HOUSE HALL	Stage 1
Wed 13th October	INT. WELL HOUSE HALL	Stage 1
Thurs 14th October	INT. WELL HOUSE HALL	Stage 1
	INT. NARROW PASSAGE	Stage 1
Fri 15th October	EXT. RAILWAY STATION, LOCATION	

Filming a day-for-night rain sequence in The Reptile *(1965).*
TOP: *The crew at work. John Gilling crouches beside the camera. Behind him is assistant director Bill Cartlidge. Arthur Grant stands to his right behind umbrella. In the hole are Michael Ripper and Ray Barrett.* BELOW: *The finished scene.*

As can be seen, on the second day of shooting the team went on location near Woking in Surrey to film the exterior cottage scenes. A dilapidated cottage (Grainger's Farm) had been found and was transformed by Bernard Robinson into 'Larkrise', the quaint Spalding home. The following day the moor scenes were shot at Frensham Ponds and on the fourth day the crew visited Oakley Court, which represented the outside of Well House, Dr Franklyn's mansion. In fact, both Gilling's Cornish films contain almost identical day-for-night shots as cast members creep up to the mansion with its characteristic, dolphin-adorned fountain in the foreground. The only actors who stayed on this time were Jacqueline Pearce, giving another haunting performance, and Hammer regular Michael Ripper, here given one of his largest parts in a Hammer movie. Joining them were two familiar faces from *The Kiss of the Vampire*, Noel Willman and Jennifer Daniel. Unlike Hammer's previous female monster, *The Gorgon*, which turned out to be an anti-climax when finally revealed, Roy Ashton's snakewoman was well worth waiting for. It is perhaps his finest work after his transformation of Oliver Reed into a werewolf. He explained, "Once more, considerable documentation was required. I read books on reptiles and went to museums to study the anatomy of the snake's head, adapting its structure to the bones of the human skull. I tried to obtain something that looked part snake and part woman. I made a model in plasticine which was all right, but I had to leave some apertures for the eyes as separate things to do. The reason for this was that I couldn't apply them directly onto Jackie Pearce; she was claustrophobic and could hardly bear to have anything on her. Once or twice, having made her up, she whipped the whole thing off because she felt so awful about it. Thus there was no other way than to put the eyes in position just before every shot, so that she wouldn't be too distressed. And even then I had to perforate little holes in them to allow her to see a little. I prepared two pairs of eyes, in fact; one pair open and one pair shut, as snakes have no lids at all.

"As to the skin, I got serpent's skin that I cast in plaster, to produce a female mould. Then I poured plastic in it and, as soon as the latter set, I could take out a perfect replica. I had literally yards of this stuff. So, if I wanted to use a bit, I only had to take some off and fix it on her hands or anywhere it was necessary. For the fangs I placed a plate in her mouth with a couple of grooves in the back of the teeth, containing glycerine. This material is very viscous; it collected together and afterwards came down in drops, like venom." [16] The arduous make-up took around two hours to complete and Pearce first appeared in it during the second week of shooting, on Tuesday 21 September, on the interior cavern set on Stage 2.

Sadly, Roy Ashton left Hammer on completion of this film. He recalled, "The last day but one on *The Reptile*, they asked me to fly to Tenerife the next morning, where the exteriors of *One Million Years BC* would be shot. 'No', I refused. 'I have been engaged almost non-stop and am going with my wife for a holiday.' I also wanted a change. I left and never returned, though I sporadically worked for them afterwards." [17] Roy would return for uncredited work on *The Devil Rides Out* (1967) and *Hands of the Ripper* (1971). His pioneering make-up work inspired many of today's experts and his creations remain classic images in horror cinema. Roy Ashton died following a long illness on 10 January 1995.

Principal photography ended on Friday 15 October after just under five weeks, ushering in post-production work at Hammer House under editors James Needs and Roy Hyde and sound editor Roy Baker. Philip Martell brought back Don Banks following completion of his score for *Rasputin the Mad Monk*. Meanwhile, it was time for Hammer's Cornish zombies to meet the BBFC. Surprisingly, given the script comments, Hammer had no problem getting the finished film past the censor. The Board viewed a black-and-white copy on 12 October and Newton Branch commented:

"Seen in black and white by JT, JC and NKB. The makers have mostly heeded our script letter and the film presents no difficulty except possibly in:

Reel 7. We want to see the episodes, in full colour and sound, in which Alice's face is 'transformed' in her coffin and Sir James decapitates her with a spade. Also the following sequence in which Peter has a nightmare, zombies emerge from their graves and attack him.

Reel 9. Resubmit sequence in which Sir James fights and kills Denver. Again with full sound and colour. The same applies to Reel 10 in which Sylvia is nearly sacrificed, zombies catch on fire and Peter rescues Sylvia. Please mark up reels 7 and 9 and resubmit 7, 9, 10. Nothing looks obviously unacceptable at present but colour may make a difference."

After a two-month pause, on 10 December Trevelyan, Audrey Field and Frank Crofts saw the final reels: "We saw Reels 7, 9, 10 in colour. They will pass."

One Million Years B.C. was hailed as Hammer's 100th production. The idea for this, Hammer's second fantasy epic, again came from Seven Arts' Kenneth Hyman, riding high on the success of *She*. The film was a straight remake of Hal Roach's *One Million B.C.* (1940) with Victor Mature, Carole Landis and Lon Chaney Jr; even some of the cavemen's rudimentary dialogue was borrowed, including such inscrutable pronouncements as 'Neetcha', 'Mekan' and 'Akeeta'.

Unlike the original, however, where the creatures were live reptiles with stuck-on fins, Hammer decided to use the talents of animation wizard Ray Harryhausen who, together with Charles Schneer, had produced a whole series of unparalleled fantasy classics for Columbia such as *The Seventh Voyage of Sinbad* (1958), *Mysterious Island* (1961) and *Jason and the Argonauts* (1963). Harryhausen's last film at the time was the British-made but not so successful *First Men in the Moon*

ONE MILLION YEARS B.C.

PRINCIPAL PHOTOGRAPHY: 18 October to 6 January 1965/66
DISTRIBUTION:
UK: Warner-Pathe; Technicolor; certificate 'A';
100 minutes
US: 20th Century-Fox; Deluxe Color; 91 minutes
UK RELEASE:
TRADE SHOW: 25 October 1966
GENERAL RELEASE: 30 December 1966, on the ABC circuit
USA RELEASE: February 21st, 1966

DIRECTOR: Don Chaffey; PRODUCER: Michael Carreras;
ASSOCIATE PRODUCER: Aida Young; SCREENPLAY: Michael
Carreras, adapted from an original screenplay by Mickell Novak,
George Baker and Joseph Frickert; ART DIRECTOR: Robert Jones;
ASSISTANT ART DIRECTOR: Kenneth McCallum Tate;
DRAUGHTSMAN: Colin Monk; SCENIC ARTIST: Bill Beavis;
DIRECTOR OF PHOTOGRAPHY: Wilkie Cooper; CAMERA
OPERATOR: David Harcourt; FOCUS PULLER: Geoffrey Glover; 2ND
CAMERA OPERATOR: Kenneth Nicholson; 2ND UNIT CAMERA:
Jack Mills; ASSISTANT DIRECTOR: Denis Beterer; 2ND ASSISTANT
DIRECTOR: Colin Lord; 3RD ASSISTANT DIRECTOR: Ray Atchelor;
SUPERVISING EDITOR: James Needs; EDITOR: Tom Simpson; 1ST

ASSISTANT EDITOR: Robert Dearberg; ASSISTANT EDITORS: Antony
Sloman, Chris Barnes; MUSIC AND SPECIAL MUSICAL EFFECTS:
Mario Nascimbene; MUSIC SUPERVISOR: Philip Martell; SOUND
RECORDISTS: Len Shilton and Bill Rowe; SOUND EDITOR: Roy
Baker and Alfred Cox; RECORDING SUPERVISOR: A W Lumkin;
MAKE-UP: Wally Schneiderman; HAIRSTYLIST: Olga Angelinetta;
PRODUCTION MANAGER: John Wilcox; CONTINUITY: Gladys
Goldsmith and Marjorie Lavelley; COSTUME DESIGNER: Carl
Toms; WARDROBE: Ivy Baker; SPECIAL VISUAL EFFECTS: Ray
Harryhausen; ANIMAL SCULPTURES: Arthur Hayward; PROLOGUE
SEQUENCE: Les Bowie; MECHANICAL SPECIAL EFFECTS: George
Blackwell; PUBLICITY DIRECTORS: Alan Thompson, Robert Webb;
STILLS PHOTOGRAPHER: Ronnie Pilgrim; PRODUCTION
SECRETARY: Eileen Mathews

Raquel Welch (Loana); John Richardson (Tumak); Percy Herbert
(Sakana); Robert Brown (Akhoba); Martine Beswick (Nupondi);
Jean Wladon (Ahot); Lisa Thomas (Sura); Malva Nappi (Tohana);
Richard James (Young Rock Man); William Lyon Brown (Payto);
Frank Hayden (1st Rock Man); Terence Maidment (1st Shell Man);
Micky De Rauch (1st Shell Girl); Yvonne Horner (Ullah)

Caveman Percy Herbert hides behind his shades on location for One Million Years B.C. (1965).

(1964); Hammer's offer came at an opportune time when he had no formal projects in preparation at Columbia. Harryhausen recalls, "I was loaned to Hammer because Charles was on a Western picture and he didn't have anything at the moment for me. I hate remakes, but I felt that we could do better than the original 1940 version."

Michael Carreras led the production, aided by associate producer Aida Young, fresh from their success with She. Carreras was dissuaded from his usual widescreen fetish by Harryhausen, who had learned vital lessons after struggling with Scope on First Men in the Moon. From Jason and the Argonauts came director Don Chaffey and cinematographer Wilkie Cooper. Camera operator David Harcourt had previously worked for Hammer on Hysteria, editor Tom Simpson on The Nanny. Continuity was supervised by both Gladys Goldsmith and Marjorie Lavelly; the latter had last worked with Hammer on The Ugly Duckling and had also worked with Ray Harryhausen on Mysterious Island.

Marjorie Lavelly recalls: "Gladys did the locations. I can only assume from memory that she had already agreed to do another picture that she couldn't get out of. Gladys was a very professional continuity girl, so it was easy to take over from her notes. I seem to remember Don Chaffey was the director, an old mate of many pictures I had worked on. Actually, because there was no dialogue, only grunts and gesticulations, it was pretty difficult to keep tabs on all the actors, because they were in animal skins with beards etc. The first couple of days was worrying, because you did not know which actor was playing what part – and you should never upset a thespian by asking him his name, because it ruins their self-confidence. Normally if you are on a picture, and you don't know the actor, you wait till he speaks, then check the script to save any embarrassment."

Like Ursula Andress before her, Raquel Welch was appointed by Seven Arts, hot on the heels of her success in Fantastic Voyage. Ray Harryhausen has always remained sceptical as to whether it was his dinosaurs or Miss Welch that made the film a success. John Richardson, the dashing hero of *She*, was brought back to play Tumak. Other notable cave persons were Martine Beswick (straight out of *Thunderball*) as Nupondi, Percy Herbert as Sakana and Robert Brown (a future 'M' in the Bond movies) as Akhoba.

Shooting began on location in Lanzarote on Monday 18 October, making good use of its barren and jagged landscape. Ray Harryhausen remembers, "I pick out the locations. I'm usually sent out months ahead and I pick out all the locations where the animation is to take place, then come back with photographs and work with the writer on the script. At first Michael Carreras wanted us to go to Iceland, but finally we decided Lanzarote and Gran Canaria would work. On location I direct my own sequences. The main job of the director is to get the best out of the actors. It's not like the European concept of the director where he creates the original film. I use a lot of storyboards. I sometimes make about 400 simple little sketches and then they are published in the scripts, so that the actors know what to look at. Then I make big production drawings to show the highlights of the picture, which we use later for publicity as well as giving the actor and director an idea of how they should react. I had already worked with Don Chaffey on *Jason*. He was an art director before and he knew of the technical realities of picture-making"

Aida Young discusses the problems encountered on location: "It was difficult terrain, which is why we chose it, because it looked volcanic and it *was* volcanic. We took a hotel up by the Teide volcano, where we shot. We went in October, which is supposed to be their best month, and of course, as usual with locations, you get rain which they haven't had for 200 years and it rained for three days. The wind knocked the trees down. Nobody could get up to the top of this mountain and so the hotel was in trouble with food and everything. One day we came down for breakfast in the morning and I noticed that the staff of the hotel were very surly and very difficult, and I couldn't understand it because previously they had been so helpful. I said to the manager, 'What's going on?' And he said, 'You know how superstitious they all are and they think that you brought the evil with you that knocked all the trees down and caused the bad weather.' I would have laughed but it was so serious. Thank goodness the rain stopped the next day because otherwise I think they would have lynched us all. But that was the only really difficult part – the weather. Other than that all locations are difficult when you're trying to film in a foreign country – I've never known a location that hasn't been difficult and it's got nothing to do with you, it's either weather or somebody hasn't turned up or the government decides you can't do this or people won't

Raquel Welch (Loana) and John Richardson (Tumak) in One Million Years B.C. (1965).

James Carreras hosted a special reception to launch One Million Years B.C. at Les Ambassadeurs, London, on 28 September 1965. Pictured are Ray Harryhausen and his wife, Michael Carreras and Raquel Welch.

co-operate. We had to choose the best time to go and I can remember poring over temperature charts and speaking to the government officials here. Apart from anything else, you couldn't afford to spend days doing nothing because our budget was very tight at Hammer."

Filming moved back to ABPC's Elstree Studios between 20 November and 6 January 1966, utilising art director Robert Jones' magnificent sets. Costume designer Carl Toms recalled: "For *One Million Years B.C.* I designed a fur bikini for Raquel Welch: she had such a perfect body that I took a very soft doe skin, we stretched it on her and tied it together with thongs – prehistoric people knew nothing of bust darts and seams. We took tiny pieces of fur and glued them at the edges of the bikini to make it appear as though Raquel was wearing two strips of fur inside out." [18] "I recall that Don Chaffey agreed with me that Raquel Welch's bikini top got smaller and smaller as the days went by, obviously to show more cleavage," says Marjorie Lavelly. "I felt very sorry for the wardrobe staff," she adds facetiously.

The Nanny was released on the ABC circuit on 7 November and shot into *Kinematograph Weekly*'s top money-maker list after two months. In the meantime, *The Reptile* (still under its original title *The Reptiles*) was on its way to the BBFC. On 3 December, John Trevelyan, Audrey Field and Newton Branch watched a black-and-white copy and Trevelyan reported back to Anthony Nelson Keys on the 6th:

"This seems basically suitable for the 'X' category, but we want one cut in it, and we shall have to see parts of certain reels again in colour before passing the film. The cut we want is in Reel 7. You should remove the close shot of the incision in Harry's neck when he returns home and is lying on the bed. The scenes which we shall want to see again in colour are as follows:

Reel 1. The sequence in which Charles is bitten and dies.

Reel 24. The sequence in which Mad Peter goes to the cottage and dies.

Reel 6. The scene in which there are close shots of Charles' face in the coffin.

Reel 7. The entire reel from the entry of Anna as the snake.

Reels 8 and 10. The entire reels."

The film was finally passed on 18 January: "The sequences were seen today by RIL/AOF with JT. The cut in Reel 7 has been made and the rest is acceptable. The film is now passed 'X'" Three days later, a file note at the Board read: "The company have checked on the title and it is in the singular *Reptile*."

As 1965 drew to a close, Ray Harryhausen was busy preparing his magic for *One Million Years B.C.* The magic was not to last, however. 1966 would see Hammer's last stand at Bray Studios.

FOURTEEN

The Curtain Falls

(1966)

As the year opened, Hammer were putting the finishing touches to *One Million Years B.C.* at Elstree and Ray Harryhausen was about to begin the arduous process of stop-motion animation. As editors James Needs and Tom Simpson, with sound editors Roy Baker and Alfred Cox, took the film into post-production (dubbing Raquel Welch with Nicolette McKenzie), Ray Harryhausen took centre stage. Harryhausen spent four months of research before deciding on what creatures to use. After countless sketches, the armatures of the models were built based on actual museum skeletons. He recalls, "I did the animation at Elstree Studios. I had a little studio in the scene dock. I went to the museums to research the dinosaurs and I had a palaeontologist called Arthur Hayward working with me. We tried to make it as accurate as possible, but we were not making pictures for professors, so we have to glamorise them a bit sometimes. First you have to model the dinosaur in clay in order to get the skin texture and that sort of thing, and then you make a mould of that and put an armature inside, and pour liquid latex into the mould, and cook it in the oven for so many hours. Then out pops a dinosaur. Well, you hope, because sometimes the rubber collapses in the oven and you have to start all over again. I make the final model myself. I have people who make the skin textures and all those things that take time. On *One Million Years B.C.*, Arthur Hayward modelled the basic dinosaur in clay and I made the actual animation model, because I like to know what's in it so that I know how far I can go during the animation period."

The animation process took a gruelling nine months; the lizard sequence was shot between 14 and 16 March, the Pteranodon between 17 March and 7 April, the Archelon between 12 and 30 April, the Allosaurus between 2 May and 3 June, the Triceratops and Ceratosaurus battle between 6 June and 15 July, and the Brontosaurus and others between 18 and 29 July.[1] It was quite frustrating for associate producer Aida Young: "Oh, it took forever! With Ray Harryhausen you couldn't ask – Ray was a God. We just sat and waited. I wasn't the producer so I didn't have to take the flak."

Despite the use of model animation, the first dinosaur we see is a real iguana. Harryhausen explains, "The theory behind it was that if you started out with a live lizard, people would believe that the animated ones were alive as well. But it seemed to do just the reverse. The lizard kept falling asleep and I wish I had animated it instead of using a real one. You have to shoot them at high speed, of course, so that you slow their movements down to give the size, and they always fall asleep under the hot lights. The lizard trainer had to sometimes move him like a hand puppet."

Hammer Productions
1966

+ *SLAVE GIRLS*
+ *THE WITCHES*
+ *THE VIKING QUEEN*
+ *FRANKENSTEIN CREATED WOMAN*
+ *THE MUMMY'S SHROUD*

OPPOSITE: Peter Cushing returns as the Baron for his last Bray outing in Frankenstein Created Woman (1966).

ABOVE: A Ray Harryhausen story-board for a One Million Years B.C. (1965) sequence that was never filmed. The escape of the prehistoric bird (Phororhacos) was intended to introduce the Allosaurus sequence.

LEFT: Triceratops versus Ceratosaurus, Harryhausen-style, in One Million Years B.C. (1965).

Time is money in animation and some proposed animation sequences never made it. "We had quite a lengthy brontosaurus sequence at the end, which we decided was too much and we shortened it down," says Harryhausen. "Budgetary reasons as well, probably. It was going to raid the cave people and they push rocks on it and cause a landslide, and then the eruption begins, but we cut that section out and just had the eruption. We shot a couple of scenes of the Brontosaurus attacking the cave people just for stills, but in the final picture we just had it walking up a hill in a short sequence. Another sequence we didn't film involved a Phororhacos. It was a prehistoric bird that was going to introduce the Allosaurus to the village. The Phororhacos was going to be kept in a cage, and Loana was going to feed it, and it gets out. The Allosaurus then jumps into the scene and grabs it, to ease him into the picture. It was cut out and we just had the Allosaurus walk into the scene. We used the idea later to introduce Gwangi [in *The Valley of Gwangi*, 1969]."

The prologue sequence was created by Les Bowie. Hammer handed him a budget of £1,100 and he managed to create the earth in just six days with an overspend of only £100! Ian Scoones recalls, "We did that at Bowie Films. I learnt a lot on that one when he had no money. Les didn't have anything at all. We used porridge naturally boiling in a frying pan, with some red food dye in it and some rubber dust from one of these places that disintegrate tyres – you get this wonderful black dust which looks good. We shot it with a diopter, which is a close-up lens, with a red filter over it, and that was the earth bubbling away. We

Evil Queen Kari (Martine Beswick) impales rebellious slave girl Gido (Carol White) in Slave Girls (1966).

also did part of the earthquake sequence with Kit West. You build a set on top of a set, which can be pulled back or pushed forwards, and as it parts, you make sure it is dressed with light, smoke, and everything else." George Blackwell worked on the rest of the miniatures and explosions, as well as the floor effects.

Now it was time to release the first double-bill from the four back-to-back pictures. Following a delay due to processing problems at Technicolor and some last-minute redubbing, *The Plague of the Zombies* was finally released in support of *Dracula Prince of Darkness* on Sunday 9 January on the ABC circuit. They took £10,190 on their opening day – double normal receipts. 20th Century-Fox released them in the US on the 12th. As a cheap gimmick, American patrons were treated to Dracula fangs for the boys and zombie eyes for the girls as they entered the theatre.

SLAVE GIRLS

PRINCIPAL PHOTOGRAPHY: 22 January to 18 February 1966
DISTRIBUTION:
  UK: Warner-Pathe; Technicolor; certificate 'A';
  74 minutes
US: 20th Century-Fox; Deluxe Color;
  US TITLE: *Prehistoric Women*; 95 minutes
Cinemascope
UK RELEASE: 7 July 1968, on the ABC circuit with *The Devil Rides Out*
US RELEASE: December 1968, with *The Devil's Bride* [ie, *The Devil Rides Out*]

DIRECTOR/PRODUCER: Michael Carreras; ASSOCIATE PRODUCER: Aida Young; EXECUTIVE PRODUCER: Anthony Hinds; SCREENPLAY: Henry Younger; ART DIRECTOR: Robert Jones; DIRECTOR OF PHOTOGRAPHY: Michael Reed; CAMERA

OPERATOR: Brian Elvin; ASSISTANT DIRECTOR: David Tringham; SUPERVISING EDITOR: James Needs; EDITOR: Roy Hyde; MUSIC: Carlo Martelli; MUSIC SUPERVISOR: Philip Martell; SOUND RECORDIST: Sash Fisher; MAKE-UP: Wally Schneidermann; HAIRSTYLIST: Olga Angelinetta; PRODUCTION MANAGER: Ross Mackenzie; CONTINUITY: Eileen Head; DRESS DESIGNER: Carl Toms; WARDROBE: Jackie Breed; CHOREOGRAPHER: Denys Palmer; SPECIAL EFFECTS: George Blackwell

Martine Beswick (Kari); Edina Ronay (Saria); Michael Latimer (David); Stephanie Randall (Amyak); Carol White (Gido); Alexandra Stevenson (Luri); Yvonne Horner (first Amazon); Sydney Bromley (Ullo); Frank Hayden (Arja); Robert Raglan (Colonel Hammond); Mary Hignett (Mrs Hammond); Louis Mahoney (Head Boy); Bari Jonson (High Priest); Danny Daniels (Jakara); Steven Berkoff (John); Sally Caclough (Amazon)

Director, producer
and writer Michael
Carreras with the
white rhino prop
from Slave Girls
(1966).

Meanwhile, as Elstree played host to a genius that January, it also housed something less inspiring – Hammer's next offering, *Slave Girls*.

Slave Girls had been announced as part of Hammer's new 11-picture deal under the title *Prehistoric Women* (which would later become the film's US title). The reason was simple. To off-set the large amount of money being poured into *One Million Years B.C.*, Hammer had planned a follow up low-budget feature to be shot back-to-back so as to re-use Robert Jones' prehistoric sets at Elstree as well as Carl Toms' sexy skinwear. Michael Carreras again steered the production, assuming the director's chair this time as well.

Carreras also wrote the script under the working title *Slave Girls of the White Rhino*, wisely hiding under his pseudonym of Henry Younger. It was the bizarre tale of an English big-game hunter who gets mixed up with two warring fractions of Amazon women, ruled over by their wicked Queen, Kari, who worships a stuffed white rhino. As Carreras recalled, "I made one terrible mistake on that film – it should have had speech bubbles because it was the perfect comic strip film. If we went back now and re-edited it, putting in balloons with the words OUCH and ARGHHHH, it would be great." [2]

Shooting started on Saturday 22 January at Elstree, with no location work apart from some opening library footage of Africa to induce false hopes. So, like *The Brigand of Kandahar* before it, the film looked cheap and claustrophobic. Joining the production from *One Million Years B.C.* were make-up artist Wally Schneidermann and hairstylist Olga Angelinetta. Lighting cameraman Michael Reed and production manager Ross Mackenzie both returned after last working on *Rasputin the Mad Monk*. Carreras also brought back Martine Beswick, this time giving her top billing as the ruthless Queen Kari.

Filming ended on Friday 18 February. Four days earlier, *Rasputin the Mad Monk* and *The Reptile* had been tradeshown, later going out on the ABC circuit from Sunday 6 March to only fair reviews. The pair also went out together in America on 6 April, this time dishing out Rasputin beards to patrons. The man whose shadow *Rasputin* had been made in, Prince Yusupov, died shortly afterwards, on 27 September 1967, aged 80.

Hammer's next offering, *The Witches*, was initiated by the star of the movie, Joan Fontaine. 49-year-old Fontaine, best actress Oscar-winner for her role in Hitchcock's *Suspicion* in 1941 (as well as having starred in the previous year's *Rebecca*), was struggling somewhat to find worthy film roles in the sixties and, following *Tender is the Night* (1962), began to concentrate on theatre. Impressed by Norah Lofts' novel *The Devil's Own* (penned under the pseudonym Peter Curtis), Fontaine bought the film rights in September 1962, eventually bringing the project to the attention

Kay Walsh
conducts a satanic
mass in The
Witches (1966).

THE WITCHES

PRINCIPAL PHOTOGRAPHY: 18 April to 10 June 1966
DISTRIBUTION:
 UK: Warner-Pathe; Technicolor; certificate 'X'
 US: 20th Century-Fox; Deluxe Color;
  US TITLE: The Devil's Own
91 minutes
UK RELEASE:
 TRADE SHOW: 14 November 1966, at Studio One
 PREMIÈRE: 21 November 1966, at the London Pavilion,
  Piccadilly Circus
 GENERAL RELEASE: 9 December 1966, on the ABC circuit
  with Death is a Woman
US RELEASE: 15 March 1967, with The Kremlin Letter

DIRECTOR: Cyril Frankel; PRODUCER: Anthony Nelson Keys;
SCREENPLAY: Nigel Kneale, based on the novel The Devil's Own
by Peter Curtis; PRODUCTION DESIGNER: Bernard Robinson; ART
DIRECTOR: Don Mingaye; DIRECTOR OF PHOTOGRAPHY: Arthur
Grant; CAMERA OPERATOR: Cece Cooney; ASSISTANT DIRECTOR:
David Tringham; SUPERVISING EDITOR: James Needs; EDITOR:
Chris Barnes; MUSIC: Richard Rodney Bennett; MUSIC

SUPERVISOR: Philip Martell; SOUND RECORDIST: Ken Rawkins;
SOUND EDITOR: Roy Hyde; MAKE-UP: George Partleton;
HAIRSTYLIST: Frieda Steiger; PRODUCTION MANAGER: Charles
Permane; CONTINUITY: Anne Deeley; WARDROBE SUPERVISOR:
Molly Arbuthnot; WARDROBE MASTER: Harry Haynes;
CHOREOGRAPHY: Denys Palmer; CASTING: Irene Lamb

Joan Fontaine (Gwen Mayfield); Kay Walsh (Stephanie Bax); Alec
McCowen (Alan Bax); Ann Bell (Sally); Ingrid Brett (Linda); John
Collin (Dowsett); Michele Dotrice (Valerie); Gwen Ffrangcon-Davies
(Granny Rigg); Duncan Lamont (Bob Curd); Leonard Rossiter (Dr
Wallis); Martin Stephens (Ronnie Dowsett); Carmel McSharry (Mrs
Dowsett); Viola Keats (Mrs Curd); Shelagh Fraser (Mrs Creek);
Bryan Marshall (Tom)

UNCREDITED: Kitty Attwood (Mrs McDowall); John Barrett (Mr
Glass); Catherine Finn (Nurse); Prudence Hyman (Stephanie's
Maid); Lizbeth Kent (1st villager); Artro Morris (Porter); Willie
Payne (Adam); Charles Rea (Police sergeant); Rudolph Walker
(Mark); Roy Desmond; Ken Robson; Brian Todd; Don Vernon; Terry
Williams (Dancers)

of Seven Arts, who took the film to Hammer in June 1964. Tony Hinds brought in Nigel Kneale to
adapt the novel and his screenplay was submitted on 19 August 1965.

 The story is a web of intrigue and it's difficult to know at times whether we're dealing with a
Sangster-style psychological thriller or a horror movie, as it comes to resemble almost a cross
between Taste of Fear and The Plague of the Zombies. There's the standard troubled heroine, Gwen
Mayfield, recovering from a nervous breakdown and apparently being deliberately driven insane

again. But in the process she uncovers a supernatural theme in the shape of a whole coven of witches. Cyril Frankel was brought in to direct, returning to Hammer after the controversial *Never Take Sweets from a Stranger*. Like many acclaimed Hollywood actresses, Fontaine insisted on 'director approval', but she was much better behaved than both Davis and Bankhead and took an immediate liking to Frankel.

Shooting began on Monday 18 April at Bray, with location work at the village of Hambledon and on the estate of Lord Hambledon, owner of the W H Smith bookshop chain. Bray regulars Arthur Grant, Cece Cooney, Bernard Robinson, Don Mingaye, James Needs, Chris Barnes, Ken Rawkins, Roy Hyde (back in his position of sound editor), Frieda Steiger and Molly Arbuthnot were back. George Partleton joined the team as regular Bray make-up artist, but the Bray crew would now lose continuity in both production managers and assistant directors.

As the official pressbook would have us believe, when Fontaine learned she was playing the role of a schoolteacher she went out and bought all nine of her costumes from the cheap shops of New York. Frankel is said to have admired her professionalism and didn't even have to change a single one. If this was the juiciest gossip Hammer's publicity machine could dig up, then excitement was clearly at a low ebb. The film continued Hammer's policy of bringing in big-name stars and Fontaine does what she can with her character, but she is completely upstaged by Kay Walsh as the laidback and malevolent witch. Hammer did their best to portray the satanic rituals but had to tread very carefully since Satanism, particularly when involving children, was still a very sensitive issue for the censor and one they were likely to come down heavily on.

Joan Fontaine cowers from the voodoo god in The Witches (1966).

Filming ended on Friday 10 June after eight weeks. Editors James Needs and Chris Barnes, with sound editor Roy Hyde, took *The Witches* to Hammer House for post-production and the customary scrutiny of the BBFC. Also in June, Hammer announced further plans for a *She* sequel – *The Return of She*. However, this time there was no mention of Ursula Andress. The same month, a press reception was held at Les Ambassadeurs in London to launch Carita, the lead in Hammer's next sexy costume adventure, *The Viking Queen*.

John Temple Smith (who had previously produced *Captain Clegg* for Hammer, as well as penning the first drafts of *She*) had been asked to produce *The Witches* when the project was still being optioned for Universal in March 1965. This was not to be but he was soon approached to produce *The Viking Queen* instead, a colourful costume adventure inspired by the legendary Queen Boadicea, telling of the tragic conflict of love and loyalty between Ancient Briton Salina and the Roman Governor General, Justinian. Hammer were obviously geared for spectacle once more, affording the film an eight-week schedule (compared with their normal six) and a budget of £350,000, which was huge by their standards, more than twice the standard amount. To put this in perspective, the four fantasy films shot back-to-back in 1965 cost only £429,648 put together, while *One Million Years B.C.* was reported to have come in at £422,816.

Like *Sword of Sherwood Forest* in 1960, the film was shot in Ireland, at the Ardmore Studios in County Wicklow. Shooting began on 15 June with an unfamiliar crew, since the regular team would be retained at Bray for the forthcoming *Frankenstein Created Woman*, due to start shooting while *The Viking*

THE VIKING QUEEN

PRINCIPAL PHOTOGRAPHY: 15 June to 18 August 1966
DISTRIBUTION:
  UK: Warner-Pathe; Technicolor; certificate 'A'
  US: 20th Century-Fox; Deluxe Color
91 minutes
UK RELEASE:
  TRADE SHOW: 6 March 1967, at Studio One
  GENERAL RELEASE: 26 March 1966, on the ABC circuit
  US RELEASE: 16 August 1967

DIRECTOR: Don Chaffey; PRODUCER: John Temple-Smith; SCREENPLAY: Clarke Reynolds, from an original story by John Temple-Smith; PRODUCTION DESIGNER: George Provis; DIRECTOR OF PHOTOGRAPHY: Stephen Dade; CAMERA OPERATOR: David Harcourt; ASSISTANT DIRECTOR: Dennis Bertera; SUPERVISING EDITOR: James Needs; EDITOR: Peter Boita; MUSIC: Gary Hughes; MUSIC SUPERVISOR: Philip Martell; SOUND RECORDIST: H L Bird,

Bob Jones; SOUND EDITOR: Stan Smith; MAKE-UP: Charles Parker; HAIRSTYLIST: Bobbie Smith; PRODUCTION MANAGER: René Dupont; CONTINUITY: Ann Skinner; WARDROBE SUPERVISOR: Hilda Geerdts; WARDROBE MASTER: Jack Gallagher; COSTUME DESIGNER: John Furniss; SPECIAL EFFECTS: Allan Bryce; MASTER OF HORSE: Frank Hayden; PRODUCTION LIASON: Lieut Col William O'Kelly

Don Murray (Justinian); Carita (Salina); Donald Houston (Maelgan); Andrew Keir (Octavian); Adrienne Corri (Beatrice); Niall MacGinnis (Tiberion); Wilfred Lawson (the King); Nicola Pagett (Talia); Percy Herbert (Catus); Patrick Troughton (Tristram); Sean Caffrey (Fergus); Denis Shaw (Osiris); Philip O'Flynn (merchant); Brendan Mathews (Nigel); Gerry Alexander (Fabian); Patrick Gardiner (Benedict); Paul Murphy (Dalan, Maelgan's son); Arthur O'Sullivan (old man at tax enquiry); Cecil Sheridan (shopkeeper at protest gathering); Anna Mannahan (shopkeeper's wife); Nita Lorraine (Nubian slave-girl); Patrick Allen (narrator)

Don Chaffey directs Carita in a sequence from The Viking Queen (1966).

Queen was still on the floor. Director Don Chaffey was back, but he was unable to instil into his Romans and Britons the same kind of savagery and brutality that had made his cavemen so fascinating in *One Million Years B.C.* Locations used included Powerscourt waterfall, Loch Tay, Wicklow Gap, Sally Gap and the Kilruddery estate. Look out for the Roman shields. They were originally made for the epic *Cleopatra* (1963) and reapperaed in *She*.

In the title role, Carita looks the part but has no real presence and can't carry the film. Seven Arts contract artist and Hollywood star Don Murray played the part of Justinian after it had been turned down by Christopher Lee, but seems drastically out of place among the film's array of British character actors. The film also wastes the talents of Andrew Keir, Patrick Troughton, Niall MacGinnis, Donald Houston and Adrienne Corri. The film's story of unrequited love presumably sounded good on paper, but even Salina's suicide at the climax (the crux of the whole film, for Heaven's sake) is handled by Chaffey as if at a distance. Hammer were perhaps just too ambitious in trying to bring off a mini-epic on what still amounted to a ludicrously low budget. As it happened, they ended up £61,000 'over'.

Shooting ended on Thursday 18 August. Meanwhile, all eyes were diverted to Bray Studios, where none other than Baron Frankenstein was up to his tricks again...

Hammer had first been interested in turning to the female of the species after *The Revenge of Frankenstein*, with a project called *And Then Frankenstein Made Woman*, clearly an in-joke regarding Roger Vadim's 1957 Brigitte Bardot opus *And God Created Woman*. This of course was the logical progression of the story, as indeed it had been for James Whale when he turned to *Bride of Frankenstein* as the first sequel in the Universal cycle. It was inevitable that one day Hammer's Baron

Frankenstein (Peter Cushing) and his bungling assistant Hertz (Thorley Walters) in Frankenstein Created Woman (1966).

FRANKENSTEIN CREATED WOMAN

PRINCIPAL PHOTOGRAPHY: 4 July to 12 August 1966
DISTRIBUTION:
UK: Warner-Pathe; Technicolor; certificate 'X'
USA: 20th Century-Fox; Deluxe Color
92 minutes [given as 86 in publicity material]
UK RELEASE:
TRADE SHOW: 15 May 1967
PREMIÈRE: 18 May 1967, at the New Victoria
GENERAL RELEASE: 18 June 1967, on the ABC circuit with
The Mummy's Shroud
US RELEASE: March 1967, with The Mummy's Shroud

DIRECTOR: Terence Fisher; PRODUCER: Anthony Nelson Keys;
SCREENPLAY: John Elder; PRODUCTION DESIGNER: Bernard
Robinson; ART DIRECTOR: Don Mingaye; DRAUGHTSMAN:
Thomas Goswell; SCENIC ARTIST: Felix Sergejak; DIRECTOR OF
PHOTOGRAPHY: Arthur Grant; CAMERA OPERATOR: Moray
Grant; FOCUS PULLER: Bob Jordan; SOUND CAMERA OPERATOR:
Al Thorne, John Soutar; ASSISTANT DIRECTOR: Douglas Hermes;
2ND ASSISTANT DIRECTOR: Joe Marks; 3RD ASSISTANT
DIRECTOR: Christopher Neame; SUPERVISING EDITOR: James
Needs; EDITOR: Spencer Reeve; 1ST ASSISTANT EDITOR: Elizabeth

Redstone; 2ND ASSISTANT EDITOR: Chris Brennan; MUSIC: James
Bernard; MUSIC SUPERVISOR: Philip Martell; SOUND
RECORDIST: Ken Rawkins; BOOM: Charles Wheeler; SOUND
MAINTENANCE: Cyril Hunt; SOUND EDITOR: Roy Hyde; MAKE-
UP: George Partleton; HAIRSTYLIST: Frieda Steiger; PRODUCTION
MANAGER: Ian Lewis; CONTINUITY: Eileen Head; WARDROBE
MISTRESS: Rosemary Burrows; WARDROBE MASTER: Larry
Stewart; CASTING: Irene Lamb; SPECIAL EFFECTS: Les Bowie;
PRODUCTION SECRETARY: Pat Sims; STILLS PHOTOGRAPHER:
Tom Edwards

Peter Cushing (Baron Frankenstein); Susan Denberg (Christina);
Thorley Walters (Doctor Hertz); Robert Morris (Hans); Duncan
Lamont (The Prisoner); Peter Blythe (Anton); Barry Warren (Karl);
Derek Fowlds (Johann); Alan MacNaughtan (Kleve); Peter Madden
(Chief of Police); Philip Ray (Mayor); Ivan Beavis (Landlord); Colin
Jeavons (Priest); Bartlett Mullins (Bystander); Alec Mango
(Spokesman)

UNCREDITED: Kevin Flood (Chief Gaoler); Lizbeth Kent (First Lady);
John Maxim (Sergeant); Stuart Middleton (Young Hans); Anthony
Viccars (Spokesman No 2); Patrick Carter; Howard Lang (Guards)

would turn his life-giving rays to the female of the species and they chose this very theme for the intrepid scientist's fourth adventure.

Anthony Hinds' draft screenplay, possibly in part inspired by A R Rawlinson's unused 'script no 1' from the aborted *Tales of Frankenstein* series, was submitted to John Trevelyan at the BBFC on 19 May. Reader Newton Branch commented on the 23rd: "I dare say this can be toned down for an 'X'. It is now a very sketchy draft script. I am not very keen on the new gimmick which seems perverse: a crippled girl, with soul of her guillotined lover transplanted to her (after she has

The rejuvenated Christina takes a cleaver to her tormentors in Frankenstein Created Woman (1966).

committed suicide), is revitalised. She becomes suddenly beautiful and tarty, luring former tormentors to make love to her and then killing them horribly before committing hara-kari. And she seems to have a male as well as a female side at times. A lot of it is ridiculous, of course, and the severed heads which clutter up the story are a real scream."

Trevelyan replied on 15 June, incorporating his reader's comments: "Basically this is typical Hammer 'X' material, but there are some elements in it that we would be unhappy about. The first point I want to make is a general one. While your new gimmick – the transplantation of a man's soul into a girl whose lover he had been – is not unacceptable, there is always the possibility that it might come out in a rather perverted way since after this 'operation' we have a kind of female-male personality, and the girl-man tempts the young men to make love to her and kills them horribly. I think you will need to exercise great care in dealing with this; otherwise both you and the Board will lay themselves open to criticism. My comments on points of detail are as follows:

Page 5. It looks as though the actual execution will be off screen which would be all right, but I am not at all sure about seeing the little boy screaming and running away, since I think that some people might find this distasteful Could you not have him with a horrified expression in the bushes frozen to the spot and not screaming wildly?

Pages 18-20. The violence in this scene should be kept to a reasonable minimum and I think you should omit the throwing of pepper into the faces of the young men. Care will need to be taken with the shot of the knife slashes on Fritz's face especially since the film will certainly be in colour.

Page 29. In view of my general comment above, sex should be kept to a minimum and this scene should therefore be discreet.

Page 32. We would not want undue violence in the attack on Kleve, certainly not 'hysterical violence' as indicated.

Page 44. Here we get the second execution and on this occasion we are to see the head of Hans. We do not like this at all and I think you should avoid showing it. Later we are to see body and head being put into the coffin; there should be no emphasis on decapitation.

Page 46. We are now to see the headless body with neck covered by blood-stained bandage. Great discretion should be used here.

<u>Pages 61-63</u>. Great care will have to be taken if the tempting and killing of Fritz are to pass. We do not like the phrase 'He opens his mouth to scream but nothing comes, only a rasping, gagging...' We shall certainly not want to see the severed head of Fritz in the basket or the policeman taking it out and stuffing it into a sack.

<u>Page 71</u>. Here Maria does it again, this time with an axe. Great care should be used, as before, and we would not want to hear a sickening crunch.

<u>Page 76</u>. The shot of the headless corpse in the coffin should be very discreet and not too macabre.

<u>Page 77</u>. I hope you will avoid the scene in which Maria has a discussion with the severed head of Hans. Surely you can find some way of making the point without emphasising what would, I think, be very nasty.

<u>Page 83</u>. There seems no need for Maria to stab Johann more than once. We are told that she brings the knife down 'again and again' which makes the scene sadistic.

<u>Page 84</u>. Here we have the head of Hans again; see my previous comments. We would not want, either, any unpleasant shot of the knife embedded in Maria's stomach."

Sadly, this is the only documentation the BBFC now holds on this film, which is frustrating since most of the above objections somehow managed to find their way into the finished movie regardless. Tony Hinds produced his shooting script in June and a number of revisions were made throughout the month. Initially, Hinds had Christina kill herself by plunging a knife into her stomach at the end. This was changed on 24 June to the familiar ending in which she throws herself into the river.

With Elstree busy, shooting started at Bray on 4 July. Terence Fisher was back, as were the Baron's complexities and quirks that were conspicuously missing in The Evil of Frankenstein. Back from The Witches after a three-week break were Arthur Grant, Bernard Robinson, Don Mingaye, James Needs, Ken Rawkins, Roy Hyde, George Partleton and Frieda Steiger. Moray Grant returned as camera operator after last working on The Reptile and Douglas Hermes returned as assistant director after his shocking experience on The Scarlet Blade with John Gilling. (Unsurprisingly, he didn't stay on for the next production, which would be directed by... John Gilling). Eileen Head was back on continuity after Slave Girls. Ian Lewis joined the team as production manager, Spencer Reeve as editor and Rosemary Burrows returned to take over wardrobe.

The team of Robinson and Mingaye once more provided the sets, which were erected two weeks before shooting, between 20 June and 2 July. The climax of the film was set in trusty Black Park and the guillotine was erected at Frensham Ponds, better known as Hammer's Dartmoor in The Hound of the Baskervilles and Cornwall in The Reptile. The village scenes were of course shot on Bray's external lot, which was a modification of the external sets for The Plague of the Zombies and The Reptile.

Peter Cushing was back as the Baron after being notably absent from Hammer's schedules in 1965. He had recently completed the Doctor Who sequel, Daleks Invasion Earth 2150 AD, for Aaru. Fisher used his old friend Thorley Walters as the perfect foil for the obstinate Baron in what amounts almost to a Holmes and Watson relationship. Susan Denberg, as the British pressbook proudly proclaimed, had progressed "from Au Pair to star in six months." Born Dietlinde Zechner in Poland in August 1944, Denberg had moved to England when she was 18 and became an au pair in London. She had joined the Bluebell Girls dance troupe and travelled to Las Vegas, where she was spotted by a Hollywood agent and given a role in Warner Bros' See You in Hell, Darling. This led to her part as Christina, which she handled, under Fisher's guidance, rather well. She celebrated her 22nd birthday on 2 August, both on set and then with a special party held at London's Playboy Club. However, she faded into obscurity afterwards, becoming a Playboy model in the August 1966 and July 1967 issues before succumbing to mental health problems.

Robert Morris, who played the Baron's new assistant Hans, remembers her vividly: "She was very sweet, very friendly; I liked her very much. She was very mixed up with that rather fast Polanski crowd, and also very much into the drug scene. She'd often arrive on the set in the mornings somewhat the worse for wear, but she was no trouble really. Her accent was pretty thick, mind you, and they decided to make out that Christina and her father were not natives of the village, so the father had to adopt an accent to match hers. Later, when they realised they'd have to dub her after all, Alan MacNaughtan had to go in and dub himself back into standard English!" He also remembers the film's 'risqué' love scene: "I don't know whether there'd been any nude bedroom scenes before that, but it was extremely discreet by later standards. One had one's briefs on, though Susan was all for taking everything off. It was my first experience of such a scene and, of course, they cleared the set as much as possible, but in fact it was more amusing than embarrassing. The cameramen would delicately lift my right arm into position over her left breast, so you couldn't see the nipple, and of course one's stuck there and one daren't move a muscle. It was most enjoyable!" [3]

Once more Les Bowie's crew were let loose on the special effects. Ian Scoones recalls, "I did a little bit with Ray Caple, who was given the job of making the aerials, those cone dishes, move. That was done at Bowie Studios. We used marble fablon from Woolworths to make the marble base of the two long rectangles of the cage. We also built a half-scale replica of the guillotine for the opening shot with Les' matted sky behind."

Robert Morris 'assisted' with further effects: "The headless body, by the way, wasn't a dummy, it was me. I wasn't scheduled to do it, but everything was going smoothly and they said, 'Why don't we use Bob's actual body?' It meant another week's wages for me, since I was called in for three or four days in the sixth week, when they did all the pyrotechnics and laboratory stuff. I just had to lie on a table with my head concealed in a well they'd built into the table, rather as magicians do." [4]

Shooting ended on Friday 12 August after six weeks; *The Viking Queen* finished six days later. Budgeted at £140,020, the Frankenstein film eventually came in at £138,595. Meanwhile, on 10 August Hammer's wardrobe lady Rosemary Burrows married stuntman Eddie Powell (who was to be the 'star' of Hammer's next movie). Editors James Needs and Spencer Reeve with sound editor Roy Hyde then took *Frankenstein Created Woman* into post-production at Hammer House. Philip Martell brought back James Bernard to compose one of his most memorable scores, including his haunting 'Christina's theme'. The music was recorded at the Anvil Studios on 14 October.

Hammer's next production, *The Mummy's Shroud*, was the last film of the current 11-picture distribution agreement. ABPC were willing to extend the programme for another six films the following year, but the same terms about studio usage applied. *The Mummy's Shroud* was to mark the end of an era.

This was the third film in Hammer's mummy series. It is a limited genre subject, but they did their best to brighten up the repetitive storyline with a whole compendium of deaths ranging from skull-crushing and burning by corrosive acid to plain old defenestration. Based on a story outline by Tony Hinds, John Gilling submitted his final shooting script on 6 September. A number of changes were to be made. Inspector Barrani was originally called 'Azi', the opening narration was expanded in the film, but the "lopping off of the head of one of Men-tah's guards" was itself axed. Sir Basil's accident was to be more graphic, inadvertently putting his hand into a nest of vipers, necessitating Paul to cut "deep into Sir Basil's arm. Black blood rushes from the wound ... Clare squeezes the wound to assist the flow of blood. Then Sir Basil raises his arm to his mouth and sucks hard on the wound, afterwards spitting out the blood."

Shooting began on Monday 12 September under the fearsome John Gilling. Back from *Frankenstein Created Woman* (after a generous four-week break) was the core team that had worked on all three films at Bray that year: Arthur Grant, Bernard Robinson, Don Mingaye, James Needs, Ken Rawkins,

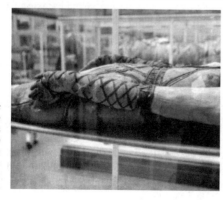

The design for the mummy in The Mummy's Shroud (1966) was based on an actual mummy in the British Museum.

Prem (Eddie Powell) attacks Paul Preston (David Buck) in The Mummy's Shroud (1966).

THE MUMMY'S SHROUD

PRINCIPAL PHOTOGRAPHY: 12 September to 21 October 1966
DISTRIBUTION:
 UK: Warner-Pathe; Technicolor; certificate 'X';
  84 minutes
 US: 20th Century-Fox; Deluxe Color; 90 minutes
UK RELEASE:
 TRADE SHOW: 3 May 1967, at Studio One
 GENERAL RELEASE: 18 June 1967, on the ABC circuit with
 Frankenstein Created Woman
US RELEASE: March 1967, with *Frankenstein Created Woman*

DIRECTOR: John Gilling; PRODUCER: Anthony Nelson Keys;
SCREENPLAY: John Gilling, from an original story by John Elder;
PRODUCTION DESIGNER: Bernard Robinson; ART DIRECTOR:
Don Mingaye; DIRECTOR OF PHOTOGRAPHY: Arthur Grant;
CAMERA OPERATOR: Moray Grant; ASSISTANT DIRECTOR: Bluey
Hill; SUPERVISING EDITOR: James Needs; EDITOR: Chris Barnes;
MUSIC: Don Banks; MUSIC SUPERVISOR: Philip Martell; SOUND

RECORDIST: Ken Rawkins; SOUND EDITOR: Roy Hyde; MAKE-UP:
George Partleton; HAIRSTYLIST: Frieda Steiger; PRODUCTION
MANAGER: Ed Harper; CONTINUITY: Eileen Head; WARDROBE
MISTRESS: Molly Arbuthnot; WARDROBE MASTER: Larry Stewart;
CASTING: Irene Lamb; SPECIAL EFFECTS: Bowie Films Ltd

André Morell (Sir Basil Walden); John Phillips (Stanley Preston);
David Buck (Paul Preston); Elizabeth Sellars (Barbara Preston);
Maggie Kimberley (Claire); Michael Ripper (Longbarrow); Tim
Barrett (Harry); Richard Warner (Inspector Barrani); Roger Delgado
(Hasmid); Catherine Lacey (Haiti); Dickie Owen (Prem); Bruno
Barnabe (Pharaoh); Toni Gilpin (Pharaoh's Wife); Toolsie Persaud
(Kah-to-Bey); Eddie Powell (The Mummy); Andreas Malandrinos
(The Curator)

UNCREDITED: John Garrie (Arab Cleaner); Darroll Richards (Sage);
George Zenios (Arab Reporter); Michael Rothwell; Terence Sewards;
Roy Stephens (Reporters)

Roy Hyde, George Partleton and Frieda Steiger. Also back from the Frankenstein film were camera operator Moray Grant, continuity Eileen Head and wardrobe staff Rosemary Burrows and Larry Stewart. Molly Arbuthnot returned to supervise wardrobe. The team went out on location for the desert scenes, which were shot at a nearby quarry at Wapsey's Wood, Gerrards Cross.

George Partleton altered the basic design of the mummy to make it look more authentic; contact sheets show that the latest creation was based faithfully on one of the exhibits in the Egyptian Rooms of the British Museum (still present today in room 60). The desiccated mummy of Kah-to-Bey was also impressive, although the original shooting script described its appearance very differently: "the perfect semblance of a human face and body. Skin, hair, etc is intact yet so opaque in appearance that one would suspect it could crumble if breathed upon."

The words of death cause Prem (Eddie Powell) to falter in his attack on Claire (Maggie Kimberley) and Paul (David Buck) in The Mummy's Shroud (1966).

The cast was first class. It's a shame that André Morell's distinguished presence is removed early on (he becomes the mummy's first victim) but Catherine Lacey gives a gorgeous performance as the evil fortune teller, Haiti. Her demented son is played by Roger Delgado (from *The Stranglers of Bombay* and *The Terror of the Tongs*), who later became notorious on BBC Television as Jon Pertwee's evil adversary, The Master, in *Doctor Who*, before his untimely death in a 1973 car crash. Michael Ripper returns as Longbarrow, the belittled manservant, and many regard this as his best performance for Hammer. Hero David Buck, who replaced the intended John Richardson, was later to marry Hammer starlet Madeline Smith. He died of cancer in February 1989. Prophetically, Elizabeth Sellars, who had starred in Hammer's first film at Bray, *Cloudburst*, was now engaged for the last.

Newly-wed Hammer stuntman and Christopher Lee double, Eddie Powell, played the actual mummy, although in the pre-credits flashback sequence Prem is played in 'life' by Dickie Owen, who had played the pot-bellied mummy in *The Curse of the Mummy's Tomb*. This was Powell's first credited performance, but he was no stranger to mummies, having previously doubled for Lee in *The Mummy*. One unpleasant moment Powell remembered was when the advancing mummy had to have acid splashed on its chest. "They wanted the effect of smoke coming off my chest and some special effects guy had this marvellous idea of throwing acid of some sort onto the front of the tunic, the mummy costume. The fumes went literally up into the mask and I was in a right old state. I couldn't breathe. I ripped the mask off, ruined it, and just rushed off the set. It was the one time I didn't wait for the director to say cut. I was away immediately, smashing my way outside. I was practically dying outside, because those fumes, once they get inside your lungs, take a bit of clearing." 5

The final dissolution of the Mummy was filmed at Bowie's studios in Slough. Ian Scoones remembers, "We completely reconstructed the set from Bray, which we put on a rostrum so we could work underneath it. The disintegration of the mummy was something we worked for weeks to perfect – we tried everything from acid to popadoms to get the right effect. In the end we used Fuller's Earth mixed with paint dust on a wax head." 6 Indeed, it is Scoones' arms and hands we see at the end of the disintegration process, poking through the rostrum and crumbling the concoction over the skull beneath.

During filming, *The Old Dark House* finally went on release in England. Hammer's original plan to release it at home as a 'U' certificate, to target the children during the 1963 Easter holidays, was blocked when the BBFC decreed that the best they could give it (at a push) was an 'A'. While Hammer released an uncut version of the film in the States (in black-and-white) with *Maniac* on 31 October 1963, they decided to persevere in England, making the cuts necessary for a 'U' certificate. However, this involved the removal of all shots where the face of a corpse could be seen, which was impossible for the continuity of the film. So Hammer finally decided to try to market it as an 'X'. Unfortunately, the exhibitors were not impressed and, with further cuts made in March 1966, Hammer managed to scramble an 'A' certificate version together and the film was released (in colour, but nine minutes shorter than the American print) on 16 September, supported by *Big Deal at Dodge City*, on the ABC circuit.

Meanwhile, shooting on *The Mummy's Shroud* ended at Bray on Friday 21 October after six weeks. James Needs and Chris Barnes now left Bray's cutting rooms for the last time to resume post-production at Hammer House and Philip Martell brought Don Banks back for another rousing score. Only a few snippets remain about the film at the BBFC, which suggests there were no undue problems for once. Audrey Field reported on 15 December and John Trevelyan wrote to James Carreras the following day: "On the incomplete print seen it looks as though this picture will be one for the 'X' category. For this category we shall need to see the scene of the death of Newton in Reel 7 with full colour and sound, and we may possibly ask you to make a cut in this scene. We shall also need to see the complete Reel 10, in which there are at present four missing scenes, which we think are probably scenes of the Mummy disintegrating." On the bottom of the letter is a handwritten note from Frank Crofts, dated 20 March 1967 after re-viewing the film with Newton Branch: "Seen today. All right for 'X'."

It was John Gilling's last film for Hammer. He remembered, "I wasn't very proud of *The Mummy's Shroud*. In fact, I thought it one of my worst! As you say, it was another worn-out theme. I agree with you over Michael Ripper's performance. I think Michael is a very neglected artist. I cast him with a view of introducing some lighter touches into the movie and I think these may have saved it from being a total disaster." [7] Gilling left England in 1970 to settle in Madrid, where he eventually became a permanent resident. He died on 22 November 1984, aged 72. Ten years before, he had made his last film in Spain, a contribution to that country's horror 'boom' called *La cruz del Diablo* (*The Devil's Cross*).

The Witches went out next (to a decidedly lukewarm reception), premiering at the London Pavilion on 21 November before going on general release on the ABC circuit from 9 December with *Death is a Woman*. Joan Fontaine, for one, was bitterly disappointed by its failure and the picture was the final nail in her ailing career. *One Million Years B.C.* went on general release on the ABC circuit from 30 December. By December 1972, the film that had cost £400,000 to make had grossed over £3,600,000 worldwide, becoming the company's most successful venture. After its initial success, Hammer entertained the possibility of remaking *King Kong*, again using the animation genius of Ray Harryhausen. However, he maintains that "It was just talk. There were legal hold-ups. They could only get the rights to a sequel, not a remake, and so they dropped the plans."

In England, *Frankenstein Created Woman* had been scheduled to go out with *Slave Girls* as late as October 1966. Then ABPC changed their minds and decided to market their latest Frankenstein feature with *The Mummy's Shroud* instead. They went on general release together on the ABC circuit from 18 June 1967. *Slave Girls* had been released in America as *Prehistoric Women* in January but would not be released in England until 7 July 1968, paired with *The Devil Rides Out* and with its US running time of 95 minutes mercifully shorn of a whopping 21 minutes. *The Viking Queen* went out on the ABC circuit from 26 March 1967 but failed to arouse much interest and proved an expensive flop.

Hammer finally moved out of Bray on 19 November 1966. They would return briefly for special effects photography on both *When Dinosaurs Ruled the Earth* and *Moon Zero Two* in 1969. Another vital chapter in Hammer's history had ended. The small family set-up at Bray, and the independence it had afforded, had given Hammer's films a style and magic that would never be replicated. Now, as the remains of Mezzera were pulled down, the external lot would lie idle and drift into a state of decay. Over the months to come, inquisitive fans would peer dolefully over the fence at the neglected sets, still just about recognisable from recent films. Sad though it was, it was little more than a sign of the times. The British film industry was in a state of collapse and to Hammer the loss of Bray seemed but a small price to pay in order to maintain a busy programme of new productions.

"I look back with tremendous nostalgia upon what I call our 'Bray period'," said Michael Carreras. "There is no question that having a permanent unit in a permanent home gave the films a uniquely personal quality, which we never recaptured once we were out in the bigger world of commercial studios." [8] And the final word can go to Michael Ripper: "The last [Hammer] film to be made at Bray Studios was *The Mummy's Shroud*. When I finished my final day on that film I must admit I was upset. To leave Bray and that period of Hammer behind was a sad moment indeed. I knew I would miss it; well of course I would, I'd made over 20 films at that old building. It was great, absolutely great. My own opinion is that all the best Hammer films were made there, especially of the horrors. It was a fine studio, everything worked smoothly and even the food was good. It was a lovely place, a dream of a studio, most efficiently run ... The unity there was unique. Everyone was so involved. Most of all, though, it had a wonderful atmosphere." [9]

FIFTEEN

Post Mortem

In closing, a few words to bring the Hammer story up to date. While many agree that Hammer's golden period corresponded to their years at Bray, several classics were still to come. The following is a list of Hammer's remaining film productions at other studios:

1967

✦ *QUATERMASS AND THE PIT*	MGM British, Borehamwood
✦ *A CHALLENGE FOR ROBIN HOOD*	Pinewood
✦ *THE ANNIVERSARY*	ABPC Elstree, Borehamwood
✦ *THE VENGEANCE OF SHE*	ABPC Elstree, Borehamwood
✦ *THE DEVIL RIDES OUT*	ABPC Elstree, Borehamwood
✦ *THE LOST CONTINENT*	ABPC Elstree, Borehamwood

1968

✦ *DRACULA HAS RISEN FROM THE GRAVE*	Pinewood
✦ *WHEN DINOSAURS RULED THE EARTH*	Shepperton, Les Bowie Studios [plus stop-motion animation at Bray Studios]

1969

✦ *FRANKENSTEIN MUST BE DESTROYED*	ABPC Elstree, Borehamwood
✦ *MOON ZERO TWO*	ABPC Elstree, Borehamwood
✦ *CRESCENDO*	ABPC Elstree, Borehamwood
✦ *TASTE THE BLOOD OF DRACULA*	ABPC Elstree, Borehamwood

1970

- THE VAMPIRE LOVERS — ABPC Elstree, Borehamwood
- THE HORROR OF FRANKENSTEIN — MGM-EMI Elstree (formerly ABPC), Borehamwood
- SCARS OF DRACULA — MGM-EMI Elstree, Borehamwood
- CREATURES THE WORLD FORGOT — Namib Desert, Africa
- LUST FOR A VAMPIRE — MGM-EMI Elstree
- COUNTESS DRACULA — Pinewood

1971

- BLOOD FROM THE MUMMY'S TOMB — MGM-EMI Elstree, Borehamwood
- HANDS OF THE RIPPER — Pinewood
- DR. JEKYLL & SISTER HYDE — MGM-EMI Elstree, Borehamwood
- ON THE BUSES — MGM-EMI Elstree, Borehamwood
- TWINS OF EVIL — Pinewood
- VAMPIRE CIRCUS — Pinewood
- DEMONS OF THE MIND — MGM-EMI Elstree, Borehamwood
- DRACULA A.D. 1972 — MGM-EMI Elstree, Borehamwood
- STRAIGHT ON TILL MORNING — MGM-EMI Elstree, Borehamwood
- FEAR IN THE NIGHT — MGM-EMI Elstree, Borehamwood

1972

- MUTINY ON THE BUSES — MGM-EMI Elstree, Borehamwood
- CAPTAIN KRONOS VAMPIRE HUNTER — MGM-EMI Elstree, Borehamwood
- THAT'S YOUR FUNERAL — MGM-EMI Elstree, Borehamwood
- NEAREST AND DEAREST — MGM-EMI Elstree, Borehamwood
- FRANKENSTEIN AND THE MONSTER FROM HELL — MGM-EMI Elstree, Borehamwood
- THE SATANIC RITES OF DRACULA — MGM-EMI Elstree, Borehamwood

1973

- LOVE THY NEIGHBOUR — MGM-EMI Elstree, Borehamwood
- MAN AT THE TOP — MGM-EMI Elstree, Borehamwood
- HOLIDAY ON THE BUSES — MGM-EMI Elstree, Borehamwood
- THE LEGEND OF THE 7 GOLDEN VAMPIRES — Shaw Brothers Studios, Hong Kong
- SHATTER — Shaw Brothers Studios, Hong Kong

1974

- MAN ABOUT THE HOUSE — MGM-EMI Elstree, Borehamwood

1975

- TO THE DEVIL A DAUGHTER — MGM-EMI Elstree, Borehamwood

1978

- THE LADY VANISHES — Pinewood

In April 1968, Hammer was awarded a prestigious Queen's Award to Industry after bringing in approximately £3 million from overseas markets in just three years. Construction manager Arthur Banks accepted the award at a special ceremony at Pinewood Studios on Wednesday 29 May 1968, during the filming of *Dracula Has Risen from the Grave*. The success continued: *Kinematograph Weekly* later reported, on 30 November: "All records were broken by *Dracula Has Risen from the Grave* on the first day of its ABC release. The film set a new circuit record by taking more money at the box-office on a Sunday than ever before." The company had reached its zenith, and the tide was about to turn.

The volatile film industry was rapidly changing. In June 1967, Eliot Hyman's Seven Arts had taken over Warner Bros at a cost of $95 million. The new company, Warner Bros-Seven Arts, continued to finance Hammer's products with ABPC and soon took over worldwide distribution of the films from 20th Century-Fox after the release of The Lost Continent in 1968. In April 1969, EMI (Electrical Musical Industries) took over ABPC and later merged with MGM. ABPC would change its name to EMI Film Productions Ltd under chairman Bernard Delfont and Elstree would now become the MGM-EMI Elstree studios.

Further shake-ups occurred in June 1969, when Warner Bros-Seven Arts merged with the Kinney National Service Corporation. Eliot Hyman, James Carreras' longstanding American business associate, retired and Ted Ashley took over the new company, which in September reverted to the name Warner Bros. However, following the commercial failure of Hammer's big budget 'space western' Moon Zero Two (1969), Ashley declined to continue the partnership with Hammer. Thus came to an end Hammer's fruitful association with their American partner; it had spanned some five years between 1965 and 1969 and embraced 23 films.

Meanwhile, there were major shake-ups in the Hammer cabinet itself. Anthony Nelson Keys left the company on completion of Frankenstein Must Be Destroyed in February 1969. In 1971 he formed Charlemagne Productions with Christopher Lee, with a view to producing a series of films based on the stories of Denis Wheatley. However, the company folded when their first film, Nothing But the Night (1972; not a Wheatley subject after all), did poorly at the box-office. An accomplished golfer, Keys died on the course from a heart attack in 1984.

Bernard Robinson also left the company after Frankenstein Must Be Destroyed and was replaced by Scott McGregor. Maybe it was the curse of Elstree, but now the sets looked cheaper and started to betray Hammer's modest budgets. Robinson collapsed and died suddenly at home, while decorating, on 2 March 1970 at the age of 58. Only minutes before he had agreed on the phone to do another Hammer horror. One imagines this must have been Lust for a Vampire, since his colleague, Don Mingaye (who had left Hammer after The Mummy's Shroud), picked up the project.

On 14 April 1969, company secretary James Dawson retired and was replaced by accountant Roy Skeggs. In 1971 Skeggs became overall production supervisor of the company and in 1972 also became a producer. Meanwhile, Tony Hinds was becoming increasingly disillusioned with the company. Following problems with a joint Hammer/Fox TV show, Journey to the Unknown, and a dispute arising from Taste the Blood of Dracula, he retired from the company on 19 May 1970.

In 1970, James Carreras was knighted in the New Year's Honours List for services to youth, in recognition of his fund-raising for the Variety Club. Later that year, he forged a new multi-picture deal with Bernard Delfont of MGM-EMI, announcing excitedly in Cinema Today on 27 March: "with 100 per cent British finance the world receipts will come direct to Britain." Meanwhile, a further rift developed between father and son when Michael Carreras declined an offer from his father to resume his old job as executive producer. A reconciliation was effected in December and James offered Michael the post of Managing Director, which he accepted after some persuasion from his mother. The appointment was formally agreed at Hammer House on 8 December and Michael took up the post on 4 January 1971. To prevent a take-over bid from Studio Film Labs, Michael finally bought the company from his father in August 1972 and officially became Chairman and Chief Executive on 31 January 1973. This finally severed Sir James' contact with the internationally acclaimed company he had helped build. He died suddenly on 9 January 1990, from a heart attack, at the age of 81.

However, it was the beginning of the end. Hammer lost the support of Bernard Delfont at EMI, and Michael was aghast to discover that Hammer's assets amounted to a meagre £200,000. The British film industry was in its final state of collapse. Hammer were finding it difficult to get finance and distribution rights to their pictures and in desperation they returned to making films of successful TV comedies. A number of pictures failed to get an American release and Hammer's last horror film, To the Devil a Daughter, a co-production with Germany's Terra Filmkunst, was released in February 1976. Despite some impressive box-office returns in the UK, Michael was powerless to halt Hammer's financial slide.

Desperate to get the company on the road again, Michael Carreras invested a lot of money, some of it his own, in a series of ambitious big-budget gambles, including *Vampirella*, *Vlad the Impaler* and *Nessie*, only to see them all die in pre-production. By the summer of 1977, Carreras was edged out of both Hammer House and Elstree and took up residence in the Coach House at Pinewood. Dipping into his own pocket to keep the company afloat, he finally set up a co-production with Rank to remake Hitchcock's *The Lady Vanishes* in December 1978. However, the picture ran over budget and Rank took Carreras off the film, forfeiting Hammer's rights in the process. In February 1979 a heartbroken Michael was informed that Hammer was to be placed in the hands of the Official Receiver; he finally resigned from the company on 30 April 1979. He died of cancer on 19 April 1994, at the age of 66.

In 1980 Hammer was re-established under former board-members Roy Skeggs and Brian Lawrence, who managed to inject some life back into the company. During the eighties and nineties Hammer produced or co-produced two anthology series (*Hammer House of Horror* and *Hammer House of Mystery and Suspense*), a compilation series of classic clips and a two-part documentary. Brian Lawrence retired in 1985, and Roy Skeggs stepped down in early 2000 when he sold the company to a private consortium which included Charles Saatchi, the co-founder of the Saatchi & Saatchi advertising agency.

Many members of Bray's team of technicians and actors have since passed away. Of particular note (apart from those already mentioned in the text) we remember the following: Arthur Grant (died 1972), Moray Grant (17 September 1977), Les Bowie (1979), Terence Fisher (18 June 1980), Don Banks (1981), Philip Martell (August 1993), Peter Cushing (11 August 1994), Michael Ripper (28 June 2000), James Bernard (9 July 2001) and Molly Arbuthnot (31 October 2001).

Meanwhile, Bray continued to provide a home for film and TV productions. When Mrs Davies died in 1968, George Davies left and the South West section they had inhabited was converted into luxury flats. In 1969 ABPC proposed that Bray should be sold, and on 11 September 1970 the following article appeared in *Today's Cinema*:

NOW BRAY IS FOR SALE

"Reports that Bray Studios, near Windsor, now temporarily closed with an hiatus in production, would be sold have been confirmed to Today's Cinema by Sir James Carreras.

'We would like to sell them' he said. 'We are so committed with our deals with Elstree and Rank that we don't have any time for the place.'

Pointing out that Bray had recently had 'two great lets' for other productions, Sir James said that they were still prepared for future lettings of the space. 'We would let tomorrow or we would sell tomorrow,' he remarked. 'At the moment nobody is there and it costs a fortune.'

What is the value of Bray Studios? 'I would say about £250,000,' said the Hammer chief.

As well as Hammer, the founders of the studio, interests are held by EMI (originally by ABPC) and Columbia Pictures."

In November 1970 Hammer finally sold the Bray freehold to Redspring Ltd for a mere £65,000. Redspring had initially intended to build a housing estate on the land, but decided to revive the studio, renaming it The Bray International Film Centre. Among the films made there were *The Music Lovers*, *The Rocky Horror Picture Show*, a disastrous spoof of *The Hound of the Baskervilles* and *Loophole*. In 1973 it was decided to demolish the existing Stage 1 and replace it with a bigger stage, the 10,200-square feet Stage 10 from the demolished MGM British Studios in Borehamwood. Hammer's old Stage 2 now became Stage 3, Stage 4 became the new Stage 2 and the ballroom Stage 3 was relegated to a viewing theatre.

On 26 March 1984, the Samuelson group of companies bought Bray for £700,000. Advertisements and pop videos were made there and Gerry Anderson made it a home for his *Terrahawks* project. Other TV shows included *Murder Most Horrid*, *Pie in the Sky* and *Poirot*. The property changed hands again in 1990 and continues to flourish as a working studio.

Despite everything, the spirit of Hammer is still alive on the stages and in the grounds of Bray Studios. The legacy will live on and continue to thrill generations to come.

Bray - Evolution of a Film Studio

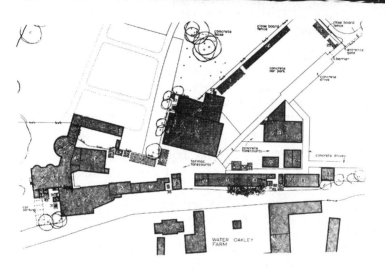

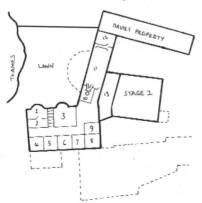

BRAY STUDIOS GROUND FLOOR PLAN

1. Canteen 1
2. Canteen 2 (originally a stage)
3. Kitchen
4. Property master, Tommy Money's office
5. Entrance/exit to rear of studio and to caretaker flat
6. Studio manager's office
7. Studio manager's secretary
8. Original switchboard
9. Mrs Tompson's kitchen
10. Restaurant dining room
11. Entrance to prop store (on two levels)
12. Entrance to Stage 3 and rear of house
13. Entrance to reception
14. Reception
15. Revamped switchboard
16. Stairwell to dressing rooms
17. Male star dressing room and conference room
18. Production office
19. Original Stage 'H' then general stores
20. Producer's office (Tony Hinds)
21. Camera department
22. Sound department
23. Stills department
24. Editing
25. Electricity transformer
26. Generator building
27. Lamp store and heating plant
28. Assistant director-unit office
29. Camera grip shed
30. Construction manager's office
31. Chief electrician's office
32. Wardrobe
33. Camera room

BRAY STUDIOS FIRST FLOOR PLAN

1. Anthony Nelson Keys' office and original stage
2. Anthony Nelson Keys' secretary (Pauline Harlow)
3. Art department office (Bernard Robinson and Don Mingaye) and original stage
4. No. 2 make-up and hairdressing
5. Hairdressing
6. Make-up room (Phil Leakey and Roy Ashton)
7. Ken Gorden's office (accounts)
8. Caretaker's flat
9. Female star dressing room
10. Viewing projection box
11. Viewing Theatre
12. Stills studio (John Jay and Tom Edwards)

Over a six-year period, Hammer converted Down Place into a working studio with four stages. While these stages were always used to maximum effect, production designer Bernard Robinson was also prolific on the back lot, creating structures which were left standing and reused with simple modifications over several productions. This pictorial appendix explores the evolution of Bray Studios and its back lot, revealing the secret to the thrifty set revamping which was central to Hammer's repertory-style approach.

1951

Hammer moves into Down Place. There are no stages – Hammer shoot their films in the rooms and grounds of the mansion.

1953

Hammer develop existing rooms into makeshift stages. The ballroom area is

converted into a rectangular stage called 'B-C-D'. Later in the year, a purpose-built brick stage is erected in the front courtyard, which is known as the 'new stage'. It is first used for *Five Days*.

1956

The Curse of Frankenstein, Hammer's first colour horror film, is shot in the house and on the new stage. The front courtyard is disguised as the prison courtyard for the opening sequence.

1957

Hammer erects a new, large 'Stage 1' on the lot, first used in *The Snorkel*. The existing stages are now renamed; the 'new stage' now becomes Stage 2 and the ballroom stage (B-C-D) becomes Stage 3. Another smaller stage, Stage 4, will soon join them on the lot. Bernard Robinson later erects an exterior castle set for *Dracula* on the lot.

ABOVE: *The front courtyard entrance to Down Place. The door in the foreground on the left side leads to Tony Hinds office. The door in the bottom left hand corner of the courtyard is the entrance to the reception area. The bottom window on the left is the studio manager's secretary's office. Above that is the window to the caretaker's flat, partly obscured by the Wisteria. The bottom right hand window is the studio manager's office. Above that is the window of the female star dressing room. The doorway in the right hand corner of the courtyard is the entrance to ballroom stage 3. Brick stage 2 is on the right.*

MIDDLE LEFT: *Bernard Robinson's exterior castle set erected on the back lot for Dracula (1957).*

BELOW LEFT: *The Dracula castle set was later revamped into the exterior of Baskerville Hall for The Hound of the Baskervilles (1958).*

TOP RIGHT: *The courtyard doubled up for the prison in The Curse of Frankenstein (1956) and the monastery in Dracula Prince of Darkness (1965).*

BELOW RIGHT: *Another view of Robinson's castle set for Dracula (1957).*

1958

The exterior castle set is disguised and re-used in *The Revenge of Frankenstein*, *The Hound of the Baskervilles* and *Further Up the Creek*.

1959

A sloping piece of ground called 'the mound' is erected on the backlot for *The Mummy*. The external *Dracula* set is re-used in *The Stranglers of* Bombay and then finally struck. In its place, Bernard Robinson erects a village square set.

1960

The village square is first used in *The Brides of Dracula*. The square becomes a Chinese waterfront for *The Terror of the Tongs* and *Visa to Canton*. It later becomes the Spanish village for *The Curse of the Werewolf*.

TOP LEFT: *The original Dracula set was finally struck and replaced with a village square for* The Brides of Dracula *(1960). The photograph shows the tunnel archway with triangular roof.*

TOP RIGHT: *The village square in* The Brides of Dracula. *To the right of the tunnel archway was a building that would become the cantina later in the year for* The Curse of the Werewolf *(1960).*

BELOW LEFT: *Another view of the village square from* The Brides of Dracula *(1960). Further to the right we now have the entrance to the village inn. This would be replaced later in the year by the bell tower for* The Curse of the Werewolf *(1960).*

BELOW RIGHT: *The village square became Hong Kong docks for* The Terror of Tongs *(1960). The mountains in the background are from a Les Bowie glass painting.*

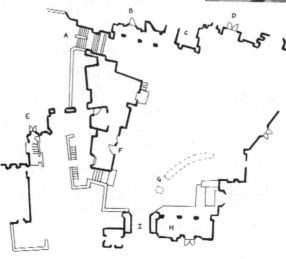

LEFT:
An adaptation of Bernard Robinson's ground plan of the village square for The Curse of the Werewolf *(1960) which also doubled as the vineyard.*

A: Original tunnel archway now with steps added for the film
B: Cantina
C: Bell Tower
D: Church
E: Carido home
F: Leon's workplace and quarters at the vineyard
G: Wall containing entrance to Don Fernando's house was added to set for vineyard revamp
H: Town Hall and jail
I: Entrance to village/vineyard

TOP LEFT:
The entrance to the village in The Curse of the Werewolf (1960)

TOP RIGHT:
The bell tower in The Curse of the Werewolf (1960). Out of sight to the left is the cantina and tunnel archway.

BELOW LEFT:
The church next to the bell tower in The Curse of the Werewolf (1960).

BELOW RIGHT:
The Carido home in The Curse of the Werewolf (1960).

1961

A fire breaks out in the main house, destroying Stage 3, in January. The village square is expanded to form two squares for Captain Clegg.

1962

A 'Gothic structure' is erected on the lot next to the mound, which becomes the entrance to both village squares. It is first used for the opening burial sequence in The Kiss of the Vampire and reappears later in the film as the lodge entrance to Ravna's chateau.

TOP LEFT:
The Huguenot stockade in The Pirates Of Blood River (1961). Note the original tunnel archway with triangular roof is visible over the fence.

TOP RIGHT:
The Gothic structure was first seen in the opening burial sequence of The Kiss of the Vampire (1962).

BELOW LEFT:
The hotel from The Kiss of the Vampire (1962) is seen here in a scene from The Devil-Ship Pirates (1963). Note more economising by Bernard Robinson: the stone pillars were cannibalised from the building next to the original archway in The Brides of Dracula (1960), which later became the cantina in The Curse of the Werewolf (1960).

ABOVE: The Gothic structure is used as the entrance to Beverley Manor in The Scarlet Blade (1963). Note Beverely Manor is the building behind the wall on the left.

1963

The village squares are modified further for *The Scarlet Blade*, *The Devil-Ship Pirates* and *The Evil of Frankenstein*. The Gothic structure becomes the entrance to Beverley Manor (*The Scarlet Blade*),

Chateau Frankenstein (*The Evil of Frankenstein*) and Castle Borski (*The Gorgon*). After *The Gorgon*, the village squares and Gothic structure are finally struck.

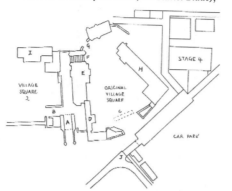

GROUND PLAN OF THE TWO VILLAGE
SQUARES FOR HAMMER'S 1963 PRODUCTIONS

A: *Gothic structure archway*
B: *Ramp leading down to village square 2*
C: *Building added for the inn in The Evil of Frankenstein (1963). Reused for the Heitz house in The Gorgon (1963)*
D: *Building added for the hotel in The Kiss of the Vampire (1962)*
E: *Timber-fronted building added for Captain Clegg (1961)*
F: *Original archway leading to village square 1*
G: *New archway entrance to village added for The Scarlet Blade (1963)*
H: *Row of tudor houses erected for The Scarlet Blade (1963)*
I: *Tudor house erected for Beverley Manor in The Scarlet Blade (1963)*
J: *Entrance gate to studio*

TOP LEFT: *Beverley Manor in village square 2 in construction for The Scarlet Blade (1963).*

TOP RIGHT: *Another view of village square 2 looking out to the back of the Gothic structure entrance and ramp down which the soldiers are riding in The Scarlet Blade (1963).*

MIDDLE LEFT: *A moat was constructed in front of the Gothic structure entrance of Beverley Manor in The Scarlet Blade (1963). It wasn't the first time water was placed here – it first appeared as the river where the scarred phantom hurls himself in The Phantom of the Opera (1961). The printing house where Herbert Lom burnt his face was in village square 2.*

MIDDLE RIGHT: *Village square 1 in The Devil-Ship Pirates (1963). Far left is the timber-fronted building introduced for Captain Clegg (1961). Next is the original tunnel archway, still with steps, from The Curse of the Werewolf (1960). To the right of that is the new archway and Tudor buildings added for The Scarlet Blade (1963).*

ABOVE: *The same view of village square 1 as seen in The Scarlet Blade (left) and The Devil-Ship Pirates (right). The only significant difference was a change to the sign outside the inn and a change of face to the Tudor building on the far right.*

TOP LEFT:
The Vandorf Sanitorium from The Gorgon (1963). This was erected between the original inn from The Kiss of the Vampire (1962) and the timber-fronted building from Captain Clegg (1961).

TOP RIGHT:
Another view of the Sanitorium (on the left) for The Gorgon (1963) in village square 1. Note the original tunnel archway with its triangular roof is still present in the centre.

BELOW LEFT:
The entrance of the Gothic structure became the entrance to Castle Borski in The Gorgon (1963).

1965
In their place Bernard Robinson erects the exterior castle set for *Dracula Prince of Darkness* and *Rasputin the Mad Monk*. This is later modified to become the sunken graveyard for *The Plague of the Zombies* and *The Reptile*.

1966
The exterior set is finally revamped into the villages for *Frankenstein Created Woman* and *The Mummy's Shroud*.

BELOW RIGHT:
Peter Cushing and Sandor Eles ride through village square 1 in The Evil of Frankenstein (1963). The inn from The Kiss of the Vampire (1962) on the left now became the police station.

LEFT AND OPPOSITE:
Two views of the castle set for Dracula Prince of Darkness (1965), which was reused in Rasputin the Mad Monk (1965). The bridge over the castle moat leads on to 'the mound', which was originally constructed for The Mummy (1959).

ABOVE: *The set was revamped into the front of a sunken graveyard for* The Plague of the Zombies *(1965).*

ABOVE: *The sunken graveyard was reused for* The Reptile *(1965).*

References

ONE
Hammer's Origins

1. A History of Horrors – The Rise and Fall of the House of Hammer; Denis Meikle; p.3; The Scarecrow Press, 1996
2. The Hammer Story; Marcus Hearn and Alan Barnes; p.8; Titan Books; 1997
3. Hammer Films – An Exhaustive Filmography; Tom Johnson and Deborah Del Vecchio; p.21; McFarland; 1996
4. A History of Horrors – The Rise and Fall of the House of Hammer; Denis Meikle; p.4; The Scarecrow Press, 1996
5. House of Hammer #16; p.31; Michael Carreras interview by John Brosnan and Dez Skinn
6. The Hammer Story; Marcus Hearn and Alan Barnes; p.9; Titan Books; 1997
7. The House of Horror: The Story of Hammer Films; Eyles; p.9; Lorrimer, 1973
8. Dark Terrors #16, p.8; Tony Hinds interview by Mike Murphy
9. Little Shoppe of Horrors #4; Edited by Richard Klemensen; p30; Michael Carreras interview
10. Little Shoppe of Horrors #3; Edited by Richard Klemensen; p.78; The works of Jack Curtis by Stephen Pickard
11. Little Shoppe of Horrors #4; Edited by Richard Klemensen, p.38; Michael Carreras interview
12. Dark Terrors #9, p.37; Francis Searle interview by Mike Murphy
13. The House of Horror: The Story of Hammer Films; Eyles; p.9; Lorrimer, 1973
14. Little Shoppe of Horrors #4; Edited by Richard Klemensen p31; Michael Carreras interview

TWO
Hammer Moves to Bray (1951-1952)

1. Hammer documentary; BBC Radio 2; 8 July, 1997
2. The House of Horror: The Story of Hammer Films; Eyles; p.13; Lorrimer, 1973
3. Do You Want It Good Or Tuesday; Jimmy Sangster; p.25; Midnight Marquee Press; 1997
4. Little Shoppe of Horrors #14; Edited by Richard Klemensen, p.68; Len Harris interview by Denis Meikle
5. Dark Terrors #10, p.25; Len Harris interview by Mike Murphy
6. Little Shoppe of Horrors #4; Edited by Richard Klemensen, p.31; Michael Carreras interview

THREE
A New Era (1953-1955)

1. Nigel Kneale interview by David Prothero; Chapter Cinema, Cardiff; 2 July, 1999
2. Little Shoppe of Horrors #10/11; Edited by Richard Klemensen, p.9; Phil Leakey letter
3. Little Shoppe of Horrors #9; Edited by Richard Klemensen, p.106; Bill Lenny interview by Al Taylor
4. Hammer Horror #7; p.33; article by Tom Edwards
5. Radio Times; 15 June, 1972; interview with Richard Wordsworth
6. Fangoria #61; p56; Michael Carreras interview by Steve Squires
7. Little Shoppe of Horrors #4; Edited by Richard Klemensen, p.36; Michael Carreras interview

FOUR
Enter Frankenstein (1956)

1. Little Shoppe of Horrors #9; Edited by Richard Klemensen,
2. Little Shoppe of Horrors #4; Edited by Richard Klemensen, p.69; Ted Marshall interview
3. Little Shoppe of Horrors #13; Edited by Richard Klemensen, p.66; Christopher Sutton interview by Bruce Hallenbeck
4. Little Shoppe of Horrors #9; Edited by Richard Klemensen, p.104; Len Harris interview by Al Taylor
5. Little Shoppe of Horrors #9; Edited by Richard Klemensen, p.93; Jack Asher interview by Richard Klemensen
6. Little Shoppe of Horrors #6; Edited by Richard Klemensen; p.16; Jack Asher tribute to Terence Fisher
7. Fangoria #11; p.37; Tony Hinds tribute to Terence Fisher courtesy of Keith Dudley
8. Little Shoppe of Horrors #3; Edited by Richard Klemensen, p.59; The Fruition of Terence Fisher by Gary Parfitt
9. The Films of Peter Cushing by Gary Parfitt; p.24; A HFCGB Publication; 1975
10. The Films of Peter Cushing by Gary Parfitt; p.37; A HFCGB Publication; 1975
11. The Films of Peter Cushing by Gary Parfitt; p.43; A HFCGB Publication; 1975
12. Little Shoppe of Horrors #6; Edited by Richard Klemensen; p36; Phil Leakey interview
13. Little Shoppe of Horrors #10/11; Edited by Richard Klemensen, p.9; Phil Leakey letter
14. Little Shoppe of Horrors #4; Edited by Richard Klemensen, p43; Anthony Nelson Keys interview
15. Little Shoppe of Horrors #3; Edited by Richard Klemensen p78; The works of Jack Curtis by Stephen Pickard
16. Little Shoppe of Horrors #4; Edited by Richard Klemensen, p40; Tony Hinds interview by Al Taylor
17. Little Shoppe of Horrors #3; Edited by Richard Klemensen, p.62; The Fruition of Terence Fisher by Gary Parfitt
18. Little Shoppe of Horrors #9; Edited by Richard Klemensen, p.88; Terence Fisher interview by Michael Caen (1964)
19. Little Shoppe of Horrors #3; Edited by Richard Klemensen, p.60; The Fruition of Terence Fisher by Gary Parfitt
20. Hammer Horror #1; p.43; Robert Urquhart interview by Alan Barnes
21. Little Shoppe of Horrors #8; Edited by Richard Klemensen, p.61; Peter Cushing interview by James Kravaal

FIVE
...and Dracula (1957)

1. Little Shoppe of Horrors #7; Edited by Richard Klemensen; p. 64; Phil Leakey interview
2. Little Shoppe of Horrors #9; Edited by Richard Klemensen, p.90; Terence Fisher interview by Michael Caen (1964)
3. Little Shoppe of Horrors #4; Edited by Richard Klemensen, p.69; Ted Marshall interview
4. Little Shoppe of Horrors #9; Edited by Richard Klemensen, p.103; Len Harris interview by Al Taylor
5. Little Shoppe of Horrors #4; Edited by Richard Klemensen, p43; Anthony Nelson Keys interview
6. Little Shoppe of Horrors #9; Edited by Richard Klemensen, p.94; Jack Asher interview by Richard Klemensen
7. A History of Horrors – The Rise and Fall of the House of Hammer; Denis Meikle; p.76; The Scarecrow Press, 1996
8. Fandom's Film Gallery #1; Terence Fisher interview by Gary Parfitt
9. The Horror People; John Brosnan; p.113; MacDonald & James, 1976

Peter Cushing
arrives in the hall
of the Count's
castle. Dracula
(1957).

10. Little Shoppe of Horrors #4; Edited by Richard Klemensen, p106; Melissa Stribling interview
11. Little Shoppe of Horrors #3; Edited by Richard Klemensen, p.51; The Fruition of Terence Fisher by Gary Parfitt
12. Photon #27, p.27; Terence Fisher interview by Ron Borst
13. Horror Elite Journal #2; Terence Fisher interview by Sue and Colin Cowie; 1975
14. House of Horror, The Story Of Hammer Films, p14; Lorrimer, 1973
15. Photon #27, p.30; Terence Fisher interview by Ron Borst
16. Photon #27, p.31; Terence Fisher interview by Ron Borst
17. Horror Films, p.75, Alan Frank; Hamlyn, 1977
18. Fangoria #41, p41; Christopher Lee interview by Lawrence French
19. House of Hammer #18, p.32; The Life And Times of Peter Cushing by Alan Frank
20. Little Shoppe of Horrors #8; Edited by Richard Klemensen, p.61; Peter Cushing interview by James Kravaal
21. Hammer International Journal #4
22. Dracula, the Complete Vampire; p.47; Christopher Lee, King of the Counts, interview by Bill Kelley
23. Famous Film Stars #1, p19; Christopher Lee interview by Gary Parfitt
24. Cinefantastique Vol. 4:3; p.26; Terence Fisher interview by Harry Ringel; 1973
25. Little Shoppe of Horrors #4; Edited by Richard Klemensen, p.107; Melissa Stribling interview
26. Scary Dreams #2, p.20; Voice over by Harry Nadler
27. Little Shoppe of Horrors #9; Edited by Richard Klemensen, p.89; Terence Fisher interview by Michael Caen (1964)

SIX
The Hound From Hell (1958)

1. Little Shoppe of Horrors #5; Edited by Richard Klemensen; Sydney Pearson interview by Al Taylor
2. Little Shoppe of Horrors #4; Edited by Richard Klemensen, p62; Roy Ashton interview
3. Little Shoppe of Horrors #4; Edited by Richard Klemensen, p97; Christopher Lee interview
4. Films & Filming, July 1964; Terence Fisher interview by Raymond Durgnat and John Cutts
5. The Peter Cushing Companion by David Miller, p.72; Reynolds and Hearn, 2000
6. Scary Dreams #2, p.11; Francis Matthews interview by Steve Laws
7. Little Shoppe of Horrors #10/11; Edited by Richard Klemensen, p.147; Oscar Quitak interview by Oscar Martinez
8. Molly's Zoo. Molly Badham and Nathalie Evans with Maureen Lawless. Simon and Schuster, 2000
9. Little Shoppe of Horrors #4; Edited by Richard Klemensen, p.35; Michael Carreras interview by Richard Klemensen
10. Dracula, the Complete Vampire; p.47; Christopher Lee, King of The Counts, interview by Bill Kelley
11. The Films of Peter Cushing by Gary Parfitt; p.43; HFCGB; 1975
12. Little Shoppe of Horrors #12; Edited by Richard Klemensen, p.42; Kenneth Hyman interview by Chris Koetting
13. Little Shoppe of Horrors #10/11; Edited by Richard Klemensen, p.56; Tony Hinds interview
14. The Films of Peter Cushing by Gary Parfitt; p.31; HFCGB; 1975
15. Little Shoppe of Horrors #3; Edited by Richard Klemensen, p.15; André Morell interview by David Soren
16. Little Shoppe of Horrors #3; Edited by Richard Klemensen, p.52; The Fruition of Terence Fisher by Gary Parfitt
17. Little Shoppe of Horrors #14; Edited by Richard Klemensen, p115; interview with John Peverall
18. John Player Lecture, 1971
19. Little Shoppe of Horrors #9; Edited by Richard Klemensen, p.103; Len Harris interview by Al Taylor
20. Little Shoppe of Horrors #9; Edited by Richard Klemensen, p.104; Len Harris interview by Al Taylor
21. The Hammer Story; Marcus Hearn and Alan Barnes; p.40; Titan Books; 1997
22. Hazel Court interview by Stephen Laws; Festival of Fantastic Films, Manchester; 1999
23. House of Hammer #2; p.41; Roy Ashton interview by John Brosnan
24. Fangoria #35; p.35; Roy Ashton interview by Philip Nutman

SEVEN
Terror from the Tomb (1959)

1. Dark Terrors #15; p.40; Yesterday's Enemy by Keith Dudley
2. Little Shoppe of Horrors #14; Edited by Richard Klemensen, p.120; John Peverall interview by Richard Klemensen
3. Little Shoppe of Horrors #9; Edited by Richard Klemensen, p.104; Len Harris interview Al Taylor
4. Little Shoppe of Horrors #9; Edited by Richard Klemensen, p.95; Jack Asher interview by Richard Klemensen
5. Little Shoppe of Horrors #14; Edited by Richard Klemensen, p.63; Roy Ashton interview by Jan Van Genechten and Gilbert Verschooten
6. House of Hammer #2; p.40; Roy Ashton interview by John Brosnan
7. Eddie Powell interview by Stephen Laws; Festival of Fantastic Films, Manchester, 1998
8. Hammer Horror #3; p.16; Eddie Powell interview by Alan Barnes
9. Peter Cushing – Past Forgetting; p.77; Weidenfeld & Nicolson, 1988
10. Little Shoppe of Horrors #14; Edited by Richard Klemensen, p116; John Peverall interview by Richard Klemensen
11. Little Shoppe of Horrors #12; Edited by Richard Klemensen, p.42; Kenneth Hyman interview by Chris Koetting
12. Cinefantastique Vol. 4:3; p.26; Terence Fisher interview by Harry Ringel; 1973
13. Films & Filming, July 1964; Terence Fisher interview by Raymond Durgnat and John Cutts
14. Little Shoppe of Horrors #9; Edited by Richard Klemensen, p.102; Len Harris interview by Al Taylor
15. Little Shoppe of Horrors #3; Edited by Richard Klemensen, p.58; The Fruition of Terence Fisher by Gary Parfitt
16. Little Shoppe of Horrors #14; Edited by Richard Klemensen, p.70; Len Harris interview by Denis Meikle
17. Dark Terrors #16; p.9; Tony Hinds interview by Mike Murphy
18. The Hammer Story; Marcus Hearn and Alan Barnes; p.48; Titan Books; 1997
19. Cinefantastique Vol. 4:3; p.24; Terence Fisher interview by Harry Ringel; 1973
20. Little Shoppe of Horrors #9; Edited by Richard Klemensen, p.89; Terence Fisher interview by Michael Caen (1964)
21. Little Shoppe of Horrors #9; Edited by Richard Klemensen, p.99; Tilly Day interview by Ton Paans and Colin Cowie

EIGHT
The Werewolf and the Censor (1960)

1. Little Shoppe of Horrors #14; Edited by Richard Klemensen, p.82; Tony Hinds interview
2. Little Shoppe of Horrors #14; Edited by Richard Klemensen, p. 85; Peter Cushing interview by Bill Kelley
3. Little Shoppe of Horrors #9; Edited by Richard Klemensen, p.95; Jack Asher interview by Richard Klemensen
4. Little Shoppe of Horrors #9; Edited by Richard Klemensen, p.102; Len Harris interview by Al Taylor
5. Little Shoppe of Horrors #9; Edited by Richard Klemensen, p.101; Tilly Day interview by Ton Paans and Colin Cowie
6. Little Shoppe of Horrors #10/11; Edited by Richard Klemensen, p.103; Malcolm Williamson interview by Sam Irving
7. The Horror People; John Brosnan; p.120; MacDonald & James, 1976
8. The Hammer Story; Marcus Hearn and Alan Barnes; p.54; Titan Books; 1997
9. Christopher Lee : The Authorised Screen History; Jonathan Rigby; p.80; Reynolds & Hearn; 2001
10. Kinematograph Weekly, 5 May, 1960
11. Little Shoppe of Horrors #14; Edited by Richard Klemensen, p117; John Peverall interview by Richard Klemensen
12. The Charm of Evil; Dixon; p.386; Scarecrow Press, 1991
13. Fangoria #74; p.53; Tony Hinds interview by Bruce Hallenbeck
14. Little Shoppe of Horrors #5; Edited by Richard Klemensen; Tony Hinds interview
15. Fangoria #75; p.55; Tony Hinds interview by Bruce Hallenbeck
16. Fandom's Film Gallery #3; Edited by Jan Van Genechten; p.32
17. Fangoria #35; p.35; Roy Ashton interview by Philip Nutman
18. Fandom's Film Gallery #3; Edited by Jan Van Genechten; p.77; Roy Ashton interview
19. Fangoria #35; p.33; Roy Ashton interview by Philip Nutman
20. Little Shoppe of Horrors #3; Edited by Richard Klemensen, p.59; The Fruition of Terence Fisher by Gary Parfitt
21. Fandom's Film Gallery #3; Edited by Jan Van Genechten
22. Little Shoppe of Horrors #15; Edited by Richard Klemensen, p.75; Catherine Feller interview by Oscar Martinez
23. The Hammer Story; Marcus Hearn and Alan Barnes; p.58; Titan Books; 1997
24. Little Shoppe of Horrors #14; Edited by Richard Klemensen, p.118; John Peverall interview
25. Fandom's Film Gallery #3; Edited by Jan Van Genechten; p.81; Roy Ashton interview

NINE
Murder at the Opera (1961)

1. Little Shoppe of Horrors #9; Edited by Richard Klemensen, p.103; Len Harris interview by Al Taylor
2. Fandom's Film Gallery #3; Edited by Jan Van Genechten; p.82; Roy Ashton interview
3. Joseph Losey; Edith De Rham; p.122; Andre Deutsch; 1991
4. Joseph Losey; Edith De Rham; p.123; Andre Deutsch; 1991
5. Little Shoppe of Horrors #14; Edited by Richard Klemensen, p.119; John Peverall interview by Richard Klemensen
6. The Hammer Story; Marcus Hearn and Alan Barnes; p.67; Titan Books; 1997
7. Little Shoppe of Horrors #4; Edited by Richard Klemensen, p43; Anthony Nelson Keys interview
8. Michael Ripper Unmasked; Derek Pykett; p.103; Midnight Marquee Press; 1999
9. What the Censor Saw; John Trevelyan; London; Michael Joseph, 1973
10. Dark Terrors #3; p.14; Len Harris interview by Mike Murphy
11. Fangoria #74; p.54; Tony Hinds interview by Bruce Hallenbeck
12. Dark Terrors #17; p.23; The Phantom of the Opera by Keith Dudley
13. Little Shoppe of Horrors #10/11; Edited by Richard Klemensen, p.62; Edward De Souza interview
14. Hammer Films – An Exhaustive Filmography; Tom Johnson and Deborah Del Vecchio; p.220; McFarland; 1996
15. Little Shoppe of Horrors #14; Edited by Richard Klemensen, p.64; Roy Ashton interview by Jan Van Genechten and Gilbert Verschooten
16. Dark Terrors #17; p.25; The Phantom of the Opera by Keith Dudley
17. Christopher Lee: The Authorised Screen History; Jonathan Rigby; pp86-7; Reynolds & Hearn; 2001

TEN
The Kiss of Death (1962)

1. Little Shoppe of Horrors #14; Edited by Richard Klemensen, p.71; Len Harris interview by Denis Meikle
2. Little Shoppe of Horrors #14; Edited by Richard Klemensen, p.67; Len Harris interview by Denis Meikle
3. Little Shoppe of Horrors #14; Edited by Richard Klemensen, p.120; John Peverall interview by Richard Klemensen
4. Janette Scott interview by Gil Lane Young; Festival of Fantastic Films, Manchester; September 1994
5. Hammer Films – An Exhaustive Filmography; Tom Johnson and Deborah Del Vecchio; p.225; McFarland; 1996
6. The Films of Freddie Francis; Dixon; p.81; The Scarecrow Press; 1991
7. Fangoria #35; p.34; Roy Ashton interview by Philip Nutman
8. The Films of Freddie Francis; Dixon; p.76; The Scarecrow Press; 1991

9. *Hammer Horror #4*; p.8; Don Sharp interview by Christopher Koetting
10. *Little Shoppe of Horrors #10/11*; Edited by Richard Klemensen, p.51; Edward De Souza interview
11. *Little Shoppe of Horrors #10/11*; Edited by Richard Klemensen, p.61; Isobel Black interview
12. *The Films of Freddie Francis*; Dixon; p.75; The Scarecrow Press; 1991
13. *The Films of Freddie Francis*; Dixon; p.83; The Scarecrow Press; 1991

ELEVEN
The Devil-Ship Disaster (1963)
1. *Little Shoppe of Horrors #9*; Edited by Richard Klemensen, p.96; Jack Asher interview by Richard Klemensen
2. *Little Shoppe of Horrors #10/11*; Edited by Richard Klemensen, p.52; Don Sharp interview by Colin Cowie
3. *Hammer Horror #4*; p.10; Don Sharp interview by Christopher Koetting
4. *House of Hammer # 2*; p39; Roy Ashton interview by John Brosnan
5. *Little Shoppe of Horrors #14*; Edited by Richard Klemensen, p.64; Roy Ashton interview by Jan Van Genechten and Gilbert Verschooten
6. *Little Shoppe of Horrors #4*; Edited by Richard Klemensen, p.47; Freddie Francis interview
7. *Little Shoppe of Horrors #4*; Edited by Richard Klemensen, p.60; Roy Ashton interview
8. *Little Shoppe of Horrors #12*; Edited by Richard Klemensen, p.48; Tony Hinds interview
9. *Little Shoppe of Horrors #9*; Edited by Richard Klemensen, p.90; Terence Fisher interview by Michael Caen (1964)
10. *Little Shoppe of Horrors #14*; Edited by Richard Klemensen, p.63; Roy Ashton interview by Jan Van Genechten and Gilbert Verschooten
11. *Little Shoppe of Horrors #7*; Edited by Richard Klemensen; p.48; Barbara Shelley interview by Al Taylor
12. *Little Shoppe of Horrors #5*; Edited by Richard Klemensen; Sydney Pearson interview by Al Taylor

TWELVE
Elstree Calling (1964)
1. *Dou Want It Good Or Tuesday*; Jimmy Sangster; p.84; Midnight Marquee Press; 1997
2. *Midnight Marquee #47*; p.79; Hammer Films Unearth The Mummy by Richard Klemensen
3. *Little Shoppe of Horrors #14*; Edited by Richard Klemensen, p.62; Roy Ashton interview by Jan Van Genechten and Gilbert Verschooten
4. *Little Shoppe of Horrors #9*; Edited by Richard Klemensen, p.95; Jack Asher interview by Richard Klemensen `
5. *Little Shoppe of Horrors #9*; Edited by Richard Klemensen, p.96; Jack Asher interview by Richard Klemensen
6. *Michael Ripper Unmasked*; Derek Pykett; p.96; Midnight Marquee Press; 1999
7. *Little Shoppe of Horrors #12*; Edited by Richard Klemensen, p.43; Kenneth Hyman interview by Chris Koetting
8. *The Films of Peter Cushing*; Gary Parfitt; p.40; HFCGB; 1975
9. *Fangoria #35*; p.34; Roy Ashton interview by Philip Nutman
10. *She/Vengeance of She* soundtrack; Sleeve notes by James Bernard; GDI Records; 2001
11. *House of Hammer #15* p22; Fanatic by John Fleming
12. *House of Hammer #15* p23; Fanatic by John Fleming

THIRTEEN
Back-to-Back at Bray (1965)
1. *Do You Want It Good Or Tuesday*; Jimmy Sangster; p.90; Midnight Marquee Press; 1997
2. *Do You Want It Good Or Tuesday*; Jimmy Sangster; p.94; Midnight Marquee Press; 1997)

3. *Do You Want It Good Or Tuesday*; Jimmy Sangster; p.96; Midnight Marquee Press; 1997
4. *Cinefantastique Vol. 4:3*; p.24; Terence Fisher interview by Harry Ringel; 1973
5. *Little Shoppe of Horrors #7*; Edited by Richard Klemensen; p.47; Barbara Shelley interview by Al Taylor
6. *Little Shoppe of Horrors #7*; Edited by Richard Klemensen; p.45; Barbara Shelley interview by Al Taylor
7. *Movie Magic*; John Brosnan; p.101; MacDonald; 1974
8. Eddie Powell interview by Stephen Laws, Festival of Fantastic Films, Manchester, 1998
9. *Hammer Horror #4*; p.11; Don Sharp interview by Christopher Koetting
10. *Little Shoppe of Horrors #7*; Edited by Richard Klemensen; p.48; Barbara Shelley interview by Al Taylor
11. Francis Matthews interview by Stephen Laws; Festival of Fantastic Films, Manchester, September 1993
12. *Little Shoppe of Horrors #4*; Edited by Richard Klemensen; p.58; John Gilling interview
13. *Dark Terrors #6*; p.17; Jacqueline Pearce interview by Mike Murphy
14. *House of Hammer #2*; p.40; Roy Ashton interview by John Brosnan
15. *Little Shoppe of Horrors #14*; Edited by Richard Klemensen, p.65; Roy Ashton interview by Jan Van Genechten and Gilbert Verschooten
16. *Little Shoppe of Horrors #14*; Edited by Richard Klemensen, p.66; Roy Ashton interview by Jan Van Genechten and Gilbert Verschooten
17. *Little Shoppe of Horrors #4*; Edited by Richard Klemensen, p.61; Roy Ashton interview
18. *Today's Cinema*; 1 October, 1971; How Mr. Berman faced up to the task of putting clothes on Hammer glamour

FOURTEEN
The Curtain Falls (1966)
1. *The Hammer Story*; Marcus Hearn and Alan Barnes; p.105; Titan Books; 1997
2. *House of Hammer #16*, p32; Michael Carreras interview by John Brosnan and Dez Skinn
3. *Hammer Horror #5*, p.10; Robert Morris interview by Jonathan Rigby
4. *Hammer Horror #5*, p.11; Robert Morris interview by Jonathan Rigby
5. Eddie Powell interview by Stephen Laws; Festival of Fantastic Films, Manchester; 1998
6. *Hammer Horror #3*, p.28; The Mummy's Shroud
7. *Little Shoppe of Horrors #4*; Edited by Richard Klemensen, p.58; John Gilling interview
8. *Fangoria #61*; p.59; Michael Carreras interview by Steve Squires
9. *Michael Ripper Unmasked*; Derek Pykett; p.121; Midnight Marquee Press; 1999

Not even an axe can halt the onslaught of Prem (Eddie Powell) in The Mummy's Shroud *(1966).*

Index

Index